Advertising

A DECISION-MAKING APPROACH

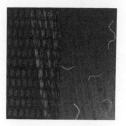

Advertising

A DECISION-MAKING APPROACH

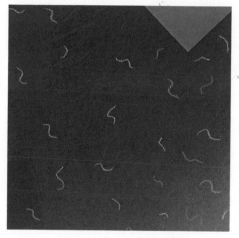

Charles H. Patti
University of Denver

Charles F. Frazer
University of Colorado–Boulder

The Dryden Press
Chicago   New York   San Francisco   Philadelphia
Montreal   Toronto   London   Sydney   Tokyo

Acquisitions Editor: Rob Zwettler
Developmental Editor: Kathryn Jandeska
Project Editor: Cate Rzasa
Design Director: Jeanne Calabrese
Production Manager: Barb Bahnsen
Permissions Editor: Cindy Lombardo
Director of Editing, Design, and Production: Jane Perkins

Text and Cover Design: Jeanne Calabrese
Text and Cover Illustrations: John Kleber
Copy Editor: Kathryn Jandeska
Indexer: Sheila Ary
Compositor: The Clarinda Company
Text Type: 10/12 Janson

Library of Congress Cataloging-in-Publication Data
Patti, Charles H.
   Advertising. a decision-making approach.

   Bibliography: p.
   Includes index.
   1. Advertising.   2. Advertising—Decision making.
I. Frazer, Charles F.   II. Title.
HF5821.P27   1988   659.1'11   87-6898
ISBN 0-03-071687-X

Printed in the United States of America
890-032-987654321

Address orders:
111 Fifth Avenue
New York, NY   10003

Address editorial correspondence:
One Salt Creek Lane
Hinsdale, IL 60521

The Dryden Press
Holt, Rinehart and Winston
Saunders College Publishing

To Judy, Greg, Mary Jo, and Chris — C. H. P.

To Kathy and Colin — C. F. F.

THE DRYDEN PRESS
SERIES IN
MARKETING

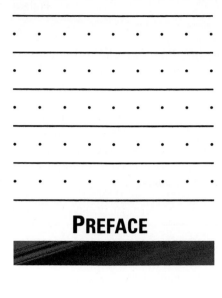

PREFACE

Why study advertising? Because advertising is part of every facet of American life. Every day, we are exposed to thousands of advertising messages. Advertising has become so much a part of our lives that we now readily acknowledge its profound impact.

Over the past decade, an increasing number of students have chosen to study advertising. This is a healthy sign. The effects of advertising are far reaching and have implications for a number of environments, including the mass media, the marketing sphere, the nation's economy, our native culture, and society as a whole.

TO THE STUDENT

This book's approach, naturally enough, has been shaped by our experiences. It has also been flavored by interaction with advertisers and advertising agencies; undergraduate and graduate students; numerous research projects in all of the key decision areas of advertising management; and colleagues who have generously shared their research, studies, and views.

We have written this text to share this approach to advertising with you. Although the book acknowledges the wide-ranging impact of advertising, it also views advertising as a business tool. The book emphasizes advertising decision making (and the sequential nature of that decision making) as its overriding theme. For example, the text discusses advertising budgets *after* the topic of advertising objectives. It shows the interrelationship of advertising decisions as well as the importance of making those decisions in a particular sequence. Throughout the book, we attempt to provide you with the tools to make the best possible advertising decisions within the internal and external environments. This is an important perspective for advertising students, for those who might be considering a career in advertising as well as those who wish to learn how marketers use advertising to meet marketing objectives.

Another reason we wrote this text was to present advertising in a way that can be easily understood by a large audience. It is important, for example, to be familiar with the advertising literature and to understand some of the controversy surrounding various topics. To broaden your knowledge, each chapter concludes with a suggested readings list. At the same time, we have intentionally avoided long discussions of theoretical issues, believing that other forums are more appropriate for such discussions. Instead, this text identifies the key decision-making areas in advertising, relating those areas to the broader issues in marketing and mass communication and illustrating key concepts with current examples and decision-making situations to stimulate involvement.

TO THE INSTRUCTOR

Advertising: A Decision-Making Approach is organized into six major parts. Each part represents a major step in understanding advertising as a marketing tool. The chapters within each part identify and explain the most important concepts, define all relevant terminology, and demonstrate the application of concepts to practical situations.

The book's organization is time tested, logical, and easy to follow. We think you'll find it helpful in presenting the discipline of advertising and its place in the marketing plan.

Part 1 (Background for Understanding Advertising) consists of four chapters that provide a backdrop for the study of advertising and identify the major components of the advertising industry. Chapter 1 discusses advertising within its historical context. Chapter 2 explains the two most important components of the advertising industry—the senders of advertising messages (advertisers) and creators of advertising messages (advertising agencies). Chapter 3 identifies the other components of the advertising business: the media and the variety of other services that support the creation and transmission of advertising to the target audiences. Chapter 4 focuses on the receivers of advertising. An understanding of how and why advertising messages are received is a critical first step in creating the advertising campaign.

Part 2 (Marketing and Advertising Planning: External Environments and Campaign Foundations) covers the external and internal environments that affect advertising decisions. One of the reasons marketers are not always successful is that their promotion efforts are constrained by the social, economic, and regulatory environments. Therefore, it is important for advertising decision makers to understand the nature of these environments and how they affect advertising. Chapter 5 discusses social and economic issues and Chapter 6 analyzes the legal and regulatory environment. Because advertising is one part of marketing, it is discussed within the context of business decisions. Chapter 7 explains exactly how advertising fits into the marketing plan. Chapter 8 focuses on one of the most important elements of both the marketing plan and the advertising campaign: the target market.

Part 3 (Advertising Decision Making: Pre-Campaign Issues) explains the three decisions that affect all other advertising campaign elements. Before an advertising campaign can be launched, the advertiser must know precisely (1) what to expect from advertising (Chapter 9); (2) what the goals of advertising are (Chapter 10); and (3) how much money to invest in the advertising campaign (Chapter 11). These three chapters cover the topics that are most crucial to the effective launching of an advertising campaign.

Part 4 (Advertising Decision Making: Campaign Development and Execution) focuses on the creation and evaluation of advertising messages. Chapter 12 explains different message strategy alternatives and shows how they are useful under different sets of circumstances. Once the guiding strategic principle for the advertising messages is established, the discussion turns to guidelines for executing the advertising message (Chapter 13). Today, few advertisers can afford high advertising costs without some assurance that their messages are communicated as intended. Why and how advertising messages are evaluated is the subject of Chapter 14.

Part 5 (Message Delivery) consists of five chapters covering the creation of the media plan, media characteristics, and evaluating the effectiveness of media plans. Chapter 15 introduces media planning, its key terms and concepts, and the relevant sources of information for media planning. Chapters 16 (Broadcast Media), 17 (Print Media), and 18 (Support Media) explain the organization, characteristics, and terminology of the media alternatives. These chapters cover all of the traditional media as well as the support media of direct response, cable television, the business press, specialty advertising, trade shows and exhibits, and several new media. Chapter 19 is the second of two research chapters in the book. The chapter explains and illustrates how the media portion of an advertising campaign is evaluated.

Part 6 (Contemporary Issues in Advertising) consists of the last chapter of the book, Chapter 20. In it, contemporary issues, the future of advertising, and career opportunities are discussed.

FEATURES OF THE BOOK

Advertising: A Decision-Making Approach offers several features that make the study of advertising interesting and relevant to decision making.

A DECISION-MAKING FRAMEWORK

A major reason for writing this text was to place advertising within the decision-making framework that we have developed over the years. This framework is introduced in Chapter 5 and appears in other parts of the book to reinforce students' understanding of the interrelationships of advertising decisions.

INTEGRATION OF TOPICS

An understanding of the key decision-making areas in advertising enables users to make sound decisions about advertising in all of its forms—for example, retail, nonprofit, business-to-business, direct response, and international. These forms obviously differ in many respects: target markets may be defined differently; the role of advertising in the promotion mix may change; creative approaches and media choices vary; and the amount of money allocated to advertising fluctuates. Although it is important to note and appreciate these differences, we believe that it is more instructive for the student to understand the *similarities* among these different forms of advertising. This text focuses on the key decisions that cut across all types of advertising. All advertisers need to set advertising objectives, create budgets, develop advertising messages, and deliver messages to their target markets. So, rather than contribute to the notion that each form of advertising must be treated separately, we want students to understand the similarities. We want the readers of this text to be able to make an equally effective decision about the advertising of a cologne, a department store, a machine tool, a museum, or computers throughout the world.

DIVERSE BACKGROUNDS OF AUTHORS

Most advertising courses are taught in either the communications/journalism or business/marketing setting. While this text is clearly a marketing, decision-making approach to advertising, the authors are sensitive to the interests and needs of both settings. One of us has spent his entire academic career in the communications setting, while the other teaches in the business setting. Without compromising the decision-making approach, we have explained advertising within the broader context of mass communication. While advertising is a marketing tool, students must also understand that advertising is a form of mass communication.

EMPHASIS ON LEARNING ELEMENTS

Advertising: A Decision-Making Approach contains a number of features that enhance students' reading enjoyment and understanding of the material.

Four-Color Visuals throughout the text illustrate key points, concepts, and procedures. Included are more than 200 diagrams, charts, tables, and ads.

Key Terms in each chapter call out the vocabulary that is essential to students' understanding. Each chapter begins with a list of the key terms, which are highlighted in boldface and defined in the chapter.

Learning Objectives identify the main goals of each chapter. Combined with the Key Terms list, they focus students' attention and prepare them for what follows.

Also part of the chapter-opening pages, an **Opening Vignette** provides a glimpse at the world of advertising and illustrates the decision topic of the chapter.

Boxed items, called **A Closer Look,** feature in-depth discussions of issues related to the chapter coverage. These treatments appear in every chapter.

An international perspective on advertising is provided in boxed items called **A Global Look.** Located in selected chapters, these boxes focus on advertising issues outside the United States and underscore the universality of advertising decision making.

Chapter Summaries provide a synopsis of the important concepts introduced in the chapter.

Experiential exercises called **You Make the Decision** provide students with an opportunity to apply what they have learned in the chapter. (Supplemental exercises appear in the *Instructor's Manual*.)

Ten **Questions for Discussion** appear at the end of each chapter, giving students an opportunity to test their understanding of important concepts.

A list of **Suggested Readings** at the end of each chapter provides sources for further exploration.

APPENDIXES AND GLOSSARY

Appendixes include Sources of Advertising Information, Media Rates, A Sample Advertising Plan, How to Compute Breakeven in Direct Marketing, and How to Make Advertising Presentations.

Appendix A (Sources of Advertising Information): Names, addresses, and telephone numbers of key places for additional information about advertising. Listed are professional associations, trade associations, media associations, sources of industry data, and trade and academic journals.

Appendix B (Media Rates): A summary of the costs to advertise in all of the major media. This appendix gives students a feel for media data, rates, and efficiencies.

Appendix C (Sample Advertising Plan: Mountain Bell, "Centron"): Designed to show students exactly how a major advertiser develops a campaign. This appendix presents a complete description of Mountain Bell's Centron campaign.

Appendix D (Calculating Breakeven in Direct Marketing): Direct marketing has become an important component of the marketing plans of a growing number of advertisers. This easy-to-follow chart allows students to calculate the breakeven point for any direct response medium.

Appendix E (How to Make Advertising Presentations): Today, almost everyone in the advertising business is called on to make presentations. Sometimes these are simple explanations to small groups, while at other times they may be carefully rehearsed group performances in front of top management. This appendix discusses fundamental principles in planning and carrying out presentations.

A helpful **Glossary** includes important terms and their definitions.

THE TEACHING/LEARNING PACKAGE

The textbook is undoubtedly the most critical element in this package. However, it is only one part. What follows represents one of the most extensive teaching/learning packages ever assembled for instructors of advertising. As teachers of this course, we are well aware of the challenges facing advertising instructors, and we have tried to create a teaching/learning package that will supplement your approach to the course.

INSTRUCTOR'S MANUAL/TEST BANK

The *Instructor's Manual* has been written by Joanne Klebba of Portland State University. We've worked closely with Professor Klebba to provide what we believe to be the most useful instructor's manual for the introduction to advertising course. The manual includes the following elements:

- Handy conversion table for former users of other leading texts
- Key Terms
- Learning Objectives
- Annotated Chapter Outlines
- Teaching notes for boxed items (A Closer Look, A Global Look)
- Teaching hints
- Lecture illustration file (anecdotal materials for classroom use)
- Teaching notes for transparency acetates
- Supplemental "You Make the Decision" exercises and possible answers
- Answers to Discussion Questions
- List of course-related videotapes, movies, and other audio-visual aids
- Discussion of appendixes and their possible uses in the course

The *Test Bank*, which appears as the second section of the *Instructor's Manual*, is authored by Professor Dennis Pitta of the University of Baltimore. This comprehensive collection of more than 1,500 items includes multiple-choice, true/false, and essay questions for each chapter. The questions have been tested in the classroom and indicate to the instructor whether each question tests applicational, definitional, or relational knowledge.

COMPUTERIZED TEST BANK

This IBM-compatible test bank allows the instructor to add or delete questions and to select questions on a random basis. It is distributed free to adopters.

FOUR-COLOR TRANSPARENCIES

Each adopter receives a set of 50 four-color acetate transparencies. Certain acetates cover key concepts in the text. The balance present an appealing and stimulating additional illustration of concepts, advertisements, and storyboards that do not appear in the book.

ACKNOWLEDGMENTS

Writing a textbook involves a great deal of pulling together of ideas, concepts, suggestions, and material from many sources. We certainly accept responsibility for the content of this book. We conceived the idea; we developed the book's framework; and we wrote it. However, we would never have been able to complete the book without the help of others.

Our first, and most important, source of material for this book is our students. Over the years, we have worked with thousands of advertising students. They are a constant source of new ideas and challenges. They identify new advertising problems, and they stimulate us to develop new ways to think about enduring advertising problems and issues. We wrote this book for advertising students, and we hope they will enjoy it and benefit from it.

We have always felt that one of the most stimulating aspects of working in the academic community is the process of reviewing each other's work. This process helps create a discipline-wide community—colleagues who share the common goal of improving the education process and the practice of advertising. We were fortunate to have the following people involved in our book. They read this manuscript and offered helpful criticism. There is no doubt that this book is better because of their willingness to help us achieve our goal.

- Alan J. Bush, Texas A & M University

- Thomas R.Gillpatrick, Portland State University

- Donald R. Glover, University of Denver

- Paul W. Jackson, Ferris State College

- William C. Lesch, Illinois State University

- Dennis G. Martin, Brigham Young University

- Milledge J. Mosby, Jr., Prince George's Community College

- Michael Munson, Santa Clara University

- Joseph Pisani, University of Florida

- Dennis A. Pitta, University of Baltimore

- Len N. Reid, University of Georgia

- Edward A. Riordan, Wayne State University

- Billy I. Ross, Texas Tech University

- Teresa A. Swartz, Arizona State University

- Ron Taylor, University of Tennessee

- Guy W. Tunnicliffe, University of Missouri—Columbia

- Lynette S. Unger, Miami University of Ohio

We wish to say thank you to the many advertising agencies, associations, companies, individuals, and media that provided us with the original artwork that we used for the illustrations, figures, and exhibits in the book.

We also want to express our appreciation to the people who helped us by offering their opinions, criticisms, and suggestions for various parts of the book and by supplying us with much of the material that was used for the book's many examples and exercises.

- Olli T. Ahtola, University of Denver

- Nancy Bettencourt

- Vincent J. Blasko, Arizona State University

- Al Dilger, Paulsen & Partners, Inc.

- R. Bruce Hutton, University of Denver

- Kathy Judd

- Steve Kanewske, Mountain Bell

- Robin I. Moore

- Sandra E. Moriarty, University of Colorado

- Laura O'Connell

- Christa Reich, Reich Communications, Inc.

- James Schirmer, Mountain Bell

- Susan M. Schoebel, International Newspaper Advertising and Marketing Executives Foundation

The success of any book depends heavily on the skill and devotion of the editorial, production, and art staffs. In this regard, we wish to thank John Kleber for his artistic contributions to this book. We also wish to express special appreciation to the following individuals of The Dryden Press: Jeanne Calabrese, Kathryn Jandeska, Cindy Lombardo, Doris Milligan, Jane Perkins, Susan Riley, Cate Rzasa, Bill Schoof, Diane Tenzi, and Rob Zwettler. Their dedication to this project created a team effort that we think has made for a better book.

Charles H. Patti
Charles F. Frazer

December 1987

ABOUT THE AUTHORS

Charles H. Patti, Ph.D., is professor and chairman of the department of marketing at the University of Denver's College of Business Administration and Public Administration. He formerly served on the faculties of Arizona State University and Elmhurst College.

Prior to his career in education, Dr. Patti spent eight years in advertising. He began his advertising career as a copywriter and designer for a book publishing company. Later, after an editorship of a large company magazine, he became director of advertising and public relations for U.S. Industries' largest operating division, USI-Clearing. Eventually, he became vice president of corporate communications for U.S. Industries, Inc. Dr. Patti continues his involvement in the advertising business through consulting.

Dr. Patti's academic research has focused on the major areas of advertising management, and his research has been published in a number of academic and trade journals, including *Journal of Advertising, Journal of Advertising Research, Journal of Marketing*, and *Industrial Marketing Management*. In addition, he has coauthored two books on advertising management.

Charles F. Frazer, Ph.D., is associate professor of advertising in the School of Journalism and Mass Communication at the University of Colorado–Boulder. He has served on the faculties of the University of Washington at Seattle and the University of Illinois at Urbana–Champaign.

After graduating from college, Dr. Frazer began working in advertising with the Eastman Kodak Company, where he planned advertising for both consumer and industrial products divisions at Kodak headquarters in Rochester, New York. He later joined the advertising agency of Young & Rubicam, where he worked in account services on large accounts such as Chrysler from Y&R offices in Detroit, New York, and Washington, D.C. Since leaving the advertising industry, he continues to work with local and regional advertisers in planning and evaluating their advertising programs.

Dr. Frazer's research and scholarly writing have covered several aspects of advertising education, especially creative strategy and evaluation, and social aspects of advertising. Reports of his work have appeared in leading mass communications journals, including *Communications Research, Journal of Communication, Journal of Advertising*, and *Journal of Broadcasting*.

CONTENTS IN BRIEF

CONTENTS

Chapter 7
The Relationship between
Advertising and Marketing *160*

P A R T 3

Advertising Decision Making: Pre-Campaign Issues *211*

**Chapter 11
Budgeting for Advertising** *256*

P A R T 4

Advertising Decision Making: Campaign Development and Execution *281*

**Chapter 12
Developing Creative
Strategy** *282*

**Chapter 13
Selecting Creative Tactics** *308*

**Chapter 14
Measuring the
Effectiveness of
Advertisements** *334*

P A R T 5

Advertising Decision Making: Message Delivery   *353*

**Chapter 18
Support Media** *440*

**Chapter 19
Evaluating Media Plans** *472*

PART 1

Background for Understanding Advertising

Because advertising has developed into such a powerful force in our society, there are many ways to approach its study. Advertising has become a social and economic force, a source of product information, a form of art, and a widely used business tool. Fundamentally, advertising is a form of mass communication; therefore, if you are to understand how advertising works, why it's used, and the effects it has, we believe it is most important to begin with examining advertising as communication.

The first four chapters of this book examine advertising as a form of mass communication. Figure 1.1 was created to help guide you through these four chapters, and to help you understand the components of the advertising communication process. As you read these chapters, refer to the figure to identify the tasks performed by each of the components. The figure also explains how the components must work together to maximize communication effectiveness.

Chapter 1 considers the **historical context** in which advertising developed and focuses on the major factors that have shaped advertising's present form. Chapter 2 describes the two groups that create advertising messages: advertisers and advertising agencies. Advertisers are identified as **sources** in the figure, and advertising agencies perform the task of **translating** objectives and ideas into visual and verbal messages, which we know as advertisements or advertising campaigns. After messages are created, they must be **transmitted** to the receivers. This is the task of the media and a variety of other related advertising services, described in Chapter 3. Chapter 4 focuses on the receivers of advertising messages. In this chapter, you will learn why we become exposed to advertising; how we process advertising; and what factors are most likely to affect what we do with advertising.

C H A P T E R 1

THE DEVELOPMENT OF MODERN ADVERTISING

Key Terms

advertising
commission system
Powers school
"reason-why" copy
preemptive claim
atmosphere copy
emulation style
comparative approach
rates of response

Learning Objectives

To describe the services offered by advertising agencies

To explain the commission system and how it works

To trace the origins of common advertising creative strategies

One of the world's best-known and most heavily advertised products was developed in 1886 by Dr. John Pemberton. Pemberton brewed a syrup in his backyard in Atlanta, Georgia, and sold it in the soda fountain of a nearby pharmacy for five cents per glass.

Pemberton's partner, Frank Robinson, suggested that the name "Coca-Cola" would look good in advertisements, and drafted the flowing script lettering used to this day to identify the brand name.

The first year's sales were not overwhelming, averaging about 13 drinks per day. Pemberton sold 25 gallons of syrup and grossed $50. He spent $73.96 on advertising, promoting the "delicious and refreshing" theme. By 1920 Coca-Cola's advertising budget had reached $2 million. In the 1930s, the firm innovated the six-pack carton. For years, it has employed consumer research in planning its creative strategy, a practice that has led to numerous imaginative (and award-winning) campaigns.

The carbonated beverage was one of the first American products to go multinational; today, it sells in more than 150 nations. Campaigns for Coke have routinely used the widest variety of media, from radio and TV to newspapers, magazines, outdoor, and specialty advertising items.

In the mid-1980s, Coca-Cola took a pioneering leap into the high-tech age by adopting what is probably the first computer-generated character to be used as a product spokesperson: the bizarre and irreverent Max Headroom, whose synthetic voice urges millions of consumers daily to "C-c-catch the wave!"

Coca-Cola's early commitment to advertising played an important role in its monumental success, and has resulted in ground-breaking innovations in the advertising field.

Source: Based on *Refreshing Facts about Coca-Cola*, Coca-Cola Company, 1982. Photographs courtesy of The Coca-Cola Company.

INTRODUCTION

Figure 1.1 illustrates the important components, processes, and "actors" in the advertising communication process. The model shows how advertisers, agencies, media, and buyers interact and communicate. It is important to note that each group has a slightly different intention in this process and that there are numerous factors that limit the effectiveness of communication. This chapter points out some of the important changes in the advertising business since its beginnings in this country. Since the advertising business of today is a direct reflection of the decisions and practices of early practitioners, much of its present nature is explained by a look at its history.

While various forms of advertising can be traced to ancient times and the earliest types of public address, we will not go back that far. Our interest is in the origin of the business of advertising as we know it today.

A DEFINITION OF ADVERTISING

Traditional definitions of advertising used in textbooks and in reference sources, such as the *Dictionary of Marketing Terms*, commonly include a number of characteristics that distinguish advertising from other forms of communication.[1]

It is paid for by the sponsor rather than run at the discretion of the medium. This distinguishes advertising from publicity material, which is not paid for. Yet, public service advertising is not paid for; the production and media costs are donated by the firms providing the services.

It is nonpersonal. That is, advertising is disseminated to a mass audience. This distinguishes it from personal selling, which is a face-to-face sales presentation. Yet some forms of direct marketing are becoming increasingly personalized, threatening to blur the line between personal selling and advertising.

It identifies the sponsor of the message. Advertising is distinguished from propaganda in that the source of the message is identified within the message itself. However, much political advertising is placed by political action committees who give themselves neutral-sounding names in the hope that their messages will be accepted as objective, rather than partisan, information.

It is carried by mass media. In the United States, advertising is identified with the mass media of communication, and plays a role in underwriting their costs. But advertising also appears in many forms that have nothing to do with mass media. The U.S. Postal Service, for example, carries a considerable amount of direct-mail advertising, but it cannot be considered a mass medium. Calendars and matchbooks carry advertising messages but are not mass media. The same is true of painted benches.

It is persuasive. Advertising is rarely designed to tell all sides of the story about a product or service; it is not designed to be objective information. Advertising is designed as a tool that organizations use to persuade people to accept products, services, or ideas. But here, too, it can be argued that certain kinds of advertising—classified advertising, for example—is not designed to be persuasive at all. It merely proposes a transaction.

FIGURE 1.1

A Model of the Advertising Communications Process

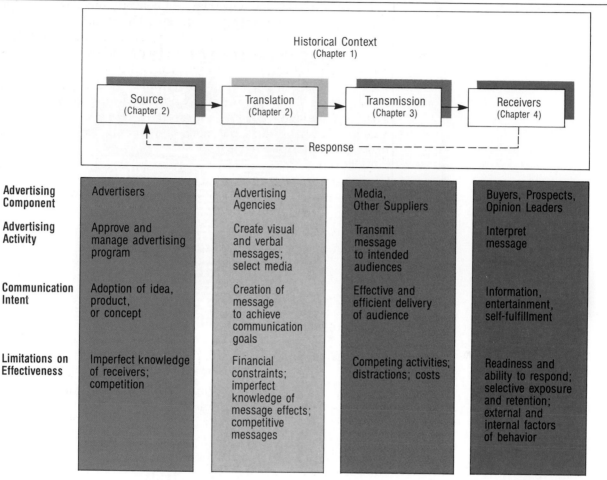

As this discussion suggests, it is difficult to arrive at a succinct definition that has no exceptions. This is true in part because the term *advertising* encompasses such a wide variety of communication forms.

This book will consider **advertising** as *planned communication activity in which messages in mass media are used to persuade audiences to adopt goods, services, or ideas.*

NATIONAL ADVERTISING AND ADVERTISING AGENCIES: A BEGINNING

The story of modern persuasive advertising is really the story of the rise of the national advertiser, which occurred in the late nineteenth and early twentieth centuries. It is also the story of the foundation and evolution of the advertising agency business. The advertising agency came about and was shaped by the needs of the national advertiser.

The term *advertisement* means news, and a good deal of early advertising simply announced the availability of goods and services, as shown in

FIGURE 1.2

An Example of Early Advertising

Figure 1.2.[2] This chapter will show that the advertising agency business quickly evolved to do much more than simply spread simple information as broadly as possible.

Around the turn of the century, the advertising agency changed from a business that simply placed commercial news items in paid space to one that took responsibility for designing ads and selecting media to give advertising messages the greatest *persuasive effects* possible. The reasons for this change are complex and related to deep changes taking place in American society.

EARLY DEVELOPMENTS, 1843–1900

During the 1830s and 1840s advertisers relied primarily on hand-bills and classified announcements in newspapers to circulate their messages. The advertising of the times was almost entirely local. It announced the goods and services of local shopkeepers and tradesmen who served small geographical communities. The growth of cities, concentrated populations, and improved printing equipment allowed the proliferation of newspapers. Even more significantly, a new type of newspaper, the penny press, emerged. Earlier types of newspapers—the party press and the mercantile press—had served the needs of their special-interest groups with very specialized information. But newspapers that reached virtually every member of the community, as they do today, simply did not exist. The penny press combined political and business news with reports of dramatic local events, often sensationally reported. But even more important was the business strategy of the publishers.

While political and mercantile papers depended mostly on subscriptions for their income (the political papers were also subsidized by politicians), the penny papers sold at considerably lower prices to a wider audience. The key to their profitability was, in part, a large number of readers; but, more importantly, advertising income rather than subscription price provided the primary source of revenue for many papers.

The rise of the penny press was the result of a number of important changes. The social and political climate favored attention to the needs and interests of the common people. The steam-powered rotary press allowed the faster and more efficient production of printed material. Increasing urbanization meant a large group of potential readers in close geographic concentration. This large market for newspapers also meant that the publication could be distributed at newsstands rather than by subscription alone.

Though the penny press provided a medium for advertising, the national advertiser did not become an important force until after the Civil War. Those who did wish to advertise their goods in more than one town or city were confronted with an overwhelming number of newspapers, some competing and most greatly exaggerating their circulation.

There were two sides to the problem of newspaper advertising. The advertiser could rarely judge the circulation claims or the fairness of the advertising rate charges made by the publisher of a paper, particularly one in a distant city. Similarly, the publisher could not assess how creditworthy a potential advertiser might be. A Philadelphian named Volney Palmer offered a partial solution to these problems in 1843 by declaring himself an "advertising agent." Though Palmer did not assume financial responsibility for the contracts of advertisers, he did provide them with rate and circulation information. A later competitor and former employee, S. M. Pettengill, was quickly successful in the newly founded advertising agency business when he guaranteed payment to publishers on advertising contracts placed through him.

The obvious benefits of increased advertising space and at least a higher probability of payment made the agency service attractive to publishers. For these reasons they were willing to sell advertising space to agencies at a discount—usually 25 percent—from their published rates. George P. Rowell made a further (and more profitable) refinement to the agency

A CLOSER LOOK

LYDIA PINKHAM AND FRIENDS: FORERUNNERS OF NATIONAL ADVERTISING

Patent (nonprescription) medicines were among the first manufacturers to use advertising heavily. A notably successful product, Lydia E. Pinkham's Vegetable Compound, proclaimed itself "the positive cure for all female complaints." Beginning in 1875, the Pinkham family employed heavy advertising—first in newspapers, then in magazines, billboards, and streetcar signs—for a product that continued to be successful through the 1930s.

Pinkham's product and advertising continued long after Lydia herself had passed away, though she continued to solicit readers' questions and dispense advice, posthumously, from the ads. Pinkham's Compound at least was not harmful. Many patent medicines of the early period contained opiates, and at least one, Peruna, could not be sold on Indian reservations because of its high alcohol content. Another, Elixir Sulfanilamide, caused the deaths of 73 people in seven states.

Though the advertising claims sound preposterous today, willing buyers sought out the products from their local druggist. Patent medicines demonstrated that advertising was an effective selling tool. At the same time, they tainted advertising with their exaggerations and their sleazy aura.

LYDIA E. PINKHAM'S VEGETABLE COMPOUND.

A Sure Cure for all FEMALE WEAK-
NESSES, Including Leucorrhœa, Ir-
regular and Painful Menstruation,
Inflammation and Ulceration of
the Womb, Flooding, PRO-
LAPSUS UTERI, &c.

Source: Otis Pease, *The Responsibilities of American Advertising* (New Haven, Conn.: Yale University Press, 1958), 124.

business by contracting ahead of time for large blocks of space (which he could buy at the lowest possible rates) and selling them as smaller and higher-priced units. In 1869 he published *Rowell's American Newspaper Dictionary* listing over 5000 newspapers in the United States and Canada. His directory also included publishers' circulation claims, with a code indicating Rowell's level of confidence in the estimate.

HOW AGENCIES SERVED ADVERTISERS

The role of the advertising agency benefited advertisers as well. In the period following the Civil War, advances in communication, transportation, and manufacturing resulted in changes in marketing and consumption. For the first time, many goods formerly made in the home—such as soap, cigarettes, candy, and bread—were offered for sale by manufacturers.[3] Increased manufacturing capacity allowed the production of more goods, but the high cost of production equipment dictated that it not sit

FIGURE 1.3

Early Ad for a Manufactured Product

ENTERPRISE

Raisin

and GRAPE

Seeder

WET THE RAISINS   NO 36

WILL SEED A POUND

IN 5 MINUTES

Takes out every seed without destroying the shape of the Raisin. So simple that a child can do it.

Saves Time, Labor, Patience.

Avoids Appendicitis.

An ingenious machine — Always ready for use — Lasts a lifetime — Never gets out of order — Easily cleaned — Made in several sizes — No. 36, for ordinary family use, seeds a pound in five minutes.

Price $1.00 at Hardware Stores.

Send two 2-cent stamps for the "ENTER-PRISING HOUSEKEEPER" — 200 recipes.

THE ENTERPRISE MFG. CO. OF PA.,
Philadelphia, Pa.

Makers of the Enterprise Meat Choppers.

idle. While rail transportation allowed goods to be shipped to distant points, fluctuations in demand and direct competition among manufactured goods were important forces confronting industrialists (see Figure 1.3).

What had happened amounted to a fundamental change in economic life for consumers, retailers, and manufacturers. Not only were new goods available in stores, but consumers had to make choices among competing brands. Advertising was the tool to perform the dual purposes of 1) informing and persuading consumers to choose the advertised brand and 2) persuading retailers they should stock the brand to satisfy brand-loyal consumers. This second point is especially important in that it gave manufacturers a new measure of influence with retailers.[4] As the result of these forces, modern persuasive advertising evolved as a tool to stimulate brand demand.[5] The commitment to expanded markets and to competition meant that manufacturers had to become national advertisers. To the advertiser, the information on costs, terms, circulation, and even names and addresses of newspapers held by the advertising agency became invaluable, especially in view of the rapid expansion of the publishing industry. One source shows that there were 254 daily newspapers in 1850, a number that grew to 2,226 by 1900.[6]

ORIGIN OF THE COMMISSION SYSTEM

By dealing directly with publishers and serving as the source of rate and circulation information for advertisers, advertising agents found themselves in a very profitable position. By assuming the role of space brokers, they could exert considerable influence both on publishers for the lowest rates and on advertisers for the highest. This led to speculation and profiteering in advertising space, with the result that agents were trusted by neither group and, according to one observer, "owed their lives to the fact that there was a law against killing them."[7]

In 1876 a modification of this arrangement was offered by F. Wayland Ayer, founder of N. W. Ayer & Sons. Ayer—who had named his business after his father to convey a sense that the business was an established family concern—announced the "open contract." According to this agreement, Ayer would disclose publication costs to his advertiser clients and work on an established commission basis. The commission was first set at 12.5 percent and later changed to 15 percent. This development not only established the basis of the **commission system** of today, but established the principle of agency service to the advertiser rather than to the publisher who actually paid the commission. The arrangement seemed to be attractive to advertisers and was profitable to Ayer. By 1884 three-quarters of Ayer's business was based on the open contract and by the 1890s his was the largest agency in the country.[8] Significantly, Ayer's innovation not only resulted in the growth of his agency, but by ending the "whatever the traffic will bear" pricing mentality, improved the level of professionalism and enhanced the service orientation of the young industry. The Ayer agency ad in Figure 1.4 appeared in *Harper's* magazine in 1893.

The young advertising industry also found it necessary to confront the distrust of both businesses and the public. The extravagant claims of mail-order advertisers, particularly for patent medicines, left audiences suspicious and skeptical. Industry spokespeople lobbied for the establishment

FIGURE 1.4

Advertisement for the N. W. Ayer
Agency, Innovators of the Open
Contract System

of college-level advertising programs to supply training and to enhance the professional status of practitioners. Then as now, the industry was divided on whether business or journalism provided the better preparation.[9]

MAGAZINES EMERGE AS AN ADVERTISING MEDIUM

Besides the evolution of the advertising agency, a second important development marked this early period: the emergence of magazines as an advertising medium. J. Walter Thompson founded his New York agency in 1878 after demonstrating literary magazines to be a valuable advertising medium. Up to that time, magazine publishers had somewhat reluctantly accepted advertisements, but had not considered them an important source of revenue. Thompson managed to sell the concept of advertising to magazine publishers and later held what he described as a "standard list" of the "best" magazines under his exclusive contract. The list included *Atlantic*, *Harper's*, *Godey's Lady's Book*, and the *North American Review*.[10] By 1885 four magazines claimed over 100,000 circulation and by the late 1880s Cyrus Curtis' newly established *Ladies' Home Journal* had surpassed 400,000 circulation. Like the penny press, the mass circulation magazine supported by advertising was a reversal of the conventional practice. Early magazines had been mostly literary and aimed at a high-brow audience. Also, like the penny press, the rise of large circulation magazines was aided by technological advances allowing cheaper, better-quality printing and better illustrations (see Figure 1.5).

THE FOUNDATIONS OF MODERN AGENCIES, 1900–1920

During the early twentieth century advertising became the tool of the nationally distributed consumer product. This change, which began before the turn of the century, resulted from the opportunity to ship goods widely and the market concentration that came about with the growth of cities. Heavy advertising expenditures characterized both industries with low manufacturing costs (such as soap and chocolate) and high costs (such as tobacco, brewing, and processed foods).[11]

Not surprisingly, the emergence of the national advertiser resulted in further changes in the advertising agency business. The majority of these changes affected the character of the advertising message itself, though important developments in agency service also occurred. While agencies had been founded primarily out of the need for information about media, the demands of large national advertisers required specialists in advertising copywriting. This marked a fundamental change in the character of advertising, a change from information to persuasion.[12] The change came about as the result of competitive pressure and the higher levels of investment necessary to sustain a national selling effort.

DEVELOPMENTS IN ADVERTISING CREATIVE STRATEGY

The period from 1900 through the early 1920s saw the formulation of several major innovations in the creative area of advertising. A good deal of earlier advertising had been characterized by the restrained and straightforward presentation of product characteristics. Leading proponents of this approach were known as the **Powers school** after John E. Powers, copywriter for Wanamaker department stores. Powers, the first full-time professional copywriter, was paid the unheard-of salary of $10,000 a year. The Powers school considered advertising copy to be product news and delivered it directly and without gimmickry. Powers' plain, truthful, and direct approach contrasted sharply with the patent

FIGURE 1.5

Godey's Lady's Book: A Leading
Magazine of the 1870s

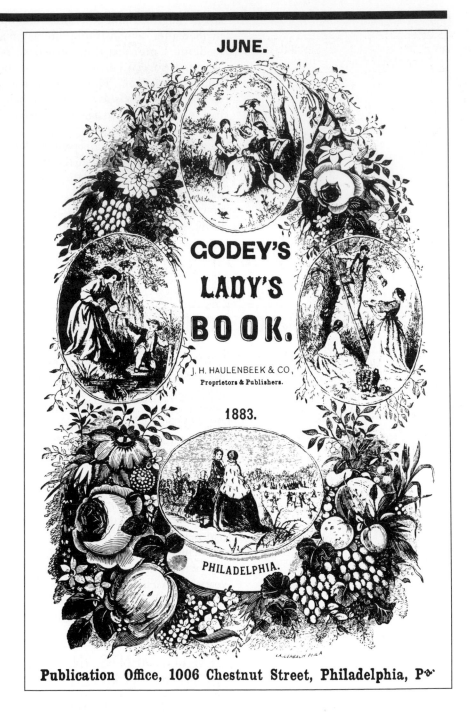

medicine advertising of the time, which was largely based on hugely exaggerated—and sometimes totally baseless—claims.

Powers was rigidly, almost fanatically truthful in all his work. He made John Wanamaker very uneasy by his tendency to use in advertisements the exact remarks that store section managers confided to him. "The neckties are not as good as they look, but they're good enough—25¢." Such unexampled frankness startled customers and usually sold out the goods promptly.[13]

FIGURE 1.6

An Example of John E. Kennedy's
"Reason-Why" Copy

My Book Is Free

My treatment too—if that fails.

But if it helps—if it succeeds,
If health is yours again,
I ask you to pay—$5.50.

The book tells all.
I send it to you free
If you but write.

And further, I will send the name of a druggist near
you who will let you take six bottles of my remedy,

Dr. Shoop's Restorative

On a month's trial.   If it succeeds, the cost to you is
$5.50.   If it fails, the druggist will bill the cost to me.

Don't Wait Until You Are Worse.

Taken in time, the suffering of this little one
would have been prevented:—

" Two years ago my little girl was sick continuously for
six months. We tried many doctors, but they failed, yet
it took only two bottles of your remedy to cure her, and
she has remained cured. You can tell others of this cure if
you so desire."   Mrs. C. H. Avery, Rockdale, N. Y.

The wife of Omer Andrus, of Bayou Chicat,
La., had been sick for 20 years. For 8 years
could do practically no work. He writes:

" When she first started taking the Restorative she
barely weighed 90 pounds; now she weighs 135, and is easily able to do all her housework."

J. G. Billingsley, of Thomasville, Ga. He
writes:

" I spent $250.00 for other medicines, and the $5.00 I
have spent with you have done me more good than all the
rest."

Both money and suffering might have been
saved.

And these are only three from over 65,000
similar cases. Such letters—many of them—
come every day to me.

How much serious illness the Restorative has
prevented I have no means of knowing, for the
slightly ill and the indisposed simply get a
bottle or two of their druggist, are cured, and I
never hear from them.

But of 600,000 sick ones—seriously sick,
mind you—who asked for my guarantee, 39
out of 40 have paid.

If I can succeed in cases like these—fail but
one time in 40 in diseases deep-seated and chronic, isn't it certain I can cure the slightly ill?

All You Need Do.

Simply write me—that is all. Tell me the
book you need. The offer I make may sound
extravagant. But it isn't. It would mean
bankruptcy to me, though, were it not for my
discovery. That discovery—the treatment of
the inside nerves—taught me a way to cure.
I do not doctor the mere organs. I doctor the
nerves that operate them—that give them
strength and power.

And failures are seldom—so seldom that I
make this offer gladly, freely—so that those
who might doubt may learn without risk.

Tell of it, please, to some sick friend. Or
send me his name. That's but a trifle—a
minute's time—a postal. He is your friend.
You can help him. My way may be his only
way to get well.

If I, a stranger, will do this for him, you
should at least write.

Drop me a postal to-day,

Simply state which
book you want and
address Dr. Shoop.
Box 3397, Racine, Wis.

Book 1 on Dyspepsia
Book 2 on the Heart
Book 3 on the Kidneys
Book 4 for Women
Book 5 for Men
Book 6 on Rheumatism

Mild cases, not chronic, are often cured with
one or two bottles. At druggists'.

Here was salesmanship in print, 1903 style. The ad was written by John E. Kennedy
when he was a highly paid copywriter for Dr. Shoop. From *Advertising Age*.

A leading innovation of the period was the development of **"reason-why" copy.** This orientation emphasized persuasion in advertising writing, viewing advertising as an argument to buy. The approach was often built around the important differentiating points of the product and is most closely associated with John E. Kennedy's work at the Lord & Thomas agency in the early 1900s. Kennedy viewed advertising as "salesmanship in print" and felt that every advertisement should "talk" like a salesman, reiterating powerful selling points (Figure 1.6).

FIGURE 1.7

An Advertisement by Claude
Hopkins, Proponent of the
Preemptive Claim

There is
no biliousness
in old beer

The beer that makes you bilious
is what we call a "green beer." It
is beer that is marketed too soon
— that is insufficiently aged.

We store Schlitz Beer for months
in refrigerating rooms, and this
fact requires a storage capacity for
425,000 barrels.

We keep it there until it is well
fermented. That adds to the cost,
of course. That is why some beers
are shipped green.

We are
that careful
all through

Careful about materials — about
cleanliness.

So careful that we filter all the
air that touches Schlitz Beer.

And when it is bottled and
sealed, we sterilize every bottle.

Your doctor will tell you to
drink Schlitz Beer, rather than
common beer; and it costs you no
more than the common.

Ask for the brewery bottling.

Source: Courtesy of the Stroh Brewery Historical Collection.

Lord & Thomas, the leading agency of the period, also contributed
the second important development in advertising strategy of the period,
the **preemptive claim.** Claude Hopkins, a successor of Kennedy at Lord
& Thomas, was apparently stumped by the need to develop a dramatic
and imaginative campaign for Schlitz beer. As the story goes, Hopkins
was struck by the bottle sterilization process while on a brewery tour and
produced the advertising theme that Schlitz bottles were "bathed in live

 A **LOSER LOOK**

IVORY SOAP:
AN EARLY NATIONAL ADVERTISER

Although Ivory soap became one of the most heavily advertised products in America by 1904, the product did not begin that way. Ivory soap, a product of the Procter & Gamble Company, appeared in 1879. By accident, a batch with more air than usual was sent to retailers and consumers found the fact that it floated quite beneficial. For one thing, it was easily located at the surface of murky dishpans and washpails. For another, it was useful in a new American custom, the Saturday night bath.

Harley Procter was able to convince his associates to invest $11,000 in advertising in 1882. Though most advertising of the time consisted of small space, classified-style notices, Procter's notion was that larger space brought more attention, greater legitimacy for his products, and greater sales. He was right.

THE "IVORY" is a Laundry Soap, with all the fine qualities of a choice Toilet Soap, and is 99 44-100 per cent. pure.

Ladies will find this Soap especially adapted for washing laces, infants', clothing, silk hose, cleaning gloves and all articles of fine texture and delicate color, and for the varied uses about the house that daily arise, requiring the use of soap that is above the ordinary in quality.

For the Bath, Toilet, or Nursery it is preferred to most of the Soaps sold for toilet use, being purer and much more pleasant and effective and possessing all the desirable properties of the finest unadultered White Castile Soap. The Ivory Soap will "float."

The cakes are so shaped that they may be used entire for general purposes or divided with a stout thread (as illustrated) into two perfectly formed cakes, of convenient size for toilet use.

The price, compared to the quality and the size of the cakes, makes it the cheapest Soap for everybody for every want. TRY IT.

SOLD EVERYWHERE.

Source: David Cleary, *Great American Brands* (New York: Fairchild Publications, 1981), 174.

steam." Untroubled by the criticism that all breweries used a similar process, Hopkins was content with the fact that Schlitz would be the first to advertise it, thus forcing others into the weak position of echoing the claim. (An example of the Hopkins style of copywriting appears in Figure 1.7.)

A third important innovation, improved design, was introduced by the Calkins and Holden agency, formed in 1900. Advertising graphics of the time were rudimentary, and even after the advent of the professional advertising copywriter, advertisements were typically sent to the printer in rough form. Typography and layout were dictated by the time and materials available and the skill of the type composer rather than the design of the agency. Earnest Elmo Calkins, however, devoted himself to improving the look of advertising. Calkins had studied the principles of in-

FIGURE 1.8

An Ad by Earnest Elmo Calkins, a
Master of Copywriting and Design

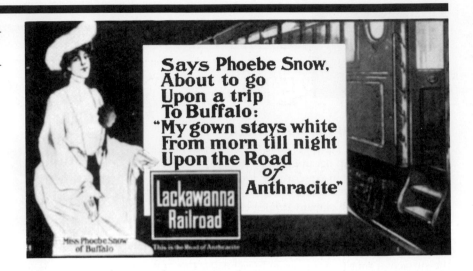

dustrial design and commercial art, designing advertisements to attract
and hold the eye.[14] The result: advertising that had a cleaner, more contemporary look (see Figure 1.8).

In 1915 one of the most widely discussed and celebrated ads of the
time appeared. The ad came to be known by its headline, "The Penalty
of Leadership," and it too represented an important new contribution to
the list of possible advertising alternatives. The ad made no product
claims and did not even mention the product (Cadillac) by name. The
writer, Theodore MacManus, described his intention as building the
impression that this product was to be preferred above all others. Mac-
Manus's contribution was called **atmosphere copy:** copy intended to surround the brand with an aura of desirability (see Figure 1.9).

The following year the J. Walter Thompson agency was purchased by
Stanley Resor. He soon married the highly respected copywriter Helen
Landsdowne, who contributed the **emulation style** to advertising prac-
tice. Under this principle, the advertising uses models that readers will
look up to or identify with, thus inducing them to buy the product.
Widely used today, this technique is seen in Landsdowne's work for
Woodbury's Facial Soap (see Figure 1.10).

A considerably more controversial technique appeared sporadically
during the period. Though many advertising people counseled against direct attacks on competitors or comparisons with them, the **comparative
approach** developed as an important and aggressive method for bringing
products to the consumer's attention. Raymond Rubicam used the comparative approach in his work for Postum in the early 1920s. However,
Rubicam was not the only one to use the approach: ads from an upstart
motor company asked readers to compare the Plymouth directly with its
competitors (see Figure 1.11).

These techniques taken together represent a considerable communications arsenal and a dramatic advance toward a body of practical alternatives for the solution of advertising problems. They seem to have developed quickly once the advertising business had established itself as an
independent enterprise. Later chapters will show that these techniques,

FIGURE 1.9

Atmosphere Copy: Surrounding a Brand with an Aura of Desirability

THE PENALTY OF LEADERSHIP

IN EVERY FIELD OF HUMAN ENDEAVOR · HE THAT IS FIRST MUST PERPETUALLY LIVE IN THE WHITE LIGHT OF PUBLICITY ❧ WHETHER THE LEADERSHIP BE VESTED IN A MAN OR IN A MANUFACTURED PRODUCT · EMULA TION AND ENVY ARE EVER AT WORK ❧ IN ART · IN LITERATURE · IN MUSIC · IN INDUSTRY · THE REWARD AND THE PUNISHMENT ARE ALWAYS THE SAME ❧ THE REWARD IS WIDESPREAD RECOGNITION · THE PUNISHMENT FIERCE DENIAL AND DETRACTION ❧ WHEN A MAN'S WORK BECOMES A STANDARD FOR THE WHOLE WORLD IT ALSO BECOMES A TARGET FOR THE SHAFTS OF THE ENVIOUS FEW ❧ IF HIS WORK IS MERELY MEDIOCRE HE WILL BE LEFT SEVERELY ALONE ❧ IF HE ACHIEVE A MASTERPIECE · IT WILL SET A MILLION TONGUES A·WAG GING ❧ JEALOUSY DOES NOT PROTRUDE ITS FORKED TONGUE AT THE ARTIST WHO PRODUCES A COMMON PLACE PAINTING ❧ WHATSOEVER YOU WRITE · OR PAINT · OR PLAY · OR SING · OR BUILD · NO ONE WILL STRIVE TO SURPASS OR TO SLANDER YOU · UNLESS YOUR WORK BE STAMPED WITH THE SEAL OF GENIUS ❧ LONG LONG AFTER A GREAT WORK OR A GOOD WORK HAS BEEN DONE · THOSE WHO ARE DISAPPOINTED OR ENVI OUS CONTINUE TO CRY OUT THAT IT CANNOT BE DONE ❧ SPITEFUL LITTLE VOICES IN THE DOMAIN OF ART WERE RAISED AGAINST OUR OWN WHISTLER AS A MOUNTEBANK · LONG AFTER THE BIG WORLD HAD ACCLAIM ED HIM ITS GREATEST ARTISTIC GENIUS ❧ MULTITUDES FLOCKED TO BAYREUTH TO WORSHIP AT THE MUSICAL SHRINE OF WAGNER · WHILE THE LITTLE GROUP OF THOSE WHOM HE HAD DETHRONED AND DISPLACED ARGUED ANGRILY THAT HE WAS NO MUSICIAN AT ALL ❧ THE LITTLE WORLD CONTINUED TO PROTEST THAT FULTON COULD NEVER BUILD A STEAMBOAT · WHILE THE BIG WORLD FLOCKED TO THE RIVER BANKS TO SEE HIS BOAT STEAM BY ❧ THE LEADER IS ASSAILED BECAUSE HE IS A LEADER · AND THE EFFORT TO EQUAL HIM IS MERELY ADDED PROOF OF THAT LEADERSHIP ❧ FAILING TO EQUAL OR TO EXCEL · THE FOLLOWER SEEKS TO DEPRECIATE AND TO DESTROY · BUT ONLY CONFIRMS ONCE MORE THE SUPERIORITY OF THAT WHICH HE STRIVES TO SUP PLANT ❧ THERE IS NOTHING NEW IN THIS ❧ IT IS AS OLD AS THE WORLD AND AS OLD AS THE HUMAN PASSIONS ENVY · FEAR · GREED · AMBITION AND THE DESIRE TO SURPASS ❧ AND IT ALL AVAILS NOTHING ❧ IF THE LEADER TRULY LEADS HE REMAINS - THE LEADER ❧ MASTER POET · MASTER PAINTER · MASTER WORKMAN · EACH IN HIS TURN IS ASSAILED · AND EACH HOLDS HIS LAURELS THROUGH THE AGES ❧ THAT WHICH IS GOOD OR GREAT MAKES ITSELF KNOWN · NO MATTER HOW LOUD THE CLAMOR OF DENIAL ❧ THAT WHICH DESERVES TO LIVE - LIVES

THIS TEXT APPEARED AS AN ADVERTISEMENT IN THE SATURDAY EVENING POST ❧ JANUARY 2ND, IN THE YEAR 1915 ❧ COPYRIGHT, CADILLAC MOTOR CAR DIVISION

Source: Used by permission of the Cadillac Motor Car Division of General Motors Corporation.

with a few additions and small refinements, form the central core of advertising creative strategy alternatives used in modern practice.

EARLY AUDIENCE AND EFFECTIVENESS RESEARCH

In addition to developments in the creative area, research became an important part of agency activities after the turn of the century. In 1900 a Records of Results department was established at Lord & Thomas. The department compiled the **rates of response** (through orders and coupon

FIGURE 1.10

How the Emulation Style Sold
Woodbury's Facial Soap

Source: Courtesy of The Andrew Jergens
Company, from the J. Walter Thompson
Company Archives.

redemption) to the ads of 600 clients in over 4,000 newspapers and magazines. The findings made it possible to evaluate the potential effectiveness of different periodicals as well as alternative advertising approaches.

In 1912 Stanley Resor commissioned a study of demographics and purchasing patterns, thus taking an important step toward understanding the consumer market and becoming a marketing as well as advertising advisor.[15] By 1919 Resor had established departments for marketing research, planning, and statistical investigations at J. Walter Thompson.

As the 1920s drew to a close, the advertising business had grown mightily. Advertising agencies had matured from merely commodity speculators in advertising space to the preparers of advertising campaigns based on research and a particular strategy.[16] Two important trade associations had been established: the Association of National Advertisers in 1911 and the American Association of Advertising Agencies in 1917. By this point the media also had become heavily dependent on advertising, with both newspapers and magazines generating about two-thirds of their income from advertising receipts.[17]

But agencies were not universally accepted. Major advertisers such as Royal Baking Powder, Singer sewing machines, and a number of patent medicines still preferred to handle their own advertising preparation and media placement. However, agencies were financially successful, leaving little doubt that the advertising agency had established itself in the American business scene, providing services that were both useful and increasingly essential. Furthermore, the advertising industry played an important and visible role in the war effort during World War I. Campaigns were directed to sell bonds, to recruit troops, to build worker morale, and to promote conservation of resources at home. One result of these patriotic efforts was to create broader understanding and more positive attitudes among the business community.[18]

THE GREAT DEPRESSION, NEW CONTROLS, AND WORLD WAR II, 1920–1946

The stock market crash of 1929 brought hardship for almost everyone, including the advertising industry. Advertising budgets proved easy targets for firms looking for ways to cut expenditures in hard times. Advertising expenditures dropped dramatically, hitting a low of $1.3 billion in 1933. This figure had been surpassed in 1915 and amounted to a mere 38 percent of the pre-Depression spending. (Examine the data in Exhibit 1.1 to appreciate the drama of this setback.) By the mid-1920s advertising had adopted the strategy of emphasizing benefits and satisfactions rather than merely product attributes.[19] But under the circumstances, such advertising appeals seemed to antagonize consumers.

The consumer movement, first established in the 1920s, grew increasingly influential during the late 1930s. It was aided by a suspicion of institutions generally, and its leaders struggled for regulation of advertising as well as other marketing practices. While the Federal Trade Commission had been established in 1914, it had no explicit power over advertising. This was remedied in 1938 by passage of the Wheeler-Lea Amendment

FIGURE 1.11

Chrysler Corporation Ads Using the Comparative Approach to Sell Plymouths

"Look at All Three!

BUT DON'T BUY ANY LOW-PRICED CAR UNTIL YOU'VE DRIVEN THE NEW PLYMOUTH WITH FLOATING POWER"

"It is my opinion that any new car without Patented Floating Power is obsolete."

THOUSANDS of people have been waiting expectantly until today before buying a new car. I hope that you are one of them.

Now that the new low-priced cars are here (including the new Plymouth which will be shown on Saturday) I urge you to carefully *compare* values.

This is the time for you to "shop" and buy wisely. Don't make a deposit on any automobile until you've actually had a demonstration.

It is my opinion that the automobile industry as a whole has never offered such values to the public.

In the new Plymouth we have achieved more than I had ever dared to hope for. If you had told me two years ago that such a big, powerful, beautiful automobile could be sold at the astonishing prices we will announce on Saturday. . . I'd have said it was absolutely impossible.

I have spent my life building fine cars. But no achievement in my career has given me the deep-down satisfaction

A STATEMENT BY WALTER P. CHRYSLER

that I derive from the value you get in this 1932 Plymouth. To me, its outstanding feature is Floating Power. We already know how the public feels about this. Last summer it was news, but today it is an established engineering achievement.

It is my opinion, and I think that of leading engineering authorities, that any new car without Floating Power is obsolete. Drive a Plymouth with Patented Floating Power, and note its utter lack of vibration . . . then drive a car with old-fashioned engine mountings and you will understand what I mean. *There's absolutely no comparison.*

We have made the Plymouth a much larger automobile. It is a BIG car. We have increased its power, lengthened the wheelbase and greatly improved its beauty.

In my opinion you will find the new Plymouth the easiest riding car you have ever driven. Yet with all these improvements we have been able to lower prices.

Again let me urge you, go and see the new Plymouth with Floating Power on Saturday. Be sure to look at all THREE low-priced cars and don't buy *any* until you do. That is the way to get the most for your money.

FIRST SHOWING NEXT SATURDAY, APRIL 2nd, AT DESOTO, DODGE AND CHRYSLER DEALERS

Source: Courtesy of the Chrysler Corporation.

empowering the FTC to police "deceptive acts and practices in commerce." In the next two years the FTC handed down 18 injunctions against major advertisers and agencies, which left Madison Avenue shaken.[20]

A good deal of the pressure to clean up advertising came from popular reaction against the usually exaggerated and often false claims of patent medicine and cosmetics advertisers. The advertising industry itself was concerned about these problems as well. *Printer's Ink*, the leading business publication of the advertising industry, drafted and circulated a model advertising statute in 1911. The law was designed to penalize deceptive advertising by making it a misdemeanor at the state level. The law was greeted with enthusiasm by advertising groups across the country, many of whom worked for the adoption of the model statute in their home states. The Associated Advertising Clubs of America formed a national committee as a watchdog for truth in advertising, and by 1914, over 100 local committees had been formed across the country. These committees evolved into what is now known as the Better Business Bureaus.[21]

In the meantime, a novel commercial medium had emerged. Radio—first dismissed as a gimmick, later considered too invasive to be allowed to carry advertising messages—grew rapidly and became an important medium. With an estimated 4,000 receivers in 1925, by 1930 there were 13,000. By 1935 the number had more than doubled. While advertisers experimented with sponsorships and various types of show formats, radio grew to surpass magazines in advertising revenues in 1938.[22]

Though the consumer movement continued to grow throughout the 1930s and early 1940s, it was eclipsed at that point by the country's entry into World War II. The industry again formed a War Advertising Council and contributed nearly a billion dollars' worth of space and time to the war effort (see Figure 1.12). Though advertising expenditures as a whole grew during World War II, they peaked at $2.9 billion in 1945 (still half a billion below the 1929 mark of $3.4 billion).[23]

POSTWAR EXPANSION

EXHIBIT 1.1

Advertising Expenditures as a Percentage of GNP, Selected Years

YEAR	ADVERTISING EXPENDITURE (in millions)	PERCENTAGE OF GNP
1900	$ 542	2.9%
1909	1,142	3.5
1915	1,302	3.4
1920	2,935	3.3
1929	3,426	3.3
1935	1,690	2.3
1945	2,875	1.4
1950	5,700	2.0
1955	9,194	2.3
1960	11,960	2.4
1965	15,255	2.2
1970	19,600	2.0
1975	27,900	1.8
1980	53,500	2.0
1985	94,750	2.4

Sources: Daniel Pope, *The Making of Modern Advertising* (New York: Basic Books, 1983), 23; U.S. Department of Commerce, Bureau of the Census, *Statistical Abstract of the United States, 1986;* and *Marketing & Media Decisions*, February 1987, 70.

The combination of relief from wartime austerity, a stepped-up economy, the baby boom, and a change from urban to suburban life-styles powered advertising to dramatic growth in the 1950s. While the basic services—and, to a large extent, the basic advertising strategies—had been established by the end of the 1920s, major new developments occurred in the postwar period.

In 1950 television emerged as a commercial medium. Its quick and nearly universal acceptance was to change the character of advertising profoundly. Television, of course, was only the first of the major advances in mass media technology that have shaped the current world of advertising. Communications satellites have made worldwide transmission of data and information a commonplace event and enable the printing and distribution of a national newspaper like *USA Today* from numerous regional locations. Combined with cable television transmission, satellite technology has allowed the growth of "superstations," which far exceed the normal limits of television broadcasting to reach audiences across the country. Both the wide variety of viewing options available to cable users and the innovation of the video cassette recorder have allowed viewers more choice and more control of their media use, as well as offering advertisers greater selectivity in reaching specific audiences.

Agency services and research continued to expand in the 1950s. At the same time, alternatives to the commission system became widespread, and alternatives to the traditional advertising agency became widely available. The brand management concept and marketing orientation were widely adopted as the organizational concepts for advertiser firms. These developments laid increased stress on the productivity of advertising and promotional activities. New and powerful personalities, including David Ogilvy, Rosser Reeves, Leo Burnett, William Bernbach, Mary Wells, and Jerry Della Femina, influenced advertising thought and marketing planning. In addition, the period saw the first full-fledged advertising

FIGURE 1.12

Wartime Advertising: Stimulating Patriotism, Encouraging a Spirit of Cooperation

agency involvement with a United States presidential election campaign conducted through broadcast advertising when Dwight D. Eisenhower committed himself to the guidance of Rosser Reeves in 1952. Since then, political candidates at all levels have relied heavily on advertising to wage a successful campaign.

Advertising techniques of course changed as well, reflecting technological and social change as well as changing business conditions. The 1950s saw the emergence of David Ogilvy's brand image school, followed in the 1960s by imaginative breakthroughs from Doyle Dane Bernbach leading to the "creative revolution" of the mid-1960s. This period was marked by innovative and exciting advertising, which many feel has rarely been equaled since. Mary Wells, a luminary of the period, achieved considerable celebrity not only for her advertising campaigns but for the considerable salary of $250,000 per year.

EXHIBIT 1.2

Timeline of Advertising
Development

1843	Volney Palmer opens first ad agency in Philadelphia.
1869	George Rowell publishes *Rowell's American Newspaper Dictionary*.
1876	N. W. Ayer & Son offers fixed commission to advertisers.
1878	J. Walter Thompson agency founded.
1880	John Wanamaker hires John E. Powers, the first full-time advertising copywriter.
1882	Ivory Soap introduced by Procter & Gamble after manufacturing accident results in too much air in soap mixture.
1893	Charles Austin Bates hired as first full-time agency copywriter.
1904	John E. Kennedy hired by Albert Lasker at Lord & Thomas.
1906	Claude Hopkins joins Lord & Thomas.
1914	Federal Trade Commission established by U.S. Congress.
1915	Theodore MacManus establishes "atmosphere advertising" with "Penalty of Leadership" ad for Cadillac.
1922	First radio ads air on New York City station.
1931	George Gallup at Young & Rubicam publishes first survey of magazine readership.
1933	Ad expenditures drop to $1.3 million, 38 percent of the 1929 expenditure.
1938	Radio passes magazines in total ad revenues.
1938	Wheeler-Lea amendment to Federal Trade Commission Act gives agency the power to police deceptive practices in commerce.
1950	Television emerges as an advertising medium.
1951	David Ogilvy's "Man in the Hathaway shirt" ad appears in *The New Yorker*.
1952	Rosser Reeves hired to advise and plan Dwight D. Eisenhower's presidential campaign.
1960	Doyle Dane Bernbach agency creates the "Think small" campaign for Volkswagen.
1965	The "creative revolution" begins.
1969	Mary Wells becomes the highest-paid ad executive at $250,000 per year.
1970	U.S. Congress bans cigarette advertising from broadcast media.
1972	"The Positioning Era" published in *Advertising Age*.
1986	Saatchi & Saatchi Compton buys Ted Bates Worldwide to form $7.6 billion mega-agency.

Many parity products in the package goods field brought a new type of advertising and marketing thinking reflected in the 1972 publication of "The Positioning Era," a set of articles in *Advertising Age*. This school of thought suggested that the brand image era was over and that a more sophisticated understanding of consumers, and how they evaluated products relative to competitors, was necessary.

The widespread use of the computer has allowed more specific analysis of audience, sales, marketing, and consumer behavior data. With greater information and control has come more sophisticated marketing efforts aimed at smaller consumer niches, while at the same time greater control and understanding of marketing variables has led to the increasing internationalization of marketing efforts, at least by major advertisers.

Innovations in technology and creative strategy were not the only changes in the business, however. Recently, agencies have also followed the trend among other large businesses to merge and expand into new spheres of operation, some becoming giant conglomerates in the process.

In addition, the constantly evolving fashions and mores of American society have led to profound changes not only in the ways products are advertised, but in the products themselves. In 1970 broadcast advertising for cigarettes was banned. It appears quite likely that in the near future all cigarette advertising will be prohibited, and equally likely that contraceptive advertising on television will become commonplace.

All of these developments have had a profound impact on modern advertising practice and will be discussed in some depth in the following chapters.

SUMMARY

The advertising agency business developed because of a host of factors, including declining costs of transportation and communication; urbanization; techological advances, especially in printing; and head-to-head competition among branded goods. Taken together, these developments created a profit opportunity for individuals with expertise in media rates and skill in price negotiations. As the commitment to a manufacturing economy grew, advertisers demanded and agencies supplied increased expertise in creating advertisements and understanding and predicting markets. Competitive pressures led to the institutionalization of the commission system of agency compensation, very much along the lines practiced by F. Wayland Ayer in the late nineteenth century. By the 1920s, the mass communication media depended upon advertising for the bulk of their revenue. The demands of advertisers and the development of agencies led to the foundation of schools of advertising thought, which formed the nucleus of advertising theory. In addition, advertising embraced both social science and marketing theory, both of which strengthened and broadened agency services and advertising practice.

Advertising weathered the pressure of reformers, and with the worst abuses curbed, emerged both improved and hardier. It readily absorbed the new radio medium and has grown steadily, generally following the growth of the gross national product.

Mass communication technology has continued to be a force shaping the advertising industry, as first television, then satellite communication, computers, cablecasting, and video cassette recorders have become central parts of American life. These innovations have both influenced the behavior of consumers and modified the ways advertisers try to reach their audiences. In addition, changing social attitudes and values have not only created markets for different types of products and services, but have changed advertising practices as well.

YOU MAKE THE DECISION

CHANGE AND DEVELOPMENT IN ADVERTISING

Visit the library and select a consumer advertisement from a publication that is at least 15 years old. Make a photocopy of the ad. Either at the library or from your own newspapers or magazines, find a current ad from the same product category and make a copy of it as well.

After giving both ads some thought, write a one-page paper comparing the two. Consider the specifics below:

- In general, do the ads seem similar or different?

- What are the most important changes reflected in the ads?

- Are they changes in products, people, usage, style, or advertising technique?

- Do the ads attempt to speak to the same consumer group?

- Does the recent ad employ more sophisticated advertising techniques than the older ad?

- Which ad do you think might have been more effective? Why?

■ ■ ■

QUESTIONS FOR DISCUSSION

1. What incentives encouraged the use of advertising agencies by publishers and advertisers?

2. What important innovation did F. Wayland Ayer bring to the advertising business?

3. How did the demands of large advertisers change the roles of advertising agencies?

4. What is the competitive significance of the preemptive advertising claim?

5. How does reason-why copy differ from the emulation style of Helen Landsdowne?

6. In addition to developments in creative strategy and new advertising media, what other agency service was established during the early period of agency development?

7. What does the effect of the Depression indicate about the nature and effectiveness of advertising?

8. How was advertising used during World Wars I and II? What effect do you think this might have had on popular acceptance of advertising?

9. Name two major social or business changes that have come about since World War II. How have they affected advertising?

10. Identify three important changes in advertising in the last five years which have come about due to innovation in mass communication technology.

NOTES

1. Irving Shapiro, *Dictionary of Marketing Terms*, 3d ed. (Totowa, N.J.: Littlefield, Adams & Co., 1981).

2. Daniel Boorstin, *Democracy and Its Discontents* (New York: Vintage Books, 1975). Boorstin's book presents an interesting discussion of the relationship of advertising and news in colonial America.

3. Daniel Pope, *The Making of Modern Advertising* (New York: Basic Books, 1983), 36.

4. Vincent Norris, "Advertising History—According to the Textbooks," *Journal of Advertising*, 9:3 (1980), 3–11.

5. Otis Pease, *The Responsibilities of American Advertising* (New Haven, Conn.: Yale University Press, 1958), 3.

6. Stephen Fox, *The Mirror Makers* (New York: William Morrow, 1984), 113.

7. Ibid., 14.

8. Pope, *Modern Advertising*, 129.

9. Quentin Schultze, "An Honorable Place: The Quest for Professional Advertising Education 1900–1917," *Business History Review*, 56:1 (1982), 16–32.

10. Fox, *Mirror Makers*, 30–31.

11. Pope, *Modern Advertising*, 33.

12. T. J. Jackson Lears, "From Salvation to Self-Realization," in *The Culture of Consumption*, ed. Stephen Fox and T. J. Jackson Lears (New York: Pantheon Books, 1983).

13. Frank Rowsome, Jr., *They Laughed When I Sat Down* (New York: Bonanza Books, 1959), 38.

14. Fox, *Mirror Makers*, 43–44.

15. William Leiss, Stephen Kline and Sut Jhally, *Social Communication in Advertising* (New York: Methuen, 1986), 108.

16. Gordon Miracle, "An Historical Analysis to Explain the Evolution of Advertising Agency Services," *Journal of Advertising*, 6:3 (1977), 24–28.

17. Pope, *Modern Advertising*, 30.

18. Roland Marchand, *Advertising the American Dream* (Berkeley: University of California Press, 1985), 5–6.

19. Richard Pollay, "The Subsiding Sizzle," *Journal of Marketing*, 49 (Summer 1985), 24–37.

20. Fox, *Mirror Makers*, 168–169.

21. Ibid., 208.

22. Ibid., 162.

23. Ibid., 170.

SUGGESTED READINGS

Atwan, Robert, Donald McQuade, and John Wright. *Edsels, Luckies, and Frigidaires: Advertising the American Way*. New York: Delta, 1979.

Gunther, John. *Taken at the Flood: The Story of Albert D. Lasker*. New York: Harper & Row, 1960.

Holland, Donald. *Volney B. Palmer (1799–1864): The Nation's First Advertising Agency Man*. Minneapolis: AEJ Publications, 1976.

Hower, Ralph. *History of an Advertising Agency: N. W. Ayer & Son at Work, 1869–1939*. Cambridge, Mass.: Harvard University Press, 1939.

Pollay, Richard. *Information Sources in Advertising History*. Westport, Conn.: Greenwood Press, 1978.

Presbrey, Frank. *History and Development of Advertising*. Garden City, N.Y.: Doubleday, 1929.

Rowell, George. *Forty Years an Advertising Agent*. New York: Printers Ink, 1906.

Rowsome, Frank. *They Laughed When I Sat Down: An Informal History of Advertising in Words and Pictures*. New York: McGraw-Hill, 1959.

Wood, James. *The Story of Advertising*. New York: Ronald Press, 1958.

ADVERTISERS AND ADVERTISING AGENCIES

Key Terms

national advertising
local advertising
cooperative advertising
corporate advertising
public service advertising
business-to-business advertising
classified advertising
direct response advertising
full-service agency
account executive
advertising plan
creative strategy
media planner
brand manager
advertising manager
agency billings
conflict of interest
house agency
creative boutique
media buying service
commission system
agency network

Learning Objectives

To list the major types and purposes of advertising

To describe the functions of an advertising agency

To analyze the roles of advertising management

To outline the reasons for using an advertising agency

To discuss the alternatives to advertising agencies

To explain how agencies are paid

During the Super Bowl broadcast in January 1984 a commercial, styled after George Orwell's novel *1984*, announced the introduction of the Apple Macintosh computer. Directed by British film director Ridley Scott, the commercial reportedly cost over $300,000 to produce and quickly became one of the most talked-about television commercials of the decade. Apple was said to have sold 50,000 units in the first few weeks after the product's introduction. The advertising industry recognized the ad with a Clio Award for the best overall commercial of the year.

The spot was the work of Chiat/Day Advertising of Los Angeles. The agency was the envy of the advertising community, not only for its outstanding work but for its innovative and interested clients, like Apple Computer and Nike Sports, who seemed willing to take the risk to develop advertising that was exciting and new.

Less than a year and a half later, the agency had lost both accounts. How did this happen? There are a number of answers, which illustrate several important points about the agency/client relationship.

▪ Despite rather heavy advertising spending—estimated at an annual $50 million—Apple was unable to crack IBM's strong grasp on the business computer market.

▪ Apple's advertising theme, "the computer for the rest of us," was illustrated with unconventional businesses and life-styles that didn't speak to the majority of business users. An advertising strategy emphasizing simplicity may not have been the right choice for business people accustomed to thinking in terms of complex systems.

▪ A bitter fight inside Apple led to the formation of two factions: those who backed company founder Steve Jobs and those who favored President/CEO John Scully. Scully came from PepsiCo, where he had worked closely with the Batten Barton Durstine & Osborn agency. Jobs had been directly involved with Chiat/Day on the development of the Macintosh campaign. By summer of 1985, Scully fired Jobs, and the following year Apple had a new ad agency: BBDO.

Agencies and clients are seldom bound together by long-term contracts. Advertising can quickly change from being the visible symbol and rallying point of a company's energies and aspirations to being an anachronistic and embarrassing reminder of earlier mistakes. In the Apple–Chiat/Day situation, major changes in management, strategy, and market conditions seemed to make the agency switch inevitable—despite the fact that Chiat/Day had produced some of the most dramatic—and, by some measures, the most effective—commercials in recent memory.

Source: Based on *Adweek*, "Chiat/Day Clings to Apple," January 20, 1986; "Core Concern: Apple Reborn," May 26, 1986; and "Life after Apple," May 26, 1986.

INTRODUCTION

This chapter will explore the roles of two of the most important participants in the advertising business: the advertiser and the advertising agency. The roles of these two participants are represented by the first two steps in the communications model pictured in Figure 1.1. Advertisers, the source of advertising messages, often choose organizations with specialized skills and abilities to translate their intended messages into advertisements and commercials. This chapter will examine source characteristics and intentions, as well as specialized abilities of translators.

The chapter will begin by describing some different types of advertising before going on to a discussion of the way advertisers and agencies are organized. After reading the chapter, you should have an understanding of the relationship between these two groups and the areas of responsibility of each in the advertising process.

TYPES OF ADVERTISING

Chapter 1 defined advertising as a form of persuasive communication that is nonpersonal, paid for by an identified sponsor, and carried in the mass media. This general definition covers many types of advertising. Advertising may be categorized using many different classification schemes. For example, it is possible to consider advertising according to the medium in which it appears or the audience it is intended to reach. Advertising can be conceived of in terms of two basic variables: 1) the scope, or scale, of the advertising effort, and 2) the purpose of the message.

The *scope* of the advertising refers to how widely the message is circulated. Is the advertising intended for large geographic regions, for example, the midwest, southern, and north central regions, or the entire country? This is considered national advertising. Is the message intended for people in a specific metropolitan area or locality? This is local advertising. Advertising that runs in different countries—often with a similar theme, though written in the native language of the home country—is called international advertising. These will be discussed later in the chapter.

The *purpose* of the advertising depends on the intention of the advertiser, as suggested in the table below. Each type of advertising is explained in detail in the text.

TYPE	PURPOSE
Corporate	To develop positive public impression for company or institution
Public service	To inform/persuade public of importance of problem or issue
Business-to-business	To offer products or services for use by other businesses
Classified	Used by small sellers to offer goods or services to small consumer groups
Direct response	To generate immediate sales or inquiries

FIGURE 2.1

National Advertising: Stimulating
Demand for a Product or Service

EXPANSIVE.

Red Lion Inns and American Express. You've Got Our Word.™

Whenever business calls in the wide-open country of the West, call a hotel with expansive services that reflect the surroundings. A Red Lion Inn. You'll find us in 38 Western cities waiting to warm you with a comforting atmosphere. Spacious rooms. Airy restaurants. Fresh native cuisine. Cozy lounges. And Red Lion's special brand of regional hospitality, big as all outdoors. Just call Red Lion at 1-800-547-8010 for a stay that will broaden your horizons next time your travels take you out West.

Expansive service with the American Express® Card.

Your Red Lion welcome will be even warmer with the American Express Card. Because even if you arrive late, an American Express® Card Assured Reservation will keep your room waiting til check-out time the next day. Just remember that if your plans change, you must cancel before 6:00 pm hotel time (4:00 pm for resorts) or you'll be billed for the first night. Be sure to keep your cancellation number in case you need to refer to it. And if you don't have the American Express Card, call 1-800-THE-CARD.

So the next time you're traveling out West, rely on the expansive services of Red Lion Inns and American Express. You've got our word.

Don't leave home without it.®

© 1986 American Express Travel Related Services Company, Inc.

NATIONAL ADVERTISING

National advertising (or general advertising) offers a product or service to the general consumer audience across the country. The advertising is most often signed by the manufacturer or provider of the product or service, though this is not always the case. The term *national advertising* can be somewhat misleading in that it may be applied to advertising campaigns that do not literally appear everywhere around the nation, but that are seen in more than one or two regions of the country (see Figure 2.1). National advertising is usually aimed at stimulating demand for the product or service.

FIGURE 2.2

Local Advertising: Projecting a
Certain Image

SPEEDY. JAZZY. UPBEAT. ART TO WEAR.

FROM LEONARD, A NERVY, MULTICOLOR, TWO-PIECE ABSTRACTION: THE LETTERS OF HIS NAME (JUST A BIT SIXTIES) ON BLACK COTTON. FULL BLOUSE
OVER ELASTIC-WAIST, STRAIGHT SKIRT. FOR 6 TO 14 SIZES, $20.00 THE DESIGNER SALON

WILSHIRE AT RODEO   PALM DESERT TOWN CENTER

Source: Courtesy of Bonwit Teller.

LOCAL ADVERTISING

By contrast, **local advertising** (also called retail advertising) is intended
to direct consumers to a specific location to obtain the product or service
advertised. Local advertising often attempts to persuade consumers that
nationally advertised items can be purchased most conveniently or economically at specific outlets. It may also be used to project a desirable
impression of an outlet, such as a fashion boutique or department store
(as shown in Figure 2.2). Local advertising tends to dominate the media
(such as newspapers and radio) that reach specific communities, and tends

Source: Courtesy of the Firestone Tire & Rubber Co., Akron, OH, © 1986.

to emphasize price more than does national advertising. Most often local advertising is not prepared by advertising agencies, for reasons that will be discussed in the following chapter.

COOPERATIVE ADVERTISING

Sometimes a manufacturer sets up a special program to encourage dealers to advertise the firm's products. Often the manufacturer allows a local dealer a certain amount of money for advertising, based on the quantity of goods the dealer purchases. These programs, known as **cooperative** (or co-op) **advertising,** are guided by strict rules about the type of advertising to be done and usually are quite specific about the emphasis to be given the manufacturer's products (see Figure 2.3).

Some programs require that manufacturer-prepared ads must be run to receive credit. The manufacturer-prepared ads allow ample space for a local dealer signature and logotype. When the local dealer supplies evidence that the ads have been run, the manufacturer credits or reimburses the dealer for a specified amount of the advertising expenditure. Though details of the programs vary widely, dealers are often reimbursed 50 percent of their cost for an approved ad.

INTERNATIONAL ADVERTISING

In the past ten years the great growth of advertising has come outside the United States. Many U.S. firms have either become multinational firms or have greatly expanded their product or service marketing abroad. While not, strictly speaking, a different type of advertising, international advertising has had a number of important effects on the advertising industry. Multinational firms often seek advertising agencies with the capabilities to create and place their advertising in the major world markets in which they do business. Some firms engage one agency to handle their international advertising and another for domestic work.

There is a continuing debate in international advertising over whether advertising should be created locally, within the culture it is designed to communicate with, or if a successful advertising theme can cross international boundaries. Figure 2.4 shows the American Express "Do you know me?" campaign, which has been run successfully in 15 countries.

CORPORATE ADVERTISING

Corporate advertising (or institutional) is designed to build good will. This type of advertising is sometimes aimed at a general audience to explain a company or institution and to suggest its positive attributes.

Corporate advertising has traditionally served one of three goals. Probably the most important goal has been *image building*. This traditional form is designed to build consumer awareness and good will. A second goal of corporate advertising is *financial relations*, aimed at informing and building confidence on Wall Street and among stockholders and potential investors, thus ensuring financial security and independence. A third, more recent goal has been *advocacy*, a type of advertising that promotes a firm's viewpoint on a controversial issue. Extremely important in the early 1980s, advocacy advertising is used less today.

A growing trend in corporate advertising involves the *corporate umbrella* concept. Usually aimed at consumers, this type of corporate advertising is designed to pave the way for sales of the company's brands. A firm strengthens new or weak brands by relating them to established, successful ones under the corporation's "umbrella."

Although corporate advertising amounts to only about 2 percent of the total advertising expenditure, it is an important combination of advertising and public relations. Exhibit 2.1 lists the top ten spenders in corporate advertising.

The advertisement in Figure 2.5 is aimed at the financial community to inform and convince them of the reasons to invest in the company. The

FIGURE 2.4

"Do You Know Me?"

This advertising campaign by American Express has been used successfully in 15 countries.

PERLMAN: (HE PLAYS SOME RAGTIME)

Do you know me?

I've taken ragtime to Vienna.

(HE PLAYS A LITTLE BEETHOVEN)

And Beethoven to Kalamazoo. And wherever I travel, I use the American Express Card.

For the same reason I use a Stradivarius.

ANNCR: To apply for a Card,

look for this display wherever the Card is welcomed.

PERLMAN: The American Express Card. (FLOURISH ON THE VIOLIN) Don't leave home without it.

EXHIBIT 2.1

Top 10 Leaders in Corporate Advertising, 1985 (in thousands of dollars)

	Seven-Media Totals	Magazines	Newspaper Supplements	Network Television	Spot Television	Network Radio	Outdoor	Cable-TV Networks
1 Ford Motor Co.	$ 50,811.8	$16,582.1	$ 420.0	$ 29,765.1	$ 341.5	$1,889.6	$ 94.6	$1,718.9
2 AT&T	44,309.0	12,929.2	—	22,490.4	2,131.5	6,347.4	—	410.5
3 General Motors	35,800.2	18,531.7	319.5	11,360.4	4,526.9	706.4	31.2	324.1
4 IBM Corp.	26,860.1	7,084.4	1,586.5	17,384.0	681.7	—	—	123.5
5 Xerox Corp.	21,829.0	210.6	—	21,044.3	88.5	—	—	485.6
6 GTE Corp.	17,666.8	5,755.0	—	8,040.5	3,696.8	—	25.6	148.9
7 Chrysler Corp.	13.954.8	3,621.2	210.0	9,012.6	1,011.0	—	—	100.0
8 ITT Corp.	13,609.7	4,890.4	—	8,383.7	188.9	—	3.2	143.5
9 Prudential Insurance Co. of America	13,180.6	3,007.2	—	9,680.0	374.2	—	—	119.2
10 Anheuser-Busch Cos. Inc.	12,196.5	2,436.1	—	8,379.9	1,065.1	—	9.8	305.6
Total	$250,218.5	$75,047.9	$2,536.0	$145,540.9	$14,106.1	$8,943.4	$164.4	$3,879.8

Source: Reprinted with permission from the December 1986 issue of the *Public Relations Journal.* Copyright 1986 by the Public Relations Society of America.

FIGURE 2.5

How McKesson Uses Corporate Advertising to Inform

Source: Courtesy of McKesson Corporation.

ad is not designed to sell the firm's products or services, but rather to assure continued operation of the organization.[1]

PUBLIC SERVICE ADVERTISING

Public service advertising has some similarity to corporate advertising in that it does not attempt to sell products. Rather, it is intended to promote noncontroversial causes, such as the prevention of forest fires or the curbing of drunk drivers (see Figure 2.6). Public service ads, and the media space or time for them to appear, are donated by the advertising industry. The campaigns are designed and coordinated by a volunteer organization, the Advertising Council.

BUSINESS-TO-BUSINESS ADVERTISING

Business-to-business advertising is the means by which one business promotes its goods or services to another. It is known by many names: some writers refer to it as "business advertising," and others occasionally (and inaccurately) call it "industrial advertising." In fact, business-to-business advertising is divided into three parts—trade, industrial, and professional—depending on the intended audience. Business-to-business ads for each kind of audience are exhibited in Figure 2.7.

Trade advertising is advertising directed to wholesalers, retailers, and others who form the link between manufacturers and buyers of products. Marketers use this form of advertising to inform these groups of special promotions and selling incentives. For example, a manufacturer about to begin the introduction of a new food product needs to communicate with those who buy food products for grocery stores. The manufacturer is likely to place trade advertising in special periodicals such as *Supermarket Business*, which circulates to grocery store buyers, in the hope of convincing readers to stock the new product.

The industrial advertiser may have a product, such as ball bearings or an electric motor, that might become a component part of some other consumer appliance, such as a washing machine or refrigerator. Industrial advertising also encompasses advertising for goods that do not ordinarily reach the average consumer directly. For example, a supplier of road maintenance equipment advertises to reach those who buy such equipment for cities and housing construction.

Professional advertising is used to communicate with decision makers in professional fields about products and services. Doctors are told of new medications and equipment, lawyers are offered office management systems and legal research tools, and so forth.

The nature of business-to-business advertising is that it serves to introduce goods and services to potential users in business, industry, and the professions. These goods or services are often very expensive or purchased in very great numbers. For this reason, advertising is usually less important in business buying decisions than are other factors that affect the buying decision, such as price and personal selling. Nonetheless, while not a huge investment, business and industrial advertising remains an important tool for these firms to communicate with potential buyers and to build brand name familiarity.

FIGURE 2.6

Public Service Advertising:
Promoting the Public Good

This Stevie Wonder poster was the
winner of an advertising competition
that sought an eye-opening poster to
help promote the Reader's Digest
Don't Drive and Drink College
Scholarship Challenge in 16,000 U.S.
high schools during 1986. The
challenge, sponsored by the Reader's
Digest Foundation, offered $500,000
in college scholarships to students
who conducted the best sober-
drinking programs.

Source: Courtesy of the Reader's Digest Foundation.

CLASSIFIED ADVERTISING

Classified advertising consists of short, simple messages usually placed
by individuals or small businesses. Traditionally, this advertising has
been placed in newspapers and has provided a very important financial

FIGURE 2.7

Business-to-Business Advertising: Telling Business about Business

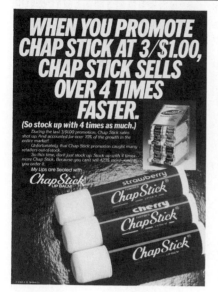

This trade ad for Chap Stick encourages retailers to stock the product.

This example of professional advertising ran in *Architectural Digest* and was aimed at architects.

This example of industrial advertising promotes the Okidata printer to business firms.

Source: Courtesy of A. H. Robins Consumer Products Division.

Source: Courtesy of John Watson Landscape Illumination.

Source: Courtesy of OKIDATA, an Oki America Company.

mainstay to the newspaper medium. However, some magazines and cable television operations also offer classified advertising.

Classified ads usually propose a specific transaction rather than offering a range of goods or services. The medium has traditionally set up the categories, or classifications, within which the ads are grouped. Classified advertising is rarely an important communications tool for large-scale advertisers.

DIRECT RESPONSE ADVERTISING

Direct response advertising is designed to urge the receiver toward an immediate purchase. For example, direct response ads on television may offer a special purchase to viewers who call a telephone number and provide their charge card number. This kind of advertising contrasts with more typical television advertising, which may provide information about a product or give a general admonition to "look for it in the frozen food section of your supermarket." Direct response advertising calls for an immediate action (usually a purchase) from the prospect, and may be carried by any medium. Figure 2.8 shows an example of a direct response ad.

While direct response advertising may be carried by any medium, direct mail is the most common. The telephone is the second most important direct response medium, and television is becoming increasingly important. At least one observer estimates that direct response will emerge as the major force in television advertising of this decade.[2]

FIGURE 2.8

Direct Response Advertising: Eliciting an Immediate Response

This highly successful print advertisement for The Franklin Mint's *Golden Caribbean Necklace* illustrates the company's consistent use of innovative direct response techniques. The ad, which appeared in prestigious fashion magazines such as *VOGUE* and *ELLE*, was produced by The Franklin Mint's in-house advertising agency, one of the largest in the world.

Money. Always in fashion.

It's only natural that the world's largest private mint should create the most spectacular example of the richest new look in fashion jewelry. The Golden Caribbean Necklace.

From The Franklin Mint—creator of the world's most beautiful coins. And that's just what these are. Real coins from the Caribbean. Uncirculated for a fresh new look and generously covered with pure 24 karat gold.

Fourteen fabulously genuine coins in all, many originally created by The Franklin Mint. Depicting some of the most romantic symbols of the tropics. And all fashionably displayed on a luxurious 18-inch chain.

Wonderfully versatile and affordably priced at $150. Available exclusively from The Franklin Mint, Franklin Center, PA 19091.

THE GOLDEN CARIBBEAN NECKLACE

- - - ORDER FORM - - -

Please mail by September 30, 1986.

The Franklin Mint
Franklin Center, Pennsylvania 19091
Please accept my order for *The Golden Caribbean Necklace.*

I need send no money now. I will be billed in five equal monthly installments of $30.* each, with the first payable in advance of shipment.
Plus my state sales tax.

SIGNATURE _____ ALL ORDERS ARE SUBJECT TO ACCEPTANCE

MR/MRS/MISS _____ PLEASE PRINT CLEARLY

ADDRESS _____

CITY, STATE, ZIP _____
79

BY THE FRANKLIN MINT

Source: © 1987 FM. Reprinted by permission of The Franklin Mint.

AGENCY SERVICES AND FUNCTIONS

As Chapter 1 pointed out, advertising agencies evolved to provide specialized information and services to marketers. While the total array of services offered varies from one agency to another, three service areas are central to the agency business. They include account service, message formulation and development (often called creative services), and media planning and buying. To be considered a **full-service agency,** an advertising agency must offer at least these services.[3] Most full-service agencies offer additional services as well, including research services, marketing consultation, sales promotion consultation, and, increasingly, public relations and direct marketing services. When a client firm wants services in addition to basic ones, these additional services are usually contracted for at negotiated rates. The basic services are usually paid for through the commission system (discussed later in this chapter).

The advertising agency usually works with the advertiser to prepare an **advertising plan,** which is a detailed, written program describing how advertising efforts are to be carried out during the planning period. The advertising plan usually covers a year and includes specification of the advertising objectives, how much is to be spent, who is to be reached, what the intended message is, and what media will be used to carry the message.

ACCOUNT SERVICES

The **account executive** is an agency employee who serves as the liaison between the advertiser, or client firm, and the others who do specialized work at the advertising agency. In addition to a grasp of the principles of effective creative and media work, account executives are expected to have special expertise in marketing and an intimate understanding of the client firm's industry and products. This background perspective allows them to discuss intelligently the client's marketing plans and the agency's capabilities within the scope of competitors' activities and prevailing market conditions. Account executives define, plan, and carry out the advertising plan developed by the agency. They usually play a role in establishing the objectives for the advertising campaign. Depending on the nature and size of the client's business, an account executive might also be involved in writing a marketing plan for a product, commissioning market research, or simply supervising the preparation of ads and buying of media for a plan already formulated by the client firm. Groups of account executives are managed by an account supervisor. While in a small agency in a city the size of Denver an account executive might be responsible for numerous small to medium-sized accounts, a large automotive account in Detroit would have numerous account executives assigned to it.

CREATIVE SERVICES

Creative services involve the formulation of the advertising **creative strategy,** a policy or guiding principle that specifies the general nature and character of messages in the advertising campaign. The creative staff is also responsible for developing the advertising message itself and supervising its production as print advertisements or broadcast commercials. Most often an agency creative department is made up of copywriters and art directors. With direction supplied by the client firm, through the account executive, the creative team formulates the creative strategy. After client approval, the creative team translates the strategy into execution in the production of advertisements and commercials. While most agencies employ specialists responsible for obtaining competitive bids, maintaining quality and accuracy, and seeing that the job proceeds on schedule, it is the creative team's responsibility to see that the original concept is maintained throughout the production process. In addition, the creative team is usually kept on-track by the need for obtaining account executive and client firm approval at various phases in production.

MEDIA PLANNING AND BUYING

When the advertising objectives have been set and the creative strategy agreed to, media planning begins. Usually the **media planner** is constrained from the beginning by a media budget. The budget is usually set during the formulation of the advertising plan, which defines a specific target audience as well. In addition, the creative strategy is likely to dictate the use of particular media that best show some important product attribute. Within these constraints the media planner must consider the most cost-efficient way to reach the specified audience. Doing this job requires the planner to be familiar with a great deal of statistical information. Media rates, audience demographics, population changes, plus variations in time of year, time of day, and discounts available represent only a few of the possible variables in considering alternatives in media selection. Once the general media plan has been set and approved, the negotiation process begins. Often this process of agreeing on price and formally contracting for media time and space is the job of a junior-level person called a media buyer. This person is responsible for placing the buy with the medium and seeing that the contracts are appropriately drawn, the client is billed, and that proof that the contract has been executed is received by the agency.

MAJOR FUNCTIONS OF THE BRAND MANAGER AND THE ADVERTISING MANAGER

Titles like *advertising manager*, *advertising director*, and *brand manager* are used to designate management people in the advertiser or client firm. The brand management form of organization has become increasingly popular in the United States, especially among consumer goods firms. Under this form of organization the **brand manager** has authority and responsibility for all marketing decisions concerning a brand (for example, all formulations of shampoo sold under the Head & Shoulders label). Marketing decision areas include 1) all aspects of the product, 2) pricing, 3) physical distribution of the product, and 4) promotion, which includes advertising. Since advertising plays a central role in the marketing of many consumer goods, it receives close attention from the brand manager. Working with the advertising agency, the brand manager assumes the following responsibilities:

- Plans the advertising effort in concert with developments anticipated for the brand

- Sets the advertising budget

- Reviews agency plans and objectives and coordinates them with all marketing elements

From this brief description it can be seen that brand managers have broader, more general responsibilities, with greater emphasis on coordination and supervision, than do account agency executives.

Conversely, the **advertising manager** or director serves a more general function and is usually responsible for several brand managers. While advertising managers approve advertising plans, they do not actually make decisions on ads or commercials, or even draft advertising plans. Because they have responsibility for advertising in several product lines, they may be less expert than a brand manager in specific situations. Ad managers usually review all advertising plans and programs for the company and coordinate their implementation.

LEADING AGENCIES AND ADVERTISERS

Exhibit 2.2 lists the 50 largest advertisers, media companies, and ad agencies in the United States based on dollar volume. As you examine the list of advertisers you will recognize that their products are quite basic to American life and are widely available: automobiles, soaps and other household products, food and drink, and a variety of other goods.

While agencies do not have sales in the normal sense of the term, they are usually compared in size based on billings. **Agency billings** are the total advertising cost billed to client firms and are generally reported on an annual basis. *Advertising Age*, one of the important magazines of the advertising industry, makes annual reports of agency size, not only in billings, but in agency income as well. Many feel that income is a more accurate benchmark since it includes revenues from agency fees in addition to media commissions.

Most of the largest agencies are headquartered in New York City, acknowledged as the capital of the communications industry. These large agencies all hold similar types of accounts: a major automotive account, food products accounts, beer and liquor accounts, and so on. This similarity exists for two reasons. First of all, these types of accounts are heavy advertisers, as suggested by the advertiser list in Exhibit 2.2. Second, agencies generally do not hold competing accounts. That is, if the agency has one automobile account, it cannot accept another. To do so would create a **conflict of interest** within the agency—that is, an untenable situation in which an agency must serve two competing clients. This prohibition on accepting competing accounts creates limits on agency growth. For example, once an agency obtains an account in each category of heavily advertised goods, the only way it can grow is by replacing the current account with a larger one from the same category. To accept the new account it would, of course, need to resign the old one.

ALTERNATIVES TO THE FULL-SERVICE AGENCY

Though the agency/brand manager relationship outlined earlier is probably most typical of the division and organization of advertising activities, there are numerous dramatically different alternatives.

One alternative favored by several major advertisers is the **house agency.** Under this system, all the specialized activities of the agency are available from a subsidiary of the advertiser firm. While in some cases the advertiser and the house agency are actually housed together, more often they are physically separated. Some house agencies do limited work for

EXHIBIT 2.2

The Elite Corps of U.S. Media and Marketing

TOP 50 ADVERTISERS		TOP 50 ADVERTISERS	
RANK ADVERTISER	ADVERTISING EXPENDITURES*	RANK ADVERTISER	ADVERTISING EXPENDITURES*
1 Procter & Gamble	$1,600	26 Bristol-Myers Co.	344
2 Philip Morris Cos.	1,400	27 International Business Machines	328
3 RJR/Nabisco	1,093	28 Nestle SA	319
4 Sears, Roebuck & Co.	800	29 Sara Lee Corp.	286
5 General Motors Corp.	779	30 Mars Inc.	276
6 Beatrice Cos.	684	31 American Cyanamid Co.	266
7 Ford Motor Co.	615	32 H.J. Heinz Co.	262
8 K mart Corp.	567	33 US Government	259
9 McDonald's Corp.	550	34 Colgate-Palmolive Co.	253
10 Anheuser-Busch Cos.	523	35 Eastman Kodak Co.	247
11 American Telephone & Telegraph	521	36 Quaker Oats Co.	246
12 Ralston Purina Co.	508	37 Sterling Drug	225
13 Dart & Kraft	489	38 Campbell Soup Co.	215
14 General Mills	484	39 CBS Inc.	208
15 Penney, JC Co.	479	40 Mobil Corp.	195
16 PepsiCo Inc.	478	41 Tandy Corp.	187
17 Pillsbury Co.	473	42 Beecham Group plc	186
18 Warner-Lambert Co.	469	43 Grand Metropolitan plc	177
19 Unilever US	414	44 Batus Industries	175
20 Johnson & Johnson	401	45 Toyota Motor Corp.	172
21 American Home Products Corp.	400	46 IC Industries	171
22 Chrysler Corp.	393	47 American Express Co.	170
23 Coca-Cola Co.	390	48 Schering-Plough Corp.	169
24 GE/RCA	373	49 Nissan Motor Co.	163
25 Kellogg Co.	364	50 Gillette Co.	161

*Dollars in millions for calendar year 1985.

accounts other than their advertiser-owners. Revlon and American Home Products are two firms who favor the house agency form of organization.

Another alternative is presented by the **creative boutique,** an ad agency that limits its services to creative work. These organizations emerged in the late 1960s and early 1970s. Though at least some of them have grown and evolved into full-service agencies, the original concept of the creative boutique was to supply strictly creative strategy and innovative communication ideas.

A **media buying service** is a complementary organization to the creative boutique. Like the boutiques, media buying services also emerged in the early 1970s, and they specialize in the buying of media at discount rates. The original concept was that through the use of large purchasing power, media could be bought at significantly lower rates. In addition, the buying services usually worked on lower rates than the full-service agency, usually at a commission of 5 to 10 percent instead of the traditional 15 percent. Though the services accepted full commission from me-

TOP 50 MEDIA COMPANIES		TOP 50 MEDIA COMPANIES	
RANK MEDIA COMPANY	MEDIA REVENUES*	RANK MEDIA COMPANY	MEDIA REVENUES*
1 Capital Cities/ABC	$3,841	26 Oklahoma Publishing Co.	411
2 CBS Inc.	3,170	27 A.H. Belo Corp.	385
3 Time Inc.	2,852	28 Central Newspapers	384
4 RCA Corp.	2,648	29 Viacom International	376
5 Times Mirror Co.	2,171	30 Thomson Newspapers	373
6 Gannett Co.	2,153	31 Affiliated Publications	366
7 Advance Publications	2,030	32 Meredith Corp.	356
8 Dun & Bradstreet	1,718	33 Multimedia Inc.	336
9 Tribune Co.	1,684	34 Turner Broadcasting Co.	332
10 Knight-Ridder Newspapers	1,679	35 Warner Communications	331
11 Hearst Corp.	1,540	36 Media General	331
12 New York Times Co.	1,394	37 Freedom Newspapers	325
13 Cox Enterprises	1,326	38 Copley Newspapers	304
14 Westinghouse Electric Co.	1,069	39 Continental Cablevision	295
15 Washington Post Co.	1,037	40 Morris Communications Corp.	284
16 McGraw-Hill	1,031	41 McClatchy Newspapers	275
17 Dow Jones & Co.	978	42 Pulitzer Publishing Co.	272
18 Scripps Howard	900	43 GFV Corp.	270
19 Kohlberg Kravis Roberts Co.	768	44 Landmark Communications	259
20 Triangle Publications	720	45 Maclean Hunter Communications	258
21 News America Publishing	584	46 Chronicle Publishing	255
22 Tele-Communications Inc.	577	47 Cowles Media	241
23 International Thomson Holdings	560	48 Donrey Media Group	237
24 Harte-Hanks Communications	550	49 A.S Abell Co.	235
25 John Blair & Co.	549	50 Ingersoll Publications	235

continued

dia, the difference was passed along to advertisers as additional savings. Even some smaller advertising agencies find it economical to use media buying services rather than do their own media buying.

In recent years, a number of large advertisers—such as Anheuser-Busch, RJR-Nabisco, and Seagram—have begun to do their own media buying. The American Association of Advertising Agencies estimates that in-house media buying amounted to about 2 percent of media spending in 1986.

Most advertisers who use this option continue to use their advertising agencies for media *planning*. The buying is done by the client firm and the agency is paid a reduced commission, usually around 12 percent.[4] Advertisers who choose this alternative usually do so because they are spending very large amounts of money in media. By consolidating under their own roof they hope to save money through volume buying and avoid a situation in which buying for their own brands drives up media prices by seeking the same availabilities. They also shorten the lines of communication for better coordination of media with changing market conditions.

EXHIBIT 2.2
Continued

TOP 50 AGENCIES			TOP 50 AGENCIES		
RANK	AGENCY	GROSS INCOME†	RANK	AGENCY	GROSS INCOME†
1	Young & Rubicam	$628.4	26	Ross Roy Inc.	62.4
2	Saatchi & Saatchi Compton Worldwide	490.5	27	Campbell-Mithun	57.1
3	Ted Bates Worldwide	486.0	28	DYR Worldwide	50.7
4	J. Walter Thompson Co.	471.0	29	Wunderman Ricotta & Kline	49.1
5	Ogilvy & Mather Worldwide	459.6	30	Lowe Marschalk	49.0
6	BBDO Worldwide	445.1	31	Chiat/Day Advertising	47.1
7	McCann-Erickson Worldwide	427.7	32	Tracy-Locke	46.2
8	DDB Needham Worldwide	375.0	33	HBM/Creamer	40.1
9	D'Arcy Masius Benton & Bowles	336.3	34	Laurence, Charles, Free & Lawson	39.4
10	Foote, Cone & Belding Communications	323.0	35	Hill, Holliday, Connors, Cosmopulos	39.4
11	Grey Advertising	309.1	36	C&W Group	38.4
12	Leo Burnett Co.	292.3	37	W.B. Doner & Co.	36.3
13	SSC&B:Lintas Worldwide	237.0	38	Ally Gargano/MCA Advertising	35.7
14	Bozell, Jacobs, Kenyon & Eckhardt	175.6	39	Geers Gross Advertising	35.0
15	NW Ayer	125.5	40	Admarketing	33.0
16	DFS Dorland Worldwide	119.6	41	Jordan, Manning, Case, Taylor & McGrath	32.7
17	HCMO	106.0	42	Doremus Porter Novelli	32.5
18	Wells, Rich, Greene	99.7	43	McCaffrey & McCall	31.0
19	Campbell-Ewald Worldwide	87.6	44	Lord, Geller, Federico, Einstein	29.4
20	Scali, McCabe, Sloves	77.5	45	Tatham-Laird & Kudner	28.5
21	Ketchum Communications	75.3	46	Sudler & Hennessey	25.5
22	William Esty Advertising Co.	75.0	47	Medicus Intercon International	24.6
23	Ogilvy & Mather Direct Response	68.0	48	Bloom Cos.	24.4
24	Backer & Spielvogel	68.0	49	Rumrill-Hoyt	23.9
25	TBWA Advertising	65.7	50	Direct Marketing Group	23.7

†Dollars in millions for calendar year 1986.
Sources: Top advertisers, *Advertising Age*, September 4, 1986; top media companies, *Advertising Age*, June 30, 1986; top agencies, *Advertising Age*, March 26, 1987. Copyright Crain Communications, Inc. Reprinted with permission.

There is currently no indication that the move to in-house media planning is a long-term trend. In fact, there seems to be continuing movement in both directions.

REASONS FOR USING AN AGENCY

With the range of available alternatives, the question "Why use an advertising agency?" naturally arises. Numerous answers to this question have been given; the most persuasive are summarized below.

SPECIALIZED KNOWLEDGE

Agencies develop considerable expertise in the areas of setting objectives, creative strategy, and media planning. While people with these skills and knowledge could be employed by the advertiser, there is some question

A CLOSER LOOK

AGENCY OR IN-HOUSE?

Each year at least one important advertiser decides to try a new arrangement for handling its advertising. In the mid-1980s three large advertisers elected to set up in-house media buying operations, or expanded existing ones. The three advertisers—R. J. Reynolds, Chesebrough-Pond's, and Anheuser-Busch, all of whom spend considerably more than $100 million per year on advertising—believe that they can save money by doing their own media buying. At this level of spending, a saving of just one or two percent can be very significant.

However, the movement goes in both directions, and each year some advertisers decide to return to advertising agencies. According to Len Matthews, President of the American Association of Advertising

Agencies, in a recent year, 68 accounts moved in-house from A.A.A.A. agencies, while 30 accounts moved to A.A.A.A. agencies from in-house. However, the accounts that moved in-house were considerably smaller. The net result was that billings of advertisers moving to A.A.A.A. agencies were greater than billings of advertisers that moved in-house.

ACCOUNT MOVEMENT SUMMARY

Total volume of A.A.A.A. agencies	$28,726,031,000	100.00%
Movement *to* A.A.A.A. agencies	85,898,000	0.30%
Movement *to* "in-house"	35,548,000	0.12%
Net movement to A.A.A.A. agencies	$ 50,350,000	0.18%.

Source: "Movement of Accounts: Full-Service Agency Is Favored," *A.A.A.A. Newsletter*, January 1986. Reprinted courtesy of the American Association of Advertising Agencies.

as to whether they could be used efficiently enough to justify the overhead. Because they work on different types of accounts as well as different brands as their assignments change, agency people accumulate experience that is often transferable to new and different products. This background knowledge and experience is something many advertisers find worth paying for.

OBJECTIVITY

Management within an advertiser firm frequently tends to become so involved with the company's plans and products that it may fail to see things as the consumer does. The agency serves to bring the consumer view to marketing management and to appraise its offerings as the public does. Agency people are involved more intimately with the public. It is their job to know popular tastes in entertainment, fashion, politics, and leisure activities. This orientation is helpful not only in the formulation of advertising strategy, but also in general counsel to the client firm.

COMMISSION SYSTEM

The commission system provides a major incentive for the use of advertising agencies. As explained in Chapter 1, commissions are paid by the media, making agency services "free" to the advertiser. In his historical examination of advertising, Daniel Pope suggests that the commission system has been the most important reason for the success of the advertising agency business.[5]

AGENCY COMPENSATION

Throughout this chapter we have alluded to the **commission system,** the means by which advertising agencies are compensated for placing advertisements in the media. Basically, the system works this way: the media publish their advertising rates in various reference publications used by agencies and on sheets known as rate cards. (A summary of rate information is shown in Figure 2.9.)

Advertising agencies—usually buying on behalf of their clients, but sometimes speculatively—contract to buy space or time with the medium involved. *Recognized advertising agencies* are billed for their purchases at the rate card price, less 15 percent. The agency in turn bills its client, the advertiser, at the full rate (the price on the rate card). When the advertiser reimburses the agency for the media buy, the commission becomes the agency's income on the transaction.

Suppose an agency placed a four-color ad for a client in a magazine that charged $16,000 for the space. The agency would bill the client $16,000 for the ad. However, the agency would pay the magazine 15 percent less:

Cost of ad (rate card)	$16,000
Less 15%	− 2,400
Agency pays magazine	$13,600

The client must pay the full $16,000 to the agency for placing the ad. As a result, the agency earns a 15-percent commission—in this case, $2,400—for its effort.

It is important to note that the discount rate is available only to recognized agencies. Others buy at the rate card rate. This arrangement gives the appearance that the services of the agency are free, or at least come at no extra cost above that of the media rates. While the situation is actually somewhat more complicated than that, this scenario conveys the general idea.

In many cases, an agency can secure additional discounts. This depends on skillful negotiation by the media buyer. Some additional discounts result from large volume buying; another, the cash discount, is given when payment is made within a specified period of time (usually 10 days). Most common in print media, these discounts help to ensure continued patronage and to encourage timely payment by agencies. Agencies almost always pass along any discount above the 15 percent agency discount to their clients. Cash discounts are usually passed along to the client on the same basis as they are offered to the agency, that is, the advertiser receives the cash discount if the bill is paid within the specified time period.

The matter of prompt payment is a subject of considerable importance for advertising agencies. As pointed out in the preceding example, it is the agency that holds the contract with the medium and is financially liable for the charges. With the huge costs of modern advertising campaigns, an agency can quickly become financially overextended if a client's payment is not quickly forthcoming.

In addition, not every agency service is paid for by a media commission. Though exactly what services are covered is a matter of negotiation between agency and advertiser, in general the commission covers the cost

FIGURE 2.9

Advertising Rate Information for *Rolling Stone*

Rolling Stone

(ABC)   MPA

Media Code 8 533 1737 8.00   **Mid 000873-000**
Published 24 times a year by Straight Arrow Publishers, Inc., 745 Fifth Ave., New York, NY 10151. Phone 212-758-3800.
PUBLISHER'S EDITORIAL PROFILE
ROLLING STONE is a magazine edited for young adults who have a special interest in popular culture, particularly music, film and politics. Regular features include state-of-the-art audio and electronics columns, record reviews, reader correspondence; interviews and photojournalism features. Special issues include Audio, Video, College, Fashion and Consumer Electronics supplements. Rec'd 5/29/84.

1. PERSONNEL
Editor—Jann S. Wenner.
Associate Publisher—Les Zeifman.
National Sales Manager—Dana Fields.
Mgr. of Adv. Traffic & Prod.—Calvin Generette.

2. REPRESENTATIVES and/or BRANCH OFFICES
Beverly Hills 90211—Bill Harper, Suite 926-929, 8500 Wilshire Blvd.   Phone 213-659-1242.
Chicago 60601—Chris Schuba, 333 N. Michigan Ave.   Phone 312-782-2366.
San Francisco 94111—Robin McKnight, 1750 Montgomery St.   Phone 415-954-8543.
Birmingham, MI—Richard Hartle Associates.

3. COMMISSION AND CASH DISCOUNT
15% to recognized agencies; 2% cash discount 10 days. Credit extended to accredited agencies only.   Billing is rendered within 5 days prior to on-sale date.   Invoices payable within 30 days of invoice date.
Carrying charge of 1% per month charged on invoice past 30 days.

4. GENERAL RATE POLICY
Publisher reserves the right to reject or cancel any ad, and to identify as "advertisement" any ad which, in his opinion, simulates editorial layout and appearance.

ADVERTISING RATES
Rates effective August 14, 1986. (Card No. 29.)
Rates received March 31, 1986.
Card received September 26, 1986.

5. BLACK/WHITE RATES

	1 ti	7 ti	13 ti	25 ti	39 ti
1 page	20,980.	20,350.	19,510.	18,460.	18,045.
3/4 page	16,785.	16,280.	15,610.	14,770.	14,435.
1/2 page	12,580.	12,205.	11,700.	11,070.	10,820.
1/4 page	7,345.	7,125.	6,830.	6,465.	6,315.
1/8 page	4,200.	4,075.	3,905.	3,695.	3,610.
Spread	41,960.	40,700.	39,025.	36,925.	36,085.
1/2 Spread	25,180.	24,425.	23,415.	22,160.	21,655.

	50 ti	75 ti	100 ti
1 page	17,205.	16,575.	15,945.
3/4 page	13,765.	13,260.	12,755.
1/2 page	10,315.	9,940.	9,560.
1/4 page	6,025.	5,805.	5,580.
1/8 page	3,445.	3,320.	3,190.
Spread	34,405.	33,150.	31,890.
1/2 Spread	20,650.	19,890.	19,135.

FREQUENCY DISCOUNT
Frequency discounts available only when a regular advertising schedule is adhered to; otherwise, frequency discounts computed at end of advertising year and a rebate or shortrate made to advertiser at that time to the nearest applicable discount.
Frequency discounts to non-contract advertisers given as earned in any 12-month period.
MULTIPLE PAGE DISCOUNTS
Advertisers purchasing 4 or more pages for one brand in a single issue will be granted a 5% multiple page discount.   Pages may run consecutively, in a single printed form, or throughout the issue.   Regular frequency discounts apply in addition to the special multiple page discount with each page counting as 1 insertion.

Source: This abbreviated rate information is taken from Standard Rate & Data Service, *Consumer Magazine and Agri-Media Rates and Data*, December 27, 1986, p. 410. Reprinted with permission.

A CLOSER LOOK

INEQUITY IN THE COMMISSION SYSTEM

The commission system of agency compensation is often criticized for not relating compensation to effort. The example below shows clearly how the same amount of work is rewarded at quite different rates, depending upon the magazine in which the ad runs.

Skiing and *Sports Illustrated* magazines are similar in size. Preparing a typical color ad for each of these magazines would require about the same amount of creative effort and production time and expense.

In part because of the differences in readership—*Skiing* has a circulation of 430,000, while *Sports Illustrated* has 2,625,000—the advertising rates are quite different.

	Sports Illustrated	*Skiing*
Page cost (4-color)	$75,370.00	$19,380.00
Agency commission	15%	15%
Agency income	$11,305.50	$ 2,907.00

Which commission would you prefer to earn?. Can you imagine that this might influence agency media recommendations?

---

of the agency's time and effort in planning a campaign, formulating advertising strategy, and planning and executing the media buy. The costs of producing advertising materials, such as print advertisements and broadcast commercials, are billed to the advertiser at cost plus a specified markup. Additional services such as research, preparation of sales promotion materials, or marketing consultation are also billed at cost plus a negotiated percentage, or at an established hourly charge.

COMMISSION SYSTEM: PROBLEMS AND ALTERNATIVES

The commission system is by all reports the most common form of agency compensation. However, the system does have serious shortcomings, from the point of view of both agencies and advertisers.[6] Perhaps the most serious criticism of commissions is that they do not relate the quality, or even the amount, of agency work to the financial reward. An agency puts in the same amount of effort to create an ad to run one time, in one publication, as it does to create an ad that might run repeatedly in a number of publications. The difference in commissions received could be staggering. Since media space and time are usually a function of audience size and quality, units of space can vary widely in price. However, the agency must do just as much work to create one magazine ad as another. Similarly, an agency derives the same commission from an ineffective ad as it does from an effective one.

In addition, the commission system provides little incentive for agencies to reduce costs. Since the agency stands to increase its revenues as the advertiser spends more, the financial interests of the agency can run counter to those of the client. For this reason, agency recommendations for increased budgets are sometimes greeted with skepticism or even hostility.

As the result of these problems, modifications and alternatives to the commission system have evolved.[7] *Fee systems* are agreements about services to be provided and rates at which they will be billed. These are attempts to add reasonable profits to the real costs of agency services. *Negotiated commissions* are based on the commission system, with the actual rate reduced in the case of large, profitable accounts and increased in the case of small or unprofitable ones. In an *incentive system*, the agency shares in the success of the advertising effort.

Criticisms and alternatives continue to develop. A 1986 study of compensation methods by the Association of National Advertisers revealed that only 43 percent of ANA members paid their agencies a straight 15% commission. The average commission for many large clients is somewhere in the neighborhood of 10 to 11 percent.[8]

AGENCY RECOGNITION

For many years, the key to whether an agency could obtain a discount from the rate card lay in its recognition by media. While the criteria for agency recognition have always been a matter of some controversy, the general standard evolved around three major criteria. Agencies seeking recognition first of all had to possess the ability to deliver professional-calibre service to advertisers. Second, they needed to be independent of advertisers and media, not simply convenient corporate entities set up to obtain media at discounts for a particular advertiser. Finally, and perhaps most important, they needed to demonstrate the financial resources to honor their commitments. In view of the role agencies play in contracting for media time and space, it is easy to see the reasons for attention to this in granting recognition.

However, formal criteria largely disappeared when in 1956 the American Association of Advertising Agencies agreed with the Federal Trade Commission to stop maintaining lists of recognized agencies. This practice, in the FTC's view, amounted to restraint of trade, by discriminating against agencies and others who were not AAAA members. The resulting agreement loosened criteria for recognition and paved the way for the development of some of the alternatives to the full-service agencies that developed in the following decades, particularly media buying services.

CRITERIA FOR SELECTING AN AGENCY

Selecting an advertising agency is one of the most important—and often the most difficult—decisions an advertiser must make. While any agency should be able to produce reasonable advertising, getting the most out of advertising depends on building a solid agency-client relationship based on mutual understanding and respect. While human factors are essential in the equation, some more objectively evaluated elements can aid in the decision.

The *range of services* offered varies considerably from one agency to another. A strong research department, an agency unit for planning and executing direct-mail advertising, or the presence of strong sales promotion or marketing expertise can be important factors in agency selection, or merely frills, depending upon the advertiser's needs.

An agency's *experience* with similar goods or services is a strong criterion for many advertisers. The special needs of industrial goods marketers have led some agencies to specialize in this type of work. Automotive and consumer package goods advertisers also consider previous experience with their categories essential for an agency.

Stability, both in terms of finance and personnel, are also important considerations. While the financial concerns are self-explanatory in view of the role of the agency in relation to media, personnel must be considered because of the trust and cooperation necessary in the agency-client relationship.

Agency philosophy is a final consideration. Some agencies are associated with particular schools of thought about the role of advertising in marketing and the ways in which it affects the consumer. These ideas ought to be considered in light of the agency task.

AGENCY NETWORKS

One way that small independent agencies have developed to compete with the services and capabilities of very large agencies with many branch offices is by joining together in agency networks. An **agency network** is an organization in which member agencies cooperate to exchange information and experience and to aid in obtaining local services. By joining together, a network of small agencies can afford syndicated research and information services that would be too expensive for a small agency by itself. They also cooperate on specific projects.

For example, suppose a small agency in Portland, Oregon, needed some research done in Portland, Maine. This task could be accomplished quickly and economically by contacting a fellow member of the agency network in that area. In addition, agencies seeking new business can contact other members of the network to take advantage of their expertise in handling similar accounts. There are currently ten advertising agency networks in the United States. In general, they allow smaller agencies to draw on a larger base of experience and expertise, much as a large agency with numerous branch offices might do.

ETHNIC ADVERTISING AGENCIES

The early 1970s saw the rise of the black advertising agency, though several black-owned agencies had been established as much as a decade earlier. What is currently the largest black advertising agency, Burrell Advertising, was founded in 1971 in Chicago by Tom Burrell. The agency was founded to serve clients who wanted to reach the black audience with messages especially designed for it. Burrell and other black agency founders have successfully demonstrated that advertising to blacks is more than just recreating white advertising with black models. To effectively reach

A CLOSER LOOK

HOW ADVERTISERS VIEW AGENCIES

In 1984 *Advertising Age* surveyed the advertising directors of 300 large firms on the subject of ad agencies. The general attitudes about agency strengths and weaknesses are indicated below. Several additional findings were important:

- Less than half of the advertisers thought that they would engage the same agency five years from now.

- Of those questioned, 65 percent of the firms had been approached by agencies seeking their business within the past three months.

- The greatest weakness attributed to agencies: a lack of knowledge about the advertiser's business.

- "Agency reputation and past awards" was the reason advertisers gave most often for considering an agency outstanding.

Agency Strengths

Know client's business 24.8%
Creative talent 36.6%
Talent to listen 2.0%
Integrity and honesty 4.0%
Organized/consistent 3.9%
Client relationship 5.9%
Quality people 10.9%
Don't know and other 10.9%

Agency Weaknesses

Lack knowledge of client business 27.0%
Don't know and other 21.9%
Bad media buying 1.0%
Don't meet deadlines 3.1%
Too much creative focus 4.2%
Inconsistent service 4.2%
Personnel turnover 4.2%
Cost estimating 11.5%
Lack creativity 8.3%
Poor account execs 7.3%
Hype and misrepresentation 7.3%

Source: Based on Joseph Winski, "Advertisers Draw Bead on Agency Reputations," *Advertising Age,* March 28, 1985, 6.

the black community, advertising must reflect the subculture's unique values and life-styles. While the largest ethnic advertising agencies concentrate on the black market, Hispanic agencies are also becoming an important part of the agency scene.

The concept of employing specialized agencies to reach specific audiences has been accepted by some major advertisers in the automobile, fast-food, and alcoholic beverage categories, as well as many others. Today, numerous large advertisers earmark a specific percentage of their budgets to reach subcultures. The leading black-owned agencies are shown on the next page.[9]

MERGERS, ACQUISITIONS, AND CONFLICT OF INTEREST

During 1985 a series of mergers occurred between a number of major advertisers. The combinations affected about 400 brand names, changed the rankings of leading advertising spenders, created some huge advertisers, and resulted in some major waves of change in the advertising business.

Leading Black-Owned Advertising Agencies

AGENCY	LOCATION	BILLINGS (In Millions)	MAJOR ACCOUNTS
Burrell Advertising	Chicago	$53	Coca-Cola, Ford, Procter & Gamble, McDonald's
UniWorld Group	New York	36	Alberto-Culver, Burger King, General Foods, General Motors
Mingo-Jones Advertising	New York	25	Goodyear Tire & Rubber, House of Seagram, Kentucky Fried Chicken, Miller Brewing
Lockhart & Pettus	New York	11	Carson Products, Hiram Walker, United Negro College Fund, U.S. Army
J. P. Martin Associates Inc.	New York	10	Anheuser-Busch

Source: Black Enterprise.

For example, Procter & Gamble, the long-time leader in advertising spending, bought Richardson-Vicks, marketer of Oil of Olay, Nyquil, and Vidal Sassoon products (who ranked 48th).[10] Sixth-ranked Philip Morris, the seller of Miller beer, Marlboro, and 7-Up, acquired General Foods (ranked 12th), the owner of Jello-O, Maxwell House, and Post cereal brands. R. J. Reynolds, the 5th-ranked marketer of such brands as Camel cigarettes, Kentucky Fried Chicken, and Del Monte, bought Nabisco, who ranked 21st nationwide.

As a result of the new combinations, some agencies suddenly found themselves holding accounts that were in direct competition. Young & Rubicam, for example, handled the Oil of Olay account for Richrdson-Vicks and the Colgate account for Colgate-Palmolive. When Procter & Gamble purchased Richardson-Vicks, however, the agency was, in effect, now working for P&G. P&G felt that Young & Rubicam's Colgate account constituted a conflict of interest with Procter & Gamble products, and pulled its $28 million Oil of Olay account from the ad agency.[11]

Few advertisers feel as strongly about competing accounts as Procter & Gamble. However, this huge advertiser insists on careful policing of a policy in which any competing products represent a potential conflict of interest for its advertising agencies. P&G insists that it will make the rules as to what constitutes a conflict of interest.

During 1986 a number of large advertising agencies followed the lead of the advertisers by merging among themselves. For example, major agency powers BBDO International, Doyle Dane Bernbach, and Needham Harper Worldwide merged to form an umbrella organization called Omnicom, with estimated billings of over $5 billion. Saatchi & Saatchi Compton, another umbrella group, acquired more than $4 billion in agency billings when it assumed control of Backer & Spielvogel ($450 million), Dancer Fitzgerald Sample ($876 million), and Ted Bates Worldwide ($3.1 billion). One result of the mergers was that the ten largest "super agencies" billed about half of the total advertising expenditures of the year's top 500 advertisers.[12]

The results of the agency mergers, however, are far from clear. The new combinations created conflicts among accounts handled by what had been distinct agencies. While some of the newly formed agency combinations consolidated to do business under a single new name, most of the large combinations will do business as independent agency networks. An umbrella organization such as Saatchi & Saatchi Compton acts strictly as a holding company without direct involvement in day-to-day business af-

EXHIBIT 2.3

Mega-Merger Fallout Highlights, 1986

CLIENT/BRAND	FROM	TO	BUDGET	PROBABLE RATIONALE
Stroh Brewery Co./Network, cable media-buying, all brands Stroh Brewery Co./Old Milwaukee, Old Milwaukee Light	BBDO	Grey Advertising	$70 million	Omnicom sister agency DDB Needham handles $100-million-plus in Anheuser-Busch
American Honda	Needham Harper Worldwide	Rubin/Postaer & Associates, L.A.	$58 million	Car conflicts at Omnicom megashop
Colgate/tooth and shaving products	Ted Bates Advertising	Young & Rubicam	$55 million	Conflicts with Procter & Gamble
RJR Nabisco/More, Now	FCB/Leber Katz Partners	Young & Rubicam	$45-$49 million	Pulling More and Now to distribute cigarette assignments among agencies
P&G/Crisco	Saatchi & Saatchi Compton	Grey Advertising	$35 million	Food group conflicts with Nabisco
Warner-Lambert/ Listermint, Trident, Bubblicious, Halls Cough Drops and Suplical	Ted Bates Advertising	J. Walter Thompson	$34 million	Conflicts with Saatchi rivals
Procter & Gamble/Oil of Olay	Young & Rubicam	Wells, Rich, Greene	$28 million	P&G exercised corporate-conflict policy
RJR Nabisco/ Cereal products	Doyle Dane Bernbach	Foote, Cone & Belding	$26 million	Consolidating cereals, conflict with General Mills at Needham
P&G/Luvs	DFS/Dorland Worldwide	Leo Burnett	$20 million	Conflict with Johnson & Johnson at Saatchi
Quaker Oats Co./ Quaker 100% Natural, Puffed, Life cereals; Puss'n Boots; new products	BBDO	Undetermined	$20 million	General Mills, DDB Needham, unwilling to coexist with Quaker, Omnicom

Source: "Mega-Merger Fallout Highlights through September 12, 1986," p. 30, September 15, 1986 issue of *ADWEEK*. Reprinted with permission of *ADWEEK* September 1986.

fairs. The architects of the large holding companies have worked hard to try to "sell" the concept of independent agency networks to client firms, though not always with great success. Many advertisers are waiting to see how well the new arrangement works, while others have already begun to switch accounts around to resolve the conflicts created when agencies merged. Exhibit 2.3 summarizes some early account changes among the giant agencies.

What the merger trend will mean for advertisers and agencies in the long term is quite difficult to say. Most believe that the trend will continue for some time. Many believe that the conflicts created by mergers will not be sorted out quickly. It may be five or more years, they say, before all potential conflict situations are resolved.

The most common rationale given for the advertiser merger trend has been new-product costs. Because the cost of launching a new consumer goods product is currently estimated at $100 million, healthy, established brands have come to be appreciated as extremely valuable properties.[13]

The result is that companies have tried to buy other consumer goods marketers because of their brand inventory, since this is cheaper than attempting to build their own new brands.

As for advertising agencies, the most frequently cited reason for merger is to provide more global service to internationally oriented marketing firms. Yet, it is not really clear how large mergers of agency networks such as Saatchi/Bates and Omnicom will result in any direct improvement in client service, either internationally or domestically. Some advertising observers suggest that the opposite may be true. They fear that increasing size and bureaucracy will stifle advertising creativity.

SUMMARY

The preceding chapter describes the roles and functions of the central partnership in the advertising enterprise, the partnership between advertiser and agency. The chapter also differentiates among the numerous types of advertising. This differentiation is based on scope—international, national, and local advertising—as well as on purpose—corporate, public service, business-to-business, direct response, and classified.

The important functions of the full-service advertising agency include account services, creative services, and media planning and buying. There are differences in functions between the advertising agency and advertising management at the advertiser firm, with the agency responsible for planning and executing advertising. The advertising manager generally has broader responsibility for overall advertising strategy and coordination of advertising with other marketing elements. Alternatives to the full-service advertising agency, such as the house agency, the creative boutique, and the media buying service, fill different needs.

The commission system remains an important form of agency compensation despite its numerous flaws. It appears that most big advertisers are moving to negotiated commissions, usually significantly below the traditional 15 percent. Other compensation plans are based on incentives or flat fees. In selecting an agency, the advertiser usually seeks one that offers the services needed, has experience with similar goods or services, is financially stable, and has a philosophy of advertising compatible with that of the advertiser.

In the past several years, mergers and acquisitions have dramatically affected the scale of operations among big advertisers and big agencies. These recombinations have created conflict-of-interest problems, which will probably have important effects on agency selection for some time into the future.

YOU MAKE THE DECISION

SELECTING AN ADVERTISING AGENCY

The Candy Council is a trade association set up to promote the giving of candy for personal occasions. The advertising manager for the council was recently hired away to become vice president of advertising at a large conglomerate. A new advertising manager, Laura Hill, was quickly hired by the council. One of Hill's first undertakings was to review past council advertising to judge its effectiveness.

One of her findings was that it was quite difficult to judge the impact of advertising on candy gift-giving. Though the amount spent on candy gifts has grown each year, the increases seem to be the result of inflation. It is difficult to say exactly what benefit came to the council members from the $5 million spent on consumer advertising.

Hill decided that she would ask for speculative presentations from several leading agencies in the medium-sized midwestern community in which the council is headquartered. (The $5 million dollar account was quite desirable and highly sought after in the community.) Hill decided that she would also invite the current agency to make a presentation. She had no concrete evidence that their past work had been ineffective (though some of the council staff felt the agency personnel were arrogant and difficult to deal with).

Interest in the Candy Council account proved to be even larger than Hill had expected, and she found that ten agencies were eager to make speculative presentations. After spending several weeks listening to and analyzing the presentations, Hill and her staff narrowed the field to three possible agencies, profiled briefly below:

Agency A has had considerable experience in the candy industry. Until last year, they handled the account of a candy manufacturer, an account about half the size of the council's. It is unclear why Agency A no longer has this account. Agency A is a full-service agency, locally owned and operated. It has a solid reputation in the local advertising community. With a staff of 50, Agency A is one of the largest in town.

Agency B currently holds the Candy Council account, and has for five years. The agency is a branch office of a national agency headquartered in New York. Agency B has a national reputation for award winning creative work, and makes no secret of the fact that it considers these awards the most important measure of advertising success. Agency B is the largest agency in town, in part because it handles the region's three largest advertisers. It has a staff of 65.

Agency C has no direct experience in the candy business, though it currently handles another trade association with notable success. The agency is locally owned and enjoys an outstanding reputation in the region for exciting creative work that produces results. Though the smallest of the group, with a full-time staff of 35, Agency C is full-service and assures Laura that the council would be their "largest and most important account."

1. What factors, controllable and uncontrollable by the council, might have influenced candy gift-giving in the past year?

2. What procedure and criteria should Laura H use in the preliminary screening of advertising agencies?

3. What do you think are the crucial factors in making a final agency selection? Would you choose agency A, B, or C?

■ ■ ■

QUESTIONS FOR DISCUSSION

1. Define the term *advertising*.

2. How does corporate advertising differ from public service advertising? How does national advertising differ from retail

advertising? How does trade advertising differ from industrial advertising?

3. Compare the services offered by full-service agencies, creative boutiques, and media buying services.

4. List the advantages and disadvantages of a house agency.

5. Explain the differences in responsibilities of the agency account executive and the client firm brand manager.

6. Explain what *billings* means, and how it is significant for agencies and media.

7. What are the alternatives to the traditional commission system?

8. For what reasons does a firm employ an advertising agency?

9. How is an ad agency paid?

10. Describe two alternatives to the commission system.

NOTES

1. For a discussion of corporate advertising, see Thomas Garbett, *Corporate Advertising: The What, The Why, The How* (New York: McGraw-Hill), 1981.

2. John Witek, *Response Television* (Chicago: Crain Books, 1981).

3. A full discussion of alternatives is to be found in *Advertising Services: Full-Service Agency, A La Carte, or In-House?* (New York: Association of National Advertisers, 1979).

4. Eileen Norris, "Clients Pluck Buying from Agencies' Grasp," *Advertising Age*, November 17, 1986, S-18.

5. Daniel Pope, *The Making of Modern Advertising* (New York: Basic Books, 1983), 152.

6. A discussion of these difficulties is found in G. A. Marken, "Agency Compensation: A Closet Problem in Client Relationships," *Marketing News*, March 10, 1985, 10.

7. See *Agency Compensation—A Guidebook* (New York: Association of National Advertisers, 1979).

8. William Claggett, "How Involved Should Clients Be in Management of Their Media?" *Advertising Age*, November 3, 1986, 20.

9. Ken Smikle, "The Image Makers," *Black Enterprise*, December 1985; and "Agency Profiles," *Advertising Age*, March 27, 1986.

10. *Advertising Age*, September 26, 1985.

11. "And, When Clients Marry . . .," *Adweek*, August 4, 1986, 10.

12. "Advertising Agency Mergers," *Journal of Advertising*, 15:3, 1986, 3.

13. "Mighty Urge to Merge," *Advertising Age*, October 28, 1985, 1.

SUGGESTED READINGS

American Association of Advertising Agencies. *What Advertising Agencies Are, What They Do, and How They Do It*. New York, 1976.

Association of National Advertisers. *Advertising Services: Full Service Agency, A La Carte, or In-House?*. New York, 1979.

———. *Current Advertiser Practices in Compensating their Advertising Agencies*. New York, 1985.

———. *Current Company Practices in the Use of Corporate Advertising*. New York, 1986.

———. *Evaluating Agency Performance*. New York, 1979.

———. *The Role of the Agency of Record*. New York, 1986.

Business/Professional Advertising Association. *Guidelines for Maintaining Healthy Agency/Client Relationships*. New York, 1983.

Garbett, Thomas. *Corporate Advertising*. New York: McGraw-Hill, 1981.

Gardner, Herbert, Jr. *The Advertising Agency Business*. Chicago: Crain Books, 1976.

Weilbacher, William. *Choosing an Advertising Agency*. Chicago: Crain Books, 1983.

C H A P T E R 3

THE MEDIA, ADVERTISING SERVICES, AND SUPPLIERS

Key Terms

Audit Bureau of Circulations
affiliate
network
network advertising
independent
spot advertising
local station advertising
narrowcasting
business papers
list broker
specialty advertising
media mix
media representative
trade association
trade press

Learning Objectives

To outline the organization of the major advertising media

To describe the special usefulness of media types

To compare variations in media use across industries

To analyze the importance of support services

To list the purposes of trade associations

The automotive industry is characterized by three different levels of advertising activity, each with its own objectives. Because of the variances in objectives, different media are employed. During 1984, the Chrysler Corporation spent about $317 million advertising its Plymouth, Dodge, and Chrysler cars and trucks. The majority was spent on television advertising designed to interest consumers in Chrysler automotive products and persuade them that these products offer significant value and competitive advantage.

The second level of advertising activity, dealer association advertising, is designed to aid consumers in finding a nearby place to buy Chrysler products. In 1984, the dealer association spent over $50 million on this task. The primary media used depend on the size of the market, the size of the dealer group, and the media available, though spot television received the largest amount of dealer association advertising dollars in 1985.

Individual dealers also advertise heavily. This advertising is designed to draw customers to do business with the specific dealer involved, and usually emphasizes the special advantage of the dealership—for example, large selection, low prices, convenient location, or service. By far the largest dollar amount of dealer advertising is placed in newspapers—about 80 percent of all dealer advertising in 1985.

The media form a vital communication link in the advertising process and, as this example illustrates, different media are used depending on the nature of the intended audience and the advertiser's objective.

Source: Courtesy of the Chrysler Corporation.

INTRODUCTION

The following chapter describes the commercial communications media and discusses the essential role they play in the advertising business. While we normally think of the media as our sources of information and entertainment, advertisers and agencies think of them as transmission channels. The commercial mass communications media carry advertising messages to consumers. Using the right media is essential to effective advertising. To choose media wisely for advertising purposes, one must understand their structure and organization. Numerous service industries also assist advertisers and agencies in the preparation and evaluation of their advertising messages. These services form an essential part of the advertising industry and understanding their roles is important as well.

When you finish reading this chapter you will better understand why advertisers use the media they do, and why some media are better suited to the needs of some types of advertisers than others. In addition, you will see that a great number of services necessary to the advertising business are not performed by advertisers or agencies, and must be obtained from other contractors or suppliers.

THE IMPORTANCE OF MEDIA

The advertising business depends on a large number of specialized services to operate effectively. While the primary function of commercial communications media for the advertising industry is to carry advertising messages, the media themselves serve other important functions for advertisers as well.

In addition to serving as a link to audiences, the entertainment content of commercial media serve to attract audiences. In most cases, media content is carefully designed to attract certain groups who are desirable to advertisers. In the case of the most popular advertising media—television, radio, newspapers, and magazines—sales of advertising provides the major source of revenue for the operators. Recent reports on cable television operations indicate that, for the first time, several cable programming originators have become profitable, largely because of increased advertising revenues.[1] Other media, such as direct mail and specialty advertising, do not have entertainment elements designed to attract audiences. In a very real sense, the medium *is* advertising. Out-of-home media such as outdoor advertising consist of physical locations or structures, but have no entertainment content without advertising messages.

In addition to attracting audiences, media supply important information to advertisers about their audiences. This information is the foundation of media planning by advertisers and agencies and provides an essential service. The descriptive information that media collect includes data on the numbers of people exposed to their content, as well as descriptions of readers and viewers in terms of demographic characteristics and in other categories useful to advertisers.

In some cases these data are compiled by the media themselves and are substantiated by some outside firm, such as the **Audit Bureau of Circulations,** a private firm that verifies the readership data released by newspapers and magazines. In the broadcast media, both potential reception and actual audience measures are made by independent research firms.

MEDIA ORGANIZATION

In the early days of the advertising industry, the media operator was an independent entrepreneur. This is rarely the case today, since chain ownership and media conglomerates dominate the scene. The following sections of this chapter will deal briefly with the organization of the major advertising media and the implications of this organization for advertising planning and decision making.

BROADCAST TELEVISION

Television broadcasting is done by local stations, which primarily carry programming produced and supplied to them from a central point of origin. These stations, called **affiliates,** are joined together in a **network** identified as the program originator. The three national networks are the American Broadcasting Company (ABC), the National Broadcasting Company (NBC), and Columbia Broadcasting System (CBS). Advertisers seeking broad national exposure for their products often contract for **network advertising,** in which a commercial is aired on all affiliated stations across the country.

Not all television stations are affiliated with a national network, however. Unaffiliated stations, called **independents,** develop their own programming, usually by buying it from program suppliers. Advertisers interested in broad national exposure sometimes contract with independent stations in major cities across the country to provide an alternative to the three major networks, or to supplement exposure on them. Often, however, local advertisers use independent stations because they are a bargain in the advertising marketplace, due to their less glamorous programming and smaller audience compared to network affiliates'. Exhibit 3.1 indicates the number of independent stations and affiliates of each major broadcast network nationally.

Independent stations are an increasingly important alternative to network advertising and, with cable TV, are eroding the large audiences that were once the province of the television networks alone. In 1985, independent television stations collected $2.5 billion in advertising revenues. That figure is expected to reach $5 billion by 1990.[2]

Many advertisers are interested in smaller, more selected audiences. Rather than advertise throughout the country, they prefer to place their commercials within a single geographic region, or perhaps in the largest cities of the country where the potential for success is greatest. Buying selected affiliates of a national network is called **spot advertising.** By using spot rather than network advertising, advertisers choose the specific locations best suited to their goals to show their messages.

EXHIBIT 3.1

Network Affiliates and Independents

NETWORK	NUMBER OF AFFILIATES
ABC	215
NBC	207
CBS	200
Independents	190

Source: Broadcasting/Cablecasting Yearbook 1986 (New York: Associated Press, 1986).

An advertiser who uses the television medium may be interested only in the exposure provided by a particular station in, for example, the Seattle market. Such an advertiser is using **local station advertising.** All of the advertisers described above have different objectives for their advertising in terms of the audience they wish to reach. The broadcast media are organized to offer a certain amount of flexibility to accommodate these needs by allowing for network, spot, and local buying.

CABLECASTING

Cable television audiences have been growing rapidly since the medium first gained a foothold against the competition of over-the-air broadcasting. The basic concept powering cable expansion has been **narrowcasting**— that is, reaching a small, but very well defined audience that is valuable to advertisers.[3] Unlike the broadcast industry, the cable industry is made up of independent operators who negotiate with a community for the franchise to wire a particular geographic area for cable reception. The cable system operator then selects program material from national, regional, and local sources to show over the channels the cable brings to subscribers' homes. At this point in its development cable advertising is primarily national in scope, though local advertising is becoming increasingly important. National advertisers contract with cable programming originators such as Music Television (MTV) or Cable Network (CBN), and their messages appear on cable systems carrying the programs of these originators. Figure 3.1 shows the leading advertising-supported cable services.

RADIO

Throughout the 1930s and 1940s network radio provided news and entertainment. With the rise of television to the status of the premier mass entertainment medium in the mid-1950s, however, radio shifted to become a more localized medium.[4] Today there are numerous radio networks, as Exhibit 3.2 indicates. While these networks provide a useful way for some advertisers to reach similar audience groups around the country, the majority of radio advertising is placed by local advertisers wishing to reach listeners in a specific market area. Most radio stations are not affiliated with a network, and compete more or less independently for audiences in the geographic area their signal reaches. Since most cities are served by many radio stations, each one tends to specialize in serving the needs and interests of a particular group of people. Thus, the programming format of the station is an important key to the audience it offers to advertisers. Most radio stations describe themselves in terms of one of the following programming formats, so that advertisers have an indication of the station's content and audience:

- Album-oriented rock
- Contemporary hits
- Soft rock
- Black programming
- Golden oldies
- Adult contemporary

- Country
- Beautiful music
- Classical
- News/talk
- Middle-of-the-road
- All news

FIGURE 3.1

Top Advertising-Supported TV Cable Services

The leading cable television programming services ranked by the number of subscribers reached through the stations carrying the programming.

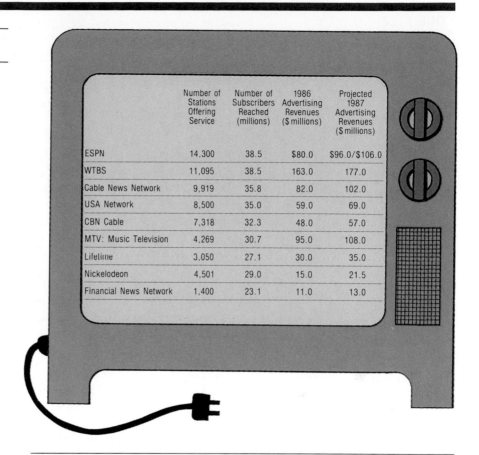

	Number of Stations Offering Service	Number of Subscribers Reached (millions)	1986 Advertising Revenues ($ millions)	Projected 1987 Advertising Revenues ($ millions)
ESPN	14,300	38.5	$80.0	$96.0/$106.0
WTBS	11,095	38.5	163.0	177.0
Cable News Network	9,919	35.8	82.0	102.0
USA Network	8,500	35.0	59.0	69.0
CBN Cable	7,318	32.3	48.0	57.0
MTV: Music Television	4,269	30.7	95.0	108.0
Lifetime	3,050	27.1	30.0	35.0
Nickelodeon	4,501	29.0	15.0	21.5
Financial News Network	1,400	23.1	11.0	13.0

Source: Reprinted with permission from *CABLE TV ADVERTISING*, Paul Kagan Associates, Inc.

NEWSPAPERS

Newspapers represent an important medium for both national and local advertisers. Although the newspaper is traditionally thought of as being tied to a specific geographical area, this is not totally the case. *The Wall Street Journal* has national circulation on a daily basis; other major papers have weekly national editions. Communication technology allowed the development of *USA Today*, which is printed and distributed across the country from content relayed by satellite. The largest and most influential newspapers, however, are metropolitan dailies.

Originally the province of the entrepreneur, the large daily newspapers are now owned primarily by chains. While advertisers seek the newspaper for its intense local coverage in the community, this feature makes the medium more important to the local advertiser than the national one. Despite the fact of chain ownership, newspaper advertising is not usually purchased through contract with chains. Today, chains own about 70 percent of all daily newspapers and almost 80 percent of all Sunday papers. These papers account for close to 80 percent of daily and about 90 percent of Sunday circulation totals.[5] Despite this dominance, the individual newspapers composing the chain are often too geographically scat-

---

EXHIBIT 3.2

Radio Stations and Networks	Radio Stations in Ten Major Metro Markets		Radio Networks and Number of Affiliates	
	METROPOLITAN AREA	**NUMBER OF STATIONS**	**NETWORK**	**NUMBER OF AFFILIATES**
	Chicago	52	ABC Radio Network	1725
	Los Angeles	48	Associated Press	1125
	New York	44	CBS Radio Network	850
	Washington, D.C.	41	Mutual Network	850
	Philadelphia	37	Transtar Radio Network	750
	San Francisco-Oakland	37	NBC Networks	664
	Dallas-Ft. Worth	33	RKO Radio Networks	575
	Detroit	30	Satellite Music Network	363
	Boston	29	National Public Radio	288
	Cleveland-Akron	29	CNN Radio Network	157
			Music Country Network	122
			Sheridan Network	100
			Wall Street Journal Report	80

Source: Broadcasting/Cablecasting Yearbook 1986 (New York: Associated Press, 1986).

Source: Broadcasting, July 23, 1984.

tered to fit advertisers' and audience objectives. The medium is most often used by national advertisers to supplement their campaigns in other media. Local advertisers find newspapers valuable for their concentrated coverage within local communities in which these merchants trade.

MAGAZINES AND BUSINESS PAPERS

There are about 10,000 magazines in the United States, ranging in character from color weeklies with circulations as high as 4,000,000 to special-interest quarterlies with circulations of only a few hundred. Before the days of television, general-interest magazines with large circulations were an important medium for the national advertiser; but television provided larger audiences at a lower cost per individual. The result was the decline of large circulation general-interest publications such as *The Saturday Evening Post*.

Today, magazines are a rather specialized medium reaching audiences with particular interests. Primarily a medium for the national advertiser, magazines reach relatively small audiences compared to television. Publishers of magazines and business papers usually offer a range of publications that provide coverage of specialized groups, and which can be combined for more generalized coverage (see Figure 3.2).

Magazines usually offer quite detailed information on their audiences, which can be very helpful for marketers of specialized products or services, such as sporting goods, gourmet food products, designer clothing, personal and financial services, and similar items.

Business papers are a special type of publication, often related to a specific industry. These periodicals carry editorial matter of interest to

A CLOSER LOOK

THE TIMES MIRROR COMPANY: HOLDINGS OF A MEDIA CONGLOMERATE

The Times Mirror Company of Los Angeles has been in the publishing business for over 100 years. The company had total revenues of almost $3 billion in 1985. It was ranked fifth in size among U.S. media companies by *Advertising Age* in 1986. More than half the sales total came from newspaper publishing.

	REVENUES	
Newspaper	$1,619,856,000	
Magazine	144,000,000	
Broadcast	128,809,000	
Cable	278,641,000	
Total media revenues		2,171,306,000
Other revenues		788,112,000
Total revenues		$2,959,418,000

Holdings

Eight daily newspapers: *Los Angeles Times, Denver Post, Greenwich Time, Stamford Advocate, Hartford Courant, Baltimore Sun, Allentown Morning Call, Dallas Times Herald, Newsday*.

Five consumer magazines: *Golf, Outdoor Life, Popular Science, Ski, The Sporting News*.

Seven broadcast TV stations: in Dallas, Austin, St. Louis, Harrisburg, Birmingham, Syracuse, and Elmira.

Over 50 cable properties: concentrated in Phoenix, Arizona; southern Orange County; and northern San Diego County, California.

The Times Mirror Company also has major land and timber holdings designed to ensure continued supplies of newsprint and significant textbook publishing operations.

Sources: Times Mirror Annual Report, 1985; and *Advertising Age*, June 30, 1986, S–68.

those in the industry and are an important means of circulating advertisements for new products and services that are useful to these businesses.

OUT-OF-HOME MEDIA

This classification includes a variety of signs, ranging from outdoor boards measuring over 10 feet high and 20 feet long, to car cards used in buses and taxis. Both national and local advertisers use outdoor advertising to reach people who are on the move, to build awareness of new products, and remind audiences of existing ones. It is usually quite difficult to obtain very specific information about the types of audiences reached by out-of-home media and the effects such ad messages have on consumption. However, the out-of-home media are important for support in many types of campaigns, usually providing very wide exposure to the advertising message in a very short amount of time. These media are usually sold by local operators who, in the case of city bus lines, bid on a franchise to operate the business much as cable television operators do. Outdoor boards are usually the property of an outdoor advertising firm, which leases or owns the space for the sign structure and prepares and posts paper signs on it for advertisers. Space is usually rented for 30-day periods. These media, too, are coming increasingly under chain ownership. The national advertiser wishing to use outdoor advertising nationwide can do so through the Institute of Outdoor Advertising. This orga-

FIGURE 3.2

Using Magazines and Business Papers to Reach a Specialized Audience

Cahners Welcomes Technical's Magazines

Technical Publishing Company is now a part of Cahners. The merger makes Cahners the largest publisher by far of specialized business magazines in the USA, with over $350 million in advertising sales. More important, the merger will enable Cahners to offer advertisers many new and important services in all of our magazines.

More Magazines in More Important Markets. With more than 60 magazines you can now look to Cahners to help you reach many more of the markets and audiences that are important to you. There are now Cahners magazines in these major markets: Building & Construction, Foodservice & Lodging, Electronics & Computers, Interior Design, Book Publishing, Printing, Medical/Health Care, Manufacturing, Power Generation,

and Industrial Research/Technology. And in the specialized consumer field, Child Care & Development.

More Marketing & Advertising Services. By utilizing the resources of both publishing companies, Cahners can now offer advertisers an even broader range of services in Marketing, Research, and other specialized services in advertising and marketing.

More People with More Skills to Serve You. Cahners Magazine Division now has over 2,000 employees. They include many of the most talented people in publishing, in the graphic arts, in circulation management, and in sales and marketing. Individually and together as a company we're dedicated to publishing the best magazines in the fields we serve.

Look to Cahners for the magazines you need to reach your target markets, and for the full range of marketing services that can extend the reach and impact of your advertising program. Now more than ever, Cahners Means Business. That's why we're the first choice of American Business in Business Magazines.

Cahners Publishing
A Division of Reed Publishing USA

For more information about Cahners Magazines, contact Fred Lubet, Vice President of Advertising.   Telephone 312/635-8800.

Source: Courtesy of the Cahners Publishing Company/A Division of Reed Publishing USA.

nization serves to coordinate the efforts and contracts of the individual firms supplying the boards to the advertiser.

DIRECT MAIL

In the case of direct-mail advertising, the medium is an envelope, card, or package carried by the U.S. Postal Service. The most attractive aspect of this form of advertising is that messages may be targeted at very specific groups of prospects who have a high likelihood of purchasing the product or service. An example of this type of mailing is shown in Figure 3.3. Equally well suited to local or national advertising, direct mail is growing in importance as sophisticated record keeping allows the construction of better, more productive mailing lists.

The phone books of most major communities contain listings for direct-mail advertising consultants. Often, these services are offered by printing firms who can also produce the materials that comprise the mailing. The heart of the direct-mail advertising effort—the prospect list—may be developed from the advertiser's records or rented from a **list broker,** a supplier who specializes in supplying this information. List brokers can supply a wide variety of mailing lists. The lists are rented for one-time use at an established rate based on the size of the list and difficulty of compiling it.

FIGURE 3.3

The Direct-Mail Package: Focusing on a Special Market

Source: Courtesy of Publishers Clearing House.

SPECIALTY ADVERTISING

Specialty advertising consists of an advertiser's name or selling message imprinted on a usable item, such as a ball-point pen or a writing tablet (see Figure 3.4). While not intended to be persuasive in themselves, specialty advertising items serve to build goodwill and remind users of the advertiser during the life of the item. The most popular specialty items are calendars, writing instruments, and matchbooks; however, new and interesting specialties are always becoming available.

Specialty advertising organizations range in sophistication from merely imprinters to knowledgeable sales promotion and advertising consultants. Outside the largest cities, the specialty advertising operator is likely to be a small business person with imprinting and heat-stamping equipment and an almost endless array of merchandise for imprinting.

VARIATIONS IN THE MEDIA MIX

The classifications of media selected by advertisers vary considerably with the needs and objectives of their advertising plans. The media included, and the relative importance of each medium in the advertising plan, is referred to as the **media mix.** Since the firms within a single product

FIGURE 3.4

Specialty Advertising

Almost any item can be the vehicle
for specialty advertising.

Source: Courtesy of Specialty Advertising Association International, Irving, TX 75038.

category often have similar advertising needs, the next section of this
chapter will examine how advertisers in different product categories allocate their dollars among the advertising media and promotional tools at
their disposal.

CONSUMER GOODS

Consumer goods advertisers depend heavily on television advertising to
deliver their selling messages. This is because such products are consumed
by the majority of Americans. For the consumer goods advertiser, reaching specialized groups within the general population is not an issue. This
is particularly true for marketers of disposable consumer goods, or *package
goods*. Package goods are low-priced, frequently purchased household and
personal items, such as health and beauty aids, soaps, and beverages.

The advertising budget for consumer *durable goods*, on the other hand,
is somewhat different from that for disposable goods, reflecting the priorities of these advertisers. Marketers of durable goods (such as refrigerators
and other major appliances) find the highest concentration of prospects for
their products among homeowners who are slightly older and better off
financially than the average television viewer. In addition, product information is important to the buying decision and often represents an important advertising component. For this reason, marketers of durable goods
concentrate their expenditures in magazines concerned with the home,
which are of interest to their target market group. In addition, these advertisers may allocate a special budget for cooperative advertising, so that
local retailers may advertise the availability of the manufacturer's products
in specific market areas.

NATIONAL RETAIL ADVERTISING

National retail chains, such as Sears, Roebuck and Company, J. C. Penney Company, and Kmart Corporation, employ a different strategy.

While catalogs are important media to Sears and Penney, these are
not, strictly speaking, advertising media. They are a form of direct re-

FIGURE 3.5

Business-to-Business Advertisers

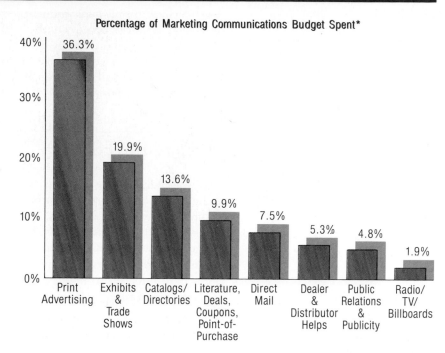

Percentage of Marketing Communications Budget Spent*

*The sum of the percentages does not add up to 100% since certain respondents chose not to respond to specific budget items, and, therefore, different bases were used.

Source: McGraw-Hill Research 1984 "Survey of Industrial Marketing Costs" based on an nth sample of marketing managers in industrial companies drawn from the circulation list of *Business Marketing* magazine.

sponse advertising and will be discussed in depth in a later chapter. The retail chains depend heavily on newspaper advertising to draw the potential buyer's attention to sales and other events at their local outlets. National retailers also depend on newspapers to distribute preprinted inserts, usually carried in the Sunday newspaper. While television is also used, it is a less significant element in the media mix of retail chains than it is for consumer goods marketers.

BUSINESS-TO-BUSINESS ADVERTISERS

Business-to-business advertisers are marketers of special goods and services consumed by other businesses. Their use of advertising is illustrated in Figure 3.5. For example, in industrial advertising, often the most important medium is print advertising in business publications. These very specialized magazines are used to reach the relatively small number of people who influence the selection of industrial goods and services. Since direct mail is also well suited to reaching selected audiences, this medium is an important one for industrial advertisers as well. On the whole, business advertisers spend very little on advertising in relation to the size of their firms. One reason for this is that industrial goods are often very expensive. Consider, for example, the cost of adding a new piece of robotic equipment to an assembly line. Because of this high cost, all selling expenses including advertising are small compared to low-priced consumer package goods. However, industrial advertising can be an effective way of reaching people who influence the decision to adopt industrial products, especially when a number of people are involved in the decision. Several studies by McGraw-Hill have shown business publications to be the only one of several marketing tools (including business publications, catalogs, direct mail, sales representatives, and trade shows) that reached all the people who influenced the purchase of industrial products.[6]

LOCAL AND NATIONAL MEDIA RATES

Newspapers usually sell their advertising space at two different rates. The higher, or *national rate*, is charged to distant advertisers who contract through advertising agencies. Lower *local rates* are charged to retailers who buy their own space, usually on a large annual contract. The local rates are usually not commissionable; that is, the papers will not discount the rate to advertising agencies. For this reason, agencies that work for retailers most often do so under a fee compensation arrangement. Exhibit 3.3 shows media revenue from local and national sources.

EXHIBIT 3.3

Media Advertising Revenue from Local and National Sources (in millions of dollars)

MEDIUM	NATIONAL	LOCAL
Newspapers	$ 3,352	$21,818
Magazines*	7,716	—
Outdoor	610	335
Direct Mail	15,500	—
Television	14,289	5,714
Radio	1,700	4,790
Cable TV	637	130
Miscellaneous	9,551	8,608
Total	$53,355	$41,395
Grand Total		$94,750

*Includes consumer, business, and farm papers.
—None
Source: Based on 1985 data from TVB and McCann-Erickson, Inc.

NATIONAL SALES REPRESENTATIVE COMPANIES

Newspapers—and other media including radio and television stations—generate some of their advertising revenues from distant advertisers who have no direct contact with the paper or station. Since it is not feasible for these media to maintain a national sales staff to call on advertising clients in New York, Chicago, Los Angeles, and so forth, there are services that do this work. **Media representatives,** or "reps," serve as the national sales force for newspapers and stations across the country. Some large rep firms maintain offices in all important advertising cities, but particularly in New York, where over half of all spot radio and television buying is done.[7] Reps are provided with the latest audience and rate information and call regularly on advertisers and agencies to interest them in the stations and newspapers they represent. Media representatives are paid on a negotiated commission basis by the organizations they represent, ranging from about 6 percent in television to as high as 20 percent in cable (a typical commission, however, is 10 percent of sales). Figure 3.6 shows an ad for one of the largest radio and television rep firms in the country.

OTHER SERVICES AND SUPPLIERS

In addition to the media that carry advertising messages, numerous other specialized services support the advertising activity in various ways.

MARKET RESEARCH

One of the most important services to advertisers, agencies, and media in planning and executing the advertising message is market research. The world's largest market research firm, A. C. Nielsen Company, posted

A CLOSER LOOK

MARKETING RESEARCH SERVICES FROM DUN & BRADSTREET CORPORATION

Advertisers need all kinds of information to help make marketing decisions. Although you might think that something like product sales data is information that the advertiser would already know, this is often not the case. While the advertiser can compile sales records to wholesalers and other middlemen in the marketing chain, the advertiser rarely has reliable information on how products are selling at the retail level. In a situation like this, the advertiser often calls for the services of an outside research firm.

For many years the A. C. Nielsen Company provided the following types of research information to many advertiser firms. In 1984, Nielsen merged with the Dun & Bradstreet Corporation, a firm that specializes in numerous other types of business research and information, such as credit reports.

Getting information on consumer acceptance and product movement is only one of the reasons a marketer might choose to use the services of a research firm. Listed below are four of Dun & Bradstreet's marketing research services commonly used in connection with advertising decision making.

Nielsen Marketing Research This division monitors consumer sales, retail inventories, and trade activities for a marketer's brand, and provides information on its competitors as well. Increasingly, this information

comes from data compiled as products bearing the Universal Product Code (UPC) are read or scanned at supermarket cash registers. Reports are made on a weekly basis. This division also provides arrangements for test marketing of different kinds, including electronic and controlled store tests. In addition to basic reports and services, custom arrangements are possible.

Nielsen Media Research Nielsen is probably best known for one of the services of this group, the Nielsen "ratings." This division provides information on TV audience tuning and viewing based on a variety of data collection methods. While this information has considerable importance to network and station management for sales and program planning, it is also vital to agencies and advertisers in planning campaigns. Audience data are also essential in determining the efficiency of an advertising campaign in reaching its intended audience.

Nielsen Clearing House Well over 200 billion coupons are circulated each year. This division redeems coupons on behalf of marketers, reimburses retailers, and provides reports to marketers evaluating the promotional activity in comparison to norms of performance.

Neodata Services This division processes and maintains the records of millions of magazine subscriptions to a wide range of consumer publications. The division produces mailing labels for the magazines themselves, as well as handling invoices, renewals, and special promotions.

Source: Courtesy of Dun & Bradstreet Corporation.

estimated revenues of $517 million in 1986.[8] Nielsen offers a broad range of research services.

Other firms may specialize in one aspect of research. For example, a firm may conduct a survey to determine the interest in a product among members of a potential target market.

Other research firms specialize in various types of testing. For example, many television commercials are screened by a test audience to determine communication and persuasive value prior to appearance on national television. This testing is carried out in special facilities under the guidance of researchers.

In addition, research firms provide general services which can be modified to meet the needs of the advertiser. A. C. Nielsen, for example, operates a coupon redemption service, in which supermarket coupons issued by advertisers are redeemed and records maintained as to redemption rates. These can then be compared to industry averages to determine the effectiveness of promotional activities.

FIGURE 3.6

Media Representatives: Selling
Space or Time Coast to Coast

Source: Courtesy of Blair Radio.

As suggested earlier, a good deal of research is used to determine the size and characteristics of media audiences. This type of research is sometimes commissioned by trade associations, by agencies or advertisers, or by the media themselves. Research activities and methods of information gathering will be discussed further in later chapters.

TRADE ASSOCIATIONS

A **trade association** has the general goal of advancing the interests of the group it represents. Trade association activities include lobbying state and federal government and regulatory agencies, raising levels of professional practice, collecting and distributing useful information to the members, and aiding the general development of the industry.

Trade associations compile large amounts of information about activities in their industry, which can be very useful to advertising and marketing planning. In addition, they maintain extensive records that may provide perspective on industry development and change. The media-related trade associations often engage in extensive research activities as well. Though the intent of this research is to obtain competitive advantages against other media, the information developed is often valuable.

There are trade associations that serve the advertising industry specifically, such as the American Association of Advertising Agencies and the Association of National Advertisers. Other trade associations are not directly concerned with advertising but may supply advertising information to their members, especially if it is an important marketing tool in the industry (the Proprietary Association, for example, serves marketers of non-prescription drugs and remedies). Media trade associations, such as the Newspaper Advertising Bureau, aid their members in selling advertising in their medium more effectively. Trade groups that supply important advertising information are included in the list of organizations in Appendix A.

THE TRADE PRESS

In addition to the information provided by trade associations, the **trade press** is composed of specialized publications that circulate to members of the advertising industry, providing a vital source of information on industry developments and up-to-the-minute news. These periodicals are not related to the trade associations, but are privately published magazines.

PRODUCTION SERVICES

Numerous other supporting services handle the production of advertisements for the print or broadcast media. Freelance artists and writers, photoengravers and printers, production houses and art studios, modeling agencies, photographers, and illustrators all provide indispensable assistance in the preparation of advertising. These services are in fact so specialized that it is difficult for agencies to keep track of them. As a result, special directories exist to organize and present the capabilities of these specialists. An ad for one, the *Adweek*/Art Directors' Index, is shown in Figure 3.7.

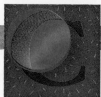

HOW BUSINESS PAPERS SERVE AN INDUSTRY: THE ADVERTISING TRADE PRESS

The advertising industry is served by a number of magazines that report and analyze events affecting the industry. Numerous agencies, advertisers, media, trade associations, and professional groups publish newsletters. Other specialized areas also have trade journals and newsletters. For example, the specialty advertising business has two trade journals of its own as well as several newsletters.

The following journals are widely read and respected in the industry:

ADWEEK General advertising weekly. Tightly focused on the advertising business with an emphasis on analysis. Edited in six regional editions.

Marketing Communications Monthly publication focusing on advertising as a promotional tool. Includes substantial coverage of sales promotion activities.

Advertising Age General advertising paper that appears weekly. Focuses on marketing and broad-scale industry developments. Large format: 11″ × 15″. Numerous special issues.

Madison Avenue Monthly publication focusing on the agency business. Large format: 11″ × 15″. Emphasizes analysis of developments affecting agencies.

Marketing & Media Decisions Monthly publication focusing on developments in media and audience behavior. Frequent case histories and guest columns on media changes.

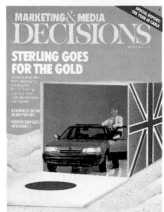

Source: Reprinted with permission of *ADWEEK*.

SUMMARY

Media serve the vital function of delivering the advertising message. For
the most part, the entertainment portion of the commercial media is very
carefully designed to attract a specific audience in whom advertisers are
interested. These days, most media are part of a large organization, either
a chain, a network, or a large conglomerate.

   Television advertising can be bought on a network, spot, or local basis, depending on the scale and needs of the advertiser. Advertising on
various cable services seems to offer great potential for reaching special-

ized audiences, but is not yet mature enough to form a mainstay for most advertisers. Like television, radio advertising is useful in reaching either a national audience (through network advertising) or a local audience (through individual station advertising). Though several national newspapers are available, newspaper advertising is primarily a local medium used by local advertisers, or a support medium for the national advertiser. Magazines are useful in reaching upscale audiences who have very specialized interests. Out-of-home and specialty advertising media are used primarily as a supplement to advertising in other media, usually for the purpose of reminding. Direct mail can be used effectively by local or national advertisers, the key being the quality of the prospect mailing list.

The relative emphasis that an advertiser gives to each of the media in the overall media plan is called the media mix. Because of differences in advertising objectives and the various advantages of each medium, the media mix of, say, a national consumer goods firm differs considerably from that of an industrial goods advertiser.

In order to sell to national advertisers, local stations and papers often employ media rep firms to represent them in major advertising cities. Information on the audiences for most major media are measured by independent research firms who sell their findings to the media and to advertisers. Almost all media are supported by trade associations, which try to advance the business interests of the media, often by attempting to point out the unique advertising advantages of using the particular medium. Considerable information on advertising industry developments and issues can be found in the trade press.

YOU MAKE THE DECISION

HEALTHWORKS, INC.

Healthworks is a regionally franchised health and fitness club that emphasizes individually designed exercise and recreation programs. The concept of the club is built around employing sophisticated computer diagnostics and sports medicine professionals at each facility. Medical advice on exercise, diet, wellness, and sports-related injuries is available at each club during afternoon and evening hours, six days a week.

The organization plans to develop a $2 million regional advertising campaign to present its concept to consumers and to stimulate interest in the local clubs, which will open soon in ten major western cities. The clubs are designed to appeal to young professionals, ages 25 to 34.

Given the information about this organization's advertising objectives, budget, and target audience, consider each of the major media discussed in this chapter and explain why you think each might or might not be useful for the Healthworks campaign.

■ ■ ■

QUESTIONS FOR DISCUSSION

1. How do advertisers and agencies normally obtain information on media audiences?

2. What differentiates the advertising potential of cablecasting from traditional broadcasting?

3. Explain the differences between network and spot television advertising.

4. What is the function of the media representative?

5. What is the function of the list broker?

6. What are the special problems of audience measurement among the out-of-home media?

7. Differentiate between package goods and consumer durables, and explain why they might be advertised in different media.

8. How and why is business-to-business advertising different from consumer advertising?

9. Outline the functions of the advertising trade associations.

10. List three advertising services contracted for outside the advertiser firm and advertising agency, and describe the function of each.

NOTES

1. Peter Kerr, "Ad Supported Cable Networks Getting Brighter Profit Picture," *The Denver Post*, August 19, 1984, 7–1.

2. James Forkan, "INTV: Indies Coming of Age," *Advertising Age*, January 6, 1986, 2.

3. See Ron Kaatz, *Cable Advertiser's Handbook* (Chicago: Crain Books, 1985), for a discussion of the status of cable narrowcasting.

4. Warren Agee, Phillip Ault, and Edwin Emery, *Introduction to Mass Communications* (New York: Harper & Row, 1985), 209.

5. "Groups Still Own Most U.S. Dailies," *Editor and Publisher*, April 28, 1984, 76.

6. McGraw-Hill Laboratory of Advertising Performance, #1032.1, 1032.2, and 1032.3.

7. Charles Warner, *Broadcast and Cable Selling* (Belmont, Calif.: Wadsworth, 1986), 307.

8. *Advertising Age*, November 24, 1986, S-4.

SUGGESTED READINGS

Agee, Warren; Phillip Ault; and Edwin Emery. *Introduction to Mass Communications*. New York: Harper & Row, 1985.

Beville, Hugh. *Audience Ratings: Radio, Television and Cable*. Hillsdale, N.J.: Lawrence Erlbaum Associates, 1985.

Bogart, Leo. *Strategy in Advertising*. 2nd ed. Chicago: Crain Books, 1984.

Kaatz, Ron. *Cable Advertiser's Handbook*. 2nd ed. Chicago: Crain Books, 1985.

McGann, Anthony, and Thomas Russell. *Advertising Media*. Homewood, Ill.: Richard D. Irwin, 1981.

Sissors, Jack, and Jim Surmanek. *Advertising Media Planning*. 2nd ed. Chicago: Crain Books, 1982.

Surmanek, Jim. *Media Planning: A Practical Guide*. Chicago: Crain Books, 1985.

Warner, Charles. *Broadcast and Cable Selling*. Belmont, Calif.: Wadsworth, 1986.

Association of National Advertisers. "Cooperative Advertising." New York, 1986.

UNDERSTANDING
BUYER BEHAVIOR

Key Terms

buyer behavior
culture
subculture
reference group
opinion leader
external conditions
situational factors
motivation
perception
selective exposure
selective distortion
selective retention
learning
personality
AIO statement
demographics
attitude

Learning Objectives

To describe the process of buyer behavior

To analyze how advertising influences buyer behavior

To discuss the major influences on how consumer and business buyers receive advertising and make buying decisions

To relate advertising to buyer behavior

Meet John and Bill, two people who are very similar but also very different. Perhaps you know people like them in your hometown. Or perhaps they're like one of your relatives or friends of your parents.

John is a 49-year-old accountant. He is married and has two teenage children. He graduated from Roosevelt University in Chicago with a B.S. in accounting and has worked for the same company since graduation. John and his wife rented an apartment for the first few years of their marriage before purchasing their home, a three-bedroom brick bungalow in the suburbs of Chicago. Recently, John and his wife celebrated the retirement of their 20-year mortgage. John's home originally cost $20,000; its current value is $58,000. Last year, John earned $55,000.

John and his wife are basically stay-at-home people. They watch a lot of television and they subscribe to the *Chicago Tribune*, *TV Guide*, *Elks Magazine*, and *Reader's Digest*. Each year, they take a family vacation to a Wisconsin lake, where they relax, fish, and boat. John also likes to bowl and he is quite proud of his latest accomplishment: a 279 game in a Chicago-area tournament.

John believes that women belong in the home. His wife is a full-time homemaker. In addition to bowling, John enjoys a weekly night out with "the boys" and shopping for bargains. He takes his wife to the an-

nual bowling banquet and occasionally they attend Friday-night fish fries at the local Elks lodge. When John has other free time, he likes to spend it working on his car.

Bill is a 48-year-old attorney. He is married and has three children. Bill holds three degrees: a B.A. in political science from the University of Chicago, an M.B.A. from Brown University, and a J.D. from Northwestern University. After finishing law school, Bill got married and worked for a large Chicago law firm. Six years later, he opened his own law practice in Cleveland.

Four years ago, Bill and his wife purchased a four-bedroom house in the suburbs of Cleveland for $149,000. Their home is currently valued at $172,000, and they have a 20-year, $100,000 mortgage. Last year, Bill earned $83,000.

Bill spends his leisure time reading, jogging, writing, and traveling. Last fall he had a short story published in the *New Yorker*. Bill's wife teaches math at a local college. Last summer they spent six weeks traveling in China. Together, they enjoy speaking to local groups on travel to exotic places. Bill and his wife have little time to watch television. Instead, they subscribe to the *Cleveland Plain Dealer*, *USA Today*, the *Wall Street Journal*, the *New Yorker*, *National Geographic*, and *Travel & Leisure*. Bill likes his work, but has knowingly sacrificed the pursuit of income for a life-style that he and his family can enjoy.

INTRODUCTION

If you were the advertising manager in charge of an advertising campaign for a new car, you would be interested in the profiles of John and Bill. Although these two people have many similar demographic characteristics—they're both in their 40s, they're married and have children, they're both college-educated, they both own a home—it's unlikely that John and Bill would be interested in the same car. In fact, they probably also shop at different stores, buy different brands of clothing, decorate their homes differently, and use differing criteria to choose such services as physicians, dentists, insurance companies, and the like.

Before an advertising campaign can be developed, the advertiser needs to know whom the campaign is directed to and what message is most likely to motivate potential buyers to take the desired action. Without knowledge about buyer behavior, an advertiser has little chance of success. For example, if all you knew about John and Bill was their age, income, and family status, imagine the potential for error in writing an advertisement and for deciding where the ad should run. Knowing how buyers are likely to respond to advertising is the foundation for advertising decision making. In Chapters 1, 2, and 3, you learned how advertising messages are affected by communications senders (advertisers) and transmitters (media). In this chapter, we are primarily concerned with how receiver characteristics influence the effectiveness of advertising messages.

WHY WE RESPOND TO ADVERTISING

As consumers, we are the buyers of most of the products and services advertised. Therefore, we already know much about why we decide to shop at a particular grocery or department store; why we prefer Coca-Cola to 7-Up; or why we prefer Dial to Irish Spring. In this context, advertising decision making seems easy—ads should contain the information we're interested in and they should appear in the media we read and watch. The problems are these: (1) very few stores, products, brands, services, or ideas satisfy everyone, and (2) our individual behavior as a buyer may not be representative of most other people. Again, recall the John and Bill profiles. How representative are their buying behaviors?

Our behavior as consumers is a subset of our overall behavior. This means that marketplace behavior is complex and is affected by many factors. As consumers, we buy products and services for a purpose—for pleasure (gourmet foods, vacations, radios, camping equipment); for satisfying physical needs (clothing, refrigerator, housing, medical services); and for psychological needs (long-distance calls to loved ones, high-fashion clothing, prestige car, etc.). Most often, the products we buy satisfy more than one purpose. Advertisers understand that our marketplace choices are based on the prospects of a particular brand to satisfy a need or to help us move from our current status to another, more desirable one. Successful marketing involves understanding what factors are relevant when we select product categories and specific brands to help move us toward our personal and professional goals.

HOW TO STUDY RECEIVERS OF ADVERTISING

All advertising is centered around translating product attributes in terms of the wants and needs of prospective buyers. Therefore, before an advertising campaign can be launched, the advertiser needs to be intimately familiar with both the product and the buyer.

Understanding the Product It's impossible to make sound advertising decisions without understanding all dimensions of the product. No two products are exactly alike. Even products that are physically identical (aspirin, sugar, salt, gasoline) have the potential for solving different types of buyer needs. Such products may vary in price, distribution, packaging, and promotion. Because price, distribution, and packaging can be copied, advertising allows marketers the possibility of differentiating their offerings by creating distinct product personalities that are difficult to copy. What we ultimately buy is both the *physical product* and the *brand personality*, or *image*.

The most effective advertising depends on thorough knowledge of the product. Product knowledge is accumulated by visiting the factory where the product is made, talking with product designers and engineers, working with wholesalers and retailers of the product, and whenever possible, selling the product to the end user. The purpose of accumulating this firsthand information is to understand what potential differentiating features the product possesses.

Because buyers are never as impressed with a particular brand as the seller is, it is equally important to understand the strengths and weaknesses of competitive brands. Marketers can learn about the competition by talking with distributors and consumers and by shopping for and using all brands in the product category.

The purpose of this type of product knowledge is to understand the product from the point of view of the buyer. Much product and market information is available through a variety of secondary sources. Although such information is useful, marketers soon realize that the market consists of individuals buying products to satisfy a complex combination of wants and needs. Published reports rarely are capable of explaining such complexities.

Think again of John and Bill, profiled at the beginning of the chapter. The key to understanding what kind of car each will buy involves two issues: (1) the physical and psychological attributes of the cars under consideration, and (2) the desired state each is attempting to reach through a new car purchase (buying motives).

Understanding the Buyer If marketers completely understood buyers, product failures would be rare. However, since product failure is a common occurrence, does this mean that marketers know very little about buyer behavior? It's naive to think that marketers will ever have a total grasp of the complexities of consumer behavior; yet, a great deal is known. Although the subject has been one of interest to marketers for a long time, an organized body of literature did not appear until shortly after World War II. This literature is based on concepts, theories, and research in the social and behavioral sciences—anthropology, sociology,

FIGURE 4.1

The Buyer Behavior Process

Problem or Need Recognition

Search for Appropriate Solutions

Evaluation of Alternative Solutions

Purchase Decision (Brand Selection)

Purchase Implementation

Postpurchase Evaluation

psychology, and social psychology. Several of these concepts will be discussed in this chapter.

As shown in Figure 4.1 **buyer behavior** is a process that includes the actions—internal and external—involved in identifying needs, and in locating, buying, using, and evaluating products and services. The fact that buying is a process has several important implications for marketers.

First, the process starts well before the actual purchase is made. Problem recognition and a search for solutions can take months. Advertisers can attempt to shorten these phases of the process by calling buyers' attention to problems, thereby increasing the relevance of the problem and the urgency to resolve it. Note, for example, how Kitty Litter brand reminds the audience of a particular problem that can be resolved through purchase (see Figure 4.2).

Second, the buyer behavior process also includes two possible postpurchase behaviors. If the product satisfies the buyers' expectations, they will likely recall the satisfactory experience at the time of repurchase. Naturally, a pleasant experience with the brand is likely to result in a repeat purchase. On the other hand, if the product does not match the buyers' expectations and/or if they receive conflicting information, buyers may feel uneasy about their purchase and they may select another brand during the next repurchase cycle.

Finally, this process can be applied to both consumer and business-to-business buying situations. However, the situations differ in many respects. The following characterize the business-to-business buying situation:

1. Purchases are often very large, both in quantity and dollar volume.

2. Buyers are usually technically trained personnel (such as purchasing agents).

3. Purchase by committee is common, particularly for capital equipment.

4. Purchases are often influenced by opinion leaders (such as engineers) and others who do not implement the purchase.

5. Multiple suppliers are used to reduce risk and to enhance satisfaction of other purchase criteria (delivery time, payment method, service, etc.).

6. Purchase criteria are usually specified in writing.

7. Products and services require personal communication between buyer and seller.

8. Advertising is used to provide prospective buyers with information, to communicate seller image, and to facilitate the personal selling effort.

9. Decision-making process usually requires months and sometimes years.

INFLUENCES ON RECEIVERS' BEHAVIOR

Every year, large numbers of people buy shirts embellished with a polo player or alligator. Many of us are willing to pay more for jeans that carry a particular label on the back pocket. In some buying situations, there

FIGURE 4.2

Problem Recognition for Cat Owners

Kitty Litter brand catches the
attention of prospective purchasers by
addressing the issue of litter box odor.

may be noticeable and important differences in the physical quality of the
merchandise we buy; however, many times, such differences are either
nonexistent or trivial (see Figure 4.3). We know, of course, that we don't
always buy products because of physical differences. A particular brand
of clothing may give us status or peer acceptance. Owning a particular
brand of television may give us a feeling of confidence that we purchased
a well-known brand.

One of the keys to understanding how receivers of advertising are likely
to behave in the marketplace is to understand why they buy. Effective
advertising depends on understanding *who* buys, *when* they buy, and
most importantly, *what* factors most strongly affect purchasing behavior.

EXTERNAL FACTORS

As shown in Figure 4.4, marketplace behavior is influenced by both external factors and internal factors. External factors include the following:
1) socio-cultural, 2) group, and 3) individual.

Socio-Cultural Factors The broadest influence on how we respond to
advertising is the socio-cultural environment. Our purchases are influenced by the culture (and subculture) in which we live as well as the social
class of which we are a part. Even though socio-cultural factors are beyond the control of the advertiser, they are important because: (1) they

FIGURE 4.3

Influences on Consumer Buying Behavior

"Generic" clothes from The Gap.   "Status" watch from Rolex.

Source: Courtesy of the Gap Stores, Inc.   *Source:* Courtesy of Rolex Watch U.S.A., Inc.

represent the basic determinants of marketplace behavior, and (2) advertising messages will be most effective if they are created within the appropriate socio-cultural context.

Culture **Culture** is the learned behavior of a society. Through interaction and involvement with such institutions as school, church, and the legal system, we learn the general values, aspirations, and behaviors of our society. In turn, these values, aspirations, and behaviors influence our entire range of activity, including what foods we eat, what clothing we wear, how we travel, and how we react to advertising. Consequently, culture has a very direct effect on the success or failure of products and services.

FIGURE 4.4

Factors Influencing Receivers' Reception of Advertising Communication

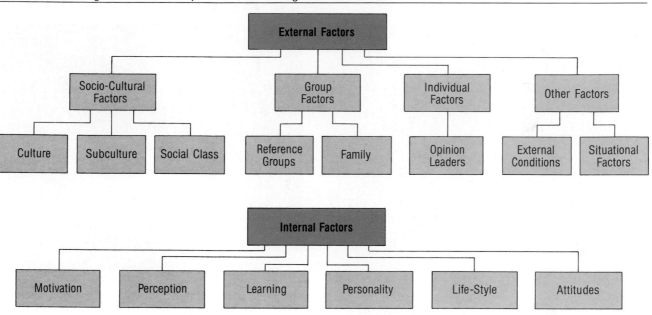

Material success, individual freedom, and youthfulness are important values in the United States. Americans frequently assume that everyone values the same things they do: doesn't everyone, for example, value material comfort, success, and physical activity? If you've ever traveled outside the United States, you may have noticed that other cultures have a set of values, aspirations, and behaviors different from what Americans are used to. Some cultures are similar to the American culture; often, however, they are considerably different. These differences account for some of the challenges in creating successful international advertising. In their book, *Management of International Advertising: A Marketing Approach*, Dean M. Peebles and John K. Ryans, Jr., identify the following cultural differences that will affect the success of advertising:

1. Religious
2. Political
3. Social habits
    a. Marriage
    b. Death
    c. Eating
    d. Alcohol
    e. Tobacco
    f. Sex
4. Racial attitudes
5. Nationalism
6. Trade customs
7. Bureaucracy[1]

FIGURE 4.5

Targeting the 1980s' American Woman

The American Express Company is aware of its market, and the firm's advertising reflects that awareness.

Source: Courtesy of American Express Travel Related Services Company, Inc.

Advertisers need to be aware of subtle shifts in changes in the culture because cultural change signals changes in marketplace behavior. One of the most significant cultural shifts in history has been the changing role of women in U.S. society. Among other things, American women's increasing entry into the work force has made a dramatic impact on a variety of shopping behaviors, and successful advertisers have sought to tailor their message to reflect this shift (see Figure 4.5). Advertisers also need to position products within the accepted codes of a culture. In the United States, for example, automobiles, clothing, and housing are widely recognized symbols of material success. However, it is inappropriate, in American culture, for women to smoke cigars.

Subculture Our behaviors are further defined and influenced by the subculture to which we may belong. A **subculture** is a division within a

EXHIBIT 4.1

The Treiman Classification: Occupational Status

Sociologist Donald J. Treiman in the early 1970s developed a "status scale" for rating more than 500 occupations. Treiman ranked the occupations on a 0-to-100 scale. Here are some of his findings.

OCCUPATION	RATING
Physician	78
University professor	78
Lawyer	75
Dentist	70
Head of large firm	70
Accountant	68
Account executive	67
Senior vice-president, investment, company	67
High-school teacher	64
Writer	62
Veterinarian	61
Manager, small business	60
Assistant manager, retail store	60
Clergy	60
Group pension plan analyst	60
Paralegal	59
Head nurse	58
Artist	57
Elementary-school teacher	57
Social worker	56
Nurse	54
Secretary	53
Real estate agent	49
Bookkeeper	49
Bank teller	48
Farmer	47
Construction worker	46
Clerk-typist	43
TV repairperson	42
Police officer	40
Soldier	39
Receptionist	38

Source: Donald J. Treiman, *Occupational Prestige in Comparative Perspective.* Orlando: Academic Press, 1977. Reprinted with permission.

culture that differs on the basis of race, nationality, religion, and/or geographic location. Advertisers have discovered significantly different purchasing behaviors in many product categories by such subcultures as blacks, Hispanics, Mormons, and some regional groups, such as New Englanders or Southerners. Currently estimated at 18 million, Hispanics represent the fastest-growing segment in the United States. Research shows that Hispanics tend to have larger families and exhibit stronger brand loyalty than the average consumer. In addition, the Hispanic income is rising steadily, leading to the prospect of more disposable income and making this ethnic group a viable marketing target.[2]

Advertisers are paying more attention to subcultures because they recognize their potential as target markets. Consequently, advertising aimed directly at subcultures is more common.

Social Class John and Bill clearly do not belong to the same social class. True, they are both married and have children; they both have college educations and hold what most would call "professional" jobs, and both men live in the suburbs of a major U.S. city. However, John's view of life and the products he buys differ greatly from Bill's.

Everyone in a society is a member of a social class. Advertisers are interested in social class because research over the years has shown that consumer behavior in the marketplace tends to generalize along such lines. That is, people of any particular social group tend to shop in the same stores, buy the same brands, pay attention to the same media, and respond similarly to advertising appeals.

Over the years, several different systems of classifying social class have been developed; however, they are all based on a number of factors that are considered relevant at a particular time. For example, one of the early social-class researchers, Lloyd Warner, used four socioeconomic indicators (occupation, source of income, house type, and dwelling area) to create six social class categories.[3] Another sociologist, Joseph Kahl, used six factors (occupation, personal performance, interactions, possessions, value orientations, and class consciousness) to determine social class.[4]

One of the most important factors in determining social class is occupation. The importance of occupations can vary over time; some may gain in prestige while others may lose status. Exhibit 4.1 presents sociologist Donald J. Treiman's ranking of occupational status.

Group Factors Group factors also help shape our behavior, and their impact is more observable than that of culture or social class. The most important group factors are reference groups and family.

Reference Groups We all belong to groups. Some are formal groups (a sorority or fraternity, a church, a professional association), and others are informal groups (friends, neighbors, the students in your advertising class, the people you work with). Many people also aspire to belong to groups, such as a country club or an "in" group of peers. A **reference group** is any group that serves as a guide in shaping an individual's behavior at a particular time. Research shows that reference groups exert influence—at times a very strong influence—on the products we use and the specific brands we select.[5]

Generally, the more conspicuous the product is, the more influence a reference group has on brand selection. An Izod or Polo shirt, for in-

FIGURE 4.6

Using Social Acceptance to Sell
Consumer Products

FIGURE 4.6

Using Social Acceptance to Sell
Consumer Products

stance, is very conspicuous. So are Cross pens, Guess jeans, Prince tennis racquets, and Swatch watches. The conspicuous display of brand
names on furniture, carpeting, and some clothing items is much less common.

One very visible way to be identified as part of a group or to be associated with a group to which you aspire is to use the products that are
most closely associated with the group. Because advertisers know this,
they frequently use advertising themes stressing social acceptance or celebrity endorsements. In Figure 4.6, Swatch watches are being advertised
on the basis of product features plus the camaraderie of an informal
group. Figure 4.7 illustrates how a reference individual is used to help sell
a product.

Family Almost all household goods and food products are shared by
members of the family, and brand choice is usually determined by one or
more members. As you might expect, the relative influence of family

FIGURE 4.7

Using a Reference Individual
to Sell Consumer Products

Source: Courtesy of Playtex Jhirmack Inc.

members depends on the specific item. Traditionally, the wife has been the main buyer of food and general household products and the husband has mainly purchased such items as life insurance, automobiles, and most durable goods. However, demographic changes, shifts in life-style, and the emergence of women in the workplace have changed this. Now, advertisers recognize that families share in making buying decisions.

Individual Factors   How we process advertising and what we buy are also determined by who we are as individuals and the influence of other individuals on us.

Opinion Leaders   Often, our decisions are strongly influenced by an **opinion leader,** a certain key individual whom we accept as having knowledge and expertise in one or more areas. If, for example, you are planning to purchase a new stereo system, you might talk with a person who you feel is knowledgeable about receivers, turntables, and tape decks. Because the opinions of this expert are likely to influence your choice of equipment, advertisers are very interested in directing advertising to opinion leaders. The result is a two-step flow of information:[6]

A ⬤LOBAL LOOK

HONG KONG'S "IN" DRINK

Question: What's the "in" drink in Hong Kong?
Answer: Cognac.

Although it may seem surprising, the Chinese in this British colony are becoming big consumers of cognac, particularly the more expensive brands. Observers say that drinking cognac marks one, in Hong Kong, as macho, successful, and of high status—all important traits in this Oriental society.

"It's a totally macho drink," says Michael Fromowitz, creative director of the Ball Partnership, which handles the account for Club cognac.

Rick Lane, creative director of DYR Inc., agency for the Remy Martin XO brand, says, "All the cognac ads [in Hong Kong] have to do with face [status] and success. It all has to do with the mark of your achievement."

Lane characterizes his agency's strategy as "trying to project an achievable fantasy. We have defined the guy in our commercials as young, smart, successful, and immoral to some degree."

Apparently the Ball Partnership agrees with this characterization. The agency chose American TV star Larry Hagman to introduce Club cognac to the Hong Kong market.

As the malevolent J. R. Ewing on the long-running "Dallas" series—which is shown both on English and Chinese channels in Hong Kong—Hagman is enormously popular and epitomizes the "macho and successful" image advertisers seek.

Although unavailable in the United States, Club cognac sells for about $25 per fifth in Hong Kong, making it a medium-priced brand in a market where fifty brands compete for annual revenues of about $51 million. Some brands cost as much as $350 per bottle.

Source: Courtesy of The Ball Partnership Hong Kong (WCRS Group).

In one print ad for Club, Hagman—dressed as J. R.—says, "Enjoy drinking it together. Obviously, there is nothing else like it."

Source: Lynn Reaves, "Hong Kong Loves Cognac," *Advertising Age*, September 22, 1986, 84.

Advertising ——→ Opinion Leader ——→ Followers (buyers)
(through   (through word-of-mouth
mass media)   communication)

Eventually, it was noted that the two-step model of communication did not totally explain the flow of communication.[7]

Followers sometimes seek and/or receive information before opinion leaders do. Furthermore, followers' information sometimes influences the

FIGURE 4.8

Influences on an Industrial Purchase

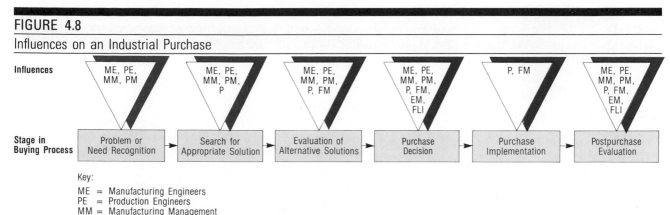

Key:
ME = Manufacturing Engineers
PE = Production Engineers
MM = Manufacturing Management
PM = Production Management
P = Purchasing
FM = Financial Management
EM = Executive Management
FLI = Financial Lending Institutions

opinions of opinion leaders. This more elaborate description of information flow is particularly relevant to business-to-business advertising because of the role that purchasing agents play in the buying process. In many business-to-business situations, the purchasing agent is *not* the opinion leader. Figure 4.8 shows how many opinion leaders participate in a purchasing agent's task of purchasing a machine tool.

In the example, the company is considering the purchase of a piece of capital equipment, a new metalcutting machine. The accepted opinion leaders (based on technical expertise and knowledge) are the manufacturing engineers; however, the purchasing agents act as gatekeepers—they gather information about alternative suppliers and they pass on their opinions to the engineers and others in the company. In this situation, the opinion leaders' decision will be influenced by the gatekeepers. Business-to-business advertisers acknowledge the role of opinion leaders, followers, and gatekeepers by directing advertising to all three groups. Indeed, business advertisers' need to communicate effectively with these various groups has in part given rise to the thousands of magazines in the business-to-business sector. It would be common, for example, for a machine tool advertiser to advertise in *Purchasing Week* (targeted at purchasing agents), *Iron Age* (top management), *Machine & Tool Blue Book* (machine operators), and *Metalworking Engineering* (opinion leader engineers).

Other External Factors   Sometimes marketplace behavior is shaped by the conditions and factors of the environment at any particular time. **External conditions** are uncontrollable aspects of the environment that influence marketplace behavior. For example, people are more likely to buy high-priced, prestige brands when their earnings are high, the economy is growing, and the prospects for their economic future are bright. Automobile manufacturers discovered a ready market for cars and luxury, add-on features when they were able to offer low interest rates to the consumer.

Consumers' choices of products and brands are also likely to vary according to the situation surrounding the purchase. **Situational factors** are

WHO ARE THE OPINION LEADERS?

For many years, marketing and advertising researchers have sought to isolate and characterize opinion leaders. Here's what studies show so far.

Opinion leaders vary widely along demographic lines. In fact, demographics alone show low correlation and are not a good predictor. Leadership depends largely on the product category under discussion. For example, young women dominate as opinion leaders in the areas of fashion and movie-going. On the other hand, market researchers interested in learning about self-esteem turn to mothers with several children.

Opinion leaders are generally gregarious people who are innovative and who relate positively to new products.

While research has shown that personality is generally not a good predictor of opinion leadership, leaders do tend to be more socially active, fashion-conscious, and independent.

Finally, in a group, opinion leaders are the individuals who tend to show greater interest in the topic under discussion. They have proven to be active searchers and information gatherers, particularly in regard to the mass media.

Source: James F. Engel, Roger D. Blackwell, and Paul W. Miniard, *Consumer Behavior*, 5th ed. (Hinsdale, Ill.: Dryden Press, 1986), 316.

time and environmental conditions that influence marketplace behavior. For example, you might pay much more attention to an advertisement for an expensive cologne if you are planning to buy the product as a gift. Or, consider the influence of time on your purchase. If you are on your way to play tennis and suddenly discover you need a can of tennis balls, price and brand name become less relevant in your selection.

INTERNAL FACTORS

Other influences on a receiver's response to advertising are internal—they exist within the individual, and marketers are not able to observe directly their influence on how advertising is received or on marketplace behavior.

Psychology has contributed to an understanding of buyer behavior through analyses of motivation, perception, learning, personality, lifestyle, and attitudes.

Motivation The basis of all behavior is **motivation**—the stimulus that causes a person to take an action. We often hear someone say, "Why did she do that?", "Why did he buy that?", or "What was the real reason they said that?". In fact, many times we don't know why we do things. We do know a *need* (some unfilled condition) existed, and we strived to satisfy that need in one or more ways. For advertisers, the interest in motivation is to understand buyer needs and to use advertising to position products as satisfactions of those needs.

Understanding Needs The most widely used classification of needs is Maslow's hierarchy of needs, a system developed by psychologist Abraham H. Maslow:[8]

1. Physiological needs (hunger, thirst, shelter)
2. Safety needs (security, protection, stability, order)

3. Love needs (affection, belonging, friendship)

4. Esteem needs (recognition, prestige, success, self-esteem)

5. Self-actualization needs (self-fulfillment and realization)

Maslow's hierarchy suggests that lower-order needs must be fulfilled before a person will have interest in higher-order needs. The implications for advertisers? A consumer who has safety needs, for example, will not be interested in an advertising message about a product that promises to satisfy esteem needs. Later in this text, you'll see how needs form a basic part of a technique used to segment markets.

Positioning Products to Fulfill Consumer Needs It is often difficult to get consumers to tell why they buy a certain product, because often they don't know all of the motivations behind their purchases, or they don't want to reveal their motivations. Nevertheless, advertising can be effective only when it is aimed at the right level of consumer motivation. Advertisers continue to learn more about consumer motivations so that they can position products and advertising within the motivation level of their prospects.

Perception Very few of us see things the same way. Some people found Wendy's "Where's the beef?" commercials of the mid-1980s very funny, while others didn't think they were funny at all. Even when two people are motivated by the same need, they might react to a commercial quite differently. The reason is a difference in **perception**—the way we organize and interpret stimuli through the five senses. The most important advertising aspect of perception is how consumers process information—they don't pay attention to all information **(selective exposure);** they interpret information in a way that is consistent with their existing opinions **(selective distortion);** and they remember only a small portion of what they are exposed to **(selective retention).**

Advertisers must create messages that will penetrate the consumer's filtering system. For example, advertising messages are more likely to be received if they:

- Relate to a current perceived need—automobile ads are more noticed by shoppers of new cars

- Are physically different—larger, better use of space, color, design, etc.

- Are consistent with the existing opinions of consumers

- Are repeated often

Learning Because consumers shop often and for a variety of products and services, they become skilled at finding products that promise to fulfill their needs. In essence, their marketplace behavior is shaped by **learning**—a process of behavioral changes based on experience. The first few times you purchase tennis balls, for instance, you might spend considerable time beforehand gathering information (perhaps talking with others, reading tennis magazines, and paying attention to advertisements for the product). After purchasing the product many times, you'll probably spend much less time thinking about your purchase because you will have learned all that is relevant to buying tennis balls. You'll have opinions and experience about brand performance, and you'll have knowledge about price, packaging, durability, and availability.

Psychologists have devoted years of study to the subject of learning, and many different theories have been introduced. However, the important implication for the advertiser remains the overall concept of receivers' abilities and inclinations to modify their behaviors as a result of advertising. For example, much advertising creates visual and verbal symbols that link the advertised product with a consumer's unfilled need. The advertiser hopes that receivers will associate satisfaction of their need (hunger, social acceptance, self-esteem, etc.) with the purchase of the advertised brand. For example, the appealing glass of Michelob beer (stimulus) in Figure 4.9 stimulates thirst. The advertiser wants the receiver to learn that his or her thirst can be satisfied in a pleasant way through the purchase of Michelob.

Personality One of the most widely researched areas of psychology is **personality**—the way one responds to the environment over a long period of time. Hundreds of studies have been conducted in an attempt to link the dimensions of personality to marketplace behavior (brand choice, media preference, message appeal, etc.). Unfortunately, the results of these works have been inconclusive.[9] Nevertheless, advertisers attempt to present products in a way that is consistent with the consumer's self-image.

It seems logical that a person's personality would determine reaction to a number of marketing stimuli, including advertising. For example, shouldn't an aggressive, self-confident personality type respond differently to a given advertisement than a compliant personality? Jim McMahon, the outspoken "punky QB" of the Chicago Bears, frequently lets his reputation precede him. Many consumers admire (and identify with) McMahon's thumbing his nose at the Establishment, a fact that makes this ad for Honda so appealing (Figure 4.10).

Despite the lack of research support, marketers maintain their interest in understanding personality and in developing advertising messages that create consistency between brand images and the self-image of the buyer.

Life-Style Another dimension of behavior is the collection of a person's activities, interests, and opinions. While a person's life-style is more temporary than personality, it tells us more about how one interacts with the environment. All people within a particular social class don't approach their environment in the same way. Marketers learn a lot about prospective buyers when they can profile them in terms of what is important to them, how they spend their time, and what they think of their world.

Life-style profiles are compiled by measuring consumers' responses to a series of statements about a large number of activities, interests, and opinions. One tool that consumer behaviorists have created to construct consumer profiles is a series of **AIO statements** (see Exhibit 4.2). By using the information compiled from an AIO questionnaire, marketers create a life-style profile, and advertisements can then be aimed at a particular life-style. We know quite a bit about the respective life-styles of John and Bill. This knowledge makes the task of writing advertising much easier.

Life-styles change over time, both for an individual and for a society. It seems natural to assume that our life-style is likely to change as we get older, make more money, change occupations, or change our family sta-

FIGURE 4.9

How Anheuser-Busch Encourages Consumers to Link Thirst Satisfaction with Michelob

Source: Courtesy of Anheuser-Busch, Inc.

FIGURE 4.10

Honda Uses Personality to Sell
Motorcycles

Source: Courtesy of America Honda Motor Co., Inc.

tus. Societal life-styles are also a function of demographic and value changes. For example, a long-term recession might well encourage a more cautious approach to discretionary spending and a stronger interest in job security. Advertisers monitor possible shifts in life-style so they can create relevant advertising.

Demographics   Another dimension of life-style is **demographics:** buyer characteristics such as age, sex, education, and income. Most of our purchases are first determined by who we are. For example, we might have a strong liking and preference for a Porsche 928, but the purchase of such an expensive car is impractical—if not impossible—at our income level. Therefore, makers of the Porsche 928 attempt to target its advertising at

EXHIBIT 4.2
AIO Statements

	FEMALES (N = 594)					MALES (N = 490)				
	SA	A	N/O	D	CD	SA	A	N/O	D	CD
VACATION RELATED										
Our family travels together quite a lot.	38%	30%	7%	16%	9%	37%	33%	7%	15%	8%
A cabin by a quiet lake is a great place to spend the summer.	44	28	10	11	7	45	30	9	11	5
I like to spend my vacations in or near a big city.	6	13	12	30	39	4	10	11	28	47
Vacations should be planned for children.	17	39	16	20	8	18	38	19	18	7
ENTERTAINMENT RELATED										
Television is our primary source of entertainment.	26%	26%	6%	23%	19%	24%	31%	6%	19%	20%
I would rather spend a quiet evening at home than go out to a party.	24	30	8	25	13	30	31	8	23	8
We do not often go out to dinner or the theater together.	20	22	8	19	31	15	25	6	22	32
SPORTING RELATED										
The best sports are very competitive.	13%	21%	31%	21%	14%	28%	28%	20%	15%	9%
I prefer to participate in individual sports more than team sports.	11	18	39	18	14	16	29	25	17	13
I like to go and watch sporting events.	18	40	13	15	14	34	37	10	12	7
LEISURE TIME RELATED										
I have enough leisure time.	14%	23%	8%	28%	27%	13%	14%	8%	31%	34%
I tend to spend most of my leisure time indoors.	16	35	6	29	14	7	22	7	32	32
My leisure time tends to be boring.	4	14	8	26	48	4	12	8	27	49
SPECIFIC ACTIVITY RELATED										
I do a lot of repair work on my car.	1%	4%	23%	7%	65%	24%	24%	5%	16%	31%
I often work on a do-it-yourself project in my home.	37	34	15	7	7	36	31	13	11	9
I am active in one or more service organizations.	12	11	19	17	41	8	10	23	18	41
GENERAL STATEMENT										
When it comes to my recreation, time is a more important factor to me than money.	23%	29%	17%	21%	10%	25%	30%	15%	19%	11%
I watch television more than I should.	21	28	7	23	21	20	29	9	24	18
My major hobby is my family.	49	30	9	9	3	35	32	14	14	5

Note: SA = Strongly agree; A = Agree; N/O = Undecided or no opinion; D = Disagree somewhat; CD = Completely disagree.
Source: Douglass K. Hawes, W. Wayne Talarzyk, and Roger D. Blackwell, "Consumer Satisfactions from Leisure Time Pursuit," in M. J. hlinger (ed.); *Advances in Consumer Research* (Chicago: American Marketing Association, 1975), 833. Reprinted by permission.

groups of buyers who *can* afford to spend $50,000 for a car. Similarly, marketers know the influence of demographic factors on the purchase of most consumer goods. Simmons Market Research Bureau is one of the leading companies in compiling product consumption/demographic data. Advertisers rely on the SMRB information to guide them as they determine the appropriate target groups for their advertising.

The popularity of products also varies by geographic location. For this reason, national advertising campaigns are often supplemented with more

EXHIBIT 4.3

Leading Markets for Selected Products

MARKET	PRODUCT
Atlanta	Antacids and aspirin
Dallas/Ft. Worth	Popcorn
Denver	Vitamins
Grand Rapids	Rat poison
Indianapolis	Shoe polish
Miami	Prune juice
New Orleans	Ketchup
New York	Laundry soaps
Oklahoma City	Motor oil additives
Philadelphia	Iced tea
Pittsburgh	Coffee
Portland	Dry cat food
Salt Lake City	Candy bars and marshmallows
Savannah	MSG and meat tenderizers
Seattle	Toothbrushes

Source: Sales & Marketing Digest, December 1985, 5. Originally published in *Fortune.*

targeted regional promotions, which appeal to the preferences of that specific geographic region. Exhibit 4.3 lists the top markets for selected products.

Because business-to-business buyers are not buying for their personal consumption, demographic factors are of much less significance. Most business-to-business buying is done by an individual or a team of people in the firm who determine needs, compile a list of possible suppliers to meet the needs, evaluate competitive bids, and then select the supplier. Business buyers are "professional" in the sense that they are hired to make the best possible purchases for their company. Their age, sex, education, and income affect the purchase decision only indirectly—to the extent that these factors impact on the buyer's interest and ability in searching for product information.

Attitudes Marketers are more interested in consumer attitudes than with any other factor influencing behavior. An **attitude** is an individual's feeling about a certain issue at a certain point in time. Attitudes are believed to be the strongest predictors of buyer behavior; therefore, advertisers' abilities to affect attitudes can mean financial success. Advertising objectives are often stated in terms of altering one or more of the components of attitudes, and virtually all measures of advertising effectiveness are concerned with attitude change.

Basically, attitudes are the mechanisms through which all other behavioral influences operate—demographic, psychological, social, and sociocultural. Attitudes are not actions; rather, they are a tendency, or predisposition, to behave or react in a consistent way.[10]

Although marketplace behavior is strongly influenced by attitudes, advertisers know that ultimately, behavior is more strongly influenced by the particular situation. For example, we may hold strongly favorable attitudes toward Arrow shirts; yet, when faced with the purchase decision, we select an alternate brand. Perhaps we could not afford the Arrow shirt; perhaps the retailer did not carry the brand; or perhaps our size was sold out.

According to the traditional view, attitudes consist of three components: the cognitive dimension (knowledge); the affective dimension (feelings); and the conative dimension (behavioral tendencies). In most buying situations, these three components are reinforcing—that is, if you have favorable information about a brand, your feelings toward the brand are likely to be positive and you are probably inclined to purchase the brand. Also, a change in any one of the dimensions will most likely result in changes in the other two in the same direction. For example, an unsatisfactory personal experience with a brand will likely create negative feelings and beliefs about it. Similarly, favorable information leads to favorable feelings, which increase the probabilities of purchase.

The goal of most advertising is to have a positive impact on as many attitude dimensions as possible. This is why most advertisers use a combination of promotional tools and a variety of messages. In Chapters 7 and 9 you will learn that some promotional tools are better at disseminating information to large numbers of people (advertising); some have a stronger impact on feelings (personal selling and public relations); and some have a stronger impact on encouraging action (sales promotion). Chapter 10 discusses attitudes within the context of setting advertising objectives.

SUMMARY

Knowledge about how buyers receive and process communication is critical to the success of an advertising message. Marketers approach the understanding of buyer behavior by first becoming thoroughly familiar with the product and what needs it can satisfy. Most of our knowledge about marketplace behavior comes from the social and behavioral sciences—specifically, anthropology, psychology, social psychology, and sociology. All buyers go through a decision-making process that begins well before an actual purchase is made and continues well after purchase; therefore, marketers stress continual communication with their customers.

Several important factors affect buyers' reception of advertising. The two major categories are external factors and internal factors. External factors include influences outside the individual—culture, social class, reference groups, the family, opinion leaders, external conditions, and situational factors. Internal factors include motivation, perception, learning, personality, life-style, and attitudes.

YOU MAKE THE DECISION

JOHN AND BILL GO SHOPPING

Early in this chapter, you read about John and Bill. You'll recall that while they shared some similarities in demographic characteristics, they were quite different in many other ways. Below is a list of products that both John and Bill would purchase. For each product, specify the brand you think each is most likely to buy.

	BRAND	
PRODUCT	**JOHN**	**BILL**
WATCH		
CAR		
VACATION		
CLOTHING (specify type and store preference)		
AFTER-SHAVE LOTION		

■ ■ ■

QUESTIONS FOR DISCUSSION

1. Explain the importance of understanding the product and the buyer to creating effective advertising.

2. What are the major contributions of the behavioral and social sciences to our understanding of buyer behavior?

3. Explain buyer behavior as a process. What are the major components of the process and what role can advertising play in moving buyers through the process?

4. List the major differences between consumer and business-to-business buying.

5. Give an example of how socio-cultural factors influence consumer buying behavior.

6. How do reference groups influence our reaction to advertising?

7. Why are demographic factors of less importance in influencing business-to-business buying behavior?

8. How can advertisers create advertising that has the best opportunity of penetrating the consumer's communications filtering system?

9. For what products will John and Bill exhibit the greatest difference in brand choice?

10. Assume John and Bill were going to shop for new cars. What advertising messages are most likely to be effective for each?

NOTES

1. Dean M. Peebles and John K. Ryans, Jr., *Management of International Advertising: A Marketing Approach* (Boston: Allyn and Bacon, 1984), 7.

2. "Business," NBC Report, February 15, 1987.

3. W. Lloyd Warner and Paul S. Lunt, *The Social Life of a Modern Community* (New Haven, Conn.: Yale University Press, 1941); and *Social Class in America: A Manual of Procedure for the Measurement of Social Status* (New York: Harper Torchbooks, 1960).

4. Joseph A. Kahl, *The American Class Structure* (New York: Holt, Rinehart and Winston, 1957), 8–10; and Dennis Gilbert and Joseph A. Kahl, *American Class Structure: A New Synthesis* (Homewood, Ill.: The Dorsey Press, 1982).

5. D. I. Hawkins and K. A. Coney, "Peer Group Influences on Children's Product Preferences," *Journal of the Academy of Marketing Science*, Spring 1974, 322–331; and J. D. Ford and E. A. Ellis, "A Reexamination of Group Influence on Member Brand Preference," *Journal of Marketing Research*, February 1980, 125–132.

6. Elihu Katz and Paul F. Lazarsfeld, *Personal Influence* (Glencoe, Ill.: The Free Press, 1955).

7. *Ibid.*, 118–119.

8. Abraham H. Maslow, *Motivation and Personality* (New York: Harper & Row, 1954).

9. H. H. Kassarjian, "Personality and Consumer Behavior: A Review," *Journal of Marketing Research*, November 1971, 409–418.

10. Based on definition in Gordon W. Allport, "Attitudes," in *A Handbook of Social Psychology*, C. A. Murchinson, ed. (Worcester, Mass.: Clark University Press, 1935), 798–844.

SUGGESTED READINGS

Arora, Raj. "Consumer Involvement: What It Offers to Advertising Strategy." *International Journal of Advertising* 4:2, 1985, 119–130.

Belk, Russell W. "Materialism: Trait Aspects of Living in the Material World." *Journal of Consumer Research*, December 1985, 281–300.

Bogart, Leo. *Strategy in Advertising*. 2d ed. Chicago: Crain Books, 1985.

Boyd, Harper W., Jr.; Michael L. Ray; and Edward C. Strong. "An Attitudinal Framework for Advertising Strategy." *Journal of Marketing* 36, April 1972.

Maloney, John C., and Bernard Silverman, eds. *Attitude Research Plays for High Stakes*. Chicago: American Marketing Association, 1979.

Moriarty, Rowland T., and Mel Patrell Furman. *Industrial Buying Behavior: Concepts, Issues, and Applications*. Lexington, Mass.: Lexington Books, 1983.

Percy, Larry, and Arch G. Woodside, eds. *Advertising and Consumer Psychology*. Lexington, Mass.: Lexington Books, 1983.

Rossiter, John R., and Larry Percy. "Advertising Communications Models." In *Advances in Consumer Research*, edited by E. C. Hirschman and M. B. Holbrook. Ann Arbor, Mich.: Association for Consumer Research, 1985.

Solomon, Jolie. "The Business of Leisure: Working at Relaxation." *The Wall Street Journal* (Special Report), April 21, 1986, 1D–24D.

Wilkie, William L., ed. *Advances in Consumer Research*. Ann Arbor, Mich.: Association for Consumer Research, 1979.

The Conference Board, Inc. "How Consumers Spend Their Money: Housing, Apparel, Transportation, Education, Recreation." New York, 1986.

D'Arcy Masius Benton & Bowles Inc. "Fears and Fantasies of the American Consumer." New York, 1986.

Mediamark Research, Inc. "Leisurestyles." New York, 1986.

The Roper Organization, Inc. "The Influential Americans." New York, 1986.

PART 2

Marketing and Advertising Planning Environments: Campaign Foundations

By now you should understand the historical background that helped shape current advertising practice; how the advertising industry is structured; and the characteristics of those who send and receive advertising messages. Part 2 helps you to understand and appreciate the major external and internal environmental factors that impact on advertising planning. We present these issues early in the book so that you will understand all of the forces that influence advertising decision making.

Part 2 consists of four chapters—Chapter 5, Social and Economic Issues; Chapter 6, The Legal and Regulatory Environment; Chapter 7, The Relationship between Advertising and Marketing; and Chapter 8, Selecting Target Markets. While we acknowledge that advertising is much more than a business tool, the purpose of this book is to help you understand advertising within a marketing environment. To accomplish our purpose, you'll need to know how social, economic, and regulatory environments and marketing decisions affect advertising decisions. The primary focus of this book is on learning how to make advertising decisions that will help fulfill the company's marketing goals. Therefore, an understanding of the external and internal environments surrounding the advertiser is critical.

In the beginning of Chapter 5 we present a decision-making framework that is to be used throughout the rest of this book. Chapters 5 and 6 deal with the environmental constraints on advertising. Chapter 7 explores the marketing/advertising relationship and how advertising decisions figure in achieving a firm's marketing goals.

One of the foundations of an effective advertising campaign is knowing how to select the campaign's audience or target market. Chapter 8 will introduce you to the various ways an advertising decision maker can look at the marketplace and select the segment which is most likely to respond to the advertised product. Later chapters will use the decision-making framework introduced in Chapter 5 to focus on creating, delivering, and measuring the effectiveness of the advertising message.

C H A P T E R 5

SOCIAL AND
ECONOMIC ISSUES

Key Terms

deceptive advertising
puffery
perceptual defenses
materialism
tasteless advertising
stereotypes
political advertising
subliminal advertising
economies of scale

Learning Objectives

To outline common social criticisms of advertising

To analyze why many people are apprehensive about advertising

To describe subliminal advertising

To identify the general social effects of advertising

To compare two competing economic models of advertising effects

To list advertising's general effects in the economy

When a new advertising campaign elicits hundreds of calls and letters of complaint as well as criticism by the ad industry itself, is it a sign of imminent disaster?

"It doesn't matter, I'm not out to offend anyone, but the ads are meant to be ambiguous—to make people stop and think. I don't want women flipping through 600 pages of *Vogue* and not even noticing my ads," says fashion designer/businessman Calvin Klein.

There doesn't seem to be much chance of that. Klein's advertising always seems to get a response, whether it's anger or admiration. Klein creates his own advertising, and he does so with the purpose of drawing attention. Sometimes he achieves this with the use of nudity or sexuality; sometimes merely with a mysterious setting.

In 1980, Calvin Klein Jeans drew attention and controversy from TV viewers with a commercial featuring a 15-year-old Brooke Shields. In the commercial Shields asked, "You know what comes between me and my Calvins? Nothing." Some

local stations—and eventually, the networks—refused to air the Klein commercials because of viewer complaints. Women Against Pornography cited Klein as particularly despicable and characterized the commercial as "aboveground child pornography."

From an artistic standpoint, the Calvin Klein ads are part of a trend some call the "New Eroticism." To

dismiss the ads as pornographic may be premature, but the effects are nonetheless disturbing to many.

"It's cerebral sex," says Barbara Lippert, an *Adweek* editor. "When we see a Calvin Klein Obsession ad on television, it's startling because it's so unlike what we're used to seeing. It's more subtle than little hammers pounding someone in the head to simulate a headache."

From a business standpoint, Calvin Klein's advertising has been a tremendous success. His 1984 sales were close to $1 billion, increasing 10 percent over the previous year. Many find his advertising a refreshing and interesting break from more traditional advertising approaches. Clearly, however, not everyone agrees.

Sources: Bernice Kanner, "The New Calvinism," *New York*, September 17, 1984, 31–36; "A Kinky New Calvinism," *Newsweek*, March 11, 1985, 65; and Marcia Froelke Coburn, "The New Eroticism," *Chicago Tribune*, November 16, 1986, sec. 18-W, 1.

INTRODUCTION

This chapter will examine numerous frequently voiced criticisms of advertising's social and economic effects. Because many of these criticisms are subjective, it is often difficult to resolve them clearly and to the satisfaction of everyone. Some criticisms are ideological in nature and spring from fundamental beliefs about the basis of society and the way it operates. We will try to present a balanced view of these issues. Many of the issues discussed here have troubled social critics, economists, and social scientists for generations and cannot be resolved by a simple analysis of the facts. Nevertheless, it is important that anyone connected with the advertising field be aware of these controversies and understand that there are differing points of view. As with other matters of social policy, we all need to develop awareness of the issues and an informed personal position.

Despite the fact that there are many perspectives on advertising's role in society, and we can't say that one is more true than another, they all serve to make up the social environment in which advertising operates. Social attitudes about advertising, as well as legal and regulatory elements considered in Chapter 6, have a profound effect on the limits and potential of advertising as a social force and as a marketing tool. Taken together, these social and legal constraints form the external environment referred to in Figure 5.1. Figure 5.1 is designed to explain the interrelationships of the many advertising decisions discussed in this text. The diagram is presented here—and again in chapters 9, 12, and 15—to highlight the concepts presented and to reinforce the idea that each advertising decision is dependent upon the preceding one.

The first two influences on advertising decision making are the environments in which advertising exists. The external environments are discussed in chapters 1, 2, 3, 5, and 6. Internal environments are discussed in chapters 7 and 8. Both influence the goals that a company realistically hopes to achieve. Because the marketing plan is created to help achieve company goals, it is subordintae to the overall goals of the company. One element of the marketing plan is the promotion plan. Its purpose is to communicate the want-satisfying qualities of the company's products or services in the hope of helping to achieve marketing goals.

The advertising plan specifies how paid media advertising will be coordinated with the other promotional and marketing tools to achieve the organization's goals. The advertising plan consists of decisions about the role of advertising, creating advertising objectives, and budgeting. After these decision areas have been addressed, the advertising manager is ready for the next series of decisions dealing with creative strategy and tactics.

The arrows between creative strategy and tactics and media acknowledge the interrelationship between these two components. Sometimes, the decision on *where* advertising will appear (media) must be made before decisions regarding creative work. In other situations, creative decisions are made first and they in turn influence media decisions.

Once all advertising decisions have been made, the campaign is delivered to the target market. Chapter 4 discusses the receivers of advertising messages. The "response" section of Figure 5.1 indicates that feedback plays a significant role in determining next year's advertising campaign.

FIGURE 5.1

A Framework for Advertising
Decision Making

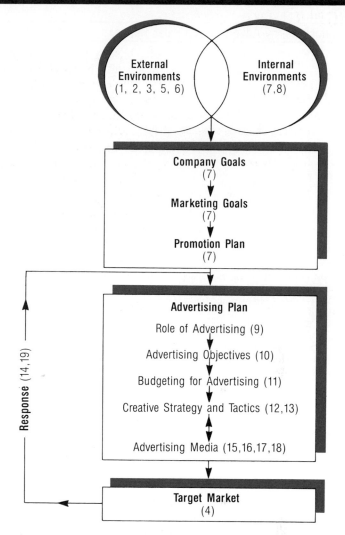

Numbers in parentheses indicate the chapter(s) in which item is discussed.

After reading this chapter, you should appreciate the positions of both defenders and critics of advertising and see the strengths and weaknesses in their arguments. These positions and opinions form an important component of the external environment in which advertising operates.

THE BASIS OF SOCIAL CONCERNS

Concerns about advertising arise for any number of reasons, but primarily due to advertising's avowed purpose of salesmanship. In a consumer society, we learn at an early age to be skeptical of the representations of a salesperson. As we shall see, this skepticism is crucial to using advertising

EXHIBIT 5.1

Top 10 Industries, by Advertising-to-Sales Ratios

RANK	INDUSTRY	PERCENT OF SALES SPENT ON ADVERTISING	PERCENT OF SALES SPENT ON ALL SELLING COSTS*	ADVERTISING AS A PERCENT OF SELLING COSTS†
1	Proprietary drugs	20.2%	35.6%	56.7%
2	Perfumes, cosmetics, and toiletries	14.6	30.5	37.9
3	Flavoring (including soft drink syrups)	13.8	27.9	49.5
4	Cutlery (including razors and blades)	12.9	23.2	55.6
5	Breakfast cereals	11.4	20.4	55.9
6	Pet foods	11.0	22.8	48.2
7	Distilled liquor	11.0	23.8	46.2
8	Periodicals	10.3	20.9	49.3
9	Cigarettes	8.8	16.8	52.4
10	Soaps and cleaners	8.0	18.5	43.2

*Includes cost of distribution, personal selling, sales promotion, and advertising.
†Calculated by determining column 1 figure as a percentage of column 2 figure.
Source: Federal Trade Commission, *Annual Line of Business Report 1977* (Washington, D.C.: U.S. Government Printing Office, 1985), 17, 27, 31, 34, and 35.

information. It is also the intention of advertising to be noticed and this intended intrusiveness evokes varying levels of hostility. In addition, many people are aware of the large sums of money spent on advertising. This, too, arouses suspicion (see Exhibit 5.1).

The billions of dollars spent on advertising last year seem a trivial sum compared to the cost of items in the U.S. defense budget. Even in the most heavily advertised product categories advertising represents an average of only about 30 percent of the total selling cost of consumer goods (other selling costs include expenses of maintaining the sales force, product distribution, sales promotion, etc.)[1] The dollar amounts spent on both commercial production and advertising time and space seem suspiciously large to many consumers. The mere size of the sums engenders the suspicion that some dramatic effect must result from advertising.

An additional factor compounds the suspicion: few consumers have an appreciation of advertisers' intentions. The public is aware that advertising agencies exist, and that they in some way assist the process of creating the ads and commercials seen on the air, but agency identities remain cloudy to the public—a kind of unseen-but-occasionally-glimpsed world of highly paid, articulate, sophisticated men and women, according to popular mythology.[2] The myths surrounding the industry are a major factor contributing to public suspicion. This mythology is fed by the occasionally flamboyant memoir, but more often by fictional characters in books and movies and on television.[3] Regardless of its origin, suspicion (or at least unease) greets both advertising and advertising people.

The following sections of this chapter will examine a number of frequently voiced criticisms about advertising. The first section will focus on charges relating to advertising and society, while the second section addresses advertising's effects in the economy. Both the basis of these criticisms and alternative interpretations will be discussed.

A CLOSER LOOK

BIG SPENDERS:
A BRIEF LIST OF INDUSTRY BENCHMARKS

Advertising is big business in the United States. As the following statistics will attest, there seems to be no limit to the amount of money advertisers will spend in an attempt to bring their product to the forefront of the American marketplace.

Expenditures of largest advertiser: Procter & Gamble, $1,600,000,000 in 1985

Billings of largest ad agency: Young & Rubicam, $2,272,000,000 in 1985

Most heavily advertised brand: McDonald's Restaurants, $311,607,000 in 1985

Total expenditures for sales promotion, 1985: $94,400,000,000

Total expenditures for advertising, 1985: $94,750,000,000

Production cost of most expensive commercial: "1984" commercial for Macintosh computer, $400,000 (agency: Chiat/Day)

Most expensive 30-second spot: Super Bowl XXI, 1987: ($550,000)

Sources: *Advertising Age*, March 27, 1986, 8 and December 22, 1986, 19; *Marketing & Media Decisions*, July 1986, 20, 172; Television Bureau of Advertising, August 1985; and *USA Today*, January 30, 1987.

ADVERTISING IS DECEPTIVE

There can be little doubt that some people are deceived by some advertisements. However, it would be a dangerous and illegal practice to design advertising with the intention of deceiving consumers, and national advertisers could not afford to embark upon campaigns of this kind. Ethical considerations aside, national advertisers depend on their reputation with consumers, both to win initial trial and to build brand loyalty. So, from a strictly business point of view, advertisers could not afford a reputation for **deceptive advertising.**

While it might seem that there should be clear standards for the identification of deceptive advertising, it is really a matter of interpretation. The Federal Trade Commission considers a claim deceptive when a reasonable consumer is misled about an important aspect of a product or service.

From the standpoint of personal integrity, it is doubtful that advertising people are any more, or any less, ethical than their colleagues in other professions. Occasionally, however, a real swindler is encountered. A "gasoline-saving device" turns out to be a bolt installed under an automobile accelerator or an "etched metal portrait" of Abraham Lincoln winds up as a penny. Such operators prey upon people looking for a deal that seems "too good to be true," and they often move so quickly that effective prosecution is impossible. However, these con men represent only a tiny fraction of the advertising community. While it is easy to judge the black-and-white situations where an ad claim is clearly honest or clearly deceptive, there is also a substantial grey area (see Figure 5.2).

The courts have held that advertisers have the right to make subjective opinion statements about their products. This exaggeration of product

FIGURE 5.2

Advertising Claims: How Consumers
Perceived Commercial Claims
for Pond's Cold Cream

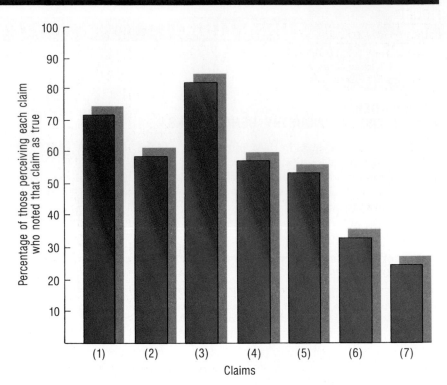

Fact Claims
(1) "Deep cleans skin and moisturizes"
(2) "Deep cleans even theatrical makeup"
(3) "Moisturizes skin"

Puff Claim
(4) "Keeps skin soft and young-looking"

Fact-Implied Claim
(5) "Removes toughest makeup"

Puff-Implied Claims
(6) "Women need to use cream to stay
    young-looking."
(7) "Women who do not use Pond's
    run the risk of aging and looking
    old."

Source: Rotfeld and Rotzoll, "Puffery versus Fact Claims," *Current Issues & Research in Advertising* 1981: 84–103.

claims is termed **puffery,** and is exemplified in statements like "the king of beers" and "the biggest name in small computers." While these imply superior quality in the brands they describe, they do not really make an explicit claim (see Figure 5.3). The courts have held that these sorts of characterizations are discounted by consumers and thus are not deceptive. Though researchers have attempted to show that consumers believe there is a factual basis for some puffery, there has not been sufficient demonstration of material deception to change puffery's legal status.

While the legality of puffery tends to blur the perception of what is allowable in advertising, the Federal Trade Commission, chief regulator of the advertising industry, has also held that advertisements and commercials must give a correct *overall* impression of the product or service. Representations in advertising must go beyond merely what is literally true; they must give a correct overall impression. For this reason, Coca-Cola's claim to be "the real thing" is allowable, since it is intended to convey a subjective evaluation of product quality. On the other hand, the

FIGURE 5.3

Puffery — or the Truth?

This campaign for the Boca Raton Hotel and Club encourages consumers to find out for themselves.

Source: Ad created for The Boca Raton Hotel and Club by Austin Kelley Advertising. Reprinted with permission.

American Dairy Association was ordered to cease use of its slogan "Milk is good for every*body*," since a significant minority in the population cannot tolerate milk in their diet.

The problem of deception is a difficult one in that people may misinterpret true information to receive a mistaken impression. In a situation like this, deception occurs without the intent of the advertiser. In a landmark study conducted in the late 1970s by consumer behaviorist Jacob Jacoby and associates, research indicated that as much as 85 percent of all televised communication is misunderstood.[4] Probably the clearest summary statement that may be made is that some false and misleading advertising does appear. It is unlikely to be major advertisers who intentionally mislead consumers, since they depend on continuing patronage. Advertising is not inherently deceptive, though it is persuasive. It is naive to regard the product information in advertising as if it were objective, and the exaggeration of puffery is something consumers must learn to see through.

ADVERTISING IS USED TO SHAPE BUYING BEHAVIOR

There are several ways of responding to this assertion, all of which suggest that it is inaccurate. First of all, consumers have strong **perceptual defenses.** As discussed in Chapter 4, they are selective in what they attend to, shutting out the majority of advertising. Selective perception and retention allow consumers to further manage and control incoming communications of all sorts. So, the consumer has a considerable resistance to receiving advertising messages in the first place.

In addition, numerous studies have shown that mass communication alone has a fairly weak effect in changing either attitudes or behavior.

When this is coupled with Jacoby's findings about misconceptions of communication messages (discussed earlier), advertising does not seem to be a very powerful force. The effects of advertising are often further reduced because consumers often cannot remember the source of an advertising message, even if they can recall the message itself. For example, several recent studies have shown that, when reminded of a commercial shown earlier, viewers tended to attribute the spot to the most visible brand in the product category rather than to the actual advertiser.

Advertisers have long realized that it is very difficult to change behavior. In fact, most advertising for existing products is targeted at those who already use this class of goods. For example, it is much easier to get a beer drinker to try a new brand of beer than it is to try to convert a consumer who either does not drink alcoholic beverages, or who prefers wine. For this reason, heavy users of a particular product category are especially sought after by advertisers. Not only do they purchase more of the product than others, but they buy more frequently. When a product is used up quickly there is less risk connected with any single purchase and thus a greater willingness to experiment with new products. The point here is that advertising is only infrequently intended to try to get consumers to behave in new and different ways. Usually it is aimed at getting them to choose a different brand in a category in which they already intend to make a purchase.

These factors, considered together, do little to support the argument that advertising is a powerful shaper of consumers' behavior. In fact, it seems that if advertising wielded such power, American society would have long ago ended forest fires; littering; racial, sexual, and age discrimination; and other problems addressed by public-service advertising created by the Advertising Council.

Though it seems that advertising has little coercive effect on the majority of American society, there are other considerations for subpopulations, both at home and abroad. Since most advertising is aimed at the middle-class consumer, advertisers often fail to consider the disadvantaged in society. Many of these individuals receive advertising messages, however, and are encouraged to make purchases that may be contrary to their self-interest. These groups include children; many of the elderly; the poor; and the relatively large population of the Third-World countries who do not have the formal education, resources, or perceptual defenses to deal with advertising and marketing techniques of the industrialized nations. Both domestic and international issues become problems of larger scale in modern times. While an in-depth discussion of the issues of advertising as they relate to these groups is beyond the scope of this chapter, it is important to note that advertising that reaches special populations deserves careful consideration and review.

It is often difficult to anticipate what might be controversial in a different culture. Nevertheless, consideration of the larger sphere of advertising's operation is one of the central responsibilities in advertising management.

ADVERTISING ENCOURAGES MATERIALISM

Many critics of advertising suggest that its everlasting repetition of what's available and its constant stress on buying creates a society that places undue importance on **materialism,** preoccupation with the possession of

A LOBAL LOOK

HOW SOCIAL VALUES AFFECT ADVERTISING IN ARAB COUNTRIES

The nine million people of Saudi Arabia love perfume. Owing perhaps to the fact that perfume is one of the few luxuries permitted in this austerely religious Islamic country, the Saudis lead the world in per capita consumption of fragrance. In fact, the kingdom ranks sixth as a world perfume market (behind the United States, Japan, Germany, France, and Italy).

Perfume marketers have found that both Saudi men and Saudi women are big purchasers of scent. Advertisers try to use their European campaigns in the Arabian countries (since a relatively high number of Saudis are frequent travelers and are acquainted with

the advertising). However, they must occasionally adjust ads to accommodate Saudi Arabia's strict moral climate.

For example, due to the Islamic taboo on drugs, the Yves St. Laurent fragrance Opium travels by plain wrapper. Opium boxes headed for Saudi Arabia are printed without the product name (although the bottles inside are labeled normally).

European ads for the Guy Laroche men's fragrance Drakkar Noir show a male hand gripping a bottle of the product, with a woman's hand holding the man's wrist. When the company realized that this approach was too sensuous for the Arab market—where physical contact in public between a man and a woman is frowned on—it directed its ad agency to reshoot the ad. Thus, in the ad that runs in Saudi Arabia, the man's arm is clothed and the woman's hand barely grazes his wrist.

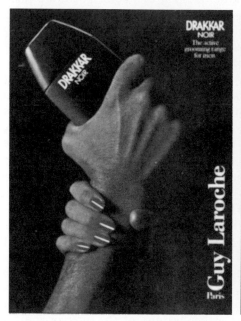

Source: Michael Field, "Fragrance Marketers Sniff Out Rich Aroma," *Advertising Age*, January 30, 1986, 10.

material things. They further suggest that these material possessions are sought not for what they do, but merely as symbols of some status attainment on the individual's part.

Like other charges surrounding advertising's social effects, this is a difficult one to answer because of the subjectivity involved in differentiating what is necessary from that which is merely emblematic, or even hedonistic. There is no question that advertising attempts to invest goods with want-satisfying qualities. It is clear that in modern consumer society our lives depend on many products that were either luxurious or unnecessary in earlier times. Turbo-charged automobiles, personal computers, blow dryers, aerobics shoes, and gourmet frozen dinners may be considered essential by many who live in modern urban environments, yet such items were virtually unavailable a generation ago. Various kinds of cosmetics and personal care products for men and women seem to be an essential part of today's living, though certainly unnecessary to sustain life.

The point is that consumers' needs and wants are really defined by the society in which they live. The dress code may be grey sweatpants or grey flannel suits, depending on the social group a person works or plays with. Simply because needs or wants are socially defined does not make them illegitimate, or any less necessary to fit and function in the social group. The problem with the materialism issue is defining what excessive or materialistic consumption is. The ad in Figure 5.4 displays a lifestyle to which many aspire. Does it display elevated, trained, sophisticated tastes, or merely hedonistic self-indulgence? While in some circles a food processor may be a badge of middle-class materialism, in others it may be regarded as an essential of a properly equipped kitchen.

There can be little question that some goods are purchased merely as trappings or badges of rank or social status. However, goods were used in this way long before the advent of advertising. For example, early American societies valued the horse as an expression of wealth. The 19th-century gentleman's silver-handled cane marked him as a personage of wealth and social stature. Advertising often tries to suggest that goods should be emblematic of certain types of social status, but unless the advertiser matches the group values closely, such attempts are doomed to failure.

Ultimately, it must be recognized that we, as a society, value goods not only for their intrinsic worth and the functions they perform, but also for their symbolic value. We satisfy a host of personal, social, and utilitarian needs when we commute to work in a Porsche. It's not just the capabilities, the expense, or the image of the Porsche that we purchase: it is all of these. And of the three, advertising plays a role only in defining the image, and even that it cannot totally shape.

MUCH ADVERTISING IS TASTELESS

Tasteless advertising refers to any message that either offends or embarrasses the receiver, either because of the topic or the way in which it is presented. The issue can arise in connection with products related to body functions (such as contraceptives, feminine hygiene products, or hemorrhoid medications), or in advertising of sensitive subjects, such as funeral arrangements. Most often, however, it deals with nudity or sexual situations in advertising.

Taste involves judgment. What appears tasteless to you, for example, might not offend another student in your class. When advertising is offensive to a large group, it is usually because advertisers didn't properly understand the attitudes and beliefs of their audience, mistargeted their messages, or simply used poor judgment. For example, Burger King spent

FIGURE 5.4

Critics of advertising may point to messages like this one when they claim that advertising encourages materialism.

Source: Courtesy of the Chubb Group of Insurance Companies.

tens of millions of dollars for an advertising campaign centered on the search for Herb, a fictional character who had never tasted a Whopper. The character was a nerd who proved to be a turn-off for most viewers.

Taste also depends on the audience. An ad that might be appropriate for *Playboy* subscribers may be totally inappropriate for readers of *Christian Century*. Thus, a marketer of suntan lotion might use a nude female, deeply tanned, to illustrate the product's benefits, but would probably not attempt to place the ad in *Christian Century*, regardless of whether those readers are heavy suntan lotion users.

A CLOSER LOOK

"IF, GOD FORBID, L.A. IS NEXT . . ."

It was all a breakdown in communication. Or so says
Rose Hills Memorial Park and Mortuary. The Whittier,
California, firm took a lot of flack after the 1985
earthquakes in Mexico, when it placed a newspaper ad
in a Los Angeles newspaper. The ad's headline read "If,
God forbid, L.A. is next, our commitment will remain
unshaken."

Critics blasted the ad, calling it "morbid" and
"tasteless," but the funeral company claims it was
misunderstood. According to Rose Hills, the ad
intended to criticize the stand taken by the Los Angeles
County Funeral Directors Association. This group had
allegedly refused to assist the Los Angeles County
coroner's office in the event of a major quake, because
the two parties had been unable to iron out the financial
details. Said Sandy Durko, Rose Hills' vice-president of
marketing: "A lot of people read the headline and didn't
understand what we were trying to say."

Still, Durko claims, the company's motives were
pure. "I would do it again," he said, "but we'd be more
explicit . . . we'd make it clearer we were responding to
the Funeral Directors Association."

However, Durko admitted, "the purpose of
advertising is to communicate. And I guess we didn't."

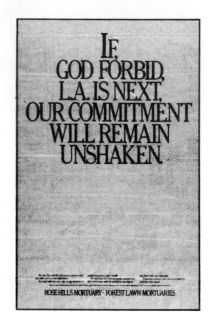

Source: Reprinted with permission from the December 2, 1985 issue of *Advertising Age*. Copyright 1985 by Crain Communications, Inc.

Finally, defining taste also has to do with the culture involved. In most
European countries, for example, nudity is not considered offensive;
hence, bare-breasted females appear in all types of advertising, from the
print media to TV to transit ads and even outdoor signs. Because nudity
is not taboo in most European cultures, it is not considered offensive in
the advertising. However, public nudity and references to sexual activity
have long been proscribed in American society.

While nudity and sex are elements of life, there is little point in dis-
playing or suggesting them when they have no relation to the product
advertised. Not only does such use suggest a sleazy image for a product,
but it runs the risk of antagonizing potential consumers. At this point in
our cultural evolution, neither nudity nor sexuality are appropriate on
broadcast television. Even if advertisers chose to use these appeals, they
would be rejected by network clearance offices, which review commercials prior to running them. No doubt American mores will change and
eventually become more liberal, but meanwhile advertisers have little to
gain by pushing actively against the barriers.

FIGURE 5.5

An Acceptable Use of Sexual Innuendo

Hello?
What are you doing?
Taking a shower.
Right now?
No, right now I'm standing in a puddle of water.
You didn't say goodbye.
I didn't want to wake you.
Who could sleep when there's a hunk with no clothes on wandering around at five in the morning, knocking over furniture?
I had to come back and dig out my sincere suit. Big meeting this morning. I get to say things like "bottom line" and "net net" with a straight face. What are you doing?
Lying here, thinking about you. You know, I can smell your Paco Rabanne. It's like you were still here.
I wish I were.
I couldn't go back to sleep, remembering everything. I wanted to hear your voice. It has the most interesting effect on me . . .
Maybe I should run over and read you a bedtime story or something.
Or something.

Paco Rabanne
For men
What is remembered is up to you

Source: Courtesy of Paco Rabanne.

Thus, tasteless advertising has much to do with the context in which it is used. Advertising approaches that *do* use nudity or explicit sexual situations are best implemented in vehicles with an adult audience. Figure 5.5 shows an ad for Paco Rabonne, one product that successfully uses the sexual innuendo in its campaigns.

MUCH ADVERTISING IS BASED ON STEREOTYPES

There is no question that this is true in many cases. It was American journalist Walter Lippmann who first applied the term **stereotype**—an oversimplified image of an individual or group—to mass communications. As Lippmann pointed out, we use stereotypes because they are an efficient way to think and speak. Communication depends upon a common sharing of understanding. Stereotypes, because they typify, are very economical ways of communicating. Since advertisers usually have such small units of time in which to get their messages across, they use the most efficient communications devices available. For this reason a host of advertising stereotypes—the harried housewife, the bumbling husband, the nosy neighbor, the unfeeling business executive, the spinster schoolteacher—have been used to set a scene in which the product drama will be played out. It should be noted that most communication depends to some degree on stereotypes as mutually understood versions of typical behavior. The real issue is the continual misrepresentation of certain groups who are never portrayed in a more meaningful way. Much analysis of media content has shown that women traditionally have been shown in primarily three roles: housewife, decorative female, or a sexually provocative figure. The lack of recognition that women can occupy roles other than these is understandably both insulting and infuriating to many people. While any particular role in a given ad or commercial is likely incidental and unintended to typify the woman's role in modern society, the sum total of all advertising presents a discouraging and extremely limiting sort of public image.

Ethnic groups have been similarly treated. Hispanics and native and black Americans have in the past been characterized by extremely negative stereotypical portrayals. Again, no advertiser intended to convey a judgment about the ethnic groups as a whole, but the stereotypes are offensive to the peoples involved. These days, it is hard to imagine that any advertiser could be so insensitive as to employ advertising that contains ethnic stereotyping, or that any advertising agency could prepare such work.

The question surrounding the portrayal of women is somewhat more complicated. Despite evidence that the majority of married women in the U.S. population are employed outside the home, a good deal of advertising continues to depend on formula portrayals of stereotypical housewives who regard a sheen on their kitchen floor or some cosmic level of brightness in the family laundry as major life goals. Such advertising is insulting, ill-advised, and unprofessional. However, it appears likely to continue, at least until the affected groups can bring market pressure to bear on the offending advertisers.

ADVERTISING EXERTS AN UNHEALTHY EFFECT ON SOCIAL VALUES

Some critics charge that advertising exerts an unhealthy effect on social values by turning consumers' attention inward toward themselves. This preoccupation with self is not only destructive to the individual, argue these critics, but deteriorates the social fabric of our culture:

ADVERTISERS' RANKING*	VALUE DIMENSION	POPULAR RANKING†
1	Personal happiness, satisfaction	4
2	Good family life	1
3	Having a nice home, car, other belongings	13
4	Having a sense of accomplishment and lasting contribution	8
5	Good physical health	2
6	Good self-image, self-respect	3
7	Having enough leisure time	15
8	Having an exciting, stimulating life	12
9	Having many friends	9
10	Living up to your full potential	6
11	Social recognition	16
12	Having a high income	14
13	Having an interesting and enjoyable job	7
14	Helping people in need	10
15	Working for a better society	11
16	Free choice to do what I want	5

EXHIBIT 5.2

The Values Displayed in Commercials: Advertisers' versus the Public's View

*Indicates values shown in commercials, ranked by frequency.
†Indicates rank order of values by the public in Gallup poll.
Source: Charles F. Frazer, "Values in Prime-Time Alcoholic Beverage Commercials," paper presented to the Association for Education in Journalism and Mass Communication, August 1983.

> In a simpler time, advertising merely called attention to the product and extolled its advantages. Now it manufactures a product of its own: the consumer, perpetually unsatisfied, restless, anxious and bored.[5]

This charge is neither supported nor refuted by empirical evidence. It is made based on an analysis of modern culture and represents one individual's opinion. The evidence, however, is open to different interpretation (see Exhibit 5.2).

As later chapters will show, advertisers target messages to groups that appear to have the highest probability of purchasing the good or service in question. In order to reach these people and persuade them to purchase, advertising attempts to detect, imitate, and mirror their values. It does not attempt to present some alternative value scheme. If the market group is inward-looking and self-involved, it is likely that the characters in advertisements will act this way. If, on the other hand, the market is inner-directed and individualistic, the advertising is likely to express such values. In short, it would not serve the purpose of advertising to contradict the value scheme of the consumers it attempts to persuade. Petit and Zakon have suggested this:

> Sociologically speaking it would be impossible for advertising to be in conflict with the value system. It is the value system which determines the nature and significance of social institutions like advertising, not the other way around.[6]

But this formulation is not quite right, for two reasons. First, in a pluralistic nation such as the United States, there can be no such thing as "the

American value system." This country is made up of countless nationalities and ethnic, racial, and religious groups, all with slightly different orientations toward what is appropriate spiritual and social behavior. Advertising certainly does not represent the values of all, or even many, of these groups. What advertising does represent is the values and life-styles of the middle and upper-middle classes, who comprise the most substantial market for the majority of mass-marketed goods in American society (and the background of most advertising people as well). Thus it seems that if advertising exerts a force on values, it is toward the norm of middle-class values. This may or may not be a socially desirable outcome, but it does not seem to be a particularly subversive one.

Michael Schudson's thoughtful analysis of this problem points out that advertising picks up values from the surrounding culture. It does not represent all of the values in our society, nor should it be taken as a representation of all that we hold important and worthwhile. Perhaps this point is the most important response to critics of the values illustrated in commercials.[7]

ADVERTISING EXPLOITS CONSUMER ANXIETIES

Since, at least, the time that Gerard Lambert brought the term *halitosis* out of the laboratory and into the vocabulary of many Americans to advertise his product Listerine, advertising has been subject to the charge that it preys on the fears and concerns of the public. While little can be said to refute the charge that advertising often presents problems to which its sponsor offers the solution, it is important to consider that advertising does not create the problems in the first place. Usually it identifies problems which are already part of the consumer's experience.

Mouthwash is sold because people know that they occasionally have bad breath. Gerard Lambert did not spontaneously create an anxiety by naming the problem "halitosis"; he identified it and suggested a solution. Few of the anxieties presented in advertising would hold any real terror if they were not based in fact. While it is not our intent to excuse advertising strategies based on exciting consumer anxiety to which products provide the solution, the fact of the matter seems to be that if there is not already an existing anxiety—and if that anxiety is in no way relieved by the product—there is little hope for sales.

Product advertising may be created based on either positive or negative aspects of a problem. For example, mouthwash advertising can use the positive: "Let people get close to you." Or it can use the negative: "Don't offend your closest friends." It seems that reference to anxiety is evident in the second message but not in the first. The advertiser's decision to suggest that the product will reduce anxiety was probably based on what is known about consumers. Do consumers use mouthwash to reduce their anxiety? to avoid offending others? to feel more confident? as part of a daily morning regimen? for the pleasant-tasting or astringent effects? or for some other reason? Since the advertising neither creates this anxiety in the first place, nor is likely to try to "peddle" an anxiety to an audience that does not already have it, this charge may be less serious than it first appears.

Nonetheless, the exploitation of people's concerns and apprehensions is not a particularly pleasant role. However, most people are not pro-

FIGURE 5.6

How Advertising Encourages "High-Tech Anxiety" in Parents of School-Age Children

Why every kid should have an Apple after school.

Today, there are more Apple® computers in schools than any other computer.

Unfortunately, there are still more kids in schools than Apple computers.

So innocent youngsters (like your own) may have to fend off packs of bully nerds to get some time on a computer.

Which is why it makes good sense to buy them an Apple IIc Personal Computer of their very own.

Send them home to a good school system.

The IIc is just like the leading computer in education, the Apple IIe. Only smaller. About the size of a three-ring notebook, to be exact.

Of course, since the IIc is the legitimate offspring of the IIe, it can access the world's largest library of educational software. Everything from Stickybear

Shapes™ for preschoolers to SAT test preparation programs for college hopefuls.

In fact, the IIc can run over 10,000 programs in all. More than a few of which you might be interested in yourself.

For example, the best-selling, AppleWorks™ 3-in-1 integrated software package. Personal finance and tax programs. Diet and fitness programs.

Not to mention

fun programs for the whole family. Like "Genetic Mapping" and "Enzyme Kinetics."

One Apple that won't leave them hungry.

The Apple IIc is easy to set up and learn. And it comes complete with most everything you need to start computing in one box.

Including a free, easy-to-use 4-diskette course to teach you all about the IIc—when your kids get tired of your questions.

As well as a long list of built-in features that would add about $800 to the cost of a smaller-minded computer.

The features include: 128K of internal memory—as powerful as the average office computer.

adding accessories, like our new ColorMonitor IIc, Image-Writer™ II printer and the Apple Personal Modem 300/1200.

A feast for their eyes.

The big 14-inch ColorMonitor IIc displays crisp, color graph-

The most popular peripherals plug right into the back of the Apple IIc.

ics or a high resolution 80-column monochrome text for word processing.

You can print sharp color graphics, too, with our new ImageWriter II. It also prints

The ImageWriter II prints high quality color graphics.

A built-in disk drive that could drive up the price of a less-senior machine considerably.

And built-in adaptors for

And speaking of high quality color, introducing ColorMonitor IIc.

near-letter-quality text in black and white, quickly and quietly. And, with its new SheetFeeder, you can switch to single sheets without

removing the sprocket paper.*

If local color isn't enough, you can talk to the rest of the world through our new wall-mounted Apple Personal Modem 300/1200. With it, you can do your banking at home, check your stocks, gain access to all kinds of information libraries and much more.

Which would all add up to a very impressive list of expandable accessories if it weren't for all the others. Like an Apple-Mouse. And an extra disk drive when the time comes.

Avoid growing pains.

So while your children's shoe sizes and appetites continue to grow at an alarming rate, there's one thing you know can keep up with them. Their Apple IIc.

To learn more about it, visit any authorized Apple dealer. Or talk to your own computer experts.

As soon as they get home from school.

Optional accessory may be purchased for ImageWriter II. © 1985 Apple Computer, Inc. Apple and the Apple logo, AppleWorks, and ImageWriter are trademarks of Apple Computer, Inc. Stickybear Shapes is a trademark of Optimum Resource. For an authorized Apple dealer near you, call (800) 538-9696. In Canada, call (800) 268-7796 or (800) 268-7637.

Source: © 1985 Apple Computer, Inc. Reprinted with permission.

pelled through life by fears and anxieties. The perception that advertising plays to these may come from its role in attempting to show how products and services solve consumer problems. Depicting problems, and how products solve them, may be construed by some as the exploitation of anxieties (see Figure 5.6).

ADVERTISING INFLUENCES THE CHARACTER OF THE MEDIA

There is little question that in our commercial society the source that underwrites a production strongly influences its makeup. Advertising's influence is probably most clearly seen in television, and it is very much the fact with all other commercial media as well.

In the case of commercial broadcast media, virtually all the revenues of the stations and networks are derived from advertising dollars. Thus they must try to supply what best satisfies the majority of advertisers.

The pricing of advertising time is established based on the audience's size and desirability to advertisers, and so advertisers can place direct financial pressure on the networks to formulate programs that attract the "right" people. Because the most desirable audiences are young married professional and managerial types who live in urban or suburban (rather than rural) areas, most prime-time programming is designed to attract this group. While this is a sensible business decision on the part of the broadcaster, the result is that important segments of the population (such as the poor, the elderly, and ethnic minority groups) have no programming designed especially for them, further isolating them from the cultural mainstream.

Though publishers derive a signficant income from subscriptions to their magazines and newspapers, it is usually far less than half their total income. Since the emergence of television as a mass medium, few magazines have been able to compete successfully for a general audience. As a result, magazines have focused on reaching specific groups by addressing themselves to certain interest areas. Examples of this specialization are the numerous periodicals dealing with personal computers, running, or adventure sports. Many publishers of enthusiast magazines regard subscription fees as simply an indication of readers' serious interest in the subject. Serious enthusiasts are, of course, the best market and most likely prospects for products related to the interest area, and many read ads as ardently as they do editorial matter.

In the case of newspapers, sections that supposedly address cooking, automobiles, and real estate often carry only a minuscule amount of editorial matter. Such sections are designed to create an environment for, and draw attention to, the advertising for grocery stores, car dealers, and real estate agencies who, not coincidentally, number among the largest advertisers in most newspapers.

It is impossible to argue that advertising does not influence the character of the commercial mass communication media. However, a more subtle question is involved as well: to what extent does advertising influence the editorial stance of the medium on particular issues? Most media observe a strict separation of editorial and advertising staffs. However, at the management level (where decisions are made as to what stories will be played and from what angle), it is probably impossible to put economic considerations totally aside.

Investigative reporters have charged that magazines, who are heavily dependent on cigarette advertising as a source of revenue, have given only minimal attention to the issue of smoking and health. Similarly, newspapers—who depend on the advertising of auto makers and dealers—have been charged with selective inattention to issues surrounding automobile safety.

In a similar way, television is frequently charged with avoiding controversial issues altogether. One reason for this is a desire to avoid the "fairness doctrine" obligation to give significant attention to opposing points of view. However, a second (and equally important) reason, is that advertisers avoid linking their products with controversial material of any kind, largely out of fear of consumer backlash.

The issues of what we don't see, hear, or read are obviously very difficult to establish and document. However, there is little question that advertising influences what we *don't* see as well as what we *do* see. It is a subtle influence, but an important one nonetheless.

It is important to keep in mind that while advertising almost certainly influences some kinds of media content, it also supports the media. As noted earlier, media come to us at a fraction of their total cost because advertisers support them. In this way advertising encourages mass communication and expands our opportunities to receive information.

ADVERTISING SUBVERTS THE DEMOCRATIC PROCESS

The application of advertising techniques to the political sphere has created a great deal of controversy. Even advertising practitioners are divided on the appropriateness of **political advertising,** using advertising techniques to sell candidates and political positions. Foote, Cone & Belding's John O'Toole characterizes the issue in this way:

> If the product doesn't work, they can take it back. If the manufacturer won't fix it or reimburse them, they can sue. What recourse do they have after "buying" a candidate on the basis of promises made in a TV spot and unfulfilled in office?[8]

The basic argument hinges on the assertion that advertising is used to create images for candidates, diverting attention from the real personalities and issues of the campaign and thus misleading voters. This situation is complicated by the fact political advertising is not subject to scrutiny, as are product and service advertising. Since a basic principle of democracy is that public debate must take place unimpeded, political advertising is totally unregulated. Its critics assert that this allows political advertising the basest sort of misrepresentation and the ability to manipulate the public through sophisticated advertising techniques (see Figure 5.7). Many advertising practitioners feel that political advertising invites public skepticism, which lowers the credibility of product advertising.

There are any number of emotionally loaded issues involved in the political advertising debate, and very little definitive research data to go on. However, there is very little in the literature to suggest that advertising has any more dramatic effect in the political sphere than in the product sphere. Conversely, increased information indicates that voters are even more skeptical of political advertising than they are of product advertising.[9]

While many critics feel that advertising demeans the democratic process, they fail to note that politics has never been an exalted affair. Charges of misrepresentation and shallowness have been a part of the political process throughout history. There is little reason to believe that the use of advertising dramatically increases the opportunity for deceit. In fact, to the extent that a candidate's expressions are made nationally through paid advertising (rather than locally through speeches to small groups), it seems likely that promises and representations are more open to public scrutiny. At least, this is true to the extent that the news media are willing and able to take candidates to task and hold them responsible for their public representations.

Among those who oppose the use of modern advertising practices by politicians, there is no consensus on which services should be restricted.

FIGURE 5.7

Memorable TV Advertising from the 1984 Presidential Election

  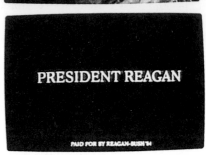

Voice Over: There is a bear in the woods. For some people, the bear is easy to see. Others don't see it at all. Some people say the bear is tame. Others say it's vicious and dangerous. Since no one can really be sure who's right, isn't it smart to be as strong as the bear? If there is a bear?
SUPER: President Reagan
Paid for by Reagan-Bush '84

Source: Courtesy of CD/CW: Hal Riney; AD: Bruce Campbell, Bernie Vangrin.

Research services that both evaluate candidates' performances and isolate pivotal groups for special attention through campaign efforts seem to be an accepted part of modern political life. Public relations practices that create events and publicity surrounding candidates also seem to form an accepted part of modern campaign practices. Few would deprive candidates of the services of media planners who calculate the most efficient ways of reaching specified target audiences with the minimum wasted coverage. What remains is the creative function: the formulation of the advertising message.

The charge that the use of advertising agents to assist the candidate in projecting a particular image or in designing a message strategy amounts to manipulation is not supported by the research literature. It also seems that a good deal of political practice, with or without the aid of paid mass-media advertising, has been aimed at exactly these goals. In concluding her study of the use of advertising in the last eight presidential elections, Kathleen Jamieson observed:

> The widespread perception that being able to present broadcast messages persuasively to a mass public would emerge as a criterion governing selection of presidential candidates is not convincingly confirmed from 1952–1980. . . . the ability to deliver televised messages artfully, while certainly an asset for those who possess it, has not become so central a qualification for the presidency that it has exiled candidates who lack it.[10]

HOW VOTERS FEEL ABOUT POLITICAL ADVERTISING

It's not just the advertising industry that's skeptical about political advertising. Many voters find political ads —especially those that attack the opponent rather than make a positive statement—tiresome and offensive.

"I would rather hear about the good things they can do. . . ."

"I dislike the battery back and forth between the candidates. . . ."

"I dislike political commercials in general, and I object to mudslinging."

According to a survey commissioned by *Adweek*, prior to the 1984 presidential election most people found political advertising only half as informative and believable as product advertising. Respondents also rated political spots lower in entertainment value.

Overall Attitude towards Television Commercials

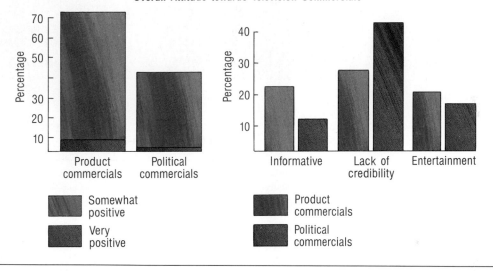

Source: Articles by Richard Morgan and Dave Vadehra in *ADWEEK*, September 10, 1984, pp. 29 and 42. Reprinted with permission of *ADWEEK*.

Regardless of the concerns that may be voiced about the role of advertising in politics, it appears that advertising will be a continuing element in the political process. "Media advisors," as they are labeled in political organizations, have become a widespread and fundamental element in political planning. Such governmental actions as the "fair campaigns practices" legislation have institutionalized advertising expenditures as a part of the election process and it appears unlikely that this will be changed. So, like it or not, political advertising appears to be here to stay.

ADVERTISING USES SUBLIMINAL TECHNIQUES TO MANIPULATE BUYERS

In the 1970s Wilson Key published a series of books on the use of subliminal communication techniques in mass communication. The first of these books (*Subliminal Seduction*) and others that followed, combined with

FIGURE 5.8

Can You Find "Sex" in the Ice Cubes?

Wilson Bryan Key used this example of a Gilbey's Gin ad to claim that the word "sex" was hidden in the ice cubes in this glass.

Key's frequent promotional appearances, gave fairly wide currency to the assumption that subliminal techniques are common in advertising.[11] **Subliminal advertising** refers to the technique of hiding messages and symbols in advertisements and commercials in such a way that they are not consciously perceived by the reader or viewer. The fact that these beliefs are so widespread makes some attention to the issues worthwhile.

Key claims that advertisers employ a conscious strategy of implanting hidden cues in advertisements and commercials. These cues, usually sexual in nature, are hidden so that they are not consciously perceived by readers or viewers. According to Key, however, those exposed receive these hidden messages unconsciously, and in this way are urged to act or to value a product in a certain way without any of the consumer's normal conscious perceptual defenses coming into play.

Key finds these hidden cues through the careful study of advertisements, sometimes turning them upside-down, or by peering intently at tiny details in the background and foreground. The ad in Figure 5.8 provides an example of such a hidden cue. In the example, Key finds the word *sex* suggested by the outlines in the ice cubes in the glass and asserts that the word was consciously embedded there by the ad's creators. This is actually a fairly simple example of the bizarre suggestions Key makes and of the unusual techniques he uses in his analysis.

While there are any number of reasons to discount Key's notions, several prominent ones bear consideration here. First of all, while some empirical evidence supports the existence of subliminal perception, there is none to suggest that baldly associating *sex* with a product is a wise or effective advertising strategy.[12]

Second, it is incredible that many readers could be expected to receive the subliminal messages, which seem to require a great deal of imagination to perceive, even when one's attention is directed to them. Even the simpler goal of merely getting consumers to notice a brand name is a very difficult job for most advertisers, since consumers have a highly developed ability to ignore advertising. The notion that they could perceive hidden elements in ads while failing to notice the most prominent elements seems most unlikely.

Third, Key's position suggests that there is some theoretical body of advertising knowledge unknown to the general public, or even social scientists. Advertising is thus a sort of "black art" of manipulating and overcoming consumer resistance. The fact of the matter is more the reverse. Advertising adopts and adapts useful theories and concepts from social science, but rarely formulates them. Advertising research is aimed at finding simple answers to such questions as who buys and when. It is almost never designed to unravel more profound questions of behavior or to build complex explanatory theories.

Finally, the advertising industry itself has standards of integrity. Advertising people realize that they depend on public tolerance. While they devote their efforts to attracting attention, finding reasons for consumer to buy, and crafting persuasive presentations, few would advocate tricking people into purchasing (see Figure 5.9).

ASSESSING THE SOCIAL EFFECTS OF ADVERTISING

Though social critics and concerned consumers raise many questions about the effects of advertising in society, it seems that many of the questions misunderstand both advertising and consumer behavior. The questions tend to emphasize the short-range effects of advertising and greatly overemphasize its power. Several authors have suggested that advertising is most likely a conservative force.[13] That is, it acts to reinforce the established and traditional norms of behavior, sometimes long after social change makes these behaviors anachronistic. Rather than making sweeping changes or pushing society in new directions, advertising thus tends to act as a break.

It is also likely that the most profound effects of advertising operate at a general social level rather than an individual one, and that these effects are felt over time rather than immediately. These sorts of effects are difficult to detect and measure, given the tools of modern social science.

FIGURE 5.9

Advertising: Another Word for Freedom of Choice

These two ads, prepared by the American Association of Advertising Agencies, refute some of the typical charges made by critics of advertising.

DESPITE WHAT SOME PEOPLE THINK, ADVERTISING CAN'T MAKE YOU BUY SOMETHING YOU DON'T NEED.

Some people would have you believe that you are putty in the hands of every advertiser in the country.

They think that when advertising is put under your nose, your mind turns to oatmeal.

It's mass hypnosis. Subliminal seduction. Brain washing. Mind control. It's advertising.

And you are a pushover for it.

It explains why your kitchen cupboard is full of food you never eat. Why your garage is full of cars you never drive.

Why your house is full of books you don't read, TV's you don't watch, beds you don't use, and clothes you don't wear.

You don't have a choice. You are forced to buy.

That's why this message is a cleverly disguised advertisement to get you to buy land in the tropics.

Got you again, didn't we? Send in your money.

ADVERTISING
ANOTHER WORD FOR FREEDOM OF CHOICE.
American Association of Advertising Agencies

IS ADVERTISING A REFLECTION OF SOCIETY? OR IS SOCIETY A REFLECTION OF ADVERTISING?

Some people say that advertising determines America's tastes.

Which is another way of saying that advertising determines *your* tastes.

Which is, in turn, another way of saying that you don't have a mind of your own.

Well, time and time again the advertising industry has found that you do have a mind of your own. If a product doesn't interest you, you simply don't buy it.

And if the product's advertising doesn't interest you, you don't buy that either.

Think of it as a sort of natural selection.

Good products and good advertising survive. Bad products and bad advertising perish. All according to the decisions you make in the marketplace.

So we've concluded that advertising is a mirror of society's tastes. Not vice versa.

Our conclusion is based on a great deal of thought. And many years of reflection.

ADVERTISING.
ANOTHER WORD FOR FREEDOM OF CHOICE.
American Association of Advertising Agencies

Source: Reprinted by permission of the American Association of Advertising Agencies.

ECONOMIC EFFECTS OF ADVERTISING

A particular group of questions about the way advertising affects our society is concerned with its effects in, and on, the marketplace. Unfortunately, there does not seem to be great precision in the answers available in this area either, though it is important to understand the kinds of questions raised, as well as the factors that militate against clear and universal answers.

Economists who have studied advertising tend to be interested in general rather than specific effects. In the effort to make general statements about the effects of advertising, they study its impact on an entire industry rather than its contribution for a particular firm or one of its brands. This very general focus of study has resulted in ambiguous findings about the effects of advertising. Imagine a study of the effects of advertising in the area of over-the-counter pain relievers. Such a study would combine data on the performance of the numerous heavily advertised brands of aspirin together with acetaminophen and other aspirin substitutes. Data would also be included on the little-advertised distributor's brands of wholesalers, supermarkets, and drug stores as well as generic products, which receive no advertising at all. While such studies may be instructive for economists looking for industry generalizations, this method of study tends to homogenize data that are extremely diverse. The results are not very instructive about the effects of advertising, which are of interest to consumers and advertisers.

SIMPLIFIED EXPLANATIONS OF ADVERTISING'S ECONOMIC ROLE

Perhaps because of this generalized approach to the study of advertising's effects, several persuasive but inaccurate general characterizations have been perpetuated.

Advertising as Economic Waste Since classical economics is based on the concept of price being determined by supply and demand, economists of this school see advertising as merely wasteful. Here, the philosophy of using advertising is directly at odds with the assumption of the economist. Marketers use advertising to differentiate and build loyalty to their products. To the extent that they are successful in doing so, they are free to raise prices above those of competitors, thus escaping the laws of supply and demand. Since the classical economist does not recognize that the consumption of advertised products may provide some additional satisfaction to the consumer, the economist sees advertising as merely raising prices and thus as economically wasteful. Contemporary economic thought provides some alternatives to this classical view, and these will be discussed later in this chapter.

Advertising and Scale Economies A second overly simplistic view of advertising's contribution is often used as a justification of advertising expenditures. This argument is illustrated in Exhibit 5.3.

Note in the example that the firm has two basic types of costs. *Fixed costs*, which are usually the firm's largest expenses, are those for which the firm is liable, regardless of the amount it produces (such as interest, rent, and taxes). *Variable costs* rise with production volume and include such elements as materials and selling costs. For the sake of simplicity in the figure, we assume the change from situation A to situation B is an increase in variable costs due to a higher expenditure for advertising. The result is that the increased expenditure for advertising results in twice as many units sold, and the firm has achieved a lower fixed price per unit of production. If this economy is passed along to retailers, and by them to consumers, the use of advertising has allowed a reduction in price. This

---

EXHIBIT 5.3

Economies of Scale

Situation A

Sales in units:	100,000	
Fixed costs:	$500,000	
Variable costs:	$100,000	
Cost per unit:	$6	(total costs divided by units)

Situation B

Sales in units	200,000
Fixed costs:	$500,000
Variable costs:	$300,000
Cost per unit:	$4

situation is referred to as **economies of scale.** In other words, increased production (in this case brought about by advertising's stimulation of demand) makes it possible to spread relatively high fixed costs over a larger number of units, lowering the cost per unit. For economies of scale to work, however, there are several important necessary conditions. The first is that the economies are achievable. To do this the firm in situation A must have excess production capacity. Second, the firm must choose to pass the economies down the line as a price decrease. Since these two conditions must be met, it makes the production scale economies suspect as a blanket justification for advertising.

In addition, rarely are such simple dynamics involved. The determination of the effect of advertising requires weighing numerous factors in a very complex setting. For the moment at least, no confirmation of the alleged effects is provided in the literature.

GENERAL ECONOMIC MODELS OF ADVERTISING EFFECTS

Recently, Mark Albion and Paul Farris offered a useful synthesis of the competing characterizations of advertising effects used by economists.[14] According to the authors, economic thought can be classified into two distinct models, or schools of thought. These competing points of view are described below and are summarized in Exhibit 5.4.

Advertising as Market Power This model reflects the traditional economic thought that advertising allows firms to build brand loyalty and increase profits by lowering price elasticity (that is, lowering consumers' sensitivity to price), thus creating market power. Under this model, firms spend large amounts on advertising, resulting in brand loyalty on the part of consumers. Small firms and new competitors are put at a disadvantage, both by the established loyalty and by the large advertising expenditures necessary to make new products visible in the marketplace. This results in a decreased number of rival firms, which lessens price competition. Marketers are thus free to raise prices, accrue monopolistic profits, and continue to spend large amounts on advertising to prevent market entry by new firms.

Advertising as Product Information The fundamental concept of this second economic model is that advertising contains product information, which reduces consumers' effort in making buying decisions. The model assumes that quality variation exists in the market. If consumers are unaware of the available alternatives, monopolistic power accrues to dominant sellers. However, advertising increases the known alternatives and makes comparisons among them possible with relatively little effort. Advertising is a means for new producers to communicate with potential buyers to tell them of product or price advantages. These better informed and knowledgeable consumers choose higher-quality products and lower prices. This results in more efficient production, lower prices, and more vigorous competition.

These two models illustrate that there are not so much *known facts* about the economic impact of advertising as there are *alternative assumptions* about how advertising operates. Economists, like other social scientists, are led to adopt a particular point of view based on their experience,

---

EXHIBIT 5.4

Competing Models of Advertising's Economic Effects

ADVERTISING AS MARKET POWER		ADVERTISING AS PRODUCT INFORMATION
Advertising affects consumer preferences and tastes, changes product attributes and differentiates the product from competitive offerings.	**ADVERTISING**	Advertising informs consumers about product attributes and does not change the way they value those attributes.
Consumers become brand loyal and less price sensitive, and perceive fewer substitutes for advertised brands.	**CONSUMER BUYING BEHAVIOR**	Consumers become more price sensitive and buy the best "value." Only the relationship between price and quality affects elasticity for a given product.
Potential entrants must overcome established brand loyalty and spend relatively more on advertising.	**BARRIERS TO ENTRY**	Advertising makes entry possible for new brands because it can communicate product attributes to consumers.
Firms are insulated from market competition and potential rivals; concentration increases, leaving firms with more discretionary power.	**INDUSTRY STRUCTURE AND MARKET POWER**	Consumers can compare competitive offerings easily and competitive rivalry is increased. Efficient firms remain, and as the inefficient firms leave, new entrants appear; the effect on concentration is ambiguous.
Firms can charge relatively higher prices and are not as likely to compete on quality or price dimensions. Innovation may be reduced.	**MARKET CONDUCT**	More informed consumers put pressure on firms to lower prices and improve quality. Innovation is facilitated via new entrants.
High prices and excessive profits accrue to advertisers and give them even more incentive to advertise their products. Output is restricted compared to conditions of perfect competition.	**MARKET PERFORMANCE**	Industry prices are decreased. The effect on profits because of increased competition and increased efficiency is ambiguous.

Source: Mark Albion, *Advertising's Hidden Effects* (Boston: Auburn House, 1983), 18.

---

training, and the individual set of problems they wish to study. Nevertheless, there is some consensus in the economics literature about enduring questions on aspects of advertising, which have been studied over time. These issues and findings are discussed in the following sections.

Effect of Advertising on Industrial Concentration Economists have long been concerned that advertising, following the market power model, results in limiting the number of competitors in an industry. The weight of the evidence indicates that industries controlled by small numbers of firms tend to have high advertising expenditures. However, there is little or no evidence to show that advertising causes this situation. It may be argued that the use of advertising and other sophisticated marketing tools has resulted in successful competitive strategies by their users. Thus the situation may reflect a triumph of more sophisticated and efficient firms over their rivals.

Effect of Advertising on Price A continual concern of consumers and public policy makers is whether the vast amounts spent on advertising by many firms results in higher prices. As suggested in the earlier discussion of scale economies, this is a complicated question that depends not only on the strategy and policy of the firm, but on those of the retailer and other intermediaries as well. Because of the difficulty of making many of the determinations of efficiencies involved, it is simply not possible to make definitive statements about the way advertising affects prices. How-

FIGURE 5.10

Two Versions of the Generalized
Advertising–Sales Response
Function

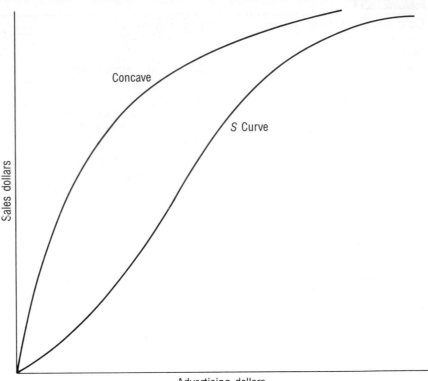

ever, observations about correlations can be made. In general, heavy advertising expenditures by manufacturers are correlated with high consumer prices. This, of course, does not mean that advertising causes high
prices. Indeed, for most sophisticated marketing firms, pricing is a strategic decision and is not immediately related to costs such as advertising.
Though a firm must cover its costs in the long run, it may be necessary
to invest large sums in marketing activities during the introductory period
when the product is new and relatively unknown. This may mean that
products are not profitable until they have been selling well for years (see
Figure 5.10).

The retail situation is somewhat different. Heavy retail advertising is
correlated with low consumer prices. In general, the whole subject of the
relationship of advertising and price awaits considerably more sophisticated research methods before it can promise more meaningful findings.

General Effect of Advertising on Consumption The literature indicates that advertising does not seem to have any powerful effect on the
general level of consumer spending. In general, other economic and social
forces have far greater effects. Studies indicate that advertising may accelerate growth trends in the economy, but it is not sufficient to stimulate
them. It seems that advertising has little effect in determining the ultimate
size of a market. In times of economic decline, advertising appears to have
little effect in counteracting the propulsive forces.

In short, it seems that advertising can affect industry sales, but only
when underlying conditions of the market, the competition, and the pre-

FIGURE 5.11

Brand Proliferation or Product
Innovation?

dispositions of consumers support an instrumental role for advertising.
Advertising's most important contribution appears to be in the role it can
play in accelerating the adoption of new products and services.

Effects of Advertising on New Product Development   A further concern of both economists and marketers is the relationship between advertising and new product development. It appears that advertising is most
frequently found in industries in which there are a large number of new
product introductions. One side has it that advertising, by accelerating
adoption, stimulates product innovation and thus has a healthy effect on
competition, consumer choice, and the economy as a whole (see Figure
5.11).

The "market power school" questions this argument. Proponents of
this position claim that it is possible for large firms to continually introduce new brands that differ in small ways from existing ones. This, they
argue, is not product innovation but brand proliferation. These tactics
essentially block the entry of new firms; thus advertising is used, along
with combative marketing techniques, to limit competition.

On the whole, it appears that advertising is related to product innovation, though the nature of the relationship is not clear. A major problem
in this area is that of definitions. Exactly what distinguishes product innovation from brand proliferation is a difficult judgment which probably
must be subjective.

ASSESSING THE ECONOMIC EFFECTS
OF ADVERTISING

It is almost as difficult to characterize advertising's economic effects as it
is to make general statements about the social effects discussed earlier in
this chapter. In fact, making determinations about advertising's economic
roles seems to be very similar in that, as in the social sphere, the conclusions reached are in part determined by the philosophical starting point.

In general, advertising seems to accentuate tendencies in the marketplace. If the market tendency is toward price rigidity, advertising tends
to solidify it. In some industries, however, advertising is associated with

price competition and tends to perpetuate that. Heavy advertising seems to be associated with consumer choice, though this may not always mean great diversity among product offerings, as the cigarette and soap industries illustrate. While advertising may result in somewhat higher prices among package goods products, it can also result in production economies among new and growing industries. This may result in lower consumer prices. Finally, advertising seems to accelerate market growth for new products, resulting in a stimulus to product development.

SUMMARY

This chapter has reviewed numerous commonly voiced criticisms of advertising. While it is most common to hear advertising condemned on social grounds and justified on economic ones, it seems that definitive information is hard to identify in either sphere. People's attitudes toward advertising seem to spring from their ideological perspectives more than from empirical evidence. Important reasons for the controversy are the visibility and intrusiveness of advertising, and the fact that most people do not clearly understand the purposes or limitations of advertising.

In addition, people are often surprised at how much money firms spend on advertising costs, particularly when the product itself may cost relatively little. The result is often a suspicion that advertisers operate in some hidden or arcane manner that manipulates consumers and justifies the huge expenditures.

Social science has generated little definitive information on the way advertising affects us socially or economically. Despite this dearth of information on how advertising works at the individual or social level, advertisers continue to use advertising because they believe that it has a positive effect on sales. Both public and private resources are expended to control advertising and to be sure that abuses feared by many critics do not go unchecked. The public and private regulatory organizations will be discussed in the following chapter.

YOU MAKE THE DECISION

DECEPTIVE OR NOT DECEPTIVE?

Consider each of the situations below and decide if you think there is deceptive advertising involved. Explain why or why not. In each case spell out what you think are the responsibilities of the advertiser and those of the consumer. Remember that the law allows advertisers to make subjective opinion statements about their products, but that ads must give an overall truthful impression of the product.

1. Sportfit athletic shoes are specially designed for aerobics. Each shoe weighs an incredibly light 2 ounces. Ads for the shoes claim they give "more bounce per ounce."
2. Morning Bugle is instant coffee that can be prepared in a microwave oven. Ads for the product claim that it is "100% safe to drink." (What expectations should a consumer have about this product? Would it be reasonable to think it was caffeine-free or had reduced caffeine? Does

the claim imply something about the methods used to remove caffeine?)

3. You receive a direct-mail offer for a "free" 14K gold chain (plus $3.99 for postage and handling). You send your check, and a few days later receive a length of gold chain—that's all, no clasp or fastener on either end.

■ ■ ■

QUESTIONS FOR DISCUSSION

1. Why do you think people are suspicious or skeptical of advertising?

2. Explain the differences between deceptive advertising and puffery.

3. What is the basis for saying that advertising has different effects on different groups of people?

4. Why does stereotyping occur in advertising?

5. How would it be possible to regulate the tastefulness of ads?

6. What are the positive and negative sides of advertising-supported communications media?

7. Does it seem possible to regulate political advertising?

8. Discuss the practical and ethical aspects of subliminal advertising.

9. Do the assumptions of the "economies of scale" argument seem to fit most large advertisers?

10. Compare and contrast the assumptions of the two competing economic models presented in this chapter.

NOTES

1. Michael Schudson, *Advertising: The Uneasy Persuasion* (New York: Basic Books, 1984), 20.

2. Charles Frazer and F. William Biglow, "Popular Perceptions of the Advertising Practitioner," in *Proceedings of the 1983 Conference of the American Academy of Advertising*, 103–107.

3. See, for example, Jerry Della Femina's memoir, *From Those Wonderful Folks Who Gave You Pearl Harbor* (New York: Simon & Schuster, 1970). Advertising people have frequently been portrayed unrealistically. Consider the following: Darren Stevens, the bewildered husband in the 1960s TV sitcom "Bewitched"; the adman role played by Jack Lemmon in the film "The Days of Wine and Roses"; and Victor Norman in the novel, *The Hucksters*.

4. Jacob Jacoby *et al.*, *Miscomprehension of Televised Communication* (New York: American Association of Advertising Agencies, 1980), 77.

5. Christopher Lasch, *The Culture of Narcissism* (New York: Warner Books, 1979), 137.

6. Thomas Petit and Alan Zakon, "Advertising and Social Values," in *Exploring Advertising*, Otto Kleppner and Irving Settel, eds. (Englewood Cliffs, N.J.: Prentice-Hall, 1970), 12.

7. Schudson, *Advertising*, 240–241.

8. John O'Toole, *The Trouble with Advertising* (New York: Chelsea House, 1981), 36.

9. *Advertising Age*, November 8, 1984, 1.

10. Kathleen Jamieson, *Packaging the Presidency* (New York: Oxford University Press, 1984), 451.

11. Wilson Key, *Subliminal Seduction* (New York: New American Library, 1973).

12. Timothy Moore, "Subliminal Advertising: What You See Is What You Get," *Journal of Marketing*, vol. 46, Spring 1982, 38–47.

13. See, for example, Ronald Berman, *Advertising and Social Change* (Beverly Hills, Calif.: Sage, 1981); and Schudson, *Advertising*. Lasch also suggests this view in *The Culture of Narcissism*.

14. Mark Albion and Paul Farris, *The Advertising Controversy* (Boston: Auburn House, 1981).

SUGGESTED READINGS

Albion, Mark. *Advertising's Hidden Effects*. Boston: Auburn House, 1983.

Albion, Mark and Paul Farris. *The Advertising Controversy*. Boston: Auburn House, 1981.

Barnouw, Erik. *The Sponsor*. New York: Oxford University Press, 1978.

Berman, Ronald. *Advertising and Social Change*. Beverly Hills, Calif.: Sage, 1981.

Courtney, Alice, and Thomas Whipple. *Sex Stereotyping in Advertising*. Lexington, Mass.: Lexington Books, 1983.

Diamond, Edwin, and Stephen Bates. *The Spot. The Rise of Political Advertising on Television*. Cambridge, Mass.: MIT Press, 1984.

Jamieson, Kathleen. *Packaging the Presidency*. New York: Oxford University Press, 1984.

Leiss, William, Stephen Kline, and Sut Jhally. *Social Communication in America*. New York: Methuen, 1986.

Schmalensee, Richard. *The Economics of Advertising*. Amsterdam: North-Holland, 1972.

Schudson, Michael. *Advertising: The Uneasy Persuasion*. New York: Basic Books, 1984.

C H A P T E R   6

THE LEGAL AND REGULATORY ENVIRONMENT

Key Terms

National Advertising Review Board (NARB)
comparative advertising
dangling comparatives
Federal Trade Commission (FTC)
consent order
cease and desist order
substantiation
affirmative disclosure
corrective advertising
trade regulation rules
residual deception
First Amendment protection

Learning Objectives

To describe the two major ways in which advertising is regulated

To explain how agency and client policies can affect ads

To outline media review procedures

To explain how industry self-regulation works

To describe the types of ads that draw scrutiny

To define the organization and activity of the Federal Trade Commission

To enumerate the major regulatory remedies of the Federal Trade Commission

To analyze the significance of corrective advertising

To trace the constitutional protection of advertising communication

An executive from Grey Advertising leaves the filming site of a commercial to make a phone call. Is the call to the client? to the main office in New York? to a film studio in LA? None of the above. The executive phones a television network clearance department to verify that a sandcastle featured in the commercial does not appear too elaborate to be the work of a child. Even after the discussion, however, the network refuses to okay the finished commercial until the child actor in the spot is brought in to demonstrate his sandcastle expertise.

Children are among the nation's most avid—and vulnerable—consumers. Some estimates place their average daily TV viewing at as much as seven hours. Correspondingly, they may be exposed to 20,000 commercials per year.

While most people agree that it's important to protect children from the unrealistic expectations sometimes encouraged by advertising, those in charge of commercial clearance at the networks come in for a

great deal of criticism. Special requirements for advertising to children tend to make commercials similar and, according to advertising people, inhibit creativity. For example, in toy commercials only ten seconds may be devoted to animation and other special effects. The closing five seconds are reserved for showing each toy individually and indicating if they are sold separately

and if batteries are included. Similarly, three seconds of every cereal ad must be used to show a balanced breakfast.

"The networks nit-pick us to death," says Jean-Claude Kaufmann of Dancer Fitzgerald Sample. One cereal ad, he recalls, featured a dog saying he really "woofed it down." The ad was rejected by the networks because they claimed it encouraged overconsumption.

In the face of such frustration, many advertisers have developed their own review procedures, including the appropriate specialists, from nutritionists and educators to psychologists and lawyers.

Source: Based on Ronald Alsop, "Watchdogs Zealously Censor Advertising Targeted to Children," *The Wall Street Journal*, September 5, 1985; and Gary Wisby, "Kids Called Walking TV Ads," *Chicago Sun-Times*, December 15, 1986.

INTRODUCTION

This chapter will consider some of the most important constraints on advertising activity: those that are explicitly designed to restrict the activities of the firm. We have already examined a number of controversies that surround advertising, so it is hardly surprising that specific institutions have been created and charged with preventing abuses in the field. In reading this chapter, you should come to appreciate the roles and perspectives of the various regulatory organizations. The chapter will also provide historical background of the two principal regulatory agencies, the Federal Trade Commission and the National Advertising Review Board.

THE SIGNIFICANCE OF ADVERTISING REGULATION

Regulation serves as a powerful constraint on advertising. In the case of television commercials, it greatly lengthens the process of producing and circulating advertising. Obviously, regulation also has an effect on the content, not just the timing, of advertising, and in some cases it affects technical aspects of the ways things are shown and where they may appear. Effective advertising mangement requires an understanding of the general intent of regulatory efforts and institutions, as well as an understanding of the limitations on regulatory powers. While advertising managers rarely deal directly with regulatory bodies, it is important for them to be aware of general constraints so as to be able to foresee and avoid potential problems. Advertising regulation has few hard-and-fast rules. As we shall see in the following sections, regulation evolves over time, responding to the social and economic environment. While some general principles have been laid down in industry codes and in case law, there are few concrete guidelines on what may or may not be done. This situation further underscores the importance of understanding regulatory bodies at a general level.

The advertising industry is guided by regulation from the inside as well as from the outside. While external regulation by federal agencies has the force of law, internal regulation, particularly by media, probably has much greater effects on day-to-day work and decision making. The following sections of this chapter will deal first with industry regulation, beginning at the most individual and informal level and moving to the most formal and structured review processes.

AGENCY AND ADVERTISER STANDARDS

Most advertising begins with a writer who devises and executes the advertising message. In a very real sense, the internal regulatory process begins at this point. Account people react to the creative ideas and present them to the client firms, who do the same. In many cases, advertisements are examined by corporate attorneys who review claims to avoid possible problems of wording and implication. Some advertisers have policies that prevent the use of certain types of appeals (such as sexual innuendo, for example). Such advertisers often avoid the use of adult magazines such as *Playboy* and *Penthouse*, also as a matter of policy.

Agencies, too, often have formal reviews of their own work. Legendary adman David Ogilvy said that the standard at his agency is that nothing is produced that "we wouldn't be proud to show our families."[1] Fairfax Cone, Leo Burnett, William Bernbach, Stanley Resor, and other notable agency heads have insisted on similar standards at their shops. In addition to these general positions about the kind of advertising that should be produced, many agencies employ a "plans board" or "creative review panel." Such units are usually composed of senior, experienced personnel, and may include top management as well as creative department representatives. The use of these review panels differs widely from agency to agency. In some they clear virtually every major piece of work that leaves the agency for concept, content, and execution, while in others they meet only periodically to provide a general assessment of the work of the creative department. In addition, most large agencies employ lawyers who review advertising prior to its presentation outside the agency. Lawyers may be permanent members of the agency staff or specialized law firms held on retainer by the agency.

While these review procedures do not amount to regulation in the formal sense, they represent very real constraints on the process of creating advertising, and in many cases they add considerably to the time necessary to produce and disseminate advertisements. For the most part, review efforts are aimed at avoiding legal problems. Few advertisers consciously choose to develop and use advertising that could incur expensive, time-consuming, and embarrassing legal problems later on.

TRADE ASSOCIATION STANDARDS

Moving beyond the level of the individual firm, numerous groups have been formed within industries to assist the development and increase the effectiveness of the firms in the industry. Often these trade associations develop advertising guidelines for member firms, particularly when advertising by the industry has been a matter of some controversy. Examples of these guidelines are seen in the standards of The Proprietary Association (the trade association for nonprescription drug marketers) and the Toy Manufacturers of America. In both cases these industry associations have taken an active role in formulating voluntary advertising codes that prohibit advertising that gives misleading impressions or distorts the satisfaction or efficacy of the products advertised.

The trade associations have an obvious interest in avoiding controversy about their members' advertising, but unfortunately, they have little power to ensure adherence to their published standards. The major trade association for the advertising agency business, the American Association of Advertising Agencies, published its Creative Code (shown in Figure 6.1) in 1956. As with other trade association codes, it sets out reasonable standards for behavior, but has no mechanism for enforcement.

FIGURE 6.1

The AAAA Creative Code

CREATIVE CODE

American Association of Advertising Agencies

The members of the American Association of Advertising Agencies recognize:

1. That advertising bears a dual responsibility in the American economic system and way of life.

To the public it is a primary way of knowing about the goods and services which are the products of American free enterprise, goods and services which can be freely chosen to suit the desires and needs of the individual. The public is entitled to expect that advertising will be reliable in content and honest in presentation.

To the advertiser it is a primary way of persuading people to buy his goods or services, within the framework of a highly competitive economic system. He is entitled to regard advertising as a dynamic means of building his business and his profits.

2. That advertising enjoys a particularly intimate relationship to the American family. It enters the home as an integral part of television and radio programs, to speak to the individual and often to the entire family. It shares the pages of favorite newspapers and magazines. It presents itself to travelers and to readers of the daily mails. In all these forms, it bears a special responsibility to respect the tastes and self-interest of the public.

3. That advertising is directed to sizable groups or to the public at large, which is made up of many interests and many tastes. As is the case with all public enterprises, ranging from sports to education and even to religion, it is almost impossible to speak without finding someone in disagreement. Nonetheless, advertising people recognize their obligation to operate within the traditional American limitations: to serve the interests of the majority and to respect the rights of the minority.

Therefore we, the members of the American Association of Advertising Agencies, in addition to supporting and obeying the laws and legal regulations pertaining to advertising, undertake to extend and broaden the application of high ethical standards. Specifically, we will not knowingly produce advertising which contains:

a. False or misleading statements or exaggerations, visual or verbal.

b. Testimonials which do not reflect the real choice of a competent witness.

c. Price claims which are misleading.

d. Comparisons which unfairly disparage a competitive product or service.

e. Claims insufficiently supported, or which distort the true meaning or practicable application of statements made by professional or scientific authority.

f. Statements, suggestions or pictures offensive to public decency.

We recognize that there are areas which are subject to honestly different interpretations and judgment. Taste is subjective and may even vary from time to time as well as from individual to individual. Frequency of seeing or hearing advertising messages will necessarily vary greatly from person to person.

However, we agree not to recommend to an advertiser and to discourage the use of advertising which is in poor or questionable taste or which is deliberately irritating through content, presentation or excessive repetition.

Clear and willful violations of this Code shall be referred to the Board of Directors of the American Association of Advertising Agencies for appropriate action, including possible annulment of membership as provided in Article IV, Section 5, of the Constitution and By-Laws.

Conscientious adherence to the letter and the spirit of this Code will strengthen advertising and the free enterprise system of which it is part.   *Adopted April 26, 1962*

Endorsed by

Advertising Association of the West, Advertising Federation of America, Agricultural Publishers Association, Associated Business Publications, Association of Industrial Advertisers, Association of National Advertisers, Magazine Publishers Association, National Business Publications, Newspaper Advertising Executives Association, Radio Code Review Board (National Association of Broadcasters), Station Representatives Association, TV Code Review Board (NAB)

Source: Reprinted with permission from the American Association of Advertising Agencies.

MEDIA STANDARDS

Except in the case of political advertising, the media may reject any advertisement. Some publishers choose to exclude the advertising of entire industries. For example, *Reader's Digest*, which once was entirely subscriber-supported and carried no advertising at all, does not currently accept advertising for either tobacco products or alcoholic beverages. Other publishers use different standards. *Good Housekeeping* magazine regularly tests products advertised on its pages. Those meeting the magazine staff's standards are awarded the *Good Housekeeping* "seal of approval," which may be displayed in advertising and packaging. Magazines like *Good Housekeeping* do this in order to protect the credibility of their editorial and advertising matter.

The broadcast media established somewhat different standards. They are prohibited by law from accepting advertising for cigarettes, though until 1971 the cigarette industry provided significant advertising revenue to broadcasters. Radio and television stations have also agreed — through their trade association, the National Association of Broadcasters (NAB) — not to air commercials for liquor, though wine and beer ads are regularly carried. As with other association codes, the NAB code has no important sanctions to apply against stations who violate its restraints. In fact, when feminine hygiene products were introduced some years ago, the commercials were judged unacceptable by stations subscribing to the NAB code. However, once the commercials began to be aired by independent, non-code stations, the code was revised to accept the commercials. The NAB code was officially suspended in March 1982, after portions dealing with the length of commercial were challenged in the courts. Despite the fact that the code is no longer in force, major portions related to advertising content have been incorporated into standards of the individual networks.

The three major television networks maintain "standards and practices" offices, which review commercials at various stages of production and give clearance for airing. After clearance by the agency and advertiser, scripts and storyboards are sent to the network clearance offices. According to one recent study, ABC alone reviews 51,000 commercials per year (see Exhibit 6.1). They accept about 65 percent and reject 3 percent. The remainder — about a third — are revised and re-reviewed.[2] While many agencies feel that network decisions tend to be arbitrary, their only alternative is to produce the commercials without sending them for clearance. Rejection of a finished commercial would be disastrous — both in terms of missing the scheduled air times and of the time and expense for any last-minute modifications needed to make the commercial acceptable. For these reasons, advertisers who feel there is the slightest risk of objection from the networks submit their commercials for review in the storyboard stage.

According to network officials, the area that advertisers most frequently must change involves matters of taste. Nudity and sexually suggestive material are the most common complaint. However, in 1987 the three major broadcast networks revised their standards to allow lingerie advertisers to show their products on live models. Before that, women's undergarments had to be displayed on mannequins, or on models in leotards. This illustrates that the standards of acceptability are constantly changing. Recently, for example, contraceptive advertising has begun to appear on broadcast media, while at the same time a ban on beer and wine advertising is under discussion. Interestingly enough, a society that

EXHIBIT 6.1

The American Broadcasting
Company's Advertising Guidelines
for Personal Care Products

1) Genital Products
   a) Representations of product fragrance and personal cleanliness/hygiene are unacceptable.
   b) These products may not be promoted for reasons of health.
   c) The use of children in advertising is unacceptable.
   d) Generalized claims of product efficacy may be acceptable, subject to taste considerations (e.g., claims of duration, "lasts", "feel fresh for hours").
   e) Products intended for external minor itching/irritation are acceptable. Male jock itch products must limit the reference to "jock itch" to three audio mentions. The feminine irritation products must limit the reference to "minor feminine irritation" to three audio mentions with the following disclosures: "If symptoms persist, see your doctor" and "for temporary relief of minor itching and irritation."
   f) Scheduling for jock itch products is limited to post 11 p.m. and Sports programming.
   g) Scheduling for feminine irritation products is limited to post 10:30 p.m. and 9 a.m. to 4 p.m. on weekdays (except in the central time zone where scheduling is limited to post 9:30 p.m. and 8 a.m. to 3 p.m. weekdays).
2) General Body and Foot Odor Products
   All representations dealing with odor problems, application demonstrations, and the use of humor should be presented in a restrained, inoffensive manner, in order to avoid playing upon fears and insecurities of individuals.
3) Products for Mouth or Denture Odor
   Representatives of mouth or denture odor should be presented in a restrained and inoffensive manner.
4) Bathroom Tissue and Related Products
   a) Direct or indirect references, graphic language, and video potrayals concerning product/body function and mechanics are unacceptable (e.g., references to cleanliness, anatomy, insertion, and application).
   b) A product's strength, softness, and absorbency must be presented in a restrained and inoffensive way.

Source: Based on *ABC Advertising Standards and Guidelines*, Section II, 24.

has traditionally accepted alcohol consumption and covert sex seems to be reversing its attitudes.

In addition to nudity, sex, and bodily functions, networks are extremely careful about clearing comparative advertising claims. Any objective advertising claim must include adequate substantiation to satisfy the reviewer.

INDUSTRYWIDE REGULATION: THE NAD/NARB

The establishment of industrywide self-regulation came in 1971 with the creation of the **National Advertising Review Board (NARB).** It works in cooperation with the National Advertising Division (NAD) of the Council of Better Business Bureaus. The NAD monitors advertising for possible abuses, receives complaints from other individuals and organizations, and attempts to bring about resolution of complaints through direct negotiation with the advertiser. The NARB is a 50-member group composed of 30 representatives from advertiser firms, 10 from advertising agencies, and 10 from the general public. The NARB serves as the appeals board for cases from the NAD. If the advertiser and the NAD can't agree about a case, five NARB members are selected to consider the findings and resolve the dispute.

There were numerous motivations for the establishment of this organization. One of the most important was to head off impending governmental regulation demanded by an active and vociferous consumer movement in the 1960s. Interestingly enough, a nearly identical mechanism (known as the Review Committee of the National Better Business Bureau) had been proposed in response to the consumerist sentiment of the 1920s, though the organization was never established.[3]

When an advertising complaint is addressed to the NARB, it is first reviewed by the National Advertising Division of the Council of Better Business Bureaus. In recent years about half the complaints have arisen from the NAD's advertising monitoring program. The remaining complaints seem to come from competitors' challenges, consumers or consumer groups, and local Better Business Bureaus, in roughly equal proportions.[4] According to the NAD, competitor challenges are an increasingly important source for investigatory direction. Competitors may provide information and test data and expertise for making determinations about advertising claims.[5] The actions of the NAD have not been closely studied, though it would be very instructive for advertisers and marketers.

Once a complaint reaches the NAD, the organization contacts the advertiser to obtain substantiation for the claim in question. If the advertiser supplies appropriate documentation, the complaint is dismissed. If, after discussion of the claim and documentation, either the NAD or the advertiser is dissatisfied with the outcome, the case may be appealed to the National Advertising Review Board. When an appeal is forwarded from the NAD, a 5-member NARB panel is selected (in the same 3:1:1 ratio as the larger group) to hear and judge the complaint.

If the panel finds in favor of the advertiser, the case is dismissed. If, however, the panel finds elements of the advertising objectionable, it urges the advertiser to modify the claims. Though the NARB has no sanctions it can impose on advertisers, it has been successful in every case to date in winning cooperation.

If the NARB panel does not receive cooperation from the advertiser, its ultimate threat is to turn its records and evidence over to the Federal Trade Commission for prosecution. The FTC has suggested that it would be particularly vigorous in its prosecution of advertisers who are uncooperative with the industry's self-regulatory efforts, but so far, such action has been unnecessary.

NARB ACTIONS

While the NAD/NARB was established to aid the industry in creating clear guidelines for what was acceptable and objectionable in advertising, this goal has since been deemed impractical. The organization has decided instead that it must deal with advertising problems on a case-by-case basis rather than in sweeping generalities. The result is that few clear principles can be identified from the NAD/NARB cases. However, some characteristics of self-regulatory action emerge. Exhibit 6.2 shows the product cat-

EXHIBIT 6.2

The Majority of NAD Cases,
by Product Category

PRODUCT CATEGORY	NUMBER OF CASES	PERCENT OF ALL CASES
Food	180	15.3%
Cosmetics	155	13.1
Household	144	12.2
Automotive	142	12.0
Appliances	89	7.5
Over-the-Counter Drugs	62	5.3

Source: Based on Gary Armstrong and Julie Ozanne, "An Evaluation of NAD/NARB Purpose and Performance," *Journal of Advertising,* vol. 12, no. 3, 1983, 24. Reprinted with permission.

egories that have generated the greatest number of NAD cases, generally indicating that more heavily advertised product categories seem to incur more complaints.

As of 1987, in the 15 years of its existence, the NAD had dealt with over 2,190 cases. These data suggest that the organization has been very effective in securing the cooperation of advertisers in modifying questionable claims, since only about 2 percent of cases (41 instances) have required hearing by an NARB panel.

Of these cases, the NARB upheld the NAD judgment in 27 instances, reversing or modifying the NAD in ten others. In four cases the investigation was dismissed without prejudice.

What specific types of advertising are most likely to run afoul of the self-regulatory process? According to the NAD, competitive challenges most often involve **comparative advertising,** messages that identify a competitor by name and suggest superiority over it. These cases have accounted for around 60 percent of the NAD caseload in recent years. After an extensive review of cases, Eric Zanot attempted to identify important principles that emerged from the NARB panel reports on advertising cases.[6] Aside from cases where no clear guidelines emerged, or where NARB simply upheld principles already established by the Federal Trade Commission, Zanot outlined the following:

1. Standards of accuracy are stringent. The NARB panels have used a strict standard of accuracy in advertising claims holding (as does FTC) that the impression received by the consumer is the standard by which advertising claims are to be judged. In several cases, panels have held that even prior review and approval of claims by FTC is not a sufficient defense when an inaccurate impression is given to consumers.

2. **Dangling comparatives,** in which a comparison is implied but the nature or conditions are not specified, are to be avoided. It is not uncommon for advertising to claim that a product is "better" without specifying what the product is better than, or under what conditions. This dangling comparative has not been clearly proscribed or restricted in panel decisions, but it is generally discouraged.

3. Puffery may be misleading. The preceding chapter discussed some of the problems of puffery, and the reluctance of regulators to act against it. While panels have noted consumers' tendency to discount puffery, they have gone farther than other regulators by noting it has a capacity for deception when used in areas that can be measured, rather than merely expressing subjective opinion.

4. Research data must be accurately represented. Several panel decisions involved examination of advertising referring to research studies. In these cases the panels reserved the right to examine the accuracy of the ad's representation of the research as well as the technical accuracy of the research itself.

5. Comparisons must be fair and accurate. As mentioned earlier, comparative advertising results in numerous complaints, particularly from competitors. While generally favoring comparative advertising as a means of providing useful information to consumers about

competing brands, panels have suggested that comparisons be based on like grade and quality of products and that claims be provable under conditions of general use, not merely in the lab. In addition, general claims of superiority should not be based on superiority of a single product feature.

THE IMPACT OF INDUSTRY SELF-REGULATION

As the foregoing discussion suggests, advertising is profoundly affected by the internal regulatory apparatus. The fact that much of this internal structure is designed for self-serving reasons—that is, to avoid offending patrons, to prevent abuses that dilute the effectiveness of advertising, or even to head off threatened governmental regulation—does not mean that the activity does not result in improved performance. The high level of cooperation with such agencies as the NAD/NARB can be taken as evidence of the industry's desire to establish fair and responsible standards for advertising execution. This effort has not escaped the attention of even federal regulators, who have termed the NAD/NARB "the most effective industry self-regulatory mechanism in operation today."

Numerous local advertising review boards have been established across the country as well. Most often these boards are headquartered in a specific metropolitan area and organized and supported jointly by the local Better Business Bureau and the advertising community. The focus of these local boards is to police local or retail advertising, which does not reach the attention of the NAD/NARB.

EXTERNAL REGULATION: THE FEDERAL TRADE COMMISSION

The **Federal Trade Commission (FTC)** has historically been the most important external influence on the advertising industry, and the organization that set the standards to which modern advertising is held.

The FTC was not established as a consumer protection agency. Rather, it was founded in 1914 to ensure healthy and vigorous competition and to protect business from unscrupulous competitors.

In its early days, the commission did not have explicit power over advertising. This was granted by Congress in 1938 through the Wheeler-Lea amendment to the Federal Trade Commission Act. Many large advertisers of the time supported the expanded powers of the FTC over advertising, feeling that regulation would reduce the abuses they believed came primarily from small-time and fly-by-night operators.

Over time, the commission's role evolved to include consumer protection, in addition to its responsibility for enforcment of antitrust and related regulation. The evolutionary process has been neither simple nor easy. At least a half dozen reports between 1924 and 1970 criticized the commission for its cumbersome procedures, preoccupation with detail, and bureaucratization. Among the challenges the commission has faced is the fact that it must receive funding from Congress, which, while critical of the FTC's inactivity, has often been either reluctant to fund the agency at appropriate levels, or has withheld the agency's funding to win changes in policy or practice. Thus the agency has reflected the social attitudes of the times. This is clearly illustrated in the recent history of the Federal Trade Commission.

In 1970, in response to the consumerist movement and reform sentiments of the late 1960s, the agency was dramatically reorganized and revitalized. During this period new approaches to advertising regulation were developed. This activist period lasted until about 1980, when the agency ran headlong into the deregulation philosophy of Ronald Reagan's presidency. Meanwhile, the FTC—which had been formulating an aggressive policy on advertising to children, as well as new rules that would have had dramatic consequences for mortuaries and used car dealers— suddenly found its funding "held captive" by a hostile Congress. Congress even went so far as to assert the right of review over FTC actions (although the federal courts later overruled this act). The FTC has maintained a low profile since then, and leadership at the commission is currently quite conservative in its view of FTC regulatory activity. In fact, recent FTC Chairmen James Miller III and Daniel Oliver have actually sought reduction of the commission's powers. It seems likely that the agency will play a considerably smaller role in advertising activity in the coming decade than it did in the 1970s.

MISSION OF THE FTC

The FTC's role is the maintenance of competition. It does this both through its role in antitrust activities and in the consumer protection field. Its regulation of advertising also serves this goal in two ways: 1) by preventing injury to legitimate advertisers arising from competitors' use of deceptive advertising, and 2) by assuring accurate information in the marketplace. Thus, in theory, the consumer chooses and rewards the firm that offers superior goods, maintaining the incentive for competitors to offer the highest quality and best value.

The FTC seeks to protect the average, or "ordinary" consumer, rather than the most or least astute. In special cases, the commission may consider the special vulnerabilities of a particular audience—such as children—when they seem likely to be affected differently and when they form an important part of the market for a product.

The commission is concerned with advertising that is deceptive, misleading, or unfair. It makes its own decision as to what deceptive advertising is, and need not demonstrate that anyone has been deceived in order to take action.

In determining deception, the commission considers the total impression given by the ad. Literal truth may not be sufficient defense for an ad that the commission considers deceptive, since it has ruled that vagueness and silence on important aspects of a product may also be deceptive. It is ironic to note that the absence of literal truth may also not draw action from the commission. The case in point is puffery, where subjective opinion statements are offered about products. While advertisers who have attempted to base their defenses on allowable hyperbole have not fared well with the commission, the FTC has not attempted to attack puffery *per se*, and the technique continues to be common on the advertising scene today, as it has been for decades.

The FTC will provide advisory opinions on specific advertisements for advertisers. While these opinions are not binding, they do represent a good-faith attempt by the FTC to interpret the law to the best of its abilities.

OPERATION OF THE FTC

The FTC is composed of five commissioners; a group of individuals who conduct hearings on advertising cases, called "administrative law judges"; a group of attorneys who investigate complaints and propose remedies, called "complaint counsels"; and the FTC staff. Complaints come to the FTC from consumers or competitors, or are generated from within the FTC. First, a staff investigation of the complaint is carried out. The case may be dismissed or a proposed complaint and consent order is written by a complaint counsel. If prepared, the proposed material is reviewed by the commissioners. The case also may be dismissed at this point; otherwise, if it has merit, it is officially conveyed to the advertiser and to the media. Since at this point the matter becomes public, the force of possible adverse public reaction is an important consideration for the advertiser.

Either the advertiser or the commissioners may find the cease and desist order unsatisfactory and choose to appeal. If this happens, the case is brought before an administrative law judge who considers the evidence to determine if "substantial evidence of a violation" exists. If the administrative law judge determines that the evidence supports the charge, a cease-and-desist order is issued. If not, the case is dismissed. If the advertiser and complaint counsel agree at this point, the case is resolved. However, either party may be dissatisfied with the outcome and may seek a hearing before the commissioners. This hearing, too, may result in agreement, dismissal, or appeal. If the outcome is unsatisfactory to the advertiser, the appeal in this case is through the federal court system. Such an appeal must be on procedural grounds rather than a dispute of the facts or issues. This process is summarized in Figure 6.2.

While the FTC has decidedly limited powers to police its rulings, it has the power to levy very stiff fines for infractions of them. For instance, it may seek fines of up to $10,000 per day for violations of cease-and-desist and consent orders. One of the FTC's most powerful weapons in seeking cooperation is probably the one with no explicit penalty: publicity. Since advertisers seek to build public trust, the news of a deceptive advertising investigation can bring literally incalculable consequences. For example, publicity surrounding the 1971 investigation of claims made against an automobile radiator antifreeze are alleged to have resulted in the death of a successful product, despite the fact that charges were eventually dismissed.[7]

FTC REMEDIES FOR DECEPTIVE ADVERTISING

During the period of vigorous enforcement and regulatory innovation of the 1970s, the FTC developed or enhanced its arsenal of regulatory tools.

The Consent Order A tool of the FTC since the early days of the agency, the **consent order** involves an agreement by the advertiser to refrain from certain advertising practices or claims. Under the consent order, the advertiser makes no admission of guilt, but simply agrees not to pursue a specified practice in the future.

FIGURE 6.2
FTC Complaint Procedure

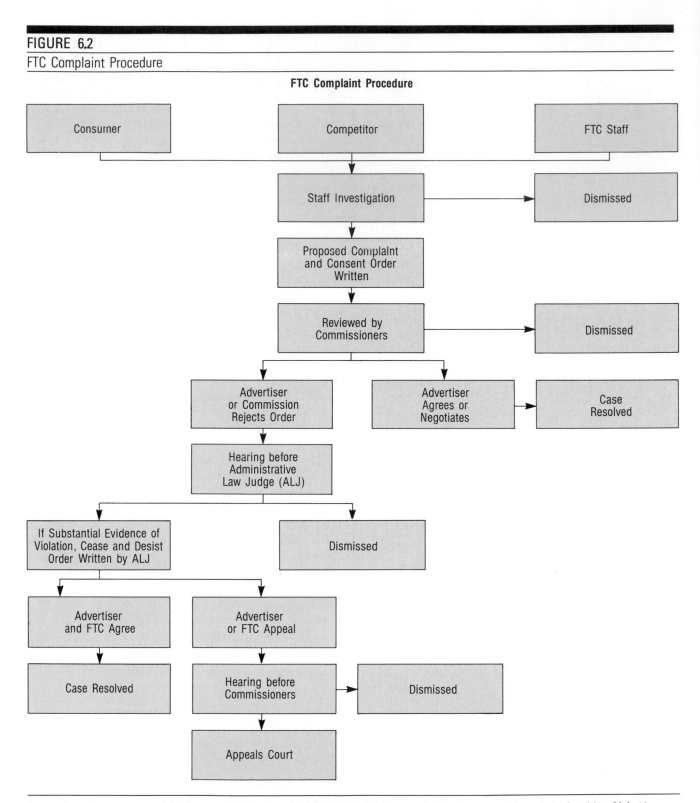

Source: Gary Armstrong and Julie Ozanne, "An Evaluation of NAD/NARB Purpose and Performance," *Journal of Advertising*, Vol. 12, No. 3, 1983, p. 24. Reprinted with permission.

The Cease and Desist Order More emphatic than a consent agreement, **the cease and desist order** requires that an advertiser stop a specified advertising claim or practice within 30 days. It, too, is a tool from the early days of the FTC, and is intended to bring a quick end to practices the commission finds objectionable. The cease and desist order involves no admission of guilt and does not require agreement by the advertiser. To respond, an advertiser must discontinue the advertising in question and pursue the FTC appeal process. Both cease and desist and consent order violations are subject to fines of up to $10,000 a day.

Substantiation For many years the FTC accepted the burden of disproving advertising claims to challenge deceptive advertising. However, the situation changed in 1971 with the advent of the FTC's **substantiation** program, under which the burden of proof shifts to the advertiser, who must supply documentation for the claims made in the advertising. This was pointed up dramatically in the Pfizer Corporation case in 1972, in which the FTC demanded evidence for Pfizer's claim that its product Unburn was effective for sunburn. This reversal of roles was dramatic and shocking to many in the advertising and over-the-counter drug industries, who had never considered that explicit evidence of effectiveness would be required, so long as a product's basic ingredients were known to be useful.

Advertisers are currently required to substantiate their claims and to be able to provide such substantiation at the request of FTC or of consumers. Where technical or scientific data are relied on, advertisers are required to provide summaries in layman's language. Former FTC chairman James Miller (appointed to the commission by Ronald Reagan) suggested that the FTC should not proceed with cases against advertisers unless it has evidence that claims are false. Current Chairman Daniel Oliver has criticized past FTC activities for being too "literalistic" and for "unreasonable disputes over the meaning of the words."[8] While this sounds like a reversal of FTC policy in the past decade, it is unlikely that it will relieve advertisers from obtaining and providing prior substantiation for advertising claims.

Affirmative Disclosure The FTC has the power not only to prevent advertisers from making statements it considers deceptive, but also to force the advertiser to say certain things. **Affirmative disclosure,** which requires advertisers to include specific kinds of information in their advertising, can be ordered when the FTC has concerns about possible harmful effects of product use. This technique has not been widely used by the FTC (warnings in cigarette ads are a result of Congressional action), but it remains a potentially important remedy.

Corrective Advertising Though cease and desist orders and the substantiation requirement can be used to stop deceptive advertising, the FTC in its activist period sought to develop a remedy that would allow redress of competitive or consumer injury that occurred as a result of deceptive advertising. From those efforts evolved the concept of **corrective advertising**, messages intended to repair mistaken impressions created by earlier messages. Needless to say, corrective advertising is a profound and far-reaching remedy. It was first ordered against ITT Continental, who had advertised its product, Profile Bread, as a dietary aid. The name, the

A CLOSER LOOK

CORRECTIVE ADVERTISING

The following messages appeared in the nation's print and broadcast media as a result of FTC rulings against some major advertisers.

Profile Bread

I'm (celebrity's name) for Profile Bread. Like all mothers, I'm concerned about nutrition and balanced meals. So, I'd like to clear up any misunderstanding you may have about Profile Bread from its advertising or even its name.

Does Profile have fewer calories than any other breads? No. Profile has about the same per ounce as other breads. To be exact, Profile has seven fewer calories per slice. That's because Profile is sliced thinner. But eating Profile will not cause you to lose weight. A reduction of seven calories is insignificant. It's total calories and balanced nutrition that count. And Profile can help you achieve a balanced meal because it provides protein and B vitamins as well as other nutrients.

"How does my family feel about Profile? Well, my husband likes Profile toast, the children love Profile sandwiches, and I prefer Profile to any other bread. So you see, at our house, delicious taste makes Profile a family affair."

(To be run in 25% of brand's advertising, for one year.)

Amstar

"Do you recall some of our past messages saying that Domino Sugar gives you strength, energy, and stamina? Actually, Domino is not a special or unique source of strength, energy, and stamina. No sugar is, because what you need is a balanced diet and plenty of rest and exercise."

(To be run in one of every four ads for one year.)

Ocean Spray

"If you've wondered what some of our earlier advertising meant when we said Ocean Spray Cranberry Juice Cocktail has more food energy than orange juice or tomato juice, let us make it clear: we didn't mean vitamins and minerals. Food energy means calories. Nothing more.

"Food energy is important at breakfast since many of us may not get enough calories, or food energy, to get off to a good start. Ocean Spray Cranberry Juice Cocktail helps because it contains more food energy than most other breakfast drinks.

"And Ocean Spray Cranberry Juice Cocktail gives you and your family Vitamin C plus a great wake-up taste. It's . . . the other breakfast drink."

(To be run in one of every four ads for one year.)

Sugar Information, Inc.

"Do you recall the messages we brought you in the past about sugar? How something with sugar in it before meals could help you curb your appetite? We hope you didn't get the idea that our little diet tip was any magic formula for losing weight. Because there are no tricks or shortcuts; the whole diet subject is very complicated. Research hasn't established that consuming sugar before meals will contribute to weight reduction or even keep you from gaining weight."

(To be run for one insertion in each of seven magazines.)

Source: William Wilkie, Dennis McNeill, and Michael Mazis, "Marketing's Scarlet Letter: The Theory and Practice of Corrective Advertising," *Journal of Marketing*, vol. 48, Spring 1984, 13. Reprinted by permission from the *Journal of Marketing*, published by the American Marketing Association.

product, and the advertising were designed to convey that Profile could help in losing weight. However, the FTC found that the product was only insignificantly different from other breads and of no special help to dieters, and therefore ordered the firm to devote 25 percent of Profile advertising for the following year to corrective messages, or to cease advertising altogether for a 12-month period.

ITT Continental chose to devote 25 percent of *each message* to corrective advertising rather than to produce one corrective ad for every three "regular" commercials. By structuring the corrective campaign in this way,

ITT Continental probably minimized its effect. Corrective advertising has been ordered in only about six national advertising cases, including the Profile Bread case. According to former FTC Chairman Robert Pitofsky, corrective advertising is a remedy that should be applied only in major cases involving material deception creating consumer misconceptions that significantly influence purchase decisions. According to Pitofsky, corrective advertising is not intended as a penalty, but rather to rectify misinformation in the marketplace.[9] Regardless of this view, corrective advertising is clearly seen as a penalty by the advertising community.

In the cases in which corrective advertising has been ordered, it has most commonly been required that 15 to 25 percent of the next year's advertising be devoted to the corrective message. In some cases, specific media have been required; in others, it was mandated that advertisers admit that earlier advertising was incorrect. In the 1977 case of Listerine antiseptic, the FTC ordered the amount spent on corrective advertising to be the average annual advertising expenditure for the brand over the previous 10 years (about $10 million). (The FTC chose ten years as a frame of reference because it estimated that the deceptive advertising occurred over a 10-year period.) Though the FTC sought an admission of "prior deception" in the commercials, this requirement was struck down by the U.S. Court of Appeals, raising the question of whether the FTC might successfully require it in the future.

Injunctions   The FTC has the power to seek injunctions, or restraining orders, from federal courts against advertising it believes to be injurious to competition or to the public. This power is not widely used and is reserved for clear violations of the law and for threats to health and safety.

Trade Regulation Rules   The Magnuson-Moss Act of 1975 gave the FTC the power to create rules for entire industries. This legislation resulted in a dramatic broadening of FTC powers. Where in the past, the FTC was required to move on a case-by-case basis, the power to develop **trade regulation rules** allows the agency to make sweeping judgments about practices in entire industries. For example, setting requirements for the use of nutritional claims is possible. Those who violate such rules are subject to the full range of FTC sanctions. While the power to formulate trade regulation rules seems immense, their publication does allow advertisers to know the FTC's position before the fact, rather than become aware of the policy as the result of prosecution.

PROBLEMS IN FEDERAL REGULATION

Though the procedures followed by the FTC can be spelled out and appear clear, the federal regulatory apparatus has some significant problems. One of the greatest of these is the pace at which the agency moves to stop deception. Advertising campaigns appear and change quickly, and while most campaigns run for 6 to 12 months, most advertising prosecutions take well over two years. This timetable puts the FTC in the position of always acting after the fact—sometimes so long after the fact that the agency's action seems irrelevant as far as the consumer is concerned.

In addition to the time element, the FTC must deal with the problem of **residual deception,** the retention of misinformation long after the ad-

A CLOSER LOOK

HOW EFFECTIVE IS CORRECTIVE ADVERTISING?

In 1975 the Federal Trade Commission began the prosecution of Warner-Lambert for deceptive advertising claims for Listerine. For over 50 years, the product had claimed to reduce chances of colds and sore throats. No medical evidence was offered to support this claim. Hearings on the matter covered four months, involved 46 witnesses, and over 4000 pages of testimony.

The FTC sought corrective advertising to remedy the misinformation in the marketplace. As it moved through the hearing and appeal process, the corrective order changed as follows:

ELEMENT	PROPOSED BY FTC	COURT OF APPEAL'S ORDER (FINAL)
REQUIRED STATEMENT:	"The Federal Trade Commission has found, contrary to the prior advertising of the Warner-Lambert Company, the makers of Listerine, that Listerine will not prevent colds or sore throats, Listerine will not cure colds or sore throats, and Listerine will not be beneficial in the treatment of cold symptoms or sore throats."	"Listerine will not help prevent colds or sore throats or lessen their severity."
SPECIFICATIONS:		
PRINT	Separated from text; type size at least as large as text, such that can be readily noticed	Same
BROADCAST	Presented in both audio and visual portions; no other sound in audio portion; in language principally employed in the ad	Same
BOTH	Nothing in ad should be inconsistent with or detract from the required disclosure	
CAMPAIGN DURATION:	Five years (plus provision to end earlier upon showing that residual effect had been dissipated)	Variable, likely one year
REQUIRED BUDGET:	Variable (to be included in every Listerine ad during the period)	Average annual expenditure 1962-72 (about $10 million)

The final settlement — over $10 million in corrective advertising — was run over a period of 16 months ending in February 1980. However, the FTC could not have been totally pleased with the results. The commission conducted a study to evaluate the effectiveness of the corrective messages. Two others were conducted by scholars in public policy research. The findings of all the studies were similar: the corrective advertising had some effect on redressing misinformation, but the effect was minimal. One study showed that seven of eight viewers had no memory of the corrective message 24 hours after seeing it.

Study of this and other corrective advertising cases has led policy researchers to a simple recommendation: If misinformation in the marketplace is to be corrected, quantified, measurable levels of public understanding should be set. Under this system, a firm would be required to advertise until the appropriate level of communication was achieved, rather than until an arbitrary amount of money had been spent.

Source: Based on William Wilkie, Dennis McNeill, and Michael Mazis, "Marketing's Scarlet Letter: The Theory and Practice of Corrective Advertising," *Journal of Marketing*, vol. 48, Spring 1984, 11–31.

vertising message appears. How long does the public retain mistaken information from advertising? Although corrective advertising offers a way of dealing with the problem, it is an extreme remedy and one the agency is hesitant to invoke in relatively minor cases.

A further problem arises in the FTC's stance on deception. In making its determination about the existence of deception, the agency has held that literal truth is not enough; the impression received by the consumer is what matters. While it is a relatively easy job to determine the truthfulness of an ad, it is more difficult, if not impossible, to determine what is in the minds of viewers. While it is understandable that the FTC must consider elements beyond literal truth, the judgment of consumer perceptions is a very difficult and controversial area.

THE CONSTITUTIONAL STATUS OF ADVERTISING

In 1942 the U.S. Supreme Court ruled in *Valentine* v. *Chrestensen* that the First Amendment to the Constitution did not afford protection to commercial advertising. The court sent a slightly different message in 1964 in *The New York Times* v. *Sullivan*. In this case, it ruled that **First Amendment protection** did extend to editorial or political advertising. Since 1975, more than a half-dozen cases have supported limited protection for advertising under the First Amendment.

Though the exact extent of constitutional protection remains far from clear, the cases of the past decade show that truthful advertising may not be regulated without regard for the rights of the speaker. A brief review of the cases will show this development.

Bigelow v. *Virginia* (1975). In this case, a Virginia newspaper publisher had run an ad from a New York women's group, which urged women in need of abortion to come to New York since abortion was illegal in Virginia at the time. The Court reversed the publisher's conviction, noting that the advertisement contained material of public interest and did not lose protection simply because it was an advertisement.

Virginia Board of Pharmacy v. *Virginia Citizens Consumer Council, Inc.* (1976). In this case, Virginia state law said that the prices of prescription drugs could not be advertised. Noting that prices of prescription drugs were as much as 650 percent higher at some pharmacies, the Supreme Court ruled that the state could not prohibit advertising for lawful transactions. It went on to note that consumers have considerable interest in commercial information, perhaps even more than in political debate, and for this reason the flow of commercial information should not be restricted.

Bates v. *State Bar of Arizona* (1977). Here the Court ruled that regulations in the legal profession forbidding virtually all advertising by lawyers, deprived consumers of needed information. While lawyers might consider advertising a shoddy or unprofessional practice, the consumer could hope to benefit from the advertising of fees for established legal services. The Court even expressed the hope that advertising might result in lower fees for basic services.

First National Bank of Boston v. *Belotti* (1978). In this case, the Court held that a business has the right to use advertising to influence opinion on issues having no direct bearing on their business activities. Specifically, the Court ruled unconstitutional a Massachusetts law that prevented the bank from publicly opposing a graduated income tax. The Court thus granted corporations the right to participate in public policy debate.

Central Hudson Gas & Electric Corporation v. *Public Service Commission of New York* (1980). This case involved the use of advertising to promote electrical consumption by the power company. The case arose during the energy crisis and the state of New York felt promoting consumption was wasteful and inappropriate and banned all promotional advertising. Again, the Court concluded that the advertising was not misleading and the activity of consuming power was legal. Thus it found the state's regulation to be overly broad in prohibiting all advertising, and thus unconstitutional.

Bolger v. *Young Drug Products Corporation* (1983). Here, the Court struck down a federal law prohibiting mass mailing of contraceptive advertising. The Court found a pamphlet mailed by Young to contain significant information on family planning and venereal disease prevention in addition to advertising its products. The value of the information contained far outweighed the importance of shielding those who might be offended by the products, according to the Court. Once again, the Court supported the notion that useful information may not be restricted by sweeping prohibitions on commercial advertising.

THE SUPREME COURT'S FOUR-PART TEST

The cases discussed above simply provide an overview of the Supreme Court's actions. They do not include all commercial speech cases, nor does the listing attempt to show the directions taken by state courts in dealing with advertising cases. However, there can be no question that the cases illustrate some directions that were almost unimaginable a decade ago. In these decisions the Court has granted protection to advertising and has forbidden blanket prohibitions of advertising to classes of advertisers and classes of goods. Further, it has granted a right of speech to corporations, not just about their products and services, but on all issues in the public sphere. In addition, it has required that any regulation of truthful advertising be specific enough so as not to restrict the flow of important and useful information to significant groups of interested consumers.

In coming to these decisions, the Court developed a four-part test to determine the constitutional protection of advertising. This was enunciated most clearly by Justice Lewis F. Powell in the *Central Hudson* case: Advertising is protected if

1. it is for lawful activity.

2. it is not false or deceptive.

Such advertising can be regulated only when regulation

3. directly advances a substantial government interest.

4. is no more extensive than necessary.

While these standards seem vague, they will doubtless become clearer as the body of case law builds and the concepts are fleshed out.[10] The Court seems to have embarked on a course that both recognizes advertising as a significant form of communication in a consumer society, and institutionalizes that status.

A LOBAL LOOK

COLA WAR STORIES

It's a jungle out there—or so it seems to the people who operate the "Pepsi Challenge" worldwide. Initially begun in the United States in the early 1980s, the Challenge went multinational after data showed Pepsi-Cola to be trailing Coca-Cola in nearly two-thirds of its markets.

In order to operate it in foreign countries, however, the Challenge had to be modified to accommodate local laws and customs in each nation. Quite often, this meant a reduction in—if not a moratorium on—comparative advertising. In Malaysia, for example, PepsiCo had to provide a third cola in the ads, so as not to imply that Coke and Pepsi were the only two colas available for Malaysian consumption.

In Mexico, the Pepsi Challenge launched an all-out cola war. The Mexican bottler of Coca-Cola installed tasting booths in front of the Pepsi Challenge booths and allocated twice the normal dollar amount for advertising. In addition, Coca-Cola management filed a complaint with the Mexican National Consumer Institute, charging that the Pepsi Challenge constituted unethical advertising.

Source: Dennis Chase, "Pepsi Uses 'Challenge' to Fight Coke Abroad," *Advertising Age*, March 25, 1985, 60–62.

DEBATE AND CONTROVERSY

While the outcome of the cases is clear enough, the debate on the status of advertising is hardly resolved. Many have grave reservations about the rights of advertisers and feel that extending constitutional protection into the marketplace weakens the First Amendment itself.

There is considerable debate especially on the right of corporations to use advertising to promote their points of view on public issues. Many feel that this essentially "signs over" the rights of the people to those with large advertising budgets. However, there are numerous reasons to believe that advertising alone—however large the expenditure—is insufficient to condition public opinion on issues of importance.

STATE AND LOCAL REGULATION

In addition to the federal apparatus described thus far, more than 40 states have laws prohibiting deceptive advertising. In addition, many states have special laws governing the advertising of significant local industries (such as textiles or automobiles). Regulations covering size and placement of signs and other forms of outdoor advertising are also quite common. Just as legal drinking ages fluctuate among states, the laws governing the advertising and promotion of alcoholic beverages also vary greatly. However, enforcement of advertising regulation is often beyond the resources of state and local governments, and few principles apply across all situations. Advertising persons, to play it safe, carefully consider state and local ordinances for communities that the advertising campaign will reach.

SUMMARY

This chapter has discussed the important regulatory forces affecting advertising, both from within the industry and outside it. The various internal regulatory processes resolve day-to-day problems, but the enduring principles of regulation are formulated at the federal level, most often through the activities of the Federal Trade Commission. This agency is subject to changes in the political environment and, at present, is considerably less involved with advertising than it has been in the recent past.

In addition, the 1970s and 1980s have seen the rise of the First Amendment doctrine of commercial speech. While the constitutional protection for advertising is not totally clear, it is becoming evident that these protections are far-reaching.

YOU MAKE THE DECISION

USING ADVERTISING TO EXPRESS CONVICTIONS

During 1986 the W. R. Grace Company developed some corporate advertising designed to express a point of view on the record high federal budget deficit. The commercial shown below is called "Deficit Trials." In it, parents who allowed an economically disastrous future to develop are put on trial by their children.

The importance of the federal budget deficit is a matter of considerable controversy. For this reason, when the television networks were approached about running the commercial, all of them refused to accept it. The commercial was eventually run on about 150 independent stations around the country in August 1986.

1. Were the networks within their rights to reject this commercial?
2. Rights of the networks aside, is it in the best interest of the American public that controversial commercials be shown?
3. Should corporations or other interest groups be able to use advertising to express their point of view without restriction?

Source: Based on information from Debbie Seaman,"Creatives: Trials Had to Be Scary," *ADWEEK*, February 10, 1986, 25. Photos courtesy of W. R. Grace & Co. Debbie Seaman, "Creatives: Trials Had to Be Scary," *ADWEEK*, February 10, 1986, p. 25.

■ ■ ■

QUESTIONS FOR DISCUSSION

1. How is regulation different from other environmental factors affecting the advertiser?

2. What are the two major types of regulation that affect advertising practice?

3. Give an example of the type of restrictions that occur at the advertiser or agency level.

4. Why do trade associations care about advertising practices?

5. Why is it important to be aware of media standards for advertising clearance?

6. What are the incentives to cooperate with the NAD/NARB?

7. How is the Federal Trade Commission affected by the political climate?

8. Consider the remedies available to the FTC in a case of deceptive advertising. Which do you think is most effective? Why?

9. As an advertiser, how would you respond to a corrective advertising order?

10. Do you think constitutional protection of advertising is likely to broaden or narrow in the next few years? Why?

NOTES

1. David Ogilvy, *Confessions of an Advertising Man* (New York: Ballantine, 1963), 46.

2. Eric Zanot, "Unseen but Effective Advertising Regulation: The Clearance Process," *Journal of Advertising*, 14:4, 1985, 48.

3. For a discussion of the consumerist movement and regulatory sentiment of the 1920s, see Otis Pease, *The Responsibilities of American Advertising* (New Haven, Conn.: Yale University Press, 1958), 68–74.

4. Ronald Smithies, National Advertising Division, Council of Better Business Bureaus, phone conversations, April 20, 1987.

5. *NAD Case Report*, National Advertising Division, Council of Better Business Bureaus, vol. 13, no. 6, New York, July 15, 1983.

6. Eric Zanot, "A Review of Eight Years of NARB Casework: Guidelines and Parameters of Deceptive Advertising," *Journal of Advertising*, 9:4, 1980, 20–26.

7. For a discussion of this case, see William Bohan and Thomas Kinnear, "Advertising Regulation via Bargaining," in *Current Issues and Research in Advertising*, James H. Leigh and Claude R. Martin, Jr., eds. (Ann Arbor, Mich.: Division of Business Research, Michigan Business School, University of Michigan, 1978), 63–80.

8. Steven Colford, "FTC's Oliver Vows No Nitpicking," *Advertising Age*, October 6, 1986, 24.

9. Robert Pitofsky, "Beyond Nader: Consumer Protection and the Regulation of Advertising," *Harvard Law Review*, 90:4, February 1977, 661–701.

10. Harold L. Nelson and Dwight L. Teeter, Jr., *Law of Mass Communications*, 5th ed. (Mineola, N.Y.: The Foundation Press, 1986), 681.

SUGGESTED READINGS

Bauer, Raymond, and Stephen Greyser. *Advertising in America: The Consumer View.* Boston: Harvard Graduate School of Business, 1968.

Clarkson, Kenneth, and Timothy Muris. *The Federal Trade Commission since 1970: Economic Regulation and Bureaucratic Behavior.* New York: Cambridge University Press, 1981.

Pease, Otis. *The Responsibilities of American Advertising*. New Haven, Conn.: Yale University Press, 1958.

Pertschuk, Michael. *Revolt against Regulation: The Rise and Pause of the Consumer Movement*. Berkeley: University of California Press, 1982.

Preston, Ivan. *The Great American Blow-Up: Puffery in Advertising and Selling*. Madison: University of Wisconsin Press, 1975.

Rohrer, Daniel. *Mass Media, Freedom of Speech, and Advertising*. Dubuque, Iowa: Kendall/Hunt Publishing Co., 1979.

Zanot, Eric. *The National Advertising Review Board 1971-1976*. Journalism Monographs, no. 59. Lexington, Ky.: Association for Education in Journalism, 1979.

THE RELATIONSHIP BETWEEN ADVERTISING AND MARKETING

Key Terms

marketing concept
marketing plan
product life cycle (PLC)
manufacturer's brand
distributor's brand
family brand
individual brand
brand extension
brand rejuvenation
intensive distribution
selective distribution
exclusive distribution
pull communication strategy
push communication strategy
push/pull communication strategy
promotion
personal selling
public relations
sales promotion
corporate advertising

Learning Objectives

To describe the suggested framework for making advertising decisions

To discuss the importance of the marketing concept

To analyze the influence of the marketing plan on advertising decisions

To link the relationship of advertising to other elements of the promotion mix

In the advertisement:

Surely, she is not telling him about our jeans.

It's also likely she's not saying that Levi's 501 jeans are made of a special denim that shrinks in the wash to fit only you. Your waist, your hips, you.

In fact, she's probably forgotten that while button-fly 501 jeans used to be made just for men, they're now also cut especially for a woman's figure. For a fit so personal, it's like having them custom tailored.

But she *is* wearing 501 jeans. And it *does* look like she's about to have a very special day.

And that's good enough for us.

In 1984, over 100 million pairs of Levi's jeans were sold. This simple product has remained essentially the same for well over 150 years, and in 1971 it won a Coty Award as America's outstanding contribution to international fashion.

The product was developed by accident. In 1850, merchant Levi Strauss found that his inventory of tent canvas was gathering dust until a miner mentioned that there were no pants strong enough to withstand the rigors of mining. Strauss immediately took his tent canvas to a tailor and told him to make a pair of pants from the sturdy material. Soon, other customers were looking for the new extra-tough workpants, first made of canvas and then of heavy denim. The pants that would become known as "the pants that won the West."

Through the years, the company made relatively few changes in the product; yet, it continued to prosper and grow. Canvas was quickly replaced by a heavy denim. Preshrunk denim was introduced in 1953. Then in 1954, Levi Strauss introduced light denim casual pants. In 1960 Sta-Prest permanent-press jeans were introduced by the company. In 1968, the company brought out Levi's for Gals.

By 1984, Levi's products were distributed worldwide and its flagship product, "Levi's 501 jeans," were sold in 85 percent of the top eastern U.S. stores, despite increased competition from both foreign and domestic manufacturers. The company's advertising budget in the mid-1980s was $150 million.

Sources: "Levi's Jeans: The Cowboy's Tailor," in David Powers Cleary, *Great American Brands* (New York: Fairchild Publications, 1981), 211–216; and Miriam Rozen, "The 501 Blues," *Madison Avenue*, November 1984, 22–26. Photo courtesy of Levi Strauss & Co.

INTRODUCTION

Levi's jeans is one of the foremost marketing success stories in American business history. The story is briefly summarized here because it demonstrates several important points about marketing and advertising. Levi Strauss's initial success was based on the ability of his product to fulfill a consumer need. In 1850, a significant portion of the population needed durable pants. Strauss created a product that satisfied that need better than any other available product. As time passed, the success of Levi Strauss Company was determined by many more variables. Some of those variables were controlled by the company—its ability to redefine its markets; to expand from local, regional, national, and eventually to international distribution; and to improve and expand its product lines. But outside forces also affected the company's success—the popularity of the American cowboy; increases in leisure time; population growth; and a social trend towards casual dress.

Certainly, advertising contributed to Levi Strauss Company's success. However, advertising comprises only one part of the company's marketing effort, and the development and success of the advertising has depended on broader marketing plans.

A FRAMEWORK FOR MAKING ADVERTISING DECISIONS

The fundamental task facing the advertising manager is making decisions about a number of advertising issues. The focus of this text is to help you understand what those decisions are and to suggest a process by which the decisions can be made. Well-managed companies don't make advertising decisions in a vacuum. They understand that success depends on their ability to identify a marketplace need and then to blend production, financial, and marketing resources to achieve company goals. As shown in Figure 7.1, advertising decisions are affected by a number of other, higher-level areas of the company. The keys to effective advertising decision making areas follows:

1. To understand how advertising is related to marketing
2. To make advertising decisions within a planning framework

The purpose of this chapter is to help you understand what decisions are made by the advertising manager; why those decisions are important; and how to approach the decision-making task.

MAKING ADVERTISING DECISIONS

Every company has its own way of making advertising decisions. As you might expect, decision making is both an art and a science. No doubt you've known people who always seem to make the right decisions; yet, they don't seem to have a system for making decisions. They seem to know intuitively what will work and what won't. Then there are those

FIGURE 7.1

Advertising's Place within a Company

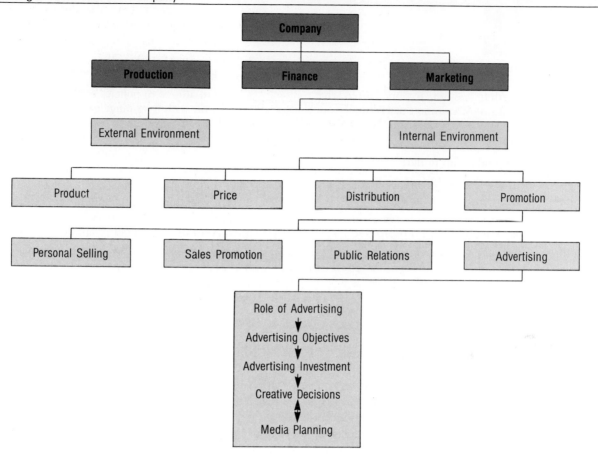

who make decisions through elaborate calculations and projections of all possible outcomes. They too can be successful. The framework presented in Figure 5.1 is based on the most current concepts and theories in marketing as well as on experiences in the advertising business. It is recommended for several reasons.

First, it views *advertising within a marketing context*. As explained in this chapter, advertising is a part of marketing; therefore, advertising decisions are directly affected by the marketing direction of the company.

Second, the framework presents *an integrative view of advertising*. It explains not only advertising's relationship to company and marketing goals, but also the interdependency of the various advertising decisions.

Finally, the framework reflects *how advertising decisions are actually made in the marketplace*. Not all advertisers follow this framework; however, many do.

In this chapter we discuss how the marketing plan is created and the relationship of marketing and promotion plans to advertising decisions.

A CLOSER LOOK

THIRTEEN MARKETING MISCUES

Market researcher Arthur Nielsen, Jr., once listed what he thought were the 13 most common marketing errors. Nielsen created this list over 25 years ago. Note how relevant they still are today.

1. Failure to keep product up to date.

2. Failure to estimate the market potential accurately.

3. Failure to gauge the trend of the market.

4. Failure to appreciate regional differences in marketing potential and in trend of market.

5. Failure to appreciate seasonal differences in your buyers' demand.

6. Failure to establish the advertising budget by the job to be done.

7. Failure to adhere to policies established in connection with long-range goals.

8. Failure to test-market new ideas.

9. Failure to differentiate between short-term tactics and long-range strategy.

10. Failure to admit defeat.

11. Failure to try new ideas while a brand is climbing.

12. Failure to integrate all phases of the marketing operation into the overall program.

13. Failure to appraise objectively your competitors' brands.

Source: "How to Reduce the Cost of 'Point-of-View' Errors," *The Nielsen Researcher*, November 1957, 2–6.

THE MARKETING CONCEPT

Recall Levi Strauss's first step toward success: responding to a consumer need. Strauss was neither the first, nor the last, person to learn that marketing success is largely determined by how well the company applies the **marketing concept**—a company orientation toward identifying and responding to the wants and needs of target markets. Marketing and advertising trade journals and textbooks are filled with examples of companies that have been either extremely successful (Levi Strauss jeans, Gerald Lambert's Listerine, Ray Kroc's McDonald's hamburgers) or unsuccessful (Ford's Edsel, DuPont's Corfam, etc.). Virtually every major product failure contains at least one example of the marketer's lack of adherence to the elements of the marketing concept. Those elements are as follows.

Orientation toward the Consumer Marketing planning should begin with understanding the wants and needs of prospects and then producing products or services that fulfill those wants and needs. In a marketplace crowded with physically similar products, a company is not likely to find success without tailoring its offerings to the desires of prospective buyers. In Figure 7.2, note how Saran Wrap* attempts to differentiate itself by using a direct comparison.

Commitment to Research Unfortunately, making and offering what buyers want does not automatically assure success. We consumers change our minds about products frequently. Our needs also change over time. The key to understanding the changing wants and needs of consumers is establishing a program of continuous research. The advertisement in Fig-

*Trademark of The Dow Chemical Company.

FIGURE 7.2

Using the Direct Comparison to Differentiate a Product from the Competition

Source: Courtesy of The Dow Chemical Company.

ure 7.3 demonstrates the positioning of a product within the context of changing needs of consumers.

A Profit (or Goal) Orientation What consumers want may not be profitable to produce. Many people would like to purchase an IBM personal computer for $500; however, it's unlikely that IBM could sell its computer for $500 and still make a profit. A company must be able to provide the right product at a price that consumers are willing and able to pay *and* still be able to make a reasonable profit.

Organizations operating in the nonprofit sector also seek to fulfill consumer needs within the context of expected return. The return for nonprofit organizations may be election (political candidates), increased usage (libraries, museums, and health care facilities), or ideas (religions and causes). Figure 7.4 shows how two nonprofit organizations use advertising to promote ideas—equal opportunity for the handicapped and planned parenthood.

Integration of Company Efforts Companies that embrace the marketing concept understand that success can be achieved only when every resource in the company is dedicated to the same objective. Successful companies are able to mount an integrated effort among all departments and units toward the satisfaction of buyers' needs.

FIGURE 7.3

How to Position the Product to
Appeal to a Consumer's Changing
Needs

Source: Courtesy of the American Honda Motor Co., Inc.

ADVERTISING AND THE MARKETING CONCEPT

In recent years, there has been much discussion about the marketing concept and its applicability to all companies.[1] The elements of the concept describe an ideal approach to business. We've all heard about enormously successful companies that don't seem to have the slightest interest in the marketing concept. For example, many companies don't do much about determining buyer wants and needs. Research is costly and time-consum-

A CLOSER LOOK

PERCEPTUAL MAPPING

Sometimes what we might want in a product may not be profitable (or even possible) for manufacturers to produce. Consider the following "perceptual map" of an individual's ideal car. While most consumers might like a low-priced car that is high in comfort/luxury, fuel efficiency, and engine performance, it is unlikely that auto manufacturers would be able to make such a car and still realize a profit. Therefore, consumers are forced to make trade-off decisions.

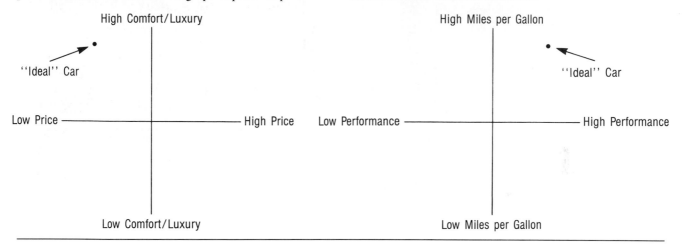

ing; therefore, it is often not done or is done poorly. Some of our own frustrations as shoppers—particularly in product delivery and/or repair service—tell us that some companies have very little integration of effort. The one element of the marketing concept that is universally adopted is *interest in profit*. Yet, an alarming number of businesses fail. For example, from 1978 to 1983, business failures increased by nearly 40 percent.[2]

Despite difficulties in using the marketing concept, many companies have adopted it, and when they do, it has important implications for advertising decision making. Companies that operate within the marketing concept view advertising in the following way.

ELEMENT OF THE MARKETING CONCEPT	IMPLICATIONS FOR ADVERTISING
Consumer orientation	Advertising is used to interpret the company's brand in terms of the wants and needs of buyers. Decisions about copy and art are largely dictated by consumer interests.
Commitment to research	Advertising decisions are made on the basis of information gathered from research among the target audience. Questions about what to say, how to say it, when to say it, and where to say it are largely answered by research.
Profit (goal) orientation	Advertising is used because it is the most effective and efficient way to communicate with the target audience. Levels of advertising investment are related to profit goals.
Integration of company effort	Advertising is coordinated with every other component of the marketing mix, including product, price, distribution, and the other elements of the promotion mix.

FIGURE 7.4

Advertising Messages with a Goal Orientation

Promoting Equal Opportunity for the Handicapped

An Appeal for Planned Parenthood

Ray Charles has a disability. Yet his abilities have enriched us all.

"35 million disabled Americans want the same things you want out of life."

We want to use our abilities to the fullest. We want to participate. That means being able to get in and out of places you want to go if you use a wheelchair; having signs in braille; getting extra help to do the job you really want.

Because this is the Decade of Disabled Persons, the National Organization on Disability urges us all to lend a hand right in our own community.

Let's put our abilities together so all Americans gain.

To find out how you can get involved, call this telephone number now:

1-800-248-ABLE

 Ad Council

NATIONAL ORGANIZATION ON
DISABILITY

"Do I look like a mother to you?"

She does if you look at the statistics.

The United States is the only industrialized nation where the teenage pregnancy rate is going up. Forty percent of all girls who are now fourteen will get pregnant before they're twenty. One million each year.

The social consequences are enormous. Because most teenage mothers are single mothers, trapped in a cycle of poverty that costs billions extra each year. In malnutrition. Disease. Unemployment. Child abuse.

But the tragic effects of motherhood on each individual teenager can't be measured in dollars and cents. And it isn't reflected in the statistics. She's robbed of her childhood and her hope.

While we must do everything we can to help *prevent* unwanted pregnancy, we must also preserve the option of safe, legal abortion.

A teenage girl shouldn't be forced to become a mother if she's not ready.

But there's an increasingly vocal and violent minority that disagrees. They want to outlaw abortions for all women, regardless of circumstances. Even if her life or health is endangered by a pregnancy. Even if she is a victim of rape or incest. And even if she is too young to be a mother.

They're pressuring lawmakers to make abortions illegal. And that's not all. They also oppose birth control and sex education—ways of *preventing* abortion. They've already tried to slash federal funding for these and other family planning programs. And to get their way, they've resorted to threats, physical intimidation and violence.

Speak out now. Or they just might succeed. Use the coupon.

The decision is yours.

This ad was paid for with private contributions. © Copyright 1985

☐ I've written my representatives in Congress to tell them I support: government programs that reduce the need for abortion by preventing unwanted pregnancy; and keeping safe and legal abortion a choice for all women.

☐ Here's my tax-deductible contribution in support of all Planned Parenthood activities and programs: ☐ $25 ☐ $35 ☐ $50 ☐ $75 ☐ $150 ☐ $500 ☐ or: $_____

NAME _____ MJ 10

STREET/CITY/ZIP _____

Planned Parenthood®
Federation of America, Inc.

810 Seventh Avenue
New York, New York 10019

Source: Photo on left courtesy of The Advertising Council; photo on right reprinted by permission of the Planned Parenthood Federation of America, Inc.

THE MARKETING PLAN

A company's marketing activities are usually guided by a written document known as the **marketing plan,** which analyzes, summarizes, and directs the actions of the marketing effort. The marketing plan covers all of the areas of marketing and represents hundreds of hours of thoughtful analysis and recommendations. The importance of the marketing plan is evidenced by the popularity of management seminars on how to create marketing plans and the growing number of books on the subject. Despite the abundance of such material, there is no single, right way to write a plan. There are, however, some common elements:

1.   Situation analysis

2.   Identification of problems and opportunities

3. Marketing objectives
4. Marketing strategy
   — Product decisions
   — Price decisions
   — Distribution decisions
   — Promotion decisions

Beyond content, effective marketing plans must also possess two other characteristics. First, the plan must go beyond a presentation of facts. The real skill is in *understanding the significance of information and in drawing appropriate conclusions.* Second, the plan must be written with enough detail to *help guide the activities of the managers who will be responsible for executing the plan.*

ANALYZING THE SITUATION

This first section of a marketing plan consists of fact and information gathering, review, and analysis of all environments surrounding the company. Sound marketing and advertising decisions cannot be made until the company knows and understands all the forces that are likely to affect decisions. The following environments are the most relevant for analysis:

1. Social/cultural/legal
   — Identification of trends
   — Specification of regulations
2. Competition
   — Who is the competition?
   — What are their strengths and weaknesses?
   — What market share do they hold?
   — How do they distribute their products?
   — What are their pricing policies?
   — What are their promotion strategies?
   — What are the advantages and disadvantages of their product offerings?
3. Market
   — What is the size of the market in annual sales dollars? Units sold? Number of heavy, moderate, and light users?
   — What are the patterns of geographic concentration?
   — What have the industry sales trends been?
   — What segment of the market is showing fastest growth?
   — What is the forecast for the industry?
   — What product type within the category has dominated the market?

IDENTIFYING PROBLEMS AND OPPORTUNITIES

The conclusions that are drawn from the situation analysis form the "Problems and Opportunities" section of the marketing plan. Facts are useful but only when they help a company understand a specific situation and indicate a course of action. A company may conclude that a market opportunity exists through identification of a dissatisfied segment. A thorough analysis of the situation may also point out the necessity to spend heavily on advertising to reach the newly identified segment.

Identifying problems and opportunities requires a great deal of skill, sensitivity, and objectivity. Too often, companies are tempted to see only opportunity without realizing the problems they will face in the marketplace.

SETTING MARKETING OBJECTIVES

This is often the shortest section of a marketing plan because marketing objectives are precisely written statements of exactly what the company wants to accomplish. As shown in Figure 7.5, marketing objectives flow directly out of the problems and opportunities, and they are usually stated in terms of sales or market share accomplishments. Ideally, marketing objectives are specific and measurable, and focus on a specific marketing element. Some examples follow.

- *Sales as an Objective:*
    The objective for our brand in the next fiscal year is to increase sales by 12 percent among the primary target market.

- *Market Share as an Objective:*
    The objective for our brand in the next fiscal year is to increase market share by 8 percent among the primary target market.

- *Product as an Objective:*
    The objective for our product in the next fiscal year is to introduce three new sizes into the product line.

- *Distribution as an Objective:*
    The objective for our brand in the next fiscal year is to expand the number of retailers stocking the brand to 500.

- *Price as an Objective:*
    The objective for our brand in the next fiscal year is to become the price leader in the product category.

- *Promotion as an Objective:*
    The objective for our brand in the next fiscal year is to spend 20 percent more on advertising than our major competitor.

CREATING MARKETING STRATEGY

This section represents the overall plan for accomplishing the objectives, and it covers each of the basic elements of marketing (product, price, distribution, and promotion). The strategy section of a marketing plan indicates the relative importance of each marketing element and guides tactical decisions that will follow. The plan usually includes one or more statements of marketing strategy. Note that tactical decisions are not made in strategy statements; however, they provide a considerable amount of guidance. Following are some hypothetical strategy statements:

- *Product Strategy:*
    During the next fiscal year our strategy is to introduce three new product sizes that will attract the business person — specifically,

FIGURE 7.5

An Outline of the Marketing Plan

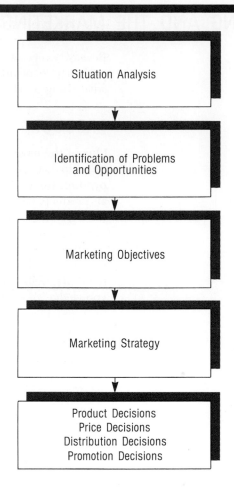

the working woman (25- to 34-year-old segment) and the business traveler (frequent flyers).

- *Pricing Strategy:*
  During the next fiscal year our strategy is to maintain a wholesale price higher than all of our major competitors and to provide a 20 percent discount to distributors.

- *Distribution Strategy:*
  During the next fiscal year our strategy is to make our product the most widely distributed brand in the product category.

- *Promotion Strategy:*
  During the next fiscal year our strategy is to allocate 60 percent of our promotion resources to advertising; 25 percent to sales promotion; 10 percent to personal selling; and 5 percent to public relations.

ADVERTISING AND THE MARKETING PLAN

Because every element of the marketing plan affects advertising, an important part of making sound advertising decisions is to understand how advertising is related to the basic elements of marketing strategy.

PRODUCT

One of the most useful concepts for understanding products and the relationship between products and the dynamics of the marketplace is the **product life cycle (PLC).** The product life cycle is based on the idea that all products (as well as individual brands within a product category) pass through stages of development in their lives, and that the stages have important implications for marketing and advertising strategy.

There are four major stages of the PLC: introduction, growth, maturity, and decline. In the introductory stage, products are just beginning their life. Sales will be very low and consumers will have little or no knowledge about the new brand. The growth stage of the PLC is marked by rapid increases in sales as well as the number of competing brands. Sales are highest during the maturity stage; by this time, consumers usually have established brand preferences. In the decline stage, the product experiences diminished sales as large segments of the market no longer want it. While it is possible for some products to become recycled, the decline stage is the "burial ground" for most brands as they are replaced by new brands that offer the promise of better fulfillment of the wants and needs of the marketplace.

Fundamentally, advertising's task is to interpret the want-satisfying qualities of products in terms that are consistent with the wants and needs of potential buyers. Most technical products need to be explained in detail. Beer, soft drinks, and cigarettes require little, if any, specific product information. Products in the early stage of their life cycle need to be explained while mature products require reminder-type advertising. Some products have been explained so well and have satisfied consumer wants so well that their manufacturers have been able to enjoy decades of profits. Here's a selected list of products that have stood the test of time.[3]

BRAND	YEAR OF INTRODUCTION
Hires Root Beer	1876
Heinz ketchup	1876
Ivory soap	1879
Wrigley's gum	1892
Campbell's soup	1897–1898
Kellogg's Corn Flakes	1898
Hershey bars	1900
Kleenex tissue	1924
Wheaties	1924

Branding Manufacturers make strategy decisions about branding and those decisions affect advertising. Does the company want to own its own

 A **LOSER LOOK**

BRANDING STRATEGY

Selection of branding strategy implies other marketing obligations. For example, here are several different types of brands and the accompanying marketing obligations of the owner of the brand. Note that brand types overlap—that is, family brands or individual brands can be owned by a manufacturer or a distributor.

TYPE OF BRAND	EXAMPLES	MARKETER'S OBLIGATIONS
Manufacturer's brand	Chevrolet	Stimulation of brand demand at the consumer level; large national advertising investment; creation and maintenance of distribution and service facilities; education of distribution channels; sales promotion directed to dealerships
Distributor's brand	Cragmont soft drinks (available only at Safeway stores)	Stimulation of demand at the consumer level; packaging and store display; minimal advertising
Family brand	Heinz, Campbell	Development of complementary products of comparable quality, price, and distribution
Individual brand	P & G's detergents (Tide, Oxydol, and others)	Creation of distinct brand personality with an appeal to a specific target market

brand (called a **manufacturer's brand** or a national brand) or does it choose to manufacture for a distributor (known as a **distributor's brand,** a private brand, or a dealer brand)? Does the company use a **family brand** (Heinz, for example), or does it use the strategy of **individual brands,** as Procter & Gamble does with its various detergent names (Tide, Oxydol, Dreft, etc.)? In each of these alternatives, advertising will play a different role—in some cases having the primary responsibility for stimulating buyer interest (manufacturer's brands) and in other cases, playing a less important role (distributor's brands). When companies decide to manufacture for distributor-branded products, they are largely relieved of the responsibilities of stimulating demand at the level of the ultimate buyer. Therefore, advertising is used: (1) to maintain interest at the distributor level (through trade advertising) and (2) to assist distributors through cooperative advertising programs.

Occasionally, a company markets both manufacturer and distributor brands. This usually happens when a company has excess production capacity and a desire to expand total market penetration. The brands of Sears Roebuck and Co. represent another alternative branding strategy. Sears brands are both manufacturer and distributor brands because many of the products that carry the Sears brand are manufactured by the Sears company and, of course, are also distributed through their retail stores and catalogs.

In the packaged goods field, building a new brand name can take up to three years and can cost as much as $500 million. Because this process is so risky, time-consuming, and costly, marketers have looked to alternatives. One alternative is **brand extension**—introducing a new product through association with an existing and successful brand name (Dole Peeled Fresh Pineapple, for example). Another strategy is **brand rejuvenation**—the process of major revitalizing of a product to strengthen consumer acceptance. This has been done with Arm & Hammer's baking soda, General Mills' Betty Crocker symbol, and Warner-Lambert's Listerine.[4]

Packaging At one time, the only reasons for packaging were to contain, protect, and identify the product. Today, packaging forms an important part of marketing strategy because good packaging allows the marketer to help build the personality, or image of a brand. Package design, once a rather small industry, now numbers more than 150 firms generating over $1 billion in annual revenue. The importance of packaging is emphasized by designer Saul Bass's statement: "Packaging is the product."[5]

Advertising has the task of calling attention to packaging features (see Figure 7.6) and of helping communicate the brand's personality. The Grey Flannel advertisement in Figure 7.7 illustrates how advertising and packaging work together to help create a brand personality.

PRICING

The style, content, and intensity of advertising must be consistent with the message that a brand's price communicates. High-priced brands must have advertising that reflects the prestige by the price. The Chateau Suisse advertisement in Figure 7.8 exemplifies the use of a prestigious environment to reflect the high price of the brand. The Johnnie Walker advertisement in Figure 7.9 is equally effective because the style of advertising and layout is consistent with the price strategy of the advertiser.

DISTRIBUTION

Advertising's role is often determined by the distribution strategy adopted by the company. The marketing plan will specify whether the company is going to use an intensive, selective, or exclusive distribution system, a decision that affects the style and role of advertising (see Figure 7.10).

In **intensive distribution,** products are available in as many outlets as possible. This is the most common distribution system for consumer convenience goods such as cigarettes, candy, and soft drinks. Such products are widely used and bought frequently; therefore, marketing success is strongly affected by the availability of the product at the retail level. The task of advertising is to help create brand awareness and to work with point-of-purchase promotions to stimulate purchase.

In **selective distribution,** products are available in less than the maximum number of outlets possible. Selective distribution is primarily used for consumer shopping goods such as stereos, some clothing items, and many appliances. Marketers know that consumers purchase such products less frequently and they need to compare product features and price. Here, the task of advertising is to create or reinforce brand preference and to inform buyers of retail locations. Cooperative advertising (between re-

FIGURE 7.6

The Importance of Packaging

Source: © Midland-Ross Corporation 1984. Reprinted with permission.

FIGURE 7.7

Special Packaging Commands
Attention and Helps Create a Brand
"Personality"

Source: Courtesy of Jacqueline Cochran, Inc.

tailer and manufacturer) is important to the success of marketers using a selective distribution system.

In **exclusive distribution,** products are available in the minimum number of outlets possible. Exclusive distribution is the opposite of intensive distribution. The strategy is to add to the prestige image of a product through scarce availability. Exclusive distribution is used by such products as expensive automobiles (Rolls-Royce), jewelry, and some clothing and cosmetics products. Because of the specialized nature and high price of such products, there is no need for a marketer to incur the costs of wider distribution systems. The task of advertising is to contribute to the

FIGURE 7.8

High-Priced Products Use a
Prestigious Environment in the
Message

Source: Courtesy of Barton's, Inc.

prestige image of the product through communicating high price and exclusivity.

PROMOTION

Of course, advertising is not the only communication tool available to
marketers. Personal selling, public relations, and sales promotion also
play an important role for most marketers. Most business-to-business marketers rely primarily on personal selling to accomplish the company's communication goals. Also, some companies decide to emphasize door-to-
door selling or telephone selling as the primary forms of communication.
In these situations, advertising is used to assist other selling efforts. Soloflex, for example, uses print advertising to assist its telephone and mail
marketing efforts (see Figure 7.11). In other situations, the majority of the
communication task is assigned to advertising and the other promotion
tools play a supporting role.

The marketing plan will also specify whether the company will use a
push strategy or pull strategy. As shown in Figure 7.12, companies

FIGURE 7.9

Using Prestige to Sell a High-Priced
Product

Source: Courtesy of Somerset Importers, LTD.

choose where to direct their communication efforts and this decision affects the task advertising is expected to fulfill.

In the **pull communication strategy,** advertising (often with the help
of sales promotion activities) is the main promotion tool. The goal is to
stimulate demand at the end buyer level. Buyer demand will then force
retailers to stock the brand, and they in turn will seek the brand from
wholesalers.

In the **push communication strategy,** the manufacturer uses the most
appropriate form of promotion (usually personal selling) to encourage sales
to the closest member of the distribution channel, the wholesaler. This
strategy then calls for the wholesaler to promote the brand to the retailer
and the retailer to promote to the end buyer. Many industrial products
are promoted through the push strategy. Advertising's role is minimal in
the "pure" push strategy.

Most marketers use the combination **push/pull communication strategy.** The manufacturer utilizes all forms of promotion with national advertising, sales promotion, and public relations aimed directly at the end
buyer and all four of the promotion tools used at the retailer and wholesaler levels. Advertising's role depends on the communication strategy

FIGURE 7.10

Three Distribution Strategies

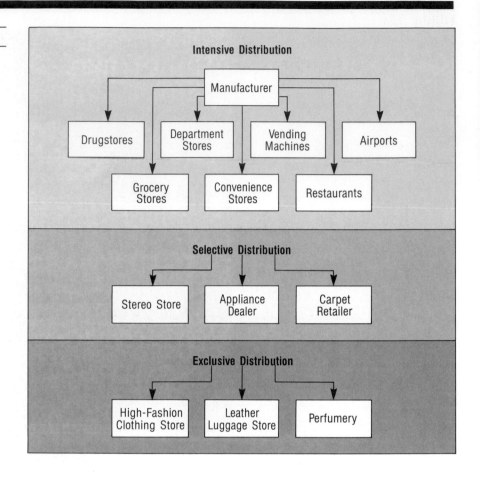

used by the marketer, the number of channel members, and the accepted practice in the particular industry.

ADVERTISING AND THE PROMOTION MIX

Promotion can be defined as that part of the marketing mix whose function is to inform and persuade.[6] The primary purpose of promotion is to help fulfill the marketing objective through communicating relevant information to the target markets. Marketers use the various tools of promotion in a mix most appropriate to the product or service being marketed. There is no single "best" promotion mix. Some companies—even those in the same industry—use widely different combinations of the four promotion tools—personal selling, public relations, sales promotion, and advertising.

Personal selling consists of oral presentations to prospective buyers for the purpose of making sales. It is usually the major promotion method for ideas, goods, or services that involve complex messages to small markets.

FIGURE 7.11

The Use of Print Advertising to
Assist in the Marketing Effort

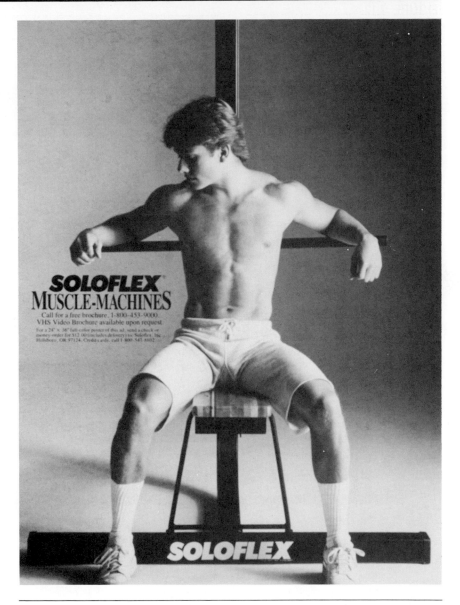

Source: Courtesy of Soloflex, Inc. Advertising Department.

Public relations includes a number of communication activities intended to promote a positive image for an individual or a firm.

Sales promotion encompasses all those promotion activities that enhance and support advertising, public relations, and personal selling. Sales promotion also helps complete and/or coordinate the entire promotion mix, and makes the marketing mix more effective.

Every company operates with different levels of resources as well as its own unique set of marketing opportunities and problems. Consider the alternatives facing a marketer attempting to compete with Levi Strauss,

FIGURE 7.12
Three Marketing Communication Strategies

Pushing Strategy

Pulling Strategy

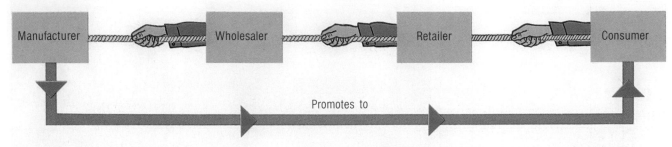

Push/Pull Strategy

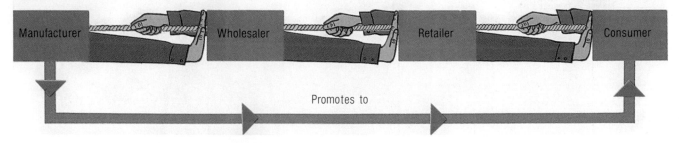

and assume the Levi Strauss decided to use the four promotion tools in the following way.

PROMOTION TOOL	PERCENTAGE OF PROMOTION BUDGET
Personal selling	25%
Public relations	15
Sales promotion	30
Advertising	30

What promotion mix should the new marketer use? Should it adopt the successful promotion mix used by Levi Strauss? The new marketer probably would not be able to use the same mix of promotion because it faces a different marketing environment. While Levi Strauss is enjoying large market share, wide distribution, and high consumer preference, a new company will have to communicate other values to the target markets.

PROMOTION SPENDING

In recent years, promotion has assumed a greater role in helping companies market their products. As the charts show, spending for promotion accounts for 65 percent of most communications budgets, which in the mid-1980s accounted for a $99.4 billion investment.

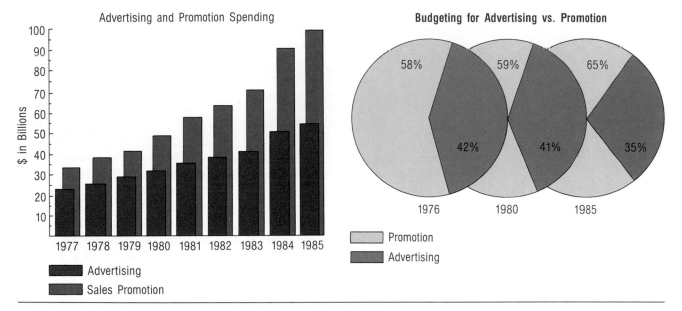

Source: Russel D. Bowman, "The Seventh Annual Advertising & Sales Promotion Report," *Marketing Communications*, vol. II, no. 7, August 1986, 7–16.

Likely alternative promotion strategies would include outspending Levi Strauss, developing a particularly effective advertising campaign, or emphasizing sales promotion activities.

INDUSTRY DIFFERENCES IN PROMOTION MIXES

Promotion mixes vary among companies and they vary even more among industries where differences in marketing environments are more pronounced. Exhibit 7.1 notes the significant differences in promotion mixes among different product categories in the business-to-business sector.

Several factors are important in determining the use of promotion tools.

Communication Task to Be Accomplished The ultimate goal of promotion is to help fulfill the company's marketing objective through communications with the target audience. For some companies, the communication task is to help alter buyer attitudes; to position (or reposition) the brand; or to help shape the brand's personality and image. Such communication tasks usually require continuous repetition of a consistent mes-

EXHIBIT 7.1

Promotional Mixes within
Business-to-Business Markets

PROMOTION TOOL	PRODUCT CATEGORY				
	MAJOR CAPITAL	MINOR CAPITAL	MATERIALS	COMPONENTS	SUPPLIES
Trade advertising	9.6%*	9.3%	8.3%	6.4%	10.1%
Technical literature	19.8	21.2	22.4	15.3	19.1
Direct mail	5.2	5.8	2.6	3.7	6.3
Sales promotion	5.4	7.6	8.6	11.8	11.6
Trade shows	12.5	7.8	4.9	6.2	4.4
Personal selling	47.5	48.3	53.2	56.6	48.5

*Percentages indicate proportion of respondents selecting the promotion tool as "most important." Sample was taken among business-to-business marketers from the five different product categories.
Source: Adapted from unpublished research conducted by Donald W. Jackson, Jr., Janet E. Keith, and Richard K. Burdick. For more information, contact Professor Donald W. Jackson, Jr., Department of Marketing, Arizona State University, Tempe, Arizona.

sage. Advertising is an ideal tool for this task and is one of the main reasons that advertising is so widely used in the promotion mixes for soft drinks, beer, cosmetics, and other personal care items.

Because so many companies realize the importance of maintaining a favorable attitude among customers and prospects, they currently spend unprecedented amounts of money on **corporate** (also known as image or institutional) **advertising**—advertising designed to communicate a positive image, or attitude, about the company or to stimulate a behavior other than product sales. While spending for such advertising declined slightly in the early 1980s, it increased by 80 percent, to $726 million, by the mid-1980s. Often, corporate advertising messages have little or no direct relationship to a firm's products or services. Sometimes it's necessary to inform the marketplace of important corporate name changes. For example, International Harvester used corporate advertising to announce that it had changed its name to Navistar. Corporate advertising is often used to promote a firm as a rewarding place to work, such as recent commercials did for Dow Chemical. Finally, many business firms use such messages to take a stance on a public policy issue. W. R. Grace & Co. has used advertising to attack the idea of a higher capital gains tax, declining productivity, and the federal deficit. United Technologies' corporate advertising provided American audiences with inspirational "sermons" in their "Aim So High You'll Never Be Bored," "The Slim Margin of Success," and "Don't Quit" campaigns.[7]

In the business-to-business sector, promotion helps fulfill marketing objectives by explaining technical product features within the context of buyers' needs. This is usually best accomplished through personal selling, although advertising and publicity are often used as important supplements to the personal selling efforts.

Size and Characteristics of the Target Market   One of the factors that guides the promotion mix is the number of people to be reached. Toothpaste, deodorant, and detergent are purchased by almost everyone, while relatively few buy large metal stamping machines, steel, or corporate jets.

Markets also vary in their use of product information; the promotion manager needs to know where buyers go for information and how they use it. The information in Exhibit 7.2 suggest that sellers do not always use the most effective promotion mix.

The primary reason for differences in promotion mixes is not just management preference. Business-to-business markets differ from consumer markets in several significant ways. As shown below, the differences in every one of the major marketing variables almost dictate a reliance on personal selling for business-to-business marketers, while advertising and sales promotion are the most logical tools for consumer goods marketers.

Major Differences between Consumer and Business Markets

BUSINESS MARKETS	CONSUMER MARKETS
Geographic concentration	Widely dispersed
Identified by Standard Industrial Classification number	Identified by demographic, psychographic, and product usage variables
Trained buyers (purchasing agents)	Buyers often know little about physical attributes of products and services
Buyer is not end user	Buyer is often end user
Many buying influences ("group buy") at one buying location	Many products selected by individual
Demand not very sensitive to changes in price or promotion	Demand comparatively elastic

The Strengths and Weaknesses of Each Promotion Tool   Some promotion tools are better suited to some tasks than others. Promotion managers need to be completely knowledgeable about the advantages and disadvantages of each tool. Equally important, they must be aware of the synergism created by using certain combinations of promotion tools. For example, one of the most important studies ever done in industrial advertising demonstrated that the total cost of selling can be *decreased* by 20 to 40 percent if advertising is used to supplement the personal selling effort.[8]

Personal selling is the most effective promotion tool for most products and services. It provides the following:

- Presents detailed information without a time or length restriction

- Is able to respond immediately to arguments

- Presents the possibility of negotiating (price, for example)

- Is capable of generating immediate feedback to the marketer

Unfortunately, personal selling is also expensive, impractical for reaching the consumer, and slow; therefore, it is not the primary promotion tool for most products. A brief summary of promotion tools and their strengths and weaknesses is presented in Exhibit 7.3.

EFFECT OF THE PROMOTION MIX ON ADVERTISING

The advertising manager must know what role advertising is to play within the total promotion mix because of the need to make decisions about the allocation of resources and the level of advertising activity. Fol-

EXHIBIT 7.2

Promotion Tool Preferences, According to Industrial Buyers and Sellers

PROMOTION TOOL	PERCENT SELECTING PROMOTION TOOL AS "MOST IMPORTANT"	
	BUYER	SELLER
Advertising in trade and industrial magazines	37%	13%
Personal selling	27	72
Trade shows	26	05
Company catalogs	10	06
Direct mail	0	04

Source: "Buyer Information Sources in the Capital Equipment Industry," by Charles H. Patti, *Industrial Marketing Management*, Volume 6, No. 4, 1977.

EXHIBIT 7.3

The Tools of Promotion: A Summary

TOOL	REPRESENTATIVE FORMS	STRENGTHS	WEAKNESSES
Personal selling	Technical sales representatives (sales engineers); missionary salespeople; clerks; door-to-door salespeople.	Most commonly used promotion tool for business-to-business products. Can tailor a message and negotiate with buyers.	Costly—recent estimates place personal sales call cost at over $200.
Sales promotion	Contests, sweepstakes, coupons, point-of-purchase materials, exhibits and trade shows, company literature.	Very important for introducing new products and for stimulating short-term activity. Objective is to complement advertising and personal selling activities. Ideal for inducing brand trial.	Difficult to sustain as buyers lose interest. Overuse can detract from brand image.
Public relations	Publicity (news releases, feature stories, press conferences, etc.); corporate advertising; sponsorships; personal appearances; seminars; company magazines and publications.	Excellent low-cost tool for both short- and long-term communications goals. Favorable publicity often has dramatic effect on internal and external publics.	Lack of control. The media decide what is aired or printed; therefore, marketer does not control content or timing of publicity.
Advertising	Types by media (tv, radio, newspaper, magazine, specialty, outdoor, transit, direct mail); market (consumer, industrial, business, trade, professional); geography (national, regional, local).	Ability to reach large numbers of people quickly and efficiently; ability to reach audiences that are too difficult to reach with other promotion tools; and control of message content and timing in hands of marketer.	Expensive, particularly to reach mass audiences. Effects often hard to measure. Benefits frequently long term.

lowing are three alternative roles for advertising and the implications for each.

Advertising is the primary promotion tool. This is common for products sold via direct response and for some convenience goods. Under this condition, advertising has the primary responsibility for accomplishing most of the communication objectives. Furthermore, the advertising effort guides the content and style of the other three promotion tools. Promotion budgets and their allocation to the promotion tools are affected by many factors; however, the tool that is expected to accomplish the most usually is allocated the greatest proportion of the financial resources.

Advertising shares importance with one or more of the promotion tools. This is common for many consumer durables and shopping goods and for many business-to-business products. Automobiles, stereo and camera equipment, and sporting goods require a balance of advertising, personal selling, sales promotion, and public relations. A balanced promotion mix requires strong coordination of message content and timing of communication efforts. Advertising should be expected to work closely with the other promotion tools toward the fulfillment of the overall communication goal.

Advertising plays a minor role within the promotion mix. This is most common for business-to-business marketers and others who determine that the most effective and efficient way to communicate to the marketplace is through personal selling. In these situations, advertising helps fulfill the promotion goal and contributes to achieving the marketing goal by generating inquiries and by contributing to a favorable company reputation. In turn, this makes the job of the personal selling staff easier.

SUMMARY

Advertising managers are required to make a number of decisions that are important in helping the company achieve its marketing objectives. The use of a planning framework can help reduce the possibility of making decision errors. This framework implies that sound decisions in advertising are based on understanding that (1) advertising is one part of the marketing plan, and (2) the components of a marketing plan must be reflected in decisions about the content, form, and style of advertising. Advertising decisions are influenced by two other factors—the degree to which the company has adopted an orientation toward the buyer (marketing concept) and the company's decisions about the composition of the promotion mix.

YOU MAKE THE DECISION

PLAS-TECH CORPORATION

Plas-Tech Corporation, a manufacturer and marketer of polyethylene film, has been in business for 15 years. Its main customers are in the construction industry. Plas-Tech's product is unbranded and unadvertised because customers buy the product by specification—that is, the customer specifies a particular thickness, size, and color. Four factors figure in Plas-Tech's success: 1) it has the production capability to meet customer demands, 2) it manufactures a quality product, 3) its prices are competitive, and 4) its service department responds quickly to customer needs.

Recently, the company has been considering entering the consumer market by introducing a line of lawn and garbage bags. Plas-Tech has the production expertise to manufacture a high-quality product, but has no experience in marketing a consumer package good.

Last year, Plas-Tech's gross sales totaled $18 million and its pre-tax profit rate stood at 10 percent. Management is attracted to the profit potential of the consumer market; however, the large advertising and promotion expenditures that seem to be required in consumer marketing have raised a concern.

What are Plas-Tech's branding options? What branding and marketing strategies would you recommend?

■ ■ ■

QUESTIONS FOR DISCUSSION

1. Figure 7.1 illustrates advertising's place within the firm. From the point of view of the advertising manager, what are the managerial implications of advertising's place?

2. Describe the influence of marketing objectives on the sequence of advertising decisions made by the advertising manager.

3. Identify three products whose success or failure has been largely

determined by factors in the external environment. Describe the influence of the external environment on the three products.

4. Identify a product or service that has failed and discuss how well the marketer used the marketing concept.

5. How does a "commitment to research" help a company market its products or services successfully?

6. From your personal experience, describe three companies who have a strong orientation toward the consumer.

7. Why do industrial companies rely on personal selling as their primary promotion tool?

8. In recent years, the investment in sales promotion has exceeded the investment in advertising. What factors have brought about this increased emphasis on sales promotion? Do you think it is likely to continue? Explain.

9. Find an example of advertisements for brands that are distributed on an intensive, selective, and exclusive basis. Identify the objective of the advertisements.

10. Describe the main strengths and weaknesses of each of the four promotion tools.

NOTES

1. John B. McKitterick, "What Is the Marketing Management Concept?" in *The Frontiers of Marketing Thought and Action* (Chicago: American Marketing Association, 1957), 71–82; Fred J. Borch, "The Marketing Philosophy as a Way of Business Life," in *The Marketing Concept: Its Meaning to Management*, Marketing Series no. 99 (New York: American Management Association, 1957), 3–5; and Theodore Levitt, "Marketing Myopia," *Harvard Business Review*, July–August 1960, 45–56.

2. David N. Allman, "The 1978–1983 Increase in U.S. Business Failures," *Federal Reserve Bank of Kansas City Economic Review*, July–August 1984, 36.

3. George Fichter, "Birth of a Nation," *Mainliner Magazine*, October 1986, 87–94.

4. Nancy L. Croft, "Marketing," *Nation's Business*, August 1986, 67; and "Trends in New-Product Marketing," *Sales & Marketing Digest*, November 1986, 10.

5. Kathleen Day, "Packaging Emerges as a Key Selling Tool," *Los Angeles Times*, March 17, 1985.

6. Ernest F. Cooke, "Defining Sales Promotion Difficult, Important," *Marketing News*, November 8, 1985, 35–36.

7. Anne B. Fisher, "Spiffing Up the Corporate Image," *Fortune*, July 21, 1986, 68–72.

8. John E. Morrill, "Industrial Advertising Pays Off," *Harvard Business Reveiw*, March/April 1970, 4–14, 159–169.

SUGGESTED READINGS

Berg, Thomas L. *Mismarketing: Case Histories of Marketing Misfires*. New York: Anchor Books, 1970.

Bernstein, David. *Corporate Image and Reality: A Critique of Corporate Communications*. London: Holt, Rinehart and Winston Ltd., 1985.

Bogart, Leo. *Strategy in Advertising*. 2d ed. Chicago: Crain Books, 1984.

Buell, Victor. *Organizing for Marketing/Advertising Success*. New York: Association of National Advertisers, Inc., 1982.

Cooper, R. G. "The Dimensions of Industrial New Product Success and Failure." *Journal of Marketing*, Summer 1979.

Farris, Paul, and Mark S. Albion. "Determinants of the Advertising-to-Sales Ratio." *Journal of Advertising Research*, February 1981.

Gardner, B. B., and S. J. Levy. "The Product and the Brand." *Harvard Business Review*, March/April 1955.

Jocz, Katherine. *Research on Sales Promotion: Collected Papers*. Cambridge, Mass.: Marketing Science Institute, July 1984.

Jones, John Philip. *What's in a Name?: Advertising and the Concept of Brands*. Lexington, Mass.: Lexington Books, 1986.

King, Stephen. *Developing New Brands*. New York: John Wiley and Sons, 1973.

Kotler, Philip. "The Major Tasks of Marketing Management." *Journal of Marketing*, October 1973.

Levitt, Theodore. *Industrial Purchasing Behavior*, Division of Research, Harvard Business School, Boston, Massachusetts, 1965.

Reiss, Craig. "Using Promotion to Get Ahead." *Advertising Age*, October 20, 1986, 80.

Robinson, William A. "12 Basic Promotion Techniques: Their Advantages — and Pitfalls." *Advertising Age*, January 10, 1977.

Rothschild, Michael. "Marketing Communciations in Nonbusiness Situations or Why It's So Hard to Sell Brotherhood Like Soap." *Journal of Marketing*, Spring 1979.

Sawyer, Howard G. *Business-to-Business Advertising*. Chicago: Crain Books, 1978.

Stewart, David C. "What Top Management Should Expect from the Advertising-Marketing Marriage." *New Directions in Marketing*. Chicago: American Marketing Association, 1965.

Sutton, Howard. *Rethinking the Company's Selling and Distribution Channels*. New York: The Conference Board, Inc., 1986.

Wood, Wally. "Costing Out Marketing." *Marketing & Media Decisions*, August 1986, 154–155.

Worcester, R. M. "Corporate Image Research Reviewed." London: Market & Opinion Research International, 1971.

———. "Why Corporate Advertising is the Key to Public Goodwill." *Campaign*, May 16, 1986, 33.

C H A P T E R   8

SELECTING TARGET MARKETS

Key Terms

target market
market segmentation
geographic segmentation
demographic segmentation
PRIZM
psychographic segmentation
VALS™
values and life-style segmentation
benefit segmentation
Standard Industrial Classification (SIC) system

Learning Objectives

To discuss the importance of market segmentation

To outline target market selection in the consumer and business-to-business markets

To analyze how advertising is tailored to market segments

The traditional attitude of American business has always been "the bigger the better." Until recently, that attitude prevailed among members of the banking industry as they measured success by the size of their assets. Today, the philosophy of scarcity, of maximizing returns, of picking opportunities where one can do best, is sweeping through U.S. banking. Banks have decided that their primary goal is not the size of deposits but profitability measured by return on assets. As a consequence, banks are now being forced to examine the profitability of each element of their operations.

Consider the challenges the banking industry has faced in recent years:

• deregulation . . . bringing on higher interest rates

• double-digit inflation, which has affected operating costs, especially in consumer banking where small accounts are personnel intensive

• competitive pressures for improved automation and operating systems, which have required new capital investment

• a market that continues to fragment. Research has shown that someone with a household income of over $20,000 often buys 38 financial products from 20 different vendors.

How will the industry adjust? Industry experts see three alternatives for banks: to become financial super-

markets, least-cost producers, or specialty firms.

Financial supermarkets offer a wide variety of financial services from a single source, often under one roof. Convenience and consumer confidence in a family of products provide the major thrust. Typically, they are marketed as offering all services to all people. Within the next few years, five or six financial supermarkets are predicted to be in operation in the United States. The prototype financial supermarket, Sears, acquired brokerage firm Dean Witter Reynolds, purchased Coldwell Banker realty, and then, with Sears's Allstate Insurance Company, combined brokerage, realty, and insurance in one organization. Citibank and Bank of America are two other firms who have the capital and other resources to become financial supermarkets in the near future.

Least-cost producers often have narrow product/service lines and focus on streamlined, low-cost banking operations and delivery systems. "Stripped-down" services and high automation, such as the extensive use of automatic teller machines, are dominant characteristics. Banks who become part of this segment must be very efficient operators who carefully target products and market segments. The money market fund is an example of a least-cost producer. Beyond high interest rates, money funds offer little service. They have no branches, allow limited withdrawals in large amounts, carry no government insurance against loss, and offer no bank officers for consultation. They are profitable with a gross margin of less than 1 percent, while the average U.S. bank has operating costs of 4 percent alone.

Specialized suppliers limit the scope of products and services and/or the market segment to whom they offer their services (for example, commercial versus consumer accounts). Often specialized suppliers will offer special added-value servicing for target segments. Specialty firms compete on service, not price. The most familiar specialized supplier is Merrill Lynch, with its elite market segment.

Source: Joyce Healy, "Survival Marketing Changes Banking," *Marketing Communications*, October 1984, 11–15.
Photo courtesy of Sears, Roebuck and Co.

INTRODUCTION

Until rather recently, marketing played an extremely limited role in the banking industry. As market observer Joyce Healy observes, "Bank marketers were regarded as frivolous people who made creative television commercials to promote the image of the bank and threw parties to open new branches."[1] Given all of the changes that have taken place in that industry, bankers (as well as most other marketers) have been forced to apply marketing in a more analytical way: to restructure their product/service offerings, to be more selective about whom they market to, and to create advertising messages that will appeal to the wants and needs of their more tightly segmented markets.

One of the first, and most important, steps in creating an advertising campaign is the selection of the **target market,** a group of people who have buying power and a common need that potentially can be satisfied through the purchase of a marketer's brand. Very few products will satisfy everyone; therefore, marketers try to divide the market into segments that might require different marketing approaches, and then select the particular target segments that they can serve best. For example, although nearly all Americans use facial soap, no one brand holds more than 20 percent of the market because there are many different wants and needs among soap buyers.[2] Some consumers are interested in deodorant protection; some, in skin conditioning. Others are interested in scent. To operate profitably, marketers must isolate a consumer need that is shared by a sufficiently large number of people.

It isn't difficult to think of a number of products that attract us and that we'd like to purchase—trips to Europe, vacation homes, sports cars, etc. Ultimately, the reason that we *aren't* part of the target market for these products may be that we don't have the financial resources to buy them. Some individuals may have the financial resources but are not sufficiently interested in the product or perhaps have other priorities for their money.

THE IMPORTANCE OF TARGET MARKET SELECTION

Selecting a target market is an important marketing decision because every facet of marketing activity needs to be precisely tailored toward the satisfaction of the target. To be successful, a company's product, price, distribution, and promotion strategies should focus on a single goal: *to encourage the target market to invest its resources in the company's product or service.* Every marketing activity should attempt to convince the target market that the company's product or service can satisfy the need better than other alternatives.

Because selecting a target market has so many implications for marketing strategy, it is usually done by someone in the marketing (rather than advertising) department. Selecting a target market is one part of a basic marketing strategy: market segmentation. Many years ago, marketing professor Wendell Smith suggested that marketers approach a market by differentiating the product or segmenting the market.[3] **Market segmentation** is a process of identifying the wants and needs of the market for the

A CLOSER LOOK

MOVIE-GOING AMERICA

How often do average Americans go to the movies in a year?

In 1946, we went 29 times. In 1984, however, we went only five times. This is a cause of deep concern to those in the movie business. Despite increases in population, disposable income, and leisure time, Americans go to the movies less frequently. Yet, multi-million-dollar movies continue to be made. What is happening in this market?

Actually, movies admissions are up. Between 1970 and 1984, for example, movie admission in the United States increased as much as 30 percent (from $920 million to $1.2 billion). The major change in this

industry is the target market. Eighty-five percent of movie admissions is accounted for by the 12-to-39 age segment. The movie industry has been able to survive by defining its target market.

The 12-to-39 age segment meets virtually all of the target-market criteria. This segment has a need for entertainment; it is interested in the social dimension of movie-going; it is a growing segment with increased buying power; the segment's age and life-style are meaningful segmentation criteria; and it can be reached through advertising.

A Newspaper Advertising Bureau study reveals that movie attendance drops off rapidly after age 35, though not because of lack of interest in the product. According to the report, older people have less time available for movies; they have a wide choice of leisure activities; and their life-style is relatively sedentary.

Sources: Joe Schwartz, "Americans Go to the Movies," *American Demographics*, September 1986, 60; and "Movie Going in the United States" (New York: Newspaper Advertising Bureau, Inc., 1985).

purpose of allocating marketing resources. Once segments have been defined, target markets can be specified.

In recent years, market segmentation has taken on increased importance because of the difficulty in creating a significantly differentiated product. There is little physical difference among brands in many product categories. Advertising is, of course, another method of differentiation; however, creating unique and relevant brand personalities is difficult and expensive. Among the most heavily advertised brands are those that possess little physical differentiation—for example, beer, liquor, cigarettes, and soft drinks. In Figure 8.1, the Canon advertisement attempts to segment the amateur photographer market through a combination of product, design, copy, and layout. Other marketers are able to rely on physical differentiation of the product in their messages (see Figure 8.2).

CHARACTERISTICS OF TARGET MARKETS

A target market must have the following characteristics:

- An identifiable common need
- An interest in the product/service
- Sufficient buying power
- Sufficient numbers of people

FIGURE 8.1

Finding a "Snappy" Way to Segment the Amateur Photography Market

Source: Courtesy of Canon U.S.A., Inc.

- An identifiable basis for segmentation

- Sufficient exposure to advertising

While some methods of segmenting markets are more widely used than others, marketers have a strong interest in finding new and useful ways. Basically, marketers need to segment the market in such a way as to provide them with a market large enough to support a marketing effort. The latest estimates of the cost to bring a new consumer packaged good to the market are $10 million.[4] To recover such costs and to earn a reasonable profit, the total size of the market segment will have to be very large. This is particularly true if the retail price and profit margins are low.

FIGURE 8.2

Using Physical Differentiation to Segment the Market

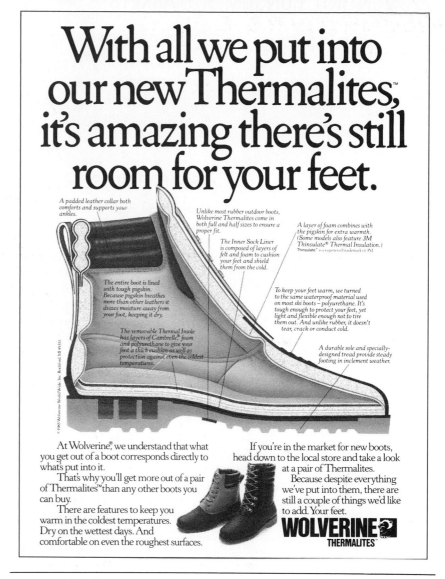

Source: Courtesy of Wolverine World Wide, Inc.

Marketers must also target a segment that is meaningful. Many methods of segmentation are not useful to the marketer because the variables do not provide marketing guidance. Segmentation by sex, for example, is useful for cigarettes and shampoos but not for aspirin or toothpaste.

Finally, marketers must isolate a segment that is reachable. It does little good to identify a segment that is difficult to reach through promotional efforts. For example, recent studies reveal that it is very inefficient to reach teenage males through print media, and that reaching women through the traditional advertising medium of television is no longer working.[5]

SEGMENTING CONSUMER MARKETS

The five most common bases of market segmentation are

1. Geographic
2. Demographic
3. Psychographic
4. Values and life-style
5. Benefit

GEOGRAPHIC SEGMENTATION

Geographic segmentation is the simplest method of segmenting the consumer market, and it involves identifying market segments according to geography. Although the United States has a large population, it is not distributed evenly across the country. Certain regions are more heavily populated than others, and the highest population density occurs in cities and metropolitan areas. Since market potential is often measured in terms of population, it is relevant for marketers to analyze markets by population concentration and growth rates (see Exhibit 8.1). While most businesses are interested in high-growth areas, some marketers find opportunity in smaller population areas or in areas of slower growth.

Another marketing consideration has to do with differences in usage patterns. A marketer of snow blowers, for example, is unlikely to advertise the product line in the South, where snow is a rare sight. Regional differences in tastes and life-styles are an important consideration for marketers.

DEMOGRAPHIC SEGMENTATION

Perhaps the most widely used method of segmentation is **demographic segmentation,** identifying market segments according to a set of quantifiable characteristics (such as age, income, and family size) of prospective purchasers. Age is a particularly relevant variable for many products, including clothing, entertainment, and health and beauty aids. The U.S. population continues to age; that is, the median age of the population is increasing, largely due to the post-World War II "baby boomers" who are now in their mid- to late thirties and early forties. As the median age of the population shifts, some products will find greater potential for success and others will find less potential for success. Particularly in the next ten years, the over-50 age groups will experience large increases, presenting an attractive marketing opportunity for some products and services. As pointed out earlier in this chapter, a chief characteristic of a target market is buying power. As the data in Exhibit 8.2 show, the older market is an increasingly affluent one.

Another useful way for marketers to segment markets is by family size and composition. The need for station wagons, five-bedroom houses, prepared foods, children's clothing, and many other products depends on the number of people in the family and whether or not both parents are employed outside the home. As shown in Figure 8.3, needs change as

EXHIBIT 8.1

The Top 25 Metro Markets in 1990

RANK, 1990	METRO MARKET	PROJECTED 1990 POPULATION (IN THOUSANDS)	PROJECTED PERCENTAGE OF CHANGE, 1985–1990
1	Los Angeles-Long Beach	8,634.9	+ 6.7%
2	New York	8,570.2	+ 1.6
3	Chicago	6,173.2	+ 0.8
4	Philadelphia	4,880.7	+ 1.5
5	Detroit	4,353.6	− 0.2
6	Boston-Lawrence-Salem-Lowell-Brockton	3,738.0	+ 0.9
7	Washington, D.C.	3,706.7	+ 6.1
8	Houston	3,637.0	+ 13.3
9	Nassau-Suffolk, N.Y.	2,787.2	+ 3.2
10	Atlanta	2,746.2	+ 11.6
11	Dallas	2,610.6	+ 13.7
12	St. Louis	2,437.9	+ 0.9
13	San Diego	2,395.1	+ 11.9
14	Baltimore	2,367.8	+ 3.3
15	Minneapolis-St. Paul	2,357.5	+ 4.6
16	Anaheim-Santa Ana, Calif.	2,292.3	+ 7.9
17	Riverside-San Bernardino, Calif.	2,196.5	+ 15.8
18	Pittsburgh	2,142.7	− 1.7
19	Phoenix	2,135.5	+ 16.0
20	Tampa-St. Petersburg-Clearwater, Fla.	2,091.8	+ 11.9
21	Oakland, Calif.	2,022.0	+ 6.2
22	Miami-Hialeah	1,902.5	+ 7.4
23	Newark, N.J.	1,881.1	n.c.*
24	Cleveland	1,845.3	− 1.5
25	Denver	1,822.9	+ 11.5

*Indicates that percent of change is less than ±0.1%.
Source: Sales & Marketing Management, October 27, 1986, 20.

EXHIBIT 8.2

Income of Households Headed by 55- to 64-Year-Olds, 1985-1995 (households in thousands; income in 1985 dollars)

	1985	1990	1995
Number of households	12,794	12,382	13,399
Less than $10,000	2,336	2,154	2,242
$10,000 to $19,999	2,822	2,619	2,736
$20,000 to $29,999	2,488	2,324	2,453
$30,000 to $39,999	1,792	1,792	1,988
$40,000 to $49,999	1,224	1,197	1,301
$50,000 to $59,999	777	851	985
$60,000 to $74,999	596	633	749
$75,000 and over	757	812	946
Median income	$24,980	$26,100	$27,020

Source: "Demographic Forecasts: Facing Retirement," *American Demographics*, September 1986, 70.

FIGURE 8.3

Average Population per Household:
1940 to Present

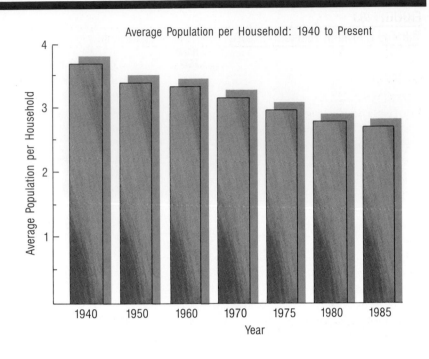

Average Population per Household: 1940 to Present

family structure changes. Recent decreases in the number of children per household and increases in the number of one-person households have presented unique market segment opportunities.

A recent innovation in demographic segmentation is the idea of *geo-demographics* — the combining of demographic characteristics with geographic location. One method of segmenting markets on a geo-demographic basis is **PRIZM** (Potential Rating Index by Zip Market), a segmentation system that classifies neighborhoods and communities into homogeneous population clusters. The PRIZM system analyzes the more than 35,000 U.S. Zip codes by over 500 different measures of five factors (education and affluence, family life cycle, mobility, ethnicity, and housing and urbanization). The analysis produces 40 homogeneous neighborhood clusters whose consumption and media habits can be crosstabulated with other existing data bases (Simmons Market Research Bureau, for example). PRIZM and other systems that analyze geo-demographic data help marketers select target markets, estimate sales potential, and buy advertising media more efficiently.[6]

PSYCHOGRAPHIC SEGMENTATION

A demographic analysis of the marketplace tells marketers exactly who buys what products, and while demographics are the most widely used data to specify markets, marketers also benefit from knowing the psychological makeup of the market.

Psychographic segmentation divides the market according to psychological characteristics of buyers. When these characteristics are measured and quantified, they can be used to specify the market in terms of life-

FIGURE 8.3

Index of Household Spending by Age of Head of Household (households in thousands)

	UNDER 25	25–34	35–44	45–54	55–64	65 AND OVER
Households	5,438	20,014	17,481	12,628	13,073	18,155
Average household size	2.3	2.9	3.4	3.2	2.4	1.8
Average household income	$16,643	$26,177	$33,389	$36,002	$30,516	$18,279
Relative Expenditures (average = 100.0)						
Total expenditures	63.4	102.8	126.1	130.9	99.6	61.6
Food	60.2	94.4	127.9	132.5	102.0	67.1
Food at home	56.3	91.8	129.2	131.1	102.5	70.6
Food away from home	72.2	102.4	124.0	136.4	100.8	56.8
Alcoholic beverages	114.0	125.7	115.7	117.2	97.2	42.6
Tobacco and smoking supplies	68.8	96.3	124.4	139.1	114.6	52.3
Housing	62.3	112.3	125.3	115.9	90.4	69.3
Shelter	69.5	122.9	127.6	111.9	82.6	61.6
Utilities, fuels, public services	46.8	87.7	119.4	130.6	108.9	83.2
Telephone	75.0	103.6	120.1	125.7	98.2	67.6
Fuel oil	18.2	53.7	91.8	129.1	128.1	142.6
House furnishings and equipment	70.1	115.8	130.2	119.7	96.4	51.5
Furniture	87.6	133.4	139.7	100.1	83.2	40.8
Major appliances	63.7	113.8	115.0	133.6	89.2	65.7
Apparel	71.1	104.0	143.1	133.8	93.2	44.2
Men's and boys'	65.0	106.4	152.1	140.4	86.0	35.4
Women's and girls'	64.4	87.6	145.8	140.9	100.1	51.8
Footwear	69.1	103.8	152.3	125.8	89.8	44.2
Transportation	74.0	105.4	124.1	141.2	102.2	48.6
Vehicles	83.2	112.6	127.4	146.6	94.4	36.6
New cars	60.0	103.0	119.6	149.9	109.8	48.1
Gasoline	70.5	104.6	124.8	137.4	103.2	51.6
Vehicle insurance	61.1	96.2	112.1	152.5	109.5	60.8
Airline fares	49.2	82.6	115.4	131.5	133.9	73.1
Health care	33.8	67.9	99.2	116.4	112.6	135.3
Health insurance	32.4	65.5	83.8	106.8	124.4	151.4
Prescription drugs	26.5	48.1	78.5	112.2	130.4	169.1
Personal care	48.0	73.9	114.8	135.3	123.1	88.8
Recreation	75.2	115.8	143.4	118.8	93.4	40.0
Fees and admissions	72.8	95.1	148.3	133.8	98.8	44.5
TVs, radios, sound equipment	95.8	117.8	125.2	123.3	91.2	47.6
Life and Personal Insurance	26.7	87.6	129.9	151.1	127.5	51.4

Source: "Spending Boom and Bust," by Fabian Linden, © *American Demographics*, October 1986, p. 4. Reprinted with permission.

style and personality characteristics. This enables the marketer to create marketing activities more effectively and efficiently. Obviously, consumers' purchases are strongly influenced by their activities, interests, and opinions. Psychographic segmentation is useful because it adds another key dimension to segmenting the marketplace. Consumer researcher Joseph Plummer's life-style dimensions listed in Exhibit 8.3 indicate the range of activities, interests, opinions, and demographics that are important in identifying key prospects.

EXHIBIT 8.3

Life-Style Dimensions

ACTIVITIES	INTERESTS	OPINIONS	DEMOGRAPHICS
Work	Family	Themselves	Age
Hobbies	Home	Social issues	Education
Social events	Job	Politics	Income
Vacation	Community	Business	Occupation
Entertainment	Recreation	Economics	Family size
Club membership	Fashion	Education	Dwelling
Community	Food	Products	Geography
Shopping	Media	Future	City size
Sports	Achievements	Culture	Stage in life cycle

Source: Joseph T. Plummer, "The Concept and Application of Life-Style Segmentation," *Journal of Marketing*, January 1974.

Several years ago, the Leo Burnett agency undertook a research project to segment the tennis racquet market into psychographic segments. Their research findings divided the tennis-playing market into four segments:

- Beginners   (30%)

- Socializers   (25%)

- Competitors   (25%)

- Buffs   (20%)

Buffs were defined as players—both men and women—who would do anything for a winning edge. The research findings were then used to help create an advertising campaign for the Wilson T-2000 tennis racket, using tennis star Jimmy Connors as the celebrity endorser. The T-2000 was marketed on the basis of extra power, a feature that the research suggested was strongly desired by the Buffs.[7]

Psychographics provides a deeper understanding of consumers, and its application to advertising lies primarily in the assistance it provides in the creation of messages that link the product to the activities, interests, and opinions of the target audience.

VALUES AND LIFE-STYLE SEGMENTATION

Closely related to psychographic segmentation is a system based on values and life-style research. The **Values and Life-Styles (VALS™)** research program of SRI International categorizes people on the basis of their attitudes, needs, and beliefs. The four major groups of the VALS segmentation system are the Integrated, the Outer-Directed, the Inner-Directed, and the Need-Driven. Also, VALS identifies nine life-styles within the four major categories.

The concept underlying the VALS research program—that our behavior in the marketplace is a result of our life-style, attitudes, and values in addition to our demographic characteristics—is sound and potentially useful to marketers. It is obviously important for marketers to know more than who buys their products, and approaches like VALS allow marke-

A CLOSER LOOK

ADVERTISING "THE DEEP"

The film version of Peter Benchley's *The Deep* was one of the few movies whose advertising campaign allocated 10 percent of the total budget to magazine advertising, and allowed for five separate full-color ads, one for each market segment. After the company examined the data that described movie audiences, it divided the potential audience for "The Deep" into five segments. Specific advertisements were created for each segment.

SEGMENT	DESCRIPTION OF AD MESSAGE
"Lusty Men"	Readers of *Playboy* and *Penthouse* were shown a spicy photograph of star Jacqueline Bisset wearing a wet, form-fitting T-shirt. Marvin Levy, the film's advertising director, called this their "excitement and sex appeal" ad.
"Romantic Women"	Readers of *McCall's, Glamour,* and *Cosmopolitan* were shown a misty closeup of Bisset about to kiss her co-star, Nick Nolte. The caption: "Their Loves and Lives at Risk."
"Love-Struck Teens"	Readers of *Seventeen* and *Teen* were given a pin-up picture of Nick Nolte along with the lines, "Their love is very new. The treasure is very old."
"Underwater Freaks"	A picture of three people in scuba gear holding an underwater torch went
"Mr. and Mrs. Front Porch America"	into *Sports Illustrated,* presumed home of well-to-do outdoor types. *Time, Newsweek,* and *People* all got an ad with the *Sports Illustrated* ad caption, "Is anything worth the terror of the deep?" However, the picture showed three people exploring the sand.

Source: "Deep Hustle," by Kenneth Turan, *Washington Post,* June 15, 1977.

ters to gain additional insight into understanding customers, how various products and services fit into their life-styles and value systems, and ultimately, why they buy.

SRI International is not the only organization interested in values and life-styles. Various firms, among them D'Arcy Masius Benton & Bowles Inc., *Sports Illustrated,* Mediamark Research Inc., and The Roper Organization, Inc., have conducted studies to obtain a better understanding of how products and services fit into life-styles. In its report, "Influential Americans," The Roper Organization found that one of every ten adults is a "trendsetter" in the marketplace. According to the report, "trendsetters" were among the first to try compact cars in the early 1970s and home computers in the 1980s. On the other hand, an "influential" is more interested in product quality than price; experiments with investments; enjoys shopping in specialty stores; and purchases often by mail.[8]

FIGURE 8.4

Segmentation Based on Values and Life-Style

Some Demographic Characteristics of the Nine VALS™ Subcategories

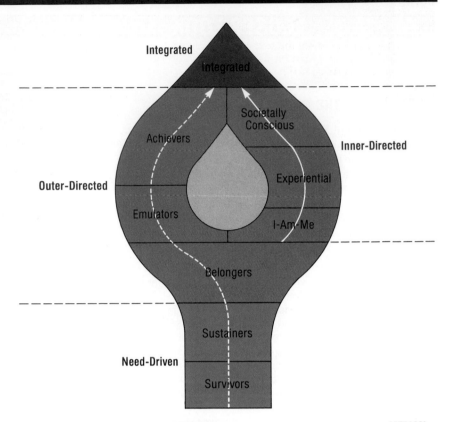

CATEGORY	PERCENT OF ALL U.S. HOUSEHOLDS	MEDIAN AGE	MEDIAN HOUSE-HOLD INCOME
Achievers	21%	42.0	$39,823
Societally Conscious	12	37.2	33,965
Belongers	38	56.5	16,285
Experiential	5	28.3	27,009
Emulators	10	27.9	21,497
I-Am-Me	3	20.1	26,014
Sustainers	7	28.4	8,303
Survivors	4	66.4	3,768
Integrated	2	*	*

*Not described by age and income.
Source: Courtesy of The Values and Lifestyles (VALS™) Program, SRI International, Menlo Park, California.

"Lifestyles," a study by Mediamark Research Inc., categorized Americans into seven groups, according to how they spend their free time.[9] These seven types, along with their favorite activities, are as follows:

- Outdoor Energetics — Sailing, downhill skiing, tennis, backpacking, hiking, and bicycling

- On Your Toes — Skating, aerobics, and health clubs

- Surf and Turf — Hunting, fishing, and boating

- Cerebrals — Chess, checkers, and backgammon

EXHIBIT 8.4

Benefit Segments of the Toothpaste Market

In the table below, we see the four benefit segments of the toothpaste market cross-referenced with demographic, personality, behavioral, and brand preference information. Russell Haley's original description of the toothpaste market was done almost 20 years ago. What brands do you think would fall into the four benefit segments today?

BENEFIT SEGMENTS	DEMOGRAPHICS	BEHAVIORISTICS	PSYCHOGRAPHICS	FAVORED BRANDS
Economy (low price)	Men	Heavy users	High autonomy, value-oriented	Brands on sale
Medicinal (decay prevention)	Large families	Heavy users	Hypochondriac, conservative	Crest
Cosmetic (bright teeth)	Teens, young adults	Smokers	High sociability, active	Aqua-Fresh, Ultra Brite
Taste (good tasting)	Children	Spearmint lovers	High self-involvement, hedonistic	Colgate, Aim

Source: Adapted from Russell I. Haley, "Benefit Segmentation: A Decision-Oriented Research Tool," *Journal of Marketing*, July 1968, 30–35; and Haley, "Benefit Segmentation: Backwards and Forwards," *Journal of Advertising Research*, February–March 1984, 19–25.

- Creatives — Painting, drawing, woodworking, and photography

- Home and Hearth — Entertaining at home, barbecuing, cooking, reading, listening to music, playing cards, and doing crossword puzzles

- Gentle Pursuits — Coin collecting, birdwatching, flower arranging, and gardening

BENEFIT SEGMENTATION

Another way to segment the market is according to the benefits sought by consumers. As with psychographic segmentation, benefit segmentation provides a deeper, more subjective understanding of the market than is provided by the purely descriptive approaches of geographic and demographic segmentation. **Benefit segmentation** cuts across geographic and demographic segments and life-style characteristics, identifying the product or service benefit reasons for purchase.

Several years ago, marketing researcher Russell Haley presented a benefit segmentation of the toothpaste market.[10] As shown in Exhibit 8.4, consumers seek four major benefits in this market: 1) sensory (flavor and product appearance); 2) brightness of teeth; 3) decay prevention; and 4) price. Benefit segmentation is a useful technique, particularly when the marketer has reason to believe that the benefit sought is more relevant to the purchase than other factors.

ADVERTISING AND SEGMENTING CONSUMER MARKETS

As stated earlier, the purpose of segmentation is to improve the profitability of all marketing activities, including product development, distribution, pricing, and promotion. This is accomplished by defining segments within a market and dividing the market into segments that have a common need. The banking industry situation described in the opening vignette of this chapter shows how at least one industry expert sees the market being segmented in the near future. Similarly, the toothpaste market has been effectively segmented by benefits sought.

The various segmentation methods help marketers identify potentially profitable target markets and suggest ways to alter the mix of product, price, distribution, and promotion to satisfy the needs of the target.

Knowledge about market segments and the target market helps advertisers make decisions about the role advertising should play in the promotion mix, the nature of advertising objectives, the size of the advertising investment, the creative approach, and media selection. Virtually every part of an advertising campaign is directly affected by the characteristics of the target market. The following information illustrates how a company's selection of a target market can affect advertising decisions. (The data provided do not necessarily reflect the market structure of the coffee industry. The information has been created to illustrate the relationship between market segments and advertising decisions.)

Influence of a Consumer Market Segment on Advertising Decisions

Product: Coffee

CHARACTERISTICS OF TARGET MARKET		IMPLICATIONS FOR ADVERTISING
Primary Benefit	Doesn't prevent sleep.	Primary message should stress the soothing aspects of the decaffeinated product.
Secondary Benefit	Economy	Secondary message should stress moderate price and high yield aspects of the brand. Consider couponing.
Sex	Female, 65%; male, 35%	Visual elements of advertising should use models in the age category of the target market.
Age	45–60	
Life-Style Characteristic	High anxiety	Show product usage followed by good night's sleep. Perhaps use testimonials to minimize anxiety.
Geographic Concentration	Top 10 U.S. markets	Moderate advertising investment because of geographic concentration.
Product Usage	Light users	Select media that match media habits and location of target market.

SEGMENTING BUSINESS-TO-BUSINESS MARKETS

Because business-to-business buyers usually do not buy for their own consumption or use, many of the segmentation techniques used in consumer markets must be modified for use in business-to-business marketing. For example, most of the demographic variables are irrelevant. A buyer's age, income, and family status won't help a business-to-business marketer select a target market because none of these variables has much to do with how or why a business product is bought. Geographic segmentation and size of plant are useful techniques in business-to-business markets. We know, for example, that automobile manufacturing takes place in Michigan; auto tire manufacturing in Ohio; and computer technology in Cali-

EXHIBIT 8.5

Analysis of the Market for Metalforming and Metalcutting Machine Tools

SIC	DESCRIPTION	PLANTS WITH 20+ EMPLOYEES	PLANTS WITH 500+ EMPLOYEES	GEOGRAPHIC CONCENTRATION
35	Metalworking	14,154	488	
3541	Metalcutting Machine Tools	698	54	Chicago, New York, Buffalo, Detroit
3542	Metalforming Machine Tools	251	11	Detroit, Chicago, Newark, Cleveland

Source: 13th American Machinist Inventory of Metalworking Equipment (New York: McGraw-Hill, Inc., November 1983).

fornia. As shown in Exhibit 8.5, relatively few geographic areas are of interest to marketers of machine tools. Also, while there are relatively few large plants of 500 or more employees, they usually account for the greatest percentage of sales. Such data enable marketers to locate targets easily, determine which geographic and size segments they want to attract, and then direct their marketing efforts efficiently.

The most useful segmentation factor in business-to-business marketing is the **Standard Industrial Classification (SIC) system,** a classification system maintained by the federal government that identifies every industry in the United States with a four-digit code. The SIC codes provide a detailed description of industries and a convenient method of segmentation. If, for example, you marketed a product that could be used in the manufacture of automobiles (steel, plastic, rubber, electrical components, etc.), the SIC system enables you to specify your best prospects. Also, total industry data (sales, shipments, employment, etc.) are available for all SIC codes through the U.S. Census of Manufacturers. The significance of the SIC data is that a business-to-business marketer can quickly identify which specific industries are major prospects. Furthermore, the circulation data of the print media designed to reach business-to-business markets are organized by SIC codes; therefore, an advertiser

EXHIBIT 8.6

The Standard Industrial Classification System and How It Works

CLASSIFICATION	SIC CODE	DESCRIPTION
Division	3 (1 of 10 divisions of U.S. economy)	Manufacturing
Major group	37	Transportation equipment
Group number	371	Motor vehicles and motor vehicle equipment
Industry number	3711	Motor vehicles and passenger car bodies
	3713	Truck and bus bodies
	3714	Motor vehicle parts and accessories
	3715	Truck trailers

Source: Standard Industrial Classification Manual (Washington, D.C.: Office of Management and Budget, 1982), 196–197.

FIGURE 8.5

Business-to-Business Marketing:
Selling a Full Range of Benefits

Source: Courtesy of Indian Industries, Evansville, IN.

can evaluate media on the basis of their ability to reach the targeted SIC industries.

Other methods that can be used to segment business-to-business markets include usage rate of the product. Government and trade association data make it possible to segment business markets into light, moderate, and heavy users of a product category.

Many business-to-business markets can be categorized by the benefits they seek. For example, an exercise equipment manufacturer may find that some segments of the market are primarily interested in low price, while others primarily seek technical expertise or service. Note how a sporting goods marketer used advertising to sell its customers and prospects a full range of benefits (see Figure 8.5).

Some business-to-business markets are segmented on the basis of buyer readiness. All buyers—consumer or business—are in various stages of readiness to buy. Some are ready to buy today; others are evaluating alternative brands or suppliers; and still others are totally unaware of a product's existence. Business-to-business marketers can identify meaningful segments by readiness stage and then create marketing efforts that will help move buyers closer to the purchase stage.

ADVERTISING AND SEGMENTING BUSINESS-TO-BUSINESS MARKETS

While we most often think of segmentation and target marketing in terms of the consumer goods we buy, the successful business-to-business marketer also depends on identifying meaningful market segments and then developing an appealing marketing mix. Although the variables used to segment business-to-business markets are somewhat different than those used in consumer markets, they serve the same purpose.

We tend to think of business-to-business marketers as product oriented; yet, the success of a business product is just as dependent upon sound marketing strategy as a consumer product is. The use of segmentation strategy and careful target market selection is of interest to business-to-business marketers because these techniques increase the efficiency of marketing programs and the opportunities for success. The following example shows the influence of segmentation on the advertising of a business-to-business product, metalforming machine tools. Metalforming machine tools are used in a large number of manufacturing industries, including the transportation, construction, furniture, appliance, fastener, and component parts industries. The information in the example indicates that the company has decided to market to three SICs. Furthermore, it has decided to segment the market further by selecting a target market of large companies (those with 500 or more employees). While there are numerous smaller companies who would be prospects for metalforming machine tools, the company has decided to focus on a more narrow segment. The segmentation strategy and target market have direct implications for the advertising decisions the firm will have to make.

Influence of a Business-to-Business Segment on Advertising Decisions	Product: Metalforming Machine Tool (capital equipment)	
	CHARACTERISTICS OF THE SELECTED TARGET MARKET	**IMPLICATIONS FOR ADVERTISING**
	Primary Benefit — Technical expertise	Primary message or theme of advertising should stress company reputation for expertise in solving manufacturing problems. Stress engineering capabilities and perhaps demonstration through case history/examples.
	Geographic Concentration — Chicago, Cleveland, Detroit, Los Angeles, and New York	Moderate advertising budget due to relatively small size of target market (plant size of 500+ and few number of companies in SICs 3711, 3713, and 3721).
	Primary SICs — 3711 (Motor vehicles and passenger car bodies) 3713 (Truck and bus bodies)	Combination of narrow target market, geographic concentration, and primary benefit sought suggests use of direct mail.
	Secondary SIC — 3721 (Aircraft)	
	Size of Buyer — 500+ employees	
	Stage of Buyer Readiness — Immediate buy	Immediate buy stage calls for action-oriented copy (perhaps seek direct response through 800 number or return card).

SUMMARY

Knowledge about who is most likely to buy is critical to the success of an advertising effort. The concept of target marketing had been the focus of a great deal of attention in marketing because of its potential benefits for marketers.

Marketers approach target market selection by first becoming thoroughly familiar with market segmentation methods and then deciding which segment(s) will provide the best opportunity for the profitable marketing of goods and services.

The rationale for market segmentation is that it is rarely possible to sell a product to everyone; therefore, sound marketing strategy calls for defining and locating a specific segment whose needs can be fulfilled. There are several techniques for segmenting markets, including geographic; demographic; psychographic; values and life-style; and benefit segmentation. While many of the same segmentation techniques can be used in both consumer and business-to-business marketing, fundamental differences between consumer and business-to-business marketing require a somewhat different analysis. For instance, many consumer demographic factors are not relevant to the business-to-business setting. At the same time, business markets can be conveniently segmented through the Standard Industrial Classification system—the business-to-business market's counterpart to demographics.

YOU MAKE THE DECISION

SUNRISE PRODUCTS, INC.

During the past six months, a group of chemists decided to go into business for themselves, an enterprise they've named Sunrise Products, Inc. They each have extensive experience working for large cosmetics firms, where they helped develop many leading cosmetic and shampoo brands. They found a partner who owns a packaging plant, and with their own money and the outside funds they've been able to raise, they decided to launch their first consumer products, Sunrise shampoo and conditioner.

Although the group has manufacturing expertise, they know very little about marketing. They would like you to help them.

1. Identify the major benefit segments in the shampoo and conditioner market. What are the major brands within each segment?

2. Which segment do you think the new company should attack? Why?

3. What are the advertising implications for the segment you have selected?

■ ■ ■

QUESTIONS FOR DISCUSSION

1. This chapter's opening vignette on the banking industry provided three possible segmentation strategies. Name three other service industries that have attempted similar segmentation strategies. Describe their segments.

2. What are the advertising implications for a firm (outside the banking

industry) that adopts the "supermarket" segmentation strategy described in the banking industry example?

3. Below is a list of products and services. Are you part of the target market for these products? Explain why or why not for each product.
   —a new Corvette
   —spray deodorant
   —a prestige-priced cat food
   —life insurance
   —clothing store specializing in country and western wear

4. Describe the benefit segments of the shampoo market. Which benefit segment offers the greatest opportunity for a new brand? Why?

5. Name three products or services that have successfully differentiated their offerings on a physical attribute.

6. Why do so many products seem so physically similar?

7. What is the difference between psychographics and life-style?

8. Explain the main differences in the variables used to segment consumer markets vs. business-to-business markets.

9. What are the limitations of relying exclusively on the SIC system for specifying business-to-business markets?

10. Can the concept of psychographics be applied to segmenting business-to-business markets? Explain.

NOTES

1. Joyce Healy, "Survival Marketing Changes Banking,"*Marketing Communications*, October 1984, 15.

2. "Facts to File," *Advertising Age*, January 1, 1986.

3. Wendell Smith, "Product Differentiation and Market Segmentation as Alternative Marketing Strategies," *Journal of Marketing*, July 1956, 3–8.

4. Richard H. Stewart, "It Costs Big Bucks to Put a New Product on the Market," *Orange County Register*, June 11–12, 1986, 34; and John R. Hauser and Glen R. Urban, *Design and Marketing New Products* (Englewood Cliffs, N.J.: Prentice-Hall, Inc., 1980), 48.

5. Valerie Free, "The Elusive Female," *Marketing Communications*, September 1985, 33–64.

6. "Dependable Data for Advertising and Marketing Decisions," Simmons Market Research Bureau, Inc., New York, 1985. Also see "We need to find out more about PRIZM . . . and Geo-Demographic Targeting," Claritas, Alexandria, Va., 1986.

7. John Peterson, "Psychographic Ads That Try to Get inside Your Head," *The National Observer*, February 26, 1977, 1, 15.

8. "Fears and Fantasies of the American Consumer," D'Arcy Masius Benton & Bowles Inc., New York, 1986; and "The Influential Americans," The Roper Organization, Inc., New York, 1986.

9. "Leisurestyles," Mediamark Research Inc., New York, 1986. Also see "Sports Poll '86," *Sports Illustrated*, New York, 1986.

10. Russell I. Haley, "Benefit Segmentation: A Decision-Oriented Research Tool," *Journal of Marketing*, July 1968, 30–35.

SUGGESTED READINGS

Aaker, David A., and J. Gary Shansby. "Positioning Your Product." *Business Horizons*, May–June 1982.

Adamec, Richard J. "How to Improve Your New Product Success Rate." *Management Review*, January 1981.

Association of American Geographers. "United States High School Sport since 1971." Washignton, D.C.: Association of American Geographers, 1986.

Bass, Frank M., Douglas J. Tigert, and Ronald T. Lonsdale. "Market Segmentation: Group Versus Individual Behavior." *Journal of Marketing Research*, May 1970, 153–158.

Bloom, David E. "Women at Work." *American Demographics*, September 1986, 25–30.

Cleaver, Joanne. "Fragmentation Enriches Problems in Reaching Group." *Advertising Age*, March 13, 1986, 11–13.

Dunn, William. "Americans on the Move." *American Demographics*, October 1986, 49–51, 73.

Gardner, Samuel R. "Successful Market Positioning—One Company Example." In *Product Line Strategies*, L. Bailey, ed. New York: The Conference Board, 1982.

Guber, Selina A. "Children as Consumers." *Advertising Age*, December 23, 1985, 12.

Kern, Richard. "USA 2000." *Sales and Marketing Management*, October 27, 1986, 8–12.

Kotler, Philip. *Marketing Management*. Englewood Cliffs, N.J.: Prentice-Hall, Inc., 1984.

Martineau, Pierre. *Motivation in Advertising*. New York: McGraw Hill, 1957.

Mitchell, Arnold. *The Nine American Lifestyles: Who We Are and Where We're Going*. New York: Macmillan Publishing Co., 1983.

Newspaper Advertising Bureau. "Psychographics: A Study of Personality, Life-Style, and Consumption Patterns." New York: Newspaper Advertising Bureau, 1973.

Nylen, David W. "The Dimensions of Industrial New Product Success and Failure." *Business Magazine*, Summer 1979.

Ozanne, Urban B., and Gilbert A. Churchill, Jr. "Five Dimensions of the Industrial Adoption Process." *Journal of Marketing Research*, August 1971.

Patti, Charles H. "The Role of Advertising in the Adoption of Industrial Goods: A Look at the Raw Materials Industry." *Journal of Advertising*, Fall 1979.

Penn, W. S., Jr., and Mark Mougel. "Industrial Marketing Myths." *Industrial Marketing Management*, 7, 1978.

Plummer, Joseph T. "The Concept and Application of Life Style Segmentation." *Journal of Marketing*, January 1974.

Robinson, Patrick J., Charles W. Faris, and Yoram Wind. *Industrial Buying and Creative Marketing*. Boston: Allyn and Bacon, 1967.

Rotzoll, Kim B. "The Effect of Social Stratification on Market Behavior." *Journal of Advertising Research*, March 1967, 22–27.

Solomon, Jolie. "The Business of Leisure: Working at Relaxation." *The Wall Street Journal*, Special Report, April 21, 1986, 1D–24D.

Sugarman, Len. "Breaking the 'Old Age' Barrier." *Advertising Age*, December 16, 1985, 18.

Webster, Frederick E., Jr. "Informal Communication in Industrial Markets." *Journal of Marketing Research*, May 1970, 186–189.

Webster, Frederick E., Jr., and Yoram Wind. *Organizational Buying Behavior*. Englewood Cliffs, N.J.: Prentice-Hall, Inc., 1972.

Wells, William D. "Psychographics: A Critical Review." *Journal of Marketing Research*, May 1975.

Wells, William D., and Douglas J. Tiger. "Activities, Interests and Opinions." *Journal of Advertising Research*, August 1971.

Wind, Yoram, and Richard Cardozo. "Industrial Market Segmentation." *Industrial Marketing Management*, no. 3, 1974, 153–166.

Woodside, Arch G., Jagdish N. Sheth, and Peter D. Bennett, eds. *Consumer and Industrial Buying Behavior*. New York: North-Holland, Inc., 1977.

Young, Shirley; Leland Ott; and Barbara Feigin. "Some Practical Considerations in Market Segmentation." *Journal of Marketing Research*, August 1978.

"Americans Change." *Business Week*, February 20, 1978.

"The Changing Role of the Consumer in the 1980s." *Marketing Review*, October–November 1980.

"Chevrolets for Women." *American Demographics*, September 1986, 22.

"Guidelines for Ads Targeting over-50 Market." *Marketing News*, February 28, 1986, 28.

"How the Changing Age Mix Changes Markets." *Business Week*, January 12, 1976.

"Market Segmentation Key to Keeping up with Today's Car Competition." *Sales and Marketing Digest*, December 1985, 2.

P A R T 3

Advertising Decision Making: Pre-Campaign Issues

If you've ever looked at an ad and asked yourself "Who are they talking to?" "What are they trying to say?" or "What do they want me to do?" it's probably because the advertiser didn't do enough thinking and planning before the advertising messages were created and delivered. Although the heart of advertising *is* the advertising message, the effectiveness of creating advertising and planning media is determined by the marketing thinking and planning that take place before an ad is ever conceived or a media schedule is developed.

This part explains the three most important pre-campaign issues. In the Framework for Advertising Decision Making (Figure 9.1), the first issue is the role of advertising. Chapter 9 presents a method for deciding what to expect from advertising. Advertising can't solve all marketing problems. Good business people know that; yet, there is a tendency to rely too much on advertising. Knowing exactly how much advertising can be expected to accomplish gives a company direction for executing an advertising campaign.

Chapter 10 makes the distinction between marketing and advertising objectives. It discusses how to create "good" objectives—objectives that guide the creation of advertising messages and media schedules, that provide for some measure of one's success or failure, and that help meet the larger goals of marketing.

Chapter 11 introduces the concept of budgeting for advertising. Determining the right amount to spend on advertising is a difficult management task—too much can be disastrous for a firm's financial picture, but too little can result in minimal impact in the marketplace. This chapter explains how major consumer and business-to-business marketers set advertising budgets, and outlines how to create advertising budgets by applying the chapter's concepts to several realistic advertising situations.

C H A P T E R   9

DETERMINING THE ROLE OF ADVERTISING

Key Terms

physical attributes
hidden qualities
powerful buying motives
generic demand trend
market potential
competitive environment
appraisal checklist
weighted evaluation procedure
factor score
factor weight
Advertising Opportunity Score (AOS)

Learning Objectives

To describe the procedure for appraising the advertising opportunity

To analyze the managerial importance of determining advertising's role in the total promotion mix

To estimate advertising's contribution to promotion objectives

To relate the appraisal of the advertising opportunity to other advertising management decisions

One of the most impressive marketing success stories in recent years is Reebok International. Operating in the highly competitive athletic-shoe market, Reebok's sales in 1983 totaled $12.5 million. A year later, sales increased 420 percent to $65 million. In 1985, Reebok grossed $307 million, nearly 25 times the 1983 mark.

In 1985, Reebok spent about $3 million on advertising, primarily in such print vehicles as *Esquire*, *Glamour*, *Rolling Stone*, and *Sports Illustrated*. In 1986, the company launched its entry into television, budgeting over $10 million for advertising.

Reebok's success isn't due entirely to advertising, however. The company achieved its goals through the careful use of a variety of promotional tools:

- **Advertising**—initially placed in specialty periodicals, gradually in broader-circulation magazines, and eventually television

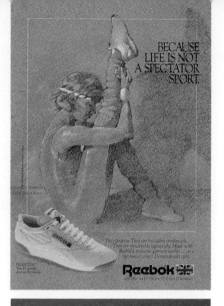

- **Celebrity endorsements**—from tennis star Hana Mandlikova and marathoner Steve Jones

- **Sales promotion and public relations**—newsletters on aerobics; research and development on injury prevention; seminars and clinics; creation of the first aerobics certification program; special price reductions to aerobics teachers

- **Personal selling**—to the product's distribution channels; the firm currently has 4,000 accounts and plans to have 5,000 in the future.

Although it will be difficult for Reebok to maintain this phenomenal rate of growth, continued success is likely. Meanwhile, areas of growth will involve the increased use of advertising; the expansion of distribution; an appeal to a larger market (walking and basketball shoes); and entering the "above-the-ankles" market (socks, hats, bags, and activewear for tennis, aerobics, and other sports).

As Reebok ventures into broader markets, it will encounter stiffer competition. Marketing costs will continue to increase and the company will be required to reexamine the role that advertising will play.

Source: Carl Weinschenk, "Setting the Pace," *Marketing & Media Decisions*, Winter 1986, 34–39. Photo courtesy of Reebok International Ltd.

INTRODUCTION

There are many ways to become successful. Although marketing has its scientific aspects, success is usually determined by the creative application of the concepts discussed in this book. Each year, thousands of new brands enter the marketplace. Most new brands are supported with an advertising campaign designed to make us aware of the brand's existence, to convince us that the brand will in some way make our life better, and to entice us to try the brand. However, a large percentage of new brands do not succeed and the losses in human and financial resources are sometimes enormous.[1]

Obviously, advertising has been (and will continue to be) an important marketing tool for Reebok. Advertising's abilities to reach mass audiences, demonstrate product features, add personality to brands, and encourage purchase are universally accepted. However, advertising does not have unlimited powers. History shows that advertising—regardless of level of spending or creative excellence—cannot assure brand success. It is the advertising manager's responsibility to determine the role advertising will play in stimulating demand for the product or service.

This chapter introduces the concept of appraising the advertising opportunity, and why some brands rely heavily on advertising and others minimize its use. The importance of this concept cannot be overstated because decisions about the role of advertising affect every other advertising decision. The basic purpose of the appraisal concept is to identify the situations within which advertising will most likely make a substantial contribution to a brand's success.

HISTORICAL DEVELOPMENT OF ADVERTISING'S ROLE

Nearly 50 years ago, researcher Neil Borden completed a major research project on the economic effects of advertising. His study included an analysis of the effects that advertising had on the demand for a large number of product categories. Although the main purpose of his study was not to evaluate advertising's role within the promotion mix, Borden was able to identify certain external and internal environmental conditions that are favorable to the use of advertising.

> . . . the opportunities for the successful use of advertising vary widely. Advertising is not a business stimulator which can be turned on and off at will with the assurance that results will be commensurate with expenditures. Successful advertising depends on the right combination of numerous factors.[2]

Borden's book, *The Economic Effects of Advertising*, was published in 1942, and although the book remains the classic study of advertising's economic effects, his observations about the conditions under which advertising is most likely to be effective have gone largely unnoticed.

In 1962, Nugent Wedding expanded the list of factors and applied them to a number of case studies.[3] And in 1971, Roy Campbell began to see the value in Borden's observations and attempted to further expand

FIGURE 9.1

A Framework for Advertising
Decision Making

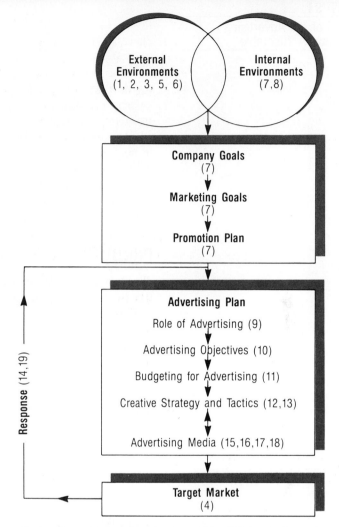

Numbers in parentheses indicate the chapter(s) in which item is discussed.

the list of conditions under which advertising might be expected to succeed.[4]

In 1974, the applicability of the Borden factors was tested within the industrial market (capital equipment industry).[5] Later, in 1977, the factors were developed into an advertising management tool, which is described in detail later in this chapter.[6] Exhibit 9.1 summarizes the historical development of this concept.

FACTORS FOR APPRAISING THE ADVERTISING OPPORTUNITY

Three major categories of factors affect the advertising opportunity: 1) product factors, 2) market factors, and 3) company factors.

EXHIBIT 9.1

Appraisal of the Advertising
Opportunity: A Timetable

1942	Publication of Neil Borden's *The Economic Effects of Advertising.* Identifies several conditions under which advertising is likely to affect both primary and brand demand.
1962	Publication of Nugent Wedding's *Advertising Management.* Expansion of appraisal factors and application to case situations.
1971	Roy Campbell authors "Why Should Products be Advertised?" Further expansion of appraisal factors.
1974	Publication of Charles H. Patti's "How to Increase Chances for Increasing Machine Tool Advertising Effectiveness" in *Industrial Marketing.* Appraisal of advertising opportunity applied to industrial market.
1977	Patti authors "Evaluating the Role of Advertising," *Journal of Advertising.* Appraisal of advertising opportunity factors developed into management decision-making model.

PRODUCT FACTORS

Three questions are appropriate in evaluating the product factors that affect the advertising opportunity.

Does the brand possess unique, relevant physical attributes? Products that lend themselves best to advertising are those having unique **physical attributes**—characteristics that physically differentiate them from competitive products—and those whose point of differentiation can be proven useful to prospective buyers. For example, at a time when consumers want fuel-efficient cars, a car that gets 50 percent better mileage than competing models is a highly "advertisable" product. Figure 9.2 shows an ad for a product whose physical differentiation becomes the key issue in the message.

Two related points are important here. First, it is possible to advertise *parity products*—that is, physically identical ones—successfully. Examples abound in such product categories as cigarettes, beer, and soft drinks. These products are differentiated primarily on the basis of their personality rather than a physical feature. And, while advertising as a communication tool is probably unsurpassed in helping shape product personality, selling a product on nonphysical attributes is an expensive, time-consuming, and risky undertaking.

Second, rarely is simply "being different" enough. The key to having an advertisable product is to be different in a way that is highly relevant to the target market, and hopefully the point of differentiation cannot be duplicated by competitors very easily (see Figure 9.3). The digital watch market has undergone rapid product development in the past few years. It is common for a digital watch to offer a number of features (time, day/date, and stop watch features, for instance). As the product category became even more competitive, watches took on even more complicated features, such as calculators, arcade-type games, pulse-taking devices, and compasses. Because of advances in the technology of the product, it would be extremely difficult to create a feature that would be both highly relevant to the target market and exclusive to one particular brand.

Does the product contain "hidden qualities"? If by viewing, feeling, tasting, or smelling the brand, the buyer can learn all there is to know about it and its benefits, advertising will be able to contribute less

FIGURE 9.2

Some products enjoy the advantage of an important physical difference.

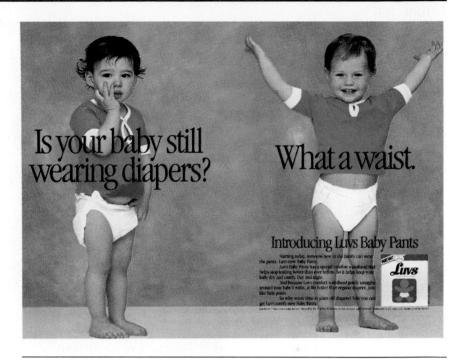

Is your baby still wearing diapers?

What a waist.

Introducing Luvs Baby Pants

Source: Courtesy of The Procter & Gamble Company.

to the stimulation of demand. Conversely, if a brand has **hidden qualities,** or benefits that are not readily apparent to the prospect, advertising has a larger role and its probability for successful use increases.

The "hidden quality" of vitamin C in oranges helps explain why Sunkist uses advertising successfully while the advertising of Chiquita lettuce failed. Vitamin C is not an attribute that can be appreciated by the physical inspection of oranges; yet, it is an important reason for buying them.

One of the reasons that products like shampoo and cosmetics can be advertised successfully is that very few of their relevant physical attributes can be appreciated by the prospective buyer's inspection of the product. While we can observe the convenience of package and scent of these two product categories, the advantages of their chemical properties need to be communicated through advertising (see Figure 9.4).

Is the product/service bought largely on the basis of powerful, emotional motives? One of the strengths of advertising is its ability to tell a story, to explain how a particular brand can solve a problem, or to contribute to the fulfillment of our personal or professional aspirations. Advertising is most effective for brands whose purchase involves **powerful buying motives**—strong emotional drives on the part of a buyer. Among the most emotional of these drives are parental affection (baby care products) and social enhancement (deodorant, cologne, toothpaste). Note how Ralston Purina uses a strong emotional appeal to advertise its product (see Figure 9.5).

Industrial goods and convenience goods do not naturally lend themselves to the use of emotional themes in advertising. It is not likely, for example, that a consumer would have an emotional motive for purchasing

FIGURE 9.3

Using Advertising That Is Highly
Relevant to the Target Market

P O R T F O L I O
SPORTSWEAR BY PERRY ELLIS

FIGURE 9.4

Communicating a Product's "Hidden
Quality": Vitamin E

Source: Reprinted courtesy of S. C.
Johnson & Son, Inc.

a flashlight; therefore, the use of an emotional advertising theme is unlikely. The Rayovac advertisement in Figure 9.6 emphasizes at least five
practical reasons for purchasing a flashlight.

MARKET FACTORS

Four questions that follow help in evaluating market factors that affect the
advertising opportunity.

　　Is the generic demand trend for the product/service favorable? Although many billions of dollars are invested in advertising annually, the
powers of advertising are not limitless. For example, if the **generic
demand trend** for a product category is negative—that is, if the category
is experiencing a long-term sales decline, it is less likely that advertising
can be used successfully for a particular brand within the category. Usu-

FIGURE 9.5

Advertising That Provokes an
Emotional Buying Motive

Source: Reprinted by permission of the Ralston Purina Company, Checkerboard Square,
St. Louis, MO. 63142.

ally, the reasons for a decline in the demand within a product category
involve a complex set of social, economic, technological, and cultural
forces. It is unrealistic to expect advertising—particularly advertising for
one specific brand—to change such forces. The best use—opportunity
—of advertising is when generic demand for the product category is increasing. For example, the increased interest in physical fitness in the
1980s has greatly helped sales in some product areas (such as athletic

FIGURE 9.6

Advertising That Focuses on
Practical Reasons for a Purchase

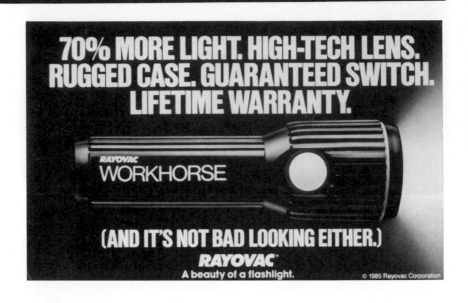

clothing, physical fitness centers, diet foods, etc.), and it has contributed
to declines in other product areas (salt, sugar, cigarettes, etc.).

Is the market potential for the product/service adequate? The use
of advertising to assist in the stimulation of demand can be expensive, and
unless the **market potential,** or opportunity for profit, is sufficiently
large, advertising should be minimized. Usually, market potential is measured in terms of profit margin and potential units or sales. The most
encouraging market conditions for a substantial advertising investment involve quite large profit margins and product use by a large segment of the
population. Most products in the personal care market fit both of these
criteria. Profit margins for cosmetics, colognes, and deodorants are comparatively large; the products are purchased frequently; and they are used
by a large segment of the population.

Is the competitive environment favorable? The **competitive
environment** refers to the size and marketing strength of competitors.
This, coupled with competitors' market share and brand loyalty, will
greatly affect the possible success of an advertising campaign. To compete
successfully against competitors like Kodak, Morton Salt, Campbell
Soup, or IBM requires considerably more marketing effort than an advertising campaign alone. These firms are large and knowledgeable. They
enjoy substantial market share and have the resources to combat attempts
to take market share away from them. E. & J. Gallo Winery, for example, sold more wine in 1985 (approximately $1 billion) than its next sev-
eral competitors combined (see Figure 9.7). Given Gallo's market share,
advertising power, and distribution system, it would be unrealistic to
expect advertising alone to take significant share away from them.[7]

This doesn't mean that industry leaders are not vulnerable; indeed,
many companies have competed very successfully in markets dominated
by a few giants. However, the opportunity for advertising to play the

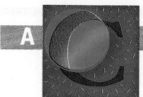

A CLOSER LOOK

MARKETING SUCCESS STORIES

Even in difficult economic times, some companies prosper. They develop new products, reposition existing brands, or implement a new marketing strategy that reaps rewards beyond their own expectations. In naming these 1986 marketing successes, *Marketing & Media Decisions* looked for companies or brands that "increased their market share in a meaningful manner; turned around a fading position through the use and execution of a canny marketing strategy; introduced a major new product that had a beneficial impact on the company, bested the competition, or kept rivals at bay; or satisfactorily accomplished some other marketing objective, such as consistently remaining at the top of an industry, regardless of business conditions."

The 1986 winners included these:

- **The Polaroid Spectra camera,** acknowledged as the "make-or-break" entry for Polaroid, whose earnings nearly tripled in 1987 to $103.5 million. Spectra gave the instant market its first sales uptick since its slide from 9 million units in 1978 to 3 million in 1985.

- **Lever's Surf detergent,** which separated itself from the competition by achieving an impressive 8 percent market share (second place nationally, behind Tide) even though it is distributed in only about 65 percent of the country. An aggressive advertising and sales promotion campaign helped the brand achieve up to an 11 percent share in the areas in which it is sold.

- **Home Shopping Network,** the biggest thing to hit direct marketing in years. The company raked in sales of $160.2 million from an estimated 1.4 million buyers, who watched and bought products from this 24-hour-a-day, direct-response television show.

- **The Ford Taurus/Mercury Sable** paid attention to consumer wants and needs, creating Ford's hottest car since the Mustang. In 1986, Ford gambled $3 billion on these two cars, and the gamble paid off— Ford is expected to top industry leader General Motors in profits for the first time in 60 years.

- **Wal-Mart Stores,** for its sustained growth during 1986. The company's ten-year compounded growth rate of 37.9 percent is unheard of in general merchandise retailing. Even though Wal-Mart stores go against the current retailing trend of appealing to the upwardly mobile, the business has grown from 30 stores in 1970 to 980 in 1986. Its sales of $11.9 billion places the company behind only Sears, Kmart, and J. C. Penney.

- **King World,** which distributes other companies' first-run TV programs on a cash/barter basis to stations around the country. During 1986, King distributed three of the top 10 shows in first-run syndication: "Wheel of Fortune" (#1), "Jeopardy" (#2), and "The Oprah Winfrey Show" (#8). Results? Revenues for 1986 totaled $145 million, a 54 percent increase over the prior year.

- **The JVC-C Camcorder** fought off the threat of 8mm, developed an improved VHS product (longer playing time, decrease of size and weight), and is considered responsible for bringing the VHS-C format to command about 20 percent of the 1.1 million-unit camcorder market in 1986. JVC leads the field with an estimated 55 percent share of the VHS-C segment.

Sources: Carol Hall, "Instant Gratification" and "Winner by a Nose"; Paula Schnorbus, "Sold!"; Rebecca Fannin, "The Road Warriors"; Toni Apgar, "The Cash Machine"; Marianne Paskowski, "Prize Packagers"; and Fred Plaff, "Cutting Rivals Down to Size," all in *Marketing & Media Decisions*, March 1987.

major role in stimulating brand demand is minimal under such conditions. Usually, a company competing with industry leaders must find success within product differentiation, market segmentation, pricing, or distribution.

Are general economic conditions favorable for the marketing of the product/service? Recent years have seen the effects of the economy on the sale of products. Interest rates drastically affect the real estate market. Increases in disposable income may bring about decisions to add luxury features to a new automobile purchase or to purchase a new stereo

FIGURE 9.7

The American Wine Market: Market Share

Despite challenges in the wine industry—decreases in consumption, a trend toward more expensive wines, and the growing popularity of wine coolers—the huge California winery of E. & J. Gallo dominates the American market.

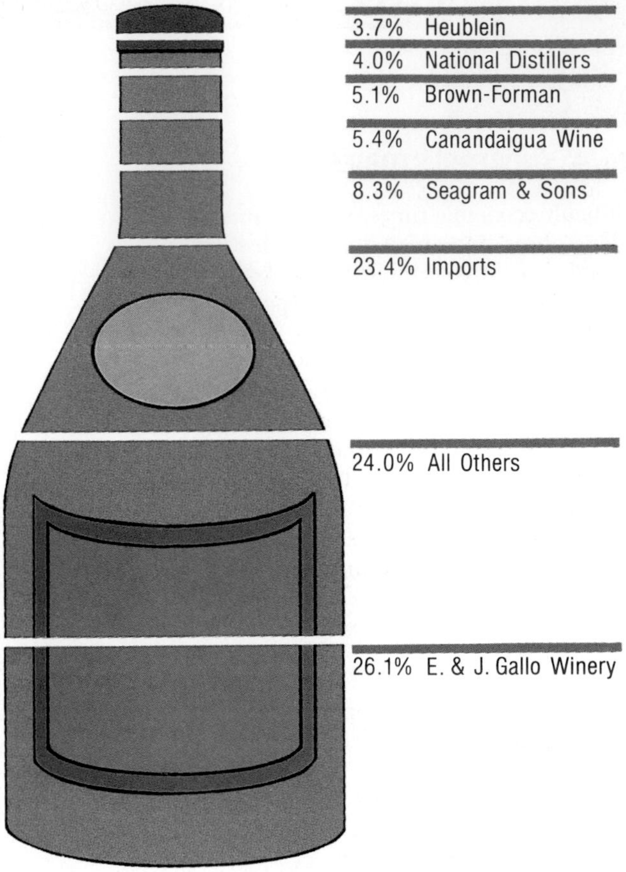

3.7%   Heublein
4.0%   National Distillers
5.1%   Brown-Forman
5.4%   Canandaigua Wine
8.3%   Seagram & Sons
23.4% Imports
24.0% All Others
26.1% E. & J. Gallo Winery

system. On the other hand, higher levels of unemployment contribute to the greater purchase of generic grocery items.

The opportunity for advertising to make a substantial contribution to demand is highest under favorable economic conditions. Advertising should not be expected to reverse the effects of the economy. It is much easier to advertise and sell luxury goods when disposable income is high. The advertising manager's task in evaluating the effects of the economy on a potential advertising campaign is to determine which specific economic conditions are applicable to the consumption of the product.

COMPANY FACTORS

The following two questions deal with the way company factors affect the advertising opportunity.

Is the company willing and financially able to spend the amount of money required to launch an advertising campaign? A company's financial commitment to an effective advertising campaign has two components. First, the company must either have, or have access to, the funds necessary to launch an advertising campaign of appropriate scale. The funds required vary widely, of course. In the mid-1980s, McDonald's

A CLOSER LOOK

CELESTIAL SEASONINGS, INC.: HOW TO BREW SUCCESS

In the beginning there were herbs.

In the early days of health foods awareness of the late 1960s and early 1970s, Moe Siegel, his wife Peggy, and their friend Wyck Hay gathered Colorado mountain herbs and sold them to local health food stores. Their objective: to provide a pleasant living for themselves and a congenial group of Boulder, Colorado, friends by selling a product that was good for people.

Their company, Celestial Seasonings, began as a relatively tranquil cottage business in which the Siegels and their friends patiently stuffed orange peel, wild cherry bark, rosehips, hibiscus flowers, lemon grass, and peppermint into hand-sewn, hand-stamped muslin teabags with instructions to buyers as to the particulars of brewing and steeping. Their first successful blend, entitled Red Zinger, quickly propelled Celestial out of the cottage and into a corporate setting. By 1982, just ten years later, Celestial required six buildings to house its manufacturing, its warehousing of herbs and spices from 35 countries, and other functions.

From the outset, Celestial espoused causes and amplified them from its cardboard packages: promoting a nonprofit foundation that protects vanishing flower species; warning about world hunger; or supporting save-the-whales efforts and other conservationist causes. Perhaps as important as its grocery-focused mission, Celestial saw itself as having an instructive, positivistic mission. "Happiness is the only thing we can give without having" and other similar messages became inherent aspects of Celestial's packaging.

After ten years in business, Celestial Seasonings' sales topped $25 million. The company held over 30 percent of the herbal tea market, milled over 4 million pounds of herbs annually, and offered some 40 different blends. Operating in an industry dominated by such giants as Lipton and Bigelow, Moe Siegel was able to compete successfully. How did he do it?

1. A health-conscious public

2. A high-quality product with readily acceptable flavor varieties

3. The distinctive and unique aspects of Celestial, including packaging, products, names, and writings

Source: Courtesy of Celestial Seasonings, Inc.

4. Professional management, mostly recruited from large, successful U.S. companies

5. Vertical integration, from raw product to finished teabag

6. Strong consumer loyalty initiated and supported by a high-quality product, unique packaging, and an innovative advertising campaign

In 1984, Celestial Seasonings was sold to Kraft for an estimated $50 million. Siegel left the company in January 1986, but the company retained much of his philosophy and management style. Kraft added some of its marketing skills, increased the investment in advertising, and helped the company move into international markets.

Listed as the smallest company in *The 100 Best Companies to Work for in America*, Celestial continues to prosper. Sales in 1983 — reported to be $23 million — have outpaced the tea market growth rate (10 percent annually) each year. The company's advertising budget is estimated at $1.5 million and current ads feature TV celebrity Mariette Hartley. Celestial's primary market includes upscale women ages 18 to 45.

Sources: From Charles L. Hinkle and Esther F. Stineman, *Cases in Marketing Management: Issues for the 1980's* (Englewood Cliffs, N. J.: Prentice-Hall, 1984), 59–78; and Sandra D. Atchison, "Kraft Is Celestial Seasoning's Cup of Tea," *Business Week*, July 28, 1986, 73.

EXHIBIT 9.2

The Top 10 Consumer Brands and Business-to-Business Advertisers, by Advertising Expenditure (in $ millions)

CONSUMER BRAND	EXPENDITURE	RANK	BUSINESS-TO-BUSINESS FIRM	EXPENDITURE
McDonald's Restaurants	$312.3	1	AT&T Co.	$49.6
Burger King	155.9	2	IBM Corp.	45.4
AT&T Residential Long Distance	*	3	General Motors Corp.	23.0
Wendy's Restaurants	86.7	4	Hewlett-Packard Co.	19.2
Chevrolet Local Dealers	*	5	American Express	18.9
Ford Local Dealers	*	6	Ford Motor Co.	17.9
Budweiser	*	7	General Electric Co.	17.4
Kentucky Fried Chicken	76.4	8	ITT Corp.	16.2
Miller Lite	*	9	Canon Inc.	14.3
Pizza Hut	64.5	10	Honeywell Inc.	14.2

*Spending for individual brand not reported. Total spending for each are: AT&T ($308.1), Chevrolet ($122.3), Ford ($120.2), Budweiser ($134.0), Miller ($152.7).
Sources: "Ninth Annual Top Brand Survey," *Marketing Communications*, June 1986; and "100 Leading Advertisers' Ad Expenditures," *Business Marketing*, July 1986.

Restaurants spent $312 million on advertising, making its fast food the most heavily advertised product in the United States.[8] Although this represents a huge sum, it is consistent with the advertising investment pattern in the fast-food category. Of the advertisers listed in Exhibit 9.2, five of the top 10 consumer advertisers are in the fast-food category. Because it's a large, highly competitive market with frequent purchase patterns, the fast-food market requires a very large investment in advertising.

On the other hand, American Telephone & Telegraph Co. (AT&T), the top business-to-business advertiser in the mid-1980s, invested only $49.6 million in advertising.[9] As the exhibit shows, business-to-business advertisers invest relatively little in advertising, compared to consumer goods advertisers.

Determining the amount of advertising required depends on factors that will be discussed in Chapter 11. Meanwhile, however, a firm should examine advertising expenditure figures for other firms in the product category. If a company wants a 10 percent market share, for example, it must be prepared to spend at least 10 percent of the total funds spent on advertising by all firms in the product category.

The second aspect of financial commitment is a company's willingness to sustain the investment in advertising. Again, as Neil Borden observed, companies too often reduce their investment in advertising too quickly. Advertising works best when it is repeated; if a company is not willing to commit an appropriate investment for at least the entire campaign period, the opportunity for advertising to make substantial contributions to demand is minimal.

Does the firm possess sufficient marketing expertise to market the product/service? Marketing involves a complex mixture of product and buyer research, product development, packaging, pricing, financial management, distribution, and promotion. A weakness in any of these areas

EXHIBIT 9.3

Checklist Model for Determining the
Role of Advertising

FACTOR	FOR ADVERTISING	AGAINST ADVERTISING
PRODUCT FACTORS		
Presence of unique, relevant physical attributes	_____	_____
Existence of "hidden qualities"	_____	_____
Possibility of using powerful, emotional motives	_____	_____
MARKET FACTORS		
Favorable generic demand trend	_____	_____
Adequacy of market potential	_____	_____
Favorable competitive environment	_____	_____
Favorable economic conditions	_____	_____
COMPANY FACTORS		
Adequacy of advertising funds	_____	_____
Sufficient marketing expertise	_____	_____

presents an obstacle to the effective use of advertising. Therefore, before a decision is made to invest heavily in an advertising effort, the company needs to conduct enough research to determine that the brand offers want-satisfying qualities; that it is priced right; that distribution channels have been developed; and that appropriate levels of service are established. One of the most frequent misuses of advertising is the attempt to market products to entirely different market sectors. For example, when companies who traditionally serve business and/or institutional markets try to market their products to consumer markets, they usually have a difficult time. The needs of the consumer marketplace are so different that the transition from business-to-business markets to consumer markets requires major changes in the marketing mix. Too often, advertising is expected to overcome these changes.

DEVELOPING AN ADVERTISING MANAGEMENT TOOL TO APPRAISE THE ADVERTISING OPPORTUNITY

Knowing the conditions under which advertising is most likely to be effective is the first step toward maximizing the use of advertising. The second step is knowing how to evaluate the conditions to assist in the management of the advertising effort.

A CHECKLIST PROCEDURE

Exhibit 9.3 presents the most basic method of determining advertising opportunity, an **appraisal checklist** for determining the role of advertising. An advertiser considers the product or service in relation to the nine questions on the checklist, with "yes" answers correlating to the "for advertising" column and "no" answers belonging in the "against advertising" column.

In situations where "no" ("against advertising") responses dominate the analysis, a decision to rely heavily on advertising will very likely fail. Conversely, whenever "yes" ("for advertising") responses dominate, advertising management should take confidence in the ability of advertising to make a substantial contribution to the marketing plan.

Unfortunately, management decisions are rarely this simple or clear-cut. Many times the checklist procedure does not provide clear direction; however, the purpose of the procedure is to assist judgment. A thorough review of the product, market, and company helps reduce the possibility of error in a very critical area of advertising management.

SHORTCOMINGS OF THE CHECKLIST PROCEDURE

There are two major shortcomings of the checklist procedure. First, a simple "yes-no"/"for-against" procedure assumes that all nine factors are of equal importance. Rarely does this accurately reflect the business environment. Usually, a company considers an advertising campaign because its management believes there is a market opportunity—one or more of the conditions appear to be extremely favorable to the marketing of the company's brand.

Because every firm operates with its own management style, objectives, competitive environments, and levels of human, financial, and physical resources, the nine-factor appraisal model described in this chapter must be adapted to the individual peculiarities of each company and the market situation it faces. Each firm must evaluate the relative importance of each factor in its own situation.

The second shortcoming of the "for-against" procedure is that it does not account for the degree or extent to which these factors exist. Business conditions are sometimes highly favorable. Some product categories experience a rapidly declining generic demand trend. Occasionally, a product is introduced that is a technological innovation (microwave ovens or low-cost personal computers, for example) and therefore possesses an unusually high degree of product differentiation. The "for-against" procedure does not allow the evaluator to make allowances for such situations.

THE WEIGHTED EVALUATION PROCEDURE

To help overcome these two problems, a **weighted evaluation procedure** was developed (see Exhibit 9.4). This system allows management to evaluate the degree to which a particular condition exists and its relative importance.

Determining Factor Scores   Each of the nine conditions are assigned a score between .00 and 1.0. The **factor score** is an expression of the extent to which the factor exists for the evaluated brand. Brands that possess little or none of a particular factor would receive a score of .00; brands that possess the highest degree of the factor would receive a score of 1.0. For example, a brand whose product category is enjoying extremely rapid growth (physical fitness equipment, for example) would receive a factor score close to 1.0 for the generic demand trend factor.

EXHIBIT 9.4

Weighted Evaluation Model for
Determining the Role of Advertising

FACTOR	FACTOR SCORE		FACTOR WEIGHT		PRODUCT (FS × FW)
PRODUCT FACTORS					
Presence of unique, relevant physical attributes	.7	×	2.0	=	1.4
Existence of "hidden qualities"	.4	×	1.0	=	.4
Possibility of using powerful, emotional motives	.8	×	2.0	=	1.6
MARKET FACTORS					
Favorable generic demand trend	.8	×	3.0	=	2.4
Adequacy of market potential	.7	×	1.0	=	.7
Favorable competitive environment	.8	×	2.0	=	1.6
Favorable economic conditions	.8	×	3.0	=	2.4
COMPANY FACTORS					
Adequacy of advertising funds	.9	×	2.0	=	1.8
Sufficient marketing expertise	.8	×	1.0	=	.8
Total			17.0		13.1

$$\text{ADVERTISING OPPORTUNITY SCORE} = \frac{\sum_{i=1}^{9} (a_i b_i)}{\sum_{i=1}^{9} (b_i)} = .77$$

Determining Factor Weights Each of the nine conditions are also assigned a **factor weight,** which reflects the relative importance of the factors in the advertiser's particular situation. In theory, factor weights can range from 0 to infinity; however, as a practical matter it is not advisable or necessary to assign factor weights higher than 5. If an advertiser felt that all the factors were of equal importance in determining the role of advertising, then each would receive a score of 1.0; however, this rarely happens and factor weights between 1.0 and 3.0 are most common.

In the example shown in Exhibit 9.4, the evaluator has assigned factor weights of 3.0 to generic demand trend and economic conditions; factor weights of 2.0 to physical attributes, powerful buying motives, competitive environment, and adequacy of advertising funds; and factor weights of 1.0 to hidden qualities, adequacy of market potential, and sufficient marketing expertise. In this example, the evaluator feels that two factors, generic demand trend and economic conditions, are three times more important for the evaluated brand than the three factors assigned a 1.0.

Calculating the Advertising Opportunity Score (AOS) An **Advertising Opportunity Score** may then be determined by multiplying each factor score by its factor weight, summing the products, and dividing by the sum of the factor weights. The AOS computed from the example is .77. By using the AOS scale in Exhibit 9.5, the advertising manager can then interpret the score. A score of .77 indicates a "very good" opportunity for advertising, and should encourage management to expect that advertising can make a significant contribution to the stimulation of brand demand.

To summarize, the Advertising Opportunity Score (AOS) is obtained as follows:

EXHIBIT 9.5

Interpreting the Advertising
Opportunity Score

ADVERTISING OPPORTUNITY SCORE (AOS)	INTERPRETATION OF ADVERTISING OPPORTUNITY	PERCENT OF SELLING TASK ASSIGNED TO ADVERTISING
.90–1.00	Extraordinary	75–100%
.80–.89	Excellent	
.70–.79	Very good	50–74
.60–.69	Good	
.50–.59	Average	25–49
.40–.49	Poor	
.30–.39	Very poor	10–24
.20–.29	Weak	
.10–.19	Extremely weak	0–9
.00–.09	Nonexistent	

1. Assign factor scores for all nine items. (Scores ranging from .00 to 1.0 should be assigned by using all available data and executive judgment.)
2. Assign factor weights. (Values should range between 1.0 and 5.0.)
3. Multiply factor scores by factor weights, obtaining nine products.
4. Total the nine products.
5. Total the factor weights.
6. Obtain AOS by dividing product total by factor weight total.
7. Interpret AOS using information in Exhibit 9.5.

MANAGEMENT GUIDELINES PROVIDED BY THE AOS

Although it is now generally accepted that communication, rather than sales, is the most legitimate short-term goal of most advertising, advertising management is concerned with the amount of the selling task that can be realistically assigned to advertising. Indeed, the basic purpose of the appraisal of the advertising opportunity concept is to help make that assessment. Therefore, general guidelines for applying the AOS to the amount of selling assigned to advertising are provided in Exhibit 9.5.

In addition to providing sales-task guidelines, the concept of appraising the advertising opportunity is of strategic importance to management because it is the first in a series of interdependent advertising management decisions.

As shown in Figure 9.8, the AOS is the main influence on the setting of advertising objectives. Budgeting for advertising can take place only after objectives have been set. In addition, decisions about creative strategy and tactics and media must be made within the constraints of the budget. The last step in the sequence, measuring advertising results, provides feedback on the degree of success and assists advertising manage-

FIGURE 9.8

How Appraisal Affects Advertising
Decisions

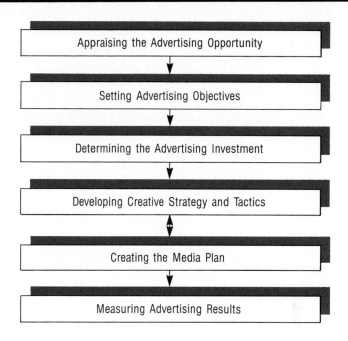

ment in reassessing the advertising opportunity for the next campaign
period.

HOW USEFUL IS ADVERTISING OPPORTUNITY APPRAISAL?

Early in this chapter, it was suggested that formal appraisal of the advertising opportunity does not currently enjoy wide use. However, most advertising managers do evaluate advertising's role within the promotion mix
by considering, instinctively and informally, the nine factors described in
this chapter. The purpose of this chapter has been to advocate the formal
use of this model because of its several advantages:

1. **It forces a management interaction.** The model works best when
   the factors are evaluated by everyone responsible for management of
   the advertising effort. This usually involves three to six people from
   the marketing and advertising departments and the advertising
   agency. The model provides a forum for discussing all of the factors
   related to the potential success of a brand.

2. **It encourages an objective look at the marketplace and the
   brand.** The intuition of experienced marketers is certainly one of the
   most valuable assets of a company; however, errors in judgment
   happen, and they are usually very costly. The structure of the
   model forces management to examine all of the relevant factors
   thoroughly and objectively, thus minimizing error.

3. **It has the greatest opportunity to affect advertising success.**
   Because the appraisal concept forms the foundation for all other

advertising decisions, it has the strongest strategic influence. No other aspect of an advertising campaign can overcome a wrong decision about advertising's role in the total promotion mix.

4. **It is a flexible management tool.** The model can be used for all products and in all industries. Like all management tools, the appraisal model is a guide to executive judgment, one that is relatively simple to understand and use, and which combines the best of objective data and executive opinion.

Summary

Appraisal of the advertising opportunity is an important step in advertising decision making. The procedure described in this chapter requires sound judgment on the part of the individual(s) determining the AOS and applying it to the guidelines. The value of the method lies in forcing decision makers to systematically consider the effects of nine major factors, which research has shown to have a direct bearing on whether or not an investment in advertising constitutes a profitable decision.

This structured procedure also provides useful strategic insights into the answers to several major questions facing a prospective advertiser. By systematically evaluating the advertising opportunity, establishing advertising objectives, and setting a budget in line with these objectives, the advertising management process can be made more rational and easier to defend to top management.

Finally, the advertising opportunity appraisal method does not simply issue a go/no-go decision on the use of advertising; it indicates the *extent* to which advertising should be used.

YOU MAKE THE DECISION

ALPHA CORPORATION

Alpha Corporation markets a line of high-quality consumer electronics products, including car and home stereo components, televisions, radios, VHS tape recorders, and portable telephones. Recently, they entered the compact disk market. The company's products are all marketed under their own brand name, "AlphaSound." Alpha has enjoyed financial success, largely due to consumer acceptance of the AlphaSound brand.

In planning the promotion program for Alpha's compact disk player, the company gathered information for determining the role of advertising. They evaluated the nine factors for appraising the advertising opportunity and determined factor scores and factor weights. Now they need your help.

Compute an Advertising Opportunity Score for Alpha's compact disk player, and make appropriate suggestions about the use of advertising, personal selling, sales promotion, and public relations.

Product: AlphaSound Compact Disk Player

FACTOR	FACTOR SCORE	FACTOR WEIGHT	PRODUCT (FS × FW)
PRODUCT FACTORS			
Presence of unique, relevant physical attributes	.2	3.0	
Existence of "hidden qualities"	.1	1.0	
Possibility of using powerful, emotional motives	.5	1.0	
MARKET FACTORS			
Favorable generic demand trend	.8	2.0	
Adequacy of market potential	.7	2.0	
Favorable competitive environment	.2	3.0	
Favorable economic conditions	.5	2.0	
COMPANY FACTORS			
Adequacy of advertising funds	.7	1.0	
Sufficient marketing expertise	.8	2.0	

■ ■ ■

QUESTIONS FOR DISCUSSION

1. Explain the meaning of the concept of appraisal of the advertising opportunity.

2. The chapter mentioned that the appraisal of the advertising opportunity concept is not widely used in industry, at least not in a formal sense. Why do you think it is not more widely used?

3. Why is it important to specify advertising's contribution to the stimulation of brand demand?

4. Explain the relationship between appraising the advertising opportunity and setting advertising objectives.

5. What factors explain the wide differences in the promotion mixes used by companies in the same industry (Avon and Revlon, for example)?

6. Which of the nine appraisal factors would seem to be most relevant to the marketing of raw materials (steel or aluminum, for example)? Which factors would seem to be the least relevant?

7. What are the main shortcomings of the weighted evaluation model for appraising the advertising opportunity?

8. What is the difference between factor scores and factor weights?

9. At least one researcher has suggested the addition of a tenth appraisal of the advertising opportunity factor—style merchandise. It was suggested that the opportunity to use advertising is greater for such products as clothing, cars, jewelry, and furniture. What do you think of this suggestion? Do these product categories seem to present a greater-than-normal advertising opportunity? If yes, is it because they represent "style merchandise"?

10. Determine the Advertising Opportunity Score for the following three brands:
    — IBM Personal Computer
    — Pittsburgh Pirates (major league baseball franchise)
    — Your college or university (assuming it is interested in attracting more undergraduate students).

NOTES

1. Thomas L. Berg, *Mismarketing: Case Histories of Marketing Misfires* (Garden City, N.Y.: Doubleday & Company, Inc., 1971), 5–7; *Management of New Products* (Chicago: Booz, Allen & Hamilton, 1968); Betty Cochran and G. Thompson, "Why New Products Fail," *National Industrial Conference Board Record*, October 1964; and David S. Hopkins and Earl L. Bailey, "New Product Pressures," *Conference Board Record*, June 1971.

2. Neil Borden, *The Economic Effects of Advertising* (Homewood, Ill.: Richard D. Irwin, Inc. 1942), xviii.

3. Nugent Wedding, *Advertising Management* (New York: The Ronald Press, 1962).

4. Roy Campbell, "When Should Products Be Advertised?" unpublished manuscript, Tempe, Arizona, 1971. Contact Charles H. Patti for additional information.

5. Charles H. Patti, "How to Appraise Chances for Increasing Machine Tool Advertising Effectiveness," *Industrial Marketing*, February 1974.

6. Charles H. Patti, "Evaluating the Role of Advertising," *Journal of Advertising*, Fall 1977.

7. Jaclyn Fierman, "How Gallo Crushes the Competition," *Fortune*, September 1, 1986, 24–31.

8. "Ninth Annual Top Brands Survey," *Marketing Communications*, June 1986, 56.

9. "100 Leading Advertisers' Ad Expenditures," *Business Marketing*, July 1986, 48.

SUGGESTED READINGS

Auer, E. "The Advertising/Marketing Union." *Journal of Advertising*, no. 2, 1974.

Abratt, Russell, and Brian I. C. van der Westhuizen. "A New Promotion Mix Appropriation Model." *International Journal of Advertising*, 4:3, 1985, 209–222.

Banks, Seymour. "Trends Affecting the Implementation of Advertising and Promotion." *Journal of Marketing*, January 1973, 19–28.

Bogart, Leo. *Strategy in Advertising*, 2d ed. Chicago: Crain Books, 1984.

Borden, Neil H. "The Concept of the Marketing Mix." *Journal of Advertising Research*, June 1964.

Bowman, Russ. "Making Peace with Advertising." *Marketing & Media Decisions*, November 1986.

Clayton, Alden G. *The Relationship between Advertising and Promotion: Some Observations, Speculations, and Hypotheses.* Cambridge, Mass.: Marketing Science Institute, 1975.

Dommermuth, William P. *Promotion: Analysis, Creativity, and Strategy.* Boston: Kent, 1984.

Dubinsky, A. J., T. E. Barry, and R. A. Kerin. "The Sales-Advertising Interface in Promotion Planning." *Journal of Advertising*, no. 3, 1981.

Jones, John Philip. *What's in a Name?: Advertising and the Concept of Brands.* Lexington, Mass.: Lexington Books, 1986.

Morrill, John E. "Industrial Advertising Pays Off." *Harvard Business Review*, March-April 1970.

Naber, James H. "The Sales Promotion Explosion." The James Webb Young Fund address series, Department of Advertising, University of Illinois, Urbana, Illinois, October 21, 1986.

Prentice, Robert M. "How to Split Your Marketing Funds between Advertising and Promotion." *Advertising Age*, January 10, 1977.

Quelch, John A., Cheri T. Marshall, and Dae R. Change. "Structural Determinants of Ratios of Promotion and Advertising to Sales." In *Research on Sales Promotion: Collected Papers*, ed., Katherine E. Joca. Cambridge, Mass.: Marketing Science Institute, July 1984.

Ray, Michael. "A Decision Sequence Analysis of Developments in Marketing Communications." *Journal of Marketing*, January 1973.

Smith, Robert E., and Robert F. Lusch. "How Advertising Can Position a Brand." *Journal of Advertising Research*, February 1976.

Smith, Robert E., and William R. Swinyard. "Attitude-Behavior Consistency: The Impact of Product Trial versus Advertising." *Journal of Marketing Research*, August 1983, 257–267.

Strang, Roger A. *The Relationship between Advertising and Promotion in Brand Strategy*. Cambridge, Mass.: Marketing Science Institute, 1975.

Sunoo, Don, and Lynn Y. S. Lin. "Sales Effects of Promotion and Advertising." *Journal of Advertising Research*, October 1978.

Swinyard, William R. "How Many Ad Exposures Is a Sales Call Worth?" *Journal of Advertising Research*, February 1979.

Wood, Wally. "Costing Out Marketing," *Marketing & Media Decisions*, August 1986.

C H A P T E R 10

SETTING ADVERTISING OBJECTIVES

Key Terms

direct objectives
indirect objectives
AIDA model
DAGMAR model
DAGMAR MOD II
learning hierarchy
low-involvement hierarchy
dissonance-attribution hierarchy

Learning Objectives

To analyze the importance of setting advertising objectives

To link advertising objectives with appraisal of the advertising opportunity

To describe the major types of advertising objectives

To define the criteria for "good" advertising objectives

Taking advantage of the latest technology in audio equipment, Oko, Inc., introduced its top-of-the-line compact disk player, The Oko, last year. The Oko features computerlike selectivity functions that enable it to be programmed to play up to 1,000 disks (or to omit their contents) in any set sequence. As many as 10 disks may be preloaded and played automatically, providing over 12 hours of continuous playing time.

Although The Oko retails at $500, discounters have been advertising it for as little as $375 during special promotional periods. In addition, a competitor has introduced a slightly lower-priced product with many of The Oko's features. While this product will challenge The Oko, the new entry is substantially lower in quality.

Oko has targeted two market segments. The primary target is employed men ages 18 to 35, with a household income of more than $25,000. This group includes both students and college grads in urban and suburban settings. The secondary market is working women ages 25 to 35 in urban or suburban settings. This group's household income totals $35,000 and up.

Although Oko has an excellent product and consumer interest in compact disk players is building, the firm realizes that the marketplace will become increasingly competitive. CD players are in the intro-ductory phase of the product life cycle, and as the product moves into the growth stage, more brands will enter the market. Also, the competition will increase advertising pressure as it fights for market share. Armed with this knowledge, Oko planned its advertising campaign. An advertising budget of $2,000,000 was established, and the firm set the following advertising objectives:

- "To increase sales by 10 percent"

- "To make a substantial contribution to our profits"

- "To create a favorable impression among the primary target market"

- "To increase brand recognition by 20 percent during the first six months of the campaign period"

Oko management realized that the next 12 to 18 months would be difficult for the firm. Yet, they were confident that the combination of a high-quality product, an excellent distribution system, and an adequate advertising budget would permit them to accomplish their advertising objectives.

INTRODUCTION

One of the most bewildering advertising management tasks is the setting of advertising objectives. For some reason, it seems easier to create a magazine advertisement or select advertising media than it is to specify precisely what advertising is expected to accomplish. Despite the millions of dollars invested in advertising each year, far too many companies manage their advertising programs with inappropriate or nonexistent advertising objectives. The setting of advertising objectives is the foundation upon which all other advertising decisions are made. As Chapter 9 pointed out, advertising objectives flow out of the appraisal of the advertising oppportunity and they have an immediate impact on the advertising investment, the creative elements in advertising, and the selection of advertising media. Therefore, the inability to articulate advertising objectives will eventually lead to:

- Investing too much or too little in advertising

- Misdirecting the creative effort

- Developing an inefficient media plan

- Measuring advertising campaign success against the wrong criteria

Well-managed organizations invest money in advertising because they expect the investment to make a contribution to financial goals. Some companies expect an immediate, or at least a short-term, return. Others see advertising as an investment that will yield results over a longer time frame. In this sense, advertising objectives are very much related to the goals of the company and, more directly, to marketing goals. Consider, for example, the direct response advertising of Doubleday Book Club. While we don't know Doubleday's exact marketing objective, we can probably assume that it involves increased sales. Advertising can help achieve this marketing objective by encouraging the target market to join the company's book club. The advertisement in Figure 10.1 illustrates Doubleday's expectations of advertising—to generate a measurable response (sales) by mail almost immediately after exposure to the advertising message. On the other hand, the advertising message in Figure 10.2 was not created to generate immediate sales. Rather, DuPont's motive in this ad was to inform the public and to create a favorable impression of the firm. This doesn't mean that DuPont does not see a relationship between its advertising and the company's marketing goals. Instead, the company is viewing the expected results of advertising in a longer time frame.

THE IMPORTANCE OF SETTING ADVERTISING OBJECTIVES

Setting advertising objectives can be deceptive. On one level, the task seems as simple as deciding what the advertising campaign should accomplish. However, this decision is often complex. Figure 10.3 helps explain the major influences on advertising objectives by illustrating the origin of

FIGURE 10.1

How a Firm Uses Advertising
to Achieve Immediate
Marketing Objectives

Source: Courtesy of Doubleday & Company, Inc.

advertising objectives and the relationship of company goals, marketing objectives, and situation analysis to advertising objectives.

There are three major reasons for setting advertising objectives:

1. **Advertising objectives are an expression of management consensus.** Advertising campaigns are rarely successful if there is disagreement among key management personnel about the goals of the campaign. A conflict is inevitable, for example, if the marketing manager believes that the purpose of the advertising campaign is to increase distribution and the advertising manager believes that the primary purpose of the campaign is to alter consumer attitudes about

FIGURE 10.2

How a Firm Uses Advertising to
Achieve Long-Term Marketing
Objectives

PATENT #4,584,240
IS THE ONE FISH STORY YOU
HAVEN'T HEARD BEFORE.

On August 1, 1985, DuPont came up with a fish
story that's so unbelievable we patented it. Patent #4,584,240 is
Prime,® the first and only cofilament fishing line. The inner
polyester filament is for low stretch. The outer nylon filament is
for flexibility.

The result? A level of sensitivity, hooksetting speed
and power that no other line can match.

Although DuPont has shown the way in nylon
fishing line from the beginning, it isn't our only sports interest.
DuPont products have brought new standards of performance to
tennis, skiing, boating, hunting, swimming, golfing and bowling.

You see, we've earned more than 80,000 patents in
the last 50 years. Some save lives, travel into space or help crops
grow. Others, like Patent #4,584,240, have a different role. They
just make your life a little more enjoyable.

BETTER THINGS FOR BETTER LIVING.

Source: Courtesy of DuPont.

the brand. A written set of advertising objectives approved by all
key management personnel minimizes conflict and helps ensure a
coordinated company effort toward a common goal.

2. **Advertising objectives help guide the budgeting, creative, and
   media phases of the advertising campaign.** As Chapter 11
   explains, the size of the advertising investment is influenced by a
   number of factors; however, the most important is the task that
   advertising is expected to accomplish. Determining the size of the
   advertising investment is always difficult. However, the task is
   simplified by knowing exactly what needs to be done, to what target
   market, and within what time frame.

FIGURE 10.3

Company Influences on Setting
Advertising Objectives

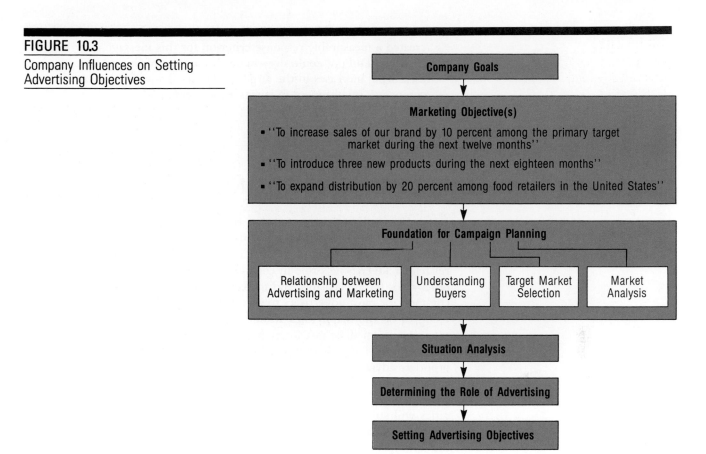

Company Goals

Marketing Objective(s)

- ''To increase sales of our brand by 10 percent among the primary target market during the next twelve months''
- ''To introduce three new products during the next eighteen months''
- ''To expand distribution by 20 percent among food retailers in the United States''

Foundation for Campaign Planning

| Relationship between Advertising and Marketing | Understanding Buyers | Target Market Selection | Market Analysis |

Situation Analysis

Determining the Role of Advertising

Setting Advertising Objectives

Direction for the creative portions of an advertising campaign also lies within the advertising objectives. A good set of advertising objectives will specify the desired position of the brand, the magnitude of the communication task, and the target audience(s).

The role of the media portion of an advertising campaign is to deliver the message to the target audience(s) efficiently and with the appropriate levels of frequency. Again, advertising objectives help media planners by detailing what audience(s) needs to be reached and by suggesting the most desirable media environments.

3. **Advertising objectives provide management with the standards against which results can be measured.** One of the major reasons that companies don't often know if a given advertising campaign has been successful is that criteria for success were not specified. The most valid measures of the effectiveness of an advertising campaign are those that correspond directly to the criterion variable (sales, profits, awareness, knowledge, etc.) of the advertising objectives. The measurement of advertising effectiveness is straightforward when the objective is clearly articulated. For example, the success or failure of the Doubleday Book Club advertisement in Figure 10.1 should be measured in terms of the number and profitability of the responses it generates. The specific objective of the DuPont

advertisement in Figure 10.2 is less clear; yet, it is possible to have created a measurable response criterion for this message also. For example, DuPont could determine the success of this ad by measuring increases in the target audience's knowledge about the company's involvement in sports equipment.

RELATIONSHIP OF ADVERTISING OBJECTIVES TO APPRAISAL OF THE ADVERTISING OPPORTUNITY

In Chapter 9, it was suggested that the most direct influence on advertising objectives is a determination of the role that advertising can play for a particular brand. Also, the Advertising Opportunity Score (AOS) was related to advertising's role in contributing to sales. There are, of course, other roles for advertising, and in recent years it has become increasingly common for most advertisers to recognize that the opportunity for advertising to be the major sales stimulant is not always high and that more modest, intermediate goals may be more realistic.[1]

Exhibit 10.1 demonstrates the relationship between the AOS and appropriate advertising goals. Notice that as the advertising opportunity becomes stronger, the suggested goals for advertising move closer to the "sales" end of the continuum. Companies with low advertising opportunities will still be able to use advertising successfully; however, advertising will play a reduced role in stimulating sales. In low AOS situations, the appropriate goals for advertising are creating awareness among the target market.

The advertisements in Figure 10.4 depict three different levels of advertising objectives. In the Centrum advertisement, the message intends to generate an immediate response. The message in the Cover Girl NailSlicks ad, however, is designed simply to convince the reader of an important point. Note that there is no specific encouragement to purchase. In the G.H. Bass advertisement, the company reinforces its image as a long-time producer of quality shoes.

EXHIBIT 10.1

The Relationship between the Advertising Opportunity Score (AOS) and Advertising Objectives

ADVERTISING OPPORTUNITY SCORE (AOS)	ADVERTISING OBJECTIVE
Extraordinary — Good	To encourage sales response from target markets
	To promote expanded use of company's brands
Average — Poor	To demonstrate a brand's want-satisfying qualities
	To generate sales leads
	To encourage target markets to request brand information
Very Poor — Extremely Weak	To communicate a favorable image throughout the distribution system
	To remind target markets of the brand's existence
	To inform target markets of company philosophies, policies, etc.

FIGURE 10.4

Communicating Different Levels of Advertising Objectives

This ad for G. H. Bass shoes reminds readers of the manufacturer's reputation for producing great shoes. It doesn't specifically urge a purchase.

Source: Courtesy of G. H. Bass.

This message for Centrum is designed to produce an immediate response.

Source: Reprinted courtesy of the American Cyanamid Company. Centrum® is a registered trademark of Cyanamid.

This Cover Girl NailSlicks ad conveys a major product attribute but does not overtly suggest purchasing the product.

Source: Courtesy of the Noxell Corporation.

TYPES OF ADVERTISING OBJECTIVES

So far, this chapter has focused on advertising objectives in terms of their intended results—to cause a specific action, to let the target market know of some important product attribute, or to reinforce or change a company or brand image. This "results-oriented" approach suggests two general types of advertising objectives—those designed to have a direct, short-term effect on the audience and those whose effects are intended to be indirect and longer term. **Direct objectives** seek an overt behavior response from the audience. Calling a toll-free number, mailing an order card, visiting a showroom, or actually purchasing a product are all examples of direct, short-term advertising objectives. **Indirect objectives** are aimed at communication tasks that must be accomplished before the ultimate, overt behavior response can be achieved.

DIRECT OBJECTIVES

Direct objectives are used when (1) the AOS is high, thus indicating a strong opportunity for advertising to make a substantial contribution to brand demand and/or (2) the nature of the advertiser's business demands that advertising be used to accomplish a specific, action-forcing activity. The Doubleday Book Club advertisment is a good example of direct objectives. Doubleday's future as a profit-oriented firm depends on persuading people to join the book club. The only method of joining the club is through advertising; therefore, advertising becomes the main selling tool.

Chapter 9 discussed the relationship of advertising to sales goals and showed that high AOS scores lead to high, direct-response expectations for advertising. The other situations in which advertising can be expected to fulfill a direct, short-term objective include retail, direct-response, sales promotion, and some business-to-business advertising situations.

Retail Advertising The primary purpose of most retail advertising is to attract prospective buyers into the store to purchase merchandise. The reason that over half the advertising revenue of most daily newspapers is derived from retailers is that newspapers provide the sense of immediacy and urgency that is conducive to short-term sales activity.[2] Figure 10.5 includes examples of two typical retail ads. Department stores and grocery stores purchase more than 30 percent of all retail newspaper advertising.[3]

Direct Response Advertising By definition, the objective of direct response advertising is to encourage an audience to take overt action. The direct response industry has been growing rapidly in recent years, and in 1985 mail-order consumer sales amounted to $58.65 billion.[4] It is difficult to estimate the total amount of goods and services sold through all forms of direct response because there are so many different forms of direct response advertising. However, the Direct Marketing Association has estimated that the total goods and services sold in the United States as a result of direct marketing is well over $150 billion per year.[5] Direct response advertisers have determined that the single most important method of selling is advertising. For example, Land's End mails its four-color catalogs of clothing and canvas goods to prospective buyers for one primary reason—to sell merchandise. If you want to purchase goods from Land's End, you must order it through the catalog and/or its toll-free telephone number. Note from Figure 10.6, that, while Land's End uses both direct mail and print advertising, the primary objective in both media is to generate an immediate response.

Sales Promotion Advertising Sales promotion advertising, like other forms of sales promotion, is designed to stimulate consumer or trade activity within a short time frame. In the Babe ad in Figure 10.7, the objective is to induce readers to enter the Babe 10th Anniversary Sweepstakes. This ad is directed at the product's primary target market and the objective is to generate near-term interest and involvement in the product.

Business-to-Business Advertising The objectives of business-to-business advertising can range from generating knowledge to affecting buyer attitudes to stimulating direct sales. Most often, business-to-business advertising is used as a support communication tool and the largest portion of the sales-generating task is assigned to personal selling. In its support role, business-to-business advertising often is called upon to produce an immediate response—usually generating leads for the personal sales force. The business advertisement in Figure 10.8 is designed to produce an immediate, direct response.

FIGURE 10.5

A Retail Advertising Objective: To Attract Purchasers

DELICIOUS
24.99

Reg. 34.00. Think peach,
banana, oyster,
aqua, red, sunshine,
blue, white.
Mouth-watering colors
in a famous-name
sweater. Short-sleeved,
boat-neck, with
seam-out detailing.
Acrylic/cotton,
S-M-L. Till April 4 in
Sportswear (d. 369),
fourth, State;
Gateway, suburbs. Call
1-800-CARSONS
or write Box AA 60690.

Source: Courtesy of Carson Pirie Scott.

Source: Courtesy of Cub Foods, Stillwater, MN.

INDIRECT OBJECTIVES

Almost all national advertising is created to contribute to brand demand, but the objective during any one campaign period is usually to accomplish one or more of the intermediate communication tasks.

In the ad in Figure 10.9, Sure deodorant is said to have useful attributes (deodorant protection and dryness). The message also attempts to convince readers that the attributes are important. Note, however, that there is no call for specific action.

Some retail advertising is also created to achieve indirect objectives. Occasionally, a retailer uses advertising to create goodwill, a good way to encourage long-term sales prospects. For example, when the Denver

FIGURE 10.6

Direct Response Advertising:
Designed to Attract Sales

To the world's shortest, strongest guarantee...

GUARANTEED. PERIOD.

Lands' End adds this short, sweet promise:

WE DELIVER!

Except for the exclamation point, the last two words are not dramatic. But what we at Lands' End mean when we say "We deliver" is setting new standards in customer service.

Consider...

A lady of our acquaintance ordered some towels from a prominent Chicago department store. She wanted them monogrammed, but other than that, it was a straightforward order.

They arrived the other day—five months after she had ordered them. With no apology. Nor did she demand one. Somehow, customers forgive retailers for delivery delays that would put us out of business in about a week.

By contrast, here in Dodgeville, when we receive an order, and the item is in stock, (which it is, the vast majority of the time), it's on its way to you in 24 hours. If the item requires monogramming or hemming,

you can add another day.

We don't know of anybody else in the mail-order business who gets orders out that fast.

In other words, at Lands' End when we say WE DELIVER!, we say it with an exclamation point for emphasis.

And now, we also say "absolutely, positively."

Yes, in our constant fight to improve customer service, we now also offer you the option of Federal Express Priority service. This absolutely, positively gets your order to you with 2 business days of the time we ship it. This new service carries an additional charge of $16.00—but when you need something at the last minute, money isn't everything.

We also offer Federal Express Standard Air shipment, which gets your order to you within 3 or 4 business days.

You'll find the full spell-out on our many delivery options in your Lands' End catalog. Or we'll be glad to explain further when you call us for a catalog—our toll-free number is 800-356-4444.

One more time, to make it crystal clear...

As we keep telling you, GUARANTEED. PERIOD. applies to every item we offer you in our catalogs. Our unconditional guarantee against anything, for the life of the item, without ifs, ands, buts or maybes.

And now we go a step beyond this emphatic guarantee of quality, with a promise of service unmatched in the mail-order business: WE DELIVER!

We invite you to put us to the test.

LANDS' END
DIRECT MERCHANTS

Please send free catalog.
Lands' End   Dept. V-52
Dodgeville, WI 53595

Name _____

Address _____

City _____

State _____ Zip _____

Or call Toll-free:
800-356-4444

Source: © Lands' End, Inc. Reprinted with permission.

Broncos won the American Football Conference championship in 1986 and advanced to the Super Bowl, the May D&F department-store chain placed this newspaper ad in Denver-area papers to publicly thank the team for an exceptional season (see Figure 10.10).

The Armco advertisement in Figure 10.11 makes no reference to specific products or services and contains no call to immediate action. Rather, its objective is to affect readers' attitudes about the company in a favorable way in the hope that when the opportunity arises, they will specify or recommend Armco as a supplier.

It is not always easy to classify an advertisement's objectives as either direct or indirect. Much advertising has multiple objectives. For example,

DIRECT RESPONSE ADVERTISIING

An important and rapidly growing component of direct marketing is direct response advertising. Direct response consists of several media, the two most important being telephone and direct mail. The following figures reflect advertising expenditures for direct response in the mid-1980s.

MEDIUM	EXPENDITURE (in millions of dollars)
Telephone	$13,608.3
Direct mail	12,692.2
Newspaper	2,850.0
Television	386.5
Magazines	188.7
Coupons	148.1
Newspapers	80.5
Business magazines	73.9
Radio	37.0
Total	$30,065.2

Source: Craig Campbell, "The Scope of Direct Marketing," in *1985 Fact Book on Direct Marketing* (New York: Direct Marketing Association, 1985), 38.

one objective of the Babe advertisement in Figure 10.7 is to generate sweepstakes entries. However, a less obvious, but important, objective is to create a closer association between the brand and the interests of the target market. Note the selection of the models, their clothing, and the tie-in with the fashionable Hard Rock Cafe. Usually, sales and/or profitability are expected outcomes of direct objectives. However, all companies are not interested in sales or profits. For example, not-for-profit organizations have increasingly used advertising during the past ten years, and these organizations do not measure success in terms of monetary gain. Nevertheless, they are often interested in the direct, short-term results of advertising. The appropriate direct advertising objective for such organizations include increases in visits (a museum, for example), enrollment (a university or health care plan), membership or attendance (a church), or votes (a political candidate or cause).

Classifying objectives as either direct or indirect is most helpful as a way to specify advertising's primary purpose. While advertisers use a variety of approaches to reach their goals (comparative advertising, testimonials, humor, etc.), a particular approach is used because it is thought to be the most effective way to achieve the objective.

CREATING "GOOD" ADVERTISING OBJECTIVES

Throughout this chapter, a hierarchical, or stair-step, approach to setting advertising objectives has been suggested. A company's long-range objective might be to increase sales or profitability, but its immediate objective for advertising is to accomplish one or more of the intermediate steps leading to brand demand stimulation. This "staircase of influence" orientation

FIGURE 10.7

This example of sales promotion advertising intends to elicit the immediate response of readers' entering Babe's 10th Anniversary Sweepstakes.

began with the simple **AIDA** (*a*ttention-*i*nterest-*d*esire-*a*ction) **model** developed in the 1920s by E. K. Strong.[6] The concept theorizes the stages before a buyer purchases a product or service. The AIDA model was refined by R. Lavidge and G. A. Steiner and others.[7] In 1961, Russell Colley operationalized the concept for advertisers in his widely known book, *Defining Advertising Goals for Measured Advertising Results*.[8] The Colley book is important because it explains the importance of the **DAGMAR model**—expressing advertising objectives in terms of communication tasks and of specifying the desired response from advertising.

FIGURE 10.8
FIGURE 10.8

Business-to-Business Ad Designed
to Produce an Immediate Response

Source: Courtesy of Douglas Turner Advertising Inc., Newark, NJ.

The hierarchy of advertising influence is intuitive—that is, to affect behavior (to generate a sale, for example), an advertiser must first implant relevant brand information, persuade the target market that the brand is worthy of purchase consideration, and then finally the desired overt behavior will take place. While this orderly approach is appealing, studies in social psychology and communications have raised several questions about the validity of the approach.[9] The most important of these questions are as follows:

1. Is the order of the steps applicable to all product categories? Does the purchase process of all products and services involve the knowledge→attitude→ action sequence?

2. Can steps in the sequence be skipped? Is it possible to generate the action component without prior conditioning of attitudes?

Both of these questions have encouraged researchers to challenge the validity of the AIDA concept, and in recent years the results of that research have helped advertisers better understand the purchase process and the role that advertising plays.[10] In pointing out the limitations of AIDA, other studies have redirected current thinking about the factors affecting

A CLOSER LOOK

PROMOTION EXPENDITURES OF BUSINESS-TO-BUSINESS ADVERTISERS

The amount a company budgets for advertising is somewhat determined by the role the company expects advertising to play. Usually, advertising plays a relatively minor role in the stimulation of demand for business-to-business goods and services; therefore, advertising receives a small proportion of the company's resources.

Until recently, little data were available on the promotion expenditures of various companies. The following table indicates the extent to which business-to-business marketers rely on advertising as well as other promotion tools to carry out communication objectives.

Promotion Expenditures (as percentage of sales)

INDUSTRY	PROMOTION TOOL							
	PRINT ADVERTISING	EXHIBITS AND TRADE SHOWS	CATALOGS AND DIRECTORIES	LITERATURE, DEALS, COUPONS, POINT-OF-PURCHASE	DIRECT MAIL	DEALER AND DISTRIBUTOR ASSISTANCE	PUBLIC RELATIONS AND PUBLICITY	TOTAL
Furniture and fixtures	0.4%	0.3%	0.3%	0.2%	0.1%	0.1%	0.1%	1.5%
Chemicals and allied products	0.6	0.2	0.2	0.2	0.2	0.4	0.04	1.84
Fabricated metal products	0.4	0.3	0.1	0.1	0.1	0.1	0.03	1.13
Machinery, except electrical	0.7	0.4	0.2	0.1	0.1	0.1	0.1	1.7
Electronic computing equipment (computer hardware)	1.1	0.9	0.04	0.2	0.1	0.1	0.5	2.94
Electrical and electronic equipment	0.8	0.3	0.4	0.1	0.1	0.1	0.1	1.9
Transportation equipment	0.3	0.3	0.2	0.1	0.1	0.1	0.1	1.2
Instruments and related products	1.1	0.6	0.3	0.3	0.2	0.2	0.1	2.8

Source: "Marketing Communications Costs Average 1.7% of Sales among Major Industrial Companies." Laboratory of Advertising Performance Report #8015.6, McGraw-Hill Publications Company, New York, 1986.

advertising objective setting. For example, Robert Smith and William Swinyard suggest the inclusion of situation-specific environment as an important variable in identifying the order through which buyers move through the AIDA framework.[11] Sandra Moriarity proposes a message-situation orientation, in which the tasks of advertising are defined within the concepts of perception, education, and persuasion.[12] David Aaker and John Myers suggest DAGMAR MOD II, an updated version of DAGMAR. **DAGMAR MOD II** emphasizes two steps: (1) identifying the sequence of decision-making steps that are applicable to each buying situation, and (2) focusing on understanding the link between such variables as image or attitude and marketplace behavior.[13]

Today, the process of creating a set of advertising objectives involves the advertising manager in the following tasks:

1. Determining which hierarchy is relevant in the purchase process for the product/service advertised

FIGURE 10.9
Communicating with
Indirect Objectives

FIGURE 10.10
A Retail Ad That
Generates Goodwill

BRONCOS!
THROUGHOUT THE 1986 SEASON YOU GAVE US:
PRIDE
EXCITEMENT
GLORY
MANIA
ANTICIPATION
ENERGY
SPIRIT
DETERMINATION
COMRADERY
TO THE 1986 AFC CHAMPIONS
THANKS FOR A GREAT YEAR!
MAY D&F

Source: Courtesy of The Procter & Gamble Company.

2. Evaluating the role advertising can be realistically expected to play in
    moving prospects through the applicable hierarchy
3. Developing a set of objectives that gives adequate direction and
    guidance for the balance of the advertising effort.

THREE ALTERNATIVE HIERARCHIES

We now know that the buying process implicit in the DAGMAR model
(knowledge→attitude→action) is not valid for all marketing situations. Research has also confirmed the existence of two other hierarchies. The three
most recognized hierarchies are as follows:

1. Learning hierarchy (DAGMAR model): Learn→Feel→Do
2. Low-involvement hierarchy: Learn→Do→Feel
3. Dissonance-attribution hierarchy: Do→Feel→Learn

The **low-involvement hierarchy** is most often associated with Herbert
Krugman and his studies on the effects of mass media. Essentially, this

FIGURE 10.11

Image Advertising: Creating a Favorable Impression

Because of Armco's expansion, they'll have more opportunities in Gainesville, Texas.

The 1975 Gainesville High graduating class numbers 185. And the investment of some of our profits in a 50 percent expansion of Armco's plant there can make a big difference to them: Job openings in the expanded plant; other employment that comes into being through its impact on local business; increased community income and buying power; a larger facility that generates more tax revenue for many purposes, including school funds for classes of the future.

Yet this major plant expansion is important far beyond Gainesville, Texas. Because this Armco facility is devoted to production of equipment used in drilling oil and gas wells. Equipment that will help us add to our energy supplies.

Jobs, buying power, tax income, more available energy. Some of the things that a few cents more profit per sales dollar make possible in our free enterprise system.

Just write us if you'd like a copy of our 1974 Annual Report. Armco Steel Corporation, General Offices, Middletown, Ohio 45043.

Responsive people in action.

Source: Courtesy of Armco.

hierarchy suggests that for some products media advertising's impact is on cognitive variables (brand recognition, recall, beliefs, etc.) that directly affect brand choice with little or no effect on, or influence from, the attitudinal component.[14]

In the **dissonance-attribution hierarchy,** the suggested sequence of purchase process is action→attitude affect→cognition. The idea is that there are some buying situations in which a buyer—after purchase has been made (Do)—experiences uncomfortable feelings (Feel) because some unchosen alternatives were better in some respects. This leads to a search for additional information (Learn) or a revision of information already in the buyer's memory in order to reduce the mental discomfort. For example, while the purchase of a new car would follow the learning hierarchy (Learn→Feel→Do), the dissonance-attribution hierachy explains much of the postpurchase behavior.[15]

Exhibit 10.2 summarizes these three hierarchies and describes the situations under which each is most likely to occur. This table is useful in

EXHIBIT 10.2

Comparing the Three Hierarchy of Effects Models

HIERARCHY	THEORETICAL SEQUENCE	CHARACTERISTICS	ADVERTISING OBJECTIVES	PRODUCT EXAMPLES
Learning hierarchy	Learn ↓ Feel ↓ Do	—clear product differentiation —greater perceived psychological and/or physical risk	—promote high awareness —encourage conviction of brand superiority —motivate action	—autos —fashion clothing —personal care items
Low-involvement hierarchy	Learn ↓ Do ↓ Feel	—lower perceived psychological and/or physical risk. —unclear product differentiation	—promote awareness understanding —encourage trial —stimulate interest	—household cleaning products —impulse good
Dissonance-attribution hierarchy	Do ↓ Feel ↓ Learn	—high psychological and physical risk —low product differentiation	—encourage purchase —build conviction —stimulate awareness	—autos —major appliances

EXHIBIT 10.3

Three Learning Models: A Summary

STAGE	MODEL		
	AIDA MODEL	HIERARCHY OF EFFECTS MODEL	INNOVATION ADOPTION MODEL
Cognitive stage (knowledge)	Attention	Awareness ↓ Knowledge	Awareness
Affective stage (feelings and emotions)	Interest ↓ Desire	Liking ↓ Preference	Interest ↓ Evaluation
Action stage (response)	Action	Conviction ↓ Purchase	Trial ↓ Adoption

Sources: E. K. Strong, *The Psychology of Selling* (New York: McGraw-Hill, 1925), 9; Robert J. Lavidge and Gary A. Steiner, "A Model for Predictive Measurements of Advertising Effectiveness," *Journal of Marketing,* October 1961, 61; and Everett M. Rogers, *Diffusion of Innovations* (New York: The Free Press, 1962), 79–86.

A GLOBAL LOOK

PEPPERONI IN PARIS?

It's difficult enough to set advertising objectives for one campaign, but Domino's Pizza, the king of the home-delivery business in the United States, faces a real challenge as it tries to reach 10,000 stores worldwide by 1990.

In 1985, Domino's added stores in Europe and Asia, creating a four-continent, $1.1 billion pizza empire. Domino's has nearly 3,000 stores throughout the world, including 24 in Canada, 16 in Australia, 3 in the United Kingdom, 2 in West Germany, and 1 in Japan. The company has sustained a 40+ percent growth rate every year since 1978, and Thomas Monaghan—founder, president, and chairman of Domino's—sees huge potential in overseas markets: "There's at least double the potential for us overseas as there is in this country. But in the startup you don't get much results for the effort you put in."

International stores sales are about half the $10,000 weekly average of U.S. units. All international stores are franchised, typically with one franchisee holding the rights to the country. In the United States, one-third of the stores are operated by the company. Advertising is funded by the international units paying 3 percent of sales to a corporate-controlled advertising fund, which directs the money into individual markets. Also, international franchises invest another 3 to 4 percent of sales on local advertising.

Domino's advertising objective? Selling the idea of home delivery in areas where there is no such tradition. To help accomplish the objective, Domino's will use separate advertising agencies in each country.

In 1986, Domino's celebrated its 25th anniversary. More than 85 percent of the company's worldwide sales of well over $1 billion come from pizza delivery.

Source: Raymond Serafin, "Domino's Pizza Finds Global Going Slow," *Advertising Age*, January 6, 1986, 12.

helping you determine which hierarchy is in operation for most product categories.

OBJECTIVES FOR DIRECTION AND GUIDANCE

After the proper buying process hierarchy has been identified and advertising's role has been determined, the advertising manager needs to develop objectives that will direct the remaining parts of the advertising campaign and provide a standard against which success can be measured. To do this, objectives must meet the following criteria:

1. Advertising objectives must be communication-oriented.

    Although there are situations in which advertising can be expected to be the major contributor to increased sales and/or profitability, advertising is only one element in the promotion mix. Most often, it is not the main sales stimulant. Therefore, for many brands, the appropriate task for advertising is the fulfillment of one or more of the intermediate communication tasks associated with the purchase process.

2. Advertising objectives must be quantifiable.

    It will be impossible to evaluate a campaign's effectiveness if the advertising objectives are not stated in quantifiable, measurable terms. Such vague objectives as "to enhance the company image" or "to make a substantial contribution to company profits" do not allow management to determine success or failure because stated levels of achievement are not measurable.

3.   Advertising objectives must be specific in terms.

Because advertising objectives provide guidance for other parts of the advertising campaign, each element of an objective needs to be specified. These elements include the communication task, the target market(s), and the time period in which the objectives are to be accomplished.

Now, if you return to the four objectives stated in the opening of this chapter, it's quite easy to see why none of them qualifies as "good" advertising objectives.

SUMMARY

Advertising objectives are a critical part of an advertising campaign, yet most companies have great difficulty in establishing objectives that give management direction and guidance. This chapter provided a series of guidelines about setting advertising objectives, the second step in the series of advertising management decisions.

There are two basic types of advertising objectives, direct objectives and indirect objectives. Direct objectives are used when the advertiser is interested in generating a specific, short-term response (sales, inquiries, location visits, votes, etc.). Indirect objectives are used when the advertiser needs to communicate information or alter attitudes before the action stage.

Companies that are primarily interested in direct, short-term results of advertising are not necessarily uninterested in longer-term communication effects. Direct response advertisers recognize the importance of goodwill and a strong, positive image; however, they choose to use marketing communication elements other than advertising to accomplish this task.

While the AIDA model is not without weaknesses, it has provided a useful framework from which to begin the objective setting process. DAGMAR MOD II and the other related research cited in the chapter are intended to help advertising managers think more analytically about the buying process and the role advertising should be expected to play within that process.

Finally, the best advertising objectives are those that are directly tied to an assessment of the advertising opportunity, are based on the knowledge of the right communication hierarchy, and meet all three criteria for "good" advertising objectives: communication-oriented, quantifiable, and specific in terms.

YOU MAKE THE DECISION

DETERMINING ADVERTISING OBJECTIVES

Below is a series of statements related to the marketing of a variety of products and services. Which of them meet the criteria for "good" advertising objectives? Defend your answers.

1.   To increase sales by 20 percent next year

2.   To build awareness of our brand's new flexible packaging among 18- to 35-year-old women

3. To increase belief by 20 percent among 25- to 34-year-old males living in California, Oregon, and Washington that our brand is the lowest-priced brand in the category

4. To generate 1,500 sales leads during the first six months of the next campaign period

5. To double the profitability of our brand during the next three-year period

6. To increase interest in brand trial by 10 percent among the target market next year

7. To increase brand preference by 15 percent

8. To expand distribution by opening 45 new retail accounts in the Southwest over the next nine months

9. To sell 3,000 units of our brand through a direct response advertising campaign on late night television

10. To improve the corporate image through sponsorship of a major PGA (Professional Golfers' Association) tournament

■ ■ ■

QUESTIONS FOR DISCUSSION

1. What are the main reasons for setting advertising objectives?

2. Explain the differences between marketing objectives and advertising objectives. Give an example of each.

3. Why do companies have such a difficult time setting advertising objectives?

4. List and explain the three criteria for setting "good" advertising objectives.

5. If the reason for investment in advertising is to contribute to the profitability of the company, why shouldn't advertising objectives be stated in terms of increases in sales or market share?

6. What is the relationship between the appraisal of the advertising opportunity and the setting of advertising objectives?

7. Explain the difference between direct objectives and indirect objectives. Give an example of each.

8. What products are most likely to fit within the low-involvement hierarchy? Which are most likely to fit within the dissonance-attribution hierarchy?

9. Brand A is a new entry in a crowded marketplace. The brand will be marketed by a company that feels that the brand's purchase will most closely follow the learning hierarchy. Create an advertising objective for brand A.

10. What are the major shortcomings of the AIDA model in terms of its application for setting advertising objectives?

NOTES

1. Russell H. Colley, *Defining Advertising Goals for Measured Advertising Results*. (New York: Association of National Advertisers, Inc., 1961).

2. "Retail Newspaper Advertising Expenditures by Category," *Newspaper Advertising Bureau*, New York, December 5, 1985; and *'85 Facts about Newspapers* (Washington, D.C.: American Newspaper Publishers' Association, 1985.

3. "Retail Newspaper Advertising Expenditures by Category," *Newspaper Advertising Bureau*, New York, December 5, 1985.

4. Arnold Fishman, *Guide to Mail Order Sales, 1985*, Mail Order Marketing Library Series, vol. 1 (Chicago: Marketing Logistics, Inc., 1986), 8.

5. Direct Marketing Association, New York, April 1987.

6. E. K. Strong, *The Psychology of Selling* (New York: McGraw-Hill Book Company, 1925), 25.

7. R. Lavidge and G. A. Steiner, "A Model for Predictive Measurement of Advertising Effectiveness," *Journal of Marketing*, vol. 25, October 1961. Also see *Sense and Nonsense in Creative Research: A Guide to Terms and Techniques* (New York: Gray Advertising, Inc., 1962); and Everett M. Rogers, *Diffusion of Innovations* (New York: The Free Press, 1962).

8. Russell H. Colley, *Defining Advertising Goals for Measured Advertising Results* (New York: Association of National Advertisers, Inc., 1961); and Colley, "Squeezing the Waste out of Advertising," *Harvard Business Review*, September–October 1962.

9. See, for example, D. J. Bem, "Self Perception Theory," in *Advances in Experimental Social Psychology*, vol. 6, ed. L. Berkowitz (New York: Academic Press, 1971); H. E. Krugman, "The Impact of Television Advertising: Learning without Involvement," *Public Opinion Quarterly*, vol. 29, Fall 1965; and Kristian S. Palda, "The Hypothesis of a Hierarchy of Effects: A Partial Evaluation," *Journal of Marketing Research*, February 1966.

10. Harper W. Boyd, Jr., Michael L. Ray, and Edward C. Strong, "An Attitudinal Framework for Advertising Strategy," *Journal of Marketing*, April 1972, 27–33; and Palda, "Hierarchy of Effects," 13–24.

11. Robert E. Smith and William R. Swinyard, "Information Response Models: An Integrated Approach," *Journal of Marketing*, Winter 1982, 81–93.

12. Sandra Ernst Moriarity, "Beyond the Hierarchy of Effects: A Conceptual Framework," in *Current Issues & Research in Advertising*, 1983, 45–55.

13. David A. Aaker and John G. Myers, *Advertising Management*, 2d ed. (Englewood Cliffs, N.J.: Prentice-Hall, Inc., 1982, 122–123).

14. Herbert E. Krugman, "The Impact of Television Advertising: Learning without Involvement," *Public Opinion Quarterly*, vol. 29, Fall 1965.

15. Elliott Arronson, "The Theory of Cognitive Dissonance," in *Advances in Experimental Social Psychology*, ed. L. Berkowitz (New York: Academic Press, 1969), and Bem, Daryl J., "Self Perception Theory," in Leonard Berkowitz, ed., *Advances in Experimental Social Psychology*, vol. 6 (New York: Academic Press, 1972), 1–62.

SUGGESTED READINGS

Anderson, R. L., and T. E. Barry. *Advertising Management: Text and Cases.* Columbus, Ohio: Charles E. Merrill Publishing Co., 1979.

Antil, John H. "Conceptualization and Operationalization of Involvement." In *Advances in Consumer Research*, vol. 11, ed. Thomas Kinnear. Ann Arbor, Mich.: Association for Consumer Research, 1984.

Leckenby, John, and Nugent Wedding. *Advertising Management: Criteria, Analysis and Decision Making.* Columbus, Ohio: Grid Publishing, Inc., 1982.

Preston, Ivan. "The Association Model of the Advertising Communication Process." *Journal of Advertising*, no. 2, 1982.

Ray, Michael L. *Advertising and Communication Management.* Englewood Cliffs, N.J.: Prentice-Hall, Inc., 1982.

———. "Marketing Communications and the Hierarchy of Effects." In *New Models for Mass Communication Research*, vol. II, ed. Peter Clarke. Beverly Hills, Calif.: Sage Publications, 1973.

Sachs, William S. *Advertising Management: Its Role in Marketing.* Tulsa, Okla.: PennWell Publishing Company, 1983.

Wilson, R. Dale, and Karen A. Machleit. "Advertising Decision Models: A Managerial Review." In *Current Issues & Research in Advertising*, vol. 2, ed. James H. Leigh and Claude R. Martin, Jr. Ann Arbor, Mich.: Graduate School of Business Administration, University of Michigan, 1985.

C H A P T E R 11

BUDGETING FOR ADVERTISING

Key Terms

advertising expenditure
advertising budget
arbitrary approaches
rule-of-thumb approaches
objective/task approach
theoretical approaches

Learning Objectives

To differentiate between the advertising expenditure and the advertising budget

To enumerate the items to be included in the advertising budget

To outline the purposes of the advertising expenditure

To discuss the variables that affect the size of the budget

To describe the methods most commonly used to determine the advertising expenditure

To outline the characteristics of an effective budget

The consumer marketplace has been anything but easy for EasyShine, a household cleaning product introduced in 1972. X/O Company developed EasyShine from one of its industrial cleaning formulas and decided to enter the consumer market with the new product. Until the introduction of EasyShine X/O's only source of revenue lay in manufacturing and selling a line of industrial cleaning solvents. Although the company has been successful, total sales for last year were just under $20 million.

Backed by a substantial advertising and promotion effort and an unconditional money-back guarantee, EasyShine achieved a significant market share (2.2 percent) within the first nine months of its introduction. Its ability to both clean and polish a floor in one application was innovative and appealing to homemakers, who have grown increasingly interested in saving time and labor.

Over the years, the marketplace became more competitive. When the huge consumer goods marketers saw the success of EasyShine, they introduced their own brands, which possessed many of EasyShine's physical properties. Although EasyShine has managed to increase its sales in

each of the past 14 years, these increases have largely resulted from market expansion and higher prices. In fact, EasyShine's market share has been slipping away as larger companies flex their marketing muscles.

In preparing for next year's advertising campaign, EasyShine's advertising manager sought to determine how much money to invest in advertising. To help guide the decision, she pulled together the following data on the market.

Brand A, the industry leader, holds an enviable position: it owns one third of the market share but less than 20 percent of the advertising share (that is, advertising spending for Brand A—$1.5 million—comprises less than 20 percent of the industry total). Like Brand A, Brand B holds 30 percent of the market; yet, though its advertising share is decreasing, Brand B's marketers still spend the most on advertising ($2.3 million, or 30.3 percent).

Brand C's position is less attractive than that of Brand A or Brand B. Holding the same advertising share as Brand A (19.7 percent), Brand C spends as much money on advertising ($1.5 million), but commands only 15 percent of the market.

EasyShine's position is even more problematic. Its market share stands at 8 percent; the firm has increased its advertising investment by $200,000, to $1.3 million; and its share of advertising, 17 percent, is more than twice its market share. What should the marketers of EasyShine do about the advertising expenditure?

Source: Photo copyright © B. E. White, 1987. All rights reserved.

INTRODUCTION

A few years ago, a panel of advertising executives met to discuss advertising budgeting. They noted four main problems:

1. ". . . the person with the power to approve budgets often lacks appreciation of the value of advertising investment."

2. ". . . budgets are the first item subject to change in business conditions. Worse, they are cut arbitrarily because the budget-cutters do not understand the function of advertising."

3. ". . . the unwillingness of clients (advertisers) to do benchmark studies to measure what is trying to be accomplished as a guide to setting realistic budgets to accomplish each objective or goal."

4. ". . . the inability to forecast with any degree of accuracy. Advertising should be tied to a profit plan or marketing plan. Once approved by management, the budget is an integral part of that plan and is changed only if, or when, the plan itself changes."[1]

These observations, when combined with the information in the Easy-Shine vignette, illustrate the fundamental problem in advertising budgeting: *the difficulty in determining the size of the advertising budget lies in the complexity of evaluating the effectiveness of advertising.*

Like all other operating budgets, the purpose of an advertising budget is to contribute to the profits of the organization. Unfortunately, specifying advertising's contribution to profits is difficult; therefore, determining advertising budget size is one of the most troublesome areas of advertising management. Yet, funds for advertising must be allocated and the advertising manager is frequently the person responsible for the recommendation. Although the budget size decision is difficult, it is important for several reasons.

First, the dollar amount involved is often very large. In the mid-1980s, the top five food franchises collectively invested nearly $700 million in advertising.[2] The amount of money invested in advertising by McDonald's alone ($312 million) is more than the annual sales of most companies. Second, look at the data in Exhibit 11.1. For many industries, advertising represents a major investment in dollars, management time, and as a percentage of sales and/or profits.

Finally, advertising potentially has an enormous impact on the success of the organization. The data in the EasyShine vignette suggests that the advertising expenditure may well be a major contributor to the success of some of the brands. Furthermore, observations of the marketplace reveal that it is nearly impossible to launch a new consumer product successfully, or to resposition a brand, without the support of a well-funded advertising effort.

Although determining budget size is difficult, an advertising campaign cannot be created without an advertising budget. And, to create a budget that has the greatest probability of contributing to the marketing goals of the firm, the advertising manager must be aware of the major issues surrounding the investment decision. The purpose of this chapter is to introduce you to those issues.

EXHIBIT 11.1

Advertising Expenditures of Top 20
Industries, As a Percentage of Sales

RANK	INDUSTRY	ADVERTISING EXPENDITURE AS PERCENTAGE OF SALES
1	Inorganic chemicals	16.7%
2	Retail — mail-order houses	13.2
3	Perfumes, cosmetics, other toiletries	13.1
4	Toys and amusements, sporting goods	10.0
5	Phonograph records	9.1
6	Motion picture production	9.0
7	Drugs	8.9
7	Prepared feeds for animals	8.9
9	Ordinance and accessories	8.7
10	Malt beverages	8.4
11	Soap and other detergents	7.9
12	Distilled beverages	7.2
13	Pharmaceutical preparations	7.1
14	Metal cans and shipping containers	7.0
15	Leather goods	6.7
16	Bottled/canned soft drinks	6.6
16	Wholesale electrical appliances, TV and radio	6.6
18	Candy and other confectionery	6.5
18	Mini and micro computers	6.5
20	Hardware	6.3

Source: *Advertising Age*, September 15, 1986.

DISTINGUISHING BETWEEN THE ADVERTISING EXPENDITURE AND THE ADVERTISING BUDGET

Too often, the terms *advertising expenditure* (or appropriation) and *advertising budget* are used interchangeably. There is an important difference. The **advertising expenditure** (sometimes called the *advertising appropriation* or *investment*) refers to the total amount of funds allocated to advertising within a given time period, usually one year. The **advertising budget** is a written plan that directs the distribution of the expenditure.

Key components of the advertising budget include the following:

1. the items to be included
2. the amount to be expended
3. the schedule of spending

The first two items will be discussed in this chapter; scheduling will be covered in Chapter 15.

ITEMS INCLUDED IN THE ADVERTISING BUDGET

There is a tendency for many companies to place in the advertising budget a large number of non-advertising expenses. For example, it is not unusual to find sales promotion, public relations, and even personal selling items in the advertising budget. The primary problem with including non-advertising items in an advertising budget is that the effects of the advertising expenditure are distorted. If advertising is to be held accountable for a certain end-result, its ability to achieve that result should not be hindered by underwriting the costs of other promotional activities. Therefore, it is important for the advertising manager to create a budget that contains only legitimate advertising items.

In 1960, *Printer's Ink* magazine submitted a list of 81 budget items to the major advertisers in the United States and asked respondents to classify each item as a "white" charge (definitely should be charged to the advertising budget), a "gray" charge (uncertain if the item should be in the advertising budget), or a "black" charge (definitely should not be charged to the advertising budget).[3] The *Printer's Ink* study was updated in 1981.[4] In 1984 the same issue was examined among business-to-business advertisers.[5] Some results of these studies are shown in Figure 11.1.

The most significant findings included the following:

1. A smaller number of items were considered "white" charges in the 1981 study (7) than in the 1960 study (14).

2. Business-to-business advertisers identified twenty items as "white" charges.

In conclusion, consumer goods advertisers have become much more selective about what items are charged to the advertising budget. On the other hand, business-to-business advertisers have been slower in creating a budget that contains only advertising expenses.

At the beginning of this chapter it was suggested that the purpose of an advertising expenditure is to contribute to the profits of the organization. This, of course, is the overall objective of every activity within profit-seeking organizations—that is, organizations invest money in plant, equipment, and people with the hope of generating an acceptable level of return on their investment. Companies invest money in advertising because they believe that each dollar invested will generate a profitable return. The difference between advertising costs and other operating costs—machinery, for example—is the difficulty in measuring the contribution of advertising to profits. This issue will be discussed more fully later in the chapter.

THE ROLE OF ADVERTISING IN DETERMINING ADVERTISING EXPENDITURES

The advertising management decision framework (illustrated throughout this text) shows that the most direct influence on the advertising budget is the advertising objectives. In Chapter 10, it was suggested that a high

FIGURE 11.1

Charges to the Advertising Budget: Three Studies

White charge refers to those items properly charged to the advertising budget.
Black charge refers to items that are properly charged to an account other than the advertising budget.
Grey charge refers to items that do not have a clearcut line in any one budget.

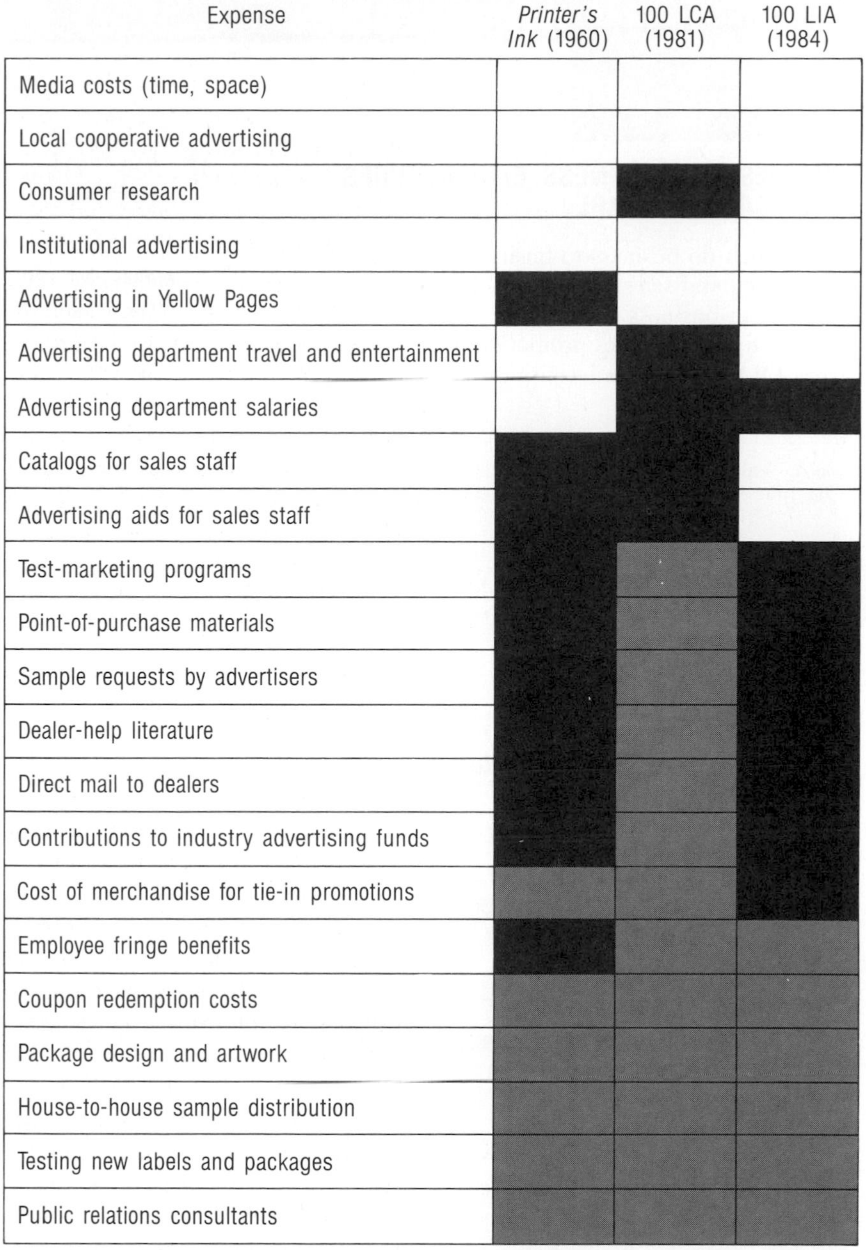

Expense	Printer's Ink (1960)	100 LCA (1981)	100 LIA (1984)
Media costs (time, space)	(white)	(white)	(white)
Local cooperative advertising	(white)	(white)	(white)
Consumer research	(white)	(black)	(white)
Institutional advertising	(white)	(white)	(white)
Advertising in Yellow Pages	(black)	(white)	(white)
Advertising department travel and entertainment	(white)	(white)	(black)
Advertising department salaries	(white)	(white)	(black)
Catalogs for sales staff	(black)	(black)	(white)
Advertising aids for sales staff	(black)	(black)	(white)
Test-marketing programs	(black)	(grey)	(black)
Point-of-purchase materials	(black)	(grey)	(black)
Sample requests by advertisers	(black)	(grey)	(black)
Dealer-help literature	(black)	(grey)	(black)
Direct mail to dealers	(black)	(grey)	(black)
Contributions to industry advertising funds	(black)	(grey)	(black)
Cost of merchandise for tie-in promotions	(grey)	(grey)	(black)
Employee fringe benefits	(black)	(grey)	(grey)
Coupon redemption costs	(grey)	(grey)	(grey)
Package design and artwork	(grey)	(grey)	(grey)
House-to-house sample distribution	(grey)	(grey)	(grey)
Testing new labels and packages	(grey)	(grey)	(grey)
Public relations consultants	(grey)	(grey)	(grey)

Sources: "Ad Budgets: A Growing Science," *Printer's Ink*, December 16, 1960; Charles H. Patti and Vincent J. Blasko, "Budgeting Practices of Big Advertisers," *Journal of Advertising Research*, December 1981, vol. 21, no. 6; and Vincent J. Blasko and Charles H. Patti, "The Advertising Budgeting Practices of Industrial Marketers," *Journal of Marketing*, November 1984.

A CLOSER LOOK

BUSINESS-TO-BUSINESS EXPENDITURES AND MARKET SHARE

How much do business-to-business marketers invest in advertising and sales promotion? The table shows that business-to-business marketers invest an average of $3.30 in advertising and sales promotion for every $1,000 of sales. Of that figure, advertising alone accounts for $1.20.

MARKETING TOOL	INVESTMENT (per $1,000 in sales)	PERCENTAGE
Media advertising	$1.20	36%
Sales promotion	$2.10	64%
Total	$3.30	100%

Source: Valerie Kijewski, "Advertising and Promotion: How Much Should You Spend," Strategic Planning Institute, Cahners Publishing Co., June 1983.

FIGURE 11.2

Advertising Management Influences on the Advertising Expenditure

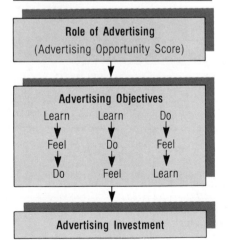

Advertising Opportunity Score (AOS) encourages advertising objectives that are closer to the action stage of the hierarchy of effects. The advantage of this orientation is that the advertising expenditure is linked directly to a specific task: the objectives of the advertising effort. Once the specific advertising task has been defined, the advertising manager can create a budget that is mission-specific (see Figure 11.2).

While this approach is theoretically sound, there are two major problems with it. First, determining the cost of accomplishing specific advertising objectives is no simple matter. If, for example, the stated advertising objective is to increase brand recognition by 15% among the primary target market during the next 12-month period, the advertising manager is put in the position of trying to estimate the cost (advertising expenditure) of accomplishing this objective. As shown in Figure 11.3, the fulfillment of the objective is influenced by several variables, not just the amount of money invested. For example, an outstanding creative effort may be able to overcome the potentially detrimental effects of a small expenditure. At the same time, a particularly ineffective creative effort will probably require a comparatively larger advertising expenditure. The point is that the advertising manager must try to recommend an advertising expenditure knowing that all of the other elements of the advertising effort will also contribute (or detract) from the achievement of the objective.

The second shortcoming is that the larger question of advertising's contribution to profits is bypassed. Ultimately, advertisers want to know if the advertising investment is profitable, and while they recognize that profits are influenced by many variables, there is strong interest in knowing more about advertising's contribution.

A second, related purpose of the advertising expenditure is to allow the company to market its offerings effectively. It has just been suggested that a primary purpose of the budget is to help fulfill the advertising objectives. A company's advertising objectives are only part of the total mar-

---

FIGURE 11.3

Influences on the Fulfillment of Advertising Objectives

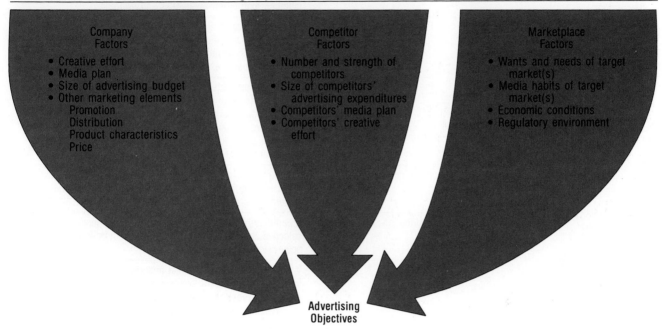

keting effort, and many of the other marketing activities are at least partially dependent on an adequately funded advertising effort. The following is a list of marketing elements and a summary of their implications for advertising expenditures. (Each of the elements are discussed in more detail later in this chapter.)

MARKETING ELEMENT	IMPLICATIONS FOR ADVERTISING EXPENDITURES
Marketing strategy	Pull strategies require large advertising expenditures as advertising becomes the main stimulant of brand demand. Push strategies demand less of advertising as other marketing mix elements (distribution, personal selling, etc.) assume larger roles.
Competition	It is usually necessary to advertise at approximately the same level as competitors; therefore, the demands of the competitive environment often dictate the level of advertising investment.
Product life cycle	Low-priced, widely distributed convenience goods require substantial advertising expenditures in the first half of the life cycle. During the introduction and growth stages, the communication tasks are to generate awareness, to stimulate distribution, and to differentiate the brand from a growing number of competitors. During the maturity and decline stages, advertising expenditures can be reduced as the product moves toward replacement.
Target market	Advertising expenditures are often a direct function of the size and characteristics of the target market. Large, widely dispersed audiences require considerably more advertising than smaller, easier-to-reach audiences.

continued

MARKETING ELEMENT	IMPLICATIONS FOR ADVERTISING EXPENDITURES
Purchase patterns	Frequently purchased products require more advertising to maintain high brand awareness and preference.
Product	The advantages of clearly differentiated brands are easier to communicate and therefore can be marketed with modest investments in advertising. Brand personalities often require larger advertising expenditures.
Price	Low-priced products with high turnover (convenience goods) often require large expenditures for advertising. Some high-priced products (autos, stereo equipment) also require large expenditures because of their large markets. Expensive industrial goods (capital equipment) usually require modest investments in advertising.
Profit margin	Larger margins allow the company the option of investing more funds in advertising to stimulate higher levels of brand preference.
Distribution	Broad distribution channels require larger expenditures. Highly selective channels or direct marketing require lower levels of advertising.
Promotion	When advertising is the least important of the promotion tools (often with business-to-business products), modest amounts of money are required for advertising. If a high AOS is present, the investment will be substantial.

Advertising can help improve the efficiency of a company's marketing effort. In the example in Figure 11.4, Pozzi Wood Windows is using advertising to help improve the efficiency of its personal selling effort. The copy is seeking inquiries from prospects who might be interested in talking with a company representative. Such an advertisement allows the company to screen prospects and thereby make better use of the personal sales staff. Screening prospects is highly desirable since the most recent estimates place the cost of a business-to-business personal sales call at well over $230.[6]

VARIABLES AFFECTING THE SIZE OF THE ADVERTISING BUDGET

When a company sets advertising objectives that meet the criteria described in Chapter 10, it is taking a major step toward helping the advertising manager determine the advertising expenditure. Good advertising objectives help the advertising manager estimate the cost of achieving the objectives by specifying several of the factors that influence budget size. Consider, for example, the ABC Company's advertising objective:

To increase preference for the ABC brand by 25 percent during the next twelve months among the primary target market. Target market characteristics include the following:

Age: 24–39
Sex: female
Marital status: married

A CLOSER LOOK

WHAT IT COSTS TO CLOSE THAT SALE

One of the main reasons that companies invest in advertising is that the cost of a personal sales call is so high. Advertising also helps close a sale by providing relevant information to prospective buyers and by creating a favorable image of the brand. Although advertising can be expensive, too, it is still a wise investment in the face of rising costs in personal selling.

Costs to Close a Business-to-Business Sale

INDUSTRY	AVERAGE NUMBER OF CALLS TO CLOSE A SALE	AVERAGE COST PER SALES CALL	TOTAL AVERAGE COST	INDUSTRY	AVERAGE NUMBER OF CALLS TO CLOSE A SALE	AVERAGE COST PER SALES CALL	TOTAL AVERAGE COST
Miscellaneous services	6.7	$328	$2,198	Stone, clay and glass products	4.8	175	840
Instruments and related products	6.2	274	1,704	Paper and allied products	5.4	143	777
Transportation equipment	7.2	227	1,637	Oil and gas extraction	4.6	165	759
Miscellaneous manufacturing	5.6	229	1,286	Business services	5.7	122	699
Chemicals and allied products	7.1	174	1,235	Insurance carriers	2.8	199	558
Machinery, except electrical	5.5	221	1,215	Rubber and miscellaneous plastic products	3.8	123	469
Transportation by air	5.7	194	1,110	Furniture and fixtures	3.3	107	354
Fabricated metal products	4.7	225	1,061	Petroleum and coal products	3.7	91	339
Banking	4.9	202	994	Wholesale trade (durable goods)	3.9	71	277
Primary metal industries	5.2	188	981	Food and kindred products	2.0	119	238
Electrical and electronic equipment	5.5	167	921				

Sources: Laboratory of Advertising Performance, McGraw-Hill Research, New York; and "Agency Biz," Paulsen & Partners, Inc., Chicago, November 1984.

Education:	high school +
Family income:	$25,000+
Household size:	4+
Geographic region:	top 50 markets
Buying habits:	heavy user of the product category (3–8 purchases per month)

Given this information, the advertising manager would be able to begin the process of recommending an advertising expenditure because many of the key influences on budget size would be known. In this ex-

FIGURE 11.4

Encouraging the Inquiry:
A Way to Refine a Firm's Personal
Selling Effort

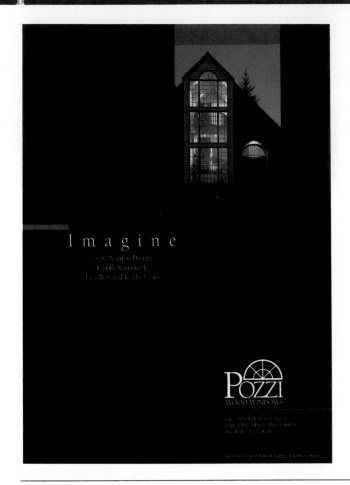

Source: Courtesy of Pozzi Wood Windows, A Division of Bend Millwork Systems/A Nortek Company.

ample, secondary research will tell the advertising manager exactly the number of people and households that match the specifications of the primary target market. With this information, the advertising manager knows how many people will have to be reached with advertising. Usually, a small target market will require a smaller expenditure. One of the reasons that business-to-business advertisers have comparatively smaller advertising budgets is that many business markets are tightly defined and contain relatively few buying prospects.

A second important piece of information in the example is the target market's buying habits or frequency of purchase. The target market purchases the product category regularly (3–8 times each month). Each time the product is purchased there is a possibility that the purchaser will switch brands; therefore, the advertising expenditure will have to be large enough to keep the brand in front of the target market regularly.

A third component that directly influences the size of the expenditure is the communication task that needs to be accomplished. In the example, the task of improving brand preference by 25 percent within twelve months sounds ambitious; therefore, a larger investment may be required.

FIGURE 11.5

Distribution Channels and Their
Implications for Advertising
Expenditures

Used by direct-response marketers for a wide variety of goods. Most common channel
for business-to-business goods (raw materials, component parts, and capital
equipment, for example). Advertising has one audience — the ultimate buyer or user.

Used by manufacturers of autos, clothing, furniture. Advertising has two audiences —
the ultimate buyer (to stimulate demand) and the retailer (to encourage stocking of
merchandise).

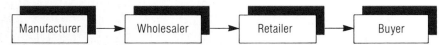

Used by manufacturers of consumer convenience goods (groceries, drugs and
cosmetics, toys, etc.) and some business-to-business manufacturers (office equipment
and supplies). Advertising has three audiences — wholesalers and retailers (to
encourage inventory stocking) and the ultimate buyer (to stimulate demand).

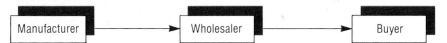

Used by some business-to-business manufacturers (raw materials and supplies).
Advertising has two audiences — wholesalers (to maintain and/or expand distribution)
and buyers (to encourage product usage and brand preference).

However, additional information from the company's marketing department may indicate that the objective is not overly ambitious. For example, company reports may indicate that the market is characterized by
low brand loyalty and that the ABC brand performed extraordinarily well
in test-markets. If this were true, we might well expect to achieve the
advertising objective with minimal advertising investment.

Other variables also affect the size of the advertising budget.

Distribution Channels   Companies using long distribution channels are
usually required to advertise to those distributors. Brands sold directly
from the manufacturer to the ultimate consumer have only one audience.
Figure 11.5 illustrates some of the more common distribution patterns and
the implications for the manufacturer's investment in advertising.

Competitive Activity   The EasyShine vignette at the beginning of this
chapter illustrates the possibility of competing successfully with a propor-
tionately smaller advertising expenditure. Most companies find it necessary to invest in advertising at about the same level as the market share
they hold. Therefore, when a brand (new or existing) finds that the major
brands in the category are investing $3 million to $5 million annually in
advertising, the required level of spending is probably within that range.

Product Differentiation   The degree and type of differentiation can dramatically affect the size of the advertising expenditure. Furthermore,

FIGURE 11.6

Differentiating a Product by Promoting a Noticeable Product Feature

some levels of differentiation argue for larger investments and others suggest comparatively easier communication tasks and thus smaller investments. The level of differentiation that requires the smallest budget is a physically differentiating feature that is obvious and simple to understand by the target market. The KitchenAid advertisement in Figure 11.6 is a good example of a brand that is physically differentiated and whose product feature is easy to understand. Note that KitchenAid claims exclusivity of its Whisper Quiet System, a feature that makes the appliance so quiet "that you can talk on the kitchen phone or entertain guests and scarcely know that your dishwasher is running."

Chivas Regal (Figure 11.7) attempts to differentiate in a different way: creating a competitive advantage by communicating a distinct brand personality. (However, personality is often more difficult to communicate because there are many subtle but relevant dimensions of personality.)

Attitudes of Company Executives   In many situations, the most important influence on the size of the advertising investment is the attitude that company executives have about advertising. Note the concern of the busi-

FIGURE 11.7

Differentiating a Product by Creating a Distinct Brand Personality

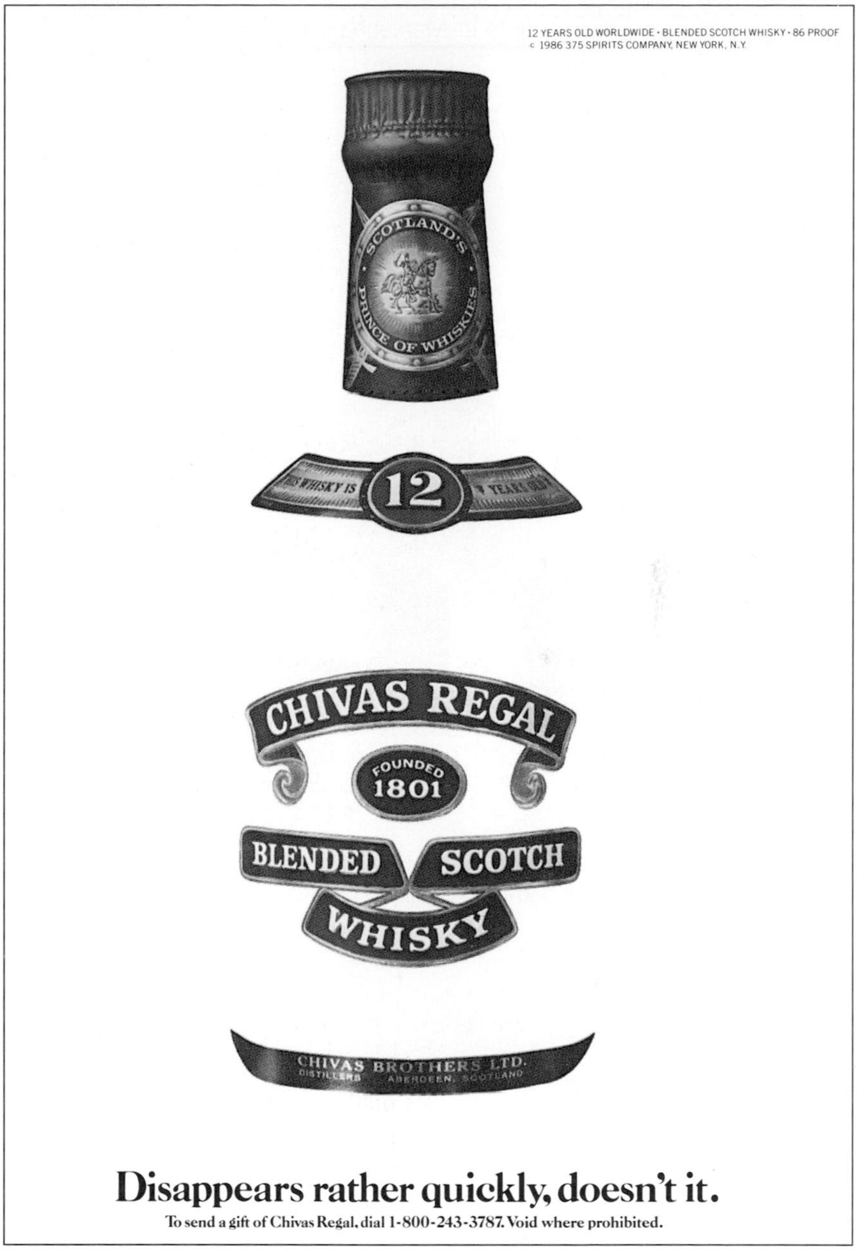
12 YEARS OLD WORLDWIDE • BLENDED SCOTCH WHISKY • 86 PROOF
© 1986 375 SPIRITS COMPANY, NEW YORK, N.Y.
SCOTLAND'S PRINCE OF WHISKIES
12
CHIVAS REGAL
FOUNDED 1801
BLENDED SCOTCH WHISKY
CHIVAS BROTHERS LTD.
Disappears rather quickly, doesn't it.
To send a gift of Chivas Regal, dial 1-800-243-3787. Void where prohibited.

Source: © 1986 375 Spirits Company, New York, NY. Reprinted with permission.

ness-to-business advertising executives: " . . . the person with the power to approve budgets often lacked appreciation of the value of advertising investment."

While this is more often an issue among business-to-business firms (where the background and training of top company executives is less likely to be marketing and advertising), the influence of company execu-

FIGURE 11.8

Percentage of Sales Investments in Marketing Costs

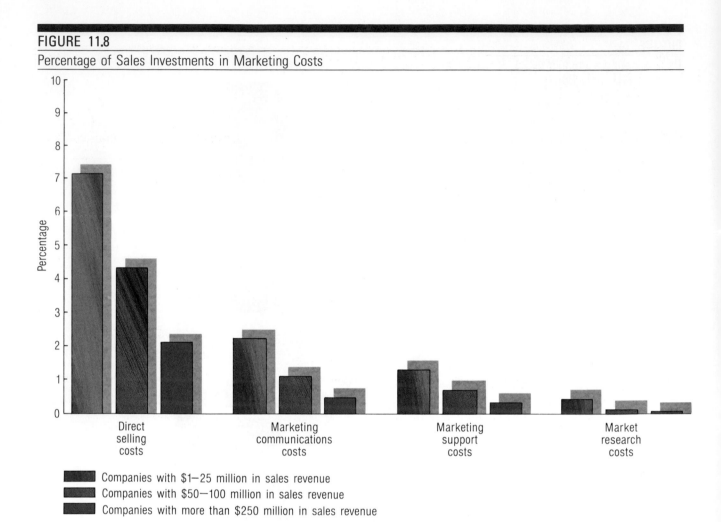

Companies with $1–25 million in sales revenue
Companies with $50–100 million in sales revenue
Companies with more than $250 million in sales revenue

tives is always a factor in determining the advertising expenditure. Eventually, the budget recommended by the advertising manager or the advertising agency must be approved by higher levels of management, and the approval process is always tempered by the beliefs and experiences of top management. If top management believes advertising can and should play a major role in accomplishing the marketing goals of the company, then larger investments are more likely to be approved. Figure 11.8 illustrates the relationship between size of company and its willingness to invest in marketing, including marketing communications. Note that as sales increase, the percentage of sales invested in marketing decreases.

Other Influences on Advertising Expenditures The above list is not all-inclusive. Each company will find its advertising investment influenced by a set of factors that may be unique to that company. The state of the economy, the amount of profit margin in the brand, the stage of the brand in its product life cycle, and the marketing strategy (push or pull) are all other factors that the advertising manager must consider.

A CLOSER LOOK

BUDGETING METHODS

How do large advertisers determine the amount they will invest in advertising? Here's a table showing the methods used by the largest consumer goods and industrial goods advertisers in the United States.

METHOD	PERCENT OF RESPONDENTS USING EACH METHOD*	
	CONSUMER GOODS	INDUSTRIAL GOODS
Affordable	20%	33%
Arbitrary	4	13
Match competitors	24	21
Objective/Task	63	74
Percent of anticipated sales	53	16
Percent of past year's sales	20	23
Per unit of sales	21	2
Quantitative	51	3

*Figures exceed 100% due to multiple responses.
Sources: Charles H. Patti and Vincent J. Blasko, "Budgeting Practices of Big Advertisers," *Journal of Advertising Research*, November 1981, vol. 21, no. 6; and Vincent J. Blasko and Charles H. Patti, "The Advertising Budgeting Practices of Industrial Marketers," *Journal of Marketing*, November 1984.

METHODS USED TO DETERMINE THE ADVERTISING EXPENDITURE

Because of the complexity of the relationship between the amount of money invested in advertising and advertising results, companies use a variety of methods to determine how much money to spend on advertising. All expenditure methods can be categorized into four approaches.

Arbitrary approaches, the least scientific in determining the advertising investment, involve an arbitrary decision by someone in the company regarding how much money will be allocated to advertising. By definition, the basis of the decision is made without a guiding principle or rule. Almost by guesswork, someone decides that a certain amount of money will be spent on advertising. Sometimes the amount is "what's left over" or "all we can afford." Sometimes the amount is "what we spent last year."

As advertising matures as a business tool, fewer companies use this approach; however, a study of the 100 largest U.S. advertisers showed that 4 percent of the respondents still use the "arbitrary" approach and another 20 percent use the closely related, "affordable" approach.[7]

Rule-of-thumb approaches involve using a guideline that the company feels is related to the advertising investment in an important way. Several of the most widely used rule-of-thumb methods are described and illustrated below.

Percentage of Past Sales Method This method consists of multiplying the company's past year's sales by a predetermined percentage. The outcome is the advertising expenditure for the next budget year.

Past year's sales	$12,500,000
Predetermined percent for advertising	× 7.5
Advertising expenditure for next year	$ 937,500

Unfortunately, the predetermined percentage is often set arbitrarily, and when this happens, the percentage of past sales method is little improvement over arbitrary methods. More often, the predetermined percentage is suggested by industry norms or company experience.

Percentage of Future Sales Method This method is identical to the one that preceded it, except that the predetermined percentage is applied to forecasted sales. Since most companies try to forecast sales at least one year in advance, the percentage of future sales method allows the company to base its advertising investment on anticipated income.

Anticipated sales for next year	$20,000,000
Predetermined percent for advertising	× 8
Advertising expenditure for next year	$ 1,600,000

Per-Unit Method The per-unit method is sometimes used by companies when their sales volume is measured in units or cases and they want to relate the cost of advertising to sales units. The amount of money spent on advertising for cars (units sold), beer (barrels or cases sold), and many food and convenience goods (cases or pounds sold) is often calculated by the per-unit method. This method applies a predetermined amount of money to be allocated to advertising for every unit or case of product sold—either in the past (last year's units/cases) or in the future (next year's units/cases). Actually, the per-unit method is another way of expressing percentage of sales; however, some companies find it more useful to relate advertising costs to units sold than to total sales.

Units/cases sold last year (next year)	700,000
Predetermined amount of advertising per unit	× $1.80
Advertising expenditure for next year	$1,260,000

Market Share Method For many companies, the ideal situation would be to specify the relationship between advertising investment and market share. Because so many variables other than advertising affect market share, most companies are unable to establish their advertising investment on the basis of desired market share. Nevertheless, many do try to specify this relationship by paying close attention to market shares and industry expenditures on advertising. Many years ago, James O. Peckham studied the sales and advertising expenditures of 34 new brands and suggested the following rule-of-thumb method of determining the advertising appropriation.

> ". . . add sufficiently skillfully applied advertising over a 24-month period to produce a share of advertising about one and one-half times that of the share of sales you plan to attain."[8]

The example below uses Peckham's rule-of-thumb method and computes the advertising investment for Brand D, a new brand that is attempting to achieve a 10 percent market share.

BRAND	MARKET SHARE	ADVERTISING (in millions)	ADVERTISING SHARE
A	20%	$ 2.5	20.5%
B	25	3.8	31.2
C	15	1.2	9.8
Others	40	4.7	38.5
Total	100	$12.2	100.0%

Desired market share for Brand D:	10%
Required share of advertising (1.5 × desired market share):	15%
Required advertising investment (15% × $12,200,000):	$1,830,000

Competition Method   One of the more frequently used rule-of-thumb methods is to use competitive spending as a guide. Once a company learns what its major competitors are spending for advertising, it is tempting to invest at a similar level. This method is a reasonable way to begin the advertising appropriation process and it also assures an equivalent "share of voice"; however, differences among company objectives, market shares, and combinations of marketing mix elements restrict the usefulness of the competition method.

The **objective/task approach** is a direct extension of setting advertising objectives and is the most widely used method among the largest advertisers in the United States.[9] The objective/task approach was briefly discussed earlier in this chapter and it is the recommended approach for determining the size of the advertising investment. Basically, this method involves (1) specifying the precise objective or task for advertising ("to increase brand awareness by 10 percent among the target market within a six-month period," for example), and (2) calculating the estimated cost of achieving that objective.

In spite of the operational difficulties with this approach, it is recommended because:

1. It is the only approach that ties advertising investment to the specific task that advertising has been assigned.

2. It overcomes the shortcomings of the arbitrary approaches (illogical) and the rule-of-thumb approaches (advertising expenditures tied to guidelines that may not yield optimal results).

Theoretical approaches rely on a theory of some kind to calculate the advertising expenditure. In recent years there has been increased interest in the development of more sophisticated approaches to the advertising investment problem. Some are based on field studies that attempt to demonstrate advertising's effects on sales. Others are based on historical data from company records. Still other approaches are based on an individual's ideas about the relationship of advertising to one or more important variables (sales, profits, market share, or brand preference).[10]

Regardless of the basis for the theory, the attempt is to specify and quantify the variables that affect sales (or some other relevant outcome). By doing this, the researcher hopes to determine the precise relationship between advertising expenditures and the company's goal.

Advertisers are certainly interested in knowing more about the effects of their investment in advertising, and the availability of data about the advertising-sales relationship is no doubt helpful in understanding the relationship. Widespread use of theoretical approaches will depend on the ability of researchers to produce valid, reliable data within a time frame that allows advertisers to make use of the data.

CHARACTERISTICS OF A GOOD ADVERTISING BUDGET

If advertising is to have an opportunity to fulfill its objective, the advertising budget must allow the effective creation of the other elements of the advertising plan — creative, media, and research.

A good advertising budget is one that

- Contains only advertising items

- Is based on the estimated cost of fulfilling the stated advertising objectives

- Is large enough to fulfill the objectives within the specified time frame

- Is dependable enough to sustain the advertising effort throughout the campaign period

- Is flexible enough to accommodate any necessary expansions or contractions in the advertising plan

A METHOD FOR DETERMINING THE ADVERTISING EXPENDITURE

Today's large advertisers — consumer, retailer, and business-to-business — use several different methods for determining the amount of money they invest in advertising. In addition, they may use several methods at the same time. In other words, it is rare that one particular method is completely satisfactory. Which method, or methods, should be used? The following method has been adapted from material developed by Cyril Freeman. It is presented here because the approach focuses on the communication tasks that advertising is expected to perform and it attempts to assess the sales dollar impact of advertising.[11]

A GLOBAL LOOK

WHEN THE JAPANESE BUDGET FOR ADVERTISING

Much like their American counterparts, when Japanese advertisers are faced with an unhealthy economy, one of the first areas they may trim is the advertising budget.

Japan's economy, according to observers, hasn't been this inert since the 1960s. "Japan's low inflation and flat business [environment] are producing results very similar to what's happening to the advertising business in the United States," said Lloyd Heibloom, executive vice-president for DDB Needham Worldwide. "Advertising budgets are following inflation and the economy."

Several Japanese firms—among them Konica Corporation and Maxell Corporation—reduced their advertising expenditures in 1986 over those of the previous year. Still others, according to Heibloom, may in fact be reallocating funds toward promotions, direct mail, and coupons.

According to Ben Katayama, managing director of Orikomi Bates in Tokyo, Japanese advertisers will be paying more attention to sales promotion and less to television advertising than they have in the past. Katayama speculated that Japanese firms will be more likely to place TV "spots" than to sponsor a special or a series.

He added, "There is no short-term solution unless the yen gets back to an acceptable rate." In 1987, the yen stood at about 150 per $1 U.S. (as compared to 240/$1 in 1985).

Source: Patricia Simmons, "Focus on Japan: While Economics Play Havoc with Ad Budgets," *Advertising Age*, October 6, 1986, 68–70. Yen exchange rate from Northern Trust Bank, Chicago, February 24, 1987.

Step 1: Determine the communication steps required to move the target market through the appropriate hierarchy of effects. (See Chapter 10 for a discussion of alternative hierarchies.) For example, an appropriate hierarchy might be the following:

1. Create brand awareness.
2. Transmit knowledge of brand's three most important physical attributes.
3. Alter attitudes about the brand.
4. Create interest in brand trial.
5. Generate trial.

Step 2: Determine the percentage of the communication process to be allocated to each of the above five steps. The percentages might be as follows:

STEP IN COMMUNICATIONS HIERARCHY	PERCENTAGE OF COMMUNICATION TASK
1. Awareness	30%
2. Knowledge	15
3. Attitude	20
4. Interest in trial	20
5. Trial generation	15

Step 3: Come to agreement on the percentage of the contribution that advertising should make to each step. This recognizes that the other three

promotional tools—personal selling, sales promotion, and public relations—will also make contributions.

For example, assume that management agreed to the following contribution for advertising.

STEP	(A) PERCENTAGE OF COMMUNICATION TASK		(B) PERCENTAGE OF CONTRIBUTION BY ADVERTISING		(C) TOTAL ADVERTISING CONTRIBUTION
1. Awareness	30%	×	80%	=	24%
2. Knowledge	15	×	50	=	8
3. Attitude	20	×	50	=	10
4. Interest in trial	20	×	25	=	5
5. Trial generation	15	×	20	=	3
					50%

Step 4: Compute advertising's total contribution by multiplying column (A) and column (B).

By following this procedure the advertising manager has a reasonably clear idea of precisely what portion of the total communication task should be assigned to advertising. With that information, it is possible to allocate to advertising an expenditure that comes closer to representing its share of the total promotion effort. In the example, advertising accounts for 50 percent of the total communication task. Using this figure as a guide, it is probably reasonable to allocate to advertising approximately 50 percent of the company's total promotion investment.

SUMMARY

Although determining the size of the advertising expenditure is one of the most complex and difficult tasks facing the advertising manager, the task is simplified by keeping certain principles in mind.

There is a difference between the advertising expenditure or investment (the total amount of funds appropriated for advertising) and an advertising budget (the specific plan for allocating the investment).

The purposes of the advertising expenditure are to contribute to the sales and/or profit goals of the company (long term) and to provide the financial resources to fulfill the advertising/communication goals (short term).

The variables that affect the size of advertising expenditure include a number of marketplace variables (competitive activity, frequency of purchase, and economic conditions) and company variables (size of the target market, distribution channels, product differentiation, and the attitudes of top management).

The methods used to determine the advertising expenditure include arbitrary approaches, rule-of-thumb approaches (percent of past and future sales, per unit/case, market share, and competition), the objective/task approach, and theoretical approaches.

An advertising budget should contain only elements that are legitimately defined as advertising. The budget should specify the amount of funds allocated to each item and provide a time schedule for expenditure.

The characteristics of a good advertising budget include these: the size of the budget is based on the cost to fulfill the advertising objectives; the budget contains only advertising items; the budget is large enough to accomplish its assigned task; and the budget is flexible enough to accommodate changes in the advertising plan.

There is no "best" method for calculating the advertising expenditure. The most satisfactory results will come from using a combination of the approaches described in this chapter. By examining data on competitive spending and calculating alternative expenditures on the basis of the rule-of-thumb approaches, a company can become more sensitive to the relationship of advertising and sales. By working with the objective/task method and becoming familiar with theoretical approaches, a firm gains valuable experience in estimating the cost of achieving both its advertising and sales goals. Determining the advertising expenditure is one of the advertising management tasks that is clearly between a science and an art.

QUESTIONS FOR DISCUSSION

1. Explain the distinction between the advertising budget and the advertising expenditure.

2. Why should an advertising manager insist on having only advertising items in the advertising budget?

3. What are the purposes of an advertising budget?

4. Explain the relationship between advertising objectives and the advertising expenditure.

5. How do executive attitudes affect the advertising expenditure?

6. This chapter explains several alternative approaches to determining the advertising expenditure. Which one do you think is best for a new consumer product? Explain.

7. What are the strengths and weaknesses of Cyril Freeman's approach to advertising budgeting?

8. Why do so many companies have difficulty in determining the size of the advertising investment?

9. In **A Closer Look** ("Budgeting Methods"), it was shown that one third of the largest business-to-business advertisers use the "affordable" method of advertising budgeting. Why is this method so widely used?

10. Explain the influence of the following marketing elements on the advertising expenditure:
    a. distribution channels
    b. amount of physical differentiation in the brand
    c. frequency of purchase of the product
    d. the stage of the brand in its life cycle

SWEET BODY DEODORANT

You're in charge of recommending the size of the advertising budget for Sweet Body, a new brand of deodorant. You've been given the information below, and you've just finished reading James O. Peckham's article on how to set advertising budgets for new consumer brands. If you develop your budget recommendation following Peckham's observations, what would be the size of your advertising budget?

Marketing Information

- Brand name: Sweet Body

- Date of introduction: January 1

- Distribution: Manufacturer→Wholesaler→Retailer→Consumer

- Desired market share: 5 percent

Market Structure

BRAND	MARKET SHARE	ADVERTISING BUDGET (in millions)	SHARE OF ADVERTISING
Competitor A	22.0%	$ 5.6	
Competitor B	18.2	6.2	
Competitor C	15.7	3.5	
Competitor D	9.0	2.0	
Others	35.1	8.6	
Total	100.0%	$25.9	

■ ■ ■

NOTES

1. "Advertising Budgeting," *White Paper Series No. 4*, Business/Professional Advertising Association, New York, 1982.

2. "Ninth Annual Top Brands Survey," *Marketing Communications*, June 1986, 56.

3. "Ad Budgets: A Growing Science," *Printer's Ink*, December 16, 1960.

4. Charles H. Patti and Vincent J. Blasko, "Budgeting Practices of Big Advertisers," *Journal of Advertising Research*, November 1981, vol. 21, no. 6.

5. Vincent J. Blasko and Charles H. Patti, "The Advertising Budgeting Practices of Industrial Marketers," *Journal of Marketing*, November 1984.

6. "Cost of an Industrial Sales Call Increases to $229.70," *Laboratory of Advertising Performance, no. 8013.8*, McGraw-Hill Publishing Company, New York, 1986.

7. Patti and Blasko, "Budgeting Practices."

8. James O. Peckham, "Can We Relate Advertising Dollars to Market Share Objectives?" in *How Much Money to Spend for Advertising*, Malcolm A. McNiven, ed. (New York: Association of National Advertisers, Inc., 1969), 30.

9. Patti and Blasko, "Budgeting Practices."

10. B. F. Butler, P. M. Thompson, and L. A. Cook, "Quantitative Relationships among Advertising Expenditures, Share of Market, and Profits," in *How Much to Spend for Advertising*, Malcolm A. McNiven, ed. (New York: Association of National Advertisers, Inc., 1969); R. Dale Wilson and Karen A. Machleit, "Advertising Decision Models: A Managerial Review," in *Current Issues & Research in Advertising*, James H. Leigh and Claude R. Martin, Jr., eds. (Ann Arbor: Graduate School of Business Administration,

University of Michigan, 1985), 99–187; and John D. Leckenby and Nugent Wedding, *Advertising Management: Criteria, Analysis, and Decision Making* (Columbus, Ohio: Grid, 1982), 219–290.

11. Cyril Freeman, "How to Evaluate Advertising's Contribution," *Harvard Business Review*, August–September 1969.

SUGGESTED READINGS

Aaker, David A., and James M. Carman. "Are You Overadvertising?" *Journal of Advertising Research*, August–September, 1982.

Ackoff, Russell L., and James R. Ernshoff. "Advertising Research at Anheuser Busch, Inc." *Sloan Management Review*, Winter 1974.

Cahners Publishing Company. "How Advertising Drives Profitability: New Facts on the Importance of Media Advertising Based on the PIMS Data Base." Newton, Mass.: Cahners Publishing Company, 1985.

———. "How Much to Spend on Advertising?: New Guidelines Based on the PIMS Data Base." Boston: Cahners Publishing Company, 1985.

———. "Work Book for Estimating Your Advertising Budget." Cambridge, Mass.: Cahners Publishing Company, 1985.

Farris, Paul, and Mark S. Albion. "Determinants of the Advertising-to-Sales Ratio." *Journal of Advertising Research*, February 1981.

Hurwood, David L. "How Companies Set Advertising Budgets." *Conference Board Record 5*, 1986.

Kelly, Richard J., ed. *The Advertising Budget: Preparation, Administration and Control.* New York: Association of National Advertisers, Inc., 1967.

Kijewski, Valerie. "Advertising and Promotion: How Much Should You Spend." Cambridge, Mass.: The Strategic Planning Institute, Cahners Publishing Co., 1983.

———. "Business-to-Business Marketing: To Advertise or Not to Advertise?" Cambridge, Mass.: Strategic Planning Institute, Cahners Publishing Co., 1985.

———. "How Advertising Drives Profitability." Cambridge, Mass.: Strategic Planning Institute, Cahners Publishing Co., 1985.

Kuehn, Alfred. "How Advertising Performance Depends on Other Marketing Factors." *Journal of Advertising Research*, March 1962.

Montgomery, David B., and Glen L. Urban. *Management Science in Marketing.* Englewood Cliffs, N.J.: Prentice-Hall, Inc., 1969.

Palda, K. *The Measurement of Cumulative Advertising Effects.* Englewood Cliffs, N.J.: Prentice-Hall, Inc., 1964.

Permut, Steven E. "How European Managers Set Advertising Budgets." *Journal of Advertising Research*, no. 17, 1977.

Parrish, T. Kirk. "How Much to Spend for Advertising." *Journal of Advertising Research*, February 1974.

Riordan, E. A., and F. W. Morgan, Jr. "A Taxonomic Evaluation of Advertising Budgeting Models." *Journal of Advertising*, no. 1, 1979.

San Augustine, Andre J., and William F. Foley. "How Large Advertisers Set Budgets." *Journal of Advertising Research*, no. 15, 1975.

Simon, Julian. *The Management of Advertising.* Englewood Cliffs, N.J.: Prentice-Hall, Inc., 1971.

Sunoo, D. H., and L. Y. S. Lin. "A Search for Optimal Advertising Spending Level." *Journal of Advertising*, no. 3, 1979.

P A R T 4

Advertising Decision Making: Campaign Development and Execution

Now that you have seen how the fundamental considerations of the advertising decision-making process are carried out, it is time to explore the process of actually creating advertising messages. On reflection, it should be obvious that beginning to make advertising decisions on messages without agreement on the preliminary issues (such as the role and purpose of advertising, who is to be reached, and the amount of resources available to create the advertising program) would be a considerable waste of time and money.

Chapter 12 explains the process of formulating advertising creative strategy—that is, coming up with the guiding principle(s) behind the advertising messages that make up the campaign. Chapter 13 discusses principles for selecting advertising tactics. Tactics, or execution, constitute the process by which the actual messages—TV commercials, magazine ads, and other advertisements—come into being. Chapter 14, the final chapter in this part, treats the subject of evaluation. No one spends money on advertising without hoping to achieve some effect, yet often these outcomes are difficult to measure directly.

DEVELOPING CREATIVE STRATEGY

Key Terms

creative objective
creative strategy
physical differentiation
psychological differentiation
selling proposition
generic strategy
preemptive strategy
Unique Selling Proposition
brand image strategy
positioning strategy
resonance strategy
affective strategy

Learning Objectives

To describe creative strategy

To differentiate strategy from tactics

To explain the importance of strategy

To outline the process of creative planning

To discuss the significance of product differentiation

To feature the important characteristics of the seven alternate strategies

To analyze the impact of the seven strategies on competitors

Establishing creative strategy is a difficult advertising decision often left to very top-level management. Its selection often involves both research data and experience or intuition. In the case of a recent television campaign for Lincoln-Mercury automobiles, the decision was made to develop a music-driven campaign based on scenes that might have been drawn directly from the popular movie, "The Big Chill."

The commercials were built around music straight out of the 1960s. Four TV spots were created, the first one based on Marvin Gaye's "Ain't No Mountain High Enough." The others were the Shirelles' "Mama Said," the Beach Boys' "Wouldn't It Be Nice?" and Steppenwolf's "Born to Be Wild."

How and why was this execution chosen? The answer is based on the strategy the agency and client developed to approach the advertising situation.

Each of these spots was targeted to a slightly different group of consumers (who were identified in terms of the VALS typology discussed in Chapter 8). Young & Rubicam, the agency that developed the spots, has extensive experience in working with VALS and in developing consumer advertising campaigns linked to it. In this case, the strategy was to de-

velop commercials that illustrated the experiences of the target audience. The VALS typology gives a way of understanding the consumers, and the strategy is based on that understanding. The execution sets the commercials in the past experience of the prospects by employing songs that are meaningful to the target audience, but that present slightly different values and social orientations so as to fit with slightly different groups. For example, the "Born to Be Wild" spot is designed to speak to a value set that revolves around freedom and independence, while the "Mama Said" spot reflects family values and relationships.

Despite these differences, all the spots were basically designed to speak to the baby boomer generation, yet each speaks in a slightly different way and to a slightly different segment of the group. However, all the spots in the campaign are tied together by the creative strategy in that each message is designed to resonate with the experience and values of a specific group of prospects.

Source: Based on Barbara Lippert, "VALS Are Driving Force in New Lincoln-Mercury Spots," *Adweek*, October 8, 1984, 51. Photo courtesy of the Lincoln-Mercury Division, Ford Motor Co.

INTRODUCTION

Previous chapters have discussed the importance of fundamental planning and information gathering activities in preparing to mount an advertising campaign. Figure 12.1 summarizes the entire decision sequence in planning an advertising campaign. This chapter examines the way some of the preliminary information is synthesized to form the guiding principle for the advertisements in the campaign: the creative strategy. The chapter will describe creative strategy and the considerations in selecting it. In addition, it will explain how the various types of creative strategies are suited to different market and competitive conditions.

FIGURE 12.1

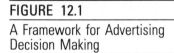
A Framework for Advertising Decision Making

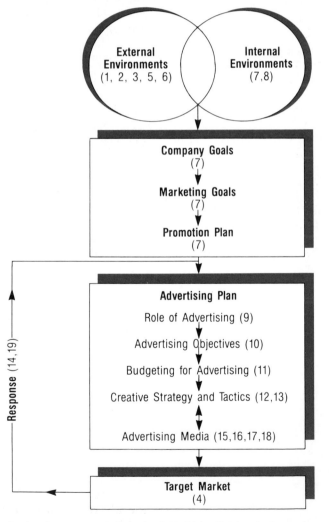

Numbers in parentheses indicate the chapter(s) in which item is discussed.

CREATIVE OBJECTIVES: A DEFINITION

The creative process in advertising involves the formulation of advertising materials: broadcast commercials, print ads, collateral materials, and so forth. All of these are designed to carry the advertising message to the intended target audience. The result of that message—the goal of successful advertising communication—is specified in the creative objectives for the ad or campaign. A **creative objective** is a statement of the communication task the advertisement or campaign is expected to carry out. Chapter 10 discussed setting objectives and the importance of objectives that are communication-oriented, quantifiable, and specific in terms. Most often senior agency planners work with advertiser management in formulating creative objectives. Depending on the size and management environment of the agency and advertiser firm, agency creative people may have a role in setting goals for the creative elements.

As suggested earlier, those who plan the goals of the advertising must not only understand consumer groups, but must understand the capabilities and limitations of advertising. Knowing and understanding consumer groups is important so that the appropriate hierarchy of advertising influence is used and realistic creative objectives are set. The planner needs to understand that only in a limited number of situations can advertising be a direct cause of sales. Advertising must be aimed at intermediate steps in the hierarchy, such as giving information, reiterating a selling point, or attaching positive emotional appeal. Once objectives have been set and agreement is reached about the task the advertising is to accomplish, creative strategy can be formulated.

CREATIVE STRATEGY AND HOW IT WORKS

In the case of most large national advertisers, the creative strategy is developed by an advertising agency, working with the advertiser. **Creative strategy** is a policy or guiding principle that specifies the general nature and character of messages in the advertising campaign. Notice that the strategy does not cover the specific way the message will be *presented* (for example, by a celebrity). Rather, it specifies how the message will be *formulated*. Alternatives in creative strategy will be presented later in this chapter.

In retail situations, the creative strategy is usually designed to reflect the store or business's general competitive position in the market. For example, consider the Gap ad in Figure 12.2. In such a campaign, the "look" and feeling of the ads are very similar over time, and are designed to convey a consistent impression about the store and the nature of the goods it sells. This consistent look and feel is a reflection of the creative strategy, which guides writers and art directors in their execution of ads for the store or business.

For the national advertiser working with a major advertising agency, the advertising planning within the agency follows the process outlined in Exhibit 12.1.

FIGURE 12.2

Creative Strategy in Retailing:
To Convey a Consistent Image

Source: Courtesy of the Gap Stores, Inc.

The account services personnel of the agency provide the creative department with the necessary background information to formulate creative strategy. This includes information on the company, its reputation and history, as well as its corporate image and philosophy. In addition, the creative department must consider important competitors in the marketplace, the types of products they offer, and the creative strategies they use. Account services people also assist the creative department in understanding the client firm's *marketing objectives and strategy* for offering a particular product or lines of goods or services. The consumer *target audience* is identified as carefully as possible by advertiser marketing efforts. This information is provided to the creative department. If the target audience is unspecified, or if little is known about it, the creative department must develop information on its own, or through the assistance of other agency departments. *Product characteristics* are also carefully analyzed to find advantages or differences not offered by competitors. Finally, and in some ways most importantly, whatever agreement has been reached about *creative objectives* is relayed to the creative people. These considerations form the guidelines and the important constraints on the creative process. Careful weighing of these types of information influences the formulation of creative strategy.

Within the agency, the creative department is usually made up of two types of individuals, copywriters and art directors. Though the names imply the functions of their jobs, they do not clarify the relationship. When a job reaches the creative department it may be assigned to a writer/artist team, or may simply be assigned to a copywriter. Regardless of the organization, it is most often the copywriter who develops the strategy. Since the copywriter is the one who works with words, it is usually he or she who works with the account people to develop the creative strategy.

EXHIBIT 12.1

Developing the Advertising
Creative Elements

1. Analyze foundation elements
   Corporate history, philosophy, reputation, resources
   Marketing objectives & strategy
   Target audience
   Creative objectives
   Product characteristics and differentiation
   Competitive situation

2. Formulate selling proposition
   "Buy this product because. . . ."

3. Select creative strategy alternative
   (one of seven alternatives)

4. Develop a central concept or advertising theme

5. Execute strategy in an imaginative and meaningful way

6. Evaluate
   Is correct message received?
   Is message appropriate for audience?

Once client approval is obtained for the concept of the creative strategy, the ideas for the executions, or tactics, are worked out. Tactics will be dealt with in Chapter 13.

CREATIVE PLANNING

The most important focus of creative planning is the consumer. Advertising creative people are specialists not only in conceiving imaginative presentations for products and services, but in understanding and empathizing with product users. Indeed, one of the most important services an advertising agency performs for a client is supplying an objective view of the firm's activities and assisting the firm in understanding the consumer viewpoint on its products and services.

Some creative people place great value on understanding the consumer through firsthand contact. Adman David Ogilvy, for instance, was said to visit supermarket aisles and gas stations regularly in an attempt to understand people's interests and the sorts of products that atracted their attention.[1] Agency creative people often use and experiment with their client's products, in part to become familiar with how they work, but more importantly, to understand the consumer's relationship with the product and experience in using it.

While the experiential approach is one way to understand consumer orientations, a more formalized way of accomplishing this is through research. Some creative people consider research to be a restrictive and inhibiting element in the creative process. In a sense, this is true: knowing more about a situation limits the range of conceivable options in dealing with it. However, once the situation is understood, those options that remain have a higher probability of success. While few would argue that

A CLOSER LOOK

"REMODELING" THE RAISIN

It was a challenge, all right, but the creative people at Foote, Cone & Belding were up to it. The assignment? To update people's perception of the lowly raisin.

Although people have eaten raisins for hundreds of years, the fruit's popularity of late has started to slip. Despite the fact that raisins are a source of potassium, phosphorus, and calcium and don't perish as quickly as fresh fruit, recent research had shown that consumer interest in raisins had flagged.

Said Alan Canton, advertising manager of the California Raisin Advisory Board: "People knew raisins were good for you, tasted good, and were natural. But on an emotional plane they did not see them as sophisticated or contemporary. People were closet raisin eaters. They didn't see them as a social food."

Thus in 1986 the Raisin Board requested its long-time advertising agency, the San Francisco office of Foote, Cone & Belding, to give raisins a "new look." The agency launched a campaign of commercials featuring the wrinkled wonders, clad in high-tops and dark glasses, dancing to "I Heard It Through the Grapevine." Appropriately enough, the second commercial first aired during the CBS mini-series "Fresno," a prime-time spoof of soap operas.

The technique used to create the dancing raisins is called "claymation." Its creator—Will Vinton of Portland, Oregon—has used the technique successfully for a variety of products. Clay figures have been featured in commercials for Kentucky Fried Chicken and Rainier Beer, as well as in rock videos such as John Fogerty's "Vanz Kant Danz." The Noid, the pizza-destroying villain in Domino's Pizza commercials, is also a claymation creation.

The technique itself involves first modeling the figure out of a special nondrying plastic clay, then moving the figure slightly and shooting one frame of film at a time. Since there are 24 frames in each second of a commercial, the process is laborious. "On a good day,"

says Marilyn Zornado, assistant producer for Vinton, "we shoot two seconds of commercial."

Why so much effort? One reason is that the commercials are aimed at an audience that is otherwise hard to reach and that normally tunes out commercials. This group of consumers is referred to as "inner-directed," and they are less influenced by traditional advertising approaches, such as celebrity endorsements and testimonials. "Inner-directeds tend to be more experimental and free-thinking," says Terese Tricamo of Stanford Research Institute, "and thus more likely to find clay-animated figures funny."

Does it work? The raisin commercial generated 25 to 35 letters per week to the California Raisin Board, and has set records for public response, according to the research firm tracking it. For a month following the ad's appearance, sales rose 1 percent. The next two months' sales rose 5 percent and 6 percent, respectively, over the previous year's performance. The commercial and its creators have been in demand for talk-show appearances, and spin-off products such as T-shirts, sweatshirts, and toys are under consideration.

Sources: Jon Berry, "Raisin Board's Grapes of Mirth," *Adweek*, October 20, 1986, 8; and "FCB's Seth Werner: Boys Just Want to Have Fun," *Adweek*, January 12, 1987, 6; David Kalish, "The Pliable Pitch," *Marketing & Media Decisions*, February 1987, 26–27; Betsy Sharkey, "Raisins Dance to No. 1 Spot," *Adweek*, January 26, 1987, 1; and Charlyne Varkonyi, "Raisins Gain Day in Sun," *Chicago Tribune*, January 22, 1987. Photo courtesy of the California Raisin Advisory Board.

creative people should be given total freedom to create advertising campaigns based on inspiration alone, many believe that research is overused and too rigidly interpreted. Regardless of the controversy, research—whether formal or informal—is an important and necessary means of understanding consumers in order to design meaningful messages to them. Research techniques will be discussed in detail in Chapter 14.

DIFFERENTIATION AND THE ISSUE OF COMPETITIVE ADVANTAGE

An earlier chapter discussed the imporance of being able to formulate convincing advertising messages for products and services. It is obvious that if an effective message cannot be devcloped, there is little reason to spend advertising dollars. However, the possibility of creating effective messages has become increasingly difficult in modern consumer society. These days, over 15,379 items crowd supermarket shelves, many of them differing from adjacent items only in label and manufacturer.[2] As an earlier chapter showed, many heavily advertised national goods (for example, airlines, toothpastes, soaps, and beer) are functionally interchangeable and thus the consumer has little reason to choose or prefer one over another. In these cases, it is the challenge to the advertising creative department to develop plausible selling appeals that are persuasive to potential consumers.

One of the first jobs in developing a selling appeal is often to seek a point of differentiation—that is, a way in which a product or service stands out from competitors. Many products are physically different: they have special features or designs that distinguish them from others on the market. In such a case, advertising can use the technique of **physical differentiation**—distinguishing a product or service on the basis of actual features or designs that make it different from competing brands. Congoleum floor covering uses this technique in Figure 12.3.

Not all products offer physical differences, however, and in such cases, advertisers use psychological differentiation to distinguish their products from the goods of other sellers. **Psychological differentiation** involves offering an emotional argument or appeal to the consumer and associating this emotional dimension with the product as an incentive to buy. Sometimes this is done by creating a "brand personality" in the advertising. In effect, a competitor may choose almost any sort of psychological differentiation since it is not based on factors inherent to the product. However, psychological appeals must be carefully designed, both to be sufficiently different from competitors and to set forth meaningful points of difference for consumers. An example of an ad based on psychological differentiation is shown in Figure 12.4.

In general, durable goods such as major appliances and automobiles tend to be differentiated and advertised based on physical characteristics, while such items as package goods products and cosmetics tend to be differentiated and advertised based on psychological ones. This is in part because the purchase of appliances is usually a more considered and expensive purchase involving close comparisons among the choices. The purchase of shampoo, on the other hand, involves considerably less risk in terms of the potential loss of money or satisfaction. In this situation

FIGURE 12.3

Physical Differentiation: Highlighting an Actual Product Feature That Distinguishes It from the Competition

Congoleum's Law:
The squirt bottle always works when it shouldn't.

So pick Congoleum with Chromabond.
It resists more household stains better than the competition's inlaid floors.

Congoleum's exclusive Chromabond® system protects its beauty better than the competition's most expensive inlaid floors. And because Congoleum® has a special double-thick layer of protection, it resists heavy traffic twice as well as competitively-priced inlaid

floors. Congoleum's Law can happen in your house. So visit your Congoleum Studio Showcase® retailer. (For the one nearest you and free literature, call 800-447-2882.) And choose Congoleum. It's made to stay beautiful longer.

Congoleum
Floors of longer lasting beauty.

Congoleum with Chromabond lines include: Ultraflor Imperial,® Pavillion™ and Pacemaker II.® Shown here: Pavillion Citadel,® style 52019.

Source: Courtesy of Congoleum Corporation Resilient Flooring Division—Grey Advertising.

FIGURE 12.4

Psychological Differentiation: Creating a "Difference" in the Receiver's Mind

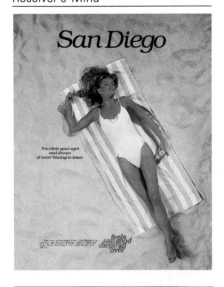

San Diego

Source: Courtesy of the San Diego Convention & Visitors Bureau (Chapman/ Warwick Advertising).

there is low risk associated with accepting an emotional argument on behalf of a product. In addition, many of these types of goods are purchased more for emotional satisfactions than physical needs.

Differentiation is a crucial element in terms of the advertisability of most products, for several reasons. First, without some difference from other competitors, the consumer is unlikely to remember the product advertised. Second, advertising a product that merely matches those currently available is unlikely to attract users who are satisfied with competitive brands. A lack of differentiation is characterized as a *"me-too" strategy*, which is generally considered a weak position by marketers, and one to be avoided. While in some cases advertisers may choose to offer a "me-too" product, it is generally for defensive reasons, such as protecting the market share of an established brand. Such products are not usually heavily advertised and are often designed to be carried by the advertising done for the established brand.

FORMULATING A SELLING PROPOSITION

To interest prospects in a product or service, the advertising message must offer the audience a reason, benefit, or reward. Psychologists have identified numerous lists of human needs and motivations. These needs and motivations often serve as the starting point for developing an ad or commercial. Advertising people don't usually think in the same terms as psychologists about the way people behave, but many advertisements are based on very similar notions about what motivates people to act.

Advertising people often think about an ad as being built around a **selling proposition,** which is the most persuasive argument that can be offered as to why prospects should buy the product. This may take the form of a simple statement such as "Buy this product and receive this benefit." While these exact words are usually not part of the finished ad, the basic idea of the selling proposition provides a structure for the advertisement. Like the creative strategy, the selling proposition guides the development of advertising ideas and executions. It is generally the most powerful and persuasive sales argument that can be made on behalf of the product. The selling proposition is part of the planning process. In the execution or tactics phase the selling proposition is artfully expressed in an original presentation designed to arrest the attention of the target audience.

Figure 12.5 shows eight examples of how selling propositions are expressed in advertisements. Note that selling propositions are often closely related to basic human motivations, such as physical comfort, emotional security, and social acceptance. Others may be based on higher needs (the price-value relationship is an example).

CONSIDERING STRATEGY ALTERNATIVES

The following seven creative strategy alternatives evolved to meet successively more complex competitive conditions. Many have existed since the earliest days of advertising, while others are more recent innovations. The strategies are suited to different types of products, services, and ideas, and require different levels of information about potential consumers. However, the factors that must be considered before implementing any strategy remain the same: company resources, competitors, marketing strategy, product characteristics, creative objectives, and the consumer.

GENERIC STRATEGY

The **generic strategy** is based on making a claim that could be made for any brand in the product category. There is no assertion of superiority, simply the claim that the product performs in a specified way. Most often

FIGURE 12.5

Selling Propositions Can Appeal to a Variety of Wants or Needs

Physical comfort

Emotional security

Social acceptance

Sensory pleasure

Sources: Courtesy of Jockey International, Inc.; Courtesy of The Procter & Gamble Company; Courtesy of Delco Electronics Corporation and Campbell-Ewald Company; and Land O' Lakes and the Indian Maiden logo are registered trademarks of Land O' Lakes, Inc. Reprinted with permission.

this type of strategy is employed by innovative products, which in effect create new product categories, or by monopolistic firms that dominate the existing market. In both cases the reasoning is the same: there is little need to attempt differentiation of the product since there is no significant competition. The advertising is designed to make the brand name synonymous with product category. This strategy requires little knowledge of the consumer beyond the fact that there is a potential consumer group for whom

Improved performance

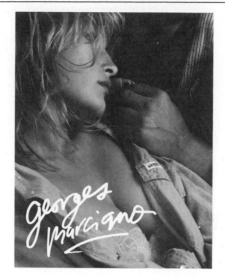

Sex appeal

Price-value relationship

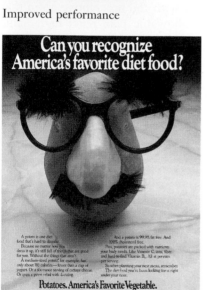

Humor

the product or service might be useful. An example of an ad based on generic strategy is shown in Figure 12.6.

PREEMPTIVE STRATEGY

Employing the **preemptive strategy** is essentially a decision to try to beat competitive products to the punch by making a claim that could be made by any of them. Claude Hopkins did exactly this in his early ads for

FIGURE 12.6

Generic Strategy

Since the Hacky Sack is an innovative product, there is little need to differentiate it from its few competitors.

THE HACKY SACK FOOTBAG.
JUST FOR KICKS.

Anytime, anywhere, in a circle or alone;
for fun, for sport, for warmups—the Hacky Sack footbag
is catching on. Give it a try. It's a kick.

HACKY SACK

Hacky Sack is a brand name and registered trademark of Wham-O.   ©1984 Wham-O

Source: Courtesy of Gardner Communications, Inc.

Schlitz Beer. In many of the ads, Hopkins claimed that the bottles were "bathed in live steam," while in fact competitors used a similar process.

The important characteristic of the preemptive strategy from the advertiser's point of view is that it places competitors in a rather awkward position. While they could devote their advertising to pointing out that they, too, have the characteristic claimed, to do so is to accept the undesirable "me-too" position. To the extent that the advertiser using the preemptive claim becomes identified with it, this advertiser is perceived by consumers as the unique source of the good or service. The basis of the preemptive claim may be either physical or psychological. Kodak has successfully used the preemptive strategy in advertising its film and cameras (see Figure 12.7). Ads for Kodak often use the words "Because time goes by," and mention capturing memories and experiences on film. Kodak's use of these "claims" makes it difficult for competitors to use them.

The preemptive strategy is most commonly used among goods where physical differentiation is difficult to achieve, in product categories such as over-the-counter pain relievers and airlines, where products are functionally interchangeable. Because it is awkward for competitors to make the same claim in their advertising, they might combat the use of the preemptive strategy with a preemptive claim of their own. For example, marketers of Pain Reliever A, when faced with the preemptive claim that Pain Reliever B contains the maximum allowable pain relief ingredient, might respond that Pain Reliever A meets the highest standards for chemical purity and is available in a tamperproof container.

UNIQUE SELLING PROPOSITION

In 1960 a leading advertising man named Rosser Reeves published a book titled *Reality in Advertising*. In it he outlined the philosophy of advertising he practiced at the Ted Bates agency. The ideas had been widely discussed in the industry for years, but the central concept—the **Unique Selling Proposition,** or U.S.P.—was one with important impact. The Unique Selling Proposition is based on some point of physical differentiation of the product. The advertising must present this difference in a meaningful and persuasive way to the consumer. Reeves asserted that advertising simply could not be effective unless it offered a distinctive reason to buy. In his view, it was the job of the agency to examine the product to find and articulate this reason to buy. According to Reeves, Unique Selling Propositions can't be developed for all products, and those without them are doomed to failure.

In many ways, the U.S.P. strategy is a descendant of the "reason-why" copy promoted by John E. Kennedy and Claude Hopkins in the early days of advertising. The product itself must offer a feature, unavailable in others, that can be made meaningful to the consumer in advertising messages. In the second ad in Figure 12.7, several physical characteristics of the Chevy S-10 truck are mentioned, which distinguish it from competitors. In general, this strategy is best suited to durable goods (like trucks), where the differentiation cannot be easily and quickly matched by competitors. In lower technology products, physical differences can be quickly imitated, undermining the advertising effort.

The decision to use the U.S.P. strategy depends, of course, on the presence of a physical difference in the product. In addition, this differ-

---

FIGURE 12.7

Preemptive and Unique Selling Proposition Strategies

Kodak's use of the phrase "Because time goes by," effectively prevents competitors from capitalizing on the idea of capturing memories on film.

The unique selling proposition strategy is particularly successful in advertising durable goods like trucks.

Source: Reprinted courtesy of Eastman Kodak Company and courtesy of the Chevrolet Motor Division.

ence must be one that the consumer will perceive as advantageous in some significant way. Competitors can do little to directly combat U.S.P. advertising so long as the point of differentiation cannot be readily matched.

BRAND IMAGE

David Ogilvy, one of the most influential advertising men of modern times, is probably best known for his ideas on the importance of the brand image. The basic goal of **brand image strategy** is to surround the product with symbols that create an attractive aura. The image created must be one that is attractive to the target market; for that reason, the symbols must be carefully chosen. Ogilvy's best-known image is probably the character of Commander Edward Whitehead, created for Schweppes Tonic (Figure 12.9). This urbane Englishman lent an air of sophistication to the product, helping to establish it as a premium-priced brand in the American market.

In some ways the brand image strategy is the counterpart of U.S.P. strategy, in that while the latter seeks to differentiate the product based

FIGURE 12.9

Brand Image Strategy

Fictional characters like Commander Edward Whitehead create a strong brand image for a product.

SCHWEPPES DISCOVERS AMERICA—AND VICE VERSA

Piutes greet Big Chief Tonic Water from over the seas!

ABOVE, demonstrating the virtues of the original and authentic Schweppes Tonic to a group of original and authentic Americans, you see Commander Edward Whitehead—heap big chief of the whole Schweppes setup in America.

The Commander first arrived on our shores eight years ago—and you can see the results of his work all around you.

Today, there's hardly a living, breathing American who doesn't know that Schweppes is the only mixer for a *real* Gin-and-Tonic. Who hasn't tasted Schweppervescence—exuberant little bubbles that last your whole drink through.

Thanks to Commander Whitehead, Schweppes Tonic is now sold in 50 states of the Union.

So whether you mix yours with gin, or vodka, or rum—or drink it straight, like our friends in the picture—make sure you get the *real stuff*.

The one and only *Schweppes* Tonic. It's curiously refreshing.

on physical attributes, brand image strategy accomplishes this through psychological ones. In fact, it seems likely that brand image strategy evolved to meet the needs of a crowded market, where physical product differentiation had become difficult to achieve and differentiation through advertising became the preferred alternative. To the extent that heavy advertising can make the symbol synonymous with the product, it creates both product differentiation *and* a powerful emotional incentive for buying. In Figure 12.10, Colombian coffee is compared with other investment opportunities to suggest its richness and great value. The effect is powerful, romantic, and culturally highbrow—if also quite exaggerated.

Using brand image strategy demands an understanding of the sorts of images and symbols that might be meaningful and persuasive to the consumer. These symbols are almost invariably symbols of high status asso-

A GLOBAL LOOK

CONDUCTING A PAN-EUROPEAN CAMPAIGN

European advertising agencies have a unique problem: how to create a campaign that can be run throughout Europe, not just in the country of origin. This issue often requires considerable advance planning and decision making by the advertiser and the agency.

For example, when Texas Instruments' European Consumer Division sought to advertise its complete line of hand-held calculators in the European markets, its agency (McCann-Erikson International of London) designed a campaign that could be implemented in 14 European countries.

McCann-Erikson had to work within several constraints: for example, students in some European countries are provided free calculators by the government. Therefore, in those countries, the market target would change from students and their parents to educators or government officials. Another consideration was that of timing. Unlike the uniform August–September back-to-school time in the United States, "back to school" in European countries varies by as much as three months. Finally, Texas Instruments' market position fluctuates from one European nation to another.

What McCann-Erikson did was to design a "modular" campaign with a "family" look. Print ads would all follow the same framework in terms of design, layout, typeface, etc. Only the numbers and

Finnish Version of a Texas Instruments Ad

types of products (and the language used in the copy, of course) would differ from nation to nation. After the agency chose a basic theme ("We'll help you do better"), it adjusted the line slightly to accommodate different market targets. For example, in nations where the government buys the calculators, educators and government authorities became the market target. The theme was modified to "We'll help them do better." Still, the underlying idea was the same: a strong message that inspired confidence in Texas Instruments products.

Source: Dean M. Peebles and John K. Ryans, Jr., *Management of International Advertising* (Boston: Allyn & Bacon, Inc., 1984), 47–54.

ciated with prestige goods. Brand image strategy does not seem to have profound effects on the competition. Competing brands are free to compete head to head using brand image strategies of their own, or to select some other creative strategy alternative.

POSITIONING STRATEGY

First described in a series of articles in *Advertising Age* in 1972, **positioning strategy** attempts to build a place for the product in the consumer's mind by relating the product to the leading competitor. This strategy developed in recognition of the fact that the consumer is confronted with innumerable advertisements on a daily basis. Since consumers receive far more than they can possibly remember—or even attend to—much advertising receives little or no conscious attention. In most product categories the best-selling brand is the one most people remember. Positioning

CREATIVE PERSONALITIES: NANCY RICE

Nancy Rice is a graduate of the Minneapolis College of Art and Design. She began her advertising career at Bozell & Jacobs, where she spent more than 11 years and reached the rank of vice-president and senior art director. In 1981 Rice left B&J to form Fallon, McElligott, Rice in Minneapolis. In 1985 she left that firm to establish — with her husband Nick, also an art director — Rice & Rice Advertising in Minneapolis.

Rice's approach to advertising involves working effectively with others: "My approach in work with people and in art direction is simple and straightforward. The best way is not to bother people with decorative elements or extra words; copy and good design work hand in hand to do that." Rice is recognized among advertising people as both a highly trained art director and a stunning graphic talent in an era when these skills are hard to come by.

Part of what makes Nancy Rice unique and successful is the freshness of her talent, which is

Nancy Rice

compelling and original. This stands out against many contemporary art directors who are not graphically talented but are merely layout people who depend on copy to carry the selling message.

Rice has been recognized by the advertising industry through numerous honors and awards. When the Art Directors Club named her 1986 Art Director of the Year, it noted that Rice had won more ADC awards in the past year than any other art director: six golds, four silvers, and five distinctive merits. These were in addition to numerous other awards, including 11 Clio awards, One Show gold and silver awards, and work showcased in various collections.

If your idea of a Rolling Stone reader looks like a holdout from the 60's, welcome to the 80's. Rolling Stone ranks number one in reaching concentrations of 18-34 readers with household incomes exceeding $25,000. When you buy Rolling Stone, you buy an audience that sets the trends and shapes the buying patterns for the most affluent consumers in America. That's the kind of reality you can take to the bank.
Source: Simmons 1984

Rolling Stone

Sources: George Lois, "She Sells Soft Sells," *Esquire*, December 1986, 105–106; and Debbie Seaman, "Art Directors Club to Induct Four into Hall of Fame," *Adweek*, Oct. 27, 1986, 27, 32. Ad from *Rolling Stone* 1986. By Straight Arrow Publishers, Inc. © 1986. All Rights Reservd. Reprinted by Permission. Agency: Fallon McElligott. Photo of Nancy Rice — photographer: Mark Hauser. Reprinted with permission.

FIGURE 12.10

Another Example of Brand
Image Strategy

Four of the best investment opportunities of the 80's.

You're probably already familiar with most of them. There's real estate. Precious metals. Objets d'art. And of course, 100% Colombian Coffee. The one investment a supermarket manager shouldn't ignore.

Discerning people everywhere have come to appreciate the delicious flavor of *the richest coffee in the world.*™ And they're more than willing to pay a premium for it.

Now, imagine how offering a 100% Colombian Coffee brand can increase your market value. Isn't there room for a product like this on your shelf? 100% Colombian Coffee. As you'll soon discover, the word is getting around.

For more information write to: 100% Colombian Coffee Program, Post Office Box 8545, New York, N.Y. 10150. Or call 800-223-3101.

Source: Property of National Federation of Coffee Growers of Colombia.

FIGURE 12.11

Positioning Strategy

Representing a calculated risk in "taking on" the market leader, positioning strategy attempts to shortcut receivers' cognitive processing.

When you're only No.2, you try harder. Or else.

Little fish have to keep moving all of the time. The big ones never stop picking on them.

Avis knows all about the problems of little fish.

We're only No.2 in rent a cars. We'd be swallowed up if we didn't try harder.

There's no rest for us.

We're always emptying ashtrays. Making sure gas tanks are full before we rent our cars. Seeing that the batteries are full of life. Checking our windshield wipers.

And the cars we rent out can't be anything less than spanking new Plymouths.

And since we're not the big fish, you won't feel like a sardine when you come to our counter.

We're not jammed with customers.

Source: Courtesy of Avis Rent-a-Car Systems, Inc.

strategy takes advantage of this by relating the advertised product to the market leader.

A classic campaign based on this approach is one for Avis (see Figure 12.11). In the campaign, ads for Avis point out how the fact that the company is not the market leader is really a benefit. Avis relates itself directly to the leading competitor in the field, something the reader already knows and understands. In effect, the strategy attempts to eliminate any necessity for cognitive processing of the message by the consumer by saying "This is the product that replaces the brand you normally buy."

The example shown in Figure 12.12 illustrates an unusual use of positioning strategy. In it, Heileman's Special Export is positioned as superior to one of the leading import beers in the United States. The ad's illustration gives equal prominence to Molson Golden, and the copy suggests that Heileman's is preferred by Canadians.

The use of the positioning strategy requires considerable knowledge of consumers. It is essential to know their mental brand hierarchy in order to know against which competing brand a product should be positioned. Making this decision also requires an understanding of competitors so that the competitive positioning is both plausible to consumers and potentially advantageous from a marketing point of view.

CREATIVE PERSONALITIES: HAL RINEY

Hal Riney graduated from the University of Washington, where he majored in art and minored in journalism/advertising. After serving in the Army, he joined the agency of Batten Barton Durstine & Osborne in San Francisco, where he worked in the mail room. In seven years he had become the agency's art director, and after 12 its vice president-creative director. He has since worked at Botsford-Ketchum (now Ketchum Advertising), and later founded the Ogilvy & Mather office in San Francisco. He formed Riney & Partners in 1976.

Riney's work is known for its warm, human quality and wry humor, both of which are evident in his work for Bartles & Jaymes Premium Wine Cooler. His advertising usually treats the consumer as someone who's just as intelligent as the writer. After 150 episodes, Riney still writes every word that comes out of Frank Bartles' mouth. Riney's commercials have been credited with an important role in taking Gallo's product from nowhere to market leadership in the crowded and highly competitive wine-cooler category.

Riney has won more than 200 advertising awards. "He's the most talked-about man in New York. People want to do Riney-style advertising," says one former employee. Riney has consciously avoided New York, preferring the quality of life on the West Coast. He notes that the sudden recognition of his work has arrived because of recent exposure on national accounts, though he's had a long series of successes for regional businesses. "Once we started working for larger national clients, our work began to be seen everywhere. It wasn't a revolution, but a revelation—at least to those who had not seen our work before. Which proves that it's easy to succeed overnight; it just takes 20 years to do it."

Hal Riney

BARTLES & JAYMES WINE COOLER

"Bagels"
:30 Commercial

FRANK: Hello. This is Frank Bartles speaking to you from New York City.

As many of you know, the Bartles & Jaymes Premium Wine Cooler is not only perfect as a refreshment, . . . but with meals as well.

Ed says it even goes with these big doughnuts they like to eat here.

I personally would not have thought Bartles & Jaymes and doughnuts would go together, much less doughnuts and fish.

But I have tried it myself, and once again, Ed is right.

So please continue to enjoy Bartles & Jaymes with all kinds of food, and we thank you once more for your support.

An Example of Riney's Work

Sources: Linda Witt, "Advantage Riney," *Sunday—The Chicago Tribune Magazine*, February 15, 1987, 8; and "How Now, Hal?" (*Wall Street Journal* ad) *Advertising Age*, January 5, 1987, 12–13. Photo of Hal Riney — photographer: Mark Thomas (San Francisco, California). Reprinted with permission.

FIGURE 12.12

Another Example of
Positioning Strategy

Import.   Export.

While the Canadians are sending us their
beer, they're importing ours. Heileman's Special
Export.
It's made with choice Bavarian hops, is now

barley, and brewed in a slow, traditional way,
called Kraeusening, for a naturally smoother flavor.
The Canadians may not brew their beer this
way. But they're happy to get one that is.

Heileman's Special Export.
You can travel the world over and never find a better beer.

Source: Courtesy of the G. Heileman
Brewing Company, Inc.

FIGURE 12.13

The Pepsi Challenge: How PepsiCo
Took on the Coca-Cola Company

Source: © Burk Uzzle 1982 for PepsiCo,
Inc. Reprinted with permission.

The competitive implications of positioning strategy are fairly profound and for that reason should be carefully considered. The decision to position a product against the market leader takes the chance of antagonizing that firm and risking whatever retaliatory measures it may employ. However, the options open to the competitor seem limited. When the Pepsi Challenge campaign (shown in Figure 12.13) positioned Pepsi as better tasting than Coke, Coca-Cola responded by finding fault with the technical basis of the comparison. Consumers seemed to find this response both silly and undignified. However, advertisers who use positioning strategy must realize that they risk having the resources of the market leader devoted to retaliation.

RESONANCE STRATEGY

While the strategies discussed above are based largely on product or market considerations, the **resonance strategy** considers primarily the consumer. The resonance principle was identified and described in the early 1970s by a political media consultant.[4] Basically, it identifies the most important aspect of a persuasive message as a presentation that is harmonious with the experience of the audience. By evoking the stored experiences of the audience, the message is more readily accepted. Advertising based on this principle does not try to convey product information or claims. Rather, it tries to present patterns of experience that match those of the audience. If the match is effective, this impression is stored and recalled when the prospect confronts the brand again in the purchase situation, making the brand more relevant than other choices and better matched to the prospect's actual or intended life-style (see Figure 12.14).

This strategy is heavily dependent on an understanding of consumers and at least a general understanding of their past experiences. Consumer research is essential to building such an understanding; this creative strategy is well matched with contemporary market segmentation techniques based on VALS analysis.[5]

An important consideration in employing the resonance strategy is that it entails a commitment to consumer research. Research is important both in designing messages and in ensuring that they communicate the desired message. Such research, though vital to effective implementation of the strategy, is expensive and time consuming. The competitive effects of the strategy depend upon the market situation and the nature and diversity of segments making up the target group. Since campaigns designed to follow the resonance strategy almost certainly address specific groups of consumers, they leave other groups unaddressed and thus open to competitors. Other creative strategies might also be employed by competitors who choose to try to attract business based on product differentiation.

AFFECTIVE STRATEGY

Some advertisers choose simply to be different. Their advertising strategy depends upon the fact that others will opt for conventional intentions and goals, while theirs is based simply on making an impression. The basis of the **affective strategy** is simply to make an emotional impact on the reader or viewer. Often advertisements based on this strategy seem unre-

FIGURE 12.14

Resonance Strategy

Presenting a message that evokes stored memories of the intended audience is the function of resonance strategy.

lated to each other and don't appear to be parts of the same campaign, in the conventional sense of the word.

The primary intention of affective strategy is simply to stand out from competitors by being bizarre, ambiguous, or avant garde, often without strong selling emphasis. Those who use this strategy often cite the necessity of achieving some sort of emotional response from the consumer. To such planners confusion, enthusiasm, or even disgust is preferable to the merely passive viewership accorded most commercials. The thought is that achieving some sort of emotional valence attached to the product is a significant achievement over the normal situation, in which the consumer merely passes over the advertising with no conscious reaction whatsoever (see Figure 12.15).

While the consumer attitude toward campaigns based on an affective strategy is often positive, it is difficult to assess the value of this sort of advertising. In addition, a marketer who intends to use affective strategy must first ascertain that the competitors are "playing it straight" in their advertising, or this unconventional presentation will lose its impact. Em-

FIGURE 12.15

Affective Strategy

Unconventional and often avant garde, affective strategy's goal is to create an impact on its receiver.

Source: Courtesy of the Kohler Co.

ploying the strategy, however, does not seem to exert any direct effect on the competitors.

THE IMPORTANCE OF CREATIVE STRATEGY

Exhibit 12.2 summarizes the seven alternative creative strategies discussed in this chapter. The discussion suggested that new advertising alternatives evolve to meet market conditions; thus any list of alternatives is not exhaustive or totally up to date. The most important point is that advertising must be guided by an established principle that is understood and agreed upon by the agency and advertiser so that the campaign is united by a consistent, underlying message policy. This understanding is important as an internal guide to those who must formulate the tactical execution of the advertising messages, but also to act as a guide in evaluating advertising effectiveness. In addition, the strategy serves as a guideline for the advertising manager, who must have a clear concept of how the advertising will be designed in order to manage it as well as the other promotional and marketing elements for maximum effectiveness.

EXHIBIT 12.2

Creative Strategy Alternatives: A Summary

STRATEGY	DESCRIPTION	MOST SUITABLE CONDITIONS	COMPETITIVE IMPLICATIONS
Generic	Straight product or benefit claim with no assertion of superiority	Monopoly or extreme dominance of product category	Serves to make advertiser's brand synonymous with product category; may be combated through higher order strategies
Preemptive	Generic claim with assertion of superiority	Most useful in growing or awakening market where competitive advertising is generic or nonexistent	May be successful in convincing consumer of superiority of advertiser's product; limited response options for competitors
Unique Selling Proposition	Superiority claim based on unique physical feature or benefit	Most useful when point of difference cannot be readily matched by competitors	Advertiser obtains strong persuasive advantage; may force competitors to imitate or choose more aggressive strategy (e.g., "positioning")
Brand Image	Claim based on psychological differentiation; usually symbolic association	Best suited to homogeneous goods where physical differences are difficult to develop or may be quickly matched; requires sufficient understanding of consumers to develop meaningful symbols/ associations	Most often involves prestige claims that rarely challenge competitors directly
Positioning	Attempt to build or occupy mental niche in relation to identified competitor	Best strategy for attacking a market leader; requires relatively long-term commitment to aggressive advertising efforts and understanding consumers	Direct comparison severely limits options for named competitor; counterattacks seem to offer little chance of success
Resonance	Attempt to evoke stored experiences of prospects to endow product with relevant meaning or significance	Best suited to socially visible goods; requires considerable consumer understanding to design message patterns	Few direct limitations on competitor's options; most likely competitive response is imitation
Affective	Attempt to provoke involvement or emotion through ambiguity, humor, or the like, without strong selling emphasis	Best suited to discretionary items; effective use depends upon conventional approach by competitors to maximize difference; greatest commitment is to aesthetics or intuition rather than research	Competitors may imitate to undermine strategy of difference or pursue other alternatives

SUMMARY

The foregoing discussion has considered the importance of creative strategy from the point of view of the advertising agency, the client firm, and the advertising message itself. Formulating advertising begins with the development of creative objectives, the goals the advertising is designed to accomplish. Once objectives have been specified, the next step is establishing the creative strategy, a policy or principle that guides the execution of the specific ads that make up the campaign. The strategy dictates how the message will be executed.

In selecting creative strategy, advertising people consider product characteristics, company resources, marketing and creative objectives, competition, and all the factors that influence consumer perception and preference. From this information they attempt to develop a way of differentiating the product from competitors' in a way that is meaningful to consumers. The next step is to develop a selling proposition for the product. Selling propositions are commonly based on satisfactions users find desirable from the product. These include physical comfort, emotional security, social acceptance, sensory pleasure, improved performance, and sex appeal. Additional possible selling propositions include price-value relationship, humor, and fashion.

Selection of an advertising creative strategy also requires an understanding of product, consumer, and competition. Seven creative strategy alternatives include generic, preemptive, Unique Selling Proposition, brand image, positioning, resonance, and affective. Successful application of each of these strategies requires certain types of market conditions and information about consumers. Each strategy has a certain type of impact on competitors. The selection of creative strategy is a complex decision requiring considerable judgment. Because creative strategy is usually not changed with every new advertising execution, and because often a great deal of money will be spent to implement the strategy, the selection decision is a particularly important one.

YOU MAKE THE DECISION

SELECTING A CREATIVE STRATEGY FOR CAJUN SPRING WATER

Cajun Spring Water is a carbonated, natural spring water flavored with jalapeño peppers. While not fiery, the water has a noticeable aroma and tangy taste. Consumers in taste tests described the drink as "zippy," "memorable," and "invigorating."

The product may be consumed by itself as a calorie-free refreshment, or used as a mixer for alcoholic beverages. Taste testers reported favoring Cajun Spring Water for traditional tonic drinks.

The product is packaged in 6-packs of 10-ounce bottles and priced between the current price leader and other national brands. It is marketed by Consolidated Foods, Inc., a major national food product producer.

Creative Platform: Cajun Spring Water

Objectives
    To create and spread awareness of this new product
    To communicate unique taste of product
    To suggest multiple uses of product

Target Audience
    Primary group is young adults 25–34. These consumers account for the majority consumption of sparkling and flavored water and set trends in drinking and eating, which often spread to other age groups. These consumers have professional/managerial jobs, live active life-styles, and are very health- and fitness-conscious.

Major Selling Idea
    The main selling point is the unique taste, which complements the growing interest in spicy cuisine. The taste is not just spicy, it's contemporary, an alternative to bland, *tasteless* refreshers.

Other Usable Benefits
   Product is readily available in supermarkets.
   Offered by firm with an established national reputation.
Creative Strategy and Rationale
   Consider the strategic alternatives suggested in this chapter in relation to Cajun Spring Water.

1. Identify the strategic alternative you think is best for the product.

2. In one sentence, explain the theme idea the advertising would follow.

3. In a paragraph or two, support the creative strategy decision you've suggested, explaining why it is superior to other possibilities.

■ ■ ■

QUESTIONS FOR DISCUSSION

1. What is meant by the term *creative strategy?*

2. What six elements must be considered in formulating creative strategy?

3. Why is differentiation important in advertising? Distinguish between physical and psychological differentiation giving an example of each.

4. What is a "me-too" product? For what reasons might a marketer offer one?

5. Why would an advertiser choose the generic advertising strategy?

6. What is the distinguishing aspect of the preemptive strategy?

7. What product characteristic is necessary to employ the Unique Selling Proposition strategy?

8. What implications does the positioning strategy have for competitors?

9. Why is special knowledge about the consumer necessary when using the resonance strategy?

10. What are the distinguishing characteristics of the affective strategy?

NOTES

1. David Ogilvy, *Confessions of an Advertising Man* (New York: Ballantine, 1963).

2. Richard Edel, "Trade Price Discounts Hold Hostages," *Advertising Age*, February 6, 1987, S-1.

3. The original articles by Al Reis and Jack Trout appeared in *Advertising Age* on April 24, and May 1 and 8, 1972. They appear, collected and updated, under the title of *Positioning: The Battle for Your Mind* (New York: McGraw-Hill, 1986).

4. Tony Schwartz, *The Responsive Chord* (New York: Anchor Books, 1972).

5. Barbara Lippert, "VALS Are Driving Force in New Lincoln-Mercury Spots," *Adweek*, October 8, 1984, 51.

SUGGESTED READINGS

Bogart, Leo. *Strategy in Advertising*. Chicago: Crain Books, 1984.

Hafer, Keith, and Gordon White. *Advertising Writing: Putting Creative Strategy to Work*. 2d ed. St. Paul, Minn.: West Publishing, 1982.

Jewler, Jerome. *Creative Strategy in Advertising*. 2d ed. Belmont, Calif.: Wadsworth Publishing, 1985.

Moriarty, Sandra. *Creative Advertising: Theory and Practice*. Englewood Cliffs, N.J.: Prentice-Hall, 1986.

Ogilvy, David. *Confessions of an Advertising Man*. New York: Ballantine, 1963.

Reeves, Rosser. *Reality in Advertising*. New York: Alfred Knopf, 1961.

Ries, Al, and Jack Trout. *Positioning: The Battle for Your Mind*. Rev. ed. New York: McGraw-Hill, 1986.

————. *Marketing Warfare*. New York: McGraw-Hill, 1986.

Schwartz, Tony. *The Responsive Chord*. New York: Anchor Books, 1972.

Young, James Webb. *A Technique for Producing Ideas*. Chicago: Crain Books, 1975.

C H A P T E R 13

SELECTING CREATIVE TACTICS

Key Terms

creative tactics
copy platform
benefit
feature
"you" attitude
headline
visual
body copy
key visual
comprehensive layout
color separations
preproduction process
shooting phase
postproduction process

Learning Objectives

To describe the creative process in advertising campaigns

To explain the point of view the agency brings to the problem

To analyze how characteristics of the message affect communication

To list the principles of effective print and broadcast ads

To contrast print ads and broadcast ads

To describe how advertisements are produced

What a great opportunity for advertising!

- big budgets

- exciting high tech clients

- highly competitive product class

Despite advertising spending estimated around $1.3 billion per year, the personal computer industry slumped in the second half of 1985. Advertisers seem to have tried both extremes of the advertising continuum. One is filling ads with arcane technical jargon. (For example, ITT claimed its Xtra XP was "25% faster than the AT on a Lotus recomputation.") The other extreme avoids any discussion of capabilities in favor of cultivating striking brand images. Neither of these alternatives seems to sell personal computers to those who don't know why they need a computer.

"People are, frankly, bewildered, and bewilderment isn't something you can overcome with flashy advertising," said one marketing manager. According to *The Wall Street Journal*, "Since the 1970's, the industry's enthusiastic marketing staffs have rushed to tell the world about the technical wizardry of their new computers—but typically haven't stopped to explain why the world needs their product."

One problem seems to be that personal computers are simply not being widely accepted for nonbusiness use at home. One estimate is that about 14 percent of U.S. households have personal computers, while others say the figure may be as low as 11 percent. Though growth is expected to continue, one source sees the market as eventually leveling off at about 35 percent of households. But, the question remains as to how to advertise personal computers in ways that are meaningful to consumers.

Wang Laboratories has opted for television strategy that emphasizes technical computer jargon. "The company defends its advertising strategy claiming that more people than you may expect understand computer terms these days. And it says viewers who don't should get the idea anyway." However, other manufacturers wonder if the ads are really telling laymen that you need a college degree to operate a computer.

These advertisers assert that "The new emphasis . . . is on benefits, trying to do a better job of showing reluctant buyers how a computer can benefit their work."

Advertising has been used to try to soften the impersonal and technological side of computers and to show that they can be useful in the home. "Personal computer advertisers have learned, in many instances the hard way, that they have to follow the same marketing rules of other advertising," says Jim D'Arezzo, vice president of corporate marketing at Compaq Computer. "Things such as brand distinction, product differentiation, appeal." Many advertisers seem to be finding that straightforwardness makes the ads easier and quicker for the target audience to understand, and thus more effective in communicating and persuading.

This situation illustrates a fundamental principle of advertising execution. To be effective, it must offer a meaningful promise or benefit to potential consumers.

Source: Based on John Marcom, Jr., "Computer Firms Confused on How to Advertise to Changing Market," *The Wall Street Journal*, Sept. 19, 1985, 33. Cheryl Spencer, "Computers That Go Home," *Personal Computing*, October, 1986, 160. "Wang Gambles on Ads Using Technical Computer Jargon," *Boulder Daily Camera*, April 12, 1987. "New Trends in Three Key Industries," *Adweek*, May 26, 1987, 22.

INTRODUCTION

This chapter examines important aspects of advertising execution and the decisions necessary to develop advertising tactics. Important principles for print and broadcast advertising are discussed, including some fundamental principles for designing and evaluating advertisements in these media.

CREATIVITY IN ADVERTISING

The concept of creativity in advertising is extremely problematic. Most industry people feel that the term is terribly overused and that it fails to accurately describe the work done in the advertising business. In spite of this, the development of advertising messages is called "creative work," the group of people who do this work are referred to collectively as the "creative department," and individually as "creatives." As ingrained as these labels are, there does not seem to be much chance of changing them.

Many outsiders imagine that creative people in advertising are exactly what the label implies. Popular novels and television have portrayed them as people with wild eyes—and imaginations to match—who merely dream up fantastic ideas about how advertisements and commercials should be executed. While this is a part of their work, the advertising creative process is a good deal more disciplined than that. Usually, extensive information gathering and considerable planning go into the formulation of the advertising message. Nevertheless, at some point in the process imagination and ingenuity are needed to translate a set of prescriptive instructions (creative strategy) about what the advertising message should contain into the message itself. In other words, **creative tactics** are how the message plan is carried out—the executional details. The constant pressure to create fresh "answers" to advertising problems sometimes results in unusual approaches, as shown in the satirical commercial illustrated in Figure 13.1.

FIGURE 13.1

The Isuzu "Liar" Campaign: An Unusual Approach to Selling Cars

He's lying. 34 MPG city, 40 highway.

Downhill in a hurricane.

House not included.

Source: Courtesy of Graham Baker.

FIGURE 13.2

General Foods International Coffees: Using Visual Similarity to Create Continuity in a Campaign

Source: GENERAL FOODS is a registered trademark of General Foods Corporation. Reprinted with permission.

Some years ago the slogan "It's not creative unless it *sells!*" became popular among some people on Madison Avenue. The slogan was a reaction against a trend to innovative, entertaining, and humorous commercials held in high regard during the 1960s. Supporters of the sales criteria held that many of the so-called "creative" commercials had very little impact on the market situation of the products advertised.[1] While of course not every advertising message is designed to have an immediate sales effect, all advertising is designed to have one, ultimately. This is the most important discipline of advertising creativity: it must succeed in its intended role in leading prospects to the adoption of the product, service, or idea. Without this success, innovation, imagination, or winning awards means very little.

THE NATURE OF ADVERTISING CAMPAIGNS

An advertising *campaign* is a set of advertisements and/or commercials united by a common theme and planned to accomplish a specific purpose. Usually advertisements or commercials in a campaign have a similar visual appearance designed to convey a feeling of continuity to the reader or viewer, and often a campaign may include special elements designed especially for specific target groups, such as retailers. While the execution of each ad in the campaign is different, all ads are based on the same fundamental purposes and planning and are usually united by a common theme.

The advertising planning process begins with the formulation of advertising objectives and strategy. Often the process of developing tactics, or actual executions in the form of advertisements and commercials, is guided by a **copy platform,** a document that serves as reminder of the earlier planning decisions. Most major agencies employ some such device to guide creative work. The document may be called by a different name (such as a creative work plan), but most contain the same basic information and are employed for the same purpose: to keep the nature of the advertising task before the creative people as they work to develop advertising executions. The general style is shown in Figure 13.3.

FOCUS OF EFFECTIVE ADVERTISING: FEATURES VERSUS BENEFITS

FIGURE 13.3

A Sample Copy Platform

KARSH & HAGAN ADVERTISING, INC.
5500 S. SYRACUSE ST. / SUITE 200
ENGLEWOOD, CO 80111-2106
303-770-8088

CREATIVE WORK PLAN

CLIENT:

1. What is the problem/opportunity?
2. What net effect do we want from advertising?
3. Who are we trying to reach?
4. What is the doubt in the mind of our prospect?
5. What or who is the competition?
6. What is our key persuasion?
7. How do we support the above?
8. How will we measure effectiveness of advertising?
9. Are there any obligatory elements to consider?

Approved by ______ Client ______ Date ______

Source: Courtesy of KARSH & HAGAN ADVERTISING.

One of the essential guiding precepts of formulating effective advertising is that it must emphasize benefits. A **benefit** is a satisfaction that the user derives from a product or service. A benefit stands distinct from a physical characteristic or component of the product, called a **feature,** built into it by the manufacturer. Good advertising emphasizes what the user gets out of the product, not what the manufacturer puts into it. This is an important point, and indeed is one of the fundamental reasons that advertisers employ agencies, as pointed out in an earlier chapter. The agency must approach the assignment with the consumer's view in mind. It is this sort of objectivity that renders the product's want-satisfying characteristics as the central focus of the advertisement. Often the advertiser firm has a tendency to consider technical aspects of the product, or of its manufacturing, to be the important and noteworthy aspect of the product. While this may be accurate in a technical sense, often such aspects are of little consequence to consumers.

John O'Toole, chairman of Foote Cone & Belding, provides an illustration of this principle as seen in the introduction of the DieHard automotive battery by Sears. Innovations in the plastics industry allowed that the case of the battery could be made thinner, meaning that in a comparably sized battery, more space could be devoted to the acid and plates that make it work. Rather than dwell on these technical aspects of the product, however, the commercials said "The DieHard. Starts your car when most other batteries won't."[2] O'Toole also points out that stressing a product's benefits is not a new concept; it goes back at least as far as the 1900s. Another example of providing reader benefits in the advertising copy is illustrated in Figure 13.4.

EFFECTIVE ADVERTISING: THE "YOU" ATTITUDE

The concept of the "you" attitude is in some ways an extension of the thinking behind benefit emphasis. Basically, the **"you" attitude** involves keeping the interest of the reader foremost and speaking to readers in terms that are meaningful for them. There is a tendency in presenting a product or service to speak in terms of how the product works, or what the service provider does. Using the "you" attitude, the information is reinterpreted and stated in terms of the improvements in the reader's life

FIGURE 13.4

Promoting Benefits in the
Advertising Copy

Source: Courtesy of The Advertising Council.

from using the product or service (see Figure 13.5). Perhaps this principle is summed up best by a quotation ascribed to an official from Scott Lawn and Garden Products: "People don't care about our seeds, they care about their lawns."

GENERAL PRINCIPLES OF ADVERTISING COMMUNICATION

Surprisingly little research information exists on general advertising effectiveness. There are several reasons for this. First, advertisers are usually concerned with a specific problem and a specific situation. In the short term, it is considerably less time-consuming and expensive to secure the information needed to solve the immediate problem than it is to try to establish enduring laws or principles. Second, the vast majority of research conducted by business is done confidentially and without publication or even wide distribution of the findings. For this reason, research does not build as it does in the scientific community. Despite these pressures of the competitive environment, some basic principles have been established through social science research. These can be organized into four general areas.

FIGURE 13.5

"You"-Oriented Advertising

Source: Courtesy of the Pantene Company, a division of Richardson-Vicks Inc.

SOURCE CHARACTERISTICS

The perceived source of advertising information has important implications for the way the information is treated by the audience. One important area of concern is source credibility, which seems to be a function of perceived expertise and perceived objectivity. Expertise seems to be generally more important to credibility than objectivity. This is the basis for the use of testimonials and product spokespeople in advertising. In addition, celebrity endorsers seem most effective in creating and sustaining brand recall. A second important dimension is source attractiveness. People tend to accept information more readily from people they consider to be like themselves (or their idealized selves).

MESSAGE PRESENTATION

The way the message is composed has a great deal to do with acceptance. Fundamental readability is very important in that difficult material is usually not read or not understood and thus cannot be recalled. Distracting and ambiguous elements result in lower readership, as do long sentences and big words. Although unusual type styles can convey mood and feel-

A CLOSER LOOK

CELEBRITY ADVERTISING

The use of celebrities to endorse products goes back a long way—at least to the early 1930s. Today, the use of celebrities is on the rise and it's big business. Approximately 10 percent of all television advertising dollars reportedly go for celebrity ads. In the mid-1980s, this amounted to well over $2 billion. Some celebrities earn more than $2 million per year for advertising products. Among the top earners are Bill Cosby, Michael Jackson, Lionel Richie, Alan Alda, and Michael Jordan.

Are celebrity advertisements effective? What advantage do they give an advertiser? Using celebrity endorsements can present problems:

• *The fragile nature of the celebrity.* Evel Knievel (Ideal Toy Corp.) was jailed in California for assault. Olympic swimmer Mark Spitz (Schick Inc.) faded from popularity long before his contract expired.

• *High cost.* Pepsi-Cola USA paid an estimated $5 million each for Michael Jackson and Lionel Richie. Alan Alda signed an estimated $2 million-per-year contract with Warner Communications' Atari. In one year, Bill Cosby received an estimated $1.5 million from General Foods (Jell-O).

• *Credibility and attention.* At least one study showed that half of all TV viewers believe that celebrities are endorsing products just for the money. Another study revealed that only 40 percent of TV celebrity ads were successful in fostering brand awareness.

• *Difficulty in choosing the right celebrity.* Market Evaluations, Inc., found that Catherine Deneuve flopped for Whitehall Labs' Youth Garde moisturing lotion because she was too intimidating. Datril discovered that people didn't believe that John Wayne, the Datril spokesman, was an expert on headache remedies.

Using celebrities in advertising can have its benefits, however:

• *Holding viewers' attention.* The move to the 15-second commercial is causing advertisers to seek every possible way to grab and hold the attention of the viewer. Viewer attention is also being fragmented by channel changing during commercials, and many advertisers feel the use of a celebrity will minimize viewers changing channels during a commercial message.

• *More enjoyable commercials.* Celebrities can make watching an ad enjoyable—particularly when they appear as entertainers (for example, Lionel Richie in Pepsi-Cola commercials).

• *Lend credibility.* Some celebrities add a dimension of trustworthiness to an advertisement. Ironically, the celebrities who are thought to be exceptionally high in credibility are those who have steadfastly refused to appear in advertising (such as Clint Eastwood, Robert Redford, Eddie Murphy, and Walter Cronkite).

• *Convincing messages.* When the right combination of product and celebrity are brought together, the message is very convincing (for example, Miller Lite beer and retired professional athletes).

Sources: Stratford P. Sherman, "When You Wish upon a Star," *Fortune*, August 19, 1985, 66–71; "The Big New Celebrity Boom," *Business Week*, May 22, 1978, 79–80; and Barbara Lippert, "Advertising: Where the Beef Is," *Saturday Review*, January/February 1985, 19.

ing, they are more difficult to read. Larger relative size and the use of color both contribute to increased attention and readership. Large visual elements in ads attract more readers who learn and recall more of the message.

MESSAGE STRUCTURE

Both the order and flow of information are important to its acceptance. Material presented first is most likely to be accepted, and thus the most relevant and persuasive information should be placed at the beginning of the ad. Repetition seems to increase positive attitudes, agreement, and perceived truthfulness, but only to the point at which disinterest and annoyance set in. Music tends to draw attention as well as form associative bonds. Thus it aids in both creating impact for the advertising message and in enhancing memorability.

LINGUISTIC CHARACTERISTICS

Concrete and specific words and phrases result in much more favorable attitudes than abstract and general references. Perceived exaggeration of claims results in negative evaluations of the ad and advertiser and lowers credibility and the willingness to buy. The use of similes and metaphors in advertising copy increases persuasiveness and credibility.[3]

DEVELOPING A CENTRAL CONCEPT OR ADVERTISING THEME

Advertising succeeds by endowing product consumption with social significance. In translating the imperatives of the creative strategy into meaningful terms for the potential consumer, a central concept or theme is developed that attempts to tie all the advertising elements together to give the consumer a coherent mental picture of the product regardless of whether the product messages are received from one mass medium, or some combination. The unity of a central concept can be provided by the artistic execution of the ad. The examples in Figure 13.2 show similar layout and copy style designed to convey a coherent impression of the product. Theme ideas often evolve over time, though a number of advertising themes have run virtually unchanged for decades—for example, the homey black-and-white campaign for Jack Daniels bourbon (Figure 13.6). An enduring theme is usually one that is well suited to the marketing situation of the product and is versatile enough to allow execution in a number of different media. Usually "soft sell" or image themes (the "Marlboro Man," for example) are most enduring, since intrusive ads tend to become irritating and wear out quickly.

PRINT ADS THAT COMMUNICATE

Print advertising is built around three basic components. These are the headline, the visual, and the body copy. The **headline** must convey the selling message as efficiently and completely as possible, since many will read no more than this. The **visual** dramatizes the selling idea and reinforces the product's promise or benefit to the reader. The **body copy** offers more detailed information, persuasion, and the urge to act. In writing or evaluating print advertising, there are certain principles that most practitioners agree make for the best readership and persuasion.

1. **Include a benefit in headline.** The headline should select prospects

FIGURE 13.6

A Successful Advertising Theme
That Has Endured over Time

Source: Courtesy of the Jack Daniel Distillery.

from the audience by offering a promise or benefit of interest to the
target group.

2. **Speak to individual readers.** No one feels moved by a general
    appeal. Focus on the self-interest of a single reader and keep the
    emphasis on "you" rather than "we."

3. **Connect the visual, headline, and copy.** These three elements
    should combine to achieve a single impression, with each enhancing
    it in a specific way.

4. **Be different, not difficult.** Novelty draws attention and contributes
    to differentiation, but ambiguity and superfluous elements distract
    from and compete with the selling message. Clichés and tired
    phrasing don't invite reading either.

5. **Write simply, directly.** Don't overload the reader with words or
    technical jargon. Communicate a single thought in a single line.

6. **Project warmth.** Warm words and empathy with the reader are
    more effective than shouting.

FIGURE 13.7

A Persuasive Print Ad

This ad for Tahiti Tourism exemplifies the principles of effective print advertising.

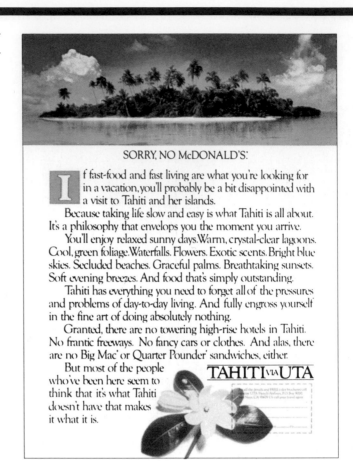

Source: Courtesy of the Tahiti Tourist Promotion Board and UTA French Airlines.

7. **Avoid puffery and bragging.** Readers are smart enough to see through exaggerated claims and superfluous adjectives, which destroy the advertisement's credibility and undermine the advertiser's integrity.

An example of a print ad that follows these guidelines is shown in Figure 13.7.

PRINCIPLES FOR EFFECTIVE COMMERCIALS

While television commercials vary considerably in complexity, cost, and intended effect, basic principles can be considered in evaluating their potential impact.

1. **Clear premise.** Behind every commercial is a single statement that sums up what the message is: the purpose of the commercial. This statement should be the standard against which the elements in the commercial are measured.

FIGURE 13.8

A Successful TV Commercial

This TV commercial for Anheuser Busch's Eagle Snacks demonstrates five principles used to evaluate effective commercials: clear premise, key visual idea, strong opening and story line, and product emphasis.

ANNCR (VO): Once you had to fly to get Eagle Snacks Honey Roast Nuts.

We're all out of Eagle Snacks.

(MUSIC) All that's changed.

Now, all you have to do . . . (MUSIC)

. . . is take a trip to your nearest store.

Eagle Snacks Honey Roast™ Nuts. The airline nut.

Source: Courtesy of Eagle Snacks, Inc; one of The Anheuser-Busch Cos.

2. **Key visual idea.** Since television is a visual medium, the bulk of the emphasis is on pictures, not words. A **key visual** is the central visual concept of what the message is about. It is the visual counterpart of the verbal premise noted above, and is the basic building block around which the commercial is constructed.

3. **Strong opening.** People watch television to be entertained, so the commercial must involve the viewers quickly or it will be tuned out.

4. **Story line.** Even though very short, the commercial must develop a story. The sense of unfolding and building is vital to maintaining viewer attention and involvement.

5. **Product emphasis.** Regardless of whether the presentation is humorous or the most serious sort of demonstration, the product must figure strongly in the commercial. As obvious as this may seem, it is often overlooked.

These principles are clearly illustrated in the popular and successful television commercial illustrated in Figure 13.8.

THE PROBLEM OF RULES FOR ADVERTISING

While general rules can be suggested to guide advertising efforts, few can be presented as irrefutable commandments. Neither the advertising nor human response to it is understood clearly enough to allow such ironclad statements. While the generalizations in the earlier sections of this chapter represent the best understanding of the situation at this time, these rules are nothing more than guidelines.

For any set of advertising rules, it will be possible to produce any number of campaigns that not only violate them, but also result in outstanding success for the advertiser in the process. The usefulness of these rules is not to treat them as imperatives, but to understand them, and violate them only with good reason.

SPECIAL CONSIDERATIONS IN PRINT ADVERTISING

Formulating print advertising tactics is based on an essential principle: Develop the strongest possible opening. This principle holds whether one is writing for magazine, newspaper, or direct mail. In magazine, the opening is most likely to be a headline, while in direct mail it might be an opening line of copy, the salutation of a letter, or a superscript on it. David Ogilvy has said that when copywriters write the headline of a print ad, they have spent $.80 of their client's advertising dollar.[4] This is because the headline must attract and involve readers, making a promise that is sufficiently strong to get them to read the body copy to learn more.

However, merely attracting attention and readership is not enough. As Leo Burnett expressed it:

> It is better to attract the serious attention of possible buyers than through an exaggerated and clever headline to attract the other possible readers who won't be interested in the message anyway.[5]

The point is that the advertisement must not merely attract curious attention by being bizarre, but should selectively attract the attention of those who can be induced to be interested, prospective buyers of the product.

Print tends to be a logical medium, one to which the reader turns for information as well as entertainment. For this reason, the reader has similar expectations of the advertisements found in magazines and newspapers. If you stop to consider your own behavior, you will probably agree that when you read specialized publications about activities you participate in, or even your daily newspaper, advertising is one of the elements you actively seek out and read. In the case of the newspaper, the advertising information may be that there is a sale at a local fashion boutique. An ad in a skiing magazine may provide interesting reading about equipment or services that make your activities safer or more exciting.

Print advertising relies on the illustration to combine with the headline to maximize the communication effectiveness. The visual portion of the print ad should also work to help select readers for the advertisement, by provoking their interest and inviting further reading. Ideally, the headline

ALTERNATIVE LAYOUT STYLES

While there are probably an infinite number of variations in the way a page of print advertising can be arranged, most designs can be considered varieties of one of the six styles below. In designing the layout the art director selects a style which is aesthetically pleasing and which best interprets the advertising idea.

Standard

Editorial

Poster

Picture-Caption

Cartoon

Picture-Cluster

and visual combine to produce a synergistic communication effect that not only selects prospects from idle scanners, but communicates far more in combination than either of the elements would singly.[6]

The body copy is the third important component of print advertising. Body copy is the words usually found in a block, or blocks, of type below the headline. The tasks of the body copy are to develop the persuasive appeal and product benefits promised by the headline and visual and offer additional reinforcing information to the reader to maximize the persuasive effect. Here, supporting detail is offered to make the claim or promise of the headline believable to the readers and offer the information and the impulsion to act on the advertisers' offer.

CHARACTERISTICS OF EFFECTIVE BROADCAST ADVERTISING

Experienced professionals agree that the first job of broadcast advertising is to arrest the attention of the target audience. Unlike the print advertising environment, the broadcast media attract viewers and listeners for passive entertainment. Since radio and television often serve a background function in the living environment, there is a special challenge to draw attention to the advertising message. Here, as in print, the opening must be strong and selective.

Radio has special challenges for the creative team in that it lacks any tangible representation of the advertising message. Though it lacks the visual dimension of print and television, radio has been called the *medium of the mind*. Imagery used in radio commercials requires the audience to create mental pictures to supplement the words; through this participation it can be especially persuasive.

Radio is also an intimate medium, in that stations draw listeners with similar interests and tastes. The radio message is personal, almost as though someone is speaking directly to you individually. Humor is often an important element in radio advertising because it builds listener involvement with the advertising message. This is shown in the radio script in Exhibit 13.1.

Television, of course, combines the elements of sight and sound to create a situation that closely approximates the presence of a salesperson in the home. While direct hard-sell tactics are quite likely to result in irritation, the medium does allow for demonstration and before/after dramatization in ways that cannot be equaled in other media. The broadcast media allow for (and seem to dictate) more emotional appeals, perhaps because more senses are involved in their apprehension, and this allows for more emotional presentation.

The combination of sight, sound, and motion in television makes it a very effective advertising medium, but also complicated and expensive to use. Recent estimates put the cost of producing even a relatively simple commercial in one day of filming at about $70,000.[7] The production process will be discussed later in this chapter. Exhibit 13.2 compares the costs of making a commercial with other television productions.[8] As the table indicates, when compared on a cost-per-minute basis, commercials are the most expensive productions seen on television. The reasons for this include intensive production and a need to have total control over every detail.

EXHIBIT 13.1

An Award-Winning Radio
Commercial: Alabama Power

Doris: Oh, Frank, not again.

Frank: Doris, please, just call Billy.

Doris: Billy! Your father has an announcement to make.

Billy: Yeah, Dad?

Frank: Son, I'm afraid we have to move again.

Billy: Oh, Dad. I just made friends.

Frank: I'm sorry, but it's Fall now and if we don't move soon, Winter will be here.

Doris: North in the Summer, South in the Winter. Sixteen moves in the last four years.

Frank: It's for our own good. To keep a constant temperature between sixty-eight and seventy-four degrees. I mean, what do you want me to do?

Billy: Dad, why don't we just get an electric heat pump?

Frank: Don't be ridic . . . what's that?

Billy: Just the most efficient all-in-one home heating and cooling system there is.

Frank: That's impossible . . . isn't it?

Billy: No, a heat pump is the perfect system for saving energy and money.

Frank: Cool in the summer?

Billy: Yep.

Frank: *And* warm in the winter?

Billy: Exactly. Everyone's converting to heat pumps.

Frank: Boy, Billy, you're smart. Isn't he smart, Doris?

Doris: Yes, he's smart.

Frank: Where'd you learn about heat pumps, Billy?

Billy: In science class at school.

Frank: Can I ask you another science question, Billy?

Billy: Sure . . .

Frank: When you erase a blackboard . . .

Billy: Oh no . . .

Frank: Where do the darn words go?

Billy: Dad, I already explained this to you . . .

Frank: I know, but they're there and they're gone.

Anncr: The electric heat pump. The all-in-one home heating and cooling system. For more details, call Alabama Power.

A BRIEF OVERVIEW OF THE PRODUCTION PROCESS

While it is not important for most people in the advertising industry to be intimately familiar with the technical aspects of production, the activity has an important impact on the shape and character of the advertising message. In addition, the production process is expensive and demands the services of outside suppliers. Both agency and advertiser need an overview of the production process in order to understand and control expenditures.

PRINT PRODUCTION

The print production process usually begins with a typewritten sheet of advertising copy (see Figure 13.9). Once approvals have been secured at the agency and advertiser, this typed copy is prepared for the typogra-

EXHIBIT 13.2

What It Costs to Produce a Commercial, in Dollars and Time

COST EFFICIENCY

PRODUCTION	COST PER EPISODE (in dollars)	MINUTES PER EPISODE	COST PER MINUTE (in dollars)
30-second commercial	$ 70,000	0.5	$140,000
Nighttime hour drama	650,000	43.0	15,116
Situation comedy	350,000	23.0	15,217
Daytime hour drama	50,000	43.0	1,162
Feature picture	10,000,000	110.0	90,900

WORK EFFICIENCY

PRODUCTION	HOURS IN PRODUCTION	MINUTES OF AIR TIME	PRODUCTION HOURS PER AIRTIME MINUTE
:30 Commercial	10	0.5	20.0
Nighttime Hour Drama	60	43.0	1.4
Situation Comedy	40	23.0	1.74
Daytime Hour Drama	10	43.0	.23

Source: Based on "How Much Should a Commercial Cost?" *Marketing Communications*, June 1983, 41.

FIGURE 13.9

The Print Production Process

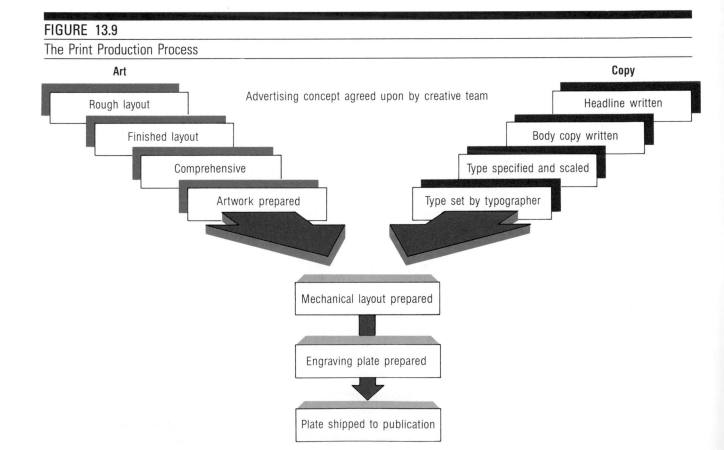

pher. This may be done by production department personnel, the copy-writer, or the art director. This person both *specifies* the typeface and the type size to be set, and *scales*, or fits, the type into the space allowed for it in the layout. The copy is then sent to a typographer, who sets the type as specified and scaled by the agency and returns proof sheets for approval.

The visual side of the production process begins with a *rough layout*, often a very simple sketch of the major elements in the ad. A *finished layout* is prepared to show the ideas in better detail once the creative team has come to agreement about how the ad will look. If the ad is to be shown to a client, a **comprehensive layout** is usually created. A comprehensive, or "comp," is a drawing of what the finished ad will look like. All elements are represented, though body copy is often represented by ruled lines, headlines are hand-lettered, and visual elements are sketched. Using the comp or finished layout as a guide, the art director commissions the artwork or photography that is to appear in the ad. This too is done by a professional or studio outside the agency. In the cases of both typography, and illustration or photography, the talents are too specialized to be part of the agency staff and it gives greater economy and versatility to buy these services from outside vendors. Usually these suppliers are selected based on competitive bidding, special abilities, or successful past work.

When the type and art have been approved and accepted, they are then put together into what is called a *pasteup*, *keyline*, or *mechanical layout*, depending on the medium. The mechanical is an exact-size replica of what the finished ad will look like, and from it a full-sized photographic negative is made. The negative in turn is used to produce a printing plate used in printing magazine ads (or a *matrix* or *stereotype*, in the case of a newspaper ad).

If the ad is to appear in color, the process is more complicated. Rather than one photographic negative, it is necessary to make four, one for each of the basic color components—red, yellow, blue, and black. The four negatives are called **color separations** and are used to make four individual printing plates. When these plates are put on a four-color press, they each lay down an impression of their respective colors successively, one on top of the other. Using four colors of ink, it is possible to achieve the look of full color in the finished printing job, as shown in Figure 13.10.

PRODUCTION OF A TELEVISION COMMERCIAL

The production process for television usually begins with an approved script or storyboard (see Figure 13.11). A script is a simple narrative much like a dramatic script, which includes the actors' lines and stage directions, while a storyboard includes the same information in pictorial form.

The script or storyboard is put out for bids among commercial production companies. These bids are evaluated by agency personnel, usually the art director in consultation with production people or an agency executive producer who is knowledgeable about the production process and keeps close watch on the production budget. As in the print process, the

FIGURE 13.10   The Four-Color Separation Process: How It Works

Source: Courtesy of Mark Oliver, Inc. Santa Barbara, CA.

A full-color advertisement must be separated into four photographic negatives—red, yellow, blue, and black—before it can be printed. Once the colors are separated, four printing plates are made and used to print the ad in full color. When the plates are put on a four-color printing press, they each lay down an impression of their respective colors in succession—one on top of the other. Using four colors of ink, it is possible to achieve the look of full color shown in the Stubbies ad.

specialized talent and equipment of the producer (the person who will actually make the commercial) are contracted for outside the agency.

After the producer is selected, the next step is the **preproduction process.** Preproduction includes all the preparations for shooting the commercial. In this phase, the location of the commercial is chosen, or the set is built; casting is done; and the necessary equipment and props are arranged for. The next phase, the actual production, or **shooting phase,** is usually the most expensive. The most crucial variable here is time. Shooting may take a day to a week and involves the use of actors and actresses as well as skilled technical people for direction, camerawork, lighting, sound recording, and so forth. While it is important that enough time be spent to get all the material needed for the finished commercial, excessive time spent in shooting adds dramatically to costs of production.

Following the shooting comes the **postproduction process.** This is the finishing stage in which the raw film or videotape is edited into a commercial; sound effects, background music, and off-camera announcers are added; and titles and optical effects are created. While agency personnel are usually involved in various stages of this process, the client firm usually is not. The client's first glimpse of the commercial is after completion of postproduction. This product, called the *answer print*, is essentially a

FIGURE 13.11

A TV Commercial: Storyboard, Script, and Answer Print Video

You Got It
30 seconds
Guy: I need that package of slides for a major presentation tomorrow at 10:30 a.m.
Competitor: You got it.
Guy: Not noon, not 3:00, 10:30 a.m.
Competitor: You got it.
Guy: Listen to me. No slides, no presentation.
Competitor: You got it.
Guy: Well, where is it?
Competitor: You'll get it.
(SFX: Barking)
Anncr: VO: Next time, send it Federal Express. Now Federal schedules delivery by 10:30 a.m. So when we say you got it, you'll get it.

finished commercial. When approved and accepted, additional prints of the commercial are prepared for distribution to networks or stations (Exhibit 13.3).

SPECIAL CONCERNS IN ADVERTISING TACTICS

One of the essential goals in selecting advertising tactics must be to achieve maximum impact on the audience. This means mustering the most dramatic and persuasive selling appeal and making the advertising presentation as outstanding and memorable as possible. However, it is possible to take this too far.

FIGURE 13.12

A Composite Storyboard: Film and Voiceover

Source: Courtesy of McDonald's.

The industry term *vampire video* refers to a presentation that is so over-whelming that it draws attention away from the product and focuses it on itself. The reader or viewer is left not with an impression of the product, but with an impression of the performance surrounding it. Showcasing products in an interesting and dramatic manner without drawing attention from them is a challenging problem that requires advertising people to walk a thin line.

A GLOBAL LOOK

WOULD YOU CARE FOR SOME CHICKEN, AMIGO?

Suppose you're running a successful campaign in an English-speaking country and you want to "convert" it for use in a Spanish-speaking one. Consider the following advertising blunders which occurred in translation from English into Spanish.

- In a recent campaign in Mexico, Braniff Airlines urged readers to relax on leather airplane seats. The ad's headline read "Sentado en cuero"; however, that can be interpreted as "Sit naked." (The $350,000 mistake, incidentally, was created in-house.)

- A recent campaign for Frank Perdue chicken created a stir when it was translated into Spanish. The Perdue slogan "It takes a tough man to make a tender chicken" became "It takes a sexually excited man to make a chick affectionate."

- Commercials for beer haven't escaped unscathed, either. In one, Budweiser seemingly underwent a sex change, going from "the king of beers" to "the queen of beers." Another beer brand was mistakenly described as "filling; less delicious."

- One candy manufacturer wanted consumers to know that the firm had been in the business for 50 years and ordered a statement to that effect to appear on the packaging. Imagine management's surprise when "n" rather than "ñ" was used in the line, resulting in the claim that the package contained 50 anuses.

- A burrito producer goofed and advertised its product as a *burrada*, which in Spanish slang means "big mistake." No kidding.

Sources: Maureen Glabman, "Oops! Braniff Ad Draws Hispanic Snickers," *Advertising Age*, February 9, 1987, 3; and "Sidelights: Marketing to Hispanics," *Advertising Age*, February 9, 1987, S–23.

EXHIBIT 13.3

Television Commercial Production: A Timetable

The time involved in producing a television commercial is considerably longer than many people realize. Ronald Harding, director of commercial production for Gillette Company (which produces about 100 commercials a year), suggests the following timetable as typical of the average commercial. (The total of about 4 months does not allow for unforeseen changes or production delays.)

Advertising agency develops creative strategy and storyboards	8 weeks
Legal clearance by agency, advertiser, and networks	2 weeks
Preproduction: including set location and construction; casting and wardrobe	2 weeks
Production: including lighting, filming, laboratory work, and sound transfers	1 week
Postproduction: including editing, screening, recording, mixing, and optical effects	3 weeks
Total	16 weeks

Source: "Cutting the Cost of Commercials," *Business Week*, February 15, 1982, 118–122.

SUMMARY

This chapter has reviewed the nature of advertising creativity and the constraints and discipline that planning brings to the campaign. Effective advertising usually emphasizes the benefits the user obtains from the product rather than the product's characteristics, called features. Advertising usually tries to adopt the attitude of the user toward the subject discussed; this is called the "you" attitude. Numerous aspects of the advertising message influence the audience response. These factors include audience perceptions about the source of the message, the manner in which the message is delivered, and the structure of the message, as well as the language used to convey the message.

Because of the complexity of advertising situations, it is almost impossible to identify inflexible rules about how advertisements should be done. However, the experience of many people, as well as some findings of research and testing, indicate that there are some important fundamental principles.

The basic elements of a print advertisement include the headline, which is designed to attract reader attention and provide a glimpse of the selling message; the visual, which dramatizes or reinforces the product benefit; and the body copy, which provides information, persuasion, and the urge to act.

Broadcast advertising is often regarded as a more emotional medium. While they can be used to demonstrate products, broadcast media are often used to tell an emotional or touching story that shows how products fit in the lives of consumers.

The production of advertisements and commercials is a time-consuming, expensive, and technical job. Mistakes at this point can mean that the carefully formulated message can be lost if the plan is not faithfully executed. To ensure that this does not happen, numerous technical people are involved in the special processes that result in a finished ad.

YOU MAKE THE DECISION

THE CONTACT SHOP

The Contact Shop offers quick replacement of lost or damaged contact lenses. The service is available through the prescription-drug departments of several large grocery store chains.

Here's how the service works: It does not substitute for prescription and fitting by an optometrist. Consumers take their contact lens prescription to the most convenient location, where it is kept on file. In the event of loss or damage, the consumer calls the Contact Shop to order a new lens or lenses. About 65 percent of contact lens prescriptions can be filled in 24 hours. Less common prescriptions can usually be replaced within a week to 10 days. Charges for replacements average 50 percent less from the Contact Shop than from other sources.

Develop a half-page newspaper ad for The Contact Shop. The ad's objective is to announce the availability of this service at local grocery stores, and to convince consumers of the savings and convenience of the service.

The target audience includes contact lens wearers and purchasers, particularly men and women who handle the family grocery shopping. Use the positioning strategy to emphasize the unique benefits of The Contact Shop.

Develop an advertising execution based on the information and direction above. On a standard-sized sheet of paper, describe the visual aspects of the ad. Below this description, write the ad's headline in capital letters. Below the head, write the advertising copy. Use a second sheet of paper for a rough layout. On the layout, sketch the visual idea and indicate the location of other major elements of the ad, such as headline, copy, subheads, etc.

■ ■ ■

QUESTIONS FOR DISCUSSION

1. How do tactics differ from strategy?
2. What is the importance of the copy platform?
3. Explain the difference between features and benefits.
4. What is the "you" attitude? Why is it important?
5. How do characteristics of the source influence message reception?
6. In what ways is readership related to effective advertising?
7. How do order and repetition affect the advertising message?
8. Why is it important to be skeptical of advertising rules?
9. What is the first challenge of creating a print ad?
10. Why are most specialized production services contracted for outside the advertising agency?

NOTES

1. For a discussion of the "creative revolution" in advertising in the 1960s, see Larry Dobrow, *When Advertising Tried Harder* (New York: Friendly Press, 1984).

2. John O'Toole, *The Trouble with Advertising . . .* (New York: Chelsea House, 1981), 98.

3. The material in this section is based in part on Larry Percy, "A Review of the Effect of Specific Advertising Elements upon Overall Communication Response," in *Current Issues and Research in Advertising—1983*, James H. Leigh and Claude R. Martin, Jr., eds., vol. II (Ann Arbor, Mich.: University of Michigan, 1983), 77–119.

4. David Ogilvy, *Confessions of an Advertising Man* (New York: Atheneum, 1963), 104.

5. Leo Burnett, *Communications of an Advertising Man* (Chicago: privately printed, 1961), 244.

6. Keith Hafer and Gordon White, *Advertising Writing*, 2d ed. (St. Paul, Minn.: West, 1982), 82.

7. "Cutting the Cost of Commercials," *Business Week*, February 15, 1982.

8. A complete discussion of TV production costs can be found in Arthur Bellaire, *Controlling Your TV Commercial Costs* (Chicago: Crain Books, 1976).

SUGGESTED READINGS

Arlen, Michael. *Thirty Seconds*. New York: Penguin Books, 1979.

Baker, Stephen. *Systematic Approach to Advertising Creativity*. New York: McGraw-Hill, 1979.

Bellaire, Arthur. *Controlling Your TV Commercial Costs*. Chicago: Crain Books, 1976.

Buxton, Edward. *Creative People at Work*. New York: Executive Communications, 1975.

Caples, John. *Tested Advertising Methods*. Englewood Cliffs, N.J.: Prentice-Hall, 1974.

Conrad, Jon. *The TV Commercial: How It Is Made*. New York: Van Nostrand Reinhold, 1983.

Higgins, Denis. *The Art of Writing Advertising*. Chicago: Advertising Publications, 1965.

Hopkins, Claude. *My Life in Advertising/Scientific Advertising*. Chicago: Crain Books, 1966.

Keil, John. *The Creative Mystique*. New York: John Wiley & Sons, 1985.

Malickson, David, and John Nason. *Advertising: How to Write the Kind That Sells*. Rev. ed. New York: Charles Scribner's Sons, 1982.

Watkins, Don. *Newspaper Advertising Handbook*. Columbia, S.C.: Newspaper Book Service, 1980.

Zeigler, Sherilyn, and J. Douglas Johnson. *Creative Strategy and Tactics in Advertising*. Columbus, Ohio: Grid, 1981.

C H A P T E R   1 4

MEASURING THE EFFECTIVENESS OF ADVERTISEMENTS

Key Terms

informal evaluation
creative review board
focus group interview
verbatim
mall intercept
concept testing
recall
inquiry
custom-designed research

Learning Objectives

To differentiate formal and informal evaluation

To focus on points in development when evaluation is useful

To enumerate the types of testing used to evaluate ad messages

To outline the principles of effective testing

To explain what makes advertising evaluation controversial

The Colorado Lottery depends on the use of advertising to let prospects know about new lottery games and to stimulate sales of lottery tickets. Not surprisingly, the lottery also depends heavily on various forms of advertising research to ensure that its efforts communicate the ad message clearly and as intended. According to Mary Brown, Marketing Director for the Colorado Lottery, "research is essential in planning our campaigns. We don't use it to tell us what kind of commercial we ought to run but to help us to avoid major problems."

The advertising managers at the Colorado Lottery are committed to using research as an integral part of their advertising efforts and spend the equivalent of 5 percent of their annual advertising budget for various research activities. For example during 1986, lottery planners developed a new lottery game based on a baseball theme. To evaluate the effectiveness of the advertising messages, lottery management contracted with an independent research firm to gather data before, during, and after the campaign.

The first step in the evaluation program was to ask prospective customers what they thought of some alternative executions of the baseball theme idea. Five alternatives, including a celebrity spokesperson and a spot based on live action baseball, were developed on storyboards and shown to focus groups. In pretesting commercial concepts, the Colorado Lottery typically uses representatives of two user groups: occasional players who buy lottery tickets less

than once a week and regular players who buy tickets more often. In this case, four focus groups, two of each user type, overwhelmingly chose the campaign execution based on the musical standard "Take Me Out to the Ball Game." As one result of reactions from the focus group, the lyrics of the song were rewritten to include mention of the top prize—important information to lottery players.

The second important component of the Colorado Lottery's evaluation program involved techniques to continuously monitor the impact of advertising once the campaign was introduced. This research used random telephone interviews to track the levels of knowledge, to record attitudes and purchase intentions, and to measure various advertising dimensions (such as recall of the advertising theme) among audience members. These studies are based on 9 interviews per night each

night of the week. Since each lottery game runs 8 to 10 weeks, the result is 500 to 600 interviews by the end of the advertising campaign for a particular game. The study supplied standards that were used to compare effectiveness from game to game and campaign to campaign. As measured in the tracking studies, the baseball campaign was again a clear winner. "An average of 65 percent of the audience was able to recall the baseball campaign," said Mary Brown, "which compared very favorably with previous games where recall levels of 35 to 40 percent were more typical."

While the techniques described above are a regular part of the Colorado Lottery's ongoing program of advertising evaluation, the lottery occasionally adds another dimension as well. Six months after the baseball campaign, the Colorado Lottery made the decision to move to a totally different style of advertising campaign. To evaluate the effectiveness of these new spots once they had been produced, the lottery once again turned to focus groups. After showing the commercials to prospective consumers, they received comments like, "the commercial showed people like me," "it looks like fun," and "I could win!" Needless to say, these reactions told management they were on target with the new commercial messages.

Source: Mary Brown, Marketing Director, Colorado Lottery, 9/30/87. Photo courtesy of KARSH & HAGAN Advertising (ad by Michael Sternagle).

INTRODUCTION

The following chapter discusses ways in which advertising concepts, advertisements, commercials, and campaigns can be evaluated. In reading it you should develop an understanding of how the measurement and evaluation processes are used in advertising, a conceptual understanding of the techniques involved, and an appreciation of the limitations of various measurement strategies.

ADVERTISING EVALUATION

The process of producing modern advertising includes considerable evaluation, both formal and informal. As Roger Wimmer and Joseph Dominick note in their mass media research text:

> . . . message research helps advertisers to answer three basic questions: (1) "What should the message say?" (2) "How should it be said?" (3) "What effect(s) did the message have?"[1]

Earlier chapters have pointed out that the advertising agency cannot proceed very far with advertising execution without approval of the client firm. Regular review of advertising alternatives and ideas can be considered a type of **informal evaluation** of the advertising campaign. In addition to the regular client reviews in setting objectives, strategies, and the steps in tactical execution, the advertising agency itself often imposes an evaluation process by means of a review panel. This panel, often called a "plans board" or **creative review board,** meets on a regular basis to review the work of the agency and to evaluate it. The panel is usually composed of senior members of the agency chosen for their wide range of experience and expertise. Approval from this group means that the advertising agency feels the advertising meets its standards and is representative of the agency's professional abilities.

An additional review of major importance is that of legal counsel. Major agencies and all reasonably sized advertiser firms rely on legal clearance. While legal reviews have little to do with improving advertising effectiveness, they remain an important aspect of advertising evaluation.

RULES OF THUMB FOR EVALUATING ADVERTISING

Some of the most important criteria for informal evaluation of advertising are based on experience. While creative people build their own store of experience throughout their career, there is also a substantial body of advertising principles that is part of the folklore of the trade. Many of these principles are found in the writing of leading practitioners, and many are simply passed along by word of mouth within the advertising organization.

It is actually somewhat surprising that there has not been greater effort by the industry to bring the principles of effective advertising together in some organized and coherent manner, but the fact is that this has not been done in any comprehensive way. David Ogilvy, who has argued in favor of this activity for years, stated:

> Some 85 percent of magazine readers do not remember seeing the average advertisement, and 75 percent of viewers cannot remember seeing the average television commercial the day after they have seen it. There can be little doubt that if more advertisements were better executed, these appalling figures would be reduced.[2]

Many in the business feel that attempts to develop an organized body of knowledge about the field are doomed to failure because by its very nature advertising is based as much on inspiration as on systematic activity. We will examine this position further in a later section of this chapter. What can be learned from the writings of a number of successful and articulate advertising practitioners also will be discussed later in this chapter.

GENERAL CRITERIA FOR EVALUATING ADVERTISEMENTS

The checklist in Exhibit 14.1 identifies some very general concerns about advertisements. These criteria might be applied by anyone with responsibilities related to the advertising function, either at the agency or the advertising firm.

Matched with Objectives While this would seem the most obvious and fundamental criterion for evaluating any advertising execution, it is often overlooked. Little can be expected from advertising efforts that do not match the goals and strategy set out for the campaign.

Clear Central Idea Evidence shows advertising designed around one central message or selling proposition is most effective. Attempting to say too much risks either confusing the prospect or inviting prospects to tune out.

Addressed to the Prospect The ad is not about the product, or even the company; it is about the satisfaction the prospect can find in the product. Ads should speak to the consumer's self-interest in terms and language that are meaningful.

Distinctive Often one of the most important goals of advertising is to achieve product differentiation. This means that the advertising must stand out, too. While difference for its own sake accomplishes little and often risks confusion, distinction is a basic requirement in both advertising concept and execution.

Tasteful While matters of taste are personal choices, advertisers have a responsibility not only to their intended audience, but to other readers and viewers as well. Though standards of popular taste change quickly, there can be little justification for offensive stereotyping and degrading portrayals, and indeed, there is considerable risk in them.

Teamwork of Elements Headline and visual in print ads, or audio and video in television commercials, must work together. They must be not merely compatible, but complementary, synergistic in effect.

EXHIBIT 14.1

General Criteria for Evaluating Advertisements

	(5) Very Good	(4)	(3) Average	(2)	(1) Very Poor
	++	+	0	−	− −
I. Concept of Ad or Campaign Is it . . .					
A. In harmony with objectives? strategy?					
B. A clear presentation of one central idea?					
C. Addressed to the prospect?					
D. Distinctive in approach?					
E. Tasteful in its appeal?					
F. Based on solid teamwork of all elements?					
II. Execution Is it . . .					
A. Imaginative in presentation?					
B. Emphatic on product/benefits?					
C. Esthetically pleasing?					
D. Convincing in its argument?					
E. Simple and clear in language?					
F. Strong in its opening and closing?					
G. Employing the medium to its fullest?					
H. A tie-in to, or development of, a continuing theme?					

Source: Charles F. Frazer, "Toward Some Criteria for Evaluating Advertisements," *Proceedings*, American Academy of Advertising.

Imaginative The ad should attempt to stand out from others and draw readers' attention through novel and intriguing presentation, while avoiding bizarre or irrelevant devices.

Emphatic The job of the ad is to present the product with maximum impact. It should give the product a vital role at the center of the presentation.

Esthetic Both the individual elements and the whole combination should come together in a pleasing and satisfying way. Awkwardness and imbalance put readers off and give the sponsor an amateurish appearance.

Convincing The job of the advertisement is to persuade the audience, not merely to assert a position. The persuasion may be logical or emotional but it should be designed to win conviction from the audience.

Clear Advertisements are not closely watched by prospects, so their messages must be unambiguous and direct. Except in special cases, technical language and abstract concepts are to be avoided.

Strong Opening and Closing Since the reader is usually not seeking advertisements, they must start in an interesting way to attract and hold attention. Closings too must be strong and positive, leaving the reader with a summary of the advertising message.

Effective Use of Medium Different advertising media offer different opportunities for persuasion. Does the advertisement make best use of the particular strengths of the media employed?

Theme Development A theme idea ties groups of advertisements together and presents a dimension of the product personality. In addition, it is often the device by which the advertised commodity is recalled. Be sure an appropriate theme idea is presented and integrated in the advertising.

These basic dimensions supply the basis for dialog between the advertising agency and the advertiser firm in informal evaluation of advertising.[3] If some of these dimensions are ignored or underplayed, this action should be taken with some explicit rationale in mind.

Though informal evaluation is an important process in the creation of the campaign, it is usually not enough of a basis on which to commit the efforts and resources of the marketer and the agency. To provide further assurances, formal evaluation of the advertising is undertaken.

WHY FORMAL EVALUATION?

Earlier chapters in this book have stressed the importance of planning and objective setting in the process of formulating the advertising campaign. The various types of measurement and evaluation described in this chapter play an important role in this process in two ways. First, by evaluating advertising ideas during their development the risk of disastrous failure is lowered. Marginal and unworkable campaign strategies can be detected early in the process before substantial dollars are committed to them.

Second, a continuous program of evaluation and testing allows the advertiser and agency to build a useful store of information about creative approaches and what can be expected to work most effectively. While in some cases this is simply a matter of becoming more experienced with a group of consumers or a product category, in others it is a matter of constructing extensive data bases that allow relatively sophisticated statistical analysis and generalizability.

WHEN TO EVALUATE

A wide variety of testing tools have evolved for the evaluation of advertising in various stages of development. Some techniques are useful at various stages in creative development, while others are best suited to particular points. Exhibit 14.2 suggests the points at which advertising ideas might be evaluated as well as techniques by which this evaluation might be carried out.

The most important element in making decisions about using evaluations is cost, in terms of time and money. While small investments of time and money at early stages can often ensure that a campaign develops along a useful and effective track, it is also quite possible to waste re-

---

EXHIBIT 14.2

Advertising Message Research: What, Why, and How

RESEARCH ACTIVITY	PURPOSE	TYPICAL TECHNIQUE
Positioning/message strategy research	Determine basic creative strategy	Analyze data from syndicated research services
Copy guidance research	Select appropriate verbal and visual elements	Conduct focus group interviews
Concept testing	Select most effective alternative	Conduct mall intercepts
Commercial pretesting	Test communication effectiveness	Perform theater testing
Campaign evaluation studies	Determine audience impact	Perform day-after recall tests

Source: Lyman E. Ostlund, "Advertising Copytesting: A Review of Current Practices, Problems and Prospects," *Current Issues and Research in Advertising*, James Leigh and Claude R. Martin, Jr., eds. (Ann Arbor: University of Michigan, 1978), 88.

sources and discourage creative personnel by continual retesting of ideas at every stage of their development. It is not recommended that every campaign be tested at every point in its execution, yet some authors have suggested that, given the importance of the advertising message, too little is spent on the development and pretesting of advertising. The following section will examine these important opportunities for evaluating advertising and discuss several alternative means of doing the evaluation.

STRATEGY FORMATION AND COPY GUIDANCE RESEARCH

At this early point in campaign development, evaluation techniques are used to check the appropriateness of advertising ideas for the desired target audience. While the audience is likely to have been specified precisely by earlier market studies and segmentation plans, it is often important for copywriters to observe real people rather than demographic categories. The most common way to do this is through a **focus group interview**, an open-ended group discussion of a product or advertising idea.

The focus group technique usually involves from 6 to 12 individuals selected as representative of the target audience and led by a trained moderator. Depending on the intention of the research, the session may take the form of a directed discussion of all products in a class and the experience of using them, or focus on the specific product and advertising being planned. Often focus groups are used to get audience reactions to strategy alternatives under consideration, or to see if the desired message is being communicated by a theme, slogan, or campaign. While multiple focus groups are often conducted, the findings from them are not generalizable in a statistical sense because of the small size of the sample of people involved. Nevertheless, focus groups are an important way of understanding the real people behind abstract demographic descriptions of target audiences. Creative people often find it valuable to observe focus group interviews to see how people talk about products and the words they use to do so. The transcripts of focus group sessions are transcribed into **verbatims**, which include notable statements and characterizations that may prove helpful in writing copy. In reviewing advertising testing methods,

A CLOSER LOOK

PACT PRINCIPLES

Evaluating advertisements often causes disagreement. Because there are few agreed-upon standards and innumerable methods of testing, it is often difficult to generalize from one test setting to another. Like the "tower of Babel," advertising people in both agencies and advertising firms have found themselves using different techniques and different vocabularies to describe their findings.

In 1982 a group of over 20 leading agencies released a position report titled "Positioning Advertising Copy Testing." The PACT report is a summary of the principles of effective message evaluation. It also represents a significant accomplishment as a cooperative dialog on a complex industrywide problem.

Following are the characteristics of a good copy testing system:

1. Provides measurements that are relevant to the objectives of the advertising

2. Requires agreement about how the results will be used in advance of each specific test

3. Provides multiple measures (because single measurements are generally inadequate to assess the performance of an advertisement)

4. Is based on a model of human response to communications—the reception of a stimulus, the comprehension of the stimulus, and the response to the stimulus

5. Allows for consideration of whether the advertising stimulus should be exposed more than once

6. Recognizes that the more finished a piece of copy is, the more soundly it can be evaluated and requires, as a minimum, that alternative executions be tested in the same degree of finish

7. Provides controls to avoid the biasing effects of the exposure context

8. Takes into account basic considerations of sample definition

9. Can demonstrate reliability and validity

Source: "PACT: Positioning Advertising Copytesting," *Journal of Advertising*, vol. 11, no. 4, 1982, 3–29.

FIGURE 14.1

Mall intercepts have become a common technique in evaluating advertising.

Source: Courtesy of the Campbell Soup Company.

researchers John Leckenby and Joe Plummer note that current research concerns seem concentrated on the issues of using research more effectively and constructively in the development stages of the advertising campaign.[4]

A second useful technique for gathering impressions and opinions in early creative planning is the **mall intercept**, in which researchers interview selected shopping mall patrons to gather responses to advertising ideas or executions. This technique, much more like a survey than the focus group, also allows the gathering of important reactions (see Figure 14.1). The technique depends upon interviewer skill in selecting appropriate respondents and has fairly severe limitations in terms of the time and depth of the interview. It does allow contact with a larger number of prospects, though results are rarely projectable.

CONCEPT TESTING AND COMMERCIAL PRETESTING

The techniques described above can often be carried out by an agency or a client firm since they do not require large resources or specialized equipment. Testing of either rough or finished commercials is a different matter, however, and usually this service is performed by a copytesting firm. While the intention of **concept testing** is to evaluate or generate ideas, advertisement or commercial testing is often performed to ensure that ad-

A CLOSER LOOK

UNDERSTANDING STARCH READERSHIP SCORES

The ad in this box has been "Starched"—that is, tested for readership using the Starch method. The tags fixed to the ad indicate the levels of attention that various elements in the ad received. In all instances in this ad the scores are preceded by a "W," indicating that the score is based on readership by women. (The ad appeared in *Woman's Day* and was targeted to female homemakers.)

Starch supplies three scores:

Noted is the percentage of readers of the issue who remembered seeing the advertisement in this issue.

Associated is the percentage of readers of the issue who saw part of the advertisement that clearly indicates the brand or advertiser.

Read Most is the percentage of readers of the issue who read 50 percent or more of the written material in the ad.

All ads in the issue are ranked according to their "associated" scores. The Miracle Whip ad did relatively well in the issue, ranking 14th among 75 ads in the magazine. This is not the entire story, however. Average scores for the product category over a two-year period are presented below.

CATEGORY	NUMBER OF ADS	NOTED	ASSOCIATED	READ MOST
Salad dressing and mayonnaise	26	60	56	16

vertisements achieve their communication goals or prove as memorable as other advertising in the category. It is sometimes used to help in deciding among alternative executions of the creative strategy.

Often this testing is carried out before final production of the advertisement or commercial is completed. This allows for revision or enhancement if important new information or critical consumer reaction is encountered in the testing process.

In print media, either representations or finished ads can be "tipped-in," or glued in place in magazines and then placed in homes of the sample recruited for the test. The usual technique is to interview readers (either in person or by phone) after 24 hours. The most common measurement is readers' recollection of important selling points in the test ad, and often their stated intentions regarding willingness to buy the product. Sample size in this type of testing is usually relatively small, rarely more than 300 people. The Starch Readership report shown in this chapter is an example of this technique.

Television testing requires more elaborate arrangements. As with print, TV commercials may be tested in either finished or rough form. The rough form, called *animatics*, usually consists of films of still pictures, much like a storyboard with a soundtrack. One of the largest suppliers of this type of service is Burke Marketing Research. The firm arranges for the telecast of the test commercial in markets specified by the advertiser. A sample of the viewers of the program in which the commercial appeared are then contacted the next day and their **recall** of the commercial's main points is recorded. The sample size is usually about 200 per market. Gallup & Robinson's In-View Service is another example of such a service, though In-View is available only in Philadelphia.

In both the techniques described above, the primary criterion for success of the advertisement is recall, usually expressed as a percentage of the total audience that remembers the element under study. Though there is considerable debate in the industry as to whether recall is the best measure of advertising effectiveness, it continues to be the most common.[5] Interpreting the raw recall score is, in itself, a difficult job. Most testing services have established norms for various product categories, and not surprisingly, there is considerable variation both within and among the categories. In relatively high interest categories, norm scores can be two to three times greater than the scores achieved in low interest categories. Comparisons with these norms provide at least a general standard for the success of ads and commercials.

Another technique for testing the communication effectiveness of commercials is the *theater test*, in which representatives of the intended target audience are invited to view test commercials in a theater setting. Commercials in theater tests are shown as part of an entertainment program to simulate the exposure the viewer has at home when viewing television. Because of the control researchers have over the environment in a theater, a variety of different sorts of information and reactions can be gathered from the audience. Difficulties with this type of testing include the unnaturalness of the exposure environment and the fact that it is very difficult to recruit representatives from some desirable audience groups.

COMPARING ADVERTISING PERFORMANCE

After the selection decisions have been made and the campaign is launched, evaluation continues to be important. Techniques like those described above are often used during the campaign to assess the comparative impact of the advertising campaign. The techniques used to evaluate relative market impact are many and varied. Often **inquiries**, reader requests generated through return of request forms or reader reply cards in print ads, serve as measures of the interest and conviction generated by advertisements. The broadcast counterpart—inquiries and orders received at toll-free telephone numbers—is also a commonly used measure of effectiveness. Such techniques of course lack norms for comparison, though many firms develop their own evaluation scales based on past experience. The weakness of this technique is that it only provides information after the fact; that is, after the advertisements have been run.

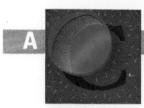

A CLOSER LOOK

WHY COMMERCIALS ARE EVALUATED

Why are commercials evaluated? When Gallup & Robinson Research (G & R) surveyed consumers about skin care product advertising, it learned some interesting things about recall. One finding was that recall of the advertising (see graph) ranged from 43 percent of viewers for the best-remembered spot to 4 percent for the least-remembered. This means that one brand's ad was remembered more than 10 times better than the least memorable. The standard of comparison for most products is the average level of recall for products in the category, called the *product norm* by G&R. In the skin care product example, one third of the campaigns scored below the norm for the category.

Recall is not the only measurable aspect of commercials. The table below shows data on recall, communication, and persuasion for two facial tissue commercials.

Softness was the key point in both commercials. Both used a slice-of-life, problem/solution presentation technique. Commercial #1 showed a woman and a man who had colds using the tissue and praising its softness, while Commercial #2 showed two women in a sad movie using the tissue to dry their tears.

Observations of Skin Care Commercials

Range
Campaign average

| Recall | High | Low | A | B | C | D | E | F | G | H | I | J | K | L |

Brand

Source: Gallup & Robinson In-View, 4–5.

Differences between Two Facial Tissue Commercials

	COMMERCIAL #1	COMMERCIAL #2	PRODUCT NORM
Percentage of audience recalling commercial	36	32	30
Percentage of recallers who remembered key point	93	95	68
Percentage who indicated increased interest in buying			
among recallers	47	25	35
among total sample	17	8	10

The data in the table show that both commercials scored above the norm in recall and communicating their key point about softness. There is considerably wider variation in willingness to buy, with commercial #1 scoring almost twice as well as #2, both among recallers and the total sample.

G&R interpreted the strength of commercial #1 as coming from the demonstration that the tissue is good when one has a cold. The application in commercial #2 was not as effectively communicated, and resulted in a less persuasive effect.

The test data show fairly wide variation in the relative effectiveness of commercials at achieving recall and affecting willingness to buy. In the struggle for market share, many advertisers feel they cannot afford to run advertising that has not been evaluated against competitors.

Custom-designed research is often used in this stage since it can be set up to monitor the exact intentions on which the campaign was based. Feedback obtained at this stage allows modification of off-target advertising, as well as helping to detect advertising wearout. It may also allow a marketer to judge the effectiveness of the campaign in relation to responses from competitors.

CAMPAIGN EVALUATION STUDIES

In some cases overlapping with the previous category, campaign effectiveness studies are primarily designed to measure the success of the advertising campaign in reaching its stated objectives. Often, such studies provide useful data not only for evaluating past performance, but for future advertising plans by providing baseline data on levels of awareness, attitudes towards products and services and so on. These sorts of campaign effectiveness measures are usually based on custom surveys since research services are not flexible enough to provide data to match varied advertising objectives. In many cases, however, leading research suppliers can also design the sorts of customized surveys that will satisfy campaign evaluation needs.

The new electronic media are also providing further opportunities for measuring advertising effectiveness. For example, Burke's ADTEL service allows direct sales effectiveness measures for advertisers. ADTEL makes sample groups available in four different market areas. In each case the sample groups are composed of two demographically matched subsamples recruited from cable television homes. The matched sample and cable hookup allows for presentation of two different test commercials. Consumer diaries of household purchases can be compared to derive estimates of the effects of different advertising treatments on purchasing patterns.

A significant advance in technique for advertising evaluation may result from a service recently offered in limited market areas by Arbitron, an audience research company. The service is based on the use of special measurement devices. These devices, called *peoplemeters*, consist of a component wired to the TV set that records the station to which the set is tuned, and a light pen (like a supermarket scanning device) that participants run across the UPC bar code on their grocery purchases. The device holds great promise for establishing correlations between the commercials viewers are exposed to and the supermarket products they buy. The acccuracy of the data depends on the cooperation of those in the sample of homes equipped with the device. Each member of the family must indicate his or her presence at the TV set to the recording device, and the family must faithfully record their purchases after every trip to the store.

INTERPRETING MEASUREMENT INFORMATION

Though the foregoing sections outline relatively sophisticated methods for evaluating advertising, some additional considerations are in order. As noted earlier, most syndicated testing services measure recall of the advertising theme or message. But recall is rarely the only goal of an advertising campaign, and is often not an explicit goal at all. One of the greatest difficulties of the advertising process is that theory in the field is not far enough advanced to specify how advertising works. In the absence of this understanding, we cannot directly measure or evaluate the effectiveness of ads or campaigns. Instead we must evaluate processes we consider related to effective advertising, such as recall of the ad message. Even these measures do not provide an absolute standard for evaluation, but must be compared with the relative standard of other ads' performances in recall tests. The ads that provide the standard may have been designed with different purposes in mind and probably were tested under slightly different market conditions.

In addition, most evaluation techniques involve making measurements of advertising effectiveness based on a single exposure to the advertisement. Few campaigns are based on a single exposure and, in fact, a basic tenet of advertising practice is that multiple exposures are essential to the advertising process. Obviously, however, the necessity for multiple exposures would dramatically increase both the time and cost of most measurement techniques. For this reason multiple exposure in testing, however desirable it may be, remains a practical impossibility in the majority of cases.

A recent publication by N. W. Ayer Advertising evaluated the general situation in modern advertising copy testing this way.

> At best, copy testing is an inexact art, therefore results should be interpreted conservatively. Copy tests cannot tell us whether a given advertising strategy is correct. However, copy testing can and should tell us whether a given piece of advertising is meeting its stated strategic objectives.[6]

After an extensive comparison of commercial copytesting services, a recent scholarly study offered the following observation:

> Validation remains a problem with virtually all of these procedures. A primary reason for the lack of progress in this area seems to be the problem of specifying what is meant by advertising effectiveness— e.g., effective at doing what? Advertising may be expected to have different effects on different respondents and on the same respondents at different times.[7]

RESEARCH VERSUS CREATIVES

Unfortunately, testing procedures and standardized methods have led to antagonism between research and creative people. Researchers charge that creatives expect their work to be accepted without question. Researchers often feel that the factual material they work to develop is ignored or disparaged by creative types, who want no restriction placed on their work and who want to be guided totally by their feelings or whatever facts happen to support their prejudices.

Creatives, on the other hand, feel that researchers present them with unnecessary strictures by unquestioning reliance on very approximate sorts of testing techniques. The creatives claim that rigid adherence to test findings would result in advertising that looks, if not identical, at least very much the same.

There seem to be elements of truth on both sides of the argument. Since day-after recall scores are the prime criterion of advertising effectiveness for some large advertisers, the creative department often feels pressure not to create what it believes is the most effective advertising, but rather that which achieves the best recall scores. There is little question that this does result in advertising that is very similar in execution. The other side of the coin is that some creative people, justly well-known for their success, become equally well-known for their egos. In some cases this results in advertising created not for the consumer (or even for the advertiser) but for their peers in the advertising world. In this situation innovation and distinction are sought for their own sakes rather than in the disciplined context of effective planning and execution. The concerns are both legitimate and important since to the extent that either extreme dominates the creative function, an inappropriate result is likely. It is equally clear that the middle ground is desirable. Both inspiration and quantifiable measurement have a role in the development of effective advertising and it is imperative that management find a balanced position in which these two areas can exchange views and establish a cooperative relationship.[8]

EXHIBIT 14.3
Comparing Testing Techniques

This chart compares three frequently used message evaluation techniques with an ideal measurement procedure. The ideal procedure specifies conditions that would give the most accurate and reliable results. As the chart indicates, each of the techniques varies considerably from the ideal, yet allows gathering of some useful information.

SIX BASIC ATTRIBUTES OF RESEARCH TECHNIQUES	IDEAL MEASUREMENT PROCEDURE	DAY-AFTER RECALL	FOCUS GROUPS	STARCH READERSHIP SERVICE
1. Scope of advertising	Multiple insertions in all media	Single ad on TV	Multiple ads Multiple media	Singe ad in magazine
2. Response measured	Natural purchase	Recall	Emotional response, communication effectiveness	Recall
3. Conditions of exposure	Natural in home	Natural in home	Forced	Natural in home
4. Conditions of measurement	Natural observation	Telephone interview	Interview-discussion	Personal interview
5. Sampling procedure	Probability sample large enough for reliability	Probability sample within limited geographic area	Very small; non-probability sample	Quota sample of 200–300
6. Norms for comparison	Alternative ad or campaign	Industry norm or alternative test commercial	Alternative ads or campaign	Industry norm or alternative test ad

Note: This chart is intended to simplify comparison of syndicated and nonsyndicated measurement techniques.
Source: Adapted from Homer M. Dalbey, Irwin Gross, and Yoram Wind, *Advertising Measurement and Decision Making*, Boston: Allyn & Bacon Inc., 1968, 38.

THE SIGNIFICANCE OF ADVERTISING EVALUATION

Most techniques for evaluating advertising are flawed in some way. Either they fail to give a complete enough picture of the advertising process or they are highly judgmental and subjective. Nevertheless, evaluation remains a centrally important advertising activity and one to which increasing resources are devoted each year.[9]

While evaluation techniques are not suited to making subtle discriminations among executions and often do not help in building an understanding of the way advertising works, this really is not their intended purpose. In most cases advertising evaluation is designed to minimize the risk of total miscalculation. The techniques, while inexact, improve the chances of avoiding totally inappropriate advertising messages. Exhibit 14.3 on the previous page presents comparisons of idealized measurement procedures with various advertising measurement techniques.

All research involves trade-offs between the comprehensiveness of the findings and the time and money allotted for completion of the project. The effort of much marketing planning is not the total elimination of risk, since the information necessary to do so would be too expensive and time consuming to gather. Rather, planning and evaluation are used to reduce the risks to a lower-than-chance level of occurrence. For this reason, evaluation of advertising is always likely to be an inexact activity operating outside the realm of certainty.

SUMMARY

This chapter has reviewed both formal and informal approaches to evaluating advertising. Informal evaluation actually begins as the agency and advertiser evaluate the commercial or advertisement based on their past experiences with similar campaigns in similar situations. The difficulty is in establishing criteria that are useful in evaluating advertising created for widely different products and market conditions.

While many feel that advertising effectiveness could be vastly improved by the proper use of evaluation, there is considerably less agreement as to the proper method for evaluation. Creative and research people are often antagonistic because of this situation. Because there is considerable risk in any advertising situation—for example, the risk of creating an unintended impression or the risk of wasting money on an ineffective presentation— pretesting of advertising messages is the rule for large advertisers.

Evaluating advertising creative materials can be done in a number of ways. There are numerous commercial research firms who have developed specialized methods for doing this testing. Evaluation is often carried out at one or more of five basic testing arenas. These include strategy formation, copy guidance, concept testing, rough or finished pretesting, and campaign evaluation studies.

Perhaps the greatest problem in evaluating creative materials is in interpreting the findings of testing. Though recall is the key test of most large-scale consumer advertising campaigns, it may or may not be the best criterion for evaluation of a specific ad.

FUNNY BUSINESS: USING RESEARCH FOR CREATIVE DECISIONS

Funny Business, a computer game marketer, is preparing the launch of a new family of adventure games. The games represent a new kind of game targeted to teenagers, and will be supported by an advertising budget of about $5 million. The majority of this budget will be spent on television.

The advertiser and its agency have reached agreement on a creative strategy based on resonance, and an advertising theme that emphasizes the fun and involvement of participation in the games.

The agency has developed two alternative executions of the concept. The first is a rather straightforward presentation of the unique aspects of the games, using close-ups of the game screens and action developments. A voice-over announcer explains what is happening on the screen. In the second execution, animation and computer simulation are used to give the viewer the experience as seen by a computer character in one of the adventure games.

The ad manager at Funny Business tends to prefer the first execution, since it explains more about the games. The agency creative people are more excited about the second execution. Both commercials are in storyboard form and production needs to begin within several weeks to make air dates already contracted. Production funds are limited and absolutely prohibit production of both spots.

1. What sort of research would you use to get some information about the possible effectiveness of the two alternatives?
2. What specific issues should be explored by research?
3. How much confidence would you have in the research findings?
4. List three or four questions that you would like to have answered by your chosen research technique.

■ ■ ■

QUESTIONS FOR DISCUSSIONS

1. What are the three basic questions that researchers suggest advertising people should be concerned about in using research to evaluate message effectiveness?
2. If you were a copywriter, would you put your faith in formal or informal evaluation of advertising concepts? What if you were a research director?
3. What sorts of things could the copywriter learn from a focus group interview?
4. What is the most important factor in doing mall intercept interviewing?
5. Is recall a good measure of advertising effectiveness? Why or why not?
6. What are the main reasons for evaluating advertising?
7. What do readership norms for product categories tell the advertising researcher?

8. What is the difference between In-View and ADTEL?

9. Why are custom surveys used for ad evaluation?

10. Do you think advertising research can or might make carefully calibrated measurements of advertising impact before the fact?

NOTES

1. Roger Wimmer and Joseph Dominick, *Mass Media Research* (Belmont, Calif.: Wadsworth Publishing Company, 1983), 297.

2. David Ogilvy and Joel Raphaelson, "Agency Boredom with Analysis Cripples Execution," *Adweek*, September 27, 1982.

3. Charles F. Frazer, "Toward Some General Criteria for Evaluating Advertisements," Proceedings of the 1977 American Academy of Advertising, 145–149.

4. John Leckenby and Joe Plummer, "Advertising Stimulus Measurement and Assessment Research: A Review of Advertising Testing Methods," *Current Issues and Research in Advertising–1983*, 135–165.

5. For a thorough discussion of the appropriateness of recall as a measure of advertising effectiveness, see David Stewart, et al., "Methodological and Theoretical Foundations of Advertising Copytesting: A Review," *Current Issues and Research in Advertising–1985*, 1–74.

6. *Evaluative Pretesting of Advertising* (New York: N. W. Ayer Advertising, undated).

7. David Stewart, David Furse, and Randall Kozak, "A Guide to Commercial Copytesting Services," *Current Issues and Research in Advertising–1983*, 1–43.

9. Richard Vaughn, "Creatives versus Researchers: Must They Be Adversaries?" *Journal of Advertising Research*, vol. 22, no. 6, January 1983, 45–48.

SUGGESTED READINGS

Flecher, Alan, and Thomas Bowers. *Fundamentals of Advertising Research*. Columbus, Ohio: Grid, 1976.

Honomichl, Jack. *Honomichl on Market Research*. Chicago: Crain Books, 1986.

Lodish, Leonard. *The Advertising and Promotional Challenge*. New York: Oxford University Press, 1986.

Stewart, David, and David Furse. *Effective Television Advertising*. Lexington, Mass.: Lexington Books, 1986.

Wimmer, Roger, and Joseph Dominick. *Mass Media Research: An Introduction*. Belmont, Calif.: Wadsworth Publishing, 1983.

Association of National Advertisers. *Advertising Research: The State of the Art*. New York: Association of National Advertisers, 1979.

———. *Marketplace Measurement: Tracking and Testing Advertising and Other Marketing Effects*. New York: Association of National Advertisers, 1986.

———. *Choosing the Best Advertising Alternative*. New York: Association of National Advertisers, 1986.

The best and most current research information is carried in the periodical literature. See especially the *Journal of Advertising* and the *Journal of Advertising Research*.

PART 5

Advertising Decision Making: Message Delivery

Advertisers have an almost endless choice of methods to deliver their advertising messages to the target market. When you total the number of newspapers, magazines, radio and television stations, and out-of-home locations, it is not surprising that media planning requires a considerable amount of data analysis. However, media planning requires much more than an ability to determine media costs and efficiencies. As you will soon learn in the next series of chapters, media planning also demands creativity and knowledge of the marketing environment.

This part of the book introduces you to the concepts and language of bringing buyer and seller together through advertising media. In Chapter 15 you will learn how and why media plans are created, including the key concepts used to evaluate the specific media alternatives discussed in chapters 16 through 18. After this foundation has been built, you will learn the important characteristics of each of the media types. Chapter 16 explains the structure, terminology, strengths, and weaknesses of the broadcast media. Chapter 17 describes the print media (newspapers and consumer and business-to-business magazines). Chapter 18 covers direct response media, outdoor and transit advertising, trade shows, specialty advertising, point-of-purchase advertising, and other forms of advertising media.

Finally, this part concludes with Chapter 19, Evaluating Media Plans. This chapter's explanation of the various methods of determining the success of media plans is consistent with the accountability approach to advertising decision making stressed throughout the book.

MEDIA PLANNING

Key Terms

media plan
reach
frequency
continuity
quantitative criteria
cost-per-thousand (CPM)
waste circulation
cost-per-thousand target market
(CPM-TM)
qualitative criteria
media schedule
gross rating points (GRP)
bartering

Learning Objectives

To describe the purposes of advertising media

To outline the process of media planning

To analyze the relationship among marketing, advertising, and media objectives

To explain who does media planning

To discuss sources of media information

When we think about the large number of competing media choices an advertiser has, it's easy to see that launching a new media vehicle is a risky business. In 1981, 31-year-old Robert Pittman thought he had a television service idea that would work. His idea, MTV*, prompted the observation, "Not since the Beatles has any one force so dramatically altered the tune of the music industry."

Certainly one of the most interesting developments in media has been the unexpected success of MTV*. In 1984, this twenty-four-hour-per-day service aimed at 12- to 34-year-olds became cable's top-rated service and brought in advertising revenues of $53 million. Predictions called for that number to continue to increase through the 1980s.

Given the obstacles that MTV* had to overcome to reach success, its impact is even more impressive. First, the innovative programming idea had to be sold to the top management of Warner Amex, the par-

ent cable company. Pittman, CEO of MTV* Networks, accomplished that in 1981. Then the concept had to be sold to the cable operators for distribution; the music industry for programming; advertisers for revenue; and, finally, to viewers.

In 1981, MTV* launched with only 1.5 million homes, but by 1982 its numbers had grown to 10.7 million. In 1983, MTV* was tuned in by 18.9 million and by the end of

1984, the service had hit the 25.2 million mark.

Over half of MTV's* audience is under 25 and nearly 90 percent is under 35. Is this a valuable audience? Media buyers are attracted to the selective, attentive audience of MTV*. "MTV* is a beautifully targeted vehicle, delivering a select audience with no spillout coverage," says Howard Nass of Cunningham & Walsh. And Greg Blaine of Foote, Cone & Belding observes that "MTV* is the ideal broadcast medium for reaching teens and young adults, and that's the beauty of it all from our viewpoint."

In looking back on what he created, Pittman says: "I think we are now institutionalized to a certain extent, and accepted. Today we're pretty much a fixture in the youth culture, pretty much the way rock radio was for 20–25 years."

---

*MTV is a registered trademark of MTV Networks. Reprinted with permission. Source: Marianne Paskowski, "Everyone Wants Their MTV," *Marketing & Media Decisions*, Spring 1985, 61–68.

INTRODUCTION

One of the main points of this chapter is that the advertising value of media is the communication link they provide. A medium must be able to deliver an attractive, attentive audience at a reasonable cost so that advertisers can offer their products and services. Figure 15.1 is reproduced here to help you understand the relevance of media to the process of creating and delivering advertising messages to target audiences.

In many ways, the most important part of an advertising campaign is media planning. Consider the following:

- More people are employed in advertising media than in any other component of the advertising business.

- Most of the money invested in advertising is allocated to advertising media.

- Product similarity emphasizes the need to attain success through effectiveness and efficiency in reaching the right people through the right media combination.

- The cost of advertising media increased an average of 68 percent from 1975 to 1985 (see Exhibit 15.1).[1] This forces advertisers to pay increased attention to media planning.

- The form and content of advertising media have undergone major changes in recent years (see Exhibit 15.2). The growth of specialty magazines, the increased success of direct mail, and the impact of cable television are just a few of the more recent changes in advertising media.

Advertisers face a number of challenges in planning advertising media. Questions about when to advertise, which media to use, who should select media, and how media schedules should be evaluated are complex management decisions. These decisions can have a dramatic effect on the company's marketing and advertising objectives. The most persuasive advertising message will be ineffective unless it is delivered to the target audience in the right environments, at the right time, and with the right levels of frequency. Given the foregoing developments, the 1980s have developed into the most interesting period in the history of media planning.

THE PURPOSES OF MEDIA PLANNING

Several times in this book, we have made the point that personal selling is the most effective promotion tool. Every advertiser would like the opportunity to talk directly with prospects, explaining product advantages, answering questions, and taking orders. We know, of course, that this isn't practical; therefore, advertisers must find other, less direct, ways to communicate.

FIGURE 15.1

A Framework for Advertising
Decision Making

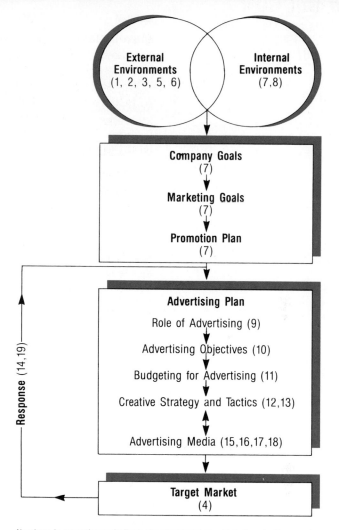

Numbers in parentheses indicate the chapter(s) in which item is discussed.

From the advertiser's point of view, the purposes of the media are to
locate target markets and to deliver the selling message to the target audience more efficiently than personal selling (see Figure 15.2).

LOCATING TARGET MARKETS

We read magazines, watch television programs, or listen to radio stations
because we're interested in what they provide—information and entertainment. The media are supported primarily by advertising income rather
than subscription income from readers, viewers, or listeners. With the

EXHIBIT 15.1

Media Costs and Media CPM
Trends: 1981–1985
(Indexed; 1967 = 100)

MEDIUM	1981	1982	1983	1984	1985
MEDIA COSTS*					
Newspapers	279	308	336	366	395†
Magazines	201	219	237	256	274
Network TV	329	365	394	441	476
Spot TV	286	317	342	376	399
Network Radio	244	268	300	327	353
Spot Radio	215	232	248	268	284
Outdoor	303	330	363	392	416
Direct Mail	263	286	290	299	319
Composite	270	297	318	344	369
MEDIA CPM					
Newspapers	263	288	314	339	366
Magazines	188	205	221	239	254
Network TV	261	292	318	353	381
Spot TV	223	248	268	291	309
Network Radio	202	220	244	264	282
Spot Radio	182	195	207	221	233
Outdoor	242	262	286	306	322
Direct Mail	263	286	290	299	319
Composite	244	267	286	307	329

Source: McCann-Erickson; data appeared in *Advertising Age*, November 29, 1984, p. 12.
*A unit in the various media listed include a single black-and-white page for newspapers, a four-color ad for magazines, 30-second spots for network and spot tv, one-minute spots for network and spot radio, a 100 showing in outdoor (100 GRPs, which is the reach and frequency of x-amount of boards per day), and 25,000 pieces of direct mail.
†1985 figures are estimated.

exception of pay cable and public radio and television, the broadcast media are completely supported by advertising revenue. The amount we pay for our daily newspaper is less than the cost of the ink used to print it.[2] And, the price we pay for magazines is only about 25 percent of the cost of production.[3] Media create information and entertainment to attract an audience that will be of interest to advertisers.

Given advertisers' interest in reaching the target market efficiently, their evaluation of media is based on how well a particular media type (television or magazines, for example) and a particular media vehicle "LA Law" or *Sports Illustrated*) can locate and deliver a desired audience. As we'll see later, efficiency is not the only criterion for media selection; however, the ability of a medium to offer an efficient substitute for personal selling is important.

Figure 15.3 is an advertisement for *Parents* magazine. This advertisement appeared in *Advertising Age* and is aimed at advertisers and advertising agencies. The copy explains the value of advertising in *Parents*—the ability to reach a specific target market. In Figure 15.4, *Medical Economics* sells its abilities to reach health care professionals.

Radio station formats are good examples of a medium's attempt to deliver different types of target audiences. Stations with classical music formats offer an attractive audience for sellers of expensive foreign cars, fine

EXHIBIT 15.2

How Advertising Dollars
Are Invested in Media

MEDIUM	INVESTMENT (Millions of Dollars)	PERCENTAGE OF TOTAL
Newspapers total	$25,170	26.6%
national	3,352	3.5
local	21,818	23.0
Magazines total	5,155	5.4
weeklies	2,297	2.4
women's	1,294	1.4
monthlies	1,564	1.7
Farm Publications total	186	0.2
Television total	20,770	21.9
network	8,285	8.7
spot	6,004	6.3
cable (nat'l.)	637	.7
local	5,714	5.7
cable (local)	130	.1
Radio total	6,490	6.8
network	365	0.4
spot	1,335	1.4
local	4,790	5.1
Direct mail total	15,500	16.4
Business papers total	2,375	2.5
Outdoor total	945	1.0
national	610	0.6
local	335	0.4
Miscellaneous total	18,159	19.2
national	9,551	10.1
local	8,608	9.1
Total national	53,355	56.3
Total local	41,395	43.7
Grand Total	$94,750	100.0%

Source: McCann-Erickson, Inc., Prepared by Newspaper Advertising Bureau, Inc., New York, New York, May 12, 1986.

FIGURE 15.2

Communication Links between
Buyers and Sellers

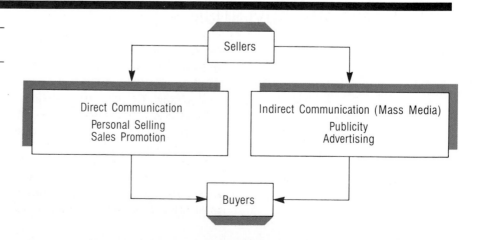

FIGURE 15.3

Promoting a Particular Media
Vehicle *(Parents Magazine)* to
the Advertising Industry

Source: Courtesy of *Parents* Magazine.

furniture, investments, and haute cuisine restaurants. Stations with coun-
try-and-western formats deliver an attractive audience for sellers of pick-
up trucks, beer and soft drinks, and fast-food restaurants.

DELIVERING THE ADVERTISING MESSAGE EFFICIENTLY

The basic task in media planning is to locate media that deliver the target
audience efficiently and effectively. No medium can sell as effectively as
the personal sales staff; however, media are far more efficient than personal selling. Examine the information in Exhibit 15.3. Note the differences in cost of "making a sales call" with personal selling and with the
most appropriate alternative advertising media, business-to-business magazines and direct mail.

While the effectiveness of a "sales call" made by personal selling is
greater than a "sales call" made by advertising, it is easy to see the value
of advertising media. Advertising is ideal for reaching large numbers of
people quickly, efficiently, and repeatedly.

THE PROCESS OF MEDIA PLANNING: DEVELOPMENT OF THE MEDIA PLAN

FIGURE 15.4

How *Medical Economics* Sells
Its Ability to Reach Health
Care Professionals

Source: Copyright © 1983 by Medical
Economics Company Inc. Reprinted with
permission.

Just as it's tempting to think of an advertising campaign as an individual advertisement, it's also tempting to think of media planning as a media schedule — a list of the media selected and the times and dates that the advertising will appear. Professional media planners realize that media planning is much more than a schedule. It is a process that begins long before the advertising campaign begins; often changes throughout the campaign; and involves every level of marketing management. The **media plan** is a course of action that specifies exactly how an advertising campaign will be delivered to the target market. This chapter presents a seven-step procedure for developing a media plan. Although there are more data available about media than any other aspect of advertising, media planning is a creative process. Media planners are constantly searching for new and exciting ways to communicate with the target audiences.[4]

STRATEGY IN MEDIA PLANNING

The media plan — just like the creative plan — consists of both strategy and tactics. The strategy component of the media plan consists of the first three steps: reviewing the marketing and advertising situation, selecting the target market, and setting the media objectives.

STEP 1. REVIEWING THE MARKETING AND ADVERTISING SITUATION

Because media planning is an extension of the company's marketing plan, the media strategy flows from a review of the marketing and advertising situation. The following outline suggests the most relevant pieces of background information for media planning.

Marketing and Advertising Situation
    A. Marketing Factors
        1. Who is the competition and what market share do they hold?
        2. What is our marketing strategy? Our marketing objective?
        3. What buyer problems does our product solve?
        4. What marketing decisions have been made about the internal marketing elements (product, price, promotion, and distribution)?
        5. What external environmental factors are influencing the marketing of our product?
    B. Advertising Factors
        1. What role is advertising expected to play in the stimulation of brand demand?
        2. What are the advertising objectives?
        3. What is the size of the advertising investment?
        4. What is our creative strategy? What are our creative tactics?

EXHIBIT 15.3

Cost-per-Thousand Comparisons

COMMUNICATION TOOL	ESTIMATED COST-PER-THOUSAND
Personal selling	$230.00
Magazines:	
Atlantic Monthly	$20.68
Cosmopolitan	$10.88
Industry Week	$32.11
Life	$22.52
Newsweek	$15.75
Progressive Farmer	$26.34
Newspapers:	
USA Today	$15.92
Wall Street Journal	$11.10
Spot radio	$9.00
Network radio	$7.50
Outdoor	$2.50
Newspapers	$10.00
Television (Prime time, network)	$7.50
Spot television (prime time)	$9.25
Direct mail	$200.00

Sources: Personal selling figure from Laboratory of Advertising Performance, McGraw-Hill Publishing Company. Direct mail figure from Direct Marketing Association. All other figures from *Media Cost Guide 1985.*

The purpose of this background review is to help guide media planning decisions. The advertising manager's role is to understand the marketing environment and to provide this understanding to those who will have responsibility for the tactical decisions.

STEP 2. SELECTING THE TARGET MARKET

Because the basic function of media planning is to select media that reach the target audience, the media planner must know the target audience with as much precision as possible. Usually, the target market is selected in the earliest stages of marketing planning; however, the media planner has a responsibility to help define the target market. The high cost of media and the need to minimize waste exposures emphasize the importance of a precise target market definition. In Chapter 7, it was pointed out that target audiences can be specified in a number of different ways, such as by using demographics, life-style, and product usage. One of the reasons we emphasized the importance of early identification of the target market is that errors in media selection are very costly. Media costs are high, and the media planner can maximize the media budget by knowing who must be reached.

STEP 3. SETTING MEDIA OBJECTIVES

Media objectives give direction to the media planner and they specify the criteria against which the media plan will ultimately be evaluated. Like all other objectives discussed throughout this book, media objectives need to be specific, measurable, realistic, and related to the company's marketing and advertising objectives.

TERMINOLOGY OF MEDIA OBJECTIVES

Because the primary purpose of media is to deliver the advertising message, media objectives should be expressed in terms of delivery ability—reaching the target audience with sufficient frequency and appropriate timing. The three terms used to express media objectives are reach, frequency, and continuity.

Reach refers to the number of different individuals, or homes, exposed to the advertising message. Generally, reach is expressed as a percentage (for example, "to reach 75 percent of all U.S. college students within the next twelve-month period").

Frequency refers to the average number of times the audience is exposed to the advertising message (for example, "to reach 75 percent of all U.S. college students an average of four times per month within the next twelve-month period").

Continuity refers to the pattern of distributing the advertising messages during the campaign period (for example, "to reach 75 percent of all U.S. college students an average of four times per month within the next twelve months with 50 percent of the exposures taking place during the first quarter of the year, 25 percent taking place during the second quarter, 15 percent during the third quarter, and 10 percent during the fourth quarter"). The three main continuity patterns (highly continuous, flighting, and pulsing) are described below.

ORIGINS OF MEDIA OBJECTIVES

The origins of media objectives are the marketing problems or opportunities facing the advertiser. Notice how media help solve the following three marketing situations.

- *Media and declining consumption*   The marketing problem facing the coffee industry is a decline in per capita consumption and low levels of consumption among young people. The media component of an advertising campaign for the coffee industry helps overcome the marketing problem by reaching the primary and secondary target markets with sufficient frequency and continuity.

- *Media and product changes*   Sales of Colgate's toothpaste container depend on the company's ability to communicate the container's advantages (see Figure 15.5). Media's role is to reach the massive market of toothpaste users.

- *Media and new product introductions*   The success of new computer software is largely dependent upon the marketer's ability to explain ease of use to the target market. Media's role is to find the communication channels that can best present the message. The main reason for the recent success of such magazines as *PC Magazine* and *PC World* is their ability to (a) provide editorials that enhance the environment for advertising, (b) deliver readers who are interested in personal computers, and (c) provide an attractive format for explaining features of computers, software, and related equipment.

FIGURE 15.5

The Colgate Pump

The Colgate-Palmolive Company used mass-circulation magazines to advertise its new packaging feature, the pump.

Source: Courtesy of the Colgate-Palmolive Company.

CONSTRAINTS ON MEDIA OBJECTIVES

Marketing, advertising, creative, and media objectives are constrained by several factors. Media planners create objectives knowing that they have a limited media budget; that competitors' media plans will need to be considered; and that knowledge about effectiveness of alternative media plans is not perfect.

- *Budget as a constraint*   The ideal goal for the media planner is to maximize reach and frequency. No company has enough money to reach every member of the target market, several times a day, every day of the year. Advertisers live within the constraints of a limited budget by making decisions between reach and frequency. An advertiser may decide that it is better to reach 25 percent of the market eight times per month than 50 percent of the market four times per month.

- *Competitors' media plans as a constraint*   Your daily newspaper contains full-page advertisements from the leading department stores, the grocery chains, the furniture stores, and the auto dealers. Your Sunday newspaper contains coupons for detergent, toothpaste, deodorant, and frozen orange juice. Although creativity is an important part of media planning, many media plans are dictated by the marketplace. There are good reasons for department stores and grocery chains to advertise in the local newspaper. We've come to use newspaper advertising as a shopping guide, noticing what is for sale and for what price. Effective media planners acknowledge this and work toward placing advertising where the target audience is—even if the competitor's advertising is on the facing page.

▪ *Imperfect media knowledge as a constraint* Media planning, like most other areas of advertising, is imprecise. Questions about the most effective levels of reach, how much frequency is enough, and when to advertise are not completely resolved.[5] Just as there is no absolute, right marketing mix, and no one, correct creative approach, there is no perfect media plan. Media objectives are constructed from the surrounding marketing and advertising environments. Ultimately, the skill, experience, and creativity of the media planner determine a winning media plan.

MARKETING INFLUENCES ON MEDIA OBJECTIVES

As suggested in an earlier section, decisions about reach, frequency, and continuity are influenced by a variety of internal and external factors. Familiarity with the marketing environment helps the media planner set media objectives. Here are some guidelines for setting media objectives within the marketing and advertising environments.

Reach Stressed over frequency when:

▪ a product is being introduced—particularly a new, consumer product that has mass appeal (soap, detergent, deodorant, cars, etc.). Reach is also stressed for retailers for sales announcements and for business-to-business advertisers who are introducing new products.

▪ a product has a large target market.

▪ the advertiser wants to influence the distribution system. Increased reach helps implement a pull marketing strategy.

Frequency Stressed over reach when:

▪ products are in the decline stage of their life cycle.

▪ products are purchased frequently and the opportunity for brand switching is high. Such products as chewing gum, candy, soft drinks, and cigarettes need to have the support of regular reminder advertising.

▪ brand loyalty is not high. Many consumer convenience goods and some business products (consumable supplies) benefit from high frequency advertising.

▪ products are sold to a relatively small target market.

▪ the advertising message is difficult to explain and repetition is important in communicating the advertising idea.

Continuity Continuity is independent of reach and frequency and refers to how advertising exposures are distributed over the campaign period. There are three basic patterns (see Figure 15.6).

Continuous Pattern Advertising exposures vary little over the campaign period. This is an appropriate pattern for products that experience little fluctuation in demand (cigarettes, facial soap, and deodorant, for example).

Flighting Pattern Advertising exposures are scheduled in waves interspersed with periods of no advertising exposures. This is an appropriate pattern for products that experience large fluctuations in demand (holiday gifts, vacation travel, and many industrial goods).

Pulsing Pattern Advertising exposures are scheduled with a continuous base supplemented by waves of increased advertising exposures. This is an appropriate pattern for products that experience a moderate amount of demand fluctuation (automobiles, beer and soft drinks, and some clothing items, for example).

TACTICS IN MEDIA PLANNING

Knowing who is to be reached (target audience) and what is to be accomplished (media objectives) guide the media planner in making tactical media decisions. These decisions begin with evaluating alternative media choices and conclude with evaluating the media plan.

STEP 4. EVALUATING MEDIA ALTERNATIVES

There are two levels of media evaluation—the first is at the media type level and the second at the media vehicle level. Media selection begins with evaluating the usefulness of alternative types of media. For example, will network television be more useful than national magazines? Should radio be used to help accomplish the frequency objective? Is there a role for outdoor advertising? Media planners answer these questions by reviewing the marketing and advertising situation; analyzing the characteristics of the product; and knowing the target audiences and the media objectives. For example, when Advil was first introduced, network television was used to introduce the brand to the consumer market because the task was to reach a large, national audience quickly and dramatically. Advil also used national magazines to help encourage product trial through cents-off coupons.

Once media types have been selected, the media planner selects media vehicles (specific magazines, newspapers, television programs, radio stations, etc.). Is *Time* magazine a better media choice than *Newsweek?* Is *Purchasing Magazine* a better media buy than *Purchasing Week?* Media vehicle analysis consumes much of the work in media planning because of the thousands of available media choices. There are, for example, nearly 3,000 magazines listed in the *Business Publications Directory* of Standard Rate & Data Service.[6] This doesn't include consumer magazines or newspapers.

FIGURE 15.6

Three Patterns of Media Exposure

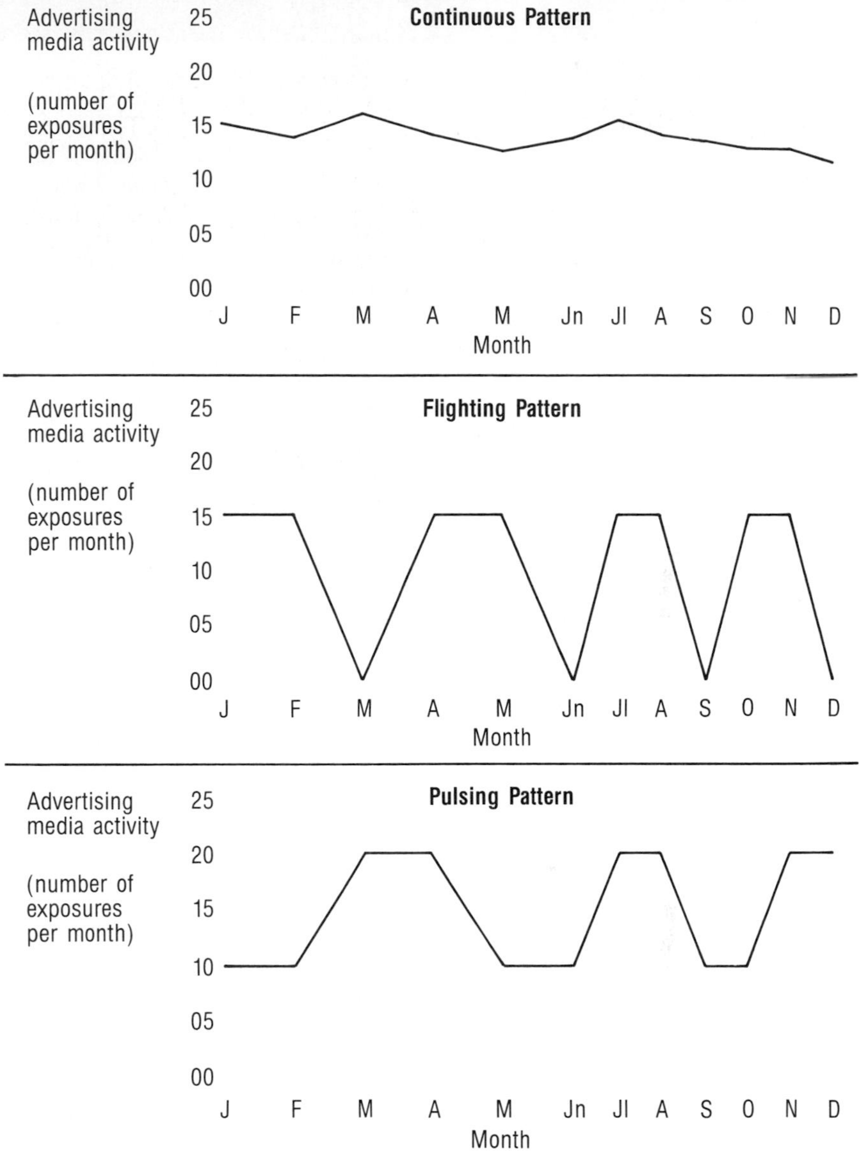

Advertising media activity

(number of exposures per month)

Continuous Pattern

Flighting Pattern

Pulsing Pattern

Media planners use a number of criteria to evaluate media vehicles. In a study conducted by John D. Leckenby and Shizue Kishi, reach, gross rating points, and frequency were the top three factors named by the sample.[7] Media vehicle analysis is based on two general criteria—quantitative and qualitative.

QUANTITATIVE CRITERIA IN MEDIA EVALUATION

Quantitative criteria are those aspects of a medium that can be measured objectively. Most of the items on the Leckenby and Kishi list are quantitative measures. It is, for example, important to know how many people will be exposed to our message; how much it costs to advertise in the

A CLOSER LOOK

EMERGING MAGAZINES

Successful media are those that adapt to cultural and economic changes—how we live, what we believe to be important, how we express ourselves, and what we spend our money on. The vitality of the media is indicated by their growth—in advertising revenue and in absolute numbers.

Think for a moment about the number of magazines that didn't exist just a few years ago—nearly all of the computer and physical fitness magazines, for example. Even in the very competitive magazine industry, over 11,000 magazines are available, with new titles emerging at a rate of more than 200 per year.

In 1985, 231 new magazines were launched—some successful and some not so successful. For example, 37 of the new magazines ran without ads. Among the magazines that carried advertising, the range of paid pages of advertising was a low of one page and a high of 87. The average was 14.9.

Some of the new titles were *Spin*, *NewLook*, *Metal Mania*, *Faces*, *Metal Muscle*, *Exercise for Men Only*, *Women's Health*, *Farm Computer News*, *Entertainment Today Magazine*, *Wrestling: The Best and the Baddest*, *Exotic Weapons*, *Vietnam Combat*, *Crime Fight*, *Outlaw Biker*, *The Psychic Inquirer*, *European Travel and Life*, *Star Hairdos*, and *Awesome*. How many of these have you read lately?

Number of Magazines, 1974–1986

YEAR	NUMBER OF U.S. PERIODICALS	INCREASE OVER PREVIOUS YEAR (in percentage)
1974	9,755	—
1979	9,719	– .3%
1984	10,809	11.2
1986	11,328	4.6

Sources: *Magazine Newsletter of Research*, Magazine Publishers Association, New York, August 1986; and Carol Hall, "Intro Redux," *Marketing & Media Decisions*, September 1986, 4.

---

vehicle, what discounts are available, how often the message will be distributed, and how efficient the vehicle is in reaching the target audience. Most of this information can be obtained directly from the medium's rate card, promotional literature, and Standard Rate & Data Service.

Comparing Media Vehicle Efficiency One of the most important factors in comparing media efficiency is known as **cost-per-thousand (CPM):** the cost to reach 1,000 people through a particular medium. Media planners use the CPM calculation because it permits a comparison of all media types and media vehicles on the same basis. A simple, convenient, and useful calculation, CPM is calculated by dividing the cost of an advertisement—(times 1,000)—by the medium's circulation:

$$\text{CPM} = \frac{\text{Cost of advertisement} \times 1,000}{\text{Total circulation}}$$

For example, suppose a magazine charged $15,000 for a black-and-white ad and its circulation totaled 500,000. To calculate cost-per-thousand, divide the product of $15,000 and 1,000 by 500,000:

$$\frac{\$15,000 \times 1,000}{500,000} = \$30$$

The cost-per-thousand is $30.

Every media vehicle has **waste circulation**—audience that falls outside the target market. One of the goals in media planning is to minimize buying waste circulation; therefore, a useful refinement to the CPM calculation is to determine the cost to reach 1,000 people who are in the target audience. In the Leckenby and Kishi study, this calculation is known as **CPM to target market (CPM-TM).** It is obtained by dividing the cost of an advertisement by the medium's circulation within the target market:

$$\text{Total circulation} = 500{,}000$$

$$\text{Circulation in target market} = 350{,}000$$

$$\text{Cost of advertisement} = \$15{,}000$$

$$\text{CPM-TM} = \frac{\text{Cost of ad} \times 1{,}000}{\text{Circulation in target market}}$$

$$\text{CPM-TM} = \frac{\$15{,}000 \times 1{,}000}{350{,}000}$$

$$\text{CPM-TM} = \$42.86$$

Although the CPM calculation is useful, it must be used carefully. First, it is a measure of efficiency, not effectiveness. The CPM tells a media planner nothing about the potential effectiveness of the message within a given media vehicle. In this sense, the CPM is comparable to the miles-per-gallon calculations that new-car buyers use when comparing models. A car that gets 50 miles per gallon may be efficient, but it may not be the best car for one's purposes.

Second, it is important to compare the CPMs of alternative media types or media vehicles on the same basis. It is unwise, for example, to compare the CPM of a one-color ad against that of a four-color ad. Magazine space is generally comparable, although full-page ads may range widely in size. For example, is a full page in *Reader's Digest* or *TV Guide* equivalent to a full page in *Sports Illustrated* or oversized *Life?*

Finally, there is the issue of intermedia comparability. What is the broadcast equivalent of a magazine page? How should outdoor advertising and direct mail be compared to print and broadcast? These questions are not totally resolved, yet CPMs are often compared among media.

QUALITATIVE CONSIDERATIONS IN MEDIA EVALUATION

Qualitative criteria are those aspects of a medium that are almost impossible to quantify and yet are important. For example, it is difficult to match the quality of advertising reproduction in *National Geographic*, the prestige of advertising in the *New Yorker*, the news value of advertising in the *Chicago Tribune*, and the business environment of the *Wall Street Journal*. Television offers unmatched demonstration and excitement possibilities while radio and outdoor give an advertiser instant local identity. Although these considerations are difficult to quantify, they are often more important than efficiency.

HOW TO EVALUATE MEDIA ALTERNATIVES

Use of Computers and Media Models The past 25 years have seen much experimenting with the use of the computer and media models to improve the media planning process. During this time, several different media models have been developed, and although there are differences among them, most media models have been designed to predict an outcome. The creator of the model exposes available media data to a set of specified relationships and assumptions. The computer then calculates the outcome. Some models are designed to produce the optimum solution to a given media problem. Linear programming models, for example, can generate a list of media vehicles that produce the greatest number of exposures within the constraints of the media budget. Non-optimizing models do not generate a media schedule, but instead evaluate predetermined, alternative schedules. Again, the evaluation criteria are usually audience exposure delivery and efficiency. Other models are formula-based and are used primarily to determine reach and frequency of alternative media vehicles.[8]

There are many different media models. However, one way to understand why they were developed is to appreciate the many complex problems facing the media planner. Exhibit 15.4 summarizes the main types of media models.

At one time, it was thought that computers and media models would take over most of the media planning process. Although much time and money have been invested in computerized media models, a great deal of media planning continues to be conducted through the personal judgment of experienced media planners. The computer's major contribution has been to minimize the time computing quantitative comparisons of media.

Non-computer Evaluations of Media The computer is not very well-suited to evaluating the qualitative aspects of media, nor can it accommodate the need for creativity in a media plan. Therefore, media planning is largely a process of evaluation of alternatives against predetermined criteria. A useful approach to media planning is for the media planner to specify and then rank the importance of each media criterion. For example, the following six-step procedure allows a media planner to evaluate alternative media choices against all relevant criteria.

1. List all of the criteria relevant to media evaluation.

   - quantitative criteria
   - qualitative criteria

2. Weight each factor according to the importance within the media needs of the brand. Using a weighting system of 1 to 5 (when 1 = very little importance and 5 = very high importance), assign importance weights to each factor.

3. Compile a list of all reasonable media choices.

4. Determine the performance of all reasonable media choices against each of the media evaluation factors listed in step 1.

   One method of doing this would be to "grade" the alternative media choices on a 0–100 scale where 90–100 = excellent; 80–89 = very

EXHIBIT 15.4
Media Models: A Summary

TYPE	WHAT IT DOES	PROBLEM IT SOLVES
Reach estimation	Calculates the net unduplicated reach of three or more media vehicles	Determines how many *different* people are reached when a number of media vehicles are used
Frequency response	Calculates how many exposures are sufficient to achieve a specified result by estimating a response curve	Determines the relationship between frequency of message (repetition) and the desired advertising effect (awareness, recall, etc.)
Media allocation	Maximizes the effect of the media budget by analyzing the variables that affect productivity of the media schedule	Determines how a predetermined media budget should be allocated among the numerous possibilities

Source: Adapted from R. Dale Wilson and Karen A. Machleit, "Advertising Decision Models: A Managerial Review," in *Current Issues and Research in Advertising 1985*, James H. Leigh and Claude R. Martin, eds., vol. 2 (Ann Arbor, Mich.: Graduate School of Business, University of Michigan, 1985), 133–151.

good; 70–79 = average; 60–69 = poor; and below 60 = unacceptable. For example:

MEDIUM (Type or Vehicle)	FACTOR	GRADE	FACTOR	GRADE
Sports Illustrated	cost	92	CPM	88
Newsweek	cost	96	CPM	64
Time	cost	84	CPM	78
U.S. News & World Report	cost	88	CPM	80

5. Calculate a total score for each alternative by multiplying the performance grades by the importance weights.

    In the example above, *Sports Illustrated* has a performance grade of 92 on the cost factor. If cost has an importance weight of 3 (out of 5), *Sports Illustrated* would have a score of 276 (3 × 92).

6. Divide the sum of the performance grades times the importance weights by the sum of the factor weights. You will then be able to compare a number of alternative media types or media vehicles against the criteria you have decided are most relevant for your brand.

STEP 5. BUILDING THE MEDIA SCHEDULE

A **media schedule** is a calendar that summarizes the evaluation of media alternatives and gives instructions to media buyers. As Figure 15.7 shows, a media schedule graphically illustrates how the media planner has decided to accomplish the media objectives. Media schedules have four major elements:

FIGURE 15.7

An Example of a Media Schedule

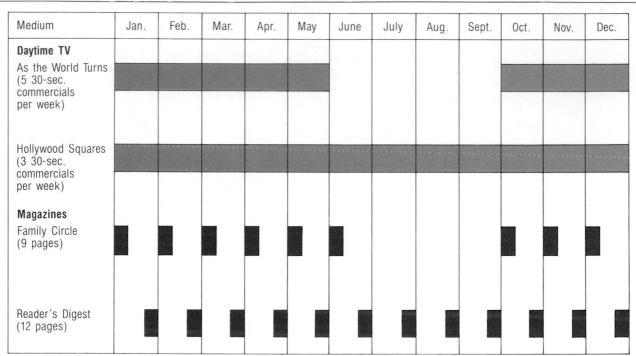

Medium	Jan.	Feb.	Mar.	Apr.	May	June	July	Aug.	Sept.	Oct.	Nov.	Dec.
Daytime TV												
As the World Turns (5 30-sec. commercials per week)												
Hollywood Squares (3 30-sec. commercials per week)												
Magazines Family Circle (9 pages)												
Reader's Digest (12 pages)												

EXHIBIT 15.5

An Example of Distribution of Media Investment by Target Market

TARGET MARKET	AMOUNT OF MEDIA INVESTMENT	PERCENTAGE OF TOTAL
PRIMARY MARKET		
Women, 24–39; Married; Employed outside home; Education, high school +; Household income, $25,000 +; Top 100 U.S. markets	$3,500,000	60.9%
SECONDARY MARKET		
Men, 35–49; Married; Education, college; Professional; Household income, $25,000 +; Top 50 U.S. markets	1,750,000	30.4
OTHER		
Women, 40–55; Professional; Household income, $35,000 +; Top 50 U.S. markets	500,000	8.7
Total	$5,750,000	100.0%

FIGURE 15.8

Distribution of Media Investment, by Geography: An Example

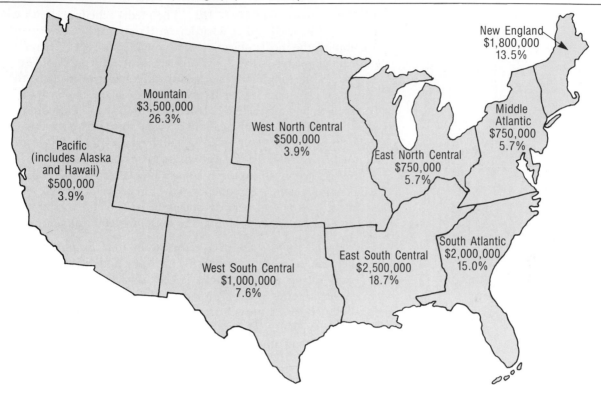

1. *When: Decisions about Continuity*   The media schedule shows how the media planner expects to meet the continuity objective of the media plan. This is usually done in two ways. First, media coverage is displayed on a 52-week calendar. This allows the media planner to see if the continuity objective is being fulfilled. It also tells the media buyer when the advertising is to be run. Second, media expenditures are summarized on a monthly and quarterly basis so that the media planner can evaluate the relationship between brand sales and advertising expenditures.

2. *Who: Decisions about Target Market*   The media schedule shows how the media planner allocates media dollars against the target markets. This is typically done by showing both total dollars and percentage of media budget against each segment of the target market (see Exhibit 15.5).

3. *Where: Decisions about Geographic Concentration*   The media schedule shows how the planner allocates advertising dollars against geographic markets. Company records and other published data sources reveal areas of sales strength and weakness. Blending this

information with the company's marketing plans, the media planner decides where to apply the greatest media pressure to support marketing objectives (see Figure 15.8).

4. *Weight: Decisions about Media Mix*   The media schedule shows what media will be used and at what levels. Rarely can an advertiser accomplish the media objectives with one media type. Therefore, most media planners use a mix of several different media. The advantages of using more than one media type are threefold: the advertiser can attain higher levels of reach; several target markets can be reached; and alternative creative executions can be used. A media plan concentrated in one medium is often appropriate for business-to-business and retail advertisers. The business press, for example, is an effective advertising medium for business-to-business advertisers who want to reach a narrowly defined target market with a moderate amount of frequency. Also, many retailers rely exclusively on newspaper advertising because of the medium's reach and frequency ability within a news-oriented environment.

Media planners find it useful to measure the total weight of a schedule so that they can estimate the impact of the reach and frequency of a given plan. **Gross rating points (GRP)** is the term used to describe media weight. A single rating point represents 1 percent of the audience. A media schedule's GRPs are calculated by multiplying the schedule's reach times its frequency. GRPs indicate the duplicated audience sizes for all the commercials and advertisements within a specific time period.

STEP 6. IMPLEMENTING THE MEDIA PLAN

A media plan is executed through a process of establishing media prices, writing media contracts, and issuing insertion orders.

Media Prices Most media have rate cards that list the cost of time or space as well as other available services (see Figure 15.9). The rate paid by the advertiser is determined by the volume and frequency of advertising: discounts are usually available for larger volume advertisers. Media rates are also sometimes negotiated, particularly in the broadcast media.

In recent years, a system of media **bartering,** or exchange, has developed. The most common types of bartering involve an advertiser exchanging goods or services for media time or space, or an advertiser or advertising agency providing programming to a television station in exchange for advertising time.

Contracts The media contract is a document that expresses the agreement between the medium and the media buyer. The contract specifies the rate earned, the amount of time or space to be purchased, the date(s) of exposure, and the total price to be paid (see Figure 15.10).

Insertion Orders An insertion order is sent to the medium along with the commercial or advertisement when the advertising is placed. The insertion order confirms the details of the contract and explains any special requirements (see Figure 15.11).

Executing Media Plans Media plans are executed through the media department of an advertising agency, a media buying service, an in-house media group, or a combination of the above.

FIGURE 15.9

A Newspaper Rate Card

Rocky Mountain News

GENERAL ADVERTISING RATE CARD #106-G EFFECTIVE JAN. 1, 1987

400 WEST COLFAX AVENUE · DENVER, COLORADO 80204 · (303) 892-5227

MARKETING SERVICES

The Marketing Services Department of the Rocky Mountain News provides advertisers with a wide range of qualitative and quantitative information. Demographic and psychographic market profiles, market penetration, readership, image and circulation figures are available. Research sources include the 1985 Simmons-Scarborough Syndicated Study, Belden Associates Study, Media Records and Audit Bureau of Circulations. Call (303)892-5258.

1. PERSONNEL

William W. Fletcher, President/General Manager
Carlos W. Boettger, Advertising Director
Paul D. Campbell, Mgr. General Advertising

2. REPRESENTATIVE

SAWYER-FERGUSON-WALKER COMPANY, INC.

3. COMMISSION AND TERMS OF PAYMENT

a. Agency Commission 15% to recognized agencies.
b. No cash discount allowed.
c. Commissions apply to this rate card only.

4. GENERAL RATE POLICY

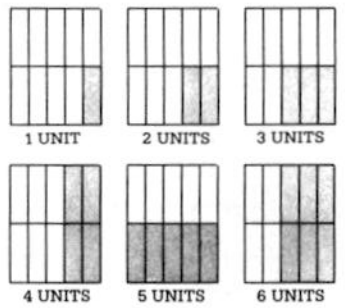

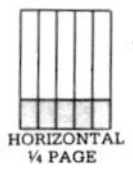

5A. GENERAL ROP RATES B/W

5B. PREPRINT INSERT RATES Sunday and Wednesday

5C. GENERAL TV DIAL RATES

6. GROUP COMBINATION RATES

Not applicable.

7A. ROP COLOR RATES

7B. FOOD FARE COLOR RATES

7C. TV DIAL COLOR RATES

8. SPECIAL ROP UNITS

9. SPLIT RUN

10. SPECIAL SERVICES

11. SPECIAL DAYS/PAGES/FEATURES

13. CONTRACT AND COPY REGULATIONS
Refer to RULES—REGULATIONS—INFORMATION

14. RETAIL DEADLINES
See bottom of this page.

15. MECHANICAL MEASUREMENTS

16. SPECIAL CLASSIFICATION RATES
Refer to 5E, 5F, 5G, 5H, 5I

17. CLASSIFIED RATES
Refer to 5J and current classified rate card.

18. SUNDAY TABLOID COLOR COMICS

19. MAGAZINES
Refer to 11A, 11B, 11C.

RULES—REGULATIONS—INFORMATION

ERRORS:

Source: Courtesy of the Rocky Mountain News.

FIGURE 15.10

A Media Contract

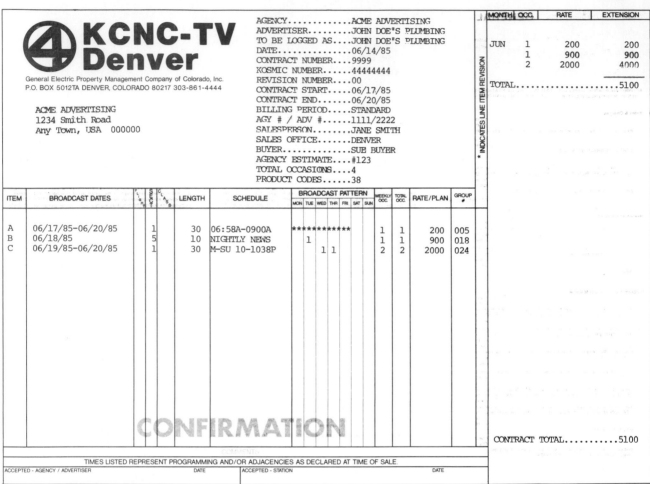

Source: Courtesy of KCNC-TV, Denver, CO, NBC Affiliate.

Media Departments of Advertising Agencies Most large, consumer-goods advertisers use a full-service advertising agency that performs all, or most, of the required media services. If the agency is compensated on the commission system, it will earn the commission rate paid by the media—usually 15 percent.

Media Buying Services A media buying service is a media wholesaler in that it purchases large amounts of media time or space and then resells it to advertisers or smaller advertising agencies who do not have their own media buying department. Media buying services can be compensated on a fee basis, on the margin between their costs for media and their selling price, or on a commission system.

FIGURE 15.11

An Insertion Order

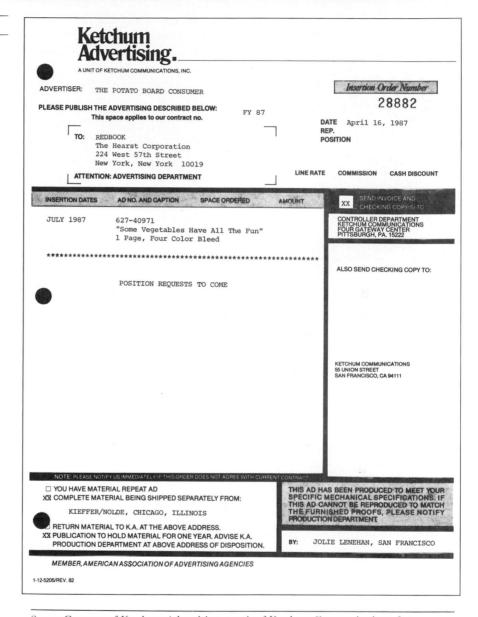

Source: Courtesy of Ketchum Advertising, a unit of Ketchum Communications, Inc.

In-House Media Group Some advertisers find it more convenient and profitable to do their own media buying. In-house media departments or groups are formed to perform all, or part of, the media planning. In some situations, the in-house group will only purchase part of the media schedule and leave other portions of the media plan to either the advertising agency or an independent media buying service. The in-house media group arrangement is very common among retailers and business-to-business advertisers. Business-to-business advertisers use relatively few media; they tend to know the media alternatives quite well; and there are fewer complexities in selecting and placing advertising.

STEP 7. EVALUATING THE MEDIA PLAN

The success of a media plan should be determined by how well it meets its objectives. Therefore, the first step in evaluating a media plan is to recall the stated objectives. Consider the following set of hypothetical media objectives:

- Reach objectives: "To reach 75 percent of all U.S. college students" (primary market)

    "To reach 50 percent of the parents of U.S. college students" (secondary market)

- Frequency objectives: "To expose the primary target market to the advertising message an average of four times per month within the next twelve-month period"

    "To expose the secondary market to the advertising message an average of three times per month within the next twelve-month period"

- Continuity objective: "To use a pulsing schedule to reach the primary market and a flighting schedule to reach the secondary market"

Exposure Pattern

TARGET MARKET	TIME PERIOD (quarter)	EXPOSURE PATTERN (number of exposures and percentage)
Primary market	1st	24 (50%)
	2nd	12 (25)
	3rd	7 (15)
	4th	5 (10)
Secondary market	1st	18 (50)
	2nd	0 (0)
	3rd	18 (50)
	4th	0 (0)

Target Market Definition

PRIMARY MARKET

Sex: 50% male, 50% female
Marital Status: single
Age: 18–24
Geographic Location: throughout United States

SECONDARY MARKET

Sex: 50% male, 50% female
Marital Status: married (one or more children attending a four-year college)
Age: 35–55
Income: $25,000 +
Education: high school +
Geographic Location: throughout United States

Given the above media objectives, exposure pattern, and target market definition, the media planner determines if the objectives have been achieved. Reach is determined by estimating audience size. If broadcast media are used, audience size can be measured by ratings services (for example, Nielsen or Arbitron for television and Arbitron and RADAR for radio). If print media are used, audience size can be measured by such services as Starch INRA Hooper and Mediamark Research, Inc., for magazines and the Audit Bureau of Circulations for newspapers. Also, Simmons Market Research Bureau measures audience size for several media types.

Frequency and continuity are determined by physical inspection (for example, driving past outdoor signs, postage receipts from direct mailings, and verifications from broadcast and print). In broadcast, verification takes the form of an affidavit signed by the station. In print, a tearsheet of the page on which the advertisement appeared is sent to the advertiser or the advertising agency. A more complete discussion of research services is included in Chapter 19.

SOURCES OF MEDIA INFORMATION

One of the most important skills that media planners must have is the ability to use available information to improve the media planning process. Because media planning involves so many aspects of marketing and advertising, every source of business and marketing information is of potential value. Consequently, media planners expose themselves to a wide range of information.

THE TRADE PRESS

Several magazines are important to the advertising business. The most widely read are *Advertising Age*, *AdWeek*, *Media & Marketing Decisions*, *Marketing Communications*, *Direct Marketing*, *Business Marketing*, and *Sales and Marketing Management*. These publications report the news and trends in the industry, and provide case histories of brand successes and failures as well as industry data, including market shares, advertising expenditures, and media spending patterns.

SCHOLARLY JOURNALS

The *Journal of Marketing*, *Journal of Marketing Research*, *Journal of Advertising*, and the *Journal of Advertising Research* are among the leading scholarly journals that regularly report the results of studies on a variety of advertising issues. Many of the articles in these journals test communication theories related to the practice of advertising.

THE MEDIA

One of the most valuable advertising services provided by the media is the information they provide to advertisers and their agencies. In addition to publishing rate cards, the media regularly conduct audience and market

FIGURE 15.12

How Leading National Advertisers Reports Media Spending

BAR/LNA MULTI-MEDIA SERVICE
CLASS/BRAND YTD $
January – December 1986

CLASS/COMPANY/BRAND	CLASS CODE	YEAR-TO-DATE ADVERTISING DOLLARS (000)							
		7-MEDIA TOTAL	LNA MAGAZINES	LNA NEWSPAPER SUPPLEMENTS	BAR NETWORK TELEVISION	BAR SPOT TELEVISION	BAR NETWORK RADIO	LNA OUTDOOR	BAR CABLE TV NETWORKS
F123 HEALTH & DIETARY FOODS (NOT ELSE CLASS) ————							CONTINUED	————	
DELMART CO INC									
FEATHERWEIGHT DIET FOODS	F123	233.1	233.1	- -	- -	- -	- -	- -	- -
ESTEE CORP									
ESTEE DIETETIC TREATS	F123	15.1	15.1	- -	- -	- -	- -	- -	- -
EXECUTIVE DISTRIBUTORS									
TROPICAL NUTRITION DIET	F123	0.4	- -	- -	- -	0.4	- -	- -	- -
HEINZ HJ CO									
WEIGHT WATCHERS DIET FOODS	F123	120.5	118.9	- -	- -	- -	- -	1.6	- -
NATURE WELL WEIGHT LOSS									
NATURAL LOSS SYSTEM/LQD	F123	4.1	- -	- -	- -	4.1	- -	- -	- -
NATURES BOUNTY INC									
NATURES BOUNTY HERBAL DIET KIT	F123	30.6	- -	- -	- -	30.6	- -	- -	- -
PILLSBURY CO									
PILLSBURY FIGURINES DIET BARS	F123	2,304.1	290.7	- -	- -	2,013.4	- -	- -	- -
SANDOZ LTD									
RESOURCE NUTRITIONAL SUPPLEMENT	F123	588.6	588.6	- -	- -	- -	- -	- -	- -
SCHERING-PLOUGH CORP									
FIBER ALL NATURAL FIBER FOOD SUPPLEMENT	F123	70.5	70.5	- -	- -	- -	- -	- -	- -
WEIDER HEALTH & FITNESS									
WEIDER DIET SUPPLEMENT DRINK POWDER	F123	135.5	40.9	- -	- -	2.3	- -	- -	92.3
COMPANY UNKNOWN									
BOOST HIGH ENERGY FOOD SUPPLEMENT	F123	13.1	- -	- -	- -	- -	- -	- -	13.1
CALBAN 3000 DIET PLAN	F123	260.2	- -	- -	- -	260.2	- -	- -	- -
CALIF TRIM DIET PLAN	F123	4.1	- -	- -	- -	4.1	- -	- -	- -
DIETERS COFFEE DIET SUPPLEMENT	F123	4.4	- -	- -	- -	3.5	- -	0.9	- -
FORMULA 75 DIET PLAN	F123	706.1	- -	- -	- -	590.4	- -	- -	115.7
GOLDEN CUP COFFEE SAVER	F123	3.9	- -	- -	- -	3.9	- -	- -	- -
MARINESS DIET SUPPLEMENT	F123	0.3	- -	- -	- -	0.3	- -	- -	- -
RICE DIET WGHT LSS PLAN	F123	1.8	- -	- -	- -	1.8	- -	- -	- -
VITACIN DIET PLAN	F123	1.2	- -	- -	- -	1.2	- -	- -	- -
WEIGHT AWAY DIET PLAN	F123	6.6	- -	- -	- -	6.6	- -	- -	- -
COMPANY TOTAL		1,001.7	- -	- -	- -	872.0	- -	0.9	128.8
F123 TOTAL		4,739.6	1,357.8	- -	- -	3,158.2	- -	2.5	221.1
F124 INFANTS FOODS ————									
GERBER PRODUCTS CO									
GERBER BABY FOODS	F124	12,467.0	5,555.6	- -	6,807.0	70.9	- -	- -	33.5
HEINZ HJ CO									
HEINZ INSTANT BABY FOOD	F124	2,954.3	493.2	- -	2,361.2	78.5	- -	- -	21.4
NESTLE SA									
BEECH-NUT FOODS FOR BABIES	F124	3,665.8	533.6	- -	- -	3,120.7	- -	- -	11.5
F124 TOTAL		19,087.1	6,582.4	- -	9,168.2	3,270.1	- -	- -	66.4

Source: Leading National Advertisers and Broadcast Advertisers Reports.

analysis studies. These studies cover media and product usage, buying influence, demographic and life-style analysis, and media preference. Most media information is provided at no cost to advertisers.

MEDIA ASSOCIATIONS

Every medium has its own association that helps promote the medium; sets standards of performance and conduct; sponsors primary research; and compiles industry statistics. Some of the leading media associations are the Newspaper Advertising Bureau, International Newspaper Adver-

FIGURE 15.13

Reading SMRB Data

0602
P-25

SUNTAN & SUNSCREEN PRODUCTS (APPLIED TO THE SKIN) – USAGE IN LAST 12 MONTHS (ADULTS)

0602
P-25

	TOTAL U.S. '000	ALL USERS A '000	B % DOWN	C % ACROSS	D INDX	HEAVY USERS TWO OR MORE A '000	B % DOWN	C % ACROSS	D INDX	MEDIUM USERS ONE A '000	B % DOWN	C % ACROSS	D INDX	LIGHT USERS LESS THAN ONE A '000	B % DOWN	C % ACROSS	D INDX
TOTAL ADULTS	169460	73820	100.0	43.6	100	31798	100.0	18.8	100								
MALES	80052	30303	41.0	37.9	87	13114	41.2	16.4	87								
FEMALES	89408	43517	59.0	48.7	112	18684	58.8	20.9	111								
18 – 24	28611	15201	20.6	53.1	122	6945	21.8	24.3	129								
25 – 34	40058	21734	29.4	54.3	125	9681	30.4	24.2	129								
35 – 44	30132	15695	21.3	52.1	120	6783	21.3	22.5	120								
45 – 54	22317	9345	12.7	41.9	96	3800	12.0	17.0	91								
55 – 64	21993	6700	9.1	30.5	70	2757	8.7	12.5	67								
65 OR OLDER	26350	5144	7.0	19.5	45	1833	5.8	7.0	37								
18 – 34	68669	36935	50.0	53.8	123	16626	52.3	24.2	129								
18 – 49	110638	57929	78.5	52.4	120	25674	80.7	23.2	124								
25 – 54	92507	46774	63.4	50.6	116	20264	63.7	21.9	117								
35 – 49	41969	20994	28.4	50.0	115	9048	28.5	21.6	115								
50 OR OLDER	58823	15891	21.5	27.0	62	6124	19.3	10.4	55								
GRADUATED COLLEGE	28689	16454	22.3	57.4	132	6875	21.6	24.0	128								
ATTENDED COLLEGE	29760	15218	20.6	51.1	117	6510	20.5	21.9	117								
GRADUATED HIGH SCHOOL	67306	30166	40.9	44.8	103	12965	40.8	19.3	103								
DID NOT GRADUATE HIGH SCHOOL	43705	11983	16.2	27.4	63	5449	17.1	12.5	66								
EMPLOYED MALES	56764	24232	32.8	42.7	98	10651	33.5	18.8	100								
EMPLOYED FEMALES	45302	26884	36.4	59.3	136	11268	35.4	24.9	133								
EMPLOYED FULL-TIME	88763	43681	59.2	49.2	113	18664	58.7	21.0	112								
EMPLOYED PART-TIME	13303	7436	10.1	55.9	128	3254	10.2	24.5	130								
NOT EMPLOYED	67395	22703	30.8	33.7	77	9879	31.1	14.7	78								
PROFESSIONAL/MANAGER	26470	15019	20.3	56.7	130	6201	19.5	23.4	125								
TECH/CLERICAL/SALES	31679	17717	24.0	55.9	128	7233	22.7	22.8	122								
PRECISION/CRAFT	12857	5223	7.1	40.6	93	2474	7.8	19.2	103								
OTHER EMPLOYED	31060	13158	17.8	42.4	97	6011	18.9	19.4	103								
SINGLE	36345	17879	24.2	49.2	113	8233	25.9	22.7	121								
MARRIED	103592	46191	62.6	44.6	102	19225	60.5	18.6	99								
DIVORCED/SEPARATED/WIDOWED	29524	9750	13.2	33.0	76	4340	13.6	14.7	78								
PARENTS	58373	30609	41.5	52.4	120	13308	41.9	22.8	121								
WHITE	147469	69504	94.2	47.1	108	29771	93.6	20.2	108								
BLACK	18302	3110	4.2	17.0	39	1513	4.8	8.3	44								
OTHER	3689	1206	1.6	32.7	75	514	1.6	13.9	74								
NORTHEAST-CENSUS	36974	17250	23.4	46.7	107	7612	23.9	20.6	110	5526	23.7	14.9	109	4113	22.0	11.1	101
NORTH CENTRAL	42557	18251	24.7	42.9	98	6459	20.3	15.2	81	6496	27.9	15.3	111	5296	28.3	12.4	113
SOUTH	57701	22186	30.1	38.4	88	11034	34.7	19.1	102	6391	27.4	11.1	81	4760	25.4	8.2	75
WEST	32228	16133	21.9	50.1	115	6693	21.0	20.8	111	4901	21.0	15.2	111	4539	24.3	14.1	128
NORTHEAST-MKTG.	38103	17544	23.8	46.0	106	7941	25.0	20.8	111	5462	23.4	14.3	104	4141	22.1	10.9	98
EAST CENTRAL	24421	10372	14.1	42.5	97	4100	12.9	16.8	89	3549	15.2	14.5	106	2724	14.6	11.2	101
WEST CENTRAL	28542	12646	17.1	44.3	102	4495	14.1	15.7	84	4476	19.2	15.7	114	3675	19.6	12.9	117
SOUTH	49737	18966	25.7	38.1	88	9327	29.3	18.8	100	5585	24.0	11.2	82	4053	21.7	8.1	74
PACIFIC	28658	14292	19.4	49.9	114	5936	18.7	20.7	110	4243	18.2	14.8	108	4114	22.0	14.4	130

HOW TO READ THIS DATA

Top Row: There were an estimated 169,460,000 adults in the U.S.

A—73,820,000 adults used suntan/sunscreen products within the last 12 months

B—Column A represents 100% of users

C—43.6% of all adults used suntan/sunscreen products (73,820,000 ÷ 169,460,000 = 43.6%)

Fourth Row: There were an estimated 28,611,000 adults ages 18–24 in the U.S.

A—15,201,000 adults use suntan/sunscreen products

B—20.6% of all users are ages 18–24

C—53.1% of all adults are users (28,611,000 × 53.1% = 15,201,000)

D—The index of usage (users compared to the population base) is 122 (53.1% ÷ 43.6% × 100 = 122)

Source: 1985 SMRB Study of Media & Markets. Reprinted with permission.

tising and Marketing Executives, the Magazine Publishers Association, the Radio Advertising Bureau, the Television Advertising Bureau, the Direct Marketing Association, the Institute of Outdoor Advertising, and the Specialty Advertising Association International. A complete list of media and advertising associations is in the Appendix.

AUDIT BUREAUS

How do you know that 20,000,000 copies of *Reader's Digest* were distributed last month? You could accept the word of the publisher, but if you are spending $100,000 for a page of advertising in the magazine, you might want more assurance than the information contained on the publisher's rate card. Audit bureaus were formed to verify media circulation. The Audit Bureau of Circulations, the Business Publications Audit, and the Traffic Audit Bureau are not-for-profit organizations that impartially verify media circulation. An individual medium agrees to have its circulation audited and pays a fee to the appropriate audit bureau for the service. The audit reports are made available to advertisers and advertising agencies.

COMPETITIVE MEDIA ACTIVITY

Because competitive activity is often an important influence on an advertiser's media plan, a market has developed for reports on media expenditures. Independent research services such as Broadcast Advertisers Reports (BAR), Leading National Advertisers (LNA), and Media Records report advertisers' expenditures by brand, media type, market, and time period. Advertisers and their agencies have access to this information by subscribing to one or more of the services.

FIGURE 15.14

Standard Rate & Data Service (SRDS)

The SRDS provides much of the information required for media evaluation and placement.

Electronic Industry Telephone Directory

Media Code 7 240 2550 7.00   Mid 002899-000
Published annually by Harris Publishing Co., 2057-2 E. Aurora Rd., Twinsburg, OH 44087. Phone 216-425-9000.

PUBLISHER'S EDITORIAL PROFILE
ELECTRONIC INDUSTRY TELEPHONE DIRECTORY is compiled for management, engineering, procurement of electronics, computer and related user industries. The Directory lists name, address, city, state, direct dial telephone number of firms engaged in: manufacture, sales or distribution of electronic components, systems and equipment, as well as computers and peripheral equipment. It contains lists of suppliers arranged under nearly 3,500 separate product and sub-product classifications. In addition to electronic and computer related suppliers, the directory lists electronic distributors, manufacturers' agents and defense users. Rec'd 8/13/82.

1. PERSONNEL
President—Robert A. Harris, Jr.
Publisher—Robert A. Harris, Sr.
Vice-Pres. & Edit. Dir.—Beatrice Harris.
Editor—Lonetta Witt.
Advertising Production—Paula Scroggy & Charlotte Frew.

2. REPRESENTATIVES and/or BRANCH OFFICES
Chatsworth, CA 91311—Ray Ginter, 11401 N. Topanga Canyon Blvd. Phone 213-341-7433.
Huntington Beach, CA 92646—Melinda Stone, 8471 Yorktown. Rd. Phone 714-968-5959.
Naperville, IL 60540—Steve Priessman, 734 Hagerman Pl. Phone 312-420-8744.
Stratford, CT 06497—Don Weil, Jeff Weil, Bob Weil, 536-B Narragansett Ln. Phone 203-377-5506.
Twinsburg (Cleveland), OH 44087—Robert Harris, Sr., 2057-2 E. Aurora Rd. Phone 216-425-9000.
Arlington, TX 76011—Catherine Coward, 1534 Stone Leigh Ct. Phone 817-261-0417.

3. COMMISSION AND CASH DISCOUNT
Banners and display space are commissionable at 15% to agencies. An Early-Bird cash discount of 4% may be earned by pre-payment of display space and/or listings. Display ads submitted by agencies requiring composition and/or cuts will be rebilled at publisher's cost. Cash discount, following publication, is 1% on net (after agency commission) if paid within 10 days of invoice. Add 1-1/2% per month for accounts over 60 days past due. Cancellations after 15 days take a 50% penalty.

4. GENERAL RATE POLICY
No cancellations of display space or paid listings will be accepted after April 15.

ADVERTISING RATES
Effective January 1, 1986.
Card received December 2, 1985.

5. BLACK/WHITE RATES
ALPHABETICAL SECTION
Extra Boldface .... 90.   Bold face type .... 45.
Mini-ads & Trade Marks may not be grouped for bulk page rates.
DISPLAY ADS
Banners (top only) .... 905.
Special position full pages .... 3295.
INFORMATION ADS
Non-commissionable.
Mini-banner (5-line) .... 295.
Mini-banner (7-line) .... 345.
YELLOW PAGES INFORMATIONAL ADS
Boldface Basic Products:
Boldface special headings .... 40.
Non-commissionable.
Mini-Ad (style A) .... 285.
Mini-Ad (style B) .... 385.
Trademark .... 430.
DISPLAY ADS
*Bulk page .... 3450.
1 page .... 3200.
2/3 page .... 2500.
1/2 page .... 2050.
1/3 page .... 1515.
1/6 page .... 970.
1/12 page .... 625.
     (*) Fractional units may be grouped for bulk page rate.
Importers receive all basic product headings in bold type and 1 bold sub-product listing for every 50.00 of display space.
Distributors receive 1 bold listing in either a basic or sub-product category for every 50.00 of display space.

6. COLOR RATES
Standard color .... 395.   4-color process .... 625.
Matched color .... 515.
Color restricted to cover positions.

7. COVERS
2nd cover (reserved for Distribution Agents).
3rd cover .... 3415.   4th cover .... 3900.

9. BLEED
Bleed confined to covers & inserts, extra .... 250.

10. SPECIAL POSITION
Specified placement adjacent to or facing product category free in yellow pages, exact placement within specific category, extra 15%

11. CLASSIFIED/MAIL ORDER
For complete data, refer to Business Publication Rates and Data - Classified.

15. MECH REQUIREMENTS
For complete, detailed production information, see SRDS Print Media Production Data.
Printing Process: Web Offset. Covers: Offset, sheetfed.
Trim size: 8-3/8 x 10-7/8; No./Cols. 3.
Binding method: Perfect.
Cover colors available: AAAA/ABP; Matched; 4-Color Process (AAAA/MPA); Metallic.

DIMENSIONS-AD PAGE			
1 7-3/4 x	10	1/3 5-1/8 x 4-7/8	
2/3 5-1/8 x	10	1/6 5-1/8 x 2-3/8	
1/2 5-1/8 x 7-1/2		1/6 2-1/2 x 4-7/8	
1/2 7-3/4 x 4-7/8		1/12 2-1/2 x 2-1/2	
1/3 2-1/2 x	10		

Top Banner .... 7-3/4   x 1
Mini-ad style A .... 2-1/2   x 1
Mini-ad style B .... 2-1/2 x 1-1/2
Trademark .... 2-1/2 x 1-1/4
Mini-banner .... 3-5/8   x 1

16. ISSUE AND CLOSING DATES
Published annually; issued in August.
Closing date for ads requiring composition April 15; for free and paid listing services in both white and yellow pages is May 1.

18. CIRCULATION
Established 1963. Single copy 40.00 plus 3.50 shipping.
SWORN 1985-86 Edition
Total   Non-Pd   Paid
99,699   23,453   76,246
Unpaid Distribution (not included above):
   Total 1,846
TERRITORIAL DISTRIBUTION 11/85—109,824
N.Eng.   Mid.Atl. E.N.Cen. W.N.Cen.   S.Atl.   E.S.Cen.
9,981   20,319 - 23,676   6,476   6,852   1,586
W.S.Cen.   Mtn.St.   Pac.St.   Canada   Foreign   Other
8,6885   4,438   22,815   2,509   638   1,846
BUSINESS ANALYSIS OF CIRCULATION
                                                          Total
Engineering 70273
Procurement 34413
Advertisers & ad agencies 2214
Book sales (exclusive of franchise) 506
Sales office 572
Undistributed 1846
Publisher's states: rates based on a circulation average of 101,000.

AUDIENCE DATA

A number of commercial services provide estimates of audience size. Simmons Market Research Bureau (SMRB) is a widely used subscription service that reports data on product, brand, and media usage by both demographic and life-style characteristics.

STANDARD RATE & DATA SERVICE

On a day-to-day basis, the most widely used source of media information is Standard Rate & Data Service (SRDS). This company sells subscriptions to its series of directories, which cover all major media except outdoor. The directories contain information on media rates, format, mechanical requirements, and audience. SRDS information is taken from information supplied by the media, primarily rate cards.

SUMMARY

This chapter introduced a seven-step process of planning media. The first three steps of the process (reviewing the marketing and advertising situation, selecting the target market, and setting media objectives) comprise the strategy component of media planning and they build on the marketing and advertising concepts discussed in earlier chapters. The best media plans develop out of marketing problems and opportunities, and their overall function is to help fulfill the company's marketing and advertising objectives.

Executing the four tactical steps of the media plan (evaluating media alternatives, building the media schedule, implementing the media plan, and evaluating the media plan) requires familiarity with the language, concepts, and resource services of media. With some understanding of the basics of media planning, you will be better able to appreciate the strengths and weaknesses of the individual media discussed in the next several chapters.

YOU MAKE THE DECISION

"BEST FRIEND"

You're the media director for an advertising agency with a client in the pet food industry. The director of advertising for the pet food company has just told you about a new product that will be introduced. Some facts about the new brand include these:

1. The product is a dog food known as "Best Friend." It will be supported by a $12 million advertising budget during its first year. (Industry averages for pet food are $7–15 million.)

2. "Best Friend" will be packaged in individual polyethylene bags, and it will be in "hamburger" form. The main selling features of the

product are that it contains more dog vitamins than any other dog food and it also contains an ingredient that promises to reduce dog mouth odor significantly.

3. "Best Friend" will be high-priced, but not significantly more than the current price leader.

4. The trend in the dog food business has been for consumers to trade down—that is, generics and store brands have been doing very well over the past few years while the brands in the middle to upper price ranges have been losing share or, at best, holding their own.

Prepare an outline of a media plan for "Best Friend."

■ ■ ■

QUESTIONS FOR DISCUSSION

1. From the point of view of the advertising manager, what are the purposes of the media?

2. Describe the seven steps of a media plan.

3. Describe the differences among marketing, advertising, and media objectives. Give an example of each.

4. Explain why an advertiser can't maximize reach and frequency within a given investment in advertising media.

5. How might a competitor's media plans affect your media plan?

6. Under what conditions would reach be stressed over frequency?

7. Describe each of the following patterns of continuity and suggest the types of products or services that would utilize each.
    a. continuous
    b. flighting
    c. pulsing

8. What is the difference between quantitative and qualitative criteria in media evaluation? Which set of criteria is more important?

9. What is the difference between CPM and CPM-TM?

10. What are gross rating points and how are they calculated?

NOTES

1. *Advertising Age*, November 29, 1984, 12; *Magazine Newsletter of Research*, no. 26, Magazine Publishers' Association, New York, August 1984; and *Marketing & Media Decisions*, August 1986, 35.

2. Newspaper Advertising Bureau, New York; and International Newspaper Advertising and Marketing Executives, Washington, D. C. (undated).

3. *Magazine Newsletter of Research*, no. 26, Magazine Publishers' Association, New York, August 1984.

4. Hubert A. Zielske and Walter A. Henry, "Remembering and Forgetting Television Ads," *Journal of Advertising Research*, April 1980; Edward C. Strong, "The Spacing and Timing of Advertising," *Journal of Advertising Research*, August 1980; and Howard Kamin, "Advertising Reach and Frequency," *Journal of Advertising Research*, February 1978.

5. Carol Hall, "Risky Business," *Marketing & Media Decisions*, October 1986, 83–90.

6. *Business Publications Directory* (Northbrook, Ill.: Standard Rate & Data Service, August 1985).

7. John D. Leckenby and Shizue Kishi, "How Media Directors View Reach/Frequency Estimation," *Journal of Advertising Research*, June–July 1982.

8. Dennis Gensch, *Advertising Planning: Mathematical Models in Advertising Media Planning* (New York: Elsevier Publishing Company, 1973); and Philip Kotler, "Toward An Explicit Model for Media Selection," *Journal of Advertising Research*, March 1964.

SUGGESTED READINGS

Barban, Arnold M.; Steven M. Cristol; and Frank J. Kopec. *Essentials of Media Planning: A Marketing Viewpoint*. Chicago: Crain Books, 1976.

Bogart, Leo. *Strategy in Advertising: Matching Media and Messages to Markets and Motivation*. 2d. ed. Chicago: Crain Books, 1984.

Dalbey, Homer M.; Irwin Gross; and Yoram Wind. *Advertising Measurement and Decision Making*. Boston: Allyn & Bacon, 1968.

Eilers, Gerald. "Snuffing out the Media Blues." *Marketing & Media Decisions*, October 1986, 110–112.

Leckenby, John D., and Nugent Wedding. *Advertising Management: Criteria, Analysis and Decision Making*. Columbus, Ohio: Grid, 1982.

McGann, Anthony F., and J. Thomas Russell. *Advertising Media: A Managerial Approach*. Homewood, Ill.: Richard D. Irwin, 1981.

Ramond, Charles. *Advertising Research: The State of the Art*. New York: Association of National Advertisers, 1976.

Selwitz, Robert. "Media Buying Moves In-House." *Marketing Communications*, September 1986, 19–23; 79; 86.

Sissors, Jack Z., and Jim Surmanek. *Advertising Media Planning*. 2d. ed. Chicago: Crain Books, 1982.

CHAPTER 16

BROADCAST MEDIA

Key Terms

affiliate
independent
network
sponsorship
participation
spot announcement
Households Using Television (HUT)
coverage
ratings
share of audience
reach
average frequency
gross rating points (GRPs)
cost per rating point (CPR)
cumulative audience
gross impressions
frequency

Learning Objectives

To describe the structure of television and radio

To explain how to use the broadcast media as advertising media

To define the terminology and concepts used in broadcast media planning

To determine when to use the broadcast media

One afternoon David Anderson, Director of Advertising for Pitney Bowes, asked his firm's advertising agency, D'Arcy-MacManus & Masius, to find an exciting new way to increase awareness of the company. Pitney Bowes wanted greater presence and impact beyond the company's traditional print media campaign. The company was widely known as the world leader in mailing systems, but not everyone knew that the company offered a complete line of office copiers and innovative concepts like postage-by-phone.

Barry Crane, Vice-President and Account Supervisor for D'Arcy-MacManus & Masius, coordinated the development and launching of a radio campaign. The campaign featured the vaudeville repartee of comedy team Gallagher and Shean, adapted for two new characters, Mr. Pitney and Mr. Bowes. The agency's radio buy used more than 100 rating points per week and consisted of both network and spot radio. The buy allowed the firm to reach 80 percent of adults more than 10 times with even greater frequency against their target audience.

Why did a business-to-business advertiser use radio? Crane explained: "Mr. Pitney and Mr. Bowes as a concept offered us great impact and the ability to personify the corporate name. And it presented us with a great vehicle capable of encompassing a variety of tailored messages within one theme. The vaudeville approach of the famous team of Gallagher and Shean offered us a natural format. The repartee and music was catchy and memorable."

Anderson said, "We knew instinctively that we had the perfect spokesmen. The campaign had excitement and entertainment value, and it pinpointed the company with an image that was ours alone."

As factors in the success of the campaign, both Crane and Anderson cited radio's unique targetability, its national and local reach, and its economic efficiency, which allowed Pitney Bowes to generate frequency for its selling message. "With radio, we were able to target our message to our key prospects and customers," Anderson said. "The commercials ran during morning and evening drive times and weekends when our target audience of managers and professionals are listening to their radios . . . on stations with news, easy listening, and sports."

"And we were able to broaden our reach to the whole country by using a combination of network buys on ABC Information, CBS, and NBC," Crane added.

Was the campaign successful? Pitney Bowes conducted a tracking study in six test markets and discovered that ad recall increased 133 percent and consumer awareness of Pitney Bowes' office copiers rose 250 percent. Also, the campaign significantly boosted the efforts of the company's sales force. "In addition to great customer feedback, the sales force remarked on how radio helped open more doors for them," Crane said. "Their customers and prospects were becoming more aware of Pitney Bowes and were beginning to sing our tune."

Source: Adapted from "Ad Recall, Consumer Awareness Increase for Pitney Bowes," *America on Radio*, Radio Advertising Bureau, Inc., New York, July 1984. Artwork provided courtesy of Pitney Bowes, Inc.

INTRODUCTION

The Pitney Bowes story is just one example of a company that has been able to maximize the benefits of the broadcast media. Many companies have enjoyed success when they took full advantage of the characteristics of the broadcast media. No other medium can match the drama created by, for example, the Apple Computer "1984" television commercial, or the humor of Monty Python's Jon Cleese in his series of radio commercials for Kronenbourg Beer.

Successful advertising—the type that makes us aware of a new brand, induces us to send in a response card, changes our opinion about a product, or makes us feel comfortable about shopping at a particular store—takes full advantage of the characteristics of the medium. Because there are so many media alternatives, media planning can be complex. It's easy to make a mistake . . . to buy a medium just because competitors use it, to select media on efficiency only, or to overlook the interaction between the message and the medium. The broadcast commercials for Pitney Bowes, Apple Computer, and Kronenbourg Beer have been successful because they work so well within the medium. This chapter helps you understand the broadcast media as carriers of advertising messages and how radio and television play a key role in helping companies meet their marketing objectives.

STRUCTURE OF TELEVISION

Television is the newest of the major advertising media, yet it is widely considered the most powerful. Less than $60 million was spent on television advertising in 1949; that figure currently surpasses $20 billion. In its relatively few years of existence, television has become our major source of entertainment and information. Volumes have been written about television's impact on our lives. Advertisers know how much we watch television and how important it has become in shaping our behavior in the marketplace. That's why they are willing to pay a half a million dollars to talk to us for a mere 30 seconds.

AFFILIATED AND INDEPENDENT STATIONS

In 1912, the Federal Communications Commission was granted the power to license broadcast stations. Stations are privately owned—either by individuals or by media conglomerates, such as Katz Radio, Tribune Broadcasting, and Group W. Some stations become affiliated with a network (**affiliates**) and others choose to remain **independents.** Network-affiliated stations agree to carry the network's programming as well as the national advertising within that programming. Additionally, network-affiliated stations sell advertising time to national and local advertisers. This advertising appears between network programming or during programming that the station itself originates.

Independent stations develop their own programming, most often in the form of original programs (news, sports, or community-interest pro-

A CLOSER LOOK

GROWTH IN TV USAGE

A whopping 87.4 million American households have a television set, and they watch an average of more than seven hours per day. When the medium of television emerged in the late 1940s and early 1950s, only nine percent of the populace owned a set. From 1950 to 1955, that number skyrocketed, with an increase to 64.5 percent, or 30.7 million households tuning in.

How we allocate those 7 + hours of viewing time is also of interest. In an average day, 4 hours 58 minutes are devoted to network television. Another hour and 35 minutes are spent watching the programming of independent stations. Pay television receives 35 minutes of viewing time, with 23 minutes for cable stations and a miniscule 15 minutes devoted to public television. (So much for culture!)

Here's how the A.C. Nielsen Company listed the top 10 prime-time shows, by the price of a 30-second spot:

Allocation of TV Viewing Time

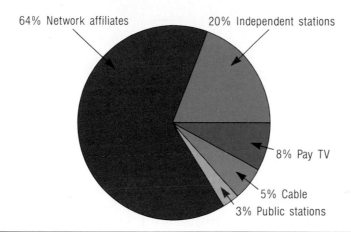

64% Network affiliates

20% Independent stations

8% Pay TV

5% Cable

3% Public stations

grams) or reruns of previously aired series and movies. Although independent stations must pay for their programming, they also have more advertising time available to sell.

NETWORKS

A **network** is a group of stations that have agreed to carry programming originated from the network and any advertising within the program. The three national networks—the American Broadcasting Company (ABC), the Columbia Broadcasting System (CBS), and the National Broadcasting Company (NBC)—broadcast the most-watched programming. Although only about 1 percent of all television commercials are carried on network television, nearly 41 percent of the total dollars invested in television advertising are spent on the three major networks.[1] Many of the top-rated, prime-time network shows reach as many as 10 to 15 million U.S. households. "The Cosby Show," for example, is the highest-priced series of all time. A 30-second commercial during the show has sold for as much as $400,000, making the program second only to recent Super Bowls in terms of the price of a commercial.[2]

EXHIBIT 16.1

Top 10 Prime-Time Television Shows, by Price of a 30-Second Commercial

RANK	SHOW	PRICE OF 30-SECOND SPOT	NETWORK	RATING	SHARE
1	Cosby Show	$380,000	NBC	35.2	53
2	Family Ties	300,000	NBC	33.3	49
3	Cheers	230,000	NBC	29.6	42
4	Moonlighting	215,000	ABC	23.8	36
5	Who's the Boss?	215,000	ABC	22.0	34
6	Night Court	206,000	NBC	25.2	38
7	Growing Pains	205,000	ABC	22.7	34
8	Miami Vice	195,000	NBC	17.4	28
9	Dynasty	185,000	ABC	17.4	27
10	Golden Girls	175,000	NBC	26.0	44

Sources: Advertising Age, December 22, 1986, 21; Television Bureau of Advertising, "Trends in Television: 1950 to Date," New York, May 1986; and "Television: 1986 Nielsen Report," A.C. Nielsen Company, Northbrook, IL.

Network television advertising is ideal for advertisers of nationally distributed products. No other medium can match network television's ability to reach large numbers of people throughout the country quickly. However, TV advertising is not inexpensive: between 1973 and 1983, the average cost of a prime-time 30-second network television commercial increased from $55,060 to $153,000 (Exhibit 16.1).[3]

Although the cost of a network commercial can be very high, network advertising's efficiency at reaching target audiences makes it the primary medium for most of the largest advertisers. For example, although a 30-second commercial during Super Bowl XXI cost $550,000, the program was watched by nearly half of all U.S. households. Two-thirds of all households that were watching television were watching the Super Bowl.[4]

The prestige of network television advertising also helps an advertiser market the product. Advertisers benefit because consumers, retailers, and distributors associate the advertised product with the prestige of a top-rated program.

Finally, network television advertising is convenient for advertisers and their advertising agencies. Once a commercial has been produced and advertising time has been purchased, the advertising message is communicated to the entire country through one business transaction. (The alternative is to advertise on one or more stations in the number of markets that are important to the advertiser. Since these markets may number 150 or more, bookkeeping and billing could be an enormous task.)

CABLE AND PAY TV

Cable TV, originally known as CATV (community antenna television), was first developed to bring improved television reception into areas where reception was difficult. Today, the popularity of cable TV is largely based on its ability to provide the subscriber a diversity of programming. In 1960, only 1 percent of all TV households subscribed to cable. By 1986, 45.6 percent of all TV households were cable subscri-

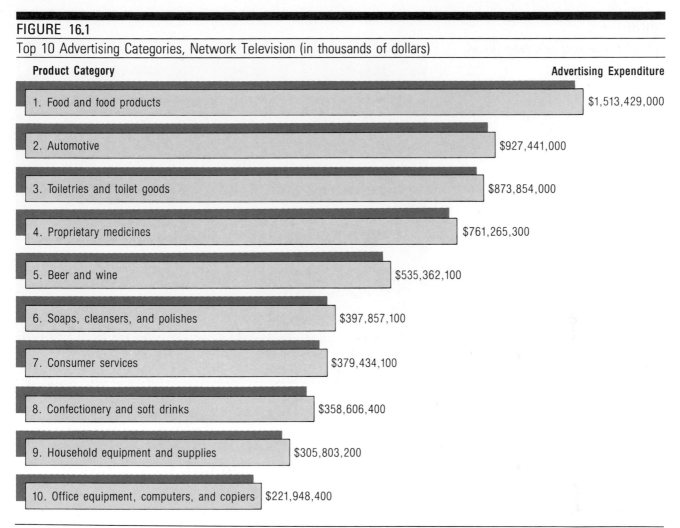

FIGURE 16.1

Top 10 Advertising Categories, Network Television (in thousands of dollars)

Product Category	Advertising Expenditure
1. Food and food products	$1,513,429,000
2. Automotive	$927,441,000
3. Toiletries and toilet goods	$873,854,000
4. Proprietary medicines	$761,265,300
5. Beer and wine	$535,362,100
6. Soaps, cleansers, and polishes	$397,857,100
7. Consumer services	$379,434,100
8. Confectionery and soft drinks	$358,606,400
9. Household equipment and supplies	$305,803,200
10. Office equipment, computers, and copiers	$221,948,400

Source: "Highlights—Local, National, Spot, & Network Commercial Television Advertising, 1986," Television Bureau of Advertising, Inc., New York, March 9, 1987.

bers.[5] A cable service provides programming from distant network affiliates, independent stations, PBS (Public Broadcasting System), one or more "superstations" (WTBS and WGN, for example), shows produced by the local cable operator, and programs supplied by one or more cable networks, such as ESPN, Cable News Network, or MTV (see Figure 16.2).

In recent years, cable systems have offered a variety of special programming (such as movies, sporting events, and children's shows), for which subscribers pay an additional fee. In 1986, 26.6% of all TV households subscribed to one or more pay cable services.[6]

Despite the growth of cable subscriptions, cable's potential as an advertising medium is unclear. As cable's popularity grew, it was thought that cable would dominate our viewing and become the main source of television advertising revenue. In 1986, however, approximately 87 percent of total television viewing was still accounted for by over-the-air television.[7]

FIGURE 16.2

Cable TV Networks and Their Reach

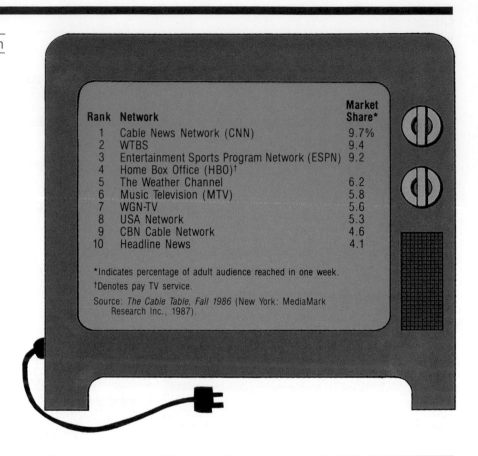

Rank	Network	Market Share*
1	Cable News Network (CNN)	9.7%
2	WTBS	9.4
3	Entertainment Sports Program Network (ESPN)	9.2
4	Home Box Office (HBO)†	
5	The Weather Channel	6.2
6	Music Television (MTV)	5.8
7	WGN-TV	5.6
8	USA Network	5.3
9	CBN Cable Network	4.6
10	Headline News	4.1

*Indicates percentage of adult audience reached in one week.

†Denotes pay TV service.

Source: *The Cable Table, Fall 1986* (New York: MediaMark Research Inc., 1987).

Source: *The Cable Table Fall 1986* (New York: MediaMark Research Inc., 1987).

Although cable's penetration has been impressive, its growth has been less than expected. It is now estimated that the 50 percent level of cable penetration will not be reached until 1989—two years later than originally predicted. The growth of pay cable has also been revised downward. The 1990 forecast now calls for 30.9 million pay cable households.[8] Exhibit 16.2 traces the growth of pay TV and cable TV since 1980.

Of greater significance to advertising management is the use of cable television as an advertising medium. While cable advertising revenue will continue to grow, its proportion of total television advertising revenue remains small. By 1990, it is estimated that total cable advertising revenue will be less than $3 billion, or less than 7% of the total over-the-air television advertising revenue.[9]

When compared to over-the-air network television, cable TV is a low-cost, efficient medium for reaching certain market segments. For example, the average cost of a 30-second, over-the-air commercial on baseball's World Series is $250,000, whereas a 30-second, prime-time commercial on ESPN costs $5,000.[10] The main reasons that cable has not yet become a major source of advertising revenue are comparatively small audiences and the lack of accurate audience measurement services.

EXHIBIT 16.2

Pay TV and Cable TV Subscriptions and Advertising Volume, 1980–1990

YEAR	NUMBER OF CABLE TV HOUSEHOLDS	PERCENTAGE OF TV HOUSEHOLDS	PAY TV HOUSEHOLDS	PERCENTAGE OF TV HOUSEHOLDS	ADVERTISING VOLUME (in Millions of Dollars)
1980	16,023,000	21%	5,341,000	7%	$ 58
1981	18,672,000	24	7,780,000	10	122
1982	22,596,000	28	11,804,000	14	227
1983	28,200,000	34	15,898,000	19	353
1984	30,300,000	36	17,877,000	21	514
1985	32,994,000	39	19,764,000	23	725
1986	36,120,000	42	21,672,000	25	995
1987	39,510,000	45	24,101,000	27	1,353
1988	41,971,000	47	26,022,000	30	1,778
1989	45,500,000	50	28,665,000	32	2,238
1990	48,256,000	52	30,883,000	33	2,765

Source: Television Bureau of Advertising, Inc., "Cable Facts," New York, 1986.

LEARNING TO USE TV AS AN ADVERTISING MEDIUM

In addition to knowing how the television industry is structured, the successful use of television depends on how well the advertising manager understands how to buy and evaluate television. The following section discusses methods of buying television commercial time; the factors that affect the cost of television time; and the terms and concepts used to estimate television audiences.

OPTIONS FOR BUYING TV COMMERCIALS

One of the advantages of television is the flexibility it offers in the length of the commercial, the geographic placement, the type of program environment, and the degree of participation in the program.

Length of Commercial Many years ago, the 60-second commercial was the most common. Today, however, the 30-second commercial accounts for nearly 90 percent of non-network commercials and nearly 75 percent of network commercials.[11] Recently, the major change in commercial length has been the availability and increased use of the 15-second commercial, which in 1985 accounted for 10 percent of all network commercials (Exhibit 16.3).

Geographic Placement An advertiser can reach a national audience through network television (over-the-air or cable), regional markets through spot television, or a single market through local television. Exhibit 16.4 shows that the amount of money invested in television advertising by the top ten product categories totaled nearly $8 billion in 1986.

EXHIBIT 16.3

Length of Television Commercials, Network and Non-Network

YEAR	10-SECOND		30-SECOND		60-SECOND		OTHER*	
	NETWORK	NON-NETWORK	NETWORK	NON-NETWORK	NETWORK	NON-NETWORK	NETWORK	NON-NETWORK
1965	0	16.1%	0	.8%	76.7%	64.0%	23.3%	19.9%
1970	0	11.8	25.1	48.1	27.0	26.5	47.9	13.6
1975	0	9.1	79.0	79.2	5.6	10.4	15.4	1.3
1980	.7	7.8	85.2	85.1	2.1	3.9	12.0	.4
1985	1.3	5.5	83.5	88.0	2.2	2.7	14.3	3.8

*In 1984, 15-second network television commercials accounted for 5.2% of the total. In 1985, that number increased to 10.1%.
Source: Television Bureau of Advertising, Inc., "Trends in Television, 1950 to Date," New York, May 1986, 12–13.

Program Environment Advertisers also select the type of program in which their advertising will run. Because various target markets have preferences for certain types of programming, an advertiser can place the advertising message in the program type that is most likely to complement the advertising message and appeal to the target market. For example, advertising Hawaiian travel services is enhanced by the physical setting of "Magnum, PI."

Degree of Participation Advertisers can assume complete or partial financial responsibility for the production of a program through sponsorship. **Sponsorship** allows the advertiser to control the content of a program, to run long commercials (60 seconds or longer), and to merchandise the sponsorship in other media.

Sponsorship—particularly sole sponsorship—is so expensive that few advertisers can afford it; therefore, the majority of network commercial time is sold on a participating basis. **Participations** allow the advertiser to adjust television advertising costs to a more modest media budget. When advertising on a participating basis, the advertiser does not pay for the production of the program and can advertise on a regular basis within one program or scatter the participation among a number of different programs.

Finally, an advertiser can purchase **spot announcements**—commercial television time that is purchased from individual stations. Unlike sponsorship and participation commercials, spot announcements appear between programs rather than within them.

COSTS OF TV COMMERCIAL TIME

Determining the cost of a television advertising schedule can be a complex job for the advertising manager. Unlike print media, the broadcast media have a fixed amount of advertising opportunities to sell. Also, broadcast time is perishable. These two factors make the cost of broadcast time subject to negotiation. Broadcasters, of course, are interested in selling the available time at the highest price possible; yet, they know that if prices are too high, the time will not be sold. Knowing the broadcaster's situa-

EXHIBIT 16.4

Top 10 Product Categories'
Spending in Spot and Local
Television Advertising, 1986

NATIONAL AND REGIONAL SPOT

RANK	CATEGORY	EXPENDITURE (in Millions of Dollars)
1	Food and food products	$977
2	Automotive	934
3	Confectionery and soft drinks	376
4	Consumer services	304
5	Beer and wine	243
6	Toiletries and toilet goods	230
6	Travel, hotels, and resorts (outside United States)	230
8	Sporting goods and toys	212
9	Publishing and media	167
10	Proprietary medicines	144

LOCAL/RETAIL

RANK	CATEGORY	EXPENDITURE (in Millions of Dollars)
1	Leisure time stores and services	$1,250
2	Automotive	483
3	Household stores	418
4	Drug and food stores	416
5	Department, discount, and variety stores	334
6	Business and financial services	294
7	Medical and health-related services	207
8	Local media	186
9	Household services	175
10	Apparel stores	167

Source: "Highlights—Local, National Spot & Network Commercial Television Advertising, 1986." Television Bureau of Advertising, Inc., New York, March 9, 1987.

tion, advertisers must decide how much they are willing to pay to be sure their advertising will run at the desired time and place. The final price paid for broadcast time depends on a number of factors, including the following:

- *When the time is bought.* Prices fluctuate more widely as air time approaches. Advertisers may be able to purchase imminent commercial time for half its preseason price.

- *Amount of time purchased.* Advertisers who consistently invest heavily in television advertising are likely to receive more favorable rates.

- *Demand for the time.* Higher prices will be paid when demand is high and supply is fixed. Advertisers will pay lower rates if they are willing to advertise in time segments and months that are less desirable and more available.

- *Rating of the program.* One of the main purposes of television advertising is to allow the advertiser to reach a large audience; therefore, programs that deliver the largest audiences command the highest advertising rates.

TERMINOLOGY AND CONCEPTS USED IN TELEVISION

Because television has become such an important medium for so many advertisers it is important for advertising managers to know the terminology and concepts of audience measurement.

Households Using Television (HUT) is a figure of audience measurement, expressed as a percentage, that denotes the number of U.S. TV households whose sets are turned on at any specific time. About 87 million households in the United States have at least one television set. If 40 million of those households turned their sets on at 9 p.m. last Sunday, the HUT figure would be 46 percent (40/87 = 46%).

HUT levels vary by the time of day, day of the week, and month of the year. TV viewing is highest during prime time and during the winter. The value of the HUT number is in helping advertisers determine the potential audience of a particular program; in evaluating the attractiveness of time periods; and in understanding viewership trends by seasons.

Coverage, another audience measurement, represents the percentage of U.S. television households that are physically able to receive a particular program. Because all network programs cannot be seen by every U.S. television household, coverage is a percentage less than 100. A program that potentially can be seen by 90 percent of U.S. television households (90 percent coverage) is likely to receive a higher rating than one that potentially can be seen by 75 percent of U.S. television households (75 percent coverage). The coverage number helps advertisers estimate audience size potential.

Ratings refer to how the broadcast media—both television and radio—express the estimate of audience size. One rating point represents 1 percent of all television households in a particular "universe" tuned to a specific program. Advertisers estimate the size of the audience to a particular program by determining its rating and then multiplying the rating figure by the number of TV households in the universe. For example, a network program that has a rating of 30.5 would deliver 26,535,000 TV households ($.305 \times 87$ million U.S. TV households = 26,535,000).

Ratings are the most widely used figures in the broadcast media because they allow advertisers to estimate how many people have been exposed to their commercial.

EXHIBIT 16.5

Top 20 Syndicated Television
Programs, 1985

RANK	PROGRAM	RATING	SHARE	NUMBER OF MARKETS	COVERAGE
1	Wheel of Fortune	18.5%	32	192	99.1%
2	Jeopardy	11.2	24	169	94.5
3	M.A.S.H.	9.2	20	165	91.6
4	New Newlywed Game	8.9	19	156	90.7
5	PM Magazine	8.8	15	53	56.0
6	Southwest Conference Football	8.7	28	20	7.5
7	Three's Company	8.6	19	154	85.9
8	Entertainment Tonight	8.4	17	141	89.9
9	Fight Back	8.0	17	27	34.3
10	Peoples Court	7.8	20	162	94.1
11	The Price Is Right	7.8	15	112	67.0
12	Honeymooners Season	7.5	14	36	25.2
13	Small Wonder	7.4	15	60	67.6
14	Different Strokes	7.3	16	126	84.0
15	Hee Haw	7.2	18	170	79.8
16	Barbara Mandrell	7.1	19	6	1.4
17	Benson	7.0	15	108	71.6
18	Serendipity Singers	7.0	27	5	1.4
19	Too Close for Comfort	6.9	14	85	74.0
20	Country Comes Alive Music Concert	6.8	12	5	2.0

Source: "Television: 1986 Nielsen Report," A.C. Nielsen Company, Northbrook, Illinois, 15.

Share of audience is expressed as a percentage of households using television that are tuned to a particular program. At any given time, not all TV households have their sets on. Therefore, the share of audience that a particular program gets can only be based on the potential audience — those that at least have their sets on. Share of audience can be calculated by dividing a program's rating by HUT. For example, if the HUT figure is 46 percent (40 million of the 87 million U.S. TV households were viewing at 9 p.m.) and Program A's rating was 30.5, the share of audience for Program A is 76.5 percent.

$$\frac{\text{Program Rating}}{\text{HUT}} = \text{Share of Audience}$$

$$\frac{30.5}{46.0} = 76.5\%$$

The value of the share of audience figure is to indicate how attractive a particular program is among the available audience. Exhibit 16.5 lists both the ratings and shares for a selected list of syndicated programs.

Although advertisers are interested in reaching the target market frequently, they also need to know how many different people are exposed to their commercials over a period of time, usually a four-week period.

Reach (also called *cumulative audience, cume, net reach,* or *unduplicated reach*) is the term used to describe that figure. Reach is determined by dividing the number of *different* households that have viewed a particular program over a four-week period, by the total number of TV households in the universe.

The value of the reach figure is that it allows the advertiser to estimate if additional media vehicles must be added to the media schedule to achieve the media plan's reach objective.

Average frequency is the average number of times each TV household is exposed to a program or series of programs over a four-week period. It is calculated by dividing the total number of times a program was viewed, by the number of different households who viewed the program during the four-week period.

Like the reach figure, the value of calculating average frequency is that it allows the advertiser to determine if a media plan's frequency objectives are being accomplished.

In Chapter 15, we defined **gross rating points (GRPs)** as the sum of the ratings of each program on a media schedule multiplied by the average frequency. GRPs gives the advertiser an estimate of the overall media weight, or pressure, that a media schedule puts against the target market. Because GRPs is a function of reach and average frequency, all three measurements can be calculated if any two are known:

$$\text{GRPs} = \text{Reach} \times \text{Average Frequency}$$

$$\text{Reach} = \frac{\text{GRPs}}{\text{Average Frequency}}$$

$$\text{Average Frequency} = \frac{\text{GRPs}}{\text{Reach}}$$

The **cost per rating point (CPRP)** is calculated to help the advertiser determine the efficiency of a media buy and to determine the number of rating points that can be purchased with a given media budget. CPRP is determined by dividing the cost of a particular media by the rating of the program. For example, if the cost of buying a 30-second commercial during the Super Bowl is $550,000 and the program generated a 50 rating, the CPRP is $11,000 ($550,000/50 = $11,000).

An advertiser with a $5 million media budget could purchase 454 rating points ($5,000,000/$11,000 = 454). If the advertiser's media plan calls for more rating points, the only options are to increase the media budget or to find programs with a lower CPRP.

WHEN TO USE TELEVISION

Television is widely considered the most powerful advertising medium because of its ability to reach large audiences with both sight and sound. Television is the best substitute for a personal sales call. It allows you to demonstrate a product right in the audience's living room. It also allows you to ask for an order. One of the most successful uses of television as a substitute for personal selling has been Home Shopping Network, a live, 24-hour, 7-day-a-week cable service through which over 8 million households watch product demonstrations and then call a toll-free number to charge a wide variety of products to major credit cards.[12] Television also allows you to reach your customers and prospects quickly and efficiently. Finally, and perhaps most importantly, television is important to us. The average American spends over seven hours a day watching it. When compared to other media, television is judged the most exciting, influential, up to date, and entertaining.[13] Why, then, don't all advertisers use television? Television should be used when:

1. **The advertiser has a large target market.** While it's possible to use television effectively to reach a local market, the medium is ideally suited to marketers of consumer package goods—products that are widely used and distributed.

2. **The advertiser wants to make an impact on the market**. Both Wendy's "Where's the beef?" campaign, and the series of "fast-talking" commercials from Federal Express made an immediate impact. We noticed those messages; they were widely discussed within the advertising industry and they helped their companies achieve marketing and advertising goals.

3. **The advertised product needs an added dimension of prestige.** Because television is so much a part of our lives, we tend to transfer our positive feelings about it to the products advertised on television.

4. **The advertiser has a media budget large enough to sustain a continuous television advertising schedule.** Television time is very expensive and most advertising messages require many repetitions to be effective; therefore, the use of television requires a substantial budget for air time and for the production of high-quality television commercials.

STRUCTURE OF RADIO

Many years ago, a familiar scene involved the entire family sitting in the living room listening to a favorite program on the family's one radio. Perhaps they were listening to a mystery, a sports event, or a musical show. Today, there are 5.5 radios per household; nearly half the rooms in a house have a radio. Radios are everywhere—in our cars, in elevators and retail stores, at work, and even in our bathrooms (nearly 10 percent of all bathrooms have radios).[14]

One of radio's primary advantages as an advertising medium is that almost everyone listens to a radio. Eighty-five percent of all households have at least one radio and radio reaches almost 95 percent of the population for an average of over three hours per day.[15]

RADIO NETWORKS AND AFFILIATED STATIONS

The structure of radio is very similar to that of television: some stations are affiliated with a network and others are not. Advertisers can use one of the national networks to reach a national audience; they can reach a

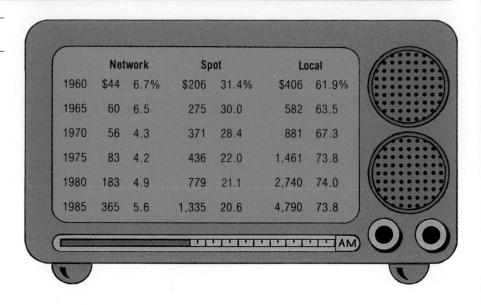

FIGURE 16.3

Radio Advertising Volume, 1960–1985

	Network		Spot		Local	
1960	$44	6.7%	$206	31.4%	$406	61.9%
1965	60	6.5	275	30.0	582	63.5
1970	56	4.3	371	28.4	881	67.3
1975	83	4.2	436	22.0	1,461	73.8
1980	183	4.9	779	21.1	2,740	74.0
1985	365	5.6	1,335	20.6	4,790	73.8

regional audience through a regional network; and they can reach a local audience through any of the more than 8,000 commercial stations throughout the country.

The four national networks (American Broadcasting Company, Columbia Broadcasting System, Mutual Broadcasting Company, and National Broadcasting Company) broadcast through affiliated stations. At one time, network radio was responsible for most radio programming and accounted for the majority of radio advertising. Today, network programming consists largely of hourly newscasts, sports programs, and special interest programming (Farm Directors Network, Spanish Language Network, etc.). In 1985, network advertising revenue accounted for less than 6 percent of radio's total.[16] Radio has become a local medium — nearly 75 percent of radio's advertising is at the local level (see Figure 16.3). Although network radio advertising volume has grown in recent years, its volume as a percentage of radio's total is still less than it was in 1960.

Network radio offers advertisers the same convenience as network television. By using one or more of the four national networks or any of the more than 100 regional networks, advertisers can reach a large audience and minimize the clerical effort.

LOCAL STATIONS AND PROGRAM FORMATS

There are nearly ten times more commercial radio stations than television stations and nearly five times more radio stations than daily newspapers. The competition for radio audiences and advertising revenue has forced radio to appeal to specific target markets. Radio has done this through a variety of formats that attract segments of a local population. Because the only source of a station's revenue is advertising, the market segment that its format appeals to must be attractive to advertisers.

A CLOSER LOOK

RADIO FORMATS

Radio has something for everyone. Just turn your dial
and you can find something to suit your taste and mood.
Here's who listens to the most common radio formats.

FORMAT	PERCENTAGE OF MALE LISTENERS	PERCENTAGE OF FEMALE LISTENERS	FORMAT	PERCENTAGE OF MALE LISTENERS	PERCENTAGE OF FEMALE LISTENERS
Adult contemporary	49%	51%	Contemporary hit/rock	49	51
All news	58	42	Country	51	49
Album-oriented rock/ Progressive	63	37	Golden oldies	61	39
			Middle-of-the-road	49	51
Beautiful music	45	55	News/talk	53	47
Black	42	58	Soft rock	51	49
Classical	60	40			

Source: *Media Cost Guide 1985*, ad forum, Inc., New York; adapted from SMRB 1984 Study of Media and Markets, 2nd
quarter 1985, 91.

LEARNING TO USE RADIO AS AN ADVERTISING MEDIUM

Like television advertising, radio commercials can be bought on a national, local, or spot basis. National advertising is bought by advertising on one or more of the national networks and is carried throughout the country through the network's affiliate stations. Nearly 40 percent of the country's commercial radio stations are affiliated with one of the four national networks. The average weekly reach of all of the four networks is about 11 percent—that is, about 11 percent of all radio households will be reached by network radio within a one-week period.[17]

Many national advertisers prefer *spot advertising*—purchasing radio time on a station-by-station, market-by-market basis. Although spot advertising requires negotiation with each station, it gives the advertiser several advantages. First, spot advertising is extremely flexible—advertisers can select individual markets, airtime, specific stations, and formats. Also, spot advertising allows the advertiser to create copy for specific markets and formats.

EXHIBIT 16.6

Top 10 Spending Categories
in Radio, 1985

NETWORK RADIO

RANK	PRODUCT CATEGORY	EXPENDITURE (in Thousands of Dollars)
1	Food and food products	$ 61,458
2	Business and consumer services	52,440
3	Retail	49,432
4	Confectionery, snacks, and soft drinks	41,058
5	Drugs and remedies	35,620
6	Automotive, accessories and equipment	32,147
7	Toiletries and cosmetics	29,021
8	Beer, wine, and liquor	18,405
9	Mail order	18,395
10	Household furnishings, appliances	15,617

SPOT RADIO

RANK	PRODUCT CATEGORY	EXPENDITURE (in Thousands of Dollars)
1	Food and food products	$275,336
2	Beer, wine, and liquor	174,666
3	Travel, hotels, and resorts	165,021
4	Automotive, accessories and equipment	148,511
5	Business and consumer services	134,950
6	Apparel, footwear, and accessories	53,836
7	Miscellaneous	53,347
8	Confectionery, snacks, and soft drinks	42,610
9	Insurance and real estate	42,290
10	Computers, office equipment, and stationery	41,670

Source: Advertising Age, September 4, 1986, 167.

The largest category of radio advertising is *local* — advertising by a local advertiser. Exhibit 16.6 shows the largest users of network and spot radio advertising, by product category. Exhibit 16.7 lists the top 10 radio advertisers in network and spot.

COSTS OF RADIO COMMERCIAL TIME

The cost of radio time is affected by most of the same factors that affect television time—the amount of time purchased, when time is bought, the rating of the station, and the demand for the time. Of course, like TV

EXHIBIT 16.7

Top 10 Radio Advertisers, 1985

NETWORK RADIO

RANK	ADVERTISER	EXPENDITURE (in Thousands of Dollars)
1	American Telephone & Telegraph Co.	$24,853
2	Sears, Roebuck & Co.	20,803
3	Warner-Lambert Co.	16,268
4	Greyhound Corp.	14,250
5	Procter & Gamble	12,770
6	RJR/Nabisco	9,334
7	Cotter & Co.	9,049
8	General Motors Corp.	9,034
9	Anheuser-Busch Cos.	8,929
10	Chesebrough-Pond's	7,969

SPOT RADIO

RANK	ADVERTISER	EXPENDITURE (in Thousands of Dollars)
1	Anheuser-Busch Cos.	$39,713
2	Van Munching & Co.	31,720
3	PepsiCo Inc.	29,925
4	General Motors Corp.	27,942
5	Philip Morris Cos.	25,808
6	Chrysler Corp.	23,549
7	Southland Corp.	19,926
8	Delta Air Lines	19,903
9	Shell Oil Co.	17,290
10	Sears, Roebuck & Co.	16,505

Source: Advertising Age, September 4, 1986, 132, 144.

stations, radio stations are interested in selling their commercial time at the highest rates possible (see Exhibit 16.8). At the same time, two factors work in the advertiser's favor—the perishable nature of broadcast time and the intense competition among radio stations. Consequently, the price of most radio time is negotiated. Stations offer discounts for advertisers who buy:

- Package plans (a number of commercials distributed throughout a station's offerings)

- Large quantities of time (dollar-volume discounts)

- Large numbers of commercials (frequency discounts)

- Time during the least attractive time segments (prime time for radio is drive time—6 a.m. to 10 a.m. and 3 p.m. to 7 p.m.; prime time in television is 8 p.m. to 11 p.m.)

- Time that can be preempted by advertisers who are willing to pay more for the time period

EXHIBIT 16.8

Cost of Network and
Spot Radio Advertising

NETWORK RADIO	AVERAGE COST PER 30-SECOND COMMERCIAL*	ADI MARKETS	AVERAGE COST PER RATING POINT (60-Second Units)†
NETWORK RADIO		**SPOT RADIO**	
Wall Street Journal Report	$2,925	Top 10	$1,263
RKO	2,250	Top 30	2,326
MBS	2,100	Top 50	2,936
CBS	2,050	Top 100	4,019
NBC	2,000		
ABC	1,800		
Sheridan Broadcasting	850	Average Cost per Rating Point:	2,100

*30-second commercials are 75 percent of the cost of a 60-second ad. Figures represent averages for all network formats and time periods.
†The cost-per-rating point figures are averages for all adults.
Source: Media Cost Guide 1985, ad forum, Inc., New York. Adapted from data supplied by the networks and *Media Market Guide, 1984*.

TERMINOLOGY AND CONCEPTS USED IN RADIO

The terms and concepts used to measure the audience of a radio advertising schedule are similar, but not identical, to those used in television.

Cumulative audience refers to the number of different people listening to a station for at least five minutes during a specified time period. Also known as *cume audience* or *cume*, this useful measurement tells the advertiser the size of the potential audience that can be exposed to a commercial.

Reach (also known as *rating* or *reach rating*) is the number of different people exposed to a specific station during a particular quarter-hour period. Reach rating is expressed as a percentage of the population being measured:

$$\text{Reach rating} = \frac{\text{Number of different persons reached}}{\text{Population}}$$

Note the difference between television's and radio's definition of reach. Recall that in television's reach, households (rather than persons) are divided by the number of TV households (rather than the total population).

Gross impressions refers to the total number of exposures to an advertiser's schedule of commercials. Although gross impressions is not a measure of the number of different people exposed, it does allow the advertiser to estimate the potential impact, or weight, of a particular radio schedule. Gross impressions are determined by multiplying the number of commercials in a given schedule by the average number of people listening:

$$\text{Gross Impressions} = \text{Average Number of Listeners} \times \text{Number of Commercials}$$

Frequency is the average number of times the audience is exposed to a commercial. The frequency measurement is useful because it tells an advertiser how many times the number of *different* people are exposed to a commercial.

$$\text{Frequency} = \frac{\text{Gross Impressions}}{\text{Reach}}$$

In radio, one rating point is equal to one percent of the population being measured. A station in Chicago with a rating of 12.0 among males 18–24 is reaching 12 percent of all males 18–24 living in the Chicago market. **Gross rating points (GRPs)** calculations are determined by multiplying a station's rating by the number of commercials in a schedule:

$$\text{Gross Rating Points} = \text{Station's Rating} \times \text{Number of Commercials}$$

The **cost per rating point (CPRP)** calculation is an efficiency measure and allows the advertiser to determine how much is being paid for each percentage of the population reached. Just as in television, CPRP is calculated by dividing the cost of the media buy by the number of gross rating points generated:

$$\text{Cost per Rating Point} = \frac{\text{Cost of Media Buy}}{\text{Gross Rating Points}}$$

WHEN TO USE RADIO

Because of its limitations, radio is not the major medium chosen by most advertisers. However, radio can be very powerful when advertisers take full advantage of its ability to stir our imagination. For example, we're listening to a baseball game, hear the crack of the bat hitting the ball, and we imagine. Two minutes later we're listening to a radio commercial, and we hear the sounds of a bottle of beer being opened and poured into a glass. Again, we're forced to imagine. We "see" a cold beer being eased down the side of a chilled glass on a hot, humid afternoon. The advertiser didn't show us anything, but we imagine what we want.

More so than television, radio competes for our attention. We listen to radio while we're driving, washing the car, or visiting with friends. Radio has become our constant companion.

Advertisers cannot demonstrate a product on the radio as they can on television. Despite its limitations, however, radio can be used effectively for almost every product. Radio should be used when:

1. **The advertiser needs to reach a specific demographic segment.**
   As the data in this chapter show, radio has become a local medium

that appeals to very specific market segments through a variety of program formats. Radio very efficiently delivers high reach within specific segments.

2. **The advertiser needs geographic flexibility within the media plan.** Because there are so many radio stations, advertisers have the flexibility of selecting the cities, time periods, and program environments that best suit the overall advertising plan.

3. **The advertiser has a limited advertising budget.** Advertising on radio can fit into the budgets of even the smallest advertisers. In many markets, a package of radio spots can be bought for a few hundred dollars. Furthermore, the cost of producing radio advertising can be very low. Announcer-read commercials, for example, may not involve any production cost.

4. **The advertiser wants high frequency in the media plan.** Because of its efficiency, frequency in a radio schedule can be built for comparatively low cost. Radio is an excellent reminder medium. The frequency of radio is particularly effective when advertisers use radio along with newspaper, television, and outdoor.

SUMMARY

This chapter has introduced the structure of the broadcast media and the terminology and concepts that are most widely used in developing a broadcast media plan. The best use of the broadcast media occurs when the media planner knows both the language of the medium as well as its persuasive powers. Television, for example, provides advertisers with the ability to demonstrate product features to large segments of the population. Radio, on the other hand, selects its audience through various programming formats, and is ideal for building frequency of exposure.

Although television and radio share many common characteristics, as advertising media they are used for very different reasons. Network television (over-the-air or cable) is essentially a national medium that has its greatest impact during the evening hours. Television is an efficient medium, but an expensive one. Radio is essentially a local medium that has its greatest impact during the driving hours. It too is an efficient medium, and it can be a low-cost way to reach selective target markets.

YOU MAKE THE DECISION

SANIBEL DEVELOPMENT COMPANY

Congratulations! You've just landed a job as a media analyst for Hufford Advertising, a full-service agency in Gulfshore, a major city in the growing resort area of southwest Florida. Your job is to analyze media and to help select the best media choices for your agency's clients.

Your first assignment involves a TV campaign for the Sanibel Development Company, builders of luxury waterfront condominiums. Gulfshore has 325,000 television households and six available television stations. Last night at 10 p.m., the television viewing pattern looked like this:

CHANNEL	PROGRAM	NUMBER OF HOUSEHOLDS	COST PER 30-SECOND COMMERCIAL
2 (Independent)	"Backyard Banter"	25,000	$500
4 (WGN)	Chicago Cubs Baseball	10,000	300
5 (NBC affiliate)	"LA Law"	18,500	450
7 (CBS affiliate)	"Falcon Crest"	27,000	750
10 (ABC affiliate)	"Hotel"	12,500	425
12 (PBS)	"Soundstage"	N/A	—

Which of the above programs represents the best buy for your client, the Sanibel Development Company? Why?

■ ■ ■

QUESTIONS FOR DISCUSSION

1. If you marketed a nationally distributed consumer product, would you be more inclined to advertise on network television or use spot television? Explain the advantages of each.

2. Why has cable TV not captured more of the investment in television advertising?

3. Explain the factors that determine the cost of buying television commercial time.

4. Sponsorship, participations, and spot announcements are three ways an advertiser can purchase television commercial time. Describe each method and explain their advantages.

5. What is the difference between a television program's rating and its share of audience?

6. Why do media planners calculate the cost per rating point?

7. When is television advertising a wise media choice for an advertiser?

8. How does an advertiser use radio to cover a national market?

9. Explain the difference in the calculation of gross rating points in radio versus television.

10. Under what conditions should radio be used as an advertising medium?

NOTES

1. *TV Basics, 1986–87*, Television Bureau of Advertising, Inc., New York, 1986; "Local Television Up 12%, National Spot Increases 9% in 1985," Television Bureau of Advertising, Inc., February 28, 1986, p. 12; "Network Television Commercial Activity: January-December 1985," Television Bureau of Advertising, Inc., 1986.

2. Verne Gay, "Cosby Smashes Upfront Records," *Advertising Age*, June 30, 1986, 1.

3. "Network TV Commercial Sales and Prices (Primetime 1983 vs. 1973)," *Advertising Age*, November 29, 1984, 12.

4. Rachel Shuster, "Giants-Broncos Rating Not as Super as Last Year," *USA Today*, January 28, 1987, 3C.

5. Television Bureau of Advertising, *Cable Facts*, New York, January 1986, 4.

6. *Ibid.*

7. "Time Spent Viewing: Over-the-Air vs. Cable in the Average TV Household," Television Bureau of Advertising, New York; and *Cable TV—A Status Report*, A.C. Neilsen (NTI), 1986.

8. "Cable TV's Projected Growth," *Cable Facts*, Television Bureau of Advertising, Inc., New York, January 1986, 7.

9. "Cable & TV Ad Volume Projections," *Cable Facts*, Television Bureau of Advertising, Inc., New York, January 1986, 8.

10. *Nielsen Sports Report, 1981 and 1982*, A.C. Nielsen Co., Northbrook, Illinois; Grey, Advertising, Inc., New York; and *Media Cost Guide 1985*, Second Quarter (April-June), ad forum, Inc., New York, 1985, 31.

11. "Trends in Television: 1950 to Date," Television Bureau of Advertising, Inc., New York, 1986, 11–12.

12. "Home Shopping Network," *American Demographics*, September 1986, 22–23.

13. *TV Basics, 1986–87.*

14. *Radio Facts*, Radio Advertising Bureau, New York, 1984, 5.

15. *Ibid.*, 4, 10.

16. McCann-Erickson, Inc., New York; prepared by Newspaper Advertising Bureau, New York, May 12, 1986.

17. *Media Cost Guide 1985*, Second Quarter (April-June), ad forum, Inc., New York, 1985, 83–87.

SUGGESTED READINGS

Bogart, Leo. *Strategy in Advertising.* 2d ed. Chicago: Crain Books, 1984.

CBS Television. *Network Television Audience Measurement: The Language and Concepts.* New York: CBS Television, 1982. "15-Second Commercial Spots Doing Well." *Sales & Marketing Digest.* July 1986, 9.

Hamilton, Jerry. "15-Second Effectiveness." *Marketing & Media Decisions.* November 1986, 90–95.

Mediamark Research, Inc. "The Cable Table." New York: Mediamark Research, 1984.

Nielsen Report on Television: 1983. Northbrook, Ill.: A.C. Nielsen Company, 1983.

Radio Advertising Bureau, Inc. "America on Radio." New York: Radio Advertising Bureau, 1984.

―――. "Inside Newspapers' Latest Claim . . . and Why Radio Is a Better Catch." New York: Radio Advertising Bureau, 1984.

―――. "Marketing, Media Mix and Your Margin: Radio's Selling Equation." New York: Radio Advertising Bureau, 1984.

―――. *The Radio Consultant's Guide to Media.* New York: Radio Advertising Bureau, 1984.

―――. "Radio Research Glossary: RAB Guide to Key Terms and Formulas." New York: Radio Advertising Bureau, 1984.

―――. "Summary of National Radio Listening Habits." New York: Radio Advertising Bureau, 1984.

Schudson, Michael. *Advertising, the Uneasy Persuasion: Its Dubious Impact on American Society.* New York: Basic Books, Inc., 1986.

"Survey Shows Most Effective Ads Appear on Television." *Sales & Marketing Digest*, November 1986, 3.

Television Bureau of Advertising, Inc. "Trends in Television: 1950 to Date." New York: Television Bureau of Advertising, May 1986.

Triangle Publications, Inc. *Television in Transition.* New York: Triangle Publications, 1982.

Vamos, Mark N. "The Coming Avalanche of 15-Second TV Ads." *Business Week*, February 11, 1985, 80.

. . . .
————————————
. . . .
————————————
. . . .
————————————
. . . .
————————————

C H A P T E R   17

PRINT MEDIA

Key Terms

total market coverage (TMC)
display advertising
classified advertising
classified-display advertising
insert
Standard Advertising Unit (SAU)
system
rate card
controlled circulation
paid circulation
flat rate
open rate
contract rate
short rate
ROP (run-of-paper)
preferred position
split run
milline rate
vertical publication
horizontal publication
gatefold
paid (noncontrolled) circulation
nonpaid (controlled) circulation

Learning Objectives

To describe the structure of newspapers and magazines

To explain how to use the print media as advertising media

To list the terminology and concepts used in print media planning

To analyze when to use the print media

"I'm just real hard-core into print advertising. I like print advertising in newspapers. It's something that the consumer can pick up and hold. It's tangible."

These are the words of retail marketing supervisor Barbara Copeland as she developed advertising plans for the opening of Faison Associates' 91-store Valley View mall in Roanoke, Virginia.

Valley View opened to great fanfare, and part of the success of its grand opening was attributed to a special 40-page cooperative advertising section appearing in the *Roanoke Times & World-News*. Valley View's use of print advertising—in this case, newspapers—is one example of how this medium helps bring buyer and seller together.

The challenge for Copeland and the *Roanoke Times & World-News* was to communicate the advertising messages of 91 different advertisers to

the Roanoke community at the same time. The paper's advertising staff worked closely with Copeland to contact all of the mall's merchants to explain the different sizes of advertisements and costs. Eventually, the

decision was made to produce a special 40-page section. Eight of the pages, including the cover, appeared in full color.

In addition to the individual advertisements, purchased by the various retailers, the section also contained a detailed color map of the two-level mall and a road map showing the mall's location. Valley View's special advertising section was preprinted, inserted, and distributed to the 129,000 subscribers of the *Roanoke Times & World-News*. Then, to ensure market saturation, an additional 50,000 copies were mailed to nonsubscribers via two other newspapers, the *Read & Shop Metro* and the *Read & Shop New River Valley*.

Source: Photo: Graphic Designer—David Graves. Reprinted with permission.

INTRODUCTION

Newspapers and magazines were the first media to carry advertising. The first U.S. newspaper advertisement appeared in 1704.[1] Magazines carried the first national advertisement in 1741.[2] Although the broadcast media have experienced more growth in advertising revenue in recent years, there are still more advertisers in the print media.

In many ways, we take print media for granted. While we are still fascinated by the comparatively recent technology of broadcasting, the print media are woven into our daily patterns. We read them, we believe them, and they are strong influences on what we buy and when we buy.

Newspapers are read in 75 percent of all U.S. households and by 63 percent of all American adults on an average weekday.[3] Newspapers are the most believable advertising medium; more people look forward to advertising in newspapers than in any other medium. Newspaper advertising has more than three times the influence on unplanned purchases than advertising in any other medium.[4]

We read newspaper advertisements before we go shoppping. We watch for the grocery store advertisements on "food day." If we need tires, the newspaper tells us who has the size we need. The inserts in the Sunday newspaper introduce us to dozens of new products and encourage us to repurchase the brand we tried last month.

Magazines serve our every possible interest. Because they provide us with useful information and entertainment, they've grown and prospered. More than 200 new magazines are born each year. Today there are over 11,000 different magazines with a combined average monthly circulation of over 300 million.[5]

In terms of the amount of money invested in national advertising, magazines rank second, behind only television.[6] Magazines are a medium of ideas. If we're interested in fashion clothing, we'll look for the fashion clothing advertisements in *Esquire*, *GQ*, *Bazaar*, or *Vogue*. If we're buying a new car, the editorial copy and advertising in *Car & Driver* may interest us. If travel is our hobby, *National Geographic* or *Travel & Leisure* will stir our imagination and help us plan our trip.

The Valley View vignette in this chapter shows how a group of retailers used print advertising successfully; however, the print media are helpful to a wide range of advertisers, including national, consumer package goods, and business-to-business advertisers. In this chapter you'll discover the marketing significance of newspapers and magazines and how they have remained major advertising forces for over 200 years.

STRUCTURE OF NEWSPAPERS

Despite the growth of television, newspapers still hold a major share of the advertising market. Advertisers still invest more of their media dollars in newspapers than in any other medium. Newspapers account for 26.4 percent of the total dollars invested in advertising.[7]

The foundation of the newspaper industry is the daily newspaper, whose purpose is to provide timely information and entertainment to its audience, usually a local community. Although the local daily newspaper remains important, other types of newspapers (Sunday, weekly, and shoppers) are important too.

In recent years, the industry has undergone a number of changes to adapt to the needs and interests of both advertisers and readers. Newspaper mergers have increased; the total number of newspapers has decreased; and the trend toward more morning papers—and away from the afternoon paper—continues. The results of these, and other changes, have created a stronger newspaper industry with increases in circulation and advertising revenue. The industry now offers advertisers more creativity, coverage, and flexibility in reaching and influencing target audiences. One example of how the marketplace impacted on the newspaper industry is the growth of direct mail. Today, newspapers compete with the mass coverage of shared mailers (packaging of two or more inserts into a single mailing piece and then distributed via third-class mail) by offering **total market coverage** (**TMC**) programs of their own. TMC programs involve distribution of a newspaper or shared mailing to nonsubscribers. Recall that the *Roanoke Times & World-News* gave the Valley View Mall 100 percent coverage by supplementing their own subscription delivery with direct mail.

CLASSIFICATIONS OF NEWSPAPERS

The major ways to classify newspapers are by geographic coverage, audience type, and frequency of issue.

GEOGRAPHIC COVERAGE

Geographic coverage can be national, regional, or local in orientation.

National Coverage The *Wall Street Journal* and *USA Today* are two of the most widely known national newspapers. Both are published each morning, Monday through Friday, and offer advertisers the opportunity to reach a national audience in a newspaper format.

Regional Coverage The circulation of some newspapers extends beyond the community in which it is published. The *Des Moines* (Iowa) *Register* and the *Arizona Republic*, for example, enjoy considerable readership throughout their respective states.

Local Coverage Most newspapers survive because they serve the interests of a local community. The dual emphasis of the local newspaper is news and advertising that appeal to a broad cross-section of the local population. High readership of a local newspaper increases its attractiveness as an advertising medium.

AUDIENCE TYPE

Some newspapers serve very specific audiences. The *Wall Street Journal* serves the interests of the business and financial reader; *Stars and Stripes* is read by those in the military. The *Sporting News* is produced for those who have a serious interest in sports statistics. College, religious, ethnic,

EXHIBIT 17.1

Growth Trends in the Newspaper Industry, 1950–1985

YEAR	CIRCULATION (in millions)				NUMBER OF NEWSPAPERS			
	A.M.	P.M.	SUNDAY	WEEKLY	A.M.	P.M.	SUNDAY	WEEKLY
1950	21.3	32.6	46.6	*	322	1,450	549	*
1955	22.2	34.0	46.5	*	316	1,454	541	*
1960	24.0	34.9	47.7	21.0	312	1,459	563	8,174
1965	24.1	36.3	48.6	25.0	320	1,444	562	8,061
1970	25.9	36.2	49.2	27.9	334	1,429	586	7,612
1975	25.5	36.2	51.1	35.9	339	1,436	639	7,612
1980	29.4	32.8	54.7	42.4	387	1,388	735	7,954
1985	36.4	26.5	58.8	50.1	456	1,196	798	7,711

*Data on weeklies not available until 1960.
Sources: "Key Facts about Newspapers and Advertising: 1987," Newspaper Advertising Bureau, Inc., New York, April 1987, 17; and *Facts about Newspapers, 1987*, American Newspaper Publishers Association, Washington, D.C., 1987, 14.

and other special-interest newspapers allow advertisers to advertise their products in an atmosphere that has high interest for specific groups.

FREQUENCY OF ISSUE

As shown in Exhibit 17.1, newspapers are classified as daily (a.m. or p.m.), weekly or Sunday publications. Although there are still almost three times more evening than morning newspapers, circulation is higher among the morning papers (and, as mentioned earlier, the number of morning papers continues to rise).

LEARNING TO USE NEWSPAPERS AS AN ADVERTISING MEDIUM

The following section discusses how newspaper advertising is purchased, the costs of newspaper advertising, and the concepts and terminology used in newspaper advertising.

HOW NEWSPAPER ADVERTISING IS BOUGHT

Although there are several different types of newspaper advertising, the two basic types are display and classified (see Figure 17.1). **Display advertising** accounts for most of the daily newspaper's advertising revenue and it is widely used by both national and local advertisers. As the name suggests, display advertising allows advertisers to illustrate merchandise in a way that will attract the interest of potential buyers.

Classified advertising, sometimes known as "want ads," represents about 30 percent of all newspaper advertising expenditures and it is one of the best-read sections of a newspaper. In a week's time, more than eight out of ten households check the newspaper classified sections.[8] A newspaper's classified advertising section is a marketplace for both buyers and sellers. Buyers can advertise under a "Wanted to Buy" listing and sellers list their merchandise under the appropriate product or service list-

FIGURE 17.1

Newspaper Advertising
Expenditures*

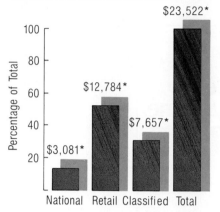

*Indicates advertising expenditures in
thousands.

Source: "Key Facts About Newspapers and
Advertising: 1987," Newspaper
Advertising Bureau, Inc., New York,
New York, April 1987, 22.

ing ("Autos," "Help Wanted," "General Merchandise," etc.). Many newspapers also offer **classified-display advertising**, which combines the marketplace feature of classified with the more attractive graphics of display. Figure 17.2 illustrates display advertising for a national advertiser, classified and classified-display advertising, and display advertising for a local advertiser.

A rapidly growing form of newspaper advertising is the **insert.** Inserts can take several different forms (single cards, individual sheets, multipage booklets, perforated coupons, etc.), and they can be either bound in the newspaper or, most often, they are free standing. While inserts are sometimes printed by newspapers, they are often produced by an advertiser and than delivered to the newspaper for insertion and delivery, either to the newspaper's entire circulation or to specific circulation zones. Inserts are particularly useful for advertisers who want to use long copy, make use of existing graphic material, or distribute coupons. In 1980, slightly more than $2 billion was invested in free-standing inserts. By 1985, the investment had grown to over $4 billion.[9] Since 1970, the circulation of inserts has increased nearly sixfold (see Exhibit 17.2).

UNITS OF NEWSPAPER ADVERTISING SPACE

Newspapers come in two basic sizes: the standard (or broadside) and the tabloid. The standard page has a print size of 13 inches wide and up to 22 1/2 inches deep. The *Wall Street Journal* and *USA Today* are standard newspapers. Tabloids have a smaller page, usually 14 inches deep with the width varying from 9 3/8 inches to just under 11 inches.

Until 1981, newspapers sold advertising space by the *agate line*, a unit of space that is one column wide and one-fourteenth of an inch deep. There are approximately 2,400 agate lines on a standard page and about 1,200 on a tabloid page. One of the problems with buying newspaper advertising space by the agate line was that the number of lines on a page varied according to the format used by the newspaper. Thus, in 1981, U.S. newspapers converted to the **Standard Advertising Unit (SAU) system.** This system simplified the production and placement of newspa-

EXHIBIT 17.2

The Use of Free-Standing
Inserts, 1970–1985

YEAR	NUMBER OF PIECES (in billions)	PERCENTAGE OF GROWTH	REVENUE (in millions of dollars)
1970	7.057	—	†
1975	15.800	2.8%	†
1980	27.733	2.2	$2.032
1981	28.708	3.5	2.289
1982	29.966	4.4	2.517
1983	35.727	19.2	3.095
1984	41.265	15.5	3.691
1985	45.379	10.0	4.179

*Revenue is based on a 12-page tabloid and includes printing and inserting.
†Not available.
Source: "Newspaper Insert Advertising Revenue," in *Key Facts about Newspapers and Advertising: 1987* (New York: Newspaper Advertising Bureau, Inc., April 1986), 32.

FIGURE 17.2

Types of Newspaper Advertising

How a National Advertiser Uses Display Advertising in a Newspaper

per advertising by creating standard units of space. Today, the newspapers who use the SAU system comprise more than 98 percent of the total daily circulation in the United States.

Under the SAU system, standard newspapers use a 6-column format for display advertising, a 13-inch print page width and a standard column width of 2 1/16 inches. Tabloids use a 5-column format with the same column widths as standards. Figure 17.3 illustrates 53 different standard advertising units of space for newspapers.

NATIONAL ADVERTISING IN THE NEWSPAPER

The newspaper has always been primarily a local medium. While there have been national newspapers for over 100 years, the popularity of a general news, daily newspaper is evidenced by the success of *USA Today*. Today, less than 15 percent of the total amount of money invested in newspaper advertising is accounted for by national advertising. Advertisers interested in reaching a national consumer market with

Classified and Classified-Display Advertising

How a Local Advertiser Uses Newpaper Display Advertising

Join our team! We are one of the most successful companies in the resort industry.

We offer:

- **Convenient Oak Brook location**
- **Opportunity to travel**
- **Excellent commission structure**
- **Paid training**

Call Steve for an interview at 495-8800

 1 South 443 Summit Avenue
Oakbrook Terrace, IL 60181
An Equal Opportunity Employer M/F

fully the field of automotive sales, call Mr. Glenn Zank for a personal appointment.
McKay Nissan-Mazda
Evanston, IL
475-8000

Sales
**ASSISTANT MANAGERS
JEWELRY SALES**
Resume or redirect your career in one of these fine opportunities with The Whitehall Company. We are seeking highly motivated individuals with a desire to fully utilize their sales ability and grow professionally. Our rapidly growing nationwide jewelry chain is seeking individuals with 1-2 years of retail sales experience, ideally in jewelry or a fashion related area. Previous retail management experience is preferred.
Currently positions are available at our beautiful CHICAGOLAND stores. In addition to growth opportunities we provide top starting salaries plus commissions, profit sharing and other fine benefits. Please call:
Sue Block
782-6800
THE WHITEHALL COMPANY
equal opportunity employer m/f

Sales
ACCOUNT EXECUTIVE
Leading service organization located in the Western suburbs has challenging opportunity for experienced salesmen. Background in meetings, conventions, and trade show industry preferred. Send resume with salary history in confidence to:
CompuSystems Inc.
PO Box 6578
Broadview, IL, 60153
Attn. Don.

Sales
**ADMISSIONS REP
40-50K per year**
Nationwide vocation school is expanding in the Chicago area is currently interviewing for career position. All leads supplied. Applicant must have excellent phone skills and minimum 1 year sales experience. For immediate consideration call between 10-2 pm, 786-0746 Mr. Craig

newspaper advertising can advertise in *USA Today*, in Sunday supplements, or in all of the newspapers that cover the appropriate geographic markets. There are now more than 150 daily newspapers just in the top 50 U.S. markets.[10]

IMPORTANT CONSIDERATIONS IN NEWSPAPER ADVERTISING

The cost of advertising in the print media can be determined from the publication's **rate card.** A newspaper's rate card is a reliable source of information about circulation, physical distribution of the newspaper, mechanical requirements, and advertising costs. Like the broadcast media, the cost to advertise in newspapers depends on the quality and quan-

WHO READS THE NEWSPAPER?

Who reads daily newspapers in America? A recent survey conducted by the Simmons Market Research Bureau showed that about 63 percent of all adult Americans read a newspaper on an average weekday. Of the men surveyed, 65 percent read the paper; among women, 61 percent. In terms of readership, the medium's audience is comprised of slightly more women than men (51 percent versus 49 percent, respectively).

Classifying newspaper readership by age groups provided some interesting findings: the 18–24 age group comprised the smallest segment of readership. Only 53 percent of these individuals read a daily newspaper; they accounted for 14 percent of the news-reading public.

The largest segment of the newspaper audience is the 25–34 age group, which makes up 22 percent of all readers. (In that group, about three-fifths reported reading the paper.)

In terms of education, college graduates were more likely to read the paper than others. Nearly 80 percent read the news, as compared to high-school graduates (65%) or those with only a grammar-school education (47%).

Correspondingly, households with higher incomes were more likely to read the newspaper than others. Seventy-five percent of the households where wage-earners made more than $40,000 per year read the newspaper. This contrasts with households whose income totals less than $10,000: only 44 percent of that group read the paper.

Surprisingly, however, the not-employed comprised a full 36 percent of a newspaper's readership. Nearly 60 percent of the non-employed surveyed said they read the newspaper.

Source: *1986 SMRB Study of Media and Markets*, Simmons Market Research Bureau.

---

tity of the audience, the amount of space purchased, the frequency of advertising, and any other special services the advertiser wishes to purchase.

Newspaper Circulation *Circulation* refers to the number of copies sold or distributed. Some newspapers are distributed free. *Shoppers* have **controlled circulation** — that is, the publisher delivers the papers to readers' homes at no cost to them. Most newspapers have **paid circulation** — readers pay for the newspaper through a monthly subscription fee or purchase it at a newsstand. In 1986, more than $7.7 billion was spent on subscriptions and newsstand sales of newspapers.[11]

How does an advertiser know how many copies of a newspaper are circulated? Many newspapers have their circulation audited by an independent organization. The Audit Bureau of Circulations (ABC) is the audit organization that confirms the circulation of paid circulation newspapers. The ABC issues audit reports to the newspaper for distribution to potential advertisers.

Advertising rates are strongly influenced by the size of a newspaper's verified circulation. When newspapers are read by more than one person the advertiser receives bonus circulation. The estimated number of adult readers per copy for weekday newspapers is 2.15 and for Sunday papers, 2.20.[12] The readers-per-copy figure is an estimate based on a survey of a sample of a newspaper's circulation. While the figure varies by market size (readers-per-copy figures tend to be higher as market size increases),

FIGURE 17.3

The Standard Advertising
Unit (SAU) System

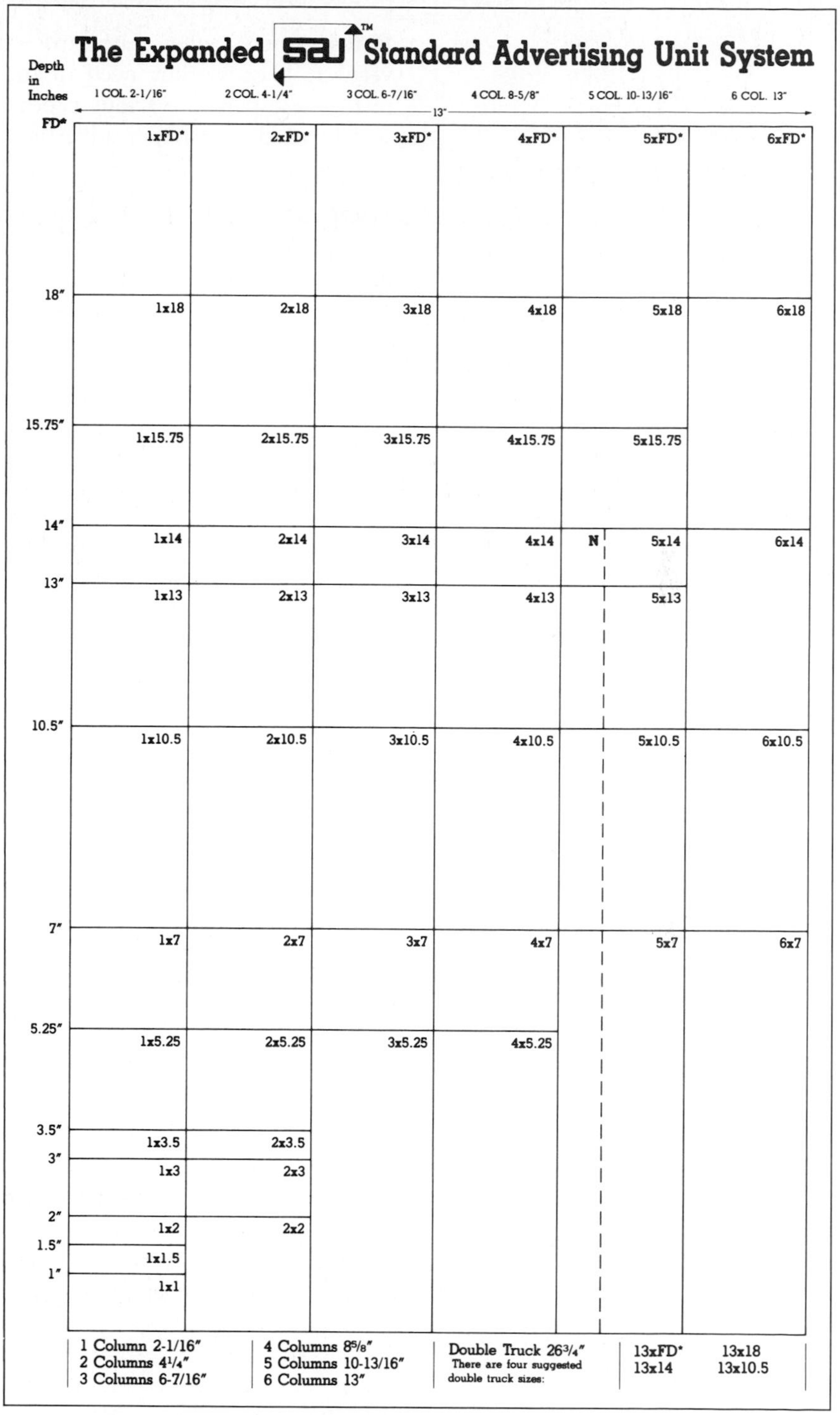

The Expanded SAU Standard Advertising Unit System

Depth in Inches	1 COL. 2-1/16"	2 COL. 4-1/4"	3 COL. 6-7/16"	4 COL. 8-5/8"	5 COL. 10-13/16"	6 COL. 13"
FD*	1xFD*	2xFD*	3xFD*	4xFD*	5xFD*	6xFD*
18"	1x18	2x18	3x18	4x18	5x18	6x18
15.75"	1x15.75	2x15.75	3x15.75	4x15.75	5x15.75	
14"	1x14	2x14	3x14	4x14	5x14	6x14
13"	1x13	2x13	3x13	4x13	5x13	
10.5"	1x10.5	2x10.5	3x10.5	4x10.5	5x10.5	6x10.5
7"	1x7	2x7	3x7	4x7	5x7	6x7
5.25"	1x5.25	2x5.25	3x5.25	4x5.25		
3.5"	1x3.5	2x3.5				
3"	1x3	2x3				
2"	1x2	2x2				
1.5"	1x1.5					
1"	1x1					

1 Column 2-1/16"   4 Columns 8⅝"   Double Truck 26¾"   13xFD*   13x18
2 Columns 4¼"   5 Columns 10-13/16"   There are four suggested   13x14   13x10.5
3 Columns 6-7/16"   6 Columns 13"   double truck sizes:

Source: Courtesy of the Newspaper Advertising Bureau, Inc.

newspaper advertisers are probably reaching at least twice the number of people indicated on the newspaper's rate card.

Rates   A newspaper's rate card is an important media buying tool for advertisers because they need to know the terms and conditions that apply to the newspaper's various types of advertising rates. Some of the most widely used newspaper advertising rate terminology is discussed in this section.

Dual Rate System   The rates charged to national advertisers are higher than those charged to local retailers. Retailers advertise in the daily newspaper more regularly and therefore provide a dependable source of revenue for the newspaper. Also, the cost of servicing national advertisers is higher. National advertisers almost always use an advertising agency to place their advertising, and the agency earns the standard 15 percent commission from the newspaper. Many newspapers do not grant an agency commission on retail advertising. Furthermore, national newspaper advertising is usually sold through sales representative firms and the individual newspapers pay these firms a sales commission.

Flat, Open, Contract, and Short Rates   Newspaper advertising rates are quoted on a line rate basis. The line rate that a particular advertiser pays depends on: (1) the advertiser's status (national or retail), (2) the frequency of advertising, and (3) the quantity of advertising. A **flat rate** is a fixed line rate offered by newspapers that do not offer discounts. When a newspaper offers discounts but an advertiser does not qualify, the rate charged is known as the **open rate.** Regular newspaper advertisers contract with the newspaper to use a specific amount of advertising space during a contract period, usually a year. The rate paid is known as the **contract rate** and it is based on the frequency and/or the quantity of advertising space planned to be used.

If advertisers do not use the amount of space contracted for, they must pay the difference between the contracted rate and the earned rate (**short rate**). For example, assume an advertiser contracts to purchase 50,000 lines during the year at a contract rate of 50 cents per line. However, the advertiser's plans change during the year and only 40,000 lines are used. The rate for 40,000 lines is 60 cents per line. How much does the advertiser pay for the space used?

$$\text{Short Rate} = \text{Earned Rate minus Contracted Rate}$$

$$40,000 \text{ lines} \times 60¢/\text{line} = \$24,000 \text{ (Earned Rate)}$$

$$40,000 \text{ lines} \times 50¢/\text{line} = \$20,000 \text{ (Contract Rate)}$$

$$\text{Short Rate} = \$24,000 - \$20,000$$

$$= \$ 4,000$$

Special Charges   Newspaper advertising rates are quoted on an **ROP** (**run-of-paper**) basis. This means that, for this rate, the advertiser cannot specify the page position or section in which the advertisement will appear; the newspaper makes the decision. However, should an advertiser want the ad to appear in a specific place in the newspaper, a higher rate is charged. This is known as **preferred position.**

In addition to this extra charge, advertisers pay special fees for other services. Running the ad in color increases the cost of advertising, although many advertisers feel the additional cost is money well invested. At one time, the use of color in ROP newspaper advertising was rare. Today, almost all newspapers offer the possibility of using color.

Some newspapers offer a **split run,** a printing and distribution service that allows an advertiser to test two different versions of an advertisement. For an additional charge, the newspaper will print and distribute half the newspapers with one version of an advertiser's message and the other half with a second version.

Insert distribution is another service now offered by nearly every daily and Sunday newspaper in the United States. Inserts are an ideal way to assure excellent color reproduction. Also, the variety of insert shapes and sizes that can be accommodated by newspapers provides advertisers maximum creative flexibility.

Comparing Newspaper Efficiency   The basic method for comparing the efficiency of alternative newspapers is to compute the milline rate. Basically, the **milline rate** is the cost to reach 1,000,000 people with one line of advertising. Like the cost-per-thousand concept discussed in chapters 15 and 16, the milline rate is useful because it allows advertisers to compare all newspapers on the same basis. It is calculated by multiplying the line rate by 1,000,000 and then dividing by the circulation:

$$\text{Milline Rate} = \frac{\text{Line Rate} \times 1,000,000}{\text{Circulation}}$$

For example, the *Chicago Tribune's* milline rate is $26.27, calculated as follows:

$$\frac{\$19.73 \times 1,000,000}{751,024} = \$26.27$$

It is also possible to compute a cost-per-thousand figure for newspapers, and this is particularly useful when an advertiser is interested in making efficiency comparisons between newspapers and other media types. Calculations of the cost-per-thousand figure in newspaper is best done by comparing the cost of a particular SAU—for example, the SAU that is closest in size to the advertising space unit used in other print media—to the cost of the space in other media. If, for example, you wanted to compare the efficiency of using full-page advertisements in *Business Week* versus newspapers, you would use the full-page cost for *Business Week* and the cost of the SAU that most closely matches the *Business Week* page size.

WHEN TO USE NEWSPAPERS AS AN ADVERTISING MEDIUM

In spite of the growth of the broadcast media, newspapers are still the number-one advertising medium in terms of annual dollars invested in advertising. As an advertising medium, the daily newspaper has survived the challenges of competition from the broadcast media and has adapted

A CLOSER LOOK

COUPONS

One of the main reasons that advertisers use print media is to distribute coupons. Recent years have seen an enormous increase in the use of coupons. In 1984, about 160 billion cents-off coupons—more than 650 per capita —were distributed. That represents a 13 percent increase over the 1983 figure and nearly 80 percent more than the 1980 figure of 90 billion.

How much do coupons cost the manufacturer?

Only about 5 percent of all coupons are redeemed. However, at the average of 25 cents each, the total redemption value is $2 billion. It is also estimated that stores and manufacturers lose another $350 million each year through fraud and redemption mistakes. In addition to the redemption value, fraud, and handling errors, there is, of course, the cost of advertising space.

Source: "Clip, Clip, Clip," *Forbes*, April 29, 1985, 15. Photo courtesy of Geo. A. Hormel & Co.

to the needs of advertisers who are constantly trying to offer their goods and services to a changing marketplace. Newspapers are successful because they offer advertisers certain advantages. Newspapers should be used when:

1. **The advertiser has a tightly defined geographic market.** With a few exceptions, newspapers are a local medium and they reach a high percentage of the adult market. Two out of three adults read one or more daily newspapers on an average day.[13] Newspapers' geographic concentration and high reach are benefits to both retailers and national advertisers. Retailers can direct their advertising messages to prospects who live in the shopping area. National advertisers can use newspapers to increase advertising pressure on key markets, to test market products, and to field-test alternative advertising executions for comparatively little money.

2. **The advertiser is interested in short-term action.** Studies show that three out of five shoppers "almost always" read newspaper advertisements before making a trip to the supermarket.[14] Because advertisers know that consumers seek sales information in the daily newspaper, newspapers have become the most popular form of distributing coupons. Over 80 percent of all coupons are distributed by newspapers. The immediacy of the news orientation of the newspaper fosters an action atmosphere that is helpful to retailers and national advertisers.

3. **The advertiser is interested in supplementary marketing support.** Although the newspaper certainly has limitations, it is a flexible medium in many ways. It provides a variety of marketing services to retail and national advertisers, low-cost (and sometimes free) creative and production assistance to retailers, and creative opportunities for the national advertiser.

Because the daily newspaper is such an important part of the local marketplace, it is often the richest source of marketing information. Most newspapers regularly monitor the buying habits, shopping patterns, and economic, social, and cultural changes of their community. Newspapers often become the central source of marketing information because their own financial well-being depends on understanding the business and social environments of their community. A good example of a newspaper that assists marketers in achieving their advertising goals is the *Los Angeles Times*. With a weekday circulation of 1,076,466 and a Sunday circulation of 1,346,343, the *Times* is the largest newspaper in the Los Angeles area and the second-largest in the country. The *Times* helps advertisers by offering a number of services:

- **Distribution of Preprinted Supplements** Advertisers can arrange to have preprinted advertising supplements distributed with any of the separate *Times* suburban sections. Preprints can also be custom-delivered to prime consumers in any specific area.

- **Selective Market Coverage (SMC)** A program designed to achieve 75 percent to 98 percent market coverage in Los Angeles, Orange, and Ventura counties and parts of Riverside and San Bernardino counties. The *Times* combines preprinted or ROP ads in the paper with mail delivery to nonsubscribers. SMC uses 129 different geographic grids, enabling an advertiser to zero in on specific areas.

- **Ad Sitters** A special telephone answering service of the classified department. Ad Sitters will answer all calls generated by an advertiser's classified ad, providing convenience and privacy at an economical cost.

- **Art and Copy Service** The *Times* has a creative graphics department that helps advertisers with their advertising copy and layout.

- **Market Research** Over 40 specialists in the *Times*' marketing research department provide definitive market and media analyses. Services include consumer/product surveys, purchasing/mobility patterns, shopping center/department store surveys, videotaped focus-group inter-

EXHIBIT 17.3

The Top 25 Newspaper Advertisers, 1985

RANK	ADVERTISER	EXPENDITURE (in thousands of dollars)
1	General Motors Corp.	$140,979
2	Philip Morris Cos.	78,031
3	Ford Motor Co.	77,295
4	RJR/Nabisco	73,321
5	American Telephone & Telegraph Co.	57,210
6	Chrysler Corp.	42,000
7	International Business Machines Corp.	30,610
8	GE/RCA	29,870
9	People Express Airlines	29,212
10	Batus Inc.	28,425
11	Eastern Air Lines	24,838
12	Pan-American World Airways	21,218
13	CBS Inc.	20,936
14	Trans World Airlines	20,870
15	Toyota Motor Corp.	20,761
16	UAL Inc.	19,987
17	AMR Corp.	19,534
18	Capital Cities/ABC	18,168
19	Daimler-Benz	18,008
20	Delta Air Lines	17,116
21	Northwest Orient Airlines	16,850
22	Nissan Motor Co.	16,504
23	NYNEX Corp.	15,133
24	Texas Air Corp.	15,075
25	American Express Co.	14,864

Source: Advertising Age, September 4, 1986, 53.

views, radius/trading area studies, competitive analyses, and advertising evaluations.[15]

Many retailers take advantage of the creative support offered by newspapers. The advertisements of smaller retailers are often planned, created, and produced with the help of the newspaper's sales representative and advertising department.

National advertisers are increasingly finding newspapers a valuable medium because of the flexibility brought about by technological improvements. The SAU program makes it easier to use newspaper space. High-quality reproduction and graphics are now widely available. Also, newspapers' ability to distribute coupons and other types of inserts are vital to the successful marketing of many consumer products.

STRUCTURE OF MAGAZINES

Although magazines account for less than 10 percent of the money invested in advertising, they remain a growing, healthy medium that provides advertisers with a creative advertising environment. Magazine cir-

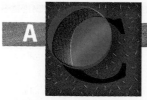

A CLOSER LOOK

NEWSPAPERS AND SATELLITES

Suppose you wanted to run a full-page advertisement in 100 different newspapers throughout the United States. After preparing the ad, you could send it by messenger or overnight mail. However, mail services sometimes experience delays, and your advertisement might be late or it might not arrive at all. The solution: AD/SAT—a satellite-transmission firm that allows an advertiser to send its ads to more than 100 different newspapers in the United States within minutes.

"It is really revolutionary," says Don Demarest of Young & Rubicam. "It makes it easier for us to adjust copy at the last minute, and we've found the quality of the facsimiles very high."

One reason why some national advertisers have been reluctant to use newspapers as a national medium is the difficulty in placing ads in dozens of newspapers scattered throughout the United States. AD/SAT promises to solve that problem. As Richard Masotta, a retail advertising executive with *The Boston Globe*, observed, "We think it should help prove newspapers an easier buy."

Currently, it costs advertisers about $70 to deliver an ad to a newspaper; however, satellite transmission will reduce the delivery cost to about $15 per ad per newspaper. AD/SAT uses microwave signals, which most newspapers can already receive through AP satellite dishes. To use the AD/SAT system, a newspaper must pay a $7,500 annual affiliation fee and purchase facsimile and message-system equipment from the network. Since its test phase in January 1987, AD/SAT users include more than a dozen advertising agencies and one major retailer, Lord & Taylor.

The 100 papers that currently are part of the system make up about 40 percent of the total daily newspaper circulation and 55 percent of Sunday circulation in the United States. Among the newspapers that have become part of AD/SAT are the *Los Angeles Times*, *New York Times*, *Washington Post*, and papers in Chicago, Detroit, Dallas, and Philadelphia.

Source: Linda Keslar, "It Came from Outer Space, or: Ads via Satellite," *ADWEEK*, April 28, 1987, 32.

culation grew nearly 90 percent from the late 1950s to the early 1980s. Advertising investment in consumer magazines has grown even more impressively: the amount invested in advertising in the mid-1980s grew nearly five times over the 1960 figure (see Figure 17.4).

Whereas newspapers are a medium that serves the needs of a broad cross-section of the local community, magazines are a national medium appealing to a variety of special interests—sports, cooking, travel, the arts, financial matters, etc. *Standard Rate & Data Service* classifies 1,751 magazines into 78 different interest categories.[16] The *SRDS Business Publications Directory* lists 2,750 magazines within 176 different categories.[17] The success of magazines is based on their ability to provide a wide range of readers the educational and entertainment information they find interesting and useful.

The ability of magazines to entertain also encourages Americans to spend considerable time reading them. During the average month, 94 percent of all adults read nearly 10 different magazines. Furthermore, each reader spends an average of 62 minutes reading an issue of a magazine and is exposed to the average page nearly twice.[18]

American consumers are involved in magazines. They read many different magazines; they spend time reading them; and they are willing to pay increasing amounts for subscriptions. It's not surprising that advertisers are investing more of their media budgets to reach consumers through magazines.

FIGURE 17.4

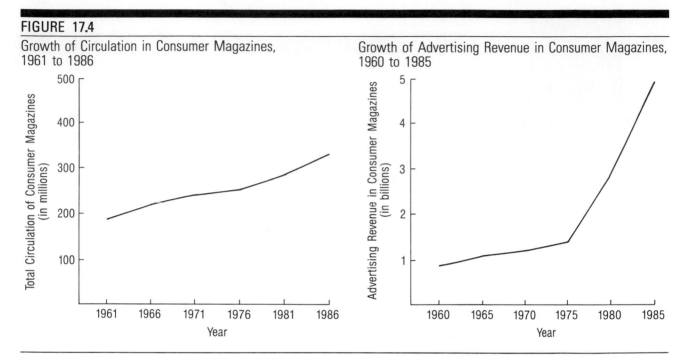

Growth of Circulation in Consumer Magazines, 1961 to 1986

Growth of Advertising Revenue in Consumer Magazines, 1960 to 1985

Source: MPA Newsletter of Research, No. 53, November 1986, pp. 1 and 2, New York: Magazine Publishers Association.

Indeed, thousands of magazines currently exist. The *IMS Directory of Publications* lists over 12,000 periodicals in the United States; however, the vast majority of magazine advertising is carried by relatively few magazines. In 1985, 142 consumer magazines accounted for nearly $5 billion of advertising and 2,760 business papers accounted for $3 billion of business press advertising.[19]

CLASSIFICATIONS OF MAGAZINES

Magazines can be classified by type of audience, geographic coverage, and frequency of issue.

AUDIENCE TYPE

Magazines serve many types of audiences. *Consumer magazines* are created to suit the tastes and interests of the general public; therefore, they cover a wide variety of topics and are usually classified in terms of their editorial focus (news, sports, women's, men's, general interest, etc.). Because consumer magazines reach so many people, they carry most of the advertising dollars invested in magazines—about two-thirds of all revenue in the mid-1980s.

Farm magazines are a separate category and appeal to the needs and interests of the farming industry. In 1985, farm magazines accounted for less than three percent of the total amount of money invested in magazine advertising.

A CLOSER LOOK

THE BUSINESS PRESS

The business press is an advertising medium often overlooked because most readers don't have much occasion to read any of the nearly 3,000 publications that comprise this important medium. The business press accounts for over 30 percent of the advertising investment in magazines and it is an important link between buyers and sellers of business-to-business goods and services.

Growth of the Business Press, 1950–1985

YEAR	NUMBER OF PUBLICATIONS	ADVERTISING PAGES	ADVERTISING REVENUE (in millions of dollars)
1950	1,772	753,000	$ 233.8
1955	1,974	1,125,000	416.0
1960	2,310	1,194,000	546.5
1965	2,548	1,205,000	682.0
1970	2,376	1,093,311	781.3
1975	2,400	1,188,000	1,020.8
1980	2,650	1,700,000	1,925.0
1985	2,760	1,810,500	3,021.0

Sources: Estimates from the Association of Business Publishers and information supplied by the American Business Press, Inc., New York, November 1986.

Business papers serve the reading interests of many different types of businesses and occupations and are often referred to as trade papers, business publications, or trade and technical journals. Some business magazines serve a specific field, industry, or trade. For example, *Advertising Age* covers advertising and marketing; *Aviation Week* focuses on independent aviation; and *Automotive Industries* deals with automotive manufacturing. These are known as **vertical publications** because they reach all job functions within a particular industry. Other business magazines serve a particular job function. For instance, *Purchasing Week* reaches purchasing agents; *Chemical Engineering* talks to engineers; and *Modern Medicine* reaches medical doctors. These are known as **horizontal publications** because they reach a single occupation across many different industries.

When we think of magazines we tend to think of those we read for our personal interest and information; yet, business papers are important because they provide a vital function for both advertisers and their target markets. For the advertiser, business papers identify, locate, and deliver advertising messages far more efficiently than any other communication alternative. At the same time, readers of business papers (advertisers' target markets) receive timely, important, and relevant information about their industry and their occupation.

Although the advertising revenue generated by business papers is somewhat less than half that of consumer magazines, many more business papers than consumer magazines are listed in *SRDS*.

GEOGRAPHIC COVERAGE

While the majority of advertising revenue is carried by magazines that reach a national audience, many successful regional or local magazines exist. *Sunset Magazine* has provided excellent coverage of the western United States since 1923 and in recent years, city magazines such as *New York*, *Texas Monthly*, *Chicago*, and others have become popular among readers and advertisers. By the mid-1980s, the ten largest city and regional magazines by circulation, were as follows:

MAGAZINE	CIRCULATION
New York	433,499
Texas Monthly	287,851
Chicago	221,728
San Francisco Focus	170,612
Los Angeles	163,896
Philadelphia	141,973
The Washingtonian	135,795
Boston	116,028
New Jersey Monthly	96,732
Ohio	87,215[20]

Most national magazines offer regional editions that enable advertisers to have their ad appear only in the specific geographic area of interest, yet the advertising is still placed within in the editorial environment of a national magazine. *Time*, for example, allows advertisers to choose from over 350 ways of buying portions of the magazine's circulation, including:

Demographic *Time*

- *Time* Top ZIPs edition (national circulation exclusively to the highest income postal ZIP codes as ranked by average household income)

- *Time* Business (all-business circulation of *Time*)

- *Time* Top Management (*Time*'s circulation among owners, partners, directors, board chairs, company presidents, and other titled officers and department heads)

- *Time* Campus (*Time*'s circulation within the college market)

Geographic *Time*

- *Time* National

- 50 Major Metros (circulation in 50 major U.S. markets accounting for 66 percent of U.S. population and 70 percent of effective buying income)

- *Time* Spot Market editions (circulation in 50 different cities are offered)

- *Time* State editions (circulation in each of the states)

- *Time* Regional editions (circulation in seven geographic regions of the United States)

- *Time* Worldwide (circulation in seven worldwide regions)[21]

FIGURE 17.5

Geographic Editions of *Time* Magazine

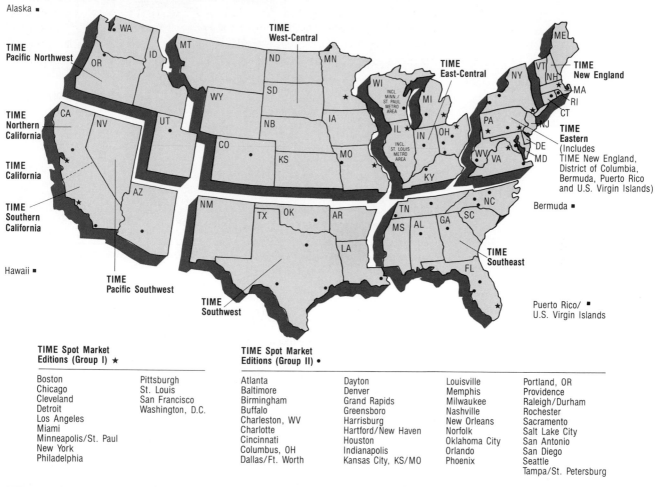

Source: Courtesy of *TIME* Magazine.

FREQUENCY OF ISSUE

While magazines are issued on many different schedules, there are more than twice as many monthlies as any other one type of magazine. Because of the variety of magazine publication schedules, advertisers have an opportunity to tie their advertising messages into current events by using weeklies, or to extend the life of their advertising through the use of quarterlies. Figure 17.6 shows the breakdown of American magazines in terms of their frequency of issue.

LEARNING TO USE MAGAZINES AS AN ADVERTISING MEDIUM

In order to use the medium of magazines, advertisers must understand how the space is bought and the relevant terminology.

FIGURE 17.6

Frequency of Issue
of U.S. Periodicals

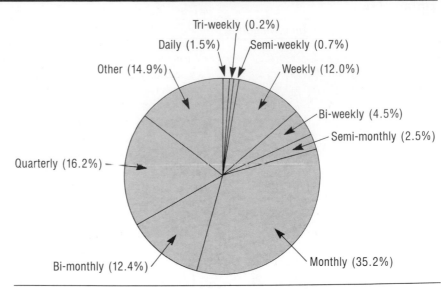

Source: 1986 IMS Directory of Publications, IMS Press, Fort Washington, Pennsylvania,
1986, p. VIII.

HOW MAGAZINE ADVERTISING IS BOUGHT

One of magazines' advantages is creative flexibility. The basic unit of advertising space is the single black-and-white page, although today nearly 70 percent of magazine advertising pages are in full color.[22] In addition to many different types of fractional pages, advertisers can purchase inserts (bound and free-standing), gatefolds, and even pop-up pages (see Figure 17.7).

Inserts are widely used in magazine advertising because they offer the advertiser maximum creative flexibility. Advertisers have used magazine inserts to bring readers multipage product catalogs, elaborate instructions on product use, and even computer disks. Advertisers are responsible for printing inserts, and they must also pay for the equivalent amount of page space. *Free-standing inserts* are used in magazines just as they are in newspapers. These unbound inserts are frequently used as subscription offers and other direct-action response devices.

A **gatefold** is a multiple-page advertisement that the reader unfolds to read. Often gatefold advertisements are used with magazine covers as one of the pages. They are used when the advertiser has a long message to tell or when the advertiser wants to create a special effect.

FIGURE 17.7

An Example of Pop-Up Advertising

Source: Courtesy of the Transamerica Corporation. Photograph copyright © B. E. White, 1987. All rights reserved.

IMPORTANT CONSIDERATIONS IN MAGAZINES

Advertisers are interested in knowing how many people read a magazine and who the readers are. A number of terms are helpful in understanding the potential effectiveness of placing an advertising campaign in a particular magazine.

Circulation refers to the number of copies distributed. Magazines are distributed by subscription, newsstand sale, or unsolicited delivery. Because everyone doesn't read every single issue of a particular magazine, a magazine's circulation figure only tells how many copies were distributed, *not* how many people read the magazine.

There are two types of circulation—paid (noncontrolled) and nonpaid (controlled). We are most familiar with **paid-circulation** magazines—that is, magazines we pay to receive. We either pay a subscription fee or we buy the magazine at a newsstand. The publishers of paid-circulation magazines have the benefit of circulation revenue; however, they have little control over who receives their magazines. Circulation is controlled only by the appeal of the editorial, the advertising content, and the ability of potential readers to purchase the magazine. **Nonpaid-circulation** magazines are distributed only to individuals who "qualify" to receive the publication—that is, to those who work in a specified industry, are part of a particular occupation, or who meet one or more other demographic characteristics. Many business publications have nonpaid circulation—that is, the circulation is controlled by the publisher. Such magazines, of course, do not provide the publisher with circulation revenue; however, controlled circulation allows the publisher to deliver a more tightly defined target market to prospective advertisers. It is not unusual for a business magazine with controlled circulation to reach 90 percent or more of a particular industry.

Audience, *total audience*, or *readership* refers to the total number of different people who read the publication. Magazines usually have an audience larger than their circulation because of "pass-along," or secondary, readers. A magazine's total audience is the sum of both its circulation (primary readers) and its secondary readers.

Average-issue audience refers to the total audience size over a number of issues, divided by the number of issues. Audience size varies from issue to issue because all readers don't read every issue. As the data below show, Magazine A has an average-issue audience of 485,667; Magazine B's is 515,000; and Magazine C's is 756,000.

Average = Issue Audience			
MAGAZINE	**JANUARY**	**FEBRUARY**	**MARCH**
A	485,000	512,000	460,000
Average Audience $= \dfrac{485,000 + 512,000 + 460,000}{3} = 485,667$			
B	550,000	575,000	515,000
Average Audience $= \dfrac{550,000 + 575,000 + 515,000}{3} = 546,667$			
C	775,000	713,000	780,000
Average Audience $= \dfrac{775,000 + 713,000 + 780,000}{3} = 756,000$			

Percent coverage refers to the percentage of a given population that reads an average issue of a magazine. The population can be any particular segment—adults, teenagers, women 18–24, etc. The percent coverage figure is computed by dividing the total population of a particular segment by a magazine's coverage of that segment. For example, if there are 50 million women between 18–24 and a particular magazine reaches 8 million

EXHIBIT 17.4

Circulation and Cost Data for Selected Magazines

Frequency (issues per year)	12	52
Circulation	440,000	480,000
Readers per copy	2.06	5.12
Median age	39.1	42.0
Median household income	$32,174	$34,032
Page rate	$9,015	$12,350
Cost per thousand	$20.49	$25.73

Source: Media Cost Guide 1985, April–June 1985, ad forum, Inc., New York.

of them, that magazine's coverage is 6.25 (50/8 = 6.25). This term is similar to "rating" used in the broadcast media.

Reach, unduplicated audience, or *net reach* estimate the number of *different* people who read a particular magazine or the number of magazines in a media schedule. Some people read more than one magazine in a given media schedule, but they are counted only once in calculating reach.

Gross impressions or *gross audience* refers to the total number of exposures in a magazine media schedule. They are determined by counting the number of times people are exposed to the same magazine more than once and the number of people who are exposed to more than one magazine in the schedule. Each exposure results in an impression that is totaled to give a gross impressions, or gross audience, figure.

Frequency refers to the number of times an individual is exposed to a magazine or a magazine schedule within a given time period. It is usually expressed in terms of the number of issues read out of the last four. *Average frequency* is calculated by dividing the gross audience by the net reach. Using our examples of magazines A, B, and C, the calculation of average frequency is shown as follows:

12	52	12
700,000	4,600,000	17,900,000
3.38	4.61	2.19
34.6	36.5	45.8
$22,441	$31,741	$24,646
$16,350	$69,650	$90,500
$23.36	$15.14	$5.06

MAGAZINE	AVERAGE AUDIENCE		NUMBER OF INSERTIONS		GROSS AUDIENCE
A	460,667	×	9	=	4,146,003
B	546,667	×	6	=	3,280,002
C	756,000	×	12	=	9,072,000
Gross Audience:					16,498,005
Net Reach:					4,180,000

$$\text{Average Frequency} = \frac{\text{Gross Audience}}{\text{Net Reach}}$$

$$= \frac{16,498,005}{4,180,000}$$

$$= 3.95$$

The main variables that affect magazine advertising rates are circulation, audience characteristics, the amount of space purchased, and the use of additional services.

As might be expected, the highest page rates are in magazines that have the highest circulation. Exhibit 17.4 lists the advertising rates for a

EXHIBIT 17.5

The Top 25 Magazine
Advertisers, 1985

RANK	ADVERTISER	EXPENDITURE (in thousands of dollars)
1	Philip Morris Cos.	$215,038
2	RJR/Nabisco	164,137
3	Ford Motor Co.	114,739
4	General Motors Corp.	107,524
5	Procter & Gamble	93,144
6	American Telephone & Telegraph Co.	88,137
7	Chrysler Corp.	73,579
8	CBS Inc.	60,405
9	GE/RCA	55,288
10	International Business Machines Corp.	52,535
11	Time Inc.	43,460
12	Beatrice Cos.	43,113
13	U.S. Government	37,651
14	Loews Corp.	36,007
15	Volkswagen of America	35,920
16	Dart & Kraft	35,723
17	American Brands	35,025
18	Capital Cities/ABC	34,898
19	American Express Co.	33,467
20	E.I. du Pont de Nemours & Co.	32,061
21	Grand Metropolitan	30,052
22	Jos. E. Seagram & Sons	29,685
23	Johnson & Johnson	29,419
24	Bristol-Myers Co.	28,435
25	Sara Lee Corp.	27,940

Source: Advertising Age, September 4, 1986, 26.

selected group of magazines. Note that as the audience becomes more specific, the rates drop, although the cost to reach a thousand people increases. The *New Yorker*, for instance, has a page rate of $12,350 and a circulation of 480,000. It is read by those interested in literature and the arts. The number of people who share that interest and who are willing to pay to read about their common interest is far fewer than the subscribers to, say, *Reader's Digest* or *TV Guide*. Also, the audience of the *New Yorker* is harder to reach; therefore, the cost per thousand will be higher.

The most common advertising rate discount in magazines is for frequency. The more often a firm advertises, the higher discount it will receive. Publishers who own more than one magazine also offer combination discounts to advertisers who want to place their ads in more than one of the publisher's magazines.

In addition to the basic black-and-white page rate, advertisers in magazines pay for any additional services they may want. The most widely used additional services are color (two colors or full color); bleed; inserts; preferred position; and split runs.

The cost-per-thousand and cost-per-thousand (target market) are the most commonly used methods of calculating the efficiency of magazines. Note the variance in the cost-per-thousand figures in Exhibit 17.4. When compared to the broadcast media, magazines are a high cost-per-thousand medium. However, the purpose of advertising in magazines is to reach a selective audience and only direct mail can be as selective as magazines.

Consider the media alternatives for reaching chemical engineers. The cost-per-thousand figure for *Chemical Week* is comparatively high, but the cost-per-thousand (target market) would be low if one were to compare *Chemical Week* with *Time, Esquire,* or *Reader's Digest,* or any broadcast media vehicle.

WHEN TO USE MAGAZINES AS AN ADVERTISING MEDIUM

Magazines were the first national advertising medium, and after two hundred years they remain an important link between buyer and seller. Although they represent a comparatively small proportion of total advertising revenue, thousands of advertisers rely on magazines to address their target markets. Magazines should be used when:

1. **The advertiser has a narrowly defined target market**. While many of the largest circulation magazines reach a mass audience, most magazines serve the special interests of a more narrowly defined audience. Advertising would be far less efficient if magazines did not exist. The business press is the clearest example of this. Without the business press' access to the target market, advertisers would be forced to use personal selling and direct mail—both far more expensive alternatives.

2. **The advertiser can take advantage of magazine's creative flexibility**. The ability to use various page sizes and formats, the excellent reproduction of color, and the availability of inserts, gatefolds, and cover advertising offer advertisers endless creative possibilities.

3. **The advertiser is interested in building a brand image**. Magazines provide specialized editorial content and a very particular, distinctive environment. Magazine advertising becomes part of that environment and the image of the magazine is transferred to the advertised brand.

4. **The advertiser wants to reach an upscale, active audience**. Magazine readership increases with education and income. Magazine readership also necessitates active participation. Readers must physically seek out magazine information. From circulation to readership, to ultimate reader action, magazines require active involvement. We must either pay to receive a magazine or request to receive it. We must read it. And, finally, our response to a magazine usually requires physical and mental action—we write to the editor; fill out a product information card; visit a retail location; use an inserted coupon; or change our attitudes about a company or a brand.

SUMMARY

This chapter has focused on the structure and usefulness of the print media in reaching target markets. Newspapers and magazines are important communication links between buyers and sellers. They are unique among advertising media because their audiences seek out the information they provide. The broadcast media only require that we flip a switch. The print media require active involvement. The print media are also important because they deliver audiences that are hard to reach. While newspaper readership is broad, it increases among more highly educated, upper-income segments of the population. The specialized editorial content of most magazines appeals to very narrowly defined target markets.

In many ways, newspapers and magazines complement each other. Newspapers are a local medium, high in a sense of immediacy, and retail-oriented. Magazines are a national medium with a long message life and a national and international editorial and advertising orientation.

Despite the growth of the broadcast media, newspapers and magazines have remained important advertising media because they continue to offer differential advantages and because they have adapted to meet the needs of their advertisers. As media technology continues to develop, the viability of the print media will continue to be challenged. The challenge for the print media is the same one they have faced for over 200 years—to provide an editorial and advertising package more efficiently and effectively than other media alternatives.

YOU MAKE THE DECISION

MAXI-BRUSH

When was the last time you bought a toothbrush? Do you remember what brand you bought? Toothbrushes just aren't a product we think about often. Though most Americans use one, they tend to spend little time thinking or talking about toothbrushes.

The Maxi-Brush Company makes just one product: soft toothbrushes. And, although it leads the soft-toothbrush market in market share, Maxi-Brush is the smallest of the four chief toothbrush makers (see Table 1). About half the market is devoted to medium-bristle toothbrushes, while hard- and soft-bristle toothbrushes each command one quarter of the market.

Recently, Maxi-Brush decided to launch a consumer advertising campaign and has chosen four possible vehicles. The target market is equally split between men and women.

TABLE 1

Toothbrush Market Shares

MANUFACTURER	MARKET SEGMENT		
	HARD	MEDIUM	SOFT
Acme	40%	50%	10%
Brushodent	50	20	5
Cariesgone	10	30	10
Maxi-Brush	——	——	75

TABLE 2

Comparison of Magazines

	MAGAZINE			
	NATIONAL GEOGRAPHIC	PEOPLE	PSYCHOLOGY TODAY	TIME
ISSUES PER YEAR	12	51	12	52
CIRCULATION	8,200,000	2,800,000	850,000	4,600,000
Readers per copy	2.62	7.96	3.88	4.61
B/W page rate (1X)	$95,000	$44,000	$17,000	$70,000
B/W page rate (6X)	$92,000	$43,000	$16,500	$68,500
B/W page rate (12X)	$88,500	$41,500	$14,750	$65,000
4/C page rate (one time)	$110,000	$57,000	$24,500	$109,000
Male/female readers (%)	55/45%	44/56%	52/48%	57/43%

Your assignment is to compare the efficiencies of the four magazines shown in Table 2. After you have determined the most efficient magazine, allocate Maxi-Brush's $3.0 million advertising media budget. Will the ads be four-color or black and white? How many ads will run, and how often? Defend your decisions.

Note: The data in the Maxi-Brush scenario are not necessarily identical to those in the toothbrush market nor within the media vehicles used. The information has been created to provide practice in applying the concepts presented in the chapter.   ■ ■ ■

QUESTIONS FOR DISCUSSION

1. Why are there so few national newspapers?

2. Newspapers are carrying an increasing number of advertising inserts in recent years. Why have inserts become more popular?

3. What is the SAU system and of what value is it to both advertisers and newspapers?

4. Explain the difference between controlled circulation and paid circulation. Why do some print media decide to use controlled circulation?

5. Explain each of the following terms:
   a. flat rate
   b. open rate
   c. contract rate
   d. short rate

6. From the advertiser's point of view, what is the main value of advertising in magazines?

7. Explain the difference between horizontal publications and vertical publications.

8. What are "pass-along readers," and of what importance are they to advertisers?

9. Define each of the following terms:
   a. average-issue audience
   b. percent coverage
   c. net reach
   d. average frequency

10. Under what conditions should an advertiser use magazines as an advertising medium?

NOTES

1. Frank Presbrey, *The History and Development of Advertising* (New York: Doubleday, Doran and Company, Inc., 1929), 124 and 127.

2. *Magazine Newsletter of Research*, August 1984, 2.

3. *Key Facts about Newspapers and Advertising: 1986* (New York: Newspaper Advertising Bureau, April 1986), 16; and *1986 SMRB Study of Media and Markets*, Simmons Market Research Bureau.

4. Ibid., 29 and 30.

5. *Magazine Newsletter of Research*, August 1986, 1–2.

6. *Newspaper Advertising Bureau: Strategic Plan Update, 1985–1987*, Newspaper Advertising Bureau, New York, 1986, 24.

7. "Total U.S. Advertising Volume," McCann-Erickson, Inc., New York, 1987.

8. "Media Myths and Facts," no. 33, Newspaper Advertising Bureau, New York, May 1985, 1.

9. "Key Facts about Newspapers and Advertising: 1986," April 1986, 35; and "Volume of Inserts in Sunday/Daily Newspapers," Newspaper Advertising Bureau, New York, 1985.

10. *Media Cost Guide 1985*, ad forum, Inc., New York, 1985; and "Total Advertising Volume in the United States: 1935–1985," Newpaper Advertising Bureau, Inc., New York, May 1986.

11. *Key Facts about Newspapers and Advertising, 1987*, April 1987, 25.

12. Ibid., 22.

13. *SMRB Study of Media and Markets* (New York: Simmons Market Research Bureau, 1983).

14. Newspaper Advertising Bureau, 1986; and *Progressive Grocer*, 1982.

15. *Los Angeles Media Facts 1986* (Los Angeles: *Los Angeles Times* Marketing Research Department, February 1986), 24.

16. *Consumer and Farm Publications Directory*, Standard Rate & Data Service, January 1, 1986.

17. *Business Publications Directory*, Standard Rate & Data Service, January 1, 1986.

18. *Magazine Newsletter of Research*, August 1986, 4.

19. *MPA Newsletter of Research*, no. 53, November 1986, Magazine Publishers Association, New York, 12; *Statistics — Business Press*, American Business Press, Inc., New York, 1987, 2.

20. Jeremy Schlosberg, "The Glittering City Magazines," *American Demographics*, July 1986.

21. *TIME* Media Kit, Time, Inc., New York, 1986.

22. *MPA Newsletter of Research*, no. 53, November 1986, Magazine Publishers Association, New York, 13.

SUGGESTED READINGS

Bearden, W. O.; J. Teel, Jr.; R. Durand; and R. Williams. "Consumer Magazines — An Efficient Medium for Reaching Organizational Buyers." *Journal of Advertising*, no. 2, 1979.

Bogart, Leo. *Strategy in Advertising: Matching Media and Messages to Markets and Motivation.* 2d ed. Chicago: Crain Books, 1984.

Grass, Robert C., and Wallace H. Wallace. "Advertising Communication: Print vs TV." *Journal of Advertising Research*, October 1974.

Larkin, E. F. "Consumer Perceptions of the Media and Their Advertising Content." *Journal of Advertising*, no. 2, 1979.

Larkin, E. F., and G. L. Grotta. "The Newspaper as a Source of Consumer Information." *Journal of Advertising*, no. 4, 1977.

Lorimor, E. S. "Classified Advertising: A Neglected Medium." *Journal of Advertising*, no. 1, 1977.

O'Keefe, Garrett J.; Kathleen Nash; and Jenny Liu. "The Perceived Utility of Advertising: A Cross-Media Analysis." *Journalism Quarterly*, Winter 1981.

Rentz, J. O., and F. D. Reynolds. "Magazine Readership Patterns." *Journal of Advertising*, no. 2, 1979.

Sissors, Jack Z., and Jim Surmanek. *Advertising Media Planning*. 2d ed. Chicago: Crain Books, 1982.

Urban, C. "Editorial and Program Choices of Heavy Media Users." *Journal of Advertising*, no. 1, 1980.

SUPPORT MEDIA

Key Terms

direct marketing
direct mail
internal (house) list
external list
direct response list
compiled list
mailing list broker
mailing list compiler
outdoor advertising
poster panel
painted bulletin
showing
transit advertising
specialty advertising
premium
point-of-purchase advertising (POP)

Learning Objectives

To explain the special role of support media in accomplishing media objectives

To describe the characteristics of direct response, out-of-home, and specialty media

To analyze when and how to use the support media

For years, Spiegel was a general merchandise, mass-market catalog marketer. The company's typical customer was the middle-class homemaker trying to stretch her husband's modest income. She sought budget merchandise, and that's what Spiegel provided.

Then one day, the company found itself facing a number of marketing pressures. Competition had increased as the average household received more and more catalogs. Big discount chains like Kmart were taking away the low-end business. Catalog giants like Sears and Montgomery Ward were intensifying their marketing efforts. Under these conditions, it's not surprising that the retailer was quickly losing market share.

Led by Ted Spiegel, vice-president of marketing, the company in 1976 began a series of changes that caused an impressive turnaround. First, Spiegel management recognized and acknowledged environmental changes. The influx of women into the work force, changing demographics, and rise in disposable income were factors affecting Spiegel's new direction.

Observed Spiegel, "We needed to pursue the market of today and tomorrow, even if it means sacrificing the market we had. After acknowledging the changing woman, we took a closer look at her. We decided the age range of our target consumer should be between 21 and 59. . . . The new woman we sought is educated. She is employed, not just on a temporary basis to make ends meet, but in a full-time career. She wants to be fashionable. Unlike her housebound predecessor, she is in the public eye every day and wants to look her best. She emerged at the same time as the consumer movement, so she looks for quality and value rather than the lowest price tag. She wants convenience. Her busy schedule and dual role as worker and mother leave her little time for casual browsing in stores."

With its new target market, Spiegel suddenly found itself up against Saks Fifth Avenue, Neiman-Marcus, Bloomingdale's, and Marshall Field's, all competing for the same customer. For Spiegel, the time was ripe for direct marketing, non-store retailing. Spiegel realized the potential of direct marketing. "Despite their efforts, the fine department stores just can't reach upscale customers in all parts of the country. At best, they reach only the upscale customer in their store locations in the larger cities. And even here, their money is spent inefficiently. Their promotional efforts reach not only the target consumer, but lower income groups who are not likely to become customers."

The advantages of direct marketing were clear—the ability to reach the top level of the market from coast to coast and to avoid the wasting of money reaching economic levels not in the target market. Over the next few years, Spiegel created a total marketing plan to attack its new customer and continued to refine the target market, raising the targeted median household from $28,300 in 1976 to $42,450 in 1984.

It also drastically changed the merchandise mix from ladies' housedresses and men's suits that could be worn four ways to offerings from the hottest designers.

By completely remodeling its "store" (the Spiegel catalog), Spiegel now considers itself "the fine department store in print." It uses the best models, graphics designers, and photographers. Spiegel made it easier for consumers to purchase goods, with an increased level of service: a 24-hour toll-free ordering line; UPS delivery to the customer's door; a complete customer guarantee; and several payment alternatives.

The results? Despite cutting catalog circulation from 40 to 20 million, Spiegel has more new customers from the upgraded market. The order response rate doubled in a six-year period, and the net order amount increased 50 percent. Also, a new, $4 million advertising program generated an estimated 20 percent of the new customer base.

The bottom line: When Spiegel first decided in 1976 to change its image to capture the upscale market, its sales stood at $268 million. In 1983, after almost eight years and a dramatic change in its catalog customer base, sales topped the $500 million mark. In 1986, revenues broke the $1 billion mark for the first time.

Acknowledging the importance of direct marketing, Ted Spiegel assessed the future for Spiegel and its competitors: "These are great times for direct marketing catalog retailing, but with a deluge of different catalogs out there crying for the U.S. consumer's dollar, it's still a time for survival tactics."

Sources: Edward Spiegel, "Spiegel's Turnaround—Net Sales Rocket to $516 Million," *Direct Marketing*, April 1984, 40–54; and Janet Key, "Cataloguing the Fresh Style of Spiegel Inc.," *Chicago Tribune*, September 1, 1986, sec. 4, 1. Photo courtesy of Spiegel Incorporated, Chicago, Illinois.

INTRODUCTION

Most people associate advertising with such media as television, radio, newspapers, and magazines. While it's true that large, national advertisers concentrate their advertising investment in these four media, many advertisers use a variety of other media to support their broadcast and print schedules or to reach their target markets more effectively and efficiently than can be accomplished through broadcast and print.

SUPPORT FUNCTION

You drive to work and notice an outdoor sign that reinforces the television commercial you saw last night. Your mail includes a package of coupons: one of them is for a new toothpaste advertised in last month's issue of *Reader's Digest*. You walk down an airport concourse and notice a large, backlit transparency for your favorite soft drink. You use a pen that is embellished with the name of the local pizzeria. In each of these situations, an advertiser is trying to extend communication to you. The media described in this chapter reinforce the advertising we see, read, and hear in broadcast and print.

REACH FUNCTION

As powerful as the broadcast and print media are, they are not perfectly suited for all advertisers, nor for all advertising tasks. Some advertisers have target markets that are best reached through direct mail. Specialty advertising might solve an advertising problem far better and for less money than would a television campaign. Trade shows and exhibits are costly, but they give an advertiser a unique communication opportunity. This chapter explains how support media are used to help meet media objectives.

DIRECT RESPONSE MEDIA: THE LANGUAGE OF DIRECT MARKETING

As shown in Figure 18.1, direct response is just one form of direct marketing. This official definition is provided by the Direct Marketing Association:

> **Direct marketing** is the total of activities by which products and services are offered to market segments in one or more media for informational purposes or to solicit a direct response from a present or prospective customer or contributor by mail, telephone, or other access.[1]

Direct marketing is a particular type of marketing—the marketing that takes place directly between buyer and seller. Of course, a market exchange cannot take place without a buyer and seller; therefore, all marketing is technically direct marketing. To clarify the distinction between direct marketing and marketing, the Direct Marketing Association excludes from its definition general over-the-counter retail sales and advertising, door-to-door selling, and other direct selling.

FIGURE 18.1

Direct Marketing: An Aspect of Total Marketing

The dashed line shows how a marketer evaluates sales when planning next year's media selection. For example, suppose a consumer ordered merchandise by telephone. The marketer might want to know what prompted that customer's order (the marketer's TV commercial, a copy of the company catalog, etc.). This information would influence the marketer's media selection the following year.

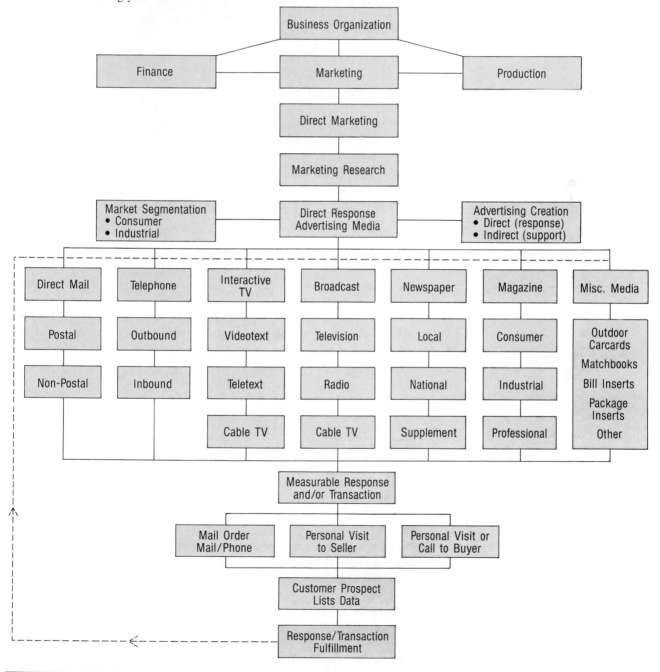

Source: Direct Marketing Magazine, 224 Seventh Street, Garden City, New York, 11530 USA. Reprinted with permission.

FIGURE 18.2

Direct Response Advertising
Expenditures, by Medium

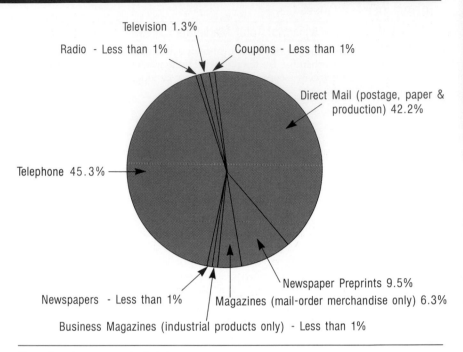

Note: Creative costs not included.
Source: Direct Marketing Association, New York.

Although direct mail and telephone account for the majority of the investment in direct response advertising, most of the major media are useful in direct marketing (see Figure 18.2). Because direct mail is the major direct response medium, however, our coverage of direct response focuses on it.

DIRECT MAIL

If it seems that your mailbox contains more catalogs, brochures, and direct-mail letters recently, you're not alone. **Direct mail**, one of the oldest advertising media, consists of advertising mailed directly to the target market. An extremely flexible medium, it now accounts for more advertising spending than any other medium, including television.

It's impossible to tell when the first advertising letter was written, but Aaron Montgomery Ward's catalog in 1872 marks the beginning of the modern era of mail order. Richard Sears started his mail-order business in 1886, and in 1912, L. L. Bean founded one of the soundest and most successful mail-order companies on the strength of a rubber-soled leather boot he had invented.[2] In 1984, the volume of charitable contributions generated directly through mail order totaled over $16 billion. Sears Roebuck and Co. sold nearly $4.5 billion of goods and services by direct marketing alone. The average household receives 2.5 direct-mail pieces each day, and 65 percent of all third-class mail is opened and read by some member of the household.[3]

THE MUSENALP EXPRESS

You might say that Othmar Beerli of Niederrickenbach, Switzerland, has his finger on the pulse of Swiss teenagers. The 42-year-old Beerli is the creator and founder of the *Musenalp Express*, a magazine aimed at the tiny nation's 15- to 21-year-old German-speaking population. What's even more unique about the magazine is that it contains a discount mail-order catalog, and because of the success of the combination magazine-catalog, Beerli's readership is extending into the over-21 market as his teen readers grow up and remain loyal.

With a circulation of 250,000 copies, the ten-year-old magazine reaches more than half of Switzerland's German-speaking 15–21 segment. The magazine is also distributed within the country's French and Italian sectors, despite the language difference.

Says Beerli: "I started thinking about what teenage readers wanted to read when I was a staffer on *Team* [a now-defunct Swiss magazine for teens]. One of the problems in any publishing house that is targeted to such a specific segment is that the editorial content, whether you want it to or not, comes out the way the editors want it, not the way the kids want it." Thus, the *Musenalp Express* is written by and for readers.

Beerli continues, "I was convinced that a magazine produced by and for young people would fly provided the editorial content was provided by the readers themselves."

Before actually publishing the *Express*, Beerli and his wife Marianne came up with the idea of a Junior Discount Club, a buying organization from which teenage consumers could purchase products and services at considerable discounts. The Junior Discount Club is what keeps the magazine afloat. Bound into every issue of the quarterly *Musenalp Express*, the Junior Discount catalog lists such products as home computers, radios, cameras, and camping equipment—discounted on an average of 15 percent off the retail price. The magazine also generates revenue by selling ad space. Some major advertisers are Agfa-Gevaert, BASF Corporation, the Coca-Cola Company, Commodore Business Machines, Eastman Kodak Company, Pentax Corporation, and Victor Technologies. A recent issue featured advertising from Swiss banks, all designed with the teen and post-teen segments in mind.

At first, Beerli had trouble attracting advertisers: "People weren't sure the idea was going to work and they were reluctant to commit themselves." Even Swiss ad agencies were skeptical about a magazine written by and for teens, until a study by Publitest, a major Swiss research firm, showed that the *Musenalp Express* was indeed an effective way to reach the market. The Publitest results were instrumental in increasing ad revenue over the years; the surge in revenue led Beerli to raise his black-and-white page rate to $8,350 in 1987.

According to Beerli, about 60 percent of the Junior Discount Club orders are placed by phone, and less than 1 percent default on payment. The mail-order operation's 1986 revenues totaled more than $12 million.

Source: John Parry, "Swiss Magazine Reaches New Heights," *Advertising Age* Special Report, October 27, 1986, S–33 and S–35.

THE APPEALS OF DIRECT MAIL TO BUYER AND SELLER

Marketers have demonstrated a growing interest in direct mail because it provides the greatest efficiency in selecting a target market. While direct mail is a very high cost-per-thousand medium (latest figures estimate its CPM to average $300), it has the least amount of waste exposures. Unlike the audiences of the mass media, the names on a carefully selected mailing list should all be interested in the marketer's offering. Marketers use direct mail for three other reasons:

1. **Direct mail is a flexible medium**. It can be used by small local advertisers with small target markets as well as by large national advertisers.

2. **Direct mail is measurable**. One of the most appealing dimensions of direct mail is that the advertiser can calculate the return on the advertising investment. The purpose of direct mail is to stimulate a short-term, direct response from the target audience; therefore, the marketer is able to determine the profitability of the effort.

3. **Direct mail works**. The response rates may not be high, but direct mail is a medium that motivates people to act.

Direct mail appeals to consumers because it is a convenient way to shop, particularly for items that may be difficult to find in retail stores. One of the reasons that some direct-mail advertisers are successful is that they offer exclusive merchandise or merchandise that is not readily available elsewhere. For example, a local retail clothing store cannot afford to stock every possible size in every style because the local market is comparatively small. A direct-mail marketer of the same clothing is selling to the entire country; therefore, potential buyers for the odd sizes are plentiful.

Direct-mail catalog operations are capable of selling more specialized products (see Figure 18.3). For example, merchandise offered in the Vermont Country Store catalog includes deerskin stretch gloves, a wooden

FIGURE 18.3

Catalogs Sell to Specialized Audiences

The Vermont Country Store carries a wide range of New England-style goods.	The Banana Republic markets travel and safari wear for globetrotters and others who appreciate high-quality, comfortable clothes.	The Gardener's Eden caters to people who love to garden and those who simply enjoy spending time in their yards.

Source: Courtesy of The Vermont Country Store, Weston, VT 05161.

Source: Courtesy of the Banana Republic Travel & Safari Clothing Co.®

Source: Courtesy of Gardener's Eden—A garden catalog from Williams-Sonoma.

A CLOSER LOOK

WHY WE SHOP BY MAIL

The growth in mail shopping has been fueled by a number of economic and environmental factors. About two-thirds of a recent sample reported that they shop by mail. The reasons were as follows:

REASON	PERCENTAGE OF RESPONDENTS*
Can't find items elsewhere	44%
Convenience	36
Fun	9
Price	7
Better quality	2
Other	2

*Approximate due to rounding.

Mail-order shopping is big business. The top ten U.S. mail-order firms alone captured a total of more than $13 million in revenues in 1985.

Top 10 Mail-Order Companies, Worldwide

RANK	COMPANY	SALES SEGMENT	SALES (in millions of dollars)
1.	Sears, Roebuck & Co.	General merchandise, insurance, auto clubs	2,809.0
2.	Time, Inc.	Books, magazine subscriptions, cable tv	1,862.6
3.	J.C. Penney Co.	General merchandise, insurance	1,769.4
4.	United Services Automobile Assn.	Insurance	1,420.9
5.	Mobil Oil Corp.	General merchandise, insurance, auto clubs	1,294.8
6.	Colonial Penn Group	Insurance	1,081.3
7.	GEICO	Insurance	1,073.0
8.	Reader's Digest Assn.	Books, collectibles, general merchandise, magazine subscriptions	1,022.0
9.	American Automobile Assn.	Auto clubs	975.0
10.	Tele-Communications Inc.	Cable tv	845.7

Sources: Adapted from Jim Kobs, *Profitable Direct Marketing* (Chicago: Crain Books, 1984); and *Fact Book on Direct Marketing* (New York: Direct Marketing Association, 1982); and *Advertising Age*, October 27, 1986, S–32.

whistle that sounds like a train, and mosquito headnets. The Banana Republic sells travel and safari clothing. Inside the pages of its catalog are bush vests, gamekeeper's bags, and desert hats—plus a variety of high-quality, reasonably priced khaki clothing for consumers on the go. Williams-Sonoma has been a successful direct marketer for a long time, and its "Gardener's Eden" catalog was created especially for those interested in gardening.

CREATIVITY IN DIRECT MAIL

Direct mail allows the advertiser to create an advertising piece that is perfectly suited to the creative needs of the product or service. With direct mail, there simply are no limits on time or space. Each mailing package is designed to take the reader through the entire sales process, from introduction of the product, to a complete explanation of benefits, to providing the mechanism for ordering.

FIGURE 18.4

Elements of a Direct-Mail Package

Elements of a Direct-Mail Package Although direct-mail packages vary widely, these basic elements are needed to take the reader through the entire sales process:

1. Outside envelope
2. Letter
3. Brochure
4. Order form
5. Return envelope

The goal is to create these five pieces to maximize response and profitability. Creativity within these pieces depends on the following factors:

- Needs of the target market
- Characteristics of the advertised product
- Competitive offerings
- Financial resources and objectives of the advertiser

The mailing package shown in Figure 18.4 is a good example of how an advertiser uses all the elements of successful direct mail.

Copy and Layout Styles A creative approach that is highly successful for one target market may be totally unsuccessful for another. Consider, for example, the style of Banana Republic. This company issues six cat-

FIGURE 18.5

An Example of Distinctive Direct Mail

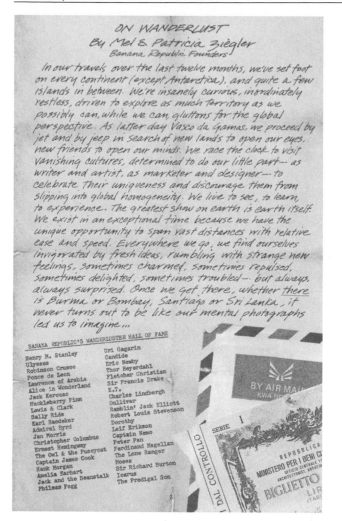

Source: Courtesy of the Banana Republic Travel & Safari Clothing Co.®

alogs a year and successfully differentiates itself with every component of its mailings. The firm's products are distinctive, and the graphics and copy are appropriately tied to its products, image, and target market. Figure 18.5 shows a two-page spread from a Banana Republic catalog.

Length of Copy How long should a direct-mail letter be? There is no "best" length. Half-page letters can be effective and so can multipage letters. Xerox Learning Systems, for example, used an eleven-page letter to help sell its Executive Advisory System. The Denver, a Colorado-based chain of department stores, used a two-paragraph letter to offer discount certificates to its preferred customers. Like most effective writing, the length of a direct-mail letter is not as important as relevance and interest to the target market.

MAILING LISTS

As important as the mailing package is, the most significant difference between direct mail and other major forms of media is the delivery to individuals. Direct mail is used so widely because it is the only advertising medium that communicates directly with a specific person or, at least, with a specific household.

Direct mail is sent to a list of people who the advertiser believes will respond to an offer. Finding the right list is crucial because the list *is* an advertiser's market. Chapter 15 pointed out that one of the main purposes of the media is to bring buyer and seller together. The broadcast and print media do this by developing programming and editorial content that attracts certain market segments. The same function is performed through mailing lists. A direct-mail piece cannot succeed without a mailing list of prospects that are likely to respond.

The best mailing lists are made up from a company's own records. Such a list is known as an **internal (house) list.** It includes current and former customers, prospective customers, people who have inquired about the company's products, contacts from the sales staff, referrals, names from warranty cards and surveys, and so forth. Internal lists are best because the names on them share some common characteristics: the most important is that they have purchased the product in the past or have expressed interest in purchasing from the firm.

A good mailing list is considerably more than a list of names and addresses. When direct-mail advertisers compile and maintain their own mailing lists, they add supplementary information that helps to identify the most likely respondents. For example, data on the date of initial purchase, frequency of purchase, dollar volume of purchase, type of products purchased, and the source from which the name was originally acquired are all important selection factors. An advertiser's prospects for maximizing profitability increase with the selectivity of the mailing list.

An **external list** is obtained from sources external to the advertiser — that is, the names are not drawn from company records. The sources of external lists can be directories, rosters, registrations, memberships, etc. There are two basic types of external lists. A **direct response list** contains names of individuals who have used the mail either to inquire about a product or to purchase it. Advertisers can acquire lists of people who have used the mail to request additional information or to purchase a wide variety of products and services (personal computers, office equipment, travel, book clubs, insurance, etc.). Direct response lists are valuable because the advertiser at least knows that the names on the list have demonstrated interest in the product category and are users of the mail for their purchases.

The other major type of external list is the **compiled list.** This type of list does not necessarily indicate prior purchase by mail, but the names on the list do share one or more common characteristic. For example, an advertiser can acquire lists of newlyweds, college students, retirees, farmers, doctors, specific businesses (food retailers, advertising agencies), and so on. The value of compiled lists is that the *common characteristic defines a market* for the advertiser. When one common characteristic is insufficient for meaningful segmentation, advertisers seek compiled lists with additional segmentation variables: for example, college students attending state universities with enrollments larger than 20,000.

FIGURE 18.6

Some of the Kinds of Lists Available from a List Broker

RETAILERS

S.I.C.	LIST	QUANT.
RETAIL TRADE BY FINANCIAL STRENGTH		
H-7	Total retailers	1,733,490
H-70	Unlisted retailers	946,950
H-71	Rated $500,000 & over	20,900
H-71S1	Headquarters	12,570
H-71S2	Branches	8,320
H-72	Rated $200,000 to $500,000	45,340
H-73	Rated $75,000 to $200,000	42,460
H-74	Rated $35,000 to $75,000	131,150
H-75	Rated $20,000 to $35,000	76,700
H-76	Rated $10,000 to $20,000	76,000
H-77	Rated $5,000 to $10,000	43,200
H-78	Rated under $5,000	22,350
H-79	Listed but unrated	328,440
H-79S1	Headquarters	298,400
H-79S2	Branches	30,040
RETAIL TRADE BY SIC		
5211+	Lumber & other building materials dlrs.	49,370
5211A+	Lumber, plywood & building mat'ls. dlrs.	29,080

S.I.C.	LIST	QUANT.
5211B+	Roofing & siding materials dealers	5,400
5211C+	Window, jalousie & door dealers	9,680
5231+	Paint, glass & wallpaper stores	42,660
5231A+	Paint dealers	31,950
5231B+	Wallpaper dealers	13,930
5251+	Hardware stores	36,210
5261+	Retail nursery & garden stores	33,330
5261A+	Nurserymen	12,970
5261B+	Garden supply stores	9,330
5261C+	Lawn mower dealers	9,220
5271+	Mobile home dealers	11,420
Department Stores		
5311+	Total department stores	29,400
5311A	Total discount department stores	9,470
5311AS4	Independent discount department stores	2,190
5311AS5/9	Chains 2 or more stores	7,280
5311AS1/20	Headquarters	340
5311AS3	Chain outlets	6,950
5311BS4+	Independent department stores	4,720
5311BS5/9	Chains, 2 or more stores	9,060
5311BS1/20	HQ & buying offices	950
5311BS3	Chain outlets	8,110
5331+	Variety stores	17,210
5331S4+	Independent variety stores	6,920
5331S5/9	Chains, 2 or more stores	8,660
5331S1/20	HQ & buying offices	760
5331S3	Chain outlets	7,900

S.I.C.	LIST	QUANT.
5399+	Misc. general mdse stores	31,530
5399A+	Army & Navy goods stores	1,100
5399B+	Salvage & surplus mdse stores	3,170
Grocery Stores **+By type of ownership—**		
5411+	Total grocery stores	175,840
5411S4+	Independent grocery stores	141,860
5411S5/9	Chains, 2 or more stores	33,980
5411S1/20	HQ & buying offices	3,710
5411S3	Chain outlets	30,270
5411A+	Delicatessens	13,250
5411B+	Gourmet shops	1,370
5411W1	Convenience food stores	19,330
5422	Freezer & locker meat purveyors	540
5423+	Meat & fish markets	29,550
5423A+	Meat markets	22,350
5423B+	Fish & seafood stores	5,170
5431+	Fruit & vegetable mkts	7,060
5441+	Candy, nut & confectionery stores	7,280
5441A+	Candy stores	5,620
5441B+	Nut stores	760
5451+	Dairy products stores	10,360
5451A+	Cheese stores	2,420
5460	Retail bakeries	16,490
5499+	Misc. food stores	6,840
5499A+	Health food stores	5,880

While it's possible for a firm to compile and maintain its own mailing list, most direct-mail advertisers acquire mailing lists from a **mailing list broker** or a **mailing list compiler**. Developing a mailing list and maintaining it (updating addresses, purchase records, and other behavioral information) require more human and financial resources than most advertisers want—or even need—to invest. Basically, mailing list brokers provide a market. They offer thousands of mailing lists that have been built through direct response and compilation. Brokers either rent or sell lists. List rentals depend on a number of factors, but they average $50 per thousand names for a one-time use (see Figure 18.6).

THE COSTS OF DIRECT-MAIL ADVERTISING

Costs of using direct mail vary widely. A one-color, one-page letter will obviously cost much less than a full-color, 64-page catalog. To help advertisers estimate direct-mail costs, the Direct Marketing Association asked 150 DMA members to complete a worksheet for the production of a "standard" direct-mail package with given components. The average figures for quantities of 10,000 to 1 million are shown in Exhibit 18.1.

Costs, of course, are only meaningful in relationship to achieving objectives. Most broadcast and print advertising is not expected to complete the entire sales process. Increasing levels of awareness or altering consumer attitudes are typical goal expectations within the broadcast and print media. Direct-mail advertising is usually expected to complete the

EXHIBIT 18.1

Average Cost-per-Thousand of Direct Mailings*

COMPONENTS	10,000	50,000	250,000	1,000,000	TOTAL
Letter-2 pages/2 colors 8½ × 11-50 lb. white	$ 35.30	$ 31.22	$ 20.63	$ 24.95	$ 26.29
Brochure–4 colors/2 sides 17 × 22 folded to 5½ × 8½ 70 lb. coated stock	320.08	137.53	64.65	63.29	117.65
Order Card–2 colors 5 × 8 perforated-7 pt. card	39.50	28.41	15.88		21.08
Reply Envelope–1 color 5½ × 5½ 24 lb. white wove	54.31	42.31	19.06	19.50	29.71
Outside Envelope-1 color 9 × 6–24 lb. white wove	56.02	34.75	27.79	24.26	33.89
Lettershop Charges	27.59	23.19	17.88	17.16	20.51
Sub Total	$532.80	$297.42	$165.49	$168.08	$249.13
House List	$3.75	$2.25	$1.17	$1.50	$2.06
Or List Rental	55.00	53.73	55.60	60.17	57.25
Merge/Purge	8.00	6.25	9.39	6.96	8.08
Postage	113.75	107.50	107.78	108.88	109.04
Additional package costs: art and preparation	0.00	0.00	13.33	9.53	11.95
Grand Total (in house)	$658.30	$413.41	$297.15	$294.94	$308.25
Grand Total (list rental)	$709.55	$464.89	$351.58	$353.61	$437.45

*Compiled from the results of a survey conducted by DMA. Includes typesetting and printing costs only. Statistics should be viewed with caution due to small respondent bases.
Source: Research Department, Direct Marketing Association, New York, 1984.

entire sales process. Therefore, direct mail's high cost per thousand is accepted by advertisers.

Appendix 4 in this text contains a worksheet illustrating how to calculate the profitability of direct-mail advertising and the number of returns necessary to break even.

WHEN TO USE DIRECT MAIL AS AN ADVERTISING MEDIUM

Despite the rising costs of third-class mailing rates and the overall high cost per thousand of direct-mail advertising, marketers have increased their usage of direct mail for the reasons of flexibility, effectiveness, and accountability. However, it is best used as an advertising medium under the following circumstances:

- **The advertiser has a narrowly defined target market.** Direct mail is the only medium that can provide both mass and individual coverage. Publisher's Clearing House, *Reader's Digest*, and book and record clubs mail millions of pieces each year. Direct mail is obviously important to them. At the same time, the value of direct mail is also appreciated by advertisers who have more narrowly defined target audiences—the trade or technical school that seeks high school graduates from a particular geographic region; the machine tool manufacturer who has less than one thousand prospects; or the new neighborhood restaurant that wants to distribute introductory coupons to a small geographic area. For advertisers like these, direct mail is the most efficient and effective medium.

- **The advertiser needs to explain a product.** Because direct mail is not constrained by time or space, it is an ideal medium for advertisers who need to explain their offerings. Relevant buying information about a trip around the world, office equipment, insurance policies, and educational programs can best be communicated through direct mail.

- **The advertiser is interested in short-term, direct response.** Although direct-mail advertising is sometimes used to say "thank you" or "welcome to our company," its power as a marketing tool is most evident when it's used to complete the sales process. To earn its way, direct mail is usually expected to get an immediate response—order a product, seek more information, enter a contest or sweepstakes, etc.

OUTDOOR ADVERTISING

Outdoor advertising consists of standardized and regulated signs that are designed to expose target markets to advertising messages when they are not at home. Although it is the oldest advertising medium, today outdoor is primarily used as a support medium for radio and television. Its comparatively slow growth is a result of the impact that the broadcast media have had on our lives. Years ago, handbills (an early form of outdoor advertising) were an important source of information. Today, we rely on the broadcast and print media. Ironically, outdoor reaches more people, faster and more efficiently than any other advertising medium. The strengths of outdoor continue to attract advertisers at both the national and local levels, and in 1986 the dollar volume invested in outdoor advertising was just under $1 billion.[4] Many of the largest advertisers invest heavily in outdoor to:

1. Help introduce new brands
2. Enhance broadcast and print advertising
3. Generate high levels of awareness within short periods of time
4. Reach the target market away from the home or business environment

Exhibit 18.2 lists the top 25 spenders in outdoor advertising.

TYPES OF OUTDOOR ADVERTISING

Every outdoor sign you see is not outdoor advertising. The distinction between outdoor advertising and the random-sized signs that are scattered throughout the landscape is one of standardization and regulation. Out-

EXHIBIT 18.2

The Top 25 Outdoor Advertisers, 1985

RANK	ADVERTISER	EXPENDITURE (in thousands of dollars)
1	RJR/Nabisco	$95,239
2	Philip Morris Cos.	66,991
3	Loews Corp.	25,171
4	Batus Inc.	22,560
5	Jos. E. Seagram & Sons	15,554
6	American Brands	7,709
7	Grand Metropolitan	7,203
8	Hiram Walker Inc.	7,073
9	McDonald's Corp.	6,914
10	National Distillers & Chemical Corp.	5,211
11	Brown-Forman Co.	5,162
12	Anheuser-Busch Cos.	5,105
13	U.S. Government	4,906
14	Rapid-American Corp.	4,528
15	Holiday Corp.	3,896
16	Coca-Cola Co.	3,852
17	Whirlpool Corp.	3,720
18	General Motors Corp.	3,633
19	PepsiCo Inc.	3,387
20	Ford Motor Co.	3,222
21	Distillers Somerset Group	3,067
22	Chrysler Corp.	3,027
23	Southland Corp.	2,908
24	Bacardi Corp.	2,840
25	Marriott Corp.	2,466

Source: *Advertising Age*, September 4, 1986, 116.

door advertising is subject to local, state, and federal laws governing sign placement. Also, sizes of outdoor advertising signs have been standardized to maintain a consistent look and to help the advertising become a part of the environment it serves.

There are two basic types of standardized outdoor advertising: the poster panel and the painted bulletin. Both types are built on leased property and then rented to advertisers by independent outdoor advertising companies.

Poster Panels A **poster panel** is a form of outdoor advertising available in three sizes: the 24-sheet, the 30-sheet, and the bleed. "Bleed" refers to a design that extends to the edge of the advertising space. The proportion of all three sizes is 2¼ to 1:

TYPE OF POSTER	DIMENSIONS
24-sheet poster	19' 6" × 8' 8"
30-sheet poster	21' 7" × 9' 7"
Bleed posters	22' 8" × 10' 5"

Poster panels give an advertiser an efficient way to build high reach and frequency within a short time. A common outdoor schedule will reach

FIGURE 18.7

Painted and Embellished Bulletins

Source: Courtesy of the Institute of Outdoor Advertising.

over 80 percent of a market within 30 days with a frequency of about 13. Average cost per thousand ranges from $.60 to $.90. Posters are an excellent way to help introduce a brand because of the strong product/package identification that can be communicated to a high proportion of the population.

Painted Bulletins A **painted bulletin** is a larger sign than a poster panel: 48 feet long by 14 feet wide. They are usually produced one at a time by an artist at the outdoor company studio, using a design provided by the advertiser. The bulletins can be put up in sections on location or they can be painted directly at the location. Some advertisers use preprinted paper *(printed bulletins)* to maintain uniformity from market to market. In any case, the design proportion is always 3½ to 1. Bulletins are sold as individual units, usually on a 12-, 24-, or 36-month basis. The *rotary bulletin* is moved every 60 or 90 days to different locations while the *permanent bulletin* remains in one location throughout the contract period.

An *embellished bulletin* is a painted bulletin that has projections extending from the basic structure. Because of the added size and flexibility of the embellished bulletin, advertisers use it to achieve special effects.

Average cost for a bulletin is $1,000 to $3,000 per month. The lease cost includes production, which is done by the outdoor company. The large format of the bulletin and the possibilities for using extensions bring an air of prestige and dominance to a product. Although bulletins are more expensive than posters (average cost per thousand ranges between $1 and $2) and require a longer time to build reach and frequency, they are an ideal way to create a powerful visual impact at key locations within a market.

HOW TO BUY OUTDOOR ADVERTISING: SHOWINGS AND GRPs

Outdoor advertising has some obvious limitations as an advertising medium; nonetheless, many advertisers recognize that outdoor can make a significant contribution to achieving media objectives. Outdoor is used when the advertiser is interested in:

- Developing high levels of awareness to a large segment of the market

- Maximizing frequency at low cost

- Maintaining or extending communication with the target market

- Bringing increased communication pressure to specific geographic markets

In most markets, poster panels are sold in a package called a **showing.** Showings are outdoor's equivalent of gross rating points. For example, a #100 showing is the media equivalent of 100 daily gross rating points. Showing sizes do not indicate the number of poster panels used but rather the percentage of the population reached. A #50 showing will expose 50 percent of the population of a given market to the message daily. On the average, a #50 showing will reach over 80 percent of a market within thirty days. An advertiser can purchase a #100 showing, a #75 showing, a #50 showing, or a #25 showing.

Advertisers first decide the degree of exposure they are interested in achieving and then purchase the appropriate showing level from the outdoor company. The number of poster panels it takes to achieve a particular showing level depends on both the size and traffic patterns of the market (see Exhibit 18.3).

EXHIBIT 18.3

Cost of 30-Sheet Poster Advertising in Top 20 U.S. Markets (#50 showing)

RANK	MARKET	NUMBER OF PLANTS	NUMBER OF POSTERS	TOTAL MONTHLY COST
1	New York	5	550	$235,724
2	Los Angeles	3	520	213,050
3	Chicago	3	298	95,608
4	Philadelphia	3	278	105,620
5	San Francisco	2	243	100,321
6	Boston	1	170	63,875
7	Detroit	1	92	43,700
8	Dallas-Ft. Worth	4	77	35,712
9	Washington, D.C.	1	26	10,180
10	Houston	1	118	33,798
11	Cleveland	2	158	52,967
12	Pittsburgh	1	98	32,004
13	Minneapolis-St. Paul	1	110	36,850
14	Miami	1	106	40,202
15	Atlanta	3	138	42,096
16	Seattle-Tacoma	1	80	30,285
17	St. Louis	1	80	32,640
18	Tampa-St. Petersburg	1	75	21,678
19	Denver	2	61	16,750
20	Sacramento-Stockton	3	77	27,925
Totals		40	3,355	$1,270,985

Source: Media Cost Guide 1985 (New York: ad forum, Inc., April-June 1985).

CREATIVITY IN OUTDOOR ADVERTISING

The obvious creative limitation of outdoor advertising is the demand for brevity. Outdoor messages are viewed from distances of 100 feet or more and by people in motion; therefore, the need for high-impact, clear communication is critical. Creators of outdoor advertising have three elements to work with: copy, design, and the outdoor structure.

In addition to brevity, outdoor copy must communicate a single, relevant point. The best outdoor designs are bold, dramatically display the brand name, and help communicate the copy. Figure 18.8 presents some

---

FIGURE 18.8

Examples of Successful Outdoor Advertising

Outdoor advertising must communicate a relevant point.

Outdoor advertising can dramatically display the brand name.

Source: Courtesy of Mars Inc.

Source: Courtesy of Heublein Inc.

In this provocative advertising, a "bite" was removed each week from the original design, over a period of 13 weeks, to convey the message.

Source: Courtesy of the Western Insecticide Company.

outstanding examples of outdoor advertising designs that enhance communication.

Dramatic effects are created in outdoor advertising by taking advantage of unusually large space, lighting or other special effects, or multiple units of space. Western Insecticide Company's four-design series in Figure 18.8 demonstrates what can be accomplished by making full use of available materials.

TRANSIT ADVERTISING

Transit advertising consists of advertising messages carried on the inside or outside of more than 70,000 vehicles (buses, subways, and taxis, etc.) and posters that are located in transportation stations (bus, rail, subway, and air). Transit advertising is similar to outdoor advertising in many ways; however, it represents a very small proportion of the amount invested in advertising. In 1985, approximately $60 million was invested in transit advertising.[5]

Like outdoor, transit requires short messages and is used to support advertising in the other major media. Also, transit is an efficient way to reach a variety of consumers with a high level of frequency. Unlike outdoor, however, transit audiences often are able to spend a considerable amount of time with the message. This has made possible the use of the *take-one*, a card or other piece of literature attached to the transit sign. Take-ones give the consumer the opportunity to request additional information or even order a product. Take-ones also give the advertiser a way to measure advertising effectiveness.

FIGURE 18.9

Transit Advertising: High Exposure, Low Cost per Thousand

TYPES OF TRANSIT ADVERTISING

A *car card* is placed inside the vehicle, usually above the windows or at the middle or end of the vehicle. Inside displays are usually sold on a monthly basis; an advertiser can purchase showings of 100 percent, 50 percent, or 25 percent of the fleet. Most transit riders travel on the same form of transportation twice a day, five days per week; therefore, the use of car cards allows the advertiser to generate high levels of frequency.

An *outside display* is placed on the sides, front, and back of buses and taxis. The displays are also bought on the basis of showings. While they reach a wider audience than car cards, they do not permit the use of take-ones.

A *station poster* is located in transportation terminals and is available in a variety of sizes and shapes. Some station posters are very large, back-lit transparencies that combine the best creative elements of outdoor with the response mechanisms of car cards. Advertisers can purchase a single poster at one location or multiple posters at a number of terminals in several geographic markets. Although posters can be purchased for a one-month period, substantial discounts are offered for longer periods.

A CLOSER LOOK

AIRPORT ADVERTISING

The growth of airline travel has created another opportunity to extend advertising communication to customers and prospects—airport advertising. This form of transit advertising is experiencing significant growth because of its ability to reach a large, affluent market.

What does it cost? Monthly figures at the Dallas-Ft. Worth Airport, for example, are as follows: four dioramas, $3,000; four two-sheet posters, $1,000; or four full cylinders, $5,600. Estimates place the monthly audience at a whopping 7 million.

Source: Courtesy of ACKERLEY AIRPORT ADVERTISING, INC.

SPECIALTY ADVERTISING

Like direct mail, specialty advertising is used to reach a tightly defined target market. **Specialty advertising** consists of articles of merchandise imprinted with an advertiser's message and distributed without obligation to the recipient. The first known use of specialty advertising took place over 100 years ago when an insurance agent discovered that his business increased among clients to whom he had given calendars imprinted with his name.[6] Today, specialty advertising is the sixth largest advertising medium, with annual billings well over $2 billion.[7] It is a widely used, flexible medium that allows advertisers to leave a lasting impression among their target audiences.

TYPES OF SPECIALTY ADVERTISING

It's estimated that over 15,000 different articles of merchandise are available as specialty advertising. The medium consists of four categories:[8]

MERCHANDISE CATEGORY	PERCENTAGE OF DOLLAR VOLUME IN INDUSTRY
Writing instruments	21%
Calendars	15
Business gifts	15
Other imprinted specialties (yardsticks, coffee mugs, notebooks, keychains, T-shirts, etc.)	49

When any of the above categories are used as an incentive to help fulfill the marketer's goals, the merchandise is known as a **premium.** The "free

FIGURE 18.10

An Example of
a Self-Liquidating Premium

gift with purchase" offers that are frequently found at cosmetic counters are examples of the use of premiums—to get the "free gift," you are obliged to purchase a product. The glass pumpkin jar in the Dunkin' Donuts ad in Figure 18.10 is a *self-liquidating premium:* a premium offered to consumers for a sum of money that covers the cost of the premium plus any handling and postage costs.

STRUCTURE OF THE SPECIALTY ADVERTISING INDUSTRY

The specialty advertising industry consists of three main components: 1) suppliers, 2) distributors or counselors, and 3) direct selling houses (see Figure 18.11). *Suppliers* are producers of the merchandise. They manufacture, import, convert, or imprint any of the merchandise categories mentioned above. *Specialty advertising distributors* are also known as *counselors* because they call on advertisers and their advertising agencies to suggest ways that specialty advertising can help achieve advertising objectives. A distributor organization can consist of as few salespeople as one or as many as several hundred. Basically, a distributor is an independent sales agent representing many different and often competing suppliers. *Direct*

FIGURE 18.11

How the Specialty Advertising
Industry Is Organized

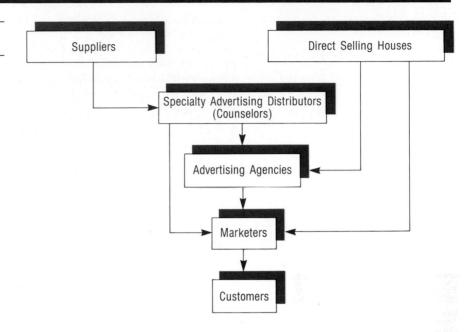

selling houses are both supplier and distributor. They produce many of their
own products and sell directly to advertisers through their own sales
staffs. There are only about a dozen direct selling houses in the United
States, and they tend to be quite large, employing hundreds of salespeople each.

WHEN TO USE SPECIALTY ADVERTISING

One of the advantages of specialty advertising is its versatility. It can be
used effectively by advertisers of all sizes and it can be used to help accomplish a number of advertising objectives. Among the most common
uses of specialty advertising are to:

- **Reinforce other media advertising.** Pilot Freight Carriers Company
  reproduced its print advertisements onto coffee mugs and then distributed the mugs to its top customers. This use of specialty advertising allowed the company to keep its primary advertising message in
  front of the target market throughout the campaign.

- **Maintain or create high levels of brand recognition.** Imprinting a
  brand name on specialty advertising merchandise and then distributing it to the target market is an ideal way to maintain high levels of
  brand awareness.

- **Stimulate customer action.** Harris Caloric Company wanted to
  draw prospective dealers of its products to the company's trade show
  booth. Prior to the show, Harris mailed executive desk folders to 240
  selected dealers. What was an otherwise attractive folder was marred
  by a message on the cover. The message read: "Come to the Harris
  booth and get your own personalized nameplate to cover this message." Sixty-three percent of the targeted audience followed the message and visited the Harris booth.

- **Build interest among the target audience.** One method of distributing specialty advertising is to use the *collection approach:* the recipient receives articles of no real value until a complete set has been accumulated. The marketer then has the opportunity to build high levels of interest among an audience that begins to anticipate the next delivery. Cooper Tire & Rubber Company used the collection approach to get new dealers. They sent three cocktail glasses etched with the likenesses of animals considered to be candidates for extinction to 282 retail and wholesale tire outlet owners and managers. A letter from the vice-president of sales accompanied the first glass, noting that although some people may think of the independent tire dealer as an "endangered species," Cooper didn't. The letter with the third glass promised that a sales representative would call the following week to bring three more glasses to complete the set. By the end of the campaign, Cooper had acquired 49 new dealers.

As Exhibit 18.4 shows, the applications of specialty advertising are almost endless. Although specialty advertising can be used successfuly as a primary medium, its comparatively high cost per thousand limits its use to mass audiences. It is, however, unmatched in its ability to deliver a lasting impression. An imprinted, disposable pen will last for a month or two, calendars deliver advertising messages for at least a year, and some specialty merchandise keeps working for the advertiser for years.

TRADE SHOWS AND EXHIBITS

Trade shows and exhibits are not technically advertising media; however, they are so strongly related to advertising decisions that they must be considered when developing the media plan. Trade shows and exhibits give the advertiser an opportunity to reach the target audience in a unique way.

In 1985, more than $10 billion was invested in over 11,000 trade shows, conventions, and exhibits. The 44 million people who attended a trade show or exhibit attest to their popularity and importance.[9] Trade shows are usually sponsored by a trade association (for example, the National Machine Tool Builders' Association, the National Home Builders' Association, or the National Housewares Association). They are important because they bring buyers and sellers together and allow face-to-face interaction. The National Machine Tool Builders' Association show, for example, consists of hundreds of exhibitors (manufacturers of machine tools) who display their products and services. The trade show environment allows the exhibitor to demonstrate products, answer questions, meet new customers, collect names for a mailing list and, in many cases, transact a sale.

Marketers participate in a trade show or exhibit by renting exhibit space from the show's sponsor. The cost of space depends on the anticipated attendance and the other costs associated with leasing the exhibit area. Some shows draw thousands of attendees and others may be quite small. Several months before the exhibit, the marketer decides if the trade show will help accomplish the marketing goals and if the exhibit costs can

EXHIBIT 18.4

Applications of Specialty Advertising

A FEW MORE OF THE MANY THINGS SPECIALTY ADVERTISING CAN DO

Revive old accounts

Serve as product container

Insure continued patronage

Stimulate ad readership

Introduce new sales personnel

Save salesperson's time

Add spice to co-op advertising

Keep sales message alive

Build convention attendance

Keep sales message visible

Symbolize success

Increase survey response rate

Smooth over hard feelings

Build unity through co-op

Facilitate policy changes

Say "Thank you"

Attract new employees

Promote safety within company

Supplement other advertising efforts

Establish prestige

Reduce prejudices

Create corporate identity

Build broadcast audience

Spotlight favorable publicity

Make customer feel important

Obtain third party endorsements

Imply third party endorsements

Introduce new service

Introduce new management

Serve as souvenir in gift shop

Build customer loyalty

Round out marketing plan

Serve as dealer loader

Symbolize friendship

Promote meeting attendance

Collect from delinquent accounts

Reduce entertainment costs

Reward sales force

Raise funds

Commemorate special occasions

Encourage quality control

Symbolize safety effort to OSHA

Stimulate window displays

Symbolize new promotional campaign

Announce marketing plans

Symbolically apologize

Discourage brand substitution

Deliver institutional message

Tell success story

Publicize company policy

Increase catalog distribution

Stimulate word-of-mouth advertising

Serve as sample holder

Produce direct sales

Educate prospects about needs

Promote early buying

Enhance direct mail response

Target message to influentials

Create new buying habits

Stimulate grand opening traffic

Reduce required sales calls

Enhance employee pride in company

Impress present stockholders

Stimulate information requests

Enhance product distinctiveness

Improve community relations

Keep company's name in buyer's mind

Encourage trial usage

Reach altogether new target groups

Strengthen brand loyalty

Give sales reps something new to discuss

Increase psychological involvement

Enlist spouse's support

Extend peak sales season

Focus appeal to a specific segment

Produce sales leads

Stimulate sample ordering

Help organize sales presentations

Get users to recommend company

Increase product usage

Spotlight product or service features

Attract new users

Reach hard-to-see prospects

Test pulling power of an ad medium

Appeal to competitor's customers

Promote multiple-unit sales

Improve employee loyalty

Attract new stockholders

Discourage competing salespeople

Boost P-O-P sales

Welcome to community

Reduce vandalism

Promote demonstrations

Encourage use of P-O-P

Project ideas for new uses

Offset competitive promotions

Offset seasonal slump

Give recognition for achievement

Encourage opening charge accounts

Reduce employee turnover

Open new distribution channels

Reduce need for price cutting

Discourage pilferage

Recognize valued suppliers

Encourage suggestions

Enhance entertainment events

Add value to business lunch

Recognize volunteers

Show sympathy

Build church attendance

Enter new territories

Encourage plant visitation

Say "Please"

Reward long-time service

Build work-group unity

Symbolize care for employees' families

Extend contest prize coverage

Involve community youth

Raise school spirit

Symbolize philanthropy

Source: Courtesy of Specialty Advertising Association International.

be justified. Once exhibit space has been rented, the marketer must also build or rent an exhibit, transport any products that should be displayed, and arrange for the staffing of the exhibit. The total cost of participating in a trade show is often quite high. When compared with other media, trade shows and exhibits also have a very high cost per thousand figure.

Nevertheless, this medium is important for many marketers (particularly for business-to-business marketers) and it is used primarily when:

1. It is important for the marketer to demonstrate products.

2. The marketer has a new product or product line and wants to introduce it to a large number of potential buyers at one time.

3. The custom of the industry is to sell merchandise in the trade show environment (the apparel industry, for example).

4. The manufacturer is seeking new distributors or distributors are seeking manufacturers.

5. Sales terms (price, delivery, quantities, credit, etc.) need to be negotiated.

POINT-OF-PURCHASE ADVERTISING

Point-of-purchase advertising (POP) involves in-store displays, usually produced at the manufacturer's expense for use by dealers of the product. The forms of point-of-purchase advertising range widely, from inexpen-

---

FIGURE 18.12

An Effective Use of Point-of-Purchase Advertising

Source: Courtesy of the Noxell Corporation, Hunt Valley, MD.

A CLOSER LOOK

TRADE SHOWS IN THE UNITED STATES

In 1985, over 125,000 companies exhibited their goods and services to more than 4 million people. These figures, however, account for only the 150 largest trade shows. Estimates for the entire industry are over $10 billion spent on over 11,000 trade shows, which were attended by over 44 million people who spent another $11 billion in the process of attending.

Following is a list of the five largest shows and some key projections on what the average trade show should look like by 1991.

The Average Trade Show in 1991	
Net square feet of exhibit space:	315,639
Number of exhibiting companies:	967
Number of attendees:	32,674
Cost per square foot:	$17.19
Average number of hotel rooms used:	7,260
Value to host city:	$14.2 million

RANK	SHOW	NUMBER OF EXHIBITING COMPANIES	EXHIBIT SPACE (in feet)	ATTENDANCE
1	International Winter Consumer Electronics Show (January)	1,411	808,000	101,665
2	International Summer Consumer Electronics Show (June)	1,323	756,000	102,731
3	Comdex/Fall (November)	1,230	701,000	85,300
4	National Hardware Show (August)	3,011	689,000	77,685
5	Print '85 (April)	726	680,000	67,000

Sources: Research Report, No. 17, January 1984, Trade Show Bureau, New Canaan, Connecticut; and "Trade Show 200," Tradeshow Week, Inc., Los Angeles, 1986, 20.

sively produced banners and small signs that can be snapped onto a shelf where the product is displayed, to large free-standing displays and exhibits that operate by means of electronic circuitry and computer hardware. The Clarion Electronic Color Consultant from Noxell Corp., Hunt Valley, Maryland (Figure 18.12), is an example of such sophisticated point-of-purchase advertising.

Point-of-purchase advertising is becoming more important as in-store purchase decisions increase. The Point-of-Purchase Advertising Institute (POPAI) estimates that more than 80 percent of supermarket shoppers make their final buying decisions in the store. In 1986, firms spent $9 billion on point-of-purchase advertising.[10]

DIRECTORY ADVERTISING

For many small retailers, the majority of their advertising budget is allocated to the Yellow Pages directory. We turn to a directory when we are ready to make a purchase and need to determine the name, address, or phone number of sellers. Although the Yellow Pages is the largest directory with 1985 advertising revenues of $6.8 billion, approximately 7,000 directories in the United States serve specific industries and product categories.[11]

The purpose of directory advertising is to place the advertiser's name, logo, main selling proposition, and retail locations before the buyer whenever the buyer seeks information about the advertiser's product category. Because there are so many directories in which an advertiser could advertise, it's important to understand which directories are most important to customers and how the directories are used. For example, we don't use a directory for most of the food and household products we buy. But, if we were making a customized industrial purchase, a product-specific directory, such as *The Machine and Tool Blue Book Directory*, would be very useful.

Directory advertising rates are largely determined by the directory's circulation. Both classified and display space can be purchased and many directories offer all of the creative flexibility of magazines — full color, inserts, and multiple pages. One of the important advantages of directory advertising is the long message life. Most directories are published annually; therefore, the advertiser's message is likely to receive multiple exposures.

EMERGING MEDIA

During the the past few years, it has become increasingly difficult and expensive for advertisers to reach customers and prospects through the traditional media. While changes in American society have been many, the following factors have strongly influenced the development of new media.

1. Broadcast audiences have become more fragmented. Increasing penetration of cable television and VCRs have cut into the network, prime-time audience. Not many years ago, most viewers had the choice of only three to six channels. Now, we can watch television with a remote-control device in our hands, selecting from among 40 or more channels.

2. The continual cost increases of advertising in the traditional media have caused advertisers to seek alternative ways to reach their target markets.

3. Finally, technological advances in printing and telecommunications are opening new ways to reach a target market that is spending more time outside the home.

MEDIA — NEW AND IMPROVED

There are two types of emerging media — the new and the improved. The new media are the result of entrepreneurs' understanding the changing marketplace and then creating a new (and often more targeted) way to reach target markets. The improved media are usually the result of improvements in the technology of existing media. Here are some of the emerging media:

Shopping by Television Ever since the coming of cable television, it has been predicted that shopping in the future would be done completely from the home. While we're a long way from that, millions of Americans are shopping on the Home Shopping Network (HSN), Cable Value Network (CVN), and other shop-at-home television programming. HSN is a live, 24-hour, 7-day-a-week cable service that recently sold $63 million in merchandise in six months' time. When viewers see something they want to buy, they simply call a toll-free number and charge their purchase to a credit card. As one observer put it: "It's the ultimate marriage of shopping and recreation. . . . Once you get hooked on the idea and learn to trust it, you'll buy anything."[12]

Thirty- and 60-Minute Commercials At the same time that the 15-second commercial is gaining in popularity among network television advertisers, other advertisers are finding ways to talk to viewers for as long as an hour. What types of products can be advertised for 30 or 60 minutes? The format tends to be the mini-seminar/commercials for home study courses (real estate, products sold through network marketing, etc.) and personal improvement products (weight gain/loss, hair growth, etc.).[13]

Card Decks Card decks are a way to shop at home, but through direct mail rather than television. The recipient receives a package of shrink-wrapped 3 × 5 cards, each offering a product or service from a different advertiser. On one side of the card is the advertising message and on the other, a reply form. It has been estimated that over $80 million has been invested in card deck advertising; more than 600 card decks are currently available.[14]

Shared Mailings Similar in concept to card decks, shared mailings are groups of advertising pieces from different advertisers, pulled together in one mailing and sent to selected households. The main difference is that shared mailings are not necessarily cards and they are sent to households within specific ZIP codes. (Card decks tend to be sent to businesses.) Advo-Systems is a leader in shared mailings, and it is able to customize mailing packages and send them to any of 36,000 different ZIP codes. Shared mailings provide an ideal way for local retailers to reach a very narrow target market.[15]

Theatre Advertising Theatre advertising is advertising (usually done on 35mm slides or film) that is shown to moviegoers before the feature film. Screenvision Cinema Network sells advertising time in movie theatres for $18 per thousand viewers of 60-second commercials. In 1986, Screenvision ran commercials in nearly 5,000 theatres, and although the advertiser stands the risk of irritating a moviegoer who has paid admission, the impact of the large screen and the uncluttered advertising environment has generated high recall scores.[16]

Grocery Carts and In-Store Advertising Several years ago, advertising began to appear on grocery carts. Now, at least one company (Interior Advertising Display & Directory Systems) is selling advertising on mini-billboards placed on the empty wall area between store shelves and the ceiling.

FIGURE 18.13

Public Telephone Advertising

Advertising on public phones allows advertisers to generate an immediate response from a targeted audience.

Source: Courtesy of American Telephone Advertising Corporation.

Public Telephone Advertising Each year, over 7,000,000,000 telephone calls are made from public telephones. An average local call lasts 3.5 minutes and an average long-distance call lasts 8 minutes. When this information is combined with the availability of advertising space on the public telephone, a potentially valuable advertising medium emerges. American Telephone Advertising, Inc. (ATA) sells advertising on the faceplates of public telephones (see Figure 18.13). Advertising on public telephones can be an effective advertising vehicle for advertisers who want to reach a tightly defined target market—ATA offers more than 20 distinct market segments—college campuses, hotels and restaurants, airports, convenience stores, etc.—and generate a direct response from the target.[17]

SUMMARY

One of the ways that a media plan can reach the target market creatively is through the support media. This chapter has introduced a group of media used to support broadcast and print media schedules and to extend the reach of other more widely used media. The support media include direct mail, outdoor advertising, transit advertising, specialty advertising, trade shows, point-of-purchase advertising, and directory advertising. These media are unique because they can play both a major and minor role for advertisers. Direct mail, for example, can be a mass medium and an individual medium. Outdoor is ideal for building high reach efficiently, and similarly, transit advertising can deliver advertising messages to out-of-home target markets at very low rates. Specialty advertising is a high cost per thousand medium, yet it is unmatched in its ability to create a long-lasting impression of an advertiser. Trade shows seldom play an important role for consumer goods marketers, but for business-to-business marketers they are an essential element in the communication mix. Point-of-purchase advertising is ideal for extending an advertiser's broadcast and/or print advertising into the retail location where the consumer has the opportunity to purchase the advertised brand. Directory advertising helps consumers locate important information at a crucial time—when they are ready to buy.

In addition to introducing the support media, this chapter has also shown how and when to best use them. The chapter has discussed how the support media are used to help introduce products, to generate a direct response from the marketplace, to reach the target audience when they are ready to buy, to help create brand recognition, and to reinforce major selling points.

The chapter also discussed newly emerging media—media that have evolved as the result of technological changes. It is difficult to tell how much impact these new media will have in the future. Will America, for instance, become a shop-at-home society? Will consumers tolerate advertising in theatres? The answers to these questions are unclear. What *is* clear is that no one medium can keep pace with changes in life-style and in the marketplace. The support media offer advertisers the flexibility to keep pace with such changes.

TRAVELPHONE COMPANY

TravelPhone is a marketer of cellular telephones. Because of the growing popularity of cellular phones, the company has done quite well over the past two years. In the last nine months, TravelPhone has opened sales and service offices in six U.S. cities and expanded its advertising efforts.

The primary objective of TravelPhone's advertising is to generate leads for the company's personal selling staff. The usual selling process involves a prospect calling the local sales office for product information. Although many prospects call to ask a question or to have product literature mailed to them, TravelPhone's inside sales staff has been trained to convince the caller to meet with a personal sales representative.

Because of the high ticket price of the product (average sale is $1,500), very few sales are made over the phone. Therefore, TravelPhone's inside sales staff works hard to set up an appointment between the caller and a TravelPhone sales representative. One of the reasons that TravelPhone has been successful is that the sales staff closes about 33 percent of the prospects they personally meet. The key to success is generating sales leads.

Recently, TravelPhone has experimented with alternative advertising media to try to lower the cost of generating leads. The company has just completed a media test and the results are shown below. Analyze the data and make a recommendation to TravelPhone. Which medium would you recommend to TravelPhone? Why?

MEDIUM	AMOUNT PURCHASED	ADVERTISING PERIOD	INQUIRIES	ADVERTISING COST	CLOSING RATE*
Outdoor	#50 showing, San Francisco	60 days	55,000	$210,000	10%
Direct mail (one mailing)	1,000,000 pieces	—	25,220	247,000	38
Public telephone advertising	10,000 ads in selected locations	60 days	31,500	200,000	30

*Refers to the percentage of inquiries converted into sales.

■ ■ ■

QUESTIONS FOR DISCUSSION

1. Explain the two basic advertising functions of the support media. Give an example of how the support media perform their functions.

2. Explain the differences among the following three terms: direct marketing, direct response, and direct mail.

3. Why is direct mail used by both small, local advertisers and large, national advertisers?

4. It has been suggested that mailing list brokers are providers of a market. In what sense is that true?

5. Why do you think the growth of outdoor advertising has been comparatively slow?

6. What is the difference between a #50 outdoor showing and 50 GRPs in the broadcast media?

7. List the main advantages and disadvantages of transit advertising.

8. Explain each of the following terms:
   a. self-liquidating premium
   b. specialty advertising distributors (counselors)
   c. direct selling houses

9. When compared with other advertising media, trade shows are a high cost-per-thousand medium. Yet, they are an important marketing tool for thousands of companies. Why do some companies place such a high value on exhibiting at trade shows?

10. Explain how point-of-purchase advertising can help make an advertiser's broadcast or print advertising campaign more effective.

NOTES

1. *Fact Book on Direct Response Marketing* (New York: Direct Marketing Association, 1982), xiv.

2. Ibid., xiv–xviii.

3. Ibid., 32.

4. "Total U.S. Advertising Volume," McCann-Erickson, Inc., New York, May 15, 1987.

5. Transit Advertising Association, January 10, 1986.

6. "The Case for Specialty Advertising," Specialty Advertising Association International, Irving, Texas.

7. Ibid.

8. Ibid.

9. *The Big "I"*, International Automotive Aftermarket Show and the Trade Show Bureau, New Canaan, Connecticut, 1985.

10. "New Ad Concept for Supermarkets," *Sales & Marketing Digest*, October 1986, 5; "In-Store Purchase Decisions Growing," *Marketing News*, September 26, 1986, 10; and "P-O-P Ad Industry Expects $9 Billion Volume in '86," *Marketing News*, September 26, 1986, 10.

11. Alan D. Fletcher, *Yellow Pages Advertising*, American Association of Yellow Pages Publishers, Chesterfield, Missouri, 1986, 5–7.

12. "Home Shopping Network," *American Demographics*, September 1986, 22–23.

13. Stan Rapp and Tom Collins, "Today's Media Market Offers 'Embarrassment of Riches,' " *Adweek*, November 10, 1986, 26, 30.

14. Ibid.

15. Ibid.

16. "Advertising on the Silver Screen Presents a Unique Situation," *Sales & Marketing Digest*, October 1986, p. 5.

17. "ATA Reaches Your Markets," American Telephone Advertising, Great Falls, Montana, February 1987, 2–4.

SUGGESTED READINGS

Ahrend, Herb. "61 Ways to Make Business Direct Mail Work Better." *Direct Marketing*, September 1984.

Bair, Martin. *Elements of Direct Marketing*. New York: McGraw-Hill, Inc., 1983.

Bingham, Darlene. "Poster Panels and Rotary Bulletins Are Efficient Forms of Outdoor Advertising." *Advertising/Communications Times*, October 1984.

Bonoma, Thomas. "Get More Out of Your Trade Shows." *Harvard Business Review*, January–February 1983.

Bowman, Russ. "Making Peace with Advertising." *Marketing & Media Decisions*, November 1986, 123–124.

Brickman, Franklin Jr. "Outdoor Advertising Has Grown Dramatically in Past Decade." *Advertising/Communications Times*, October 1984.

Cohen, William A. *Direct Response Marketing: An Entrepreneurial Approach*. New York: John Wiley & Sons, Inc., 1984.

"Coupons May Be Heading for a Fall." *Sales & Marketing Digest*, August 1986, 4.

Decent Exposure. Specialty Advertising Association International. Irving, Texas, 1984.

Dougherty, Philip H., "$1 Billion in Outdoor Billings." *New York Times*, February 16, 1984.

Duffy, Martin, and Melinda Skaar. *An Econometric Analysis of the Trade Show Industry*. Data Resources, Inc., Lexington, Massachusetts, September 30, 1981.

Dugas, Christine. "Ad Space Now Has a Whole New Meaning." *Business Week*, July 29, 1985, 52.

Ebel, Richard G. "Specialty Advertising: 9½ Ways to Use a Powerful Marketing Tactic." *Industrial Marketing*, February 1982.

Eicoff, Alvin. *Or Your Money Back*. New York: Crown Publishers, Inc., 1982.

Fisher, J. A. "Are Trade Shows Worth It?" *Advertising and Publishing News*, 1979.

The Guide to Mail Order Sales 1985. Garden City, N.Y.: Hoke Communications, 1986.

"Inside Report: Trade Show Marketing." *Marketing News*, May 10, 1985, 12–15.

Johnson, Lewis. "Trade Show Marketing—Adjusting to the Needs of a Changing Market Place." Trade Show Bureau, New Canaan, Connecticut, 1985.

Kessler, Felix. "The Costly Coupon Craze." *Fortune*, June 9, 1986, 83–84.

Konikow, Robert B. "Exhibiting at Trade Shows." *Management Aids for Small Manufacturers*. U.S. Small Business Administration, MA 245, Fort Worth, Texas, March 20, 1975.

Krugman, Dean M. "Evaluating the Audiences of the New Media." *Journal of Advertising* 14, April 1985, 21–27.

Lipman, Joanne. "As Network TV Fades, Many Advertisers Try Age-Old Promotions." *Wall Street Journal*, August 26, 1986, 1, 15.

Mee, William W. "How to Use the Trade Show as a Marketing Tool." *Creative Magazine*, February 1979.

Morrissey, William R. "Gain Competitive Edge with Data-Based Direct Marketing." *Marketing News*, March 15, 1985.

Reece, Chuck. "Marketers Finally Check Out Simple Idea." *Adweek*, September 30, 1985, 50.

Robins, J. Max. "Making Point-of-Purchase More Pointed." *Adweek*, November 10, 1986, 8.

Stone, Bob. *Successful Direct Marketing Methods*. 2d ed. Chicago: Crain Books, 1979.

"Trade Shows—Essential Factor in the Marketing Mix." White Paper Series no. 10, Business/Professional Advertising Association, New York, June 1982.

"Trends in Outdoor Advertising." Institute of Outdoor Advertising, New York, 1984.

Yellow Pages Update. vol. 1, no. 2, American Association of Yellow Pages Publishers, Chesterfield, Missouri, Fall 1986.

EVALUATING MEDIA PLANS

Key Terms

Standard Rate & Data Service (SRDS)

Mediamark Research, Inc. (MRI)

Simmons Market Research Bureau, Inc. (SMRB)

Insight Retrieval System

Media Imperatives

Leading National Advertisers, Inc. (LNA)

Broadcast Advertisers Reports, Inc. (BAR)

A. C. Nielsen Company

Audimeter

Arbitron Ratings Company

Area of Dominant Influence (ADI)

Donovan Data Systems Company

Audit Bureau of Circulations (ABC)

Business Publications Audit of Circulation, Inc. (BPA)

calibration survey

map recall method

Traffic Audit Bureau (TAB)

Exhibition Validation Council (EVC)

Learning Objectives

To create a framework for evaluating media plans

To outline the major sources of media data and their specific uses

To describe how to evaluate the effectiveness of the media plan

If you watch a sports program on television, chances are you'll be exposed to one or more commercials for beer. A combination of the right environment and the ability to reach the target market has made television the primary advertising medium for beer advertisers.

Though one of the largest spenders in the product category, Detroit-based Stroh Brewing Company found its $31 million budget dwarfed by that of industry leaders:

BRAND	EXPENDITURE (in millions of dollars)	PERCENTAGE OF CATEGORY
Miller	153	24.8
Budweiser	134	21.8
Michelob	67	10.9
Coors	59	9.5
Stroh's	31	5.1
All others	172	27.9

Like the other major advertisers in the beer category, Stroh Brewing had traditionally allocated approximately 80 percent of its budget to television. By 1985, however, Stroh management was concerned about its media schedule, particularly about its reliance on television. The firm's concerns involved the lack of media weight against competitors' much larger television budgets and the changes that were taking place within television viewing (audience fragmentation and declining viewer attention as a result of increased use of remote controls, commercial clutter, and VCRs). Stroh management decided to explore the effectiveness

IT TOOK GENERATIONS OF UNBUSINESSLIKE DECISIONS TO GET US WHERE WE ARE TODAY.

of increasing the use of newspapers as a medium. The objective of the proposed test was to determine if a combination of TV and newspapers would be more effective than TV alone.

First, the company compiled a list of 15 markets in which the Stroh brand was strong. The list included such major cities as New York, Philadelphia, and Detroit as well as less populated Oklahoma City, Louisville, and Little Rock. The company then approved a weekly gross rating point level consistent with its TV-buying pattern. The test would be aimed at Stroh's target market: 18- to 54-year-old blue-collar men with an annual household income of less than $35,000. The objective was to compare an all-spot TV campaign with campaigns that combined TV spots and newspaper advertising. Creative units included 30-second TV spots and quarter-

page newspaper ads. The combination campaigns were tested over a four-week period in fall and winter, using the same budget of $2.4 million. The test plan detailed reach and frequency, impressions, gross rating points, and cost per thousand for both types of campaigns.

The results were eye-opening: the use of television and newspapers in combination created a significant increase in all measured criteria. Increases in unduplicated reach and frequency ranged from 8 to 15 percent. GRP levels improved as much as 184 points, and the number of gross impressions under the combination campaigns rose by as much as 29 million. The media combination also proved to be more efficient, lowering the cost per thousand reach and cost per thousand impressions. Interestingly, newspapers generated more gross rating points than TV for the dollars invested. Although the combination plan budgeted only 25 percent for newspaper advertising, newspapers delivered 38 percent of the total gross rating points across all three demographic characteristics.

Sources: "1985 Top Ten Advertising Categories and Their Top Brand Families," *Marketing & Media Decisions*, June 1986, 58; and Roy G. Blackfield, "NASA Proposes Combination Newspaper, TV Campaign for Stroh's," *INAME News*, September 1986, 35–36. Photo courtesy of P. Blum—Historian, Stroh Brewery Co.

INTRODUCTION

One of the most important aspects of a media plan is an evaluation of its effectiveness. Because such a large percentage—as much as 70 to 80 percent—of the advertising budget is allocated to media, evaluating the effectiveness of a media plan is particularly important. Unfortunately, the task is not a simple one. It's complicated for the following reasons:

1. **Advertisers must make intramedia comparisons.** Is a 60-second television commercial as effective as a full-page magazine advertisement? Does a 30-second radio commercial have the same exposure capability of an outdoor sign? Is a direct-mail brochure more valuable than a newspaper advertisement? The answers to these questions are, of course, difficult to know, and their difficulty complicates the assessment of media plans. In Chapters 16 and 17 it was pointed out that gross rating points are determined differently for different types of media. Therefore, a gross rating point in television is not exactly the same as one in outdoor.

2. **Advertisers must make intermedia comparisons.** Is a page in the oversized *Life* magazine the equivalent of a full page in *Reader's Digest* or *TV Guide?* How about the differences among radio formats, television programs, and daily newspapers? Although circulation and audience size can be determined easily enough, a broader concept of effectiveness must also consider the psychological effects of media placement. For example, the editorial environment of *National Geographic* enhances the credibility of and interest in advertisements for vacation spots and travel-related products and services.

3. **Advertisers lack standardized media measurements.** One of the problems in measuring the effectiveness of media plans is that there are so many different techniques to use. Some services have been around for a long time; however, the complexities of managing media data and measuring media effectiveness have encouraged the development of new approaches to measurement. As you will see in this chapter, there is no one, accepted measure for all media types. While this lack of a universally accepted measure may be justified, it further complicates the assessment of media plans.

   Despite these obstacles, there are many valid, reliable ways to approach the measurement of media effectiveness. This chapter acquaints you with several of the most important services that are used by advertisers and advertising agencies.

A FRAMEWORK FOR EVALUATING MEDIA PLANS

The approach for evaluating media plans is straightforward: The most appropriate measure of effectiveness is the one that provides the most valid and reliable measure of the objectives. The guide for assessment of media plans should be the media objectives—the degree to which the

A CLOSER LOOK

WHO DOES THE RESEARCH?

How much money is invested annually in measuring the effectiveness of media? Recent estimates indicate that revenues of 136 research companies of the Council of American Survey Research Organizations totaled $2.1 billion in 1986, a 15.1 percent increase over 1985. Most marketing/advertising research firms perform a range of research services, including market feasibility studies, focus group studies, surveys, copytesting, and media effectiveness studies. Here's a list of the 25 largest marketing/advertising research organizations in the United States.

The Top 25 Research Organizations, 1986

RANK	ORGANIZATION	TOTAL REVENUES (in millions of dollars)	PERCENTAGE OF NONDOMESTIC REVENUES	RANK	ORGANIZATION	TOTAL REVENUES (in millions of dollars)	PERCENTAGE OF NONDOMESTIC REVENUES
1	A. C. Nielsen Co.	$615.0	60.0%	14	YSW/Clancy Shulman	22.0	—
2	IMS International	245.4	45.6	15	Walker Research	21.3	—
3	SAMI/Burke	174.5	3.5	16	Chilton Research	19.5	—
4	Arbitron Ratings Co.	137.2	—	17	ASI Market Research	17.1	—
5	Information Resources	93.6	4.0	18	Decisions Center	15.6	—
6	MRB Group	52.0	37.0	19	Louis Harris and Associates	15.5	43.0
7	M/A/R/C	47.5	—	20	Opinion Research Corp.	15.2	—
8	NFO Research	36.7	—	21	Ehrhart-Babic Group	14.5	—
9	Market Facts	36.0	—	22	National Analysts	13.3	—
10	NPD Group	35.5	1.4	23	Harte-Hanks Marketing Services Group	12.2	—
11	Westat	35.2	—	24	Mediamark Research	11.1	—
12	Maritz Marketing Research	32.9	—	25	Data Development Corp.	10.5	—
13	Elrick and Lavidge	26.7	—				

*Includes revenues for research activities only.
Source: Jack J. Honomichl, "Top 46 Companies' Growth Is Partly Illusion," *Advertising Age*, May 11, 1987, S-1–S2.

media plan delivers the desired reach, frequency, and continuity. Increases in sales and market share are achieved by skillful management of specific marketing activities (product development, pricing strategies, distribution, and promotion). The media plan is one part of the advertising element within promotion; therefore, it should be held accountable only for those tasks that it is capable of performing: locating and reaching the target markets. Exhibit 19.1 shows the relationship between marketing, advertising, and media objectives.

The data sources discussed in this chapter are useful for two purposes:

1. **To understand the relevant media environments.**

    Media plan development requires a great deal of data. Good media plans require knowledge about:

    ▪   the target market, particularly its demographics, life-styles, and media habits

EXHIBIT 19.1

Relationship and Measurement
of Marketing, Advertising,
and Media Objectives

TYPE OF OBJECTIVE	OBJECTIVE	APPROPRIATE MEASURE
Marketing	To increase sales among primary target market by 10 percent during next 12 months	Change in sales levels
Advertising	To increase awareness among primary target market by 20 percent during next 12 months	Change in awareness levels
Media	To reach 75 pcrccnt of primary target market with an average frequency of 10 times per month during the next 12 months (750 GRPs)	Determine GRP levels delivered in each month during the campaign year

- the competition's media investment patterns
- all possible media alternatives and their abilities to help fulfill the media objectives

2. **To measure the effectiveness of the media plan.**

Although there are many different sources of media information, most of those discussed in this chapter are designed to help advertisers determine:

- if the media they selected reached the designated target market
- if the media plan delivered the desired levels of reach and frequency
- if the media plan was efficient

UNDERSTANDING THE MEDIA ENVIRONMENT

Standard Rate & Data Service (SRDS) publishes a set of media directories that are widely used by both advertising agencies and advertising departments (see Exhibit 19.2). SRDS pulls together information that has been published elsewhere, organizes the information in a way that is most useful for media planners, and then makes the information available in directories that are updated on a regular basis. SRDS directories provide a convenient source of basic information about media. Media planners use SRDS for the following tasks:

1. **To determine the most appropriate media vehicles within a media type.** For example, a media planner trying to reach the top 50 U.S. markets by radio could look in SRDS' Spot Radio directory for profiles of all stations as well as their rates and other pertinent buying information.
2. **To compare the costs and efficiencies of alternative media vehicles and schedules.** For example SRDS' three print directories

---

EXHIBIT 19.2

Publications of the Standard
Rate & Data Service

—Newspaper: Rates and Data

—Co-op Source Directory

—Spot Television: Rates and Data

—Business Publication: Rates and Data

—Community Publication: Rates and Data

—Direct-Mail List: Rates and Data

—Spot Radio Small Markets Edition

—Spot Radio: Rates and Data

—Consumer Magazine and Agri-Media:
  Rates and Data

—Business Publication (Classified)

—Print Media: Production Data

—Canadian Advertising: Rates and Data

—International: Rates and Data

Source: The Books Professionals Depend On (Wilmette, Ill.: Standard Rate & Data Service, 1986).

(Business Publication, Newspaper, and Consumer Magazine and Agri-Media) contain circulation data as well as costs for all units of advertising space; therefore, a media planner can compare total costs as well as costs per thousand.

3. **To locate markets.** For instance, when a business-to-business advertiser wants to market a new product, the SRDS Business Publication directory provides a convenient way to locate the print media that serve any of 175 different markets.

Mediamark Research, Inc. (MRI) provides a comprehensive source of media/product information. Formed in 1979, the company offers advertisers and advertising agencies a number of research services; however, its most valuable service is the data collected from its large-scale surveys. MRI's surveys consist of two sets of 10,000 interviews taken among adult Americans selected in a probability sample. In a personal interview setting, respondents supply data about their use of the print and broadcast media. They are then asked to complete a comprehensive questionnaire about their usage of products and brands. The MRI data base is a combination of data from the personal interviews and from the questionnaire booklets. Because the company gathers the data twice a year, it is able to offer updated information every six months.

The MRI reports are useful because they allow media planners to learn more about the media habits of target markets. For example, the respondents' readership of 214 magazines are cross-tabulated with the consumption of nearly 6,000 different brands of products. Figure 19.1 shows part of a sample page from an MRI report.

Simmons Market Research Bureau, Inc. (SMRB) provides advertisers and advertising agencies with a variety of information about media and markets. In 1987, SMRB published its 24th annual *Study of Media and Markets*, 43 volumes of data that media planners use to make decisions. Thirteen of the volumes deal specifically with the measurement of audiences of newspapers, magazines, television, cable TV, radio, outdoor, and Yellow Pages. The media audiences are described in terms of 27 characteristics, including age, sex, income, education, occupation, marital status, number of children, geographic region, county size, and value of residence.

Another 13 SMRB volumes are devoted to consumption and purchasing data for over 800 product categories and 3,900 brands cross-tabulated by demographics and by media (see Exhibit 19.3). These data allow the media planner to make intermedia comparisons of heavy, medium, and light readers, viewers, and listeners by various demographic variables. Like MRI data, SMRB data can be combined with other data bases, such as VALS (for values and life-styles), PRIZM (for ZIP code segmentation), and ClusterPlus, to help marketers make better management decisions in marketing, advertising, and media.

In addition to their large data-based volumes on media and markets, both SMRB and MRI offer a number of other syndicated research services. SMRB's **Insight Retrieval System** is one of those services. Insight Retrieval allows marketers to analyze: 1) the demography of product users, 2) the geography of product sales, 3) the attitudes and life-styles of product user segments, and 4) the most effective media to reach market segments.

FIGURE 19.1

MRI Reports

Mediamark Research, Inc. provides valuable data to media planners.

DENTAL FLOSS   47

------------------ TIMES IN LAST 7 DAYS ------------------

BASE: ADULTS	TOTAL U.S. '000	ALL A '000	B % DOWN	C % ACROSS	D INDEX	HEAVY MORE THAN 7 A '000	B % DOWN	C % ACROSS	D INDEX	MEDIUM 3 - 7 A '000	B % DOWN	C % ACROSS	D INDEX	LIGHT LESS THAN 3 A '000	B % DOWN	C % ACROSS	D INDEX
ALL ADULTS	170599	87088	100.0	51.0	100	13741	100.0	8.1	100	47346	100.0	27.8	100	26001	100.0	15.2	100
QUINTILE I - NEWSPAPERS	34120	19008	21.8	55.7	109	3097	22.5	9.1	113	10683	22.6	31.3	113	5229	20.1	15.3	101
QUINTILE II	34125	17714	20.3	51.9	102	2882	21.0	8.4	105	9751	20.6	28.6	103	5082	19.5	14.9	98
QUINTILE III	34108	17881	20.5	52.4	103	2589	18.8	7.6	94	9929	21.0	29.1	105	5362	20.6	15.7	103
QUINTILE IV	34101	17293	19.9	50.7	99	2502	18.2	7.3	91	9378	19.8	27.5	99	5412	20.8	15.9	104
QUINTILE V	34145	15193	17.4	44.5	87	2672	19.4	7.8	97	7605	16.1	22.3	80	4916	18.9	14.4	94
QUINTILE I - RADIO	34130	17779	20.4	52.1	102	2825	20.6	8.3	103	9627	20.3	28.2	102	5328	20.5	15.6	102
QUINTILE II	34110	18456	21.2	54.1	106	3117	22.7	9.1	114	10048	21.2	29.5	106	5292	20.4	15.5	102
QUINTILE III	34125	18188	20.9	53.3	104	3240	23.6	9.5	118	9587	20.2	28.1	101	5361	20.6	15.7	103
QUINTILE IV	34116	17320	19.9	50.8	99	2444	17.8	7.2	89	9596	20.3	28.1	101	5281	20.3	15.5	102
QUINTILE V	34117	15344	17.6	45.0	88	2116	15.4	6.2	77	8488	17.9	24.9	90	4740	18.2	13.9	91
QUINTILE I - TV (TOTAL)	34121	14331	16.5	42.0	82	2642	19.2	7.7	96	7809	16.5	22.9	82	3880	14.9	11.4	75
QUINTILE II	34100	16432	18.9	48.2	94	2821	20.5	8.3	103	8956	18.9	26.3	95	4655	17.9	13.7	90
QUINTILE III	34130	18713	21.5	54.8	107	2612	19.0	7.7	95	10212	21.6	29.9	108	5890	22.7	17.3	113
QUINTILE IV	34128	18598	21.4	54.5	107	2853	20.8	8.4	104	10085	21.3	29.6	106	5659	21.8	16.6	109
QUINTILE V	34119	19014	21.8	55.7	109	2813	20.5	8.2	102	10283	21.7	30.1	109	5918	22.8	17.3	114
RADIO WKDAY: 6-10:00 AM CUME	101798	53574	61.5	52.6	103	8530	62.1	8.4	104	29224	61.7	28.7	103	15820	60.8	15.5	102
10:00 AM - 3:00 PM	65278	34403	39.5	52.7	103	5813	42.3	8.9	111	18574	39.2	28.5	103	10015	38.5	15.3	101
3:00 PM - 7:00 PM	70134	37971	43.6	54.1	106	5861	42.7	8.4	104	20543	43.4	29.3	106	11568	44.5	16.5	108
7:00 PM - MIDNIGHT	39071	21125	24.3	54.1	106	3546	25.8	9.1	113	10824	22.9	27.7	100	6755	26.0	17.3	113
RADIO AVERAGE WEEKDAY CUME	138824	72647	83.4	52.3	103	11797	85.9	8.5	106	39300	83.0	28.3	102	21549	82.9	15.5	102
RADIO WKEND: 6-10:00 AM CUME	61913	30838	35.4	49.8	98	5087	37.0	8.2	102	16824	35.5	27.2	98	8927	34.3	14.4	95
10:00 AM - 3:00 PM	68838	36866	42.3	53.6	105	5911	43.0	8.6	107	20297	42.9	29.5	106	10658	41.0	15.5	102
3:00 PM - 7:00 PM	51242	27942	32.1	54.5	107	4414	32.1	8.6	107	15359	32.4	30.0	108	8168	31.4	15.9	105
7:00 PM - MIDNIGHT	31504	17070	19.6	54.2	106	2764	20.1	8.8	109	8803	18.6	27.9	101	5503	21.2	17.5	115
RADIO AVE. WEEKEND DAY CUME	112759	59152	67.9	52.5	103	9363	68.1	8.3	103	32124	67.8	28.5	103	17665	67.9	15.7	103
RADIO FORMATS: ADULT CONTEMP	45567	25598	29.4	56.2	110	3780	27.5	8.3	103	13701	28.9	30.1	108	8117	31.2	17.8	117
ALBUM ORIENTED ROCK (AOR)	21669	12675	14.6	58.5	115	1848	13.4	8.5	106	6682	14.1	30.8	111	4146	15.9	19.1	126
ALL NEWS	8313	4444	5.1	53.5	105	854	6.2	10.3	128	2477	5.2	29.8	107	1112	4.3	13.4	88
BLACK	5666	2848	3.3	50.3	98	688	5.0	12.1	151	1437	3.0	25.4	91	722	2.8	12.7	84
CLASSICAL	5168	3322	3.8	64.3	126	544	4.0	10.5	131	1759	3.7	34.0	123	1020	3.9	19.7	130
CHR/ROCK	29416	17331	19.9	58.9	115	2243	16.3	7.6	95	9520	20.1	32.4	117	5568	21.4	18.9	124
COUNTRY	31484	15121	17.4	48.0	94	2323	16.9	7.4	92	8137	17.2	25.8	93	4661	17.9	14.8	97
EASY LISTENING	16382	9014	10.4	55.0	108	1748	12.7	10.7	133	5005	10.6	30.6	110	2261	8.7	13.8	91
GOLDEN OLDIES	5074	2800	3.2	55.2	108	417	3.0	8.2	102	1472	3.1	29.0	105	912	3.5	18.0	118
JAZZ	1596	838	1.0	52.5	103	*99	.7	6.2	77	478	1.0	29.9	108	*262	1.0	16.4	108
MOR/NOSTALGIA	10148	5242	6.0	51.7	101	914	6.7	9.0	112	3043	6.4	30.0	108	1285	4.9	12.7	83
NEWS/TALK	12624	6857	7.9	54.3	106	1188	8.6	9.4	117	3819	8.1	30.3	109	1850	7.1	14.7	96
RELIGIOUS	5604	2871	3.3	51.2	100	429	3.1	7.7	95	1461	3.1	26.1	94	981	3.8	17.5	115
URBAN CONTEMPORARY	6395	3374	3.9	52.8	103	662	4.8	10.4	129	1725	3.6	27.0	97	987	3.8	15.4	101

Source: Spring 1986 Mediamark Research Inc. Reprinted with permission.

One part of the Insight Retrieval System is SMRB's **Media Imperatives,** which helps advertisers determine appropriate media strategies by identifying individuals' media orientation. Media planners know that combinations of media are usually more effective than the use of a single medium. The question is, how much more effectiveness can be achieved by using different media combinations? Media Imperatives allows a media planner to determine the proportion of product users that would be added if the brand's media schedule were supplemented with another medium. In the example shown in Figure 19.2, television is the primary medium for many brands in the yogurt category. The bars indicate the proportion

EXHIBIT 19.3

A Sample of the Data SMRB Provides to Advertisers

TYPES OF MEDIA MEASURED

Magazines and Sunday Newspaper Supplements
American Photographer
Atlantic
Audio
Barron's
Better Homes & Gardens
Boating
Bon Appétit
Business Week
Car and Driver
Changing Times
Colonial Homes
Consumers Digest
Cosmopolitan
Country Living
Cuisine
Cycle

Cycle World
DCI: Creative Ideas for Living
Discover
Ebony
Esquire
Essence
Family Circle
Family Handyman
Family Weekly
Field & Stream
Flying
Food & Wine
Forbes
Fortune
Gentlemen's Quarterly
Glamour
Golf Digest
Golf Magazine

Good Housekeeping
Harper's Bazaar
Health
Newspapers
New York Times
Wall St. Journal
USA Today
Television
(Audience Composition)
Average Half-Hour Segments
Weekday Daytime Network
   Programs
Weekend Daytime Network
   Programs
Evening Network Programs
Weekday Local Evening News
TV Sports Events
Special Events Programming

Radio
(Average Daily CUME)
Dayparts
Station Formats
Wired Networks
Non-Wired Networks
Cable
Major Systems
Outdoor
30 Day Reach and
Frequency for:
   100 Showing
   50 Showing
   25 Showing
Yellow Pages
Frequency
Products/Services

PRODUCT & SERVICE CATEGORIES REPORTED

Apparel—Men (P-13)
Clothing bought for a woman
Coats
Jackets
Jeans & slacks
Shirts
Shoes, boots & sneakers
Sports apparel
Suits
Sunglasses
Sweaters
Banking, Investments, Memberships, Public Activities & Contributions (P-5)
Accounting services
Auto loans
Brokerage account
Checking accounts
Farm ownership
Gold/silver
I.R.A. or Keogh plan

Memberships
Mortgages
NOW Accounts
Personal loans
Public activities
Contributions to public TV
Retirement &
   investment property
Safe deposit boxes
Savings accounts
Savings certificates
Securities
Treasury bills
Trust agreements
Vacation/weekend homes
Cereals, Rice, Pasta, Pizza, Mexican Foods, Fruits & Vegetables (P-20)
Baked beans
Breakfast cereals
Complete packaged prepared
   dishes & dinner mixes
Fruits/canned or jarred,
   fresh or dried

Pizzas
Potatoes/frozen,
   packaged, instant
Rice
Spaghetti & macaroni products
Spaghetti sauce
Tomato paste
Tomato sauce
Vegetables/canned or
   jarred, frozen
Home Furnishings & Home Improvements (P-9)
Clocks: Wall, Mantle,
   Desk, Standing
Dinner & tableware
   Glassware
   Crystalware
   Fine china
   Flatware
   Other dinnerware
Fluorescent & incandescent
   lighting

Home furnishings &
   household durables
   Beds/other bedroom furniture
   Blankets, electric/other
   Comforters/quilts
   Curtains & draperies
   Dining room furniture
   Mattresses
   Pianos & organs
   Telephones & telephone
      answering machines
   Pillowcases
   Sheets
   Towels
Travel (P-4)
Domestic travel
Foreign travel
Hotels & motels
Passports
Tour package
Travelers cheques
   Business, vacation, other
   purpose

of users that could be added if a brand were to supplement a TV schedule with advertising in one of the other media.

One of the major influences on a media plan is competitive spending, or knowing the volume and placement of competitive media investment. Two of the most widely used sources of this information are **Leading**

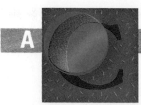

A **C**LOSER LOOK

MEDIA IMPERATIVES: WHAT ARE THEY?

The Media Imperatives system provides a way of looking at individuals in terms of their media orientation. In comparing newspapers and television, for example, a *Newspaper Imperative* is someone who is both a heavy newspaper reader and a light television viewer. *Television Imperatives* are both heavy television viewers and light readers. The *Dual Audience* group is comprised of heavy consumers of both media and the *Lightly Exposed* are lightly exposed to both media.

Among all adults, Newspaper Imperatives lead Television Imperatives by 6 percent, but among adults with an income of $30,000 or more, the newspaper-oriented have a 4-to-1 lead over the TV-oriented.

Newspapers versus Television

	Occupation: Professional/ Technical	Grade: College Graduate	Household Income: $40,000+	Individual Income: $30,000+	Total Adults
Heavy Television/ Light Newspaper	15%	13%	14%	14%	30%
Heavy Newspaper/ Light Television	51%	53%	50%	54%	33%
Heavy Television/ Heavy Newspaper	19%	21%	22%	20%	21%
Light Television/ Light Newspaper	15%	13%	14%	12%	16%

Source: 1986 SMRB Study of Media & Markets. Reprinted with permission.

FIGURE 19.2

Media Imperatives for Advertising Yogurt

Media Imperatives can help in determining appropriate media strategies. Marketers have discovered that combinations of media are usually more effective than the use of a single medium.

Insight Retrieval Systems show advertisers the added effectiveness that can be achieved by using different media combinations.

Television is the primary medium for many brands in the yogurt category. Listed is the proportion of users that could be added if a brand were to supplement a TV schedule with advertising in one of these other media:

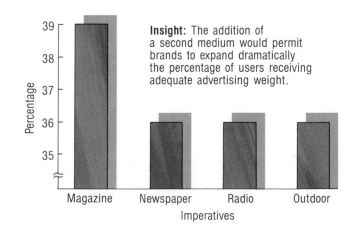

Insight: The addition of a second medium would permit brands to expand dramatically the percentage of users receiving adequate advertising weight.

Source: 1985 SMRB Study of Media & Markets. Reprinted with permission.

National Advertisers, Inc. (LNA) and **Broadcast Advertisers Reports, Inc. (BAR).** These two services compile and report media expenditures for companies, products, and specific brands.

LNA reports media expenditures for national advertisers in magazines, newspaper supplements, network TV, spot TV, network radio, and outdoor. The LNA data represent six-month activity patterns and cover product category, company, and brand. LNA enables a media planner to see where competitive media dollars are being invested.

BAR offers several services, each telling the media planner the amount of money invested, number, frequency, and timing of broadcast commercials. In spot television, BAR monitors over 300 stations in 75 top U.S. markets. In New York, Chicago, and Los Angeles, the monitoring is continuous and full-time. In the other 72 markets, BAR monitors one full week every month. Each week approximately one-fourth of the markets are monitored so that over the course of a month, all 75 markets are covered. The monitoring schedule varies and stations do not know when they are being recorded. One of the reasons that these data are important to advertisers is that more than three-fourths of all U.S. television households are located in these markets and approximately 85 percent of the spot television advertising dollars are spent in monitored markets.

BAR also monitors three broadcast television networks (ABC, CBS, and NBC), four cable television networks (CNN, ESPN, USA, and WTBS), and three radio networks (ABC, CBS, and NBC). The microwave or satellite transmissions of the network signals are recorded for the entire broadcast day, every day of the year.

MEASURING THE EFFECTIVENESS OF MEDIA PLANS

Experience, judgment, and much hard work go into developing a media plan. The data sources described above are only a sampling of the tools available to help the media planner understand the target market and the available media options. In spite of analyzing millions of statistics, the media planner never knows if the media plan will do what it is intended to do. Proof of accomplishment of the media objectives is still elusive. Because there is no one method of determining success, media planners use a number of techniques and services to estimate how well their media schedule accomplishes the stated goals. This section describes several of the most widely used services.

SYNDICATED SERVICES

Determining the effectiveness of the broadcast portion of a media schedule means knowing if the media vehicles selected delivered the desired number of gross rating points. To determine this, it's necessary to know the ratings (reach) of the broadcast schedule. The A. C. Nielsen and Arbitron Ratings companies are the two most widely used broadcast rating services. Advertisers, advertising agencies, and the media subscribe to these services so that they can determine which programs deliver the most audience. When viewer and listener data are combined with cost data, the media planner can determine how efficient specific broadcast programs are in reaching selected target markets.

Though the **A. C. Nielsen Company** offers 125 marketing and advertising services to companies throughout the world, it is probably best known for its "Nielsen Ratings"—estimates of audience size of network television programs. The *Nielsen Television Index (NTI)* service provides estimates of the size and composition of the audience to national television. Data are collected through the *Storage Instantaneous Audimeter*, which is installed in 1,750 TV households throughout the United States. The **Audimeter** is a device that automatically records and stores minute-by-minute tuning changes (both on-off and channel selection) for each television set in the home. Nielsen computers retrieve the data over telephone lines and compute program ratings.

Records from the metered households are supplemented by a separate panel of households that keep weekly diaries of viewing activity for each individual in the household. These tuning and viewing records are available to Nielsen subscribers through a number of reports (see Figure 19.3). Nielsen's *Metered Market Service* is similar to the National NTI service and covers 12 major markets: New York, Los Angeles, Chicago, San Francisco-Oakland, Philadelphia, Boston, Detroit, Washington, D.C., Dallas-Ft. Worth, Houston, Miami-Ft. Lauderdale, and Denver.

The *Nielsen Station Index (NSI)* measures local television audiences in approximately 220 markets. For each four-week, all-market measurement cycle, the computer draws a sample of over 200,000 telephone households. Trained operators contact these households from seven WATS centers, asking their cooperation in keeping a diary of their viewing. Cooperating families fill out one diary for each TV set in the home. Nielsen then compiles these records, market by market, and publishes detailed reports for use by advertisers and agencies in buying time, and by stations and their representatives for purposes of time sales and program evaluation.

The Nielsen *Telephone Coincidental Service* also uses telephone surveys and measures the audience size during specific telecasts, viewing of new shows, specials, etc. Nielsen operators place calls during the actual telecast and the Nielsen clients normally receive the research results within two days.

Nielsen's *HomeVideo Index (NHI)* provides measurement services for the cable television industry and conducts customized audience measurements for cable satellite networks, local cable systems, pay-TV services, and program suppliers. Among the syndicated reports offered, the national *Pay Cable Report* (which measures viewing in pay cable households), is released four times a year in conjunction with each NSI all-market measurement cycle. A one-time-only complementary release, the *Cable/Non-Cable Report*, provides viewing estimates for basic cable-only households and for non-cable households. NHI has also released surveys on VCR usage.

For over 35 years, the **Arbitron Ratings Company** has been providing the advertising community with audience measurement research (see Exhibit 19.4). Today, more than 9,000 clients use Arbitron research to help sell air time and to plan, buy, and evaluate advertising media schedules. Like Nielsen, Arbitron offers a number of research services; however,

FIGURE 19.3

Nielsen Station Index

The Station Index helps media planners determine who's watching what.

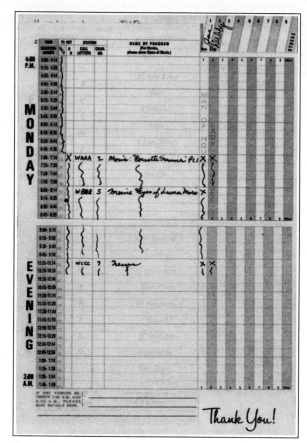

Source: Courtesy of Nielsen Media Research.

EXHIBIT 19.4

A Brief History of Arbitron

1949	American Research Bureau (ARB) begins operations in Washington, D.C. It measured television viewing in three markets: Washington, D.C., Philadelphia, and Baltimore.
1953	ARB expands surveys to 35 cities.
1961	ARB merges with C.E.I.R., a software company.
1965	ARB enters radio audience measurement business.
1967	ARB acquired by Control Data Corporation.
1973	Company name changed to The Arbitron Company.
1976	Arbitron first begins ongoing measurement of television audiences by electronic meter systems.
1982	Company name changed to Arbitron Ratings Company.
Today	Company maintains offices in 16 cities throughout the United States. Measures radio, television, and cable audiences in over 200 local markets.

Source: "Arbitron Ratings Today," Arbitron Ratings Company.

A CLOSER LOOK

THE AUDIMETER: HOW TV SHOWS ARE RATED

Ever wonder how your favorite television programs are rated? Here's a brief history of the famous Audimeter.

The A. C. Nielsen Company began its efforts in the area of broadcast audience research in 1936, when it acquired a device known as the "Audimeter" from two professors, Robert F. Elder and Louis Woodruff, from the Massachusetts Institute of Technology. The device provided a mechanical link between the tuning dial on a radio receiver and a moving roll of paper in such a way that a permanent record of dial positon (i.e., station tuned to) was produced (see photo).

In 1942, after more than six years of costly technical and pilot testing, a commercial audience measurement service for network radio, the Nielsen Radio Index (NRI), was launched. By today's standards, the first service was very basic; at the time, however, it represented the most advanced technological, statistical, and data processing methods and equipment available.

The initial sample consisted of 1,000 Audimeter homes in nine Eastern and Central states. Due to wartime restrictions on the manufacturing of the Audimeter, NRI service covered only about 25 percent of all U.S. radio homes. Each of these homes was visited once a month by a full-time field representative who had the technical training necessary to change the tapes on which the listening records were maintained.

By 1948, Audimeter design had advanced to the point where it required very little in-field maintenance. More important, participants could mail tuning records rather than be visited by a technician. Insignificant as this step may seem, it allowed the Nielsen Company to expand the sample into areas that had previously been

The first version of the Audimeter used by A. C. Nielsen Company

Source: Courtesy of Nielsen Media Research.

inaccessible. Perhaps of even greater importance was that this development aided in expanding the Nielsen efforts into another newly developing area: television.

The Nielsen Television Index (NTI) began providing network audience estimates early in 1950, when only 9 percent of U.S. homes had television sets. As TV ownership increased, the NTI service changed and expanded.

Small and unobstrusive, the Audimeter is installed out of sight in a closet, basement, or cabinet. Its electronic memory records exactly when each set is turned on and off, how long it stays on the channel tuned, and all channel switchings. Each Audimeter home is connected to a special phone line used only by the Nielsen Company. At least twice a day, a central office computer dials each home unit and retrieves the stored information. The entire process is automatic and requires no work on the part of the sample household. After the data have been analyzed by Nielsen's central office computer, a report is issued documenting the viewing patterns of television programming.

Source: "The Measurement of Broadcast Audiences," in *The Nielsen Ratings in Perspective*, A. C. Nielsen Company, Northbrook, Illinois, 1980, 6, 16; and "1985 Updates," A. C. Nielsen Company, 1986.

the following services focus on the company's measurement of radio and television.

Television Audiences Arbitron uses both a metered service and diaries to estimate the size of television audiences. Their metered service provides 24-hour, 7-days-a-week, year-round viewership data for all telecasts in 11 cities: New York, Los Angeles, Chicago, San Francisco, Philadelphia, Dallas/Ft. Worth, Washington, D.C., Detroit, Miami, Houston, and Boston. Based on the data generated by the hundreds of meters in each

FIGURE 19.4

Arbitron TV Market Reports

Source: Copyright Arbitron Ratings Company. Reprinted with permission.

market, Arbitron subscribers receive *Daily Meter Reports*, which include quarter-hour HUT (Homes Using Television) estimates, station ratings, and shares for the previous 24-hour period. *Meter Weeklies* provide subscribers with audience estimates by time period and program averages by Area of Dominant Influence (ADI) household. **Area of Dominant Influence (ADI)** is an Arbitron term that refers to a geographical area made up of the counties in which local stations receive the bulk of the viewing time. In addition to the Individual Day section, the report contains Monday–Friday averages, Program Audience, and Daypart sections.

Arbitron's diary methodology surveys approximately 211 television markets across the country four times a year for four weeks in November, February, May, and July. Larger markets are surveyed again in October, January, and March. After collection and tabulation of the diary data, Arbitron issues *Television Market Reports*, which gives subscribers estimates and share trends by daypart, time period, and program averages for each of the 211 ADI markets (see Figure 19.4). In Arbitron's metered markets, the diary and meter information is integrated.

Radio Audiences The cornerstone of Arbitron's radio research is the *Radio Market Report*. Like the Television Market Reports, the Radio Market Reports are based on diary data and they provide estimates for all stations in a market for a specific survey period. Each report includes a wide variety of demographics and dayparts listening data, including away-from-home listening. The reports are produced from one to four times each year, depending on the size of the market. A total of 260 of the country's most populated areas receive listening reports from Arbitron's spring survey. Surveys are also conducted during the fall in over 125 markets; the largest markets receive survey information on an almost continuous basis, with winter and/or summer surveys.

All audience rating services collect much more information than is reported in their market reports. The data that are not reported on a regular basis are used to produce custom reports for clients. For example, Arbitron's *Radio and Television AID* can analyze any station's audience by selected demographics, specific geography, or nonstandard time periods. This capability allows subscribers to select audience data that best meet their needs. (Similarly, Nielsen's *NSI Plus Service* supplements the various syndicated reports and offers clients a broad range of computerized special studies.)

HOW TO COMPARE MEDIA RESULTS AGAINST MEDIA OBJECTIVES

The process of evaluating media plans begins with establishing media objectives and concludes with integrating the postcampaign evaluation into next year's plans (see Figure 19.5). How the media evaluation process is performed is a management decision. The following two approaches are possible.

Measurement against Precampaign Audience Data Once a media planner has stated media objectives, the assumption is made that the objectives will be achieved by scheduling placement in the media vehicles, time slots, and geographic locations that have historically produced the desired audience size and frequencies. This approach minimizes the cost of evaluation because it does not require data collection beyond the precampaign stage. The sources of this information include Nielsen, Arbitron, SRDS, and the various auditing bureaus.

Measurement against Postcampaign Audience Data This approach involves determining the success of the media plan against the actual performance of the purchased media schedule. The advertiser has two options for collecting measurement data: collect the data internally or use a data processing firm to perform the task. The first option requires that the advertiser collect media performance data from the various sources described in this chapter, and then compare that data gainst the media objectives. For example, an advertiser's objective for a particular network TV vehicle might have been to deliver 250 GRP against the target market. However, a postcampaign analysis of Nielsen data might reveal that the vehicle achieved a 20.0 rating; therefore, the media objective was not achieved.

FIGURE 19.5

Evaluating Media Plans:
The Process

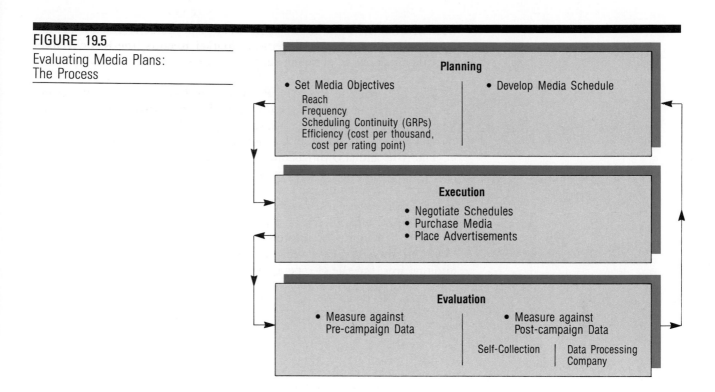

	250 GRP
▪ Advertiser Media Vehicle Objective	250 GRP
▪ Planned Vehicle Reach (rating)	25.0
▪ Planned Frequency	10
▪ Delivered Vehicle Reach (rating)	20.0
▪ Delivered Frequency	10
▪ Delivered GRP	200.0
▪ Percentage of Objective Achieved	80.0% (200/250)

The second option for evaluating the media schedule against actual media performance is to use a data processing company that specializes in media recordkeeping. **Donovan Data Systems Company** is one of the leaders in this field and offers advertisers and their agencies a variety of media recordkeeping, accounting, and evaluation services. For example, Donovan's SPOTPAK, PRINTPAK, and NETPAK systems can compare media schedule objectives with actual media schedule performance data.

EVALUATING PRINT MEDIA

The cornerstone of analyzing newspapers and magazines is circulation. Advertising rates are primarily based on circulation, and media planners hope to achieve print media objectives by selecting print media that will deliver the target audiences. The advertising industry realized the importance of circulation data. Thus in 1914, advertisers, advertising agencies, and publishers joined together to form the **Audit Bureau of Circulations**

(ABC). This agency, with its more than 5,000 members, maintains circulation auditing standards, verifies circulation data through field auditors' examinations of pertinent records, and issues standardized reports of circulation data.

The ABC and the **Business Publications Audit of Circulation, Inc. (BPA)** supply the advertising industry with reports used in both pre- and postcampaign evaluations of print media. Both organizations issue publisher's statements and audit statements.

The ABC audits both paid and controlled circulation print media. The majority of its members are newspapers, although it also audits consumer and farm publications as well as the business press. The BPA is the leading auditing service for business and professional journals, auditing all-paid, all-controlled, or any combination of paid and controlled circulation for over 1,000 industrial and technical publications, professional journals, and other special-interest magazines. Both organizations are supported by auditing fees, the sale of reports, and membership dues.

THE VALUE OF AUDITING SERVICES

The services of the auditing bureaus are valuable to media planners for several reasons:

1. **Verification of Circulation Data** The financial independence of the ABC and the BPA assures media planners that circulation data are accurately and objectively reported.

2. **Standardization of Circulation Data** Both the ABC and the BPA maintain standardized formats and strict definitions in the reporting of circulation data. Each organization's reports allow media planners to compare media easily.

3. **Factual Basis for Media Research** Audit statements give the media planner a convenient way to compare a large number of relevant pieces of information, including:

   - Reach (circulation)

   - Efficiency (CPM and CPM-TM)

   - Circulation trends

   - Circulation distribution (geographic concentration, industry concentration, job title, plant size, etc.)

   - Circulation quality (renewal rates and duration, methods of subscription, quantities sold through newsstands, bulk copies distributed, source of circulation qualification, etc.)

4. **Evaluation of Media Objectives** Because audit statements are confirmation of circulation, they allow the media planner to determine how successfully each print medium delivered the target market. In their own way, audit statements are the print counterparts of Nielsen and Arbitron broadcast data. Unfortunately, audit statements are usually published only once a year and in some cases only if specifically ordered by the publisher. Publisher's statements are issued every six months and although the data are not

necessarily subjected to an audit, they are widely accepted as reliable estimates of circulation.

MEASURING THE EFFECTIVENESS OF SUPPORT MEDIA

A variety of other means are used to measure the effectiveness of support media such as direct mail, specialty advertising, outdoor advertising, transit advertising, and trade shows.

DIRECT MAIL

One surefire way to know exactly how successful a media plan is, is to invest solely in direct mail. Because the purpose of direct mail is to get a response, the most legitimate measure of its performance is the number of responses received.

The closest thing to an "auditing bureau" for direct mail is proof of postage—confirmation that a specific number of pieces were mailed on a specific date. Delivery is virtually assured; therefore, the only other measure is the response itself. Direct-mail users maintain comprehensive records of response, noting the number, size, and profitability of orders, as well as the demographics of customers.

SPECIALTY ADVERTISING

Because specialty advertising is used for so many different reasons, the techniques used to measure its contribution to the advertising plan vary widely. Circulation (distribution of specialty merchandise) is confirmed through distribution—either personal or mail distribution. Frequently, specialty advertising is used to enhance an advertiser's image or to increase brand recognition. Appropriate measures of the success of these objectives include brand recognition and recall tests and measures of improvements in company image, including increased receptivity of the advertiser's personal sales staff.

OUTDOOR ADVERTISING

Outdoor circulation can be determined in two ways. One method, the **calibration survey,** measures respondents' actual frequencies of exposures to outdoor signs and then relates these frequencies to demographic characteristics and travel behavior. The mathematical model developed from the calibration data is then applied to the annual SMRB survey of 15,000 people to produce national reach-frequency estimates for outdoor. The second technique, the **map recall method,** involves the respondents' recalling each trip out of home and physically drawing a travel route on a separate map for each trip. Coders then tally the number of outdoor sign exposures that each of the respondents' trips would have generated.

The **Traffic Audit Bureau (TAB)** also verifies outdoor circulation. The TAB audits every sign location in a market by counting traffic in areas adjacent to poster locations. To estimate the value of a location, the TAB gives each poster *Space Position Value Rating (SPV)*. Because the value of any given poster is a function of circulation and visibility, the SPV evaluates obstruction to visibility, angle to traffic flow, number of signs in a location, and speed of traffic.

The most important circulation data for planning an outdoor campaign are found in the audit statements of the Traffic Audit Bureau, SMRB's *Guide to Media and Markets,* and the *Buyer's Guide to Outdoor Advertising,* which includes rates, circulation, and other useful scheduling information. Determining the contribution of outdoor to media objectives is a bit more problematic. The audit statements produced by the TAB are updated every three years; therefore, verified estimates of circulation on a year-to-year basis for a particular market are not available. How, then, can an advertiser determine if media objectives have been achieved? The primary method is to request the local outdoor operator to perform a *postbuy analysis.* A postbuy analysis uses the most current, audited circulation data to compare the gross rating points achieved against the stated objective. Occasionally, an advertiser's message appears on more locations and for a longer time than the terms of the media contract. This can occur when sign locations are substituted and when locations are not leased immediately after a contract date expires. The advertiser in the table below achieved 1.4 percent "bonus signs."

MARKET	SHOWING	NUMBER OF SIGNS PURCHASED	NUMBER OF SIGNS RECEIVED	PERCENTAGE OF GOAL ACHIEVED
Chicago	#50	850	872	102.6
St. Louis	50	540	535	99.1
San Francisco	50	575	586	101.9
Totals		1,965	1,993	101.4

TRANSIT ADVERTISING

Unfortunately, little documented information exists about the circulation of transit advertising. Unlike print and outdoor, transit circulation is not audited. Audience figures are based on estimates of the number of passengers riding the carrier or moving through the transportation terminal. Occasionally, a study is undertaken in a single market—sometimes by an owner of a transit franchise or by an advertiser.

TRADE SHOWS

Prior to entering a trade show, advertisers can contact the show sponsor for information on the previous year's attendance. This information can then be used to project the current year's attendance. Although the attendance to some shows is audited, the figure that is most relevant to exhibitors is attendance to their own booth. For this reason, advertisers invest a considerable amount of money and energy to motivate booth attendance and to maintain records of every visitor.

In 1981, the Trade Show Bureau introduced a marketing report by the **Exhibition Validation Council (EVC),** a group dedicated to standardizing trade show attendance reporting and simplifying comparisons between shows. The EVC report is completed by the exhibition manager, and its purpose is to provide accurate, consistent data about trade show attendence. The report consists of 24 questions that must be answered for validation and another 17 optional questions. The questions fall into seven areas: general exhibition information, exhibitor, attendance, audience profile, marketing data, admission policy, and program.

After the EVC report is filled out, it is reviewed by the Exhibition Validation Council for completeness and consistency. If the information meets the established standards, the Council applies its seal of approval to the report and exhibition managers are then able to use the certification for promotion purposes. The EVC report is a major step toward providing marketers with meaningful data on their investment in trade shows.

SUMMARY

The measurement of the effectiveness of a media plan is a complex task —one that begins with understanding the objectives of the plan and involves a search for valid, reliable circulation data. Media measurement, like other areas of advertising, is often frustrating. The inherent problems with inter- and intra-media comparison, the lack of audience data, and in some cases, unreliable data all contribute to the frustration. Some media types have a long history of documenting audience size and characteristics: The print media (through the ABC and the BPA) and the broadcast media (through Nielsen and Arbitron) are good examples. Other media types—direct mail and to some extent, specialty advertising— have a more direct measure of effectiveness: direct response from the audience. Finally, transit advertising and trade shows either do little to measure circulation or their audits are of little value to advertisers.

YOU MAKE THE DECISION

ROCKY MOUNTAIN MUSEUM OF ART

Six years ago, the Rocky Mountain Museum of Art opened the doors to its new eight-story home. The museum is a 128-year-old institution that has built a national reputation for its collection of American Indian art. Over the years, the RMMA collection has grown in size and stature. Unfortunately, museum usage and membership have not grown at the same rate. In fact, since the move into its new home, membership has dropped off by 9 percent. And, while such factors as the economy and growing competition from other cultural and entertainment entities have no doubt contributed to the membership decline, the museum's management remains convinced that the main problem is lack of knowledge about the museum and what it offers. Consequently, the RMMA has decided to launch an advertising campaign. The overall purposes of the campaign are to communicate basic, relevant information about the museum and to convince a large number of prospects to purchase a $30 annual membership.

The museum developed the following marketing plan:

Target Market

- Adults, 35–49

- Household income: $35,000+

- Attended college

- Denver metro area residents

Marketing Objectives

- To increase the number of new adult visitors by 12 percent

- To sell 9 percent more memberships

Advertising Objectives

- To increase awareness of the RMMA's location, hours of operation, and main attractions by 50 percent

- To convince 30 percent of the target market that membership in the RMMA is a "good entertainment value"

Media Objective

- To reach 75 percent of the target market an average of four times per month for each of the next six months

Media Plan

January:
- ¼-page, b/w advertisement in *Denver Magazine* (monthly)
- ⅛-page, b/w advertisements in the *Rocky Mountain News* (one per week)

February
- ¼-page, b/w advertisement in *Denver Magazine*
- ½-page, b/w advertisement in *Colorado Business Magazine* (monthly)
- ⅛-page, b/w advertisements in the *Rocky Mountain News* (one per week for first two weeks of month)
- ⅛-page, b/w advertisements in the *Denver Post* (one per week for second two weeks of month)

March:
- ¼-page, b/w advertisement in *Denver Magazine*
- ⅛-page, b/w advertisement in the *Denver Post* (one per week)

April:
- ½-page, 4-color advertisement in *Denver Magazine*
- ½-page, b/w advertisement in the *Rocky Mountain News* (first week of month)
- ½-page, b/w advertisement in the *Denver Post* (second week of month)
- Full-page, 4-color advertisement in *Colorado Business Magazine*
- Direct mailing of Events Calendar to 50,000 households in Denver metro area

May:
- ½-page, 4-color advertisement in *Denver Magazine*
- ¼-page, b/w advertisements in the *Rocky Mountain News* (one per week)
- ¼-page, b/w advertisements in the *Denver Post* (one per week)
- Full-page, 4-color advertisement in *Colorado Business Magazine*

June:
- Full-page, 4-color advertisement in *Denver Magazine*
- Full-page, 4-color advertisement in *Colorado Business Magazine*
- ¼-page, b/w advertisements in the *Rocky Mountain News* (one per week)
- ¼-page, b/w advertisements in the *Denver Post* (one per week)

Based on the preceding information, how should the Rocky Mountain Museum of Art determine the effectiveness of its media plan?

■ ■ ■

QUESTIONS FOR DISCUSSION

1. Why is the evaluation of the effectiveness of a media plan so difficult?

2. Explain this chapter's framework for evaluating media plans.

3. How are the following services most commonly used?
   a. Standard Rate & Data Service
   b. Mediamark Research, Inc.
   c. Simmons Market Research Bureau

4. What is a "media imperative" and what is its relationship to media planning?

5. Explain the value of Leading National Advertisers and Broadcast Advertisers Reports data for media planners.

6. What are the possible shortcomings of the Audimeter system?

7. What advantages do diaries offer over the Audimeter in terms of measuring the size of a television audience? Which method is more reliable? Why?

8. Explain the value of the services provided by the Audit Bureau of Circulations and the Business Publications Audit of Circulation.

9. From the point of view of the advertiser, in which medium is it easiest to assess effectiveness? Why?

10. In addition to the information contained in an Exhibition Validation Council report, what other factors would be important in determining the effectiveness of a particular trade show?

SUGGESTED READINGS

Although there are no endnotes for this chapter, there is an abundance of literature on the topic of measuring the effectiveness of media. The most heavily researched topics within media effectiveness involve the effects of message repetition (frequency) and scheduling of media (continuity). Also, there are hundreds of studies documenting the effectiveness of the various media. A few of these are cited below; however, most have been conducted through the media associations.

For additional information on the topic of measuring the effectiveness of media plans, contact the media associations listed in the Appendix to this text as well as those described in this chapter; review the trade literature, particularly *Advertising Age, Adweek, Marketing & Media Decisions*, and *Marketing Communications*; and review the scholarly literature, particularly the *Journal of Advertising, Journal of Advertising Research, Journal of Marketing*, and the *Journal of Marketing Research*. The following list of articles and books provides a good grasp of the main issues and approaches used to measure the effectiveness of media.

Bearden, W. O.; J. Teel, Jr.; R. Durand; and R. Williams. "Consumer Magazines—An Efficient Medium for Reaching Organizational Buyers." *Journal of Advertising*, no. 2, 1979.

Boyd, Marsha M., and John D. Leckenby. "Random Duplication in Reach/Frequency Estimation." In *Current Issues & Research in Advertising*, James H. Leigh and Claude R. Martin, Jr., eds. Ann Arbor, Mich.: University of Michigan, Graduate School of Business Administration, 1985.

Cannon, Hugh M. "A Method for Estimating Target Market Ratings in Television Media Selection." *Journal of Advertising*, no. 2, 1986, 21–26.

Craig, C. Samuel, and Vithala R. Rao. "Measurement of Subjective Trade-offs in Media Allocation Decisions." In *Current Issues & Research in Advertising*, James H. Leigh and Claude R. Martin, Jr., eds. Ann Arbor, Mich.: University of Michigan, Graduate School of Business Administration, 1980.

Effective Frequency: The State of the Art. Proceedings of the Advertising Research Foundation's Conference on Advertising Repetition, 1982.

Gensch, Dennis. *Advertising Planning: Mathematical Models in Advertising Media Planning*. New York: Elsevier Publishing Company, 1973.

Headen, R.; J. Klompmaker; and J. Teel, Jr. "Increasing the Informational Content of Reach and Frequency Estimates." *Journal of Advertising*, no. 1, 1976.

Kamin, Howard. "Advertising Reach and Frequency." *Journal of Advertising Research*, February 1978.

Kreshel, Peggy; Kent M. Lancaster; and Margaret A. Toomey. "How Leading Advertising Agencies Perceive Effective Reach and Frequency." *Journal of Advertising*, no. 3, 1985, 32–38, 51.

Lancaster, Kent M.; Peggy Kreshel; and Joya R. Harris. "Estimating the Impact of Advertising Media Plans: Media Executives Describe Weighting and Timing Factors." *Journal of Advertising*, no. 3, 1986, 21–29, 45.

Mogg, J., and B. Enis. "Assessing Media Effectiveness via Network Flowgraphs." *Journal of Advertising*, no. 3, 1974.

Naples, Michael J. *Effective Frequency: The Relationship between Frequency and Advertising Effectiveness*. New York: Association of National Advertisers, 1979.

Palda, Kristian S. *The Measurement of Cumulative Advertising Effects*. Englewood Cliffs, N.J.: Prentice-Hall, Inc., 1964.

Rust, Roland T., Robert P. Leone, and Mary R. Zimmer. "Estimating the Duplicated Audience of Media Vehicles in National Advertising Schedules." *Journal of Advertising*, no. 3, 1986.

Schultz, D.; M. Block; and S. Custer. "A Comparative Study of Radio Audience Measurement Methodology." *Journal of Advertising*, no. 2, 1978.

Sissors, Jack Z. "Vehicle Exposure Measurements and Beyond." In *Current Issues & Research in Advertising*, James Leigh and Claude R. Martin, Jr., eds. Ann Arbor, Mich.: University of Michigan, Graduate School of Business Administration, 1978.

Strong, Edward C. "The Spacing and Timing of Advertising." *Journal of Advertising Research*, August 1980.

Teel, J., Jr.; R. Durand; and W. Bearden. "Weekly Variation in Audience Delivery of TV Advertising Schedules." *Journal of Advertising*, no. 4, 1977.

Wilson, R. Dale, and Karen A. Machleit. "Advertising Decision Models: A Managerial Review." In *Current Issues & Research in Advertising*, James H. Leigh and Claude R. Martin, Jr., eds. Ann Arbor, Mich.: University of Michigan, Graduate School of Business Administration, 1985.

Zielske, Hubert A., and Walter A. Henry. "Remembering and Forgetting Television Ads." *Journal of Advertising Research*, April 1980.

PART 6

Contemporary Issues in Advertising

Previous sections of this book have dealt with advertising as it has developed and as it is now. This final chapter will deal with advertising as we imagine it will respond to foreseeable trends in business and society. The chapter deals with three different areas: ethical dimensions of advertising practice; future developments affecting the industry; and possibilities and skills for an advertising career.

Also included in this part are five appendixes, which should prove useful. Appendix A provides sources of advertising information. Appendix B lists media rates to estimate the cost of bringing an advertising campaign to a target market. Appendix C presents a sample marketing plan for Mountain Bell. Appendix D discusses how to calculate the breakeven point in direct marketing. Appendix E explains how to make an advertising presentation.

THE FUTURE OF ADVERTISING/ADVERTISING CAREERS

Key Terms

cable television
premium service
video cassette recorder (VCR)
zipping
time-shift
zapping
narrowcasting
split-30
infomercial
underwriting
internship program
copywriter
art director
portfolio
media buyer
research assistant
account executive
brand manager
resume
cover letter
interview
entry-level position

Learning Objectives

To present technological changes in communication media

To analyze the impact of cable services

To determine how VCRs change viewing

To examine the responses of advertising to media changes

To outline the types of jobs available in advertising

To explain where most advertising work is carried out

To describe the best preparation for an advertising career

To explain how to assess your abilities for an advertising job

To describe the process of job hunting

The 1980s saw a host of changes in American culture, not the least of which stemmed from fears of an AIDS epidemic in America. At first, few people knew much about AIDS. After the deadly disease claimed the lives of some well-known Americans, however, the federal government took steps to learn more. U.S. Surgeon General C. Everett Koop, in a pioneering move, called for the use of condoms as a way to halt the spread of AIDS. Testifying before a House subcommittee investigating the health problem, Koop asserted that TV advertising of condoms would "have a positive public health value."

Ironically, for years American condom manufacturers had sought in vain to use television advertising, but were consistently turned away. Now, a major public official not only advocated the use of condoms nationwide, but pledged to meet with condom marketers to forge a way to advertise the product effectively.

After years of attempting to market their product as a contraceptive, condom advertisers "found" a new product feature: disease control. Yet, the networks refused to reverse their long-standing policy.

At least one political figure objected to the networks' position. Rep. Henry Waxman (D., Calif.) called the networks "so hypocriti-

cally priggish that they refuse to describe disease control as they promote disease transmission. While portraying thousands of sexual encounters each year in programming and while marketing thousands of products using sex appeal, TV is unwilling to give the life-saving information about safe sex and condoms."

Said an ABC spokesperson: ". . . The advertising of contraceptives is an issue that deals with many social, religious, and ethical considerations. More than involving only the question of taste, a significant portion of our audience finds these products inappropriate for advertising on a medium with such powerful reach into American homes."

NBC agreed with ABC, saying that condom ads "would offend the moral and religious sensitivities" of its audience: "We want to be responsive to our affiliates, many of whom have indicated that they don't want such advertising."

Surprisingly, however, some of the affiliates refuted this claim. A station in San Francisco was the first to accept condom commercials; Indianapolis and Detroit affiliates soon followed. Other stations have followed suit, in numbers that have surprised even the condom advertisers.

Says Jeanne Findlater, vice-president and general manager of ABC affiliate WXYZ-TV in Detroit: "Commercials work. They supply encapsulated information. You can discuss concepts and you can change practices. I don't think these ads corrupt morality. It's evident that people need to know."

Sources: Nancy Giges, "AIDS Scare Could Lead Nets to Run Ads for Condoms," *Advertising Age*, December 15, 1986, 1, 101; Patricia Winters, "TV Stations Embrace Condom Spots," *Advertising Age*, February 2, 1987, 4; Steve Daley, "TV Barriers to Condom Ads Breaking Down," *Chicago Tribune*, February 15, 1987, sec. 5, 1, 6; and Steven W. Colford, "Nets Take Flak on Condom Ads," *Advertising Age*, February 16, 1987, 79. Ad courtesy of the Mentor Corporation.

INTRODUCTION

This chapter discusses ethical issues sometimes faced by the media, advertisers, and agencies, and some important developments and trends that affect the industry. Some of these will have implications for future employment in the industry; others simply reflect the natural pressures of evolution in society and business.

Finally, the chapter focuses on advertising career opportunities, the skills and preparation needed to enter the field, and the basics of how (and where) to seek an advertising job.

THE FUTURE OF ADVERTISING: THE ETHICS ISSUE

These days we are very concerned with ethical behavior. The conduct of people in public life is being scrutinized as never before. However, all activities where outcomes affect others involve ethical consideration. Advertising people, involved as they are in mass communication and persuasion, clearly must be aware of the ethical dimensions in which they operate.

The vignette at the beginning of this chapter describes a situation in which numerous ethical issues are raised. A major public health problem occurs and those who control the most effective medium for calling attention to it refuse to acknowledge the problem because they fear offending their viewers. Is it really the viewers' sensibilities they fear, or are they afraid of adverse effects on advertising revenues? Which is the stronger obligation—the obligation not to offend, or the obligation to provide health information?

These questions are complicated by strong religious and moral views. Does encouraging condom use condone sexual promiscuity? Where television stations have accepted condom advertising, they have insisted that it be based on disease control only. No mention of birth control is allowed. Does this seem a realistic restraint? Many have argued with the format requirements stations have imposed. Most condom spots that have been accepted are clinical in nature—that is, a straight discussion of the use of condoms with little use of advertising's usual dramatic emphasis. In addition, most stations have required that such advertising be carried only after 10 or 11 p.m. These combined restrictions have led critics to charge that those who most need to have information about condoms are least likely to receive it or, if they are exposed, will tune it out due to its dull presentation.

These issues are not restricted to television; newspapers have had to contend with the AIDS problem as well. Before early 1987, the *New York Times* did not accept contraceptive advertising. AIDS forced the paper to reconsider its advertising policy and eventually to accept the ad shown in Figure 20.1. However, the ad was not accepted until the paper was assured that it bore no reference to contraception. In addition, the original headline "I enjoy sex, but I'm not ready to die for it" was revised to "I'll do a lot for love, but I'm not willing to die for it" at the paper's insistence.[1]

FIGURE 20.1

One of the First Condom Ads to
Run in an American Newspaper

"I'll do a lot for love, but I'm not ready to die for it."

"I never thought having an intimate relationship with someone could be a matter of life or death. But with everything I hear about AIDS these days, I'm more than uncomfortable. I'm afraid."

AIDS isn't just a gay disease, it's everybody's disease.

And everybody who gets it dies.

AIDS is transmitted from one sexual partner to another, often by a mate who has contracted the disease without even knowing it.

But what we find so alarming about this terrible disease is that people are doing so little to try to prevent it.

Especially since the Surgeon General recently stated, "The best protection against infection right now, barring abstinence, is use of a condom."

It's for this reason that we at LifeStyles® say that the proper use of a LifeStyles Brand Condom can greatly reduce the chances of you or your partner contracting AIDS.

Because a LifeStyles condom acts as a shield that helps prevent the transfer of the AIDS virus. So the likelihood of getting this disease is dramatically diminished. And LifeStyles Brand Condoms, when properly used, help prevent other sexually transmitted diseases like herpes and gonorrhea.

LifeStyles condoms are manufactured by Ansell International, America's largest manufacturers of condoms. Tinton Falls, NJ 07724. © Ansell, Inc. 1987.

Source: Courtesy of Ansell Americas, Tinton Falls, NJ USA.

Condom manufacturers are not totally altruistic either. The president of the company that manufactured the product shown in Figure 20.1 was quoted in a newsmagazine as calling AIDS "a condom marketer's dream." The agency that created the campaign, Della Femina, Travisano & Partners, promptly resigned the account, saying the statement "is contrary to everything we believe in . . . and we choose not to work with anyone who believes otherwise."

But the AIDS issue, as important as it is, serves here only as an illustration of the complex ethical problems encountered in advertising practice. They are farreaching and surface in many aspects of advertising practice. For example, as noted above, many newspapers prohibit condom advertising, yet they accept ads for handguns. While editorializing against alcohol and tobacco, they readily accept advertising for both. The issues here are complicated and involve conflicts among the rights of individuals and corporations, and social good. Individuals who hope to work in the advertising industry must realize the complexity of these problems and be prepared to deal with them in a responsible, ethical manner.

THE FUTURE OF ADVERTISING: DEVELOPMENTS IN MEDIA

Almost daily, we are reminded of the growth and development taking place in the technology of mass communications. From interactive personal computer information links to teleconferencing, new communications capabilities seem ever present and always growing. Despite the long list of possible communications capabilities for the future, the real issue is which systems will prove economically viable. While the answer to this question is far from clear, most mass communications systems will probably depend on advertising support in one way or another. The media most likely to obtain that support are those that offer audiences attractive to advertisers.

Though interactive data systems, low power television, direct broadcast satellite, and other capabilities are technologically possible, both large investments and practical limitations seem likely to slow wide offering and adoption of these services. For the next five to ten years it seems most probable that the greatest impact on established advertising media will come from cable television services and from selective use of devices like home video cassette recorders. Though the growth in cable adoption has not been close to the optimistic projections of the early 1980s, it seems obvious that cable is, and will be, the most likely new competitor for advertising dollars in the late 1980s and the 1990s. With this growth will come a greater need at agencies and advertisers for specialists who understand how to use this medium. The competition for sales among media indicates a continuing need for effective sales people.

THE IMPACT OF CABLE

In discussing **cable television** as an advertising medium, it is important to keep in mind that the medium actually covers several different types of audiences. At the most general level, it encompasses both those who subscribe to simple community antenna systems that provide local signals with improved quality of reception, and those with 40 or more signals from both local and distant points of origin. It may also include subscribers to a **premium service**, such as Home Box Office or the Playboy channel. The point is that the term "cable audience" actually describes a wide range of subscribers, many of whom spend a relatively large amount of money for specialized programming.[2] Though cable is conceived by viewers as an alternative to commercial broadcasting, few in the industry believe that it will continue this way for long. Most industry observers believe that once cable audiences have grown to a critical point and been identified in terms of important market segmentation criteria, cable television will rapidly commercialize. Though some cable subscribers are

A CLOSER LOOK

THIRTEEN CHANGES

In his 1983 book, *Ogilvy on Advertising*, David Ogilvy offered the following speculations about the future of the advertising business:

I have never been a futurist, and with every passing year my interest in the future declines. However, my publisher insists that I take a shot at predicting the changes that you, gentle reader, will see in the advertising business. So here goes:

1. The quality of research will improve, and this will generate a bigger corpus of knowledge as to what works and what doesn't. Creative people will learn to exploit this knowledge, thereby improving their strike rate at the cash register.

2. There will be a renaissance in print advertising.

3. Advertising will contain more information and less hot air.

4. Billboards will be abolished.

5. The clutter of commercials on television and radio will be brought under control.

6. There will be a vast increase in the use of advertising by governments for purposes of education, particularly *health* education.

7. Advertising will play a part in bringing the population explosion under control.

8. Candidates for political office will stop using dishonest advertising.

9. The quality and efficiency of advertising overseas will continue to improve—at an accelerating rate. More foreign hares will overtake the American tortoise.

10. Several foreign agencies will open offices in the United States, and will prosper.

11. Multinational manufacturers will increase their market-shares all over the non-Communist world, and will market more of their brands internationally. The advertising campaigns for these brands will emanate from the headquarters of multinational agencies, but will be adapted to respect differences in local culture.

12. Direct-response advertising will cease to be a separate specialty, and will be folded into the 'general' agencies.

13. Ways will be found to produce effective television commercials at a more sensible cost.

Source: Reprinted from *Ogilvy on Advertising*, p. 217. Copyright © 1983 by David Ogilvy. Compilation copyright © 1983 by Multimedia Publications (UK) Ltd. Used by permission of Crown Publishers, Inc.

EXHIBIT 20.1

Projected Growth of Cable Network Advertising

YEAR	ALL TV HOMES (millions)	CABLE AD HOMES (millions)	CABLE VIEWING SHARE (%)	=	ACTUAL CABLE VIEWING (millions)	CABLE NETWORK REVENUE (billions)	PERCENTAGE CHANGE
1984	85	24.0	16		1.92	$0.460	51.9%
1985	87	27.5	17		2.34	0.606	31.7
1986	89	30.5	18		2.75	0.800	32.0
1987	91	33.5	19		3.18	1.048	31.0
1988	93	36.5	20		3.65	1.338	27.7
1989	94	38.5	21		4.04	1.669	24.7
1990	96	40.5	22		4.46	2.084	24.9
1991	98	42.5	23		4.89	2.508	20.4
1992	99	44.5	24		5.34	3.038	21.1
1993	100	46.5	25		5.81	3.667	20.7
1994	101	48.5	25		6.06	4.241	15.7

Source: Based on *Marketing and Media Decisions*, Fall 1985 Special Issue, p. 46.

likely to be unhappy with this development, many seem more willing to accept commercials than increased fees for cable services.

At the moment cable networks seem unable to offer persuasive audience research data to most large advertisers. Nonetheless, General Foods Media Director Don Miceli offers a response typical of many large advertisers who are keeping a close watch on cable: "We've been involved with cable for the past five years and most likely will accelerate our participation as cable continues to mature."[3] Available data indicate dramatic growth in advertising revenues for cable, which indicates increasing advertiser interest in the medium. The potential contribution of advertising to underwriting the costs of the medium, both for cable system operators and for viewers, makes it clear that cable will be a commercial medium in the near future.

VIDEO CASSETTE RECORDERS

Another important development in media technology is the widespread distribution of the **video cassette recorder (VCR).** Consumer interest in these machines has lead to rapid scale economies and price reductions, which have accelerated their adoption. VCRs have affected media habits in three important ways:

1. The use of the device allows viewing of programs that might otherwise be missed, since timers can be preset to record shows while viewers are away.

2. Shows that are replayed are subject to **zipping**—the industry term for using the fast-forward control to skip through commercials and thus avoid the advertising messages.

3. The wide adoption of VCRs has led to numerous video rental services where both movies and other forms of entertainment and instruction are available.

All three of these developments are quite significant for the advertising community. Figure 20.2 indicates how VCR's are being used in American homes.

Use of VCRs for **time-shift**—that is, to see programs that the viewer would normally miss—can result in a gain of audience for the station and for the advertiser. This of course is desirable, and the result is often that viewers who are particularly sought after are added to the audience in this way. Those who use VCRs are often more affluent, and attracted by particular types of programs, but their demanding schedules often do not fit with normal television programming. Thus these audience members are a bonus to broadcasters and to advertisers.

However, the problem of zipping is one to which the industry has little response. By some estimates, as much as 65 percent of the time-shift audience zips through commercials, cancelling out the majority of the audience gained through VCR use.[4] Remote control units on VCRs and TV sets create the related problem of **zapping,** avoiding commercials by changing channels. The use of VCRs as player units for prerecorded programs is also a problem from the advertising and media industry points of view. By the end of 1986, 40 percent of U.S. households had VCRs. It is currently estimated that every U.S. household will have a VCR by the

FIGURE 20.2
VCR Activity: When, How, and What

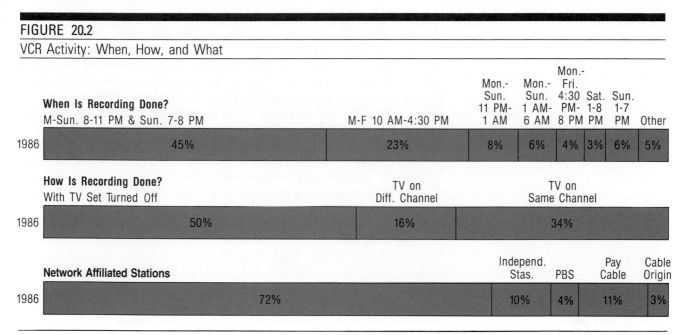

Source: A.C. Nielsen Company, *Television: 1986 Nielsen Report*, 12.

end of 1990.[5] If this proves to be the case, and VCRs are heavily used to play prerecorded material, the likely result is lower demand for cable services, particularly movie programming. It is also likely that they will affect television viewing. Some industry experts believe, as the result of competition from VCRs and cable, the average network show rating—currently 16—will drop to 10 by the year 2000, a reduction of nearly 40 percent. All of this has led advertisers to consider tape cassettes as advertising vehicles. Canon and Nikon, for instance, have produced how-to cassettes on photography. More commercials on rental cassettes, as Pepsi did in the video cassette release of "Top Gun," as well as video-store promotions for advertisers are among the related activities advertisers are experimenting with.[6]

VCRs aside, there is increasing competition from other communications media for viewers' attention. A good deal of mass media research indicates that consumers have a finite amount of time to devote to mass media each day, and that, as the alternatives increase, the proportion of their attention to each alternative decreases. One industry analyst believes that the number of media vehicles—that is magazines, television and cable channels, radio stations, etc.—will double by the year 2000.[7] There can be little doubt that there will be considerable competition for the consumer's attention, with the result meaning small audiences who spend less time with each alternative.

THE MASS MEDIA AUDIENCE

Jane Zenaty, Director of Media Research for the Leo Burnett agency, characterized the options facing the media audience in the year 2000 as containing three features: choice, control, and interactivity.[8] The choice will be allowed by the wide variety of program sources from a combination of traditional media and the options offered through cable and other alternatives. The control comes about through such techniques as time-shift, zipping, and zapping. Interactivity will be available to those with personal computers who use them to link up with various data suppliers to select special programming on a pay-per-view basis, or to use this media link for electronic shopping, or other kinds of domestic and financial services. These services might range from routine banking deposits and withdrawals to bill paying and investing.

Zenaty suggests that 80 percent of U.S. households will have cable available in 2000 (though no more than 55% are likely to subscribe), but that the remaining 20 percent of the country may never have this option. This seems quite a believable suggestion in that cable wiring has two important imperatives. One is the cost of physically installing the cable. This is balanced against the second imperative, the desirability of the audience who receives the signal. The wiring of many urban areas requires tremendous expense, often with fairly low concentrations of desirable audiences for the franchise owner and advertiser.

It is important to keep in mind that, while there will be continued emphasis on extending cable hookups in the next decade, the emphasis is likely to be on securing desirable audiences rather than on providing complete coverage. It also seems that these desirable audiences will receive a considerably larger number of advertising messages than at any time in the past. As a matter of fact, a survey of advertising professionals indicated that they expected the number of messages directed to upscale target audiences to double by the year 2000.[9]

A likely result of this massive increase in advertising messages is that audiences will develop further defenses to shelter them from advertising messages. To some extent these defenses will probably be technological (such as zipping and zapping). In addition, viewers' powers of selective perception are likely to become more highly developed as well. Many consumers may consider it a plus that advertising is forced to offer tangible consumer benefits as a way of attracting and holding consumer attention in a crowded and increasingly "noisy" advertising marketplace.

THE ADVERTISER AND AGENCIES

All industry observers expect that advertising volume will grow in the coming decade. While this is quite likely, few expect that the traditional national/retail split of 60/40 respectively of total ad volume to change dramatically. In addition, while advertising expenditures are expected to grow, few observers see any significant change in advertising expenditures as a percentage of annual consumer spending, or of the gross national product. All of this means that advertising dollars will be spread more thinly among a larger number of media. Exhibit 20.2 illustrates the expected growth in advertising expenditures among media.

The cable advertising industry's response to the fragmentation of the audience has been to emphasize the concept of **narrowcasting.** The aim of narrowcasting is to reach a narrowly defined target audience rather than a broad, undifferentiated one. Narrowcasting was originally what made

EXHIBIT 20.2

Advertising Dollar Volume
Projections, 1980–2000

MEDIUM	YEAR				
	1980	1985	1990	1995	2000
Newspapers	$15.9	$24.8	$ 35.5	$ 50.0	$ 74.2
Magazines	3.4	5.8	9.2	14.4	21.0
Television	12.4	22.8	38.7	64.3	98.9
Radio	3.8	6.0	8.9	13.0	17.8
Direct Mail	7.6	11.3	15.8	21.6	27.5
Business & Farm	1.9	2.8	3.9	5.4	7.0
Outdoor & Transit	.6	.8	1.0	1.2	1.3
Totals	$45.6	74.3	113.0	169.9	247.7

Note: Media categories exclude miscellaneous.
Source: Advertising Age, April 30, 1980.

the cable audience salable to advertisers. Narrowcasting may have a very important impact on the advertising industry if it turns its attention from large homogeneous television audiences to specific interests and specialization among cable viewers. However, the cable industry seems to be moving away from the narrowcasting concept toward more general audience entertainment.[10]

UNCONVENTIONAL MEDIA UNITS

There is little question that more advertisements will assault the consumer making the job of delivering any specific message that much more difficult. This will become increasingly difficult with such broadcasting trends as the **split-30,** the practice of dividing a 30-second commercial into two 15-second messages for different products. In 1986, the networks accepted freestanding 15-second commercials for the first time. Despite early industry estimates that 15-second spots would soon amount to 40 percent of all ad units sold, actual figures for 1986 were much closer to 20 percent.[11] However, this still means significantly more messages to the consumer in the same amount of time.

The 15-second commercial isn't the only departure from the conventional, however. More commercials means that advertisers and agencies are seeking any new way to communicate that promises impact. Longer broadcast spots, from the informative two- to ten-minute **infomercial** to the 90- to 120-second units commonly used by direct marketers, are very much in evidence. In print, new ways of using color in newspapers and pop-up ads in magazines are innovative communication tools.

Because of stepped-up competition for the consumer's attention, agencies and advertisers will increasingly need to focus their attention on the *quality* of the advertising message rather than depend upon repetition to get the sales point across. A study by a media trade association showed that while the number of commercials appearing on television has increased 140 percent over a 15-year period, the number of ads *actually noticed* by viewers increased only 78 percent.[12] Competition for attention is the rule in sales promotion as well. Figure 20.3 illustrates the vast growth couponing has experienced in recent years.

FIGURE 20.3

The Growth in Couponing,
1980–1986

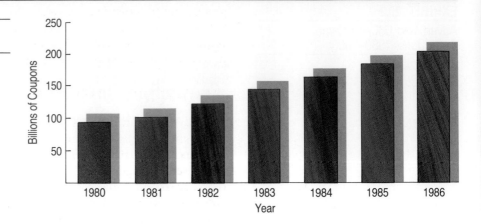

It seems likely that this increased emphasis on the content of commercials may actually result in different forms of commercials, especially in such media as cable. Here, extended forms of advertising messages such as informercials are possible. This concept combines attention-getting material and a sales pitch with hard product information, and may range up to 10 minutes, or even more in length. Many advertisers are also looking to producing specialized programming for cable channels in which product messages and consumer information are so closely intertwined that zipping or zapping is not possible. Examples might be an investment series sponsored by Merrill-Lynch or a cooking program sponsored by Beatrice Foods. This strategy seems to be the only one open to advertisers to escape zipping. General Foods estimated that zipping cost the firm $1 million in viewers from its 1984 media buys.

As the media become more selective and it becomes more efficient to reach audiences locally, it seems likely that advertisers will select local agencies to carry out their advertising. Thus mastery of the local media audience composition and how it fits into the national picture will provide important growth opportunities for regional agencies. It also seems likely that personal selling at the retail level will continue to decline. This will increase the importance of "preselling" through mass media—that is, advertising's importance in the retail market will continue to grow.

Some observers suggest that by the year 2000, as much as one third of national advertising will be aimed to generate direct response.[13] Certainly the increasing ease of getting information and making comparisons among products and services through mass communication systems make this believable. In recent years, direct marketing has grown at about 12 percent to 15 percent per year, about double the growth of total ad spending. Significant career opportunities will exist for people with a quantitative orientation and a desire to see tangible results. An understanding of computers helps, as does a good head for details.

If analysts are correct and the trend is to communicating with increasingly smaller, better defined, more affluent target audiences, the overall cost of advertising will almost certainly go up. It is a basic truism of the industry that the more select the target audience, the higher the cost per thousand. However, this need not be a barrier as long as advertising productivity is high. Clearly, the future calls for more sophisticated concepts and methods in audience and avertising research to identify consumer groups and to measure advertising effectiveness. This will require individuals with the training and experience to interpret research findings and to translate them into strategic action plans. These people will understand mass communication concepts as well as business imperatives.

THE AGENCY BUSINESS

The advertising trade press currently reminds us of several major issues facing the advertising business. The first of these, discussed in Chapter 2, concerns the mergers and acquisitions that have taken place among advertisers and agencies. (Will this result in important changes in the business?) A second is the continuing decline of agency personnel per million dollars of billings. (Will the pressure on the agency to operate more efficiently never cease?) A third has to do with the increasing number of agencies and client firms that work on a cost-plus or fee system of compensation. (Is this the end of the commission system?)

The answers to all these questions seem to be the same: While the events are in the news now, they have always been important issues in the industry. The Interpublic Group of companies (a group of advertising agencies) long ago pioneered the concept of noncompeting agency groups under a holding company. The decline in people/$million billing began in the 1950s. And, though there is constant pressure for more efficient agency operation, billings are growing fast enough that there is no actual decline—in fact, there is real growth—in agency employment. As to the commission system, criticisms and alternatives are as old as the system itself. Modern profit pressures and sophisticated accounting tools make it possible to develop workable alternatives that solve at least some of the problems. It is likely that all of these issues will continue in importance as the industry evolves.

A more fundamental question is the relative importance of advertising in the future. As Figure 20.4 indicates, the past decade has seen a relatively slow but important shift of promotional dollars from advertising to sales promotion. Does this indicate that advertising in the future will be less important as a marketing communication tool? Probably not. The most likely explanation for the shift of promotional dollars to sales pro-

FIGURE 20.4

Ad Promotion Allocations:
A Ten-Year History

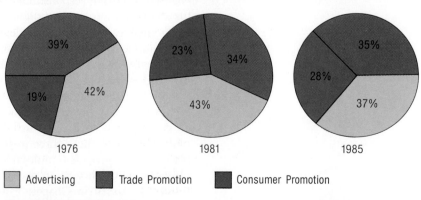

Source: Donnelley Marketing Annual Survey

motion is that it is a response to economic conditions. In other words, with the economy down, marketers have tended to shift dollars into programs aimed at immediate stimulation of sales. As economic conditions improve, it is likely that they will begin to shift funds back toward advertising, which gives long-term value to the brand.

There is little doubt that the advertising business currently faces important challenges and inexorable pressures to change. These factors combine to make the field an exciting and dynamic one—one where exciting individual achievement, rewarding team effort, innovation, and satisfaction are all possible.

THE ADVERTISING EMPLOYERS: WHO ARE THEY?

Earlier chapters of this text describe the work done by the central employers of the advertising industry: agencies, advertisers, media and suppliers of various specialized services. Advertising agencies, of course, employ a large number of specialized personnel to carry out the preparation and dissemination of advertising campaigns. It is important to keep in mind, however, that the advertising agency business is not a huge employer. While the country's largest advertising agency reports over 4,600 people in its 41 U.S. offices, the "typical" advertising agency is much smaller. The U.S. Bureau of the Census estimates that about 200,000 people are employed in the advertising agency business nationwide. This means that the agency business is really rather small and, consequently, that jobs are not easy to find.

Though advertisers, or client firms, constitute much greater numbers than agencies, they employ far fewer people in advertising-related work than even the medium-sized advertising agencies. For instance, the nation's *leading* national advertiser, Procter & Gamble, employs a number of people with important direct responsibilities for advertising activities, though few with advertising titles.

The commercial media employ a relatively large number of people directly involved with advertising. Most of these people are involved in the selling of commercial time and space to advertisers and agencies. While many of these employees spend some time in the development of advertising and promotional ideas for their clients (especially for retail advertisers), their primary responsibility is for sales. Most are paid a base salary plus a commission on their sales volume. The commission incentive is one reason they cannot afford to devote a great deal of time to developing advertising executions. Support from the business community is becoming increasingly important to public radio and television stations as well. The term **underwriting** is used to describe financial support rather than sponsorship or advertising. Publicly supported media represent a growing opportunity for employment for those with an understanding of advertising and the needs of sponsoring firms.

In addition to these three important employers, the innumerable support services provide employment opportunities. Printers, audio and video production houses, research firms, and the numerous other support services discussed in Chapter 3 are involved with the development and execution of advertising ideas. These smaller firms often require that people have more than one set of interests and abilities. For some, this is a stimulating environment where they can be involved in numerous projects at various levels. Others prefer the specialization necessary in a larger firm.

New goods and services are continually appearing on the scene and provide new challenges and opportunities for advertising people. The growth of high-tech industries in such fields as information technology and communications has resulted in dramatically increased advertising expenditures on behalf of these products and services. No doubt this trend will continue meaning that advertising people must be attuned to developing technology and the personal and business opportunities it represents.

Existing industries—such as health care—are awakening to the benefits of using marketing, promotional, and advertising techniques and concepts. Traditional public services (such as the United Way) as well as private charitable organizations are awakening to the importance and value of paid mass communications as a way of reaching the public and increasing participation. The important lesson here is that the techniques of persuasive communication in mass media can be applied to virtually any field or activity, and more and more groups are realizing that an understanding of advertising principles can result in more efficient and effective communication. As society becomes both larger and more complex, the opportunities for those who understand the strategy and tactics of persuasive communication likely will continue to increase.

THE ADVERTISING OPPORTUNITIES: WHERE ARE THEY?

There is little question that the advertising agency business is headquartered in New York City. New York is followed in prominence by Chicago, Los Angeles, and Detroit, with the other important metropolitan areas of the country following roughly in order of population size. Exhibit 20.3 lists the top 25 cities according to mid-1980s advertising billing. The overwhelmingly large numbers are from the top four cities. This is significant for several reasons. First, these cities are likely to remain the leaders of the agency business for some time. The presence of large agencies and large clients means that the most sophisticated advertising planning and people are likely to be found there. Second, the larger agency advertising community means more jobs, more turnover in them and, consequently, greater employment opportunity for those seeking a first job.

The advertiser community follows a similar geographical distribution. Exhibit 20.4 shows the corporate location of the 25 leading national advertisers. Major advertisers also tend to be found in or near large cities, though not at quite the same level of concentration.

These observations do not mean that New York is the only place to find an advertising job. In fact, countless opportunities exist in communities all across the country. One of the best ways to learn more about

EXHIBIT 20.3

Top 25 U.S. Cities
by Agency Billings

RANK	CITY	SHOPS REPORTING	TOTAL DOMESTIC BILLINGS		PERCENTAGE OF CHANGE
			1986	1985	
1	New York City	179	$19,974.7	$18,330.4	9.0
2	Chicago	71	4,908.3	4,644.2	5.7
3	Los Angeles	56	2,953.7	2,699.9	9.4
4	Detroit	27	2,436.0	2,196.3	10.9
5	San Francisco	24	1,265.9	1,186.3	6.7
6	Dallas	17	968.5	865.3	11.9
7	Boston	22	842.5	649.0	29.8
8	Minneapolis	16	832.2	747.0	11.4
9	Atlanta	20	594.7	666.1	(10.7)
10	Philadelphia	27	554.1	480.6	15.3
11	Cleveland	12	461.5	440.1	4.9
12	St. Louis	8	442.6	436.3	1.4
13	Houston	15	379.1	353.0	7.4
14	Pittsburgh	9	300.2	272.0	10.4
15	Washington	8	266.5	234.6	13.6
16	Baltimore	8	262.8	224.7	17.0
17	Milwaukee	11	222.5	198.3	12.2
18	Seattle	7	175.0	175.3	(0.2)
19	Kansas City	7	170.1	140.0	21.5
20	Columbus, Ohio	4	133.2	110.9	20.1
21	Rochester, N.Y.	5	130.6	118.6	10.1
22	Akron, Ohio	3	126.1	117.3	7.5
23	Denver	9	116.5	113.7	2.5
24	Greenville, S.C.	3	111.9	112.4	(0.4)
25	Richmond, Va.	3	111.9	71.3	56.9

Note: Dollars in millions. Where possible, billings of large agencies were apportioned to individual offices. Some estimates were used. Agency universe is the Ad Age 500. *Advertising Age,* April 20, 1987, 40.

opportunities in your local community is to contact the local advertising club. Their address can be obtained from the American Advertising Federation (listed in Appendix A of this book).

PREPARING FOR AN ADVERTISING CAREER

The answer to the question, "How should I prepare for a career in advertising?" is controversial and depends on the nature of your career goal and the background of the person you ask. Despite the fact that a great number of people have enjoyed successful and rewarding advertising careers without any specific training—or even a college degree—the chances of this happening these days is slight.

The question above elicits two common responses from advertising practitioners. One group claims that business training is essential. They

EXHIBIT 20.4

Top 25 National Advertisers

RANK	COMPANY	HEADQUARTERS	TOTAL ESTIMATED SPENDING
1	Procter & Gamble	Cincinnati	$1,600,000
2	Philip Morris Cos.	New York	1,400,000
3	RJR/Nabisco	Winston-Salem, N.C.	1,093,000
4	Sears, Roebuck & Co.	Chicago	800,000
5	General Motors Corp.	Detroit	779,000
6	Beatrice Cos.	Chicago	684,000
7	Ford Motor Co.	Dearborn, Mich.	614,600
8	Kmart Corp.	Troy, Mich.	567,000
9	McDonald's Corp.	Oak Brook, Ill.	550,000
10	Anheuser-Busch Cos.	St. Louis	522,900
11	American Telephone & Telegraph	New York	521,318
12	Ralston Purina Co.	St. Louis	508,365
13	Dart & Kraft	Northbrook, Ill.	489,349
14	General Mills	Minneapolis	484,146
15	J.C. Penney Co.	New York	478,892
16	PepsiCo Inc.	Purchase, N.Y.	478,372
17	Pillsbury Co.	Minneapolis	473,220
18	Warner-Lambert Co.	Morris Plains, N.J.	469,339
19	Unilever U.S.	New York	413,623
20	Johnson & Johnson	New Brunswick, N.J.	401,217
21	American Home Products Corp.	New York	399,516
22	Chrysler Corp.	Highland Park, Mich.	393,400
23	Coca-Cola Co.	Atlanta	390,000
24	GE/RCA	New York	373,336
25	Kellogg Co.	Battle Creek, Mich.	364,299

Source: *Advertising Age*, September 4, 1986, 12.

reason that today's advertising person must understand the assumptions and the imperatives of the client's business and must also grasp the business operation of the agency. While these facts do not rule out a non-business student from an advertising career, business students *are* able to start more quickly and learn more rapidly. Some advertiser and agency training programs are geared to business graduates, and some to those who hold the Master's of Business Administration (MBA) degree.

A second school of thought holds that the best preparation for advertising work is through a professionally oriented program in mass communications, based on broad exposure to the arts, sciences, and humanities. In this view, the practice of advertising is considered less the application of business principles and more the understanding of American people and culture. Broad training in liberal arts, with some professional coursework at the junior/senior level, is seen as providing the background and knowledge base to draw upon and build through experience on the job. Communication program advocates also claim that the ability to express oneself clearly and succinctly in speaking and writing is better fostered in smaller liberal arts disciplines than in large business schools.

As suggested at the outset, there is no clear answer as to the best preparation for an advertising career, though from the foregoing discussion, it should be obvious that an understanding of business activities and procedures and the ability to communicate clearly and effectively are both essential.

There is an increasing emphasis on graduate degrees in management training programs, not only in advertising but also in other segments of the business world. MBA's have been highly sought after by industry. Though those who hold master's degrees in advertising, or in liberal arts fields like psychology and English can often be competitive in getting jobs, it is difficult for them to command the same salaries as the MBA grad. In short, advanced degrees are becoming more important, but the same two schools of thought exist about what sort of preparation is best.

Of course, other kinds of knowledge and abilities are also useful in the advertising business. One is experience in a related industry or business. Agency experience can be a distinct asset for an advertising manager. Experience in broadcast sales gives a firm foundation for a position as agency media buyer, while experience with a commercial research firm might be an important qualification for the research director at an agency or client firm. Not many college students have the opportunity to acquire work-related experience, though considering a position related to your eventual career objective might be good advice in choosing a first job, or in finding summer employment.

Finally, an **internship program** is another possibility. Many colleges and universities maintain such programs with industry, through which students often can get university credit for supervised part-time work in jobs related to their career goals. Such programs offer students a chance to get firsthand experience in the working world and often allow them to make more accurate judgments about their career and employment objectives.

WHAT JOB IS RIGHT FOR ME?

To be seriously interested in a career in advertising, you should be willing to accept long working hours for results that are sometimes difficult to measure, and a highly competitive environment for finding that first job. If you are willing to accept these ground rules, there are many rewards. These can include the satisfaction of seeing your work in the media and the sense of accomplishment in designing plans that contribute in a large way to the successful marketing of products and services. Direct contact with interesting and imaginative people in the communications industry is major satisfaction for many. Not the least of the satisfactions, of course, is the financial reward possible. Exhibit 20.5 shows the average salaries for advertising positions reported to *Adweek* in 1987. While six-figure salaries are not unheard of in the advertising business—and often go to people in their 30s—such salaries are certainly not typical.

The first step in determining where to start in the advertising business is to make an honest inventory of your own talents, interests, and abilities. The following suggestions can help to guide you in your analysis.

EXHIBIT 20.5

The 1987 Salary Survey Results
(in thousands of dollars)

CORPORATE MARKETING/ADVERTISING	MEN	WOMEN	TOTAL
GENERAL/CORPORATE MANAGEMENT			
Chairman, President, Exec./Sen. VP, Vice Pres., Supervisor, "Director of"	$75.0	$39.0	$70.0
MARKETING/BRAND MANAGEMENT			
Executive/Senior VP, Vice President, Supervisor, "Director of"	70.0	37.0	59.7
Marketing Manager, Brand Manager	46.2	35.5	39.0
SALES/SALES MANAGEMENT			
Supervisor, "Director of," Manager	39.5	—	42.5
SALES PROMOTION			
Vice President, Supervisor, "Director of," Manager	50.0	40.0	43.7
ADVERTISING MANAGEMENT			
Vice President, Supervisor, "Director of"	54.0	38.3	50.8
Advertising Manager	45.9	32.0	42.2
Writer, Planner	34.0*	34.5*	34.5
OTHER CORPORATE POSITIONS			
Media Buying/Media Planning	40.0	28.0	34.0
Public Relations/Public Affairs	41.2	35.0	40.0
Advertising Research/Marketing Research	56.2	30.5	42.5
▪TOTAL: CORPORATE MARKETING/ADVERTISING	50.4	35.6	43.7
AGENCIES			
Chairman, President, Chief Executive Officer, Chief Operating Officer	62.5	50.8	57.9
Executive Vice President, Senior Vice President	81.7	42.2*	70.0
Vice President, Assistant VP, Supervisor, "Director of," Manager	58.1	40.0	50.0
▪TOTAL: GENERAL MANAGEMENT	62.4	42.9	56.0
Chairman, President, Vice Chairman, Exec./Sen. VP, Vice President	75.0	—	73.3
Assistant Vice President, Supervisor, Director, Manager	35.7	29.0*	34.7
Copywriter, Art Director	28.5	27.0	27.8
▪TOTAL: CREATIVE DEPARTMENT	44.5	27.9	39.7
Executive Vice President, Senior Vice President, Vice President	73.0	80.0*	74.2
Assistant Vice President, Supervisor, Director	45.0	45.0	45.0
Manager, Account Representative	32.5	32.2	32.3
Assistant Account Representative	—	19.4*	19.4
▪TOTAL: ACCOUNT MANAGEMENT DEPARTMENT	49.0	32.5	39.0
Executive Vice President, Senior Vice President, Vice President	72.5*	47.5	61.7
Assistant Vice President, Supervisor, Director	—	32.5	32.0
Manager, Buyer, Planner	25.5	25.0	25.0
Assistant Buyer, Assistant Planner	—	19.4*	19.4
▪TOTAL: MEDIA DEPARTMENT	35.0	31.0	32.2
Public Relations/Public Affairs	47.5	34.7	40.6
Advertising Research/Marketing Research	48.7	31.0*	45.0
Production/Traffic	40.0*	21.7	27.0
Administration/Financial	38.0	17.2*	33.3
▪TOTAL: ADVERTISING AGENCIES	49.0	32.2	41.4
▪TOTAL: CORPORATE PLUS AGENCIES	$49.5	$33.5	$42.1

*Small sample size. Note: All salaries are medians for job classifications. If no salary number is reported, it is because the number of responses was insufficient to be statistically significant.
Source: "Money and Power" Special Report, *Adweek*, May 18, 1987, MP23.

A CLOSER LOOK

YOUNG ADVERTISING PROFESSIONALS

Following are some brief profiles of former advertising students who have gone on to careers in the advertising industry. After their graduation from the University of Colorado—Boulder, the three took widely dispersed career paths. All of them currently work outside the traditional "advertising capital" of New York.

Diana Haytko is from Northglenn, Colorado. After graduating from Colorado in 1985, she earned a master's degree in advertising from the University of Illinois at Urbana-Champaign.

Diana works for The Bloom Agency in Dallas, where she began as an account assistant on the Maybelline account. Since then, she has worked on a number of brands, including Tropical Blend, Solarcaine, and Di-Gel. In 1987 she became Assistant Account Executive on the Zales Jewelry account.

Her advice to students seeking advertising jobs: "Do not expect a job to find you. Be aggressive and willing to take risks, and compromise. Take all things into consideration when looking at an agency: size, types of accounts, opportunity for promotion, and location."

Diana's long-term objective is to build a solid base of business experience, then return to school for a Ph.D. and teach advertising at a major university.

Pat Wallace graduated with two degrees: one in journalism (advertising major) and the other in business (marketing major). He moved to the West Coast and quickly found a job as an assistant account executive with Phillips-Ramsey Advertising, a well-known agency in San Diego. Since joining the agency he's been involved in everything from print production to strategic planning, as well as media, research, direct marketing, and public relations.

He advises students seeking advertising jobs to "know what you want to do and what you can do. Employers need people who can jump in and go to work. Be prepared to work hard and don't forget you'll be paying dues for awhile (with clerical stuff and behind-the-scenes work). Team play is very important, so handling interpersonal relationships is critical. Self-confidence always helps."

Pat's long-term goal is to establish his own marketing communications firm specializing in international business-to-business marketing.

Amy Lutz is originally from San Francisco. After graduation, she chose from among several advertising job offers to take a position selling newspaper space for the *Longmont Times-Call* in Longmont, Colorado.

Amy began as an advertising telemarketing representative, cold-calling new accounts and reactivating smaller existing accounts. After three months she was promoted to Account Executive, and assigned a large list of major accounts, which she assisted in planning and scheduling advertising efforts. After 14 months at the *Times-Call*, Amy joined the *Denver Post* as an account executive in retail advertising.

She says, "In all my interviews with agencies and newspapers, no one was interested in my transcript, but everyone was interested in my resume. Most schools have internship programs as well as newspaper

WRITING AND VISUALIZATION: THE CREATIVE AREA

While clear writing is a skill that everyone in advertising should possess, it is essential for anyone who hopes to become a **copywriter.** Mere writing skill is not enough, however; it must be an interest and facility at combin-

Patrick Wallace

and radio stations at which you can gain experience. Keep your eyes and ears open for businesses and organizations that need no-pay advertising positions filled. Take advantage of any and all advertising-related experience you can find. You're competing not only against other students, but possibly against people who have been 'out there' a while. Make the effort to make yourself an obvious asset to any company, and good luck!"

Amy's long-term career goal: to become an advertising director or publisher of a national publication.

Diana Haytko

Amy Lutz

ing words and pictures and harnessing their communication power. If you are fascinated by the impact and nuance of words and the ways that they can be used to convince a cynic or to evoke an emotion, and if you are willing to work and rework words so that the minimum number have the maximum impact, you may have the interests and skills for copywriting.

Visualization is the fundamental skill of the **art director.** This ability to imagine the visual part of the advertising message in a way that enhances and enlivens the message is an indispensable talent. It can often be cultivated through training in fine or commercial art programs. However, it is essential that individuals bring an understanding of design, layout, and aesthetics as well as an interest in visual arts and fashions. If the creative areas of advertising are your interest, you should begin to assemble a **portfolio** while in college. This is essentially a sample book containing your work. Writers should include samples of various kinds of writing, especially advertising concepts (published or unpublished). Artists should include illustrations and designs of either published material or speculative layouts.

ANALYSIS, ORGANIZATION, AND PLANNING

If you are not intimidated by numbers and are willing to apply some brain power to making comparisons among them, using both simple formulas and statistical calculations, then media planning or research are strong career possibilities. Both these areas require broad knowledge developed through experience and a willingness to toy with numerical data in search of undiscovered combinations. These positions increasingly require an understanding of computer applications, both for data processing and in the use of various kinds of applied models. Because of the importance of experience in making media planning and research decisions, these jobs are rarely a starting point for new employees. More often, people with these skills begin as a **media buyer** or a **research assistant.** These positions involve the execution of programs planned by senior-level personnel.

The ability to make poised presentations, to grasp complex marketing problems quickly, and to apply analytical thinking to advertising situations are characteristics of the **account executive.** This individual must also be able to organize and coordinate the work of the agency staff. Usually those interested in account work begin as assistant or junior account executives, or come up through the training program of a large advertising agency. While some agencies hire only MBAs for account positions, others subscribe to the liberal arts school of thought discussed earlier. Regardless of educational background, electives in business—especially marketing—are helpful preparation for positions in account work.

Those who are more interested in the overall planning, organization, and administration of the advertising program than in its development are better suited to work with the advertiser firm. Work as a **brand manager** usually includes responsibility for the overall marketing efforts of products or groups of products. Effective work as a brand manager can lead to the position of advertising manager, which entails supervisory responsibility for the advertising activities of a number of brands or product groups. It is more and more the rule that people filling these positions hold an MBA degree, usually with emphasis in marketing.

Some people are fascinated by the behind-the-scenes work: the technical, artistic, and mechanical aspects of preparing advertising and related materials. Many opportunities exist in these areas; they require special technical expertise, especially in the areas of production. These specialists work with both advertisers and agencies to translate strategies and ideas into the finished versions on advertisements seen by the public. Some

A CLOSER LOOK

THE JOB SEARCH: WHAT WORKS

In *Ogilvy on Advertising*, the agency leader offers the following observations about the job hunt: Don't telephone—*write* to three or four agencies, and enclose your curriculum vitae. Be sure to *type* your letter, and take a lot of trouble with it. In their book *Writing that Works*, my partners Kenneth Roman and Joel Raphaelson offer this golden advice:

1   Spell all names correctly

It's astonishing how often job applicants misspell the names of the agencies they want to work for. The message that gets through, right off the bat, is: 'This applicant can't be seriously interested in working here; he didn't even take the trouble to find out how to spell our name.'

2   Identify the sort of job you're applying for

State it clearly and at once. Say what led you to apply —a want ad, a recommendation from a friend, whatever. A letter applying for a job as a research analyst started in this mysterious way:

> Dear Ms. Smith:
> It's spring already—a time to think about planting seeds. Some seeds are small, like apple seeds. Others are bigger. Coconuts, for example. But big or little, a seed can grow and flourish if it's planted in proper soil.

The applicant would have done better to start like this:

> Dear Ms. Smith:
> I understand that you are looking for a research analyst.

Ms. Smith doesn't have time to play guessing games with her mail.

3   Be specific and factual

Once you've made clear what job you want, then touch on your chief qualifications. Avoid egotistical abstractions like: 'Ambition mixed with a striving for excellence is one of my strongest assets.'

4   Be personal, direct and natural

You are a human being writing to another human being. Neither of you is an institution. You should be businesslike and courteous, but never stiff and impersonal.

The more your letter sounds like *you*, the more it will stand apart from the letters of your competitors. But don't try to dazzle your reader with your sparkling personality. You wouldn't show off in an interview, so why show off in a letter? If you make each sentence sound the way you would *say* it across a desk, there will be plenty of personality in your letter.

5   Propose a specific next step

Close your letter with a clear and precise statement of how you wish to proceed toward an interview. Avoid such mumblings as:

> 'Hoping to hear from you soon.'

> 'Thank you for your time and consideration.'

> 'I'm looking forward to the opportunity of discussing a position with you.'

All such conclusions place the burden of the next step on your busy prospective employer. Why make *him* work in *your* interest? Do the job yourself, like this:

> 'I'll call your office on Wednesday afternoon to see if you'd like me to come in for an interview.'

> 'I'm free for an interview every morning until 8:45, and Thursday after 2:30. I'll call your office on Wednesday afternoon to find out if you would like to get together at any of those times.'

At this stage a phone call makes things easy for the person at the other end. If you don't call him, he has to go to the trouble of calling or writing to you. The idea is to make it as simple as you possibly can for your prospective employer to set up an appointment at a time that's convenient to you.

---

colleges offer preparation in broadcast production, for example, which provides a good foundation for starting out.

SELLING AND ACCOUNT SERVICE

An essential part of the mass-media industry is selling. As suggested above, this applies to public broadcasting as well as to commercial stations and print media. To be effective in selling media you need self-confidence, good interpersonal skills, and a high level of self-motivation. There are, and will continue to be, numerous opportunities for people with these characteristics in mass-media sales. While it was formerly the case that sales people started in smaller markets and worked their way up, these days there are opportunities in even the largest markets for those with enthusiasm and ability.

Media sales is a competitive job. There is every indication that it will grow more so as new media become available and competition for the advertiser's dollar increases. Many media sales organizations, particularly rep firms, start new employees as support, research, or account service people within the organization. This is often a good way to learn the business and how to assemble the information necessary to make a sale.

HOW DO I FIND A JOB IN ADVERTISING?

Finding a first job in a highly competitive area is often the result of careful preparation, tenacity, and a certain measure of good luck. Although part of the preparation involves college coursework and the knowledge and perspective gained there, the job search has other aspects as well. As mentioned earlier, a carefully chosen internship can provide useful experience and demonstrate to an employer that you are sincerely interested in the field. Thinking through your skills, interests, and abilities is also essential to organizing a productive job search.

Once you've determined your job objective, you will need to consider other factors and limitations, such as your willingness to relocate to a distant city. With this planning done, you can identify the market of potential employers. Most college libraries and many public ones have reference books that can be quite useful in the job search. These include the *Standard Directory of Advertising Agencies*, the *Standard Directory of Advertisers*, *Editor and Publisher Yearbook*, and *Broadcasting Yearbook*. These publications contain considerable information about potential employers, including the names of people in key positions, numbers of employees, location of offices, etc.

RESUMES AND COVER LETTERS

After identifying your market, you will need to develop the basic tool of job hunting, the **resume.** Basically, a resume is a communication device between you and your potential employer. It emphasizes your accom-

A CLOSER LOOK

BEHIND THE JOB-HUNTING FACADE

In *Creative Management*, William Marsteller suggests the kind of questions he likes to ask of job applicants in an interview.

Most managers, when they're interviewing prospective new employees, ask questions like "Are you honest? Do you drink to excess? Did you get good grades in school? Why did you leave your last job?"

Such a waste of time. Do you expect someone to admit being a dumb alcoholic thief who got canned for incompetence and sloth?

Good interviewing combines an element of surprise with some off-beat questions that probe beyond the obvious.

Here are some I use:

- If you come to work here, what do you expect to be doing in five years? In 20 years?

- What did you do last Saturday and Sunday? Take me through those days.

- What do you most admire about your wife (husband, tentmate)?

- In your opinion, what's the best museum in town? Why?

- What were the last two books you've read?

- Who are your two closest friends? Tell me about them.

- Here's paper and pencil. Take five minutes to write down the adjectives that best describe you.

- What school would you rather have gone to than the one you did? Why?

- What do you think the economic situation will be a year from today?

- If you could just get in a car and drive for 30 days, where would you go?

- What's the greatest honor you've ever had?

- What did you learn from the last person you worked for on how to get along with people?

- What would you hope your children would do when they're grown?

- Can you type?

- What television programs interest you most?

- Of all the people you've been associated with, whom did you dislike most? Why?

- What do you remember most happily from your childhood?

- If you were me, why would you hire you?

Now, aren't you glad I didn't interview you?

Source: William Marsteller, *Creative Management*, pp. 66–67. Copyright © 1981 Crain Books (National Textbook Company). Reprinted with permission.

plishments and intentions as well as your distinctive characteristics. Keep in mind that employers may receive hundreds of resumes a week during peak job search times. Any that are unclear or messy, or that contain spelling errors or other sloppy mistakes are discarded without further attention. Usually a resume is no more than a page in length and includes a statement of a career objective at the outset. Your resume should be straightforward and factual and include your full name, address, and phone. In addition, it should summarize your educational and employment experience.

Numerous books can guide you in writing your resume; some of them are mentioned at the end of this chapter. Your college placement office may also help you.

The introduction to the resume is contained in a **cover letter.** In this device you introduce yourself to your prospects and explain your reason for contacting them. Your letter should also convey your interest in the employer and why you would be an asset to the firm. The cover letter offers you a chance to make a specific and personalized proposition to each reader.

Your goal in writing cover letters and circulating your resume is usually to get an **interview** at some future time, since it is most unlikely that any employer will respond to your resume with a job offer. At the interview you will probably have the opportunity to talk with members of the personnel department as well as some who work in the area in which you have expressed an interest. Again, preparation is important. During your identification of the target market you should make an effort to learn as much as you can about the firms you contact. Who are their major clients? What are their most successful brands? How is their business affected by recent trends in economics, society, or regulation? The effort to learn a bit about the important developments affecting the business can pay big dividends in the interview situation. First of all, an understanding of the company is an indication to interviewers of your seriousness about working for them. Secondly, it is flattering to interviewers that you would take an interest in them and their activities and concerns, and you will find that it eases conversation to know enough to ask intelligent questions about business operations and developments.

INTERVIEWING

Remember that hiring decisions are about half rational and half emotional. Though interviewers are interested in your skills and abilities, they are also collecting their personal responses to very subjective measures of your personality, your poise, and your compatibility as a coworker. Time spent in anticipating interviewer questions and in formulating questions of your own can help considerably in managing the impression you make in an interview situation. Remember also that interviewing is itself a skill that improves with practice. While it is understandable to be nervous in your first efforts, try to cultivate your own abilities to relax and be yourself. After all, you are not interested in getting a job in a situation where you have to spend a majority of your effort simply trying to fit in. Remember that the choosing process works two ways, and that you are trying to make a determination about whether you can be happy and successful in the environment in which you are interviewing.

Most often college graduates interview for an **entry-level position** — a job in which people without experience are employed. These include positions such as media buyers and account trainees at agencies, and assistant brand managers or sometimes field sales positions in advertiser firms. It is important to realize that you may have to consider a job that does not at first seem to be in line with your career objective. For example, Proctor & Gamble, the nation's leading advertiser, rarely accepts people into advertising and marketing positions without experience in field sales.

Many large advertising agencies start those interested in account work in positions in the traffic department. This is a staff department that expedites work through the steps of the production process within the advertising agency. The reason for this is that management feels it provides an intimate understanding of the activities most basic to the operation of the company. This understanding is believed to be fundamental to making intelligent management decisions later in one's career. Smaller agencies and advertisers have different approaches, and it is sometimes possible to find opportunities that seem closer to your career objectives by starting with them. The decision of how to approach your career is of course yours alone, but many successful advertising people have found that it was beneficial for them to accept a first job that simply got them into the advertising industry. Once they accumulated some experience in an entry-level position, they were either promoted or found jobs that brought them closer to their eventual objective.

SUMMARY

This chapter has suggested that advertising mirrors the controversies and problems in society. Condom advertising was used as an example to suggest some of the possible ethical conflicts that can arise among media, advertisers, and advertising agencies.

The future of advertising is likely to be shaped by trends we can see today. These will include increasing use of cable television and VCRs. More sophisticated communications technology, while available, is not likely to become a major force in the near future. Innovations in form, such as the 15-second spot and infomercials, are likely to continue. As the economy changes, it is likely that the balance between advertising and other forms of promotional expenditures will continue to shift.

In seeking an advertising career, it is important to be honest with yourself about your talents, interests, and abilities, and try to match these with the needs of employers. Although the largest employers are in major cities, many people build rewarding careers in smaller communities. Advertising employment is competitive, and the best chance of finding it comes from good educational preparation, job experience through summer work or internship, and a carefully written resume.

QUESTIONS FOR DISCUSSION

1. Should media have the right to restrict condom advertising as they have? Why or why not?

2. Does it seem likely that many new forms of mass communication technology will become important ad media? Does there seem to be advertising potential in these systems?

3. Distinguish between cable service and premium services. Why is the difference important to advertisers?

4. Describe two important viewer activities connected with the use of VCRs. What is important to advertisers about these behaviors?

5. Explain the concept of narrowcasting.

6. What is a split-30?

7. How do you think audiences might respond to the increase in advertising messages expected in the coming years? How will advertisers respond?

8. Would you prefer to take a job in advertising in your hometown or in a major advertising city? What are the advantages of each?

9. Do you think business or mass communication provides the best preparation for an advertising career? Does it make a difference which area of advertising you choose?

10. Describe the difference in purpose between a cover letter and a resume.

NOTES

1. "Agency Drops Condom Work," *Advertising Age*, February 23, 1987, 8.

2. For a discussion of audience characteristics, see Dean Krugman, "Evaluating the Audiences of the New Media," *Journal of Advertising*, vol. 14, no. 4, 1985, 21–27.

3. "A Conversation with Don Miceli," *Marketing and Media Decisions*, vol. 12, no. 12, Fall 1985, 46.

4. Estimates were made by A.C. Nielsen Company and reported in the *Los Angeles Times*, September 2, 1984.

5. "VCR Sales Explosion Shakes Up Industry," *Advertising Age*, January 9, 1986, 14.

6. Tom Delaney, "Follow the Zapper," *Adweek*, August 18, 1986, 6.

7. Leo Bogart, "War of the Words: Advertising in the Year 2010," *Across the Board*, January 1985, 21.

8. "Advertising in the Year 2000," *AAAA Newsletter*, American Association of Advertising Agencies, December 1984.

9. Bogart, "War of the Words."

10. "Cable Puts a Lid on Rises as It Redefines Its Base," *Marketing and Media Decisions*, vol. 20, no. 12, Fall 1985, 43–45.

11. Dennis Freeman, "Heyday of 15-Second Spot Falls behind Schedule," *Advertising Age*, November 17, 1986, S–13.

12. Bogart, "War of the Words," 23.

13. For a discussion of the growing role of direct response, see John Witek, *Response Television* (Chicago: Crain Books, 1981).

SUGGESTED READINGS

The following books should be quite helpful to anyone interested in finding a job in advertising. With the exception of the first book listed (which is a general guide to job hunting and career planning), all refer specifically to the advertising industry.

Bolles, Richard. *What Color Is Your Parachute?* Berkeley, Calif.: 10 Speed Press, 1985.

Deckinger, E. L., and Jules Singer. *Exploring Careers in Advertising*. New York: Rosen Publishing Group, 1985.

Haas, Ken. *How to Get a Job in Advertising*. New York: Art Direction Book Co., 1979.

Katz, Judith. *The Ad Game*. New York: Harper & Row, 1984.

Kirkpatrick, Frank. *How to Get the Right Job in Advertising*. Chicago: Contemporary Books, 1982.

Paetro, Maxine. *How to Put Your Book Together and Get a Job in Advertising*. New York: Hawthorn Books, 1980.

Pattis, William. *Opportunities in Advertising Careers*. Chicago: National Textbook Co., 1984.

Rogers, Ed. *Getting Hired*. Englewood Cliffs, N.J.: Prentice-Hall, 1984.

Young, James Webb. *How to Become an Advertising Man*. Chicago: Crain Books, 1963.

Zimmermann, Caroline. *How to Break into the Media Professions*. Garden City, N.Y.: Doubleday, 1981.

The Advertising Career Directory–1987. New York: Career Publishing, 1987.

Advertising–A Guide to Careers in Advertising. New York: American Association of Advertising Agencies, 1975.

APPENDIXES

ADVERTISING ASSOCIATIONS

Advertising Council
825 Third Avenue
New York, New York 10022
(212) 758-0400

Advertising Research Foundation
(Publisher of *Journal of Advertising Research*)
3 East 54th Street
New York, New York 10022
(212) 751-5656

American Academy of Advertising
(Publisher of *Journal of Advertising*)
Robert L. King, Executive Secretary
The Citadel
Charleston, South Carolina 29409
(803) 792-7089

American Advertising Federation
1400 K Street, NW Suite 1000
Washington, D.C. 20005
(202) 898-0089

American Association of Advertising Agencies
666 Third Avenue
13th Floor
New York, New York 10017
(212) 683-2500

American Marketing Association
(Publisher of *Journal of Marketing, Journal of Marketing Research, Marketing News*)
250 S. Wacker Drive
Chicago, Illinois 60606-5819
(312) 648-0536

Association of National Advertisers, Inc.
155 E. 44th Street
New York, New York 10017
(212) 697-5950

Business/Professional Advertising Association
205 E. 42nd Street
New York, New York 10017
(212) 661-0222

International Advertising Association
475 Fifth Avenue
New York, New York 10017
(212) 684-1583

National Advertising Division
Council of Better Business Bureaus
845 Third Avenue
New York, New York 10022
(212) 754-1358

National Advertising Review Board
845 Third Avenue
New York, New York 10022
(212) 832-1320

MEDIA ASSOCIATIONS

American Business Press, Inc.
205 East 42nd Street
New York, New York 10017
(212) 661-6360

Cabletelevision Advertising Bureau
767 Third Avenue
New York, New York 10017
(212) 751-7770

Direct Marketing Association
Six East 43rd Street
New York, New York 10017
(212) 689-4977

Institute of Outdoor Advertising
485 Lexington Avenue
New York, New York 10017
(212) 986-5920

International Newspaper Advertising & Marketing
   Executives, Inc.
11600 Sunrise Valley Drive
Reston, Virginia 22091
(703) 620-0090

Magazine Publishers Association
575 Lexington Avenue
New York, New York 10022
(212) 752-0055

National Association of Broadcasters
1771 N Street, NW
Washington, D.C. 20036
(202) 293-3500

National Yellow Pages Service
999 W. Big Beaver Road
Troy, Michigan 48084
(313) 362-3300

Newspaper Advertising Bureau, Inc.
485 Lexington Avenue
New York, New York 10017
(212) 921-5080

Outdoor Advertising Association of America
342 Madison Avenue
New York, New York 10173
(212) 986-5920

Point-of-Purchase Advertising Institute, Inc.
60 East 42nd Street
New York, New York 10017
(212) 682-7041

Radio Advertising Bureau, Inc.
485 Lexington Avenue
New York, New York 10017
(212) 599-6666

Specialty Advertising Association International
1404 Walnut Hill Lane
Irving, Texas 75062
(214) 258-0404

Television Bureau of Advertising, Inc.
485 Lexington Avenue
New York, New York 10017
(211) 661-8440

Trade Show Bureau
49 Locust Avenue
New Canaan, Connecticut 06840
(203) 966-7133

Transit Advertising Association
1899 L Street, NW
Washington, D.C. 20036
(202) 293-4708

DIRECTORIES AND MAGAZINES

Advertising Age
740 N. Rush Street
Chicago, Illinois 60611
(312) 649–5200

Adweek
820 Second Avenue
New York, New York 10017
(212) 661–8080

The IMS Ayer Directory of Publications
426 Pennsylvania Avenue
Fort Washington, Pennsylvania 19034
(215) 628–8590

Business Marketing
740 N. Rush Street
Chicago, Illinois 60611
(312) 649–5260

Editor and Publisher Market Guide
575 Lexington Avenue
New York, New York 10022
(212) 675–4380

Madison Avenue
369 Lexington Avenue
New York, New York 10017
(212) 972–0600

Marketing Communications
475 Park Avenue South
New York, New York 10016
(212) 725–2300

Marketing & Media Decisions
1140 Avenue of the Americas
New York, New York 10036
(212) 391–2155

The Media Book
75 East 55th Street
New York, New York 10022
(212) 751–2671

Media Market Guide
Bethlehem Publishing, Inc.
Box 19
Bethlehem, New Hampshire 03514
(603) 869–2418

Standard Directory of Advertisers
5201 Old Orchard Road
Skokie, Illinois 60077
(312) 441–2193

Standard Directory of Advertising Agencies
5201 Old Orchard Road
Skokie, Illinois 60077
(312) 470–3404

Standard Rate & Data Service
5201 Old Orchard Road
Skokie, Illinois 60077
(312) 256–6067

OTHER SOURCES OF ADVERTISING DATA

A.C. Nielsen Company
Nielsen Plaza
Northbrook, Illinois 60062
(312) 498–6300

The Arbitron Company
1350 Avenue of the Americas
New York, New York 10019
(212) 887–1300

Audit Bureau of Circulations, Inc.
900 North Meacham Road
Schaumburg, Illinois 60173
(312) 885–0910

Broadcast Advertisers Reports, Inc.
500 Fifth Avenue
New York, New York 10036
(212) 221–2630

Business Publications Audit of Circulation, Inc.
360 Park Avenue South
New York, New York 10010
(212) 532–6880

Gallup & Robinson
Research Park
Princeton, New Jersey 08540
(609) 924–3400

Leading National Advertisers, Inc.
515 Madison Avenue
New York, New York 10022
(212) 725–2700

Marketing Science Institute
14 Story Street
Cambridge, Massachusetts 02138
(617) 491–2060

MediaMark Research, Inc.
341 Madison Avenue
New York, New York 10017
(212) 599–0444

National Retail Merchants Associations
100 W. 31st Street
New York, New York 10001
(212) 244–8780

Public Relations Society of America
845 Third Avenue
New York, New York 10022
(212) 826–1750

Simmons Market Research Bureau
219 East 42nd Street
New York, New York 10017
(212) 867–1414

Starch INRA Hooper, Inc.
566 E. Boston Post Road
Mamaroneck, New York 10543
(914) 698–0800

The Survey of Buying Power Data Service
633 Third Avenue
New York, New York 10017
(212) 986–4800

Media planning and buying is a complex task: there are thousands of media options, costs change often, and prices are frequently negotiated. The following media data are provided as a convenience in estimating the cost of bringing an advertising campaign to the target market.

The authors wish to thank Christa Reich and the staff of Reich Communications in Aurora, Colorado, for compiling the information in this appendix.

Magazines

MAGAZINE	FREQUENCY OF ISSUE	CIRCULATION (in thousands)	PAGE RATE B/W	PAGE RATE 4-C	FOUR-COLOR PAGE CPM
WOMEN'S					
Cosmopolitan	Monthly	2,935	$32,170	$43,290	$14.75
Good Housekeeping	Monthly	5,142	66,965	84,025	16.34
Ladies' Home Journal	Monthly	5,121	52,300	64,300	12.56
McCall's	Monthly	5,275	51,400	63,300	12.00
Parents Magazine	Monthly	1,729	29,870	38,235	22.12
Redbook	Monthly	3,891	43,875	58,020	14.91
Seventeen	Monthly	1,804	21,100	30,575	16.95
True Story	Monthly	1,444	13,355	17,360	12.02
Woman's Day	Monthly	5,632	53,465	64,000	11.36
Woman's World	Weekly	1,337	11,600	13,900	10.39
HOME SERVICE					
Better Homes/Gardens	Monthly	8,012	$82,025	$99,215	$12.38
Country Home	Monthly	811	18,700	26,700	32.93
Country Living	Monthly	1,580	24,640	33,720	21.34
Family Handyman	Monthly	1,221	16,550	23,745	19.45
Home	Monthly	900	12,680	16,880	18.76
House Beautiful	Monthly	828	19,235	24,620	29.73
Metropolitan Home	Monthly	721	19,665	27,825	38.61
1001 Home Ideas	Monthly	1,527	21,630	26,095	17.09
Southern Living	Monthly	2,272	32,400	45,680	20.10
Sunset	Monthly	1,440	21,696	30,198	20.98

Magazines (continued)

MAGAZINE	FREQUENCY OF ISSUE	CIRCULATION (in thousands)	PAGE RATE B/W	PAGE RATE 4-C	FOUR-COLOR PAGE CPM
GENERAL					
Changing Times	Monthly	1,392	$ 20,125	$ 30,000	$ 21.55
Life	Monthly	1,622	39,630	52,470	32.35
Modern Maturity	Monthly	13,597	138,100	153,000	11.25
Money	Monthly	1,773	34,595	54,130	30.53
National Enquirer	Monthly	4,505	30,360	38,270	8.50
National Geographic	Weekly	10,691	94,620	123,000	11.51
Reader's Digest	Monthly	17,300	87,001	104,600	6.05
Smithsonian	Monthly	2,289	28,855	36,155	15.79
The Star	Weekly	3,560	24,680	30,450	8.55
Yankee	Monthly	1,002	11,660	15,625	15.60
NEWS					
Insight Weekly	Weekly	311	$ 14,000	$ 20,000	$ 64.31
Jet	Weekly	790	9,905	13,810	17.47
Newsweek	Weekly	3,054	54,095	70,975	23.24
People	Weekly	2,846	50,820	65,505	23.01
Sports Illustrated	Weekly	2,877	57,350	89,470	31.10
Sporting News	Weekly	716	14,080	17,730	24.75
Time	Weekly	4,832	73,695	92,140	19.07
TV Guide	Weekly	16,874	81,300	95,900	5.68
Us	Biweekly	1,008	16,410	21,180	21.02
U.S. News & World Report	Weekly	2,256	36,400	55,300	24.51
FASHION					
Bazaar	Monthly	725	$ 17,100	$ 24,720	$ 34.08
Elle	Monthly	472	12,657	18,982	40.23
Glamour	Monthly	2,228	29,540	36,560	16.41
Mademoiselle	Monthly	1,204	18,840	23,120	19.20
Vogue	Monthly	1,191	20,440	24,030	20.18
MEN'S					
Playboy	Monthly	3,901	$ 38,955	$ 54,550	$ 13.98
Penthouse	Monthly	2,701	36,695	41,140	15.23
Field & Stream	Monthly	2,002	32,455	48,810	24.38
Esquire	Monthly	692	18,190	27,200	39.31
Gentlemen's Quarterly	Monthly	615	13,780	20,700	33.67
BUSINESS & FINANCIAL					
Business Weekly	Weekly	876	$ 34,570	$ 52,550	$ 60.01
Forbes	Biweekly	727	23,790	36,180	49.75
Fortune	27X/Year	745	29,440	45,040	60.42
Inc.	Monthly	601	25,105	33,890	56.34
Industry Week	Biweekly	360	11,190	12,890	35.78
Nation's Business	Monthly	867	18,430	22,990	26.52
Real Estate Today	9X/Year	666	12,960	17,020	25.57
Savvy	Monthly	369	9,225	13,800	37.41
Sylvia Porter's Personal Finance	10X/Year	351	7,670	11,400	32.44
Venture	Monthly	330	15,250	19,055	57.66

Magazines (continued)

MAGAZINE	FREQUENCY OF ISSUE	CIRCULATION (in thousands)	PAGE RATE B/W	PAGE RATE 4-C	FOUR-COLOR PAGE CPM
FARM					
Farm Futures	11X/Year	162	$ 8,310	$10,760	$66.48
Farm Industry News	11X/Year	301	8,195	10,770	35.76
Farm Journal	14X/Year	813	24,000	33,500	41.23
Progressive Farmer	Monthly	536	16,480	23,200	43.28
Successful Farmer	14X/Year	495	19,485	27,865	56.31
YOUTH					
Boy's Life	Monthly	1,362	$11,860	$16,560	$12.16
Careers	3X/Year	602	10,585	14,820	24.62
Fast Times	9X/Year	525	13,125	19,125	36.43
Junior Scholastic	Bi-weekly	763	7,865	11,505	15.09
Sesame Street	10X/Year	1,159	27,600	30,000	25.89
BUSINESS-TO-BUSINESS					
Advertising Age	Weekly	89	$8,470	$10,781	$121.22
Asta Travel News	Monthly	20	2,500	4,135	206.91
Chronicle of Higher Education	Weekly	76	3,625	N/A	47.84
Communication's Week	Weekly	62	6,500	7,490	120.91
Dental Management	Monthly	102	3,900	5,175	50.61
Hospital Practices	18X/Year	189	4,045	5,355	28.27
Metalworking Digest	Monthly	102	7,060	8,060	79.35
Office	Monthly	163	4,350	5,300	32.57
Progressive Grocer	Monthly	72	7,950	10,750	148.96
Women's Wear Daily	Daily	64	7,490	9,970	155.35

Source: Consumer Magazines, Business Publications Standard Rate & Data Service, January 1987.

Newspapers

NEWSPAPER	CIRCULATION (in thousands)	SAU PAGE RATE	1X PAGE CPM
New York Daily News	1,271	$22,498	$17.70
Los Angeles Times	1,086	27,605	25.42
New York Times	1,002	34,359	34.29
New York Post	804	17,780	22.11
Philadelphia Inquirer/News	787	26,907	34.19
Washington Post	748	30,360	40.59
Chicago Tribune	745	27,099	36.37
San Francisco Chronicle/Examiner	697	23,901	34.29
Detroit News	681	25,019	36.74
Detroit Free Press	656	27,796	42.37

Source: Marketer's Guide to Media, 2nd Quarter 1987.

National Supplements

SUPPLEMENT	CIRCULATION (in thousands)	PAGE RATE B/W	PAGE RATE 4-C	FOUR-COLOR PAGE CPM
Parade	31,640	$252,500	$311,700	$ 9.85
Sunday Magazine	20,339	175,880	215,367	10.59
Dawn Magazine	900	13,244	18,359	20.40
USA Weekend	14,200	114,300	131,900	9.29
Vista	786	21,900	27,000	34.35

Source: Marketer's Guide to Media, 2nd Quarter 1987.

Television
Network Television*

TIME PERIOD	AVERAGE COST PER 30-SECOND COMMERCIAL	AVERAGE HOUSEHOLD RATING
Daytime	$ 17,175	5.4
Early News	48,975	11.9
Prime Time	112,775	14.6
Late Evening	21,725	4.3
Weekend Children's Shows	18,200	4.5

*Average of quarterly data, 1987.
Source: Marketer's Guide to Media, 2nd Quarter 1987.

Spot Television: Average Cost per Home Rating Point*

MARKET	DAYTIME	EARLY FRINGE	EARLY NEWS	PRIME TIME	LATE NEWS	LATE FRINGE
New York	$189.88	$191.00	$208.88	$626.50	$500.63	$228.13
Los Angeles	221.25	206.25	232.88	666.75	480.63	235.75
Chicago	109.88	110.75	126.50	303.38	271.00	135.50
Philadelphia	99.13	94.38	126.63	257.70	226.00	129.63
San Francisco	117.25	132.13	168.38	335.75	281.63	175.88
Boston	107.50	119.25	150.75	320.00	293.63	189.88
Detroit	52.00	67.75	77.13	168.75	125.88	94.50
Dallas	89.00	94.13	118.25	260.00	192.25	122.50
Washington	74.13	74.75	84.88	181.75	135.63	80.75
Houston	74.13	94.63	106.75	256.75	174.75	113.88
Cleveland	40.38	44.38	59.50	117.63	95.88	65.00
Atlanta	57.50	77.00	91.63	166.63	137.38	119.39
Pittsburgh	39.88	55.88	64.75	127.00	93.25	70.00
Miami	57.13	74.63	99.00	214.50	116.50	96.88
Minneapolis-St. Paul	62.13	65.00	71.26	138.00	121.13	78.88
Seattle-Tacoma	58.25	54.13	67.38	177.88	116.25	85.00
Tampa-St. Petersburg	58.13	57.13	65.00	139.38	117.88	89.13
St. Louis	44.00	45.38	55.00	103.00	72.75	55.75
Denver	46.63	47.63	65.88	120.13	87.63	84.13
Sacramento-Stockton	41.00	50.88	58.13	104.88	73.13	62.38

*1st/2nd Quarter 1987 Average (30-Second Spot).
Source: Media Market Guide, 1st Quarter 1987.

Cable Television (National): Cost per Daypart (30-Second Spot)

CABLE NETWORK	EARLY MORNING	MORNING	AFTERNOON	EARLY EVENING	PRIME TIME	LATE EVENING
			TIME OF DAY			
A&E	$600	............$300............		$500*	$300 – 1,500	$600 – 800
BET					$500 – 600	$450 – 550
CBN Cable	..................$525..................			$1,800	$2,225	1,125
CMT	$200	............$250............		$200	$300	$150
CNN/HI. News	$400 – 1,600	.........$500 – 800		$700 – 900	$1,500 – 2,500	$400 – 1,800
ESPN	............$1,500............		........$1,500 – 3,000*		$6,000	$1,500
FNN	$530	............$750............		$1,000		
FNN SCORE				............$300............		$300
FNN TelShop		............$200............				$200
LIF	$200 – 300	$400 – 500	$500 – 600	$600 – 700	$800 – 1,200	$600 – 800
MTV	....$3,000..					
Nickelodeon	.......................$750 – 2,000					
NICK AT NITE					$500 – 750	$450 – 500
TDC	....$250 – 750					
Tempo	...........$120		$200	............$300............		$120
TNN	.........$250 – 750..........		........$300 – 1,000		$1,000 – 5,000	$300 – 1,500
TWC	............$650		$400	............$500............		$300
UNIVISION	...........$1,200............		$3,000	$8,000	$9,000	$500
USA	$300 – 500	$500 – 800	$800 – 1,100	$1,200 – 2,000	$2,000 – 5,000	$1,000 – 1,700
VH-1	....$300 – 1,000..					
WTBS	$500 – 9,500	$1,650 – 1,950	$1,400 – 1,350	$3,850 – 6,400	$4,450 – 7,650	$700 – 2,200

*Weekend rates.
Source: Marketer's Guide to Media, 2nd Quarter 1987.

Radio
Network Radio, Daypart Rates (per 30-second spot, run of station)

NETWORK	AVERAGE COST
ABC Contemporary	$2,900
ABC Direction	1,500
ABC Entertainment	2,500
ABC FM	2,400
ABC Information	2,700
ABC Rock	2,100
ABC Talk	600
CBS Radio Talk	2,600
CBS RADIORADIO	2,000
CMN	750
CNN	1,500*
MBS	2,700
NBC	____**
NBC "The Source"	3,500
NBC Talknet	750
Satellite	1,600
Sheridan Broadcasting	1,200
Transtar	1,500*
United Stations One	3,000
United Stations Two	2,500
United Stations Programming	2,000 – 8,000
Wall Street Journal Report	4,250†

Note: These are general rates, subject to specific negotiation and package buys.
*CNN and Transtar sold as one unit.
**NBC sold as follows: 6 – 10 a.m., $2,500; 10 a.m. – 3 p.m., $1,500; 3 – 7 p.m., $1,800; and 7 p.m. – Midnight, $650.
†Sold as 60-second units; 30's are 75 percent of 60's.
Source: Marketer's Guide to Media, 2nd Quarter 1987.

Spot Radio: Cost per Metro Rating Point (60-Second Spots)

MARKETS	MEN			WOMEN			TEENS
	18+	18–34	25–54	18+	18–34	25–54	12–17
Top 10	$1,638	$1,081	$1,617	$1,481	$1,075	$1,453	$ 602
Top 20	2,386	1,597	2,372	2,207	1,615	2,146	937
Top 30	2,984	2,004	2,987	2,786	2,019	2,714	1,238
Top 40	3,431	2,261	3,429	3,198	2,286	3,092	1,415
Top 50	3,808	2,503	3,803	3,544	2,534	3,416	1,592
Top 60	4,079	2,673	4,062	3,780	2,694	3,643	1,737
Top 70	4,340	2,825	4,340	4,032	2,851	3,892	1,860
Top 80	4,531	2,937	4,512	4,200	2,952	4,046	1,952
Top 90	4,669	3,022	4,647	4,320	3,025	4,159	2,023
Top 100	4,807	3,104	4,773	4,445	3,098	4,272	2,088

Source: Media Market Guide, 1st Quarter 1987.

Outdoor

30-Sheet ADI Market Area Poster Costs (#50 Showing)

MARKET AND OUTDOOR SUPPLIERS	POPULATION (in thousands)	NUMBER OF POSTERS	MONTHLY COST
New York			
Winston Network	7,179	134	$ 70,350
Seaboard	7,072	186	97,650
Los Angeles			
Gannett	10,600	250	115,991
Patrick	12,120	250	117,062
Chicago			
Patrick	6,029	164	75,976
Philadelphia			
H. A. Steen	3,592	78	31,200
San Francisco-Oakland-San Jose			
Patrick	4,304	121	53,837
Gannett	4,746	122	53,480
Boston			
Ackerley	4,566	170	68,995
Detroit			
Gannett	4,100	92	46,920
Dallas-Ft. Worth			
Patrick	1,981	64	20,440
Washington, D.C.			
Rollins	3,426	102	44,880
Houston			
Patrick	3,475	118	38,008
Cleveland			
Patrick	2,659	106	44,786
Pittsburgh			
Patrick	2,577	100	37,246
Minneapolis-St. Paul			
Naegele	2,200	110	42,570
Miami/Ft. Lauderdale			
Ackerley	3,875	106	43,428
Atlanta			
Turner	2,320	60	21,380
Patrick	2,320	60	22,632
Seattle-Tacoma			
Ackerley	2,360	80	32,715
St. Louis			
Gannett	2,296	80	36,320
Tampa-St. Petersburg			
Patrick	1,788	75	24,636
Denver			
Gannett	1,504	39	15,200
Sacramento-Stockton			
Gannett	997	27	11,430
Patrick	1,062	30	13,835

Source: Marketer's Guide to Media, 2nd Quarter 1987.

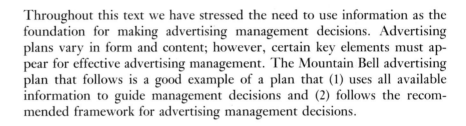

APPENDIX C

A SAMPLE ADVERTISING PLAN: MOUNTAIN BELL, "CENTRON"

Throughout this text we have stressed the need to use information as the foundation for making advertising management decisions. Advertising plans vary in form and content; however, certain key elements must appear for effective advertising management. The Mountain Bell advertising plan that follows is a good example of a plan that (1) uses all available information to guide management decisions and (2) follows the recommended framework for advertising management decisions.

BACKGROUND

Since the mid-1970s, Mountain Bell of Denver, Colorado, has been promoting and selling customer-premise switching systems (PBXs) and smaller-sized key systems to meet the telecommunication needs of business customers. In 1983, Mountain Bell's concentration on the sale of new customer-premise equipment came to an end with the advent of Computer Inquiry II.[1] In 1984, Mountain Bell reintroduced Network and Switching Center (NSC)-based services as its primary communications service offering. These services offered most of the calling features found on PBX and key systems, but the equipment is located in Mountain Bell's Network and Switching Center rather than at the customer's premises.

Mountain Bell has four basic offerings in its NSC-based services line:

- Centron Custom (300+ line customers)

- Centron 300 (30–299) line customers)

- Centron 30 (7–29 line customers)

- Centron 6 (2–6 line customers)

These four services are the backbone of Mountain Bell's communications offering and provide services for all customer sizes.

Centron was originally introduced under the name Centrex in the 1960s. In 1984, Centron was offered to small, medium, and large busi-

Source: Information and advertisments courtesy of Mountain Bell, Department of Advertising, Denver, 1986.

nesses (2 to 10,000 lines) in all market segments. Although the bulk of the business market is covered by on-premise electronic key and PBX systems, Centron offers business customers a flexible, cost-effective, reliable alternative.

NEED FOR CENTRON

Businesses change every day and so do their communications needs. Whether it involves sudden expansion or consolidation, a NSC-based system like Centron offers the flexibility to reshape and update a communications system at minimum cost. This makes NSC-based services preemptive because other PBX and key systems cannot match Centron's flexibility. Designed to match the dynamics of modern business, Centron provides for unlimited growth. Yet, the service is affordable because customers pay only for the services they need—adding or subtracting capability and/or features to meet their changing communications requirements.

Centron 6 and 30, which tie as many as 30 lines together, require no additional premise equipment other than touch-tone telephones. They are flexible in that features (beyond those included in the basic package) can be added individually to meet specific needs.

The addition of Centron 6 and 30 to the product line offers a major opportunity to gain new revenue from existing technology in market segments where NSC features were previously unavailable. It improves the profitability of the target markets, while developing two new market opportunities—multipremise and business/residence combinations. Further, Centron 6 and 30 can stem the tide of business customers' moving

---

TABLE 1

Concerns of Business Customers

CONCERN	PERCENTAGE OF RESPONDENTS MENTIONING
Little flexibility in selecting telephone features	44%
A telephone system that is not adaptable to newly developed features	42
A telephone system that has to be replaced due to customer growth	41
A telephone system not flexible enough to adapt to changing business needs	39
The quality of in-house communications	36
Lack of knowledge and understanding about features purchased	30
The amount of time it takes employees to keep telephone equipment operating properly	27
Features on a system that are not paying for themselves	25
Telephone equipment occupying potential office space	23
Features purchased because it was thought they were needed, but in actuality not used	22
Features on a system that were paid for, but not used	21
A system that is underutilized because of decrease in business	20

to small key systems and prepare them for new applications of future NSC offerings from Mountain Bell. In essence, what we will be selling are "smart lines," not "smart sets."

CONCERNS OF BUSINESS CUSTOMERS

Mountain Bell has approximately 500,000 business customers, 60 percent of which have the potential to be served by an NSC-based service. If Mountain Bell is to retain its position as a market leader in the communications market, it must actively pursue the introduction and sale of NSC-based services to all customers.

In a recently completed study, the following items of concern were cited by the 1,200 business customers interviewed.[2]

These findings indicate that many of the concerns identified by customers can be overcome by our NSC technology. And with enhancements being made to NSC capabilities all the time, our ability to meet customer needs should improve.

COMPETITION

The competition for NSC-based services comes from all marketers of customer-premise PBX, electronic communications systems, and key systems. An analysis of the major competitors within each of the four basic NSC offerings follows.

CENTRON 300 AND CENTRON CUSTOM

Northern Telecom offers everything from small key systems to advanced switching systems capable of handling the needs of the largest customers.

AT&T's Dimension System 85 is another competitor. Since 1977, Mountain Bell has sold Dimension systems by positioning them as the technology of the future to displace Centrex systems. Through this sales strategy, Mountain Bell was successful in eroding the Centrex base to a mere 170 systems. We are now in a position where we have to approach the first- and second-generation Dimension PBX customers and convince them that Centron (formerly Centrex) is *not* antiquated technology, but rather a modern cost-effective alternative for customers who currently have Dimension systems.

Rolm continues to grow in the PBX market, focusing primarily on the mid-sized customer (70–100 lines). Their position will be further enhanced by their joint venture with IBM. This project plans to integrate a digital voice communications system with an office computer system.

Current Centron technology is not capable of competing with the advanced third- and fourth-generation PBXs offered by the competition. Mountain Bell will be forced to focus on earlier vintage PBX and key system customers until more sophisticated, state-of-the-art features are available.

CENTRON 6 AND 30

Some small customer-premise equipment systems—including Comkey, Horizon, and other key equipment—perform many of the same functions as Centron 6 and 30. AT&T is test-marketing a new product, Merlin, designed for small businesses with two incoming lines and up to six stations. Merlin can be rented or purchased. This system appears to present some stiff competition for Centron 6 because of its feature superiority and relatively low costs.

TARGET MARKET

The target market for NSC-based services is segmented into the four service offerings: Centron Custom, Centron 300, Centron 30, and Centron 6. The target market is composed of customers who:

- Need a system with a high degree of flexibility—the ability to expand capacity and features without replacing equipment

- Conduct business in an area served by a Network and Switching Center

- Are willing to consider Mountain Bell services whether or not we provide or install the terminal equipment

An analysis of four metropolitan areas (Denver, Phoenix, Salt Lake City, and Albuquerque), indicates the size of the potential market for all four Centron services to be approximately 30,000 businesses.

Additional characteristics of the target market follow.

Sex:	Male
Age:	25–54
Income:	$20,000+
Job Title:	Telecommunications manager/owner
Industry:	Education Health care Insurance Manufacturing Media Processing Services and utilities
Location:	Arizona (Phoenix, Tucson) Colorado (Denver, Colorado Springs) Idaho (Boise) New Mexico (Albuquerque) Utah (Salt Lake City) Wyoming (Casper)
Other:	Target companies must have two or more telephone lines and be serviced by NSC.

MARKETING OPPORTUNITIES

- Unlimited line capacities and extensive feature capabilities make NSC services available to all sizes of customers.

- Steady growth in the number of NSCs capable of offering certain Centron features will make these services available to increasing numbers of customers.

- NSC-based services can be configured to meet the needs specified by the customer. It is not necessary to purchase features that are neither needed nor used.

- NSC-based services will not become outdated. As new features and systems are developed, customers can add them without costly equipment changes.

- NSC-based services are anticipated to be competitively priced with customer-premise systems.

- NSC-based services are located at Mountain Bell facilities; consequently, unlike PBXs and key systems, they do not use costly office floor space.

- NSC-based services are extremely reliable and have 24-hour repair service because they are located in constantly monitored Mountain Bell Electronic Switching System offices.

- NSC-based services will be the flagships of the Mountain Bell product line and will have the backing of the entire sales force as well as the Business Service Centers.

- Mountain Bell is viewed as a capable, high-technology vendor of telecommunications services.[3]

MARKETING CHALLENGES

- Mountain Bell has spent the last several years positioning customer-premises equipment (key and PBX) as the state-of-the-art replacement for NSC-based services. This marketing strategy worked, and premise-based equipment has gained a high presence in the marketplace.

- Because Mountain Bell will now be selling "smart lines" rather than "smart sets," customers cannot see or relate to equipment not on their desks.

- Most NSC-based technology dates to the 1960s and currently is not as advanced as the customer-premise systems offered by competitors.

- Competition in the business communications systems market is intense.

- NSC-based systems are available through lease only. Customers can purchase *or* lease premise systems.

- NSC services eliminate the need for most multibutton key sets including Touch-a-matics and electronic customer telephone sets that are perceived as office "status symbols."

MARKETING OBJECTIVES

Based on the opportunities and challenges before us, the following marketing objective has been established.

Support Mountain Bell's combined Network and Switching Center services forecast of 109,576 station lines/features worth approximately $8.9 million in annualized revenues.[4]

ADVERTISING OBJECTIVES

1. Positively shift target market attitudes 5 percent by year-end that Mountain Bell's Centron Systems can meet the communications needs of the target market.

2. Increase awareness/recall levels among the target markets by 15 percent by year-end.[5]

3. Increase sales point efficiency among the target market by 15 percent by year-end.[6]

4. Achieve a 1 percent response rate from direct-mail advertising.[7]

CAMPAIGN BUDGET

The budget for this campaign was created through a combination of the objective-task and percent-of-projected-revenue methods. Because the Centron advertising campaign was charged with the responsibility of introducing a new product concept, we anticipated a somewhat higher than normal amount of advertising investment. The objective-task method allowed us to estimate the cost of accomplishing the advertising objectives we felt would be necessary to support the marketing objective. Once an

TABLE 2

Centron Advertising Budget

CATEGORY	AMOUNT	PERCENTAGE OF TOTAL
Advertising media	$2,700,000	76.1%
Advertising production	420,000	11.8
Direct marketing	350,000	9.8
Sales promotion and publicity	50,000	1.4
Research	30,000	.9
TOTAL	$3,550,000	100.0

estimated budget was determined, we examined it as a percentage of anticipated revenue. When we found that percentage to be consistent with company and industry norms, the budget was approved.

ADVERTISING CREATIVE STRATEGY

Communicate the message that Centron is a flexible communications system that gives you (1) feature selection, (2) line growth, and (3) the ability to add new technology. Centron is the only system that does not tie its users to bulky equipment. The tone of the message should be professional and compelling, and should reflect Mountain Bell's leadership role. The desired response from the target market should be, "Mountain Bell's Centron Systems are far more flexible and adaptable than any other. I will contact them for more information."

ADVERTISING TACTICS

The advertising creative strategy will be communicated to the target market through twelve separate executions:

- Two 30-second television commercials
- Two 60-second radio commercials
- Three 1,200-line newspaper advertisements
- One full-page, four-color magazine advertisement
- Four direct mailings

The executions are shown in Figures 1 through 10.

MEDIA PLAN

TARGET MARKET (See Target Market section.)

MEDIA OBJECTIVES

1. Reach 90 percent of the target market with an average frequency of 10 during January through November.
2. Primary media weight should be placed during the first six months of the campaign period.

MEDIA SELECTION CRITERIA

- Media mix must maximize the generation of Centron's awareness as the most flexible in communications systems for all size businesses.

FIGURE 1

Mountain Bell

"SALESMAN & ASSISTANT"

COMM'L NO.: MBT 3533

LENGTH: 30 SECONDS

SALESMAN: The newest communications technology is right here.

COMMUNICATIONS MANAGER: Are you sure?
SALESMAN: Ah. For really state-of-the-art communications,

just add this...
(SFX: CLUNK)

COMM. MGR.: But what about...

SALESMAN: There's an even more advanced dual pack...
(SFX: CLUNK)
ANNCR: (VO) Mountain Bell has a better idea.

(SFX: PUSH)
The Centron Systems.

Only Centron can offer you the newest technologies

without equipment changeouts.
(SFX: PHONE RINGS)

Because only Centron doesn't tie you down to equipment.

SALESMAN: But it was state-of-the-art this morning.

ANNCR: (VO) Centron from Mountain Bell. Technology made simple.

FIGURE 2

Mountain Bell
"DON'T NEED THAT"

COMM'L NO.: MBT 3513

LENGTH: 30 SECONDS

SALESMAN: State-of-the-art communications.

This has Tri-Levular Modulating feature...
COMMUNICATIONS MANAGER: But, I don't need that.

SALESMAN: The Multitron

Autofeed-in feature...
COMM. MGR.: I don't need that.

SALESMAN: Auto Digitron Relay...

ANNCR: (VO) Instead of getting stuck with communication features that come in packages...
(SFX: PUSH)

Mountain Bell has a better idea.

The Centron Systems.

Only Centron lets you pick just the communications features you want.

Because only Centron doesn't tie you down to equipment.

COMM. MGR.: Now, that's what I need.
ANNCR: (VO) Centron from Mountain Bell. Technology made simple.

FIGURE 3

Mountain Bell

"FATHER & SONS"

COMM'L NO.: MBT 3523

LENGTH: 30 SECONDS

SALESMAN: This communications system is just what you need.

SON 1: What about our busy season?

SALESMAN: You'll need more lines. Then I'd recommend. . .
(SFX: CLUNK)

SONG 2: But our slow season?

SALESMAN: Fewer lines.
(SFX: CLUNK)

(SFX: PUSH)
ANNCR: (VO) Mountain Bell has a better idea.

The Centron systems. Only Centron lets you add

or subtract as many lines as you want. Because only Centron doesn't tie you down to equipment.

SONS 1 & 2: Good thing I thought of Centron,

huh, Dad?

ANNCR: (VO) Centron from Mountain Bell. Technology made simple.

TECHNOLOGY MADE SIMPLE

Mountain Bell

FIGURE 4

PRODUCTION ORDER NO.	PJ# 41861
COPY PREPARED FOR	Mountain Bell
PUBLICATION	Centron/Features
DATE OF ISSUE	12/1/83
SPACE TO BE USED	Radio :60

SECRETARY:	Mr. Robbins, the communications system salesperson is here to see you.
ROBBINS:	Is he from Mountain Bell?
SECRETARY:	No.
ROBBINS:	Well, send him in anyway.
AVO:	One of the most important decisions a communications manager can make is which system is right for his company.
SALESMAN:	This communications system is our best. It has absolutely everything.
ROBBINS:	But I don't need everything.
SALESMAN:	Duotone Autotrak Monitoring.
ROBBINS:	But, I don't need that.
AVO:	Instead of getting stuck with communication features that come in packages, Mountain Bell has a better idea. The Centron Systems.
SALESMAN:	Triplex Readout Forwarding.
ROBBINS:	But, I don't need that.
AVO:	Only Centron lets you pick just the features you want. Because only Centron doesn't tie you down to equipment.
SALESMAN:	Regulatory Callback Blipping?
ROBBINS:	But, I don't need that.
SALESMAN:	Bilevular Integrated Advance? Macro Call Intercept? Trans-regional Wa-Wa?
ROBBINS:	No. No. No.
SALESMAN:	Mr. Robbins, what exactly do you need?
ROBBINS:	I need Centron.
AVO:	The Centron Systems from Mountain Bell. Technology Made Simple.

- Media must provide a quality environment appropriate for Mountain Bell's position as a market leader.

- Media must be able to reach business prospects in eight primary markets.

MEDIA TACTICS

Television provides the necessary reach, environment, and prestige; therefore, it is the primary medium in this campaign. Accounting for 60 percent of the total media investment, television is scheduled for 19 weeks in four flights (January, March, May, and July-August). It is estimated that 94 percent of the target audience will be reached an average of eight times by television. Both over-the-air and cable programming will be used, with emphasis on programs most appropriate to the target—sports and news.

Radio is used to increase frequency of the message among the target audience. It is scheduled for 20 weeks at a level of 175 GRP/week and

FIGURE 5

PRODUCTION ORDER NO.	PJ# 41861
COPY PREPARED FOR	Mountain Bell
PUBLICATION	Centron/Line Capacity
DATE OF ISSUE	12/1/83
SPACE TO BE USED	Radio :60

SECRETARY: Mr. Robbins, another communications system salesperson is here to see you.

ROBBINS: Is *this* one from Mountain Bell?

SECRETARY: I'm afraid not.

ROBBINS: (VERY DISAPPOINTED) oh . . .

SECRETARY: He said to go right in.

AVO: It's unfortunate that most communications systems tie you down to a specific line capacity.

SALESMAN: This communications system would just be perfect for your needs.

ROBBINS: But during our busy season our needs triple.

SALESMAN: Well, here's just what you need. It's triple that capacity. And . . .

ROBBINS: That means during my slow season I'd be paying for triple what I can use.

AVO: Mountain Bell has a better idea. The Centron Systems. Only Centron lets you add or subtract as many lines as you want. Because only Centron doesn't tie you down to equipment. You pay for only what you can use.

SALESMAN: Mr. Robbins, with your changing needs and seasonal fluctuations, I'd say go with this system. It's a Rolls Royce. So who cares if you only drive it on Sundays.

ROBBINS: I think I'd prefer a Rolls Royce that I can drive all the time. I'll go with Centron.

AVO: The Centron Systems from Mountain Bell. Technology Made Simple.

uses 60-second commercials in five four-week flights (January, March, April, and June). The estimated reach is 64 percent and the average frequency is 10. Radio accounts for 20 percent of the media investment.

Newspapers are used to support the broadcast schedule and to provide a format appropriate to explaining Centron. The media schedule calls for 1,200-line advertisements in the business sections of daily newspapers. The 34 newspaper insertions represent 17 percent of the media investment.

Magazines provide a prestige environment and supplement the broadcast schedule. One-page, four-color advertisements will appear in individual state editions of *Time, U.S. News & World Report*, and *Newsweek* during a four-month period. Magazines represent 3 percent of the media investment.

Direct mail is used to place product information directly in the hands of the target audience so they can move toward purchase quickly and efficiently. Fifty percent of the direct-mail packages will be mailed before the mass media campaign and the remaining 50 percent after the creation

FIGURE 6

PRODUCTION ORDER NO.	PJ# 41861
COPY PREPARED FOR	Mountain Bell
PUBLICATION	Centron/New Technology
DATE OF ISSUE	12/9/83
SPACE TO BE USED	Radio :60
	Rev. 1

SECRETARY: Mr. Robbins, the communications systems salesperson is here.

ROBBINS: Terrific, wonderful, what perfect timing. I'm so glad he's here.

SECRETARY: Mr. Robbins, he's *not* from Mountain Bell.

ROBBINS: Uh, can you say I'm out to lunch.

SECRETARY: At 10 a.m., sir? I'm sorry, no.

AVO: Everyone promises state-of-the-art communications. But who really delivers it?

SALESMAN: Mr. Robbins, here's our newest communications system. Oh, wait a minute, just let me check the manual. Uh huh, just as I thought, this has been replaced with this even more state-of-the-art system.

AVO: Only Mountain Bell can deliver state-of-the-art communications that stay that way. Communications that will never become obsolete.

SALESMAN: I think we have a system with newer technology. Here it is.

AVO: Only Mountain Bell's Centron Systems can offer you the newest technologies without equipment changeouts. Because only Centron doesn't tie you down to equipment.

SALESMAN: Now, if you really want the most advanced system, just wait a few months and we have one coming out that will . . .

ROBBINS: You know, you're right.

SALESMAN: I am??

ROBBINS: Yes, I really do want the most advanced communications. But I want them to stay that way. So I'm going with Centron.

SALESMAN: But, but . . . I don't sell Centron. Only Mountain Bell does.

ROBBINS: I know.

AVO: The Centron Systems from Mountain Bell. Technology Made Simple.

of awareness. Direct mail accounts for 10 percent of the total advertising budget.

OTHER FORMS OF PROMOTION

To assist in accomplishing the stated marketing goals of Centron and to complement the advertising campaign, a variety of other forms of promotion will be used.

TRADE SHOWS AND DISPLAYS

"Alex," the robot, will be a graphic representation of Centron for use at trade shows in five headquarter cities. Audio-visual tapes will be devel-

FIGURE 7

oped for use in "Alex." Mountain Bell's 15th Street (Denver) office window will contain a display of Centron.

COLLATERAL MATERIAL

Collateral sales aid materials will be developed for use at trade shows. These materials include invitations, giveaways, brochures, and trade show information packets.

INTERNAL PROMOTIONS

Centron posters will be produced and distributed to Mountain Bell's marketing personnel.

The advertising newsletter, "AdNotes," will be mailed to all Mountain Bell salespeople to inform them of the Centron advertising campaign.

FIGURE 8

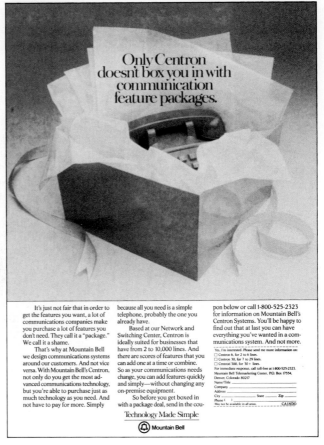

MBT-6734-41873-R4X1-CAINDO
"Only Centron Doesn't CF
Prepared by Tracy-Locke Advertising, Inc.
7503 Marin Drive, Englewood, CO 80110

PRODUCT PUBLICITY

Feature articles will be developed for placement in national industry trade publications.

Trade articles will be developed for state business and industry publications.

The individual state public relations staffs of Mountain Bell will be provided with articles for placement in state business and industry publications.

The opportunities for favorable publicity for Centron will be expanded to include state events, such as Chamber of Commerce anniversaries, trade shows, or conventions.

A press kit will be developed for editors of trade publications.

A publicity schedule will be developed to include press releases and talk-show appearances.

FIGURE 9

FIGURE 10

FIGURE 11

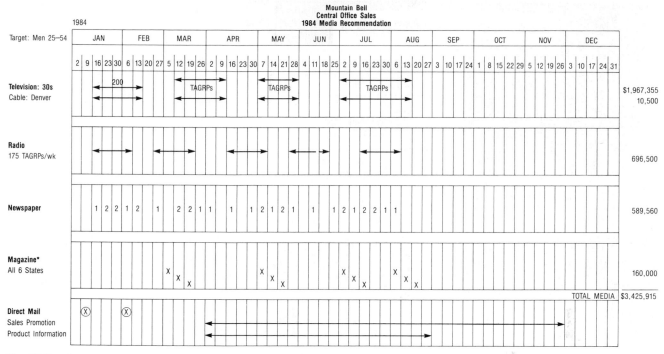

*Time, U.S. News, Newsweek

Markets include Phoenix, Tucson, Denver, Colorado Springs, Boise, Albuquerque, Salt Lake, Casper

NOTES

1. Until January 1, 1984, Mountain Bell was one of the 26 telephone companies of AT&T. Mountain Bell provides telephone service to the more than five million households and businesses in a seven-state area. Computer Inquiry II is a ruling against AT&T by the Federal Communications Commission. This ruling required that AT&T separate its competitive services from its monopoly services, thereby requiring the equipment division of AT&T to become a separate entity. The result of this ruling was American Bell.

Computer Inquiry II took effect on January 1, 1983, and was the precursor to divestiture on January 1, 1984. Under divestiture proceedings, AT&T was prohibited from using the "Bell" name. Consequently, American Bell evolved into the current AT&T Information Systems.

2. "Centron Feasibility Study," MTB 82-12-052, Mountain Bell, Denver, Colorado, June 1983.

3. "Corporate Identity Study," The Sherman Group, Inc., Great Neck, New York, November 1983.

4. "Annualized revenue" is the projected revenue for one calendar year based on some portion of that year. For example, if a program runs from July through February, annualized revenue would refer to the projected revenue for the period from July through December only. If the company has revenue figures for the first three months of that program, and those figures are estimated to be a valid and reliable representation, the figure is multiplied by two to determine annualized revenue.

5. "Awareness" refers to a customer's recognition of the Centron brand. "Recall" refers to a customer's ability to cite one or more of Centron's main customer benefits.

6. Sales point efficiency and sales point recall are measured through telephone surveys taken among a representative sample of the target market. In measuring net point recall, members of the sample who can recall the campaign are identified. Net point recall is the percentage of the group that can list at least one major benefit of the product. Sales point efficiency, however, is the percentage of the entire target market that can cite one or more major benefits of the product.

7. "Response" is defined as either a telephone or mail response seeking additional service information, an order for service, or a request for a personal sales call.

CALCULATING BREAKEVEN IN DIRECT MARKETING

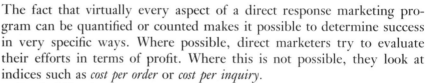

The fact that virtually every aspect of a direct response marketing program can be quantified or counted makes it possible to determine success in very specific ways. Where possible, direct marketers try to evaluate their efforts in terms of profit. Where this is not possible, they look at indices such as *cost per order* or *cost per inquiry*.

Profitability in direct response marketing is a function of the interrelationships between:

- Promotional cost (the direct marketer's selling cost)

- Contribution to promotional cost and profit

- Response

PROMOTIONAL COST

Promotional cost incorporates the total variable cost of distributing the offer. Where a mailing is involved, this amount includes printing, lists, postage, lettershop, etc.

This cost is usually expressed in terms of the cost of reaching 1,000 persons. It varies greatly with the particular medium being used. For example, a small advertisement in a magazine may cost less than $1 per thousand, whereas a package insert or cooperative mailing may cost $25 to $45 per thousand, and a catalog or brochure sent by third class mail may cost $150 to $500 or more per thousand.

Start-up programs, or tests, which usually are run on a small scale will incur higher costs per thousand in almost any medium. When small-scale programs are used, it is important to evaluate the results on the basis of the costs that would be incurred if the program were expanded to a volume commensurate with the level of acceptable risk and available funds.

One-time costs of creation and production should be recognized as a budget item, but it is usually best to consider them separately from the variable promotional costs.

CONTRIBUTION TO PROFIT

Contribution to profit and marketing is the amount of money available from each sale or average order after *all costs* of merchandise, operations, administration and overhead are subtracted from net sales. Note that promotional costs are *not included* when determining contribution.

The calculation of contribution must be very careful and thorough. Every applicable cost should be included. It is advisable to use a prepared form as a checklist to assure that all potential cost centers are considered. Frequencies with which costs such as those associated with returns, credit sales, bad debts, etc., should be accurately determined so that their cost is properly allocated to the units that stay sold, or to net revenues. In other words, if 100 orders are shipped and seven are then returned, the costs of processing all 100 orders together with all costs and losses associated with the seven returns must be borne by the 93 orders that were sold, that is, by the net sales.

RESPONSE

When we know the cost per 1,000 and the contribution, we can determine the response rate at which we break even (e.g., recapture promotional costs). We can also determine profit or loss results at other response rates. The following examples show the calculation of breakeven.

CALCULATION OF BREAKEVEN POINT IN A DIRECT MAIL PROGRAM

Average selling price	$ 107.22	
Total costs (excluding promotional cost)	71.65	
Contribution to promotional cost and profit	$ 35.57	
If total cost per thousand in the mail is	$ 250.00	$ 185.00
and that amount is divided by the contribution of	35.57	35.57
then required orders per thousand to break even		
equals	7.0	5.2
which is equivalent to a net response % of	0.7%	0.5%

If actual orders (net after returns) in the examples cited above were 1%, or ten orders per thousand pieces mailed, the profit could be calculated as follows:

Net sales per thousand (10 × $107.22)	$1,072.20	$1,072.20
Actual net orders per thousand	10.0	10.0
Less required orders per thousand to break even	7.0	5.2
Orders in excess of breakeven	3.0	4.8
Times contribution to promotional cost & profit	35.57	35.57
Pre-tax profit per thousand	106.11	170.74
Pre-tax profit as % of sales	9.9%	15.9%

It can be readily seen that, as the value of the average order rises and the average contribution per sale rises along with it, the number of orders needed to break even drops. Thus, an item carrying a $5 contribution would require 37 net sales, or 3.74% response to break even with a promotional cost of $185 per thousand, while an item with a $50 contribution would require only 3.7 net sales or 0.37% to break even.

OTHER PROGRAMS

The same approach of relating contribution and response to promotional cost may be applied to other types of programs.

Where, for example, inquiries are sought and then converted to sales, the cost of producing 1,000 inquiries is added to the promotional cost. Thus, if a $3,000 advertisement produces 1,000 inquiries, this is equivalent to increasing the promotional cost of the conversion mailing by $3,000 per thousand to reflect the cost of acquiring the inquiry list. Since the conversion mailing would cost about $3200 per thousand, its breakeven would rise to about 90 sales or 9% conversion rate.

When a series or continuity program is involved, it is advisable to calculate separately the contribution associated with each shipment in the series. Weighting each of these individual contributions by the number of each kind of shipment typically made to each starter and then adding these weighted contributions together, will determine the average contribution per starter. This average contribution can then be compared to the cost of acquiring starters to assess profitability.

When thinking about a direct marketing program, therefore, do not ask: "What is a typical response to a mailing?". Instead, determine how many orders you need in order to make your targeted profit.

Source: Fact Book on Direct Response Marketing: 1981 Statistical Update. Courtesy of the Direct Marketing Association.

MAKING AN ADVERTISING PRESENTATION

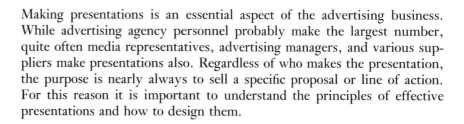

Making presentations is an essential aspect of the advertising business. While advertising agency personnel probably make the largest number, quite often media representatives, advertising managers, and various suppliers make presentations also. Regardless of who makes the presentation, the purpose is nearly always to sell a specific proposal or line of action. For this reason it is important to understand the principles of effective presentations and how to design them.

TYPES OF PRESENTATIONS

A presentation can be as simple as a direct, extemporaneous explanation of an idea to a coworker or supervisor. These sorts of informal presentations are a common part of all business. The advertising business frequently involves the use of elaborate formal presentations, in which a number of people are assigned specific roles. Often these presentations are carefully organized and scripted to be sure that essential material is covered in a coherent way and with a minimum of overlap. Such presentations are also designed to be as persuasive as possible in order to sell the line of action recommended by the presenters. One common type of presentation made regularly by agencies is the speculative presentation to a potential user of the agency's services. Though such presentations vary greatly in content and complexity, they typically include attention to marketing, creative, media, and research areas. Sometimes these areas are covered by specialists who have prepared the plans, and sometimes by agency management who has supervised it.

Exactly how far an agency goes in preparing advertising materials for a potential new account depends on the importance and demands of the advertiser. In some cases agencies are either compensated for out-of-pocket expenses or paid a fee to help defray the preparation costs. Such presentations can be quite expensive, involving large amounts of time from agency specialists, research, costs of slides, charts, videotape, and other visual materials.

ESSENTIAL ELEMENTS OF EFFECTIVE PRESENTATIONS

Despite the fact that presentations represent a central part of the advertising business, they are frequently marred by fundamental oversights and mistakes. While there is little clear consensus among experts as to exactly how ad presentations should be made, few would dispute the central importance of the following principles.

Be Clear about Your Purpose Robert Marker, himself a seasoned agency presenter and now a consultant on agency selection and making presentations, cites purpose as the most profound problem of any presentation.[1] Be sure you are absolutely clear about what you are being asked to present, and for what reason. While this may take some prying on your part, to do less is to risk looking foolish, incompetent, or both.

Prepare and Organize Carefully Most presentations proceed from identification of a problem through analysis of the problem dimensions to a proposed solution. A logical sequence of well-organized information leaves the audience with a sense that they have been presented with a coherent and competent solution. A well-organized presentation is easier to understand and thus has a better chance of being remembered and preferred among alternatives. In addition, a fundamental scheme of organization ensures that the important elements will be covered and the extraneous material pruned out.

The AAAA booklet, "What Every Young Account Executive Should Know about Oral Presentations," suggests three purposes for organization: to spotlight important ideas, to help the presenter move directly through his ideas, and to anticipate and answer audience questions as they arise.[2]

Though most professional presentations look casual and easy, they get this way through preparation and practice. Rehearsal and mastery of your material is the best way to ensure that you can relax during the presentation enough to attend to physical aspects of your delivery and to be sensitive to the overall impact of the presentation.

Advertising people are often asked to prepare presentations of a specified length. Do not *under any circumstances* exceed the assigned length. Be aware that the tendency is always to include too much and to run too long. It is much more difficult to be succinct. Make every effort to respect the time and needs of the audience.

Know Your Audience Any communicator knows that the message will be most effective if it closely matches the needs, understanding, and biases of the audience. This important point applies to presentations as well. Burson-Marsteller's Presentation Skills Workshop Notebook makes the point simply: "In any presentation or discussion, the well-prepared speaker is one who understands and is sensitive to his audience."[3] In preparing for a presentation, devote considerable effort to learning the background of the company and its marketing and advertising history and corporate philosophy. Information about key decision makers and their employment backgrounds and experience in marketing and advertising will help you in planning the level of address, the amount of detail, and the style of presentation you plan to make.

Never assume that because a presentation was a "hit" in one situation it will be successful in another. Recognize that different audiences will have different needs and interests, and modify your presentation to speak to these individual concerns.

Consider another fundamental communication principle as well: The "you attitude" means considering the audience's self-interest. Gear your presentation to the interest of the audience. Though the presentation may be designed for selecting an agency, it is rare that an advertising firm is interested in lengthy descriptions of agency organization, management policy, or advertising philosophy. More direct concerns are what the agency feels it can do for the advertiser, what sort of insight the agency can develop on current marketing problems, and principles of agency compensation.

Persuade and Convince Merely telling people information or asserting an interpretation of facts is not persuasive. A presentation should be designed as a sort of argument that leads to a specific set of recommendations. Thus, a presentation is a sales pitch. It should reiterate important points, anticipate and answer potential objections, and marshall evidence that supports the course of action recommended.

Advertising presentations often cover a good deal of relatively complex information in a short time. Such presentations also usually contain specialized jargon that may not be understood by decision makers from outside the marketing field. The presenter must be prepared to clarify quickly and simply when necessary. The presentation should be designed in such a way that emphasis is given to the central elements without a bewildering array of details to confuse and divert. In general, your presentation should be designed to make your point, present credible supporting evidence, and summarize your recommendation. Keep in mind that because a point has been made once in a presentation does not mean that it has been accepted, understood, or even heard by the audience. Summarize frequently and emphasize your central points.

Use Visual Aids Appropriately Visual aids can be used to give emphasis to important points and to present a great deal of information economically. Graphs, for example, can instantly convey a pattern in advertising expenditures over time that would be ponderously complex to explain using only words and statistics.

Using visual aids can also have its drawbacks. Complex technical presentations often seem to dehumanize what should be a chance for people to meet, interact, and make judgments about each other. In addition to the possibility of breakdown, heavy reliance on equipment cuts the possibility of spontaneity in presentations.

Jerry Schorin, advertising man and educator, suggests that "Color should be used *carefully*. Important materials can be underscored in a bold color, but too much color in a chart or graph makes it look like a peacock."[4]

Good visual aids—whether slides, overheads, or flip charts—should be used to enhance the presenter's message. When using them the presenter should identify the aid and explain its significance. Visual material that is merely decorative should be eliminated. Aids are especially important in building conviction and persuading because they involve two senses, increasing memorability. In designing charts and slides the presenter should keep them as simple as possible, using as few as five to seven words. With some sorts of material such as media flow charts or budget breakdowns this is impossible, but attention should be given to designing these complex and important elements so that the visual impression is appropriate.

Andrew Kershaw of Ogilvy & Mather suggests, "A presenter makes his life much easier if he sticks to just one kind of visual aid—to switch from slides to charts to film is asking for trouble."[5]

Prepare for Questions Few things convey a worse impression than a mumbled or fumbled response to questions from the audience. For this reason professional presenters often devote a good deal of time to anticipating questions and organizing their answers. While it's essential to have responses on the general elements of your plan, and even its nuances, it's also important to be ready for general questions about advertising and marketing terminology. Outsiders who observe your presentation rehearsals can often be very helpful in anticipating questions that may arise.

Creative director Ron Hoff makes the following suggestion:

> The day before the presentation, gather everybody on the team and spend at least one hour anticipating questions you may get. Write them down. Make sure you have strong, factual answers—not flabby generalities.[6]

The most important point in dealing with questions is to listen carefully to be sure you understand what is being asked. A long-winded, irrelevant response is both an annoyance and a waste of time. If you don't know the answer, say so. Then find out and respond to the questioner as soon as possible. Bluffing your way through is usually obvious.

Develop Your Skills Like any other skill, the ability to make successful presentations improves with practice. The more experience you have, the more you learn to cope with the inevitable nervousness. One authority says:

> Don't worry about being nervous. Speakers who say they aren't nervous before a speech are either lying or don't really care about the audience. Direct that nervous energy into a positive image and enthusiastic manner and delivery.[7]

Through practice you'll become more proficient at "thinking on your feet." Your organizational skills and judgment will sharpen as well. If possible, record yourself on videotape so that you can see and evaluate your strengths and weaknesses. This will help you to be even more effective.

Physical appearance is an important element in making presentations as well. While different business cultures will call for different dress, a business presentation is not the place to call attention to yourself by flamboyant attire. Reserve revealing necklines and plaid sport coats for strictly social occasions. The same is true of other fashion elements that can raise questions about judgment in the minds of the audience.

SOME SPECIFIC TECHNICAL SUGGESTIONS

1. Scout the room in advance.
2. Keep lights high enough for eye contact.
3. Make your opening interesting and memorable.
4. Talk to people, not the room.
5. Emphasize the benefits of your recommendation.
6. Be sure your audio-visual materials are visible and readable.
7. Carry spare bulbs, cords, markers, etc.
8. If presenting in a group, give a "team" impression.
9. On time is not good enough; be early.
10. Don't hand out written material until you're finished.
11. Use showmanship, but avoid exotic staging.
12. Don't turn your back on the audience.
13. Check materials for typos.
14. Use colorful and interesting language.
15. Rehearse, rehearse, rehearse.
16. Either thoroughly understand your equipment or bring an expert with you.
17. Make your closing strong, positive, and memorable.
18. Ask for the order.

NOTES

1. Robert S. Marker, "The Art of Better Presentations," Denver Advertising Federation, April 18, 1985.

2. "What Every Young Account Executive Should Know about Oral Presentations," American Association of Advertising Agencies, New York, 1977, 6.

3. Presentation Skills Workshop, March 1984, Burson-Marsteller, 1 East Wacker Drive, Chicago, 3.

4. Gerald Schorin, "Notes on Advertising Presentations," unpublished paper, 7.

5. Andrew Kershaw, "How to Make Agency Presentations," Ogilvy & Mather, 1976, 26.

6. Ron Hoff, "What's Your Presentation Quotient?" *Advertising Age*, January 16, 1978, 94.

7. G. A. Marken, "Getting More Out of a Speech," *Marketing Communications*, October 1985, 93.

GLOSSARY

Account executive an advertising agency employee who serves as the liaison between the advertiser (client firm) and the others who do the specialized work of the agency

A. C. Nielsen Company the world's largest market research firm, which provides a wide variety of audience and market data to the advertising industry

Advertising A planned communication activity in which messages in mass media are used to persuade audiences to adopt goods, services, or ideas. Advertising is distinguished from other promotional activities in that it is paid for by an identified sponsor, nonpersonal, carried by mass media, and designed to be persuasive.

Advertising appropriation See **Advertising expenditure**

Advertising budget a written plan that directs the distribution of the advertising expenditure

Advertising expenditure the total amount of funds allocated to advertising within a given time period, usually one year (also called *advertising appropriation* or *advertising investment*)

Advertising investment See **Advertising expenditure**

Advertising manager in the client firm (advertiser), the employee who is responsible for the overall management and direction of the advertising campaign

Advertising Opportunity Score (AOS) a calculation, expressed as a number between 0 and 1.0, that predicts the effectiveness of advertising in a given marketing situation

Advertising plan a detailed, annual program describing how the advertising efforts are to be carried out, including objectives, budget, target audience, and creative and media strategies

Advocacy advertising a type of corporate advertising that promotes the firm's viewpoint on a controversial issue

Affective strategy a creative strategy based on making an emotional impact on the audience, often by being bizarre, ambiguous, or avant garde and usually without strong selling emphasis

Affiliate a television or radio station that carries programming produced and supplied to it by a central point of origin

Agency billings the total amount of money an agency spends on behalf of all its clients; a measurement of agency size

Agency network an organization in which member agencies cooperate to exchange information and experience, and to aid in obtaining local services

Agency philosophy a general statement or policy in an ad agency regarding the role of advertising in marketing and the ways in which it affects the consumer

Agency recognition the status that the mass media grant an advertising agency, which allows the agency to buy media at discounted rates

AIDA (*attention-interest-desire-action*) **model** in setting advertising objectives, a theory that suggests that a buyer progresses through stair-step "stages" before taking the action recommended in advertising

AIO statement a consumer behavior tool that helps to measure an individual's activities, interests, and opinions

Animatics in TV commercial testing, films of the still pictures that will make up the commercial

Appraisal checklist a nine-factor model for determining the role of advertising in marketing a product or service

Arbitrary approach one of a number of methods of budgeting for advertising, in which a decision on the level of advertising investment is made without the benefit of a guiding principle or rule

Arbitron Ratings Company a market research firm that provides information to the advertising industry, largely focusing on radio and television usage

Area of Dominant Influence (ADI) an Arbitron term that refers to a geographic area made up of the counties in which local stations receive the bulk of viewing time

Art director an advertising agency employee responsible for the visual portion of an advertising message

Atmosphere copy advertising copy intended to surround the product with an aura of desirability

Attitude an individual's feeling about a certain issue at a certain point in time; a tendency or predisposition to behave or react in a consistent way

Audimeter a device that automatically records and stores minute-by-minute tuning changes (both on-off and channel selection) for each television set in a respondent's home

Audit Bureau of Circulations (ABC) a private firm that maintains circulation auditing standards, verifies the readership data released by newspapers and magazines, and issues reports of circulation data

Average frequency in print media, the average number of times an audience is exposed to a media schedule; calculated by dividing gross audience by net reach

Average frequency in television, the average number of times each household is exposed to a program or series of programs over a four-week period

Bartering the exchange of goods or services for media time or space

Benefit a satisfaction that the user derives from the product or service

Benefit segmentation identifying markets according to the benefit or use derived from the marketer's product or service

Body copy in print advertising, a group of words or sentences that provides information, persuasion, and the urge to act

Brand extension the process of introducing a new product through the association with an existing and successful brand name

Brand image strategy a creative strategy based on surrounding the product with symbols that create an attractive aura

Brand manager in the client firm (advertiser), the employee who has responsibility and authority for all marketing decisions regarding a specific brand

Brand rejuvenation the process of revitalizing a brand to strengthen consumer acceptance

Broadcast Advertisers Reports, Inc. (BAR) a research firm that reports on media expenditures for companies, products, and specific brands

Business paper a publication designed to appeal to the needs and interests of a specific occupation or industry (also called *trade paper*, *business publication*, and *trade* or *technical journal*)

Business publication See **Business paper**

Business Publications Audit of Circulation (BPA) a research firm that audits circulations of business and professional journals

Business-to-business advertising the means by which one business promotes its goods or services to another

Buyer behavior a process that includes the actions—internal and external—involved in identifying needs,

and in locating, buying, using, and evaluating products and services

Cable television a medium that is transmitted to viewers by subscription, over a coaxial cable

Calibration survey in outdoor advertising, a research technique that measures exposures to signs and mathematically relates them to demographic characteristics and travel behavior of the respondents

Car card in transit advertising, a sign placed inside a vehicle, usually above the windows or at the middle or end of the vehicle

Cease and desist order an action by the Federal Trade Commission, which requires an advertiser to stop a specified advertising claim or practice within 30 days

Circulation in the print media, the number of copies sold or distributed

Classified advertising short, simple messages, most common in print media, usually placed by individuals or small businesses

Classified-display advertising in newspapers, advertising that combines the feature of classified advertising with the more attractive graphic capabilities of display advertising

Cognitive dissonance a postpurchase feeling of unease that results when a product does not meet a buyer's expectations

Collection approach in specialty advertising, a technique through which buyers receive articles of no real value until a complete set is accumulated

Color separations the four or more negatives that are used to make the printing plates for four-color advertisements

Commission system a possible form of agency compensation in which the agency retains a portion (usually 15 percent) of the money its client spends for advertising

Comparative advertising a message that identifies a competitor or competing product and suggests superiority over it

Comparative approach an advertising technique in which the product is directly compared with one or more competitors

Competitive environment one of nine factors for appraising the advertising opportunity; indicates the size and marketing strength of a brand's competitors

Compiled list in direct mail, a collection of names with one or more common characteristics, such as marital status, income level, etc.

Comprehensive layout a drawing of what a finished ad will look like

Concept testing an evaluation technique used to measure how effectively an advertisement achieves its communication goals

Conflict of interest an untenable situation in which an ad agency is faced with serving two competing clients

Consent order a tool of the Federal Trade Commission, under which an advertiser, while making no admission of guilt, agrees to refrain from certain advertising practices or claims

Consumer magazine a publication designed to appeal to the tastes and interests of the general public or a specific subgroup

Continuity the pattern of distributing the advertising messages during the campaign period; a term used in expressing media objectives

Continuous pattern in media planning, the practice of varying the distribution of an advertising message very little over the campaign period

Contract rate in newspapers, the rate paid by an advertiser who has arranged to use a specific amount of advertising, with a certain frequency and over a given period of time

Controlled circulation the free distribution of print media to an audience that "qualifies" for such distribution by virtue of certain demographic or professional characteristics

Cooperative advertising special advertising program set up by a manufacturer to encourage dealers to advertise the firm's products

Copy platform a document used by an agency's creative department as a reminder of the earlier planning decisions in a campaign

Copywriter an advertising agency employee who writes the verbal parts of an advertising message

Corporate advertising messages designed to communciate a positive image, or attitude, about a firm or to stimulate a behavior other than product sales; also called *image advertising* or *institutional advertising*

Corporate umbrella a type of corporate advertising techinque in which a firm strengthens new or weak brands by relating them to established, successful ones marketed by the firm

Corrective advertising a message, ordered as a remedy by the FTC, intended to repair mistaken impressions created by earlier messages

Cost per rating point (CPRP) in media buying, one method of measuring the efficiency of a media buy; calculated by dividing the cost of the media buy by the ratings of the media used

Cost per thousand (CPM) the cost to reach 1,000 people through a particular medium or vehicle; calculated by dividing the cost of the media buy by the ratings of the media used

Cost per thousand to target market (CPM-TM) the cost of reaching 1,000 persons in the target audience

Counselor See **Specialty advertising distributor**

Cover letter a document that accompanies a resume, usually also providing specific reasons why the applicant is suited to the job being sought

Coverage a media measurement, expressed as a percentage of a market reached by a particular medium

Creative boutique an advertising agency that limits its services to creative work

Creative objective a statement of the communication task the advertisement or campaign is expected to carry out

Creative review board a group of people within an advertising agency that meets regularly to review and evaluate the agency's work (also called a *plans board*)

Creative strategy a policy or guiding principle that specifies the general nature and character of messages in the advertising campaign

Creative tactics how the message plan is carried out; the executional details of an advertising campaign

Culture the learned behavior of a society

Cume See **Reach**

Cumulative audience in radio, the number of different people listening to a station for at least five minutes during a specified time period (see also **Reach**)

Custom-designed research in advertising testing, an examination process specially designed to measure the effectiveness of a particular message or campaign

DAGMAR model a concept that suggests the expression of advertising objectives in terms of communication tasks and specifies the desired response from the target audience; acronym for *Defining Advertising Goals for Measured Advertising Results*

DAGMAR MOD II an extension of DAGMAR that identifies the sequence of decision-making steps applicable to each buying situation and focuses on understanding the link between such variables as image or attitude and marketplace behavior

Dangling comparatives The advertising practice of implying a comparison between one's product and a competing product, without stipulating the nature or conditions of the comparison

Deceptive advertising a message that misleads a consumer about an important aspect of a product or service

Demographic segmentation identifying market segments according to a set of quantifiable characteristics (such as age, income, and family size) of prospective purchasers

Demographics buyer characteristics such as age, sex, education, and income

Differentiation distinguishing a product or service from competing brands

Direct marketing the total of activities by which products and services are offered to market segments in one or more media for informational purposes or to solicit a direct response from a present or prospective customer or contributor by mail, telephone, or other access

Direct objective an advertising goal that seeks an overt behavior response (e.g., brand purchase, store visit, inquiry) from the audience

Direct response advertising messages designed to urge the receiver toward an immediate action (purchase or inquiry)

Direct response list a list that contains names of individuals who have used the mail either to inquire about a product or to purchase it

Direct selling house in specialty advertising, a firm that manufactures and sells its merchandise

Display advertising in newspapers, advertising that allows advertisers to illustrate and explain products and services in a way that will attract the interest of potential buyers

Dissonance-attribution hierarchy a learning theory suggesting that buyers sometimes make purchase decisions without sufficient product knowledge or attitudes about the product, which leads to attitude formation and learning about the product after its purchase

Distributor's brand a brand owned and marketed by one firm but often manufactured by another (also called a *private brand* or a *house brand*)

Donovan Data Systems Company a data processing company that offers advertisers and agencies a variety of media recordkeeping, accounting, and evaluation services

Economies of scale a situation in which increased production makes it possible to spread relatively high fixed costs over a larger number of units, lowering the cost per unit

Embellished bulletin in outdoor advertising, a painted sign that has projections extending from the basic structure

Emulation style advertising principle of using models that the audience will look up to or identify with, thus inducing them to buy the product

Entry-level position a job in which individuals with little or no job-related experience are usually employed

Exclusive distribution a marketing situation in which the marketer intentionally limits and minimizes the number of outlets available for purchase of a particular brand

Exhibition Validation Council (EVC) a research group dedicated to standardizing trade show attendance reporting and simplifying comparisons between shows

External conditions uncontrollable aspects of an environment that influence marketplace behavior (e.g., the economy, government regulation, the weather)

External list a mailing list that is drawn from sources outside the firm

Factor score in evaluating the role of advertising, a numerical expression of the extent to which a product, market, or company factor exists for the brand under evaluation; scores range between 0 and 1.0

Factor weight in evaluating the role of advertising, a quantitative expression of the relative importance of the product, market, and company factors in the marketing situation; suggested weights range between 1.0 and 3.0

Family brand a brand that has several products carrying its name (e.g., Heinz, Del Monte, etc.)

Farm magazine a publication designed to appeal to the needs and interests of individuals in the farming industry

Feature a physical characteristic or component of a product or service

Federal Trade Commission the principal federal agency that regulates the advertising industry

Fee system an agreement about services to be provided by an ad agency and the rates at which those services will be billed

Fixed costs expenses for which a firm is responsible, regardless of its amount of production

Flat rate a fixed line rate offered by a newspaper that does not allow a discount

Flighting pattern in media planning, the practice of scheduling the advertising message in waves, interspersed with periods of no advertising exposures

Focus group interview an open-ended group discussion of a product or advertising idea, for use in advertising planning

Free-standing insert an unbound advertisement appearing in a newspaper or magazine (e.g., coupon offers)

Frequency the average number of times the audience is exposed to the advertising message

Full-service agency an advertising agency that offers account service, message formulation and development (creative services), and media planning and buying

Gatefold a multipage advertisement that a reader must unfold to read

General advertising See **National advertising**

Generic demand trend one of nine factors for appraising the advertising opportunity; indicates the sales trends of a particular product category

Generic strategy a creative strategy based on making a product claim without an assertion of superiority

Geographic segmentation identifying market segments according to the geographical location of prospective purchasers

Gross audience See **Gross impressions**

Gross impressions the total number of exposures to an advertiser's schedule of advertisements (in magazines, also called *gross audience*)

Gross rating points (GRP) a calculation used to determine media weight; arrived at by multiplying reach times frequency; one GRP equals 1 percent of the audience

Headline in print advertising, a word or group of words designed to attract the reader's attention and provide a glimpse at the selling message

Hidden quality one of nine factors for appraising the advertising opportunity; indicates a product benefit that is not readily apparent to the prospective buyer upon physical inspection of the product

Horizontal publication a business magazine that reaches a single occupation across many different industries

House agency an organization in which all the specialized activities of an agency are provided by a subsidiary of the advertiser firm

Households Using Television (HUT) a figure of audience measurement, expressed as a percentage, that denotes the number of TV households in the United States whose sets are turned on at any specific time

Image advertising See **Corporate advertising**

Incentive system a form of ad agency compensation, whereby the agency shares in the success of the advertising effort

Independent a radio or television station that is not affiliated with a network

Indirect objective an advertising goal aimed at a communication task that must be accomplished before the ultimate, physical behavior response can be achieved (e.g., change in knowledge or attitudes)

Individual brand one of several brands within a product category, all marketed by the same firm

Infomercial a two- to ten-minute commercial message

Informal evaluation the regular review of advertising alternatives and ideas that takes place before the advertising is exposed to the public

Inquiry a request for additional information, generated through the return of a request form, a reader reply card, a store visit, or a phone call to an 800 telephone number

Insert in print advertising, an advertisement that is literally inserted into the newspaper or magazine, either free-standing or bound

Insertion order a document that confirms the details of a media contract and explains any special requirements

Insight Retrieval System an SMRB research service that allows marketers to analyze the demographics of a market, the geographic sales of a product, the attitudes and life-styles of product users, and the most effective media to reach the target audience

Institutional advertising See **Corporate advertising**

Intensive distribution a marketing situation in which the marketer tries to maximize the number of outlets available for purchase of a particular brand

Internal (house) list a mailing list that is compiled from a firm's own records

Internship program an academic program under which a student may earn college credit for performing supervised part-time work in a job related to his or her area of study

Interview a one-on-one meeting between a job applicant and a prospective employer, usually for the purpose of discussing a job opening

Key visual in TV commercials, the central visual concept of what the message is about

Keyline See **Mechanical layout**

Leading National Advertisers, Inc. (LNA) a research firm that reports on media expenditures for companies, products, and specific brands

Learning a process of behavior change based on experience

List broker See **Mailing list broker**

Local advertising advertising that directs consumers to a specific location to obtain a product or service (also called *retail advertising*)

Local rate in newspaper advertising, a lower rate charged to retailers who buy their own space, usually on a large annual contract

Local station advertising the practice of buying media time on a particular station in a particular market

Low-involvement hierarchy a learning theory suggesting that for some products and media, the impact of advertising is on cognitive variables that directly affect brand choice, with little or no effect on, or influence from, attitudes

Mailing list broker an advertising supplier who sells or rents mailing lists to advertisers for direct-mail campaigns

Mall intercept an information-gathering technique, in which researchers interview selected shopping-mall patrons to learn their opinions about advertising ideas or executions

Manufacturer's brand a brand name owned by a manufacturer (also called a *national brand*)

Map recall method in outdoor advertising, a research technique in which respondents recall trips away from home and draw a travel route for each trip

Market potential one of nine factors for appraising the advertising opportunity; indicates the opportunity for profitable sale of a particular brand

Market segmentation a process of identifying the wants and needs of the market for the purpose of allocating marketing resources

Marketing concept a company orientation toward identifying and responding to the wants and needs of target markets

Marketing plan a written document that analyzes, summarizes, and directs the actions of the marketing effort

Materialism a philosophy that places undue value on the possession of material things

Mechanical layout an exact-size replica of what the finished ad will look like; used to make a full-sized photographic negative, from which the finished ad is made (also called a *keyline* or *pasteup*)

Media buyer an advertising professional who negotiates and purchases advertising time and/or space

Media buying service a firm that specializes in the planning, buying, and placing of media at discount rates

Media contract a document that expresses the agreement between the medium and the media buyer

Media Imperatives an SMRB research service that allows advertisers to determine appropriate media strategies by identifying individuals' media orientation

Media mix the variety of media used in the media portion of the advertising campaign

Media plan a course of action that specifies exactly how an advertising campaign will be delivered to the target market

Media planner an advertising professional who formulates the most effective and efficient way of reaching the target market with the advertising message

Media representative an advertising employee who sells media time and space to advertisers throughout the country

Media representative firm (rep firm) a business that specializes in selling advertising space or time for a number of noncompeting publications or stations that are located outside the major advertising communities

Media schedule in an advertising campaign, a list of the media selected and the times and dates that the advertising will appear

Mediamark Research, Inc. (MRI) a research firm that publishes information about consumers' use of print and broadcast media and various products and brands

"Me-too" strategy a generally undesirable creative strategy in which a product is not differentiated from its competitors

Milline rate in newspapers, the cost to reach one million people with one line of advertising

Motivation the stimulus that causes an individual to take a certain action

Narrowcasting the practice of reaching a narrowly defined market target as opposed to a broad, undifferentiated one

National advertising advertising that offers a product or service to the general consumer audience across the United States (also called *general advertising*)

National Advertising Review Board a 50-member group, comprised of members of advertiser firms, ad agencies, and the general public, that serves as the self-regulatory body of the advertising industry

National brand See **Manufacturer's brand**

National rate in newspaper advertising, the higher rate charged to distant advertisers who place their advertising through ad agencies

Negotiated commission a form of agency compensation in which the actual amount of payment is raised or lowered to provide a reasonable profit for the agency

Net reach See **Reach**

Network a group of radio or television stations that have contractually agreed to carry the same programming and any advertising within that programming

Network advertising messages that are carried on all affiliated stations across the United States

Noncontrolled circulation See **Paid circulation**

Non-paid (controlled) circulation distribution of a magazine or newspaper to subscribers who do not pay because they are "qualified" by virtue of their occupation or title

Objective/task approach one of a number of methods of budgeting for advertising, in which the decision on the level of advertising investment is made by setting an objective for advertising and then calculating the cost of reaching the objective

Open rate in newspapers, the rate charged to advertisers who do not qualify for a discount

Opinion leader a key individual with knowledge and/or expertise in a certain area

Outdoor advertising displays of messages on standardized and regulated structures that reach target markets when they are out of home

Outside display in transit advertising, a sign placed on the side, back, or front of a bus or taxi

Paid (noncontrolled) circulation distribution of a magazine or newspaper to individuals who pay a fee to receive the publication

Painted bulletin a sign 48 feet long by 14 feet wide, on which outdoor advertising is displayed

Participation in television or radio, an arrangement in which an advertiser may advertise on a regular basis within a program (or several programs), but is not responsible for the program's production costs

Pasteup See **Mechanical layout**

Peoplemeter an audience measurement device used by Arbitron to collect data on audience viewing and supermarket purchasing behavior

Percent coverage in magazines, the percentage of a population that reads an average issue

Perception the way we organize and interpret stimuli through the five senses

Perceptual defenses consumers' abilities to be selective in their attention to an advertising message

Permanent bulletin in outdoor advertising, a sign that remains in one location throughout the contract period

Personal selling oral presentations to prospective buyers for the purpose of making sales

Personality the way in which an individual responds to one's environment over a long period of time

Physical attribute a characteristic that physically differentiates a product from its competition

Physical differentiation the practice of distinguishing a product or service on the basis of actual features (shape, design, or appearance) that make it different from competitors

Plans board See **Creative review board**

Point-of-purchase advertising the use of in-store displays, usually produced at the manufacturer's expense for dealers of the product

Political advertising the use of advertising techniques to sell candidates and political positions

Portfolio a collection of samples of an artist's or writer's work, which is displayed during an interview

Positioning strategy a creative strategy based on building a place for the product in the consumer's mind by relating the product to the leading competitor

Poster panel a form of outdoor advertising sign available in three sizes: the 24-sheet, and 30-sheet, and the bleed

Postproduction the final phase of commercial production, in which sound effects, titles, etc., are added to the film or tape

Powerful emotional motive one of the nine factors for appraising the advertising opportunity; indicates a brand's appeal to strong inner drives on the part of prospective buyers

Powers school an advertising approach named for early retail copywriter John E. Powers, characterized by the restrained and straightforward presentation of product features

Preemptive claim an advertising technique that emphasizes a product feature that is common to all brands in the product category, placing competitors in the weak position of echoing the claim

Preemptive strategy a creative strategy based on the making of a claim of superiority based on a characteristic common to all brands in the category

Preferred position in print advertising, a placement policy that permits an advertiser to specify a certain position for its ad, often at an additional charge

Premium merchandise that is given away as an incentive for a buyer to purchase a particular brand

Premium service on cable television, those services that are offered to subscribers for additional fees beyond the basic subscriber fee

Preproduction process the tasks involved in preparing to shoot a TV commercial; includes choosing a location, building a set, casting, and arranging for props and equipment

Printed bulletin in outdoor advertising, a sign comprised of preprinted paper

Private brand See **Distributor's brand**

PRIZM a segmentation system that classifies neighborhoods and communities into homeogeneous population clusters

Product life cycle (PLC) a marketing concept that suggests that all products pass through four stages of development in their life: introduction, growth, maturity, and decline

Promotion one of the four basic elements of the marketing mix, whose function is to communicate the want-satisfying qualities of a brand; includes advertising, personal selling, public relations, and sales promotion

Psychographic segmentation identifying market segments according to the psychological characteristics of prospective purchasers

Psychological differentiation the advertising technique of distinguishing a product or service from competing brands by offering an emotional argument or appeal to the consumer and associating this emotional dimension with the product or service as an incentive to buy

Public relations communication activities intended to promote a positive image for an individual or a firm

Public service advertising advertising that promotes noncontroversial causes and is usually donated by the advertising industry

Puffery the exaggeration of a product claim

Pull communication strategy a marketing strategy that stimulates demand from the end buyer, who encourages the retailer to stock a certain brand, thus "pulling" goods through the distribution system

Pulsing pattern in media planning, the practice of scheduling a continuous base of advertising, supplemented by waves of increased exposures

Push communication strategy a marketing strategy that stimulates demand from the wholesaler, who promotes the brand to the retailer, who in turn sells to the consumer, thus "pushing" goods through the distribution system

Push/pull communication strategy a promotion strategy that stimulates demand at all levels: wholesaler, retailer, and end buyer

Qualitative criteria in media evaluation, those aspects of a medium that are difficult to quantify yet are important to evaluate

Quantitative criteria in media evaluation, those aspects of a medium that can be measured objectively

Rate card a document that contains pertinent data about the costs, mechanical requirements, and audience for a media vehicle

Rates of response advertising data that specify the effectiveness of advertising

Rating See **Reach (radio)**

Ratings in television and radio, an estimate of audience size, expressed as a percentage of a particular market

Reach the number of different people exposed to a particular media vehicle over a certain period of time (also called *cumulative audience, cume, net reach, unduplicated audience,* and *unduplicated reach*)

Reach in magazine advertising, the number of different people who read a particular magazine or a group of magazines in a media schedule (also called *unduplicated audience* or *net reach*)

Reach in radio, the number of different people exposed to a specific station during a particular quarter-hour period (also called *rating* or *reach rating*)

"Reason-why" copy an advertising technique characterized by persuasive copy that presents an argument for buying the product

Recall a reader or viewer's ability to remember an advertisement or portions of it

Recognition See **Agency recognition**

Reference group a group that serves as a guide in shaping an individual's behavior at a particular time

Research assistant an entry-level position in the research department of a large agency or advertiser

Residual deception the retention of misinformation long after an advertising message appears

Resonance strategy a creative strategy based on designing messages to match the stored experience of the intended audience

Resume a communication device between the job seeker and the prospective employer; outlines the applicant's credentials, achievements, and skills

Retail advertising See **Local advertising**

ROP (run-of-paper) in newspaper advertising, a placement policy in which the physical location of the ad within the newspaper is determined by the publication

Rotary bulletin in outdoor advertising, a sign that is moved to a different location every 60 to 90 days

Rule-of-thumb approach one of a number of methods of budgeting for advertising, in which the decision is made using some guiding principle, such as a percentage of sales

Sales promotion all those promotion activities that enhance and support advertising, public relations, and personal selling

Selective attention a sensory mechanism that permits individuals to shut out stimuli that are not of interest to them

Selective distortion the interpreting of information in a way that is consistent with a consumer's existing opinions

Selective distribution a marketing situation in which the marketer intentionally limits the number of outlets available for purchase of a particular brand

Selective exposure the incomplete processing of information by consumers

Selective perception a sensory mechanism that permits individuals to unconsciously perceive only those messages that are of interest to them

Selective retention a sensory mechanism that permits individuals to attend to certain stimuli and block out others

Self-liquidating premium in specialty advertising, an offer of merchandise to consumers for a sum of money that covers the cost of the item plus postage and handling charges

Selling proposition the most persuasive argument that can be offered for why prospects should purchase a product or service

Shooting phase the period of time in which a commercial is filmed or taped

Shopper a newspaper that consists mostly of classified and display advertising; usually distributed free

Short rate in newspapers, the amount that an advertiser must pay when the advertising space used does not equal or exceed the amount contracted for

Showing in outdoor advertising, an expression of the percentage of the population reached by a certain collection of outdoor locations

Simmons Market Research Bureau, Inc. (SMRB) a research firm that publishes information about the media, their audiences, and product consumption

Situational factors time and environmental conditions that affect marketplace behavior

Specialty advertising the practice of imprinting an advertiser's name or message on a usable item (such as a ball-point pen or a t-shirt) for the purpose of helping achieve the advertising objective

Specialty advertising distributor a salesperson who helps to sell specialty advertising to client firms

Split run a testing technique that allows an advertiser to test alternative versions of an ad at the same time

Split-30 the practice of dividing a 30-second commercial into two 15-second ones

Sponsorship in television or radio, an arrangement in which an advertiser assumes complete or partial financial responsiblity for the production of a program

Spot advertising the practice of purchasing broadcast advertising time on a station-by-station, market-by-market basis

Standard Advertising Unit (SAU) system in newspapers, the system by which advertising space is measured and purchased in more than 98 percent of the newspapers in the United States

Standard Industrial Classification (SIC) system a classification system, maintained by the federal government, to identify every industry in the United States with a four-digit code

Standard Rate & Data Service (SRDS) a research firm that publishes media information for use by the advertising industry

Station poster in transit advertising, a sign placed in a transportation terminal

Stereotype a mold used in printing a newspaper ad

Stereotypes oversimplified images of an individual or a group

Storyboard in TV commercials, a combination of illustrations and script, usually pasted onto a board, that indicates the audio and video portions of the commercial

Subculture a group within a culture that differs on the basis of race, nationality, religion, and/or geographic location

Subliminal advertising the technique of hiding messages and symbols in advertisements in such a way that they are not consciously perceived

Substantiation a policy of the Federal Trade Commission, which requires advertisers to supply documentation for the claims made in the advertising

Supplier in specialty advertising, the producer of merchandise to be used for specialty advertising purposes

Take-one in transit advertising, a card or other piece of literature attached to a transit sign

Target market a group of people who have buying power and a common need that potentially can be satisfied through the purchase of a marketer's brand

Tasteless advertising any message that either offends or embarrasses the receiver

Technical journal See **Business paper**

Theater test in TV commercial testing, a technique in which test participants view the commercials in a theater setting

Theoretical approach one of a number of methods of budgeting for advertising, in which the decision on the level of advertising investment is made based on a particular theory of how advertising works

Time-shift the practice of using a video cassette recorder to tape a TV program for the purpose of watching it at a time other than its broadcast time

Total market coverage (TMC) in newspaper advertising, a program that offers distribution of a newspaper or shared mailing to nonsubscribers

Trade association a group whose goal is to advance the interests of a specific industry

Trade journal See **Business paper**

Trade paper See **Business paper**

Trade press a collective term for the publications that serve a particular industry

Trade regulation rules ordinances, established by the Federal Trade Commission, that control trade practices in an entire industry

Traffic Audit Bureau (TAB) a research firm that verifies outdoor advertising circulation

Transit advertising the practice of carrying a message on the inside or outside of public transportation vehicles and their stations

Underwriting the process of providing financial support for a TV or radio program without the larger dollar investment involved in sponsorship

Unduplicated audience See **Reach**

Unique Selling Proposition a creative strategy based on some point of physical differentiation of the product, presented to the consumer in a meaningful and persuasive way

VALS (*Values and Life-Styles*) a research program, conducted by SRI International, that characterizes consumers on the basis of their attitudes, needs, and beliefs

Vampire video an industry term for an ad that is so overwhelming that it draws attention away from the product and focuses it on itself

Variable costs expenses that rise with production volume

Verbatim a document prepared from transcripts of focus group interviews, containing notable statements and characterizations that may prove helpful in writing advertising copy

Vertical publication a business magazine that reaches all job functions within a particular industry

Video cassette recorder (VCR) a device used to record and play back television programming and other materials

Visual in print advertising, an illustration or image that dramatizes the selling idea and reinforces the product's premise or benefit to the reader

Waste circulation that portion of the audience that falls outside the target market

Weighted evaluation procedure a quantitative method for determining the role of advertising in marketing a product or service

"You" attitude a style of writing based on keeping the interest of the reader foremost and speaking to the reader in terms that are meaningful for him/her

Zapping the practice of using the remote-control device on a TV set or video cassette recorder to switch channels and avoid commercials

Zipping the practice of using the fast-forward button on a video cassette recorder to avoid the advertising messages in recorded television programming

NAME INDEX

SUBJECT INDEX